CANCELLED

Sir James
Martin

As part of our ongoing market research, we are always pleased to receive comments about our books, suggestions for new titles, or requests for catalogues. Please write to: The Editorial Director, Patrick Stephens Limited, Sparkford, Nr Yeovil, Somerset BA22 7JJ.

Sir James
Martin

The authorised biography of the
Martin-Baker ejection seat pioneer

SARAH SHARMAN
Foreword by HRH The Duke of Edinburgh

PSL

Patrick Stephens Limited

First published in 1996

British Library Cataloguing-in-Publication Data:
A catalogue record for this book
is available from the British Library

ISBN 1 85260 551 0

Library of Congress catalog card no. 96 075168

Patrick Stephens Limited is an imprint
of Haynes Publishing, Sparkford, Nr Yeovil,
Somerset, BA22 7JJ

Designed and typeset by G&M, Raunds, Northamptonshire
Printed and bound in Great Britain by
Biddles Limited, Guildford and King's Lynn

Contents

Foreword

by HRH The Duke of Edinburgh

James Martin was one of those rare people who
combined an exceptionally creative and fertile
imagination with the pragmatism of a practical
engineer. He was also single-minded in the pursuit of
his ambitions. Like so many great inventors and
innovators, he could not understand nor tolerate
bureaucracy and he suffered fools not at all.

This is a fascinating book about a man who was
devoted to finding elegant and simple solutions to what
others considered to be baffling problems. The story of
the origin, development and achievements of the
Martin-Baker Company makes gripping reading and the
evolution of its greatest success, the ejection-seat,
reveals the utter dedication of James Martin to making
life safer for military pilots all over the world.

The author has captured the essence of this
remarkable and contradictory character - intolerant,
yet considerate; uncooperative, yet always ready to
learn from trial and error; immensely hard-working, yet
with little interest in financial reward. His success
brought him many well-deserved honours, yet it probably
gave him more satisfaction to hear from a pilot whose
life had been saved by one of his ejection-seats.

Acknowledgements

Sir James Martin shunned publicity and would not have countenanced the publication of his biography in his lifetime. I am therefore very grateful to his widow, Lady Martin, and his sons and daughters, John and James Martin, Jane Livesey and Anne Hess, for their permission to write this book, and to Lady Martin in particular for her interest and enthusiasm, and for allowing me access to Sir James's personal correspondence. I would also like to give my sincere thanks to Sir James's niece and nephew, Joan Holt and Denis Burrell, for their invaluable help and support.

This book would not have been possible without the full co-operation of the Martin-Baker Aircraft Company, and I would like to thank the directors, Denis Burrell and John and James Martin, for allowing me access to their staff, their numerous files and records, to use their brochures as the source of the technical information in this book, and to use so many of their photographs. I would like to express my appreciation in particular for the help given to me by Basil Macnab, Brian Miller and Eric Thomas; also to Richard Holt, Del Holyland, Peter Stevens, David Taylor and Keith Wilson. Among the retired employees of the company and other colleagues of Sir James I would like to thank: Gladys Aspinwall, Arthur Bates, James Elliott, Stewart Fifield, the late Clifford Gaskell, Owen Gilbert, the late Bryan Greensted, Peter Hodgkiss, Anne Mower, Ken Neil, Jack Scott, Helen Taylor, and Francis Francis's widow, Patricia Francis.

I am most grateful for the whole-hearted assistance of Sir James's friends: Lord Kings Norton, Bill Bedford, Margaret Fenn, John Francis, Air Vice-Marshal Peter Howard, Margaret Loudon, Dr. Gerhard Sedlmayr, Ivy Snell and the late Patricia Webb, and also to Sir George Edwards, Sir Peter Masefield, Sally Alexander, Jo Corr, Bessie and Jack Coulter and Adeline Mathers.

I contacted many people during the course of my research, and I would like to acknowledge with thanks the willing co-operation and help of Constance Babington-Smith, Jock Bryce , Rear Admiral Tom Cruddas, Air Marshal the Reverend Sir Patterson Fraser, Ben Gunn, Barney Hallam, Lt. Linda Hyde, Jo Lancaster, Capt. Colin Little, the late Sir

Wylie McKissock, Lt. Meier, Lt. Cdr. Muir, Philip Murphy, Kate Nightingale, and Capt. S.G. Orr.

My thanks to Ron Kennett, the Director of the Royal Aeronautical Society, for his help with contacts and for his constructive comments on the manuscript; to Mike Evans at Rolls-Royce Heritage Trust for his valuable contribution from the Rolls-Royce archives and for his kind permission to use that archive material in this book; to John Aldington for his research on my behalf at the Frazer-Nash Archives; and to Air Vice-Marshal Tim Jenner, Air Commodore Rick Peacock-Edwards, Capt. Joe Hart and Stephen Bomes for their help along the way.

I also appreciate the help that I received from John Golley, Arnold Nayler, Brian Riddle, Jack Pierce, Dominic Malocco, Derek Beardsell, Joan Phillipson, Stephanie Zarach, Victor Bryant, S.J. Anglim, Eric McCleary, Tom Wylie, Deirdre Armstrong, Louis Malcolm and John McGiffert.

I would like to thank *Air International, Flight International* and *Aircraft Engineering* for their kind permission to quote from their periodicals, and the RAF Museum at Hendon for their kind permission to quote from Amy Johnson's letters which are held in their archives. I have quoted from the 19 December 1934, 30 November 1945 and 9 January 1948 editions of *Aeroplane* with the kind permission of *Aeroplane Monthly*. Crown Copyright material in the Public Record Office is reproduced by permission of the Controller of HMSO: files AVIA 18/660(MB2), AVIA 15/1341 and AIR 19/491(MB3 and MB5), AVIA 15/449 (cable cutters), AVIA 18/584 (blast tubes) and AVIA 15/2051–2060 (ejection seats).

My thanks to Ally Sharman for her research at the Patent Office for me; Yvonne Lord for typing my taped interviews; Maureen Piner for her help in typing the manuscript; Judy Alderton for her help with my computer; and Spectrum Capital for the use of their offices when the builders took over my house.

A special thank you to Bill Gunston for introducing me to Darryl Reach, the Editorial Director of Patrick Stephens Ltd, and for his interest and comments on the manuscript. My thanks, of course, to Darryl Reach and his colleagues who published this book, and I would like to express my real appreciation for all those who worked on this book for Haynes and who have all been such a pleasure to work with.

Finally, thanks to my husband John for his interest and support, and for his unaccustomed patience and forbearance while living with the writing of this book.

Chapter One

Eject or Die

It was another routine test flight for John Lancaster, usually known as Jo, the new deputy chief test pilot for Sir W.G. Armstrong Whitworth Aircraft Limited. That afternoon, on 30 May 1949, he was preparing for his third flight in the second AW52, the experimental tailless aircraft or flying wing being developed by Armstrong Whitworth. Lancaster thought it was a beautiful aircraft to look at. He admired its aerodynamically clean lines and its swept-back wings with the laminar flow profile. It was certainly an unusual-looking flying machine, with a wing span of 90 ft and an overall length of only 37 ft 4 in; a huge expanse of wing with a small, pressurized cockpit at the front. It was a pity, he thought, that its unharmonized controls, which were exceedingly heavy and sluggish laterally, and conversely light and responsive fore and aft, made it such a horror to fly.

His brief that day was to investigate the general handling of the aircraft and to explore its response at speeds from 270 mph up to 350 mph. It was a lovely day, with large towering cumulus providing half cover. He climbed into the cockpit and strapped himself into the seat. It was one of an early type of Martin-Baker ejection seat, the aircraft ejection seat which had only been accepted for service in the Royal Air Force and for use by test pilots like himself in 1947. He thought nothing of it. No-one had ever used an ejection seat in an emergency in England, and the ejection seat was not often discussed among the test pilots, who all operated on the basis that: 'It won't happen to me'.

Lancaster took off and flew up through the clouds. For 45 minutes he explored the flying characteristics of the prototype at the lower end of the speed range, and then climbed to 10,000 ft so that he could gain speed in the descent and investigate its performance at higher speeds. He descended through a gap in the clouds to 5,000 ft, by which stage the aircraft had reached 320 mph.

Suddenly, the aircraft encountered turbulent air conditions and began shaking violently. Within seconds, the rapid pitching oscillation increased and became severe and extreme. Lancaster's head was thrown about by the shaking aircraft, and he could not focus on anything. His vision blurred and the instruments became unreadable. He felt weak and his perception of light began to fade. He thought that the aircraft must be breaking up, but beyond that he could not think straight. He was aware only of the noise and the shaking and the fact that he could not control the aircraft. Disorientated and confused, he instinctively elected to eject, although he can remember nothing of the ejection process, and his next recollection is of plummeting rapidly towards the ground, still strapped into his seat, which was tilted forward at an angle of about 45°, just enough to give him an unnerving view of the world below him.

He tried to re-order his thoughts and remember his emergency procedures. Clearly he needed to disengage himself from his seat and pull the ripcord on his parachute. He was sitting in an elementary type of ejection seat, very different from the fully automatic seats of later years which leave nothing for the pilot to do once he has initiated the ejection process. There were two harness release buckles, one which would release him from the seat and the other which would release him from the parachute. He concentrated hard to make sure that he operated the correct one, and as he released his seat harness, he literally fell out of the seat. He pulled the ripcord, the parachute streamed, and he felt the jerk on his parachute harness as it opened. There was no time to feel relief. Instead he got an abrupt shock as the ejection seat fell past him, rather too close for comfort and safety. He looked down and realized with alarm that he was heading for a canal. He had no wish to land in the water and drown under the enveloping folds of the parachute canopy. He remembered his rudimentary air force parachute training, that he could control the direction of his fall by pulling on the parachute lines. He reached upwards for the parachute lines, pulled hard and initiated an alarming swing. He was quite out of control again. He stopped pulling, hoped the swinging would stop, and knew that it would not as the ground seemed to accelerate upwards to meet him. He crashed through a hedge and landed hard on his back.

He lay there for a minute, stunned by the drama of the preceding minutes. He watched the water meandering through the canal, just a few feet away, and felt thankful that he had landed on dry land. Disordered thoughts jumbled through his mind. He heard a voice, turned his head, and saw a man coming towards him. He had landed just the other side of the road from a farmhouse in Long Itchington in Warwickshire, and the owner, Mr Shepherd, helped him to his feet and back to the farmhouse where he was soon sitting at the kitchen table drinking a cup of tea. Lancaster telephoned the test pilots' office at the Armstrong Whitworth headquarters at Baginton to let them know what had happened and so that they could organize what was to happen next. Then he had another cup of tea and waited for someone to come and pick him up.

He was taken to hospital where examinations revealed a chip to the knuckle joint of his shoulder, cracks to his first lumbar vertebra, and a lot of bad bruising, although it was impossible for the doctors to decide which injuries had been caused by the buffeting in the cockpit, which by the ejection and which by the hard landing.

The days that followed blurred together for Lancaster. Waves of relief and happiness at being alive alternated with his concern about what had gone wrong with the aircraft and the shock of the experience. He tried to remember exactly what had happened, what he had done, and what could have been the cause of it all. He realized that everything had happened very quickly, and that only about 15 seconds had elapsed from the onset of the shaking until he left the aircraft. He had very little coherent recollection of what he had done. 'Obviously, subconsciously I would have closed the throttles and tried to control it. That would have been instinctive', he says, but he cannot remember doing so. He remembers feeling like 'a pea in a matchbox' as he was shaken about in the aircraft. He recalls: 'It was harsh, hard, noisy shaking, and I knew that if I did not get out straight away I wouldn't be conscious enough to do anything at all'. He can remember recalling that he must operate the hood jettison control before initiating the ejection but he cannot remember performing either function. He cannot remember the controlled explosion as the cartridge under the ejection seat fired, the enormous acceleration as the seat ejected, the wind blast on leaving the aircraft, or the deceleration due to the opening of the stabilizing drogue parachute.

The crash investigation concluded that an asymmetric flutter had developed in one wing tip and had quickly spread across the whole wing span so that the entire aircraft had been subjected to uncontrollable pitching oscillation. The frequency of the oscillation was estimated at between $1^1/2$ and 2 cycles per second, with a total angular movement of $20°$. Ironically, the blast of the ejection had interrupted and stopped this flutter, and the aircraft had flown on for a short while on its own before crashing in open country.

The investigations were unable to establish whether Lancaster had correctly followed the pre-ejection emergency procedures and it was uncertain whether he had released the control column by means of the explosive charge attached to it (the pilot's legs went underneath the spectacle-type control column, and the theory was that it would cut off the pilot's legs if he tried to eject with the column in place), and whether he had placed his feet on the heel rests attached to the base of the ejection seat which were there to ensure that he was in the correct position for ejection so as to minimize the risk of back injury. In the event it had not mattered and he had survived with both legs bruised but intact. But if the circumstances in the cockpit had rendered Lancaster, a professional test pilot, incapable of remembering what he had done, and incapable of remembering his escape, what chance of survival would he have had without an ejection seat?

Could he have climbed out of the cockpit and parachuted to safety on his own? Whichever way he viewed it, and however many times he went over the drama in his mind, Lancaster remained convinced of one thing: the pitching had built up so violently and so quickly, and its effect had been so debilitating, that without the ejection seat escape would have been impossible. Of this he was sure. His thoughts turned to Martin-Baker and the man who had designed the seat, James Martin. Lancaster had had one ride on the ejection seat training tower at the Martin-Baker factory, but he had not met James and knew very little about him. He was slightly surprised that James, the man who had made his escape possible, was the one man he did not meet during the weeks of meetings after the crash. He wondered why he had not wanted a first-hand account of his product, but then, Lancaster supposed, it had worked as it should have done, and James would have received copies of the reports prepared by the Ministry and the RAF Institute of Aviation Medicine. He nevertheless owed his life to this man, and decided to write to him and thank him.

When recounting his experience of over 40 years ago, Lancaster was sure, because of his firm belief, then and now, that James's ejection seat had saved his life, that he had written that letter within days of his ejection. He was surprised to find, when he unearthed his memorabilia concerning his ejection, the photographs and the newspaper cuttings, that it was seven weeks after the event before he had written. It reminded him of how distracted he had been by the debriefing sessions and crash investigation meetings, and how long it had taken him to absorb the enormity of his experience.

He sent the letter, and a week later was overwhelmed by the reply he received from James:

Thank you for your letter dated 13th July. It was exceedingly nice of you to write to me and I am more than glad that the seat did its stuff effectively.

In point of fact I had intended to write to you long ago congratulating you on using the seat but I felt that you would probably be so worried by kind people asking you stupid questions that I would only have been one of the queue.

So I would now like to take the opportunity of telling you how exceedingly glad I am that it was possible for you to get out of your predicament without any serious physical damage to yourself. I feel quite certain that it will be possible for a large number of pilots to save their lives by this method. Unfortunately machines with these seats fitted are only very slowly getting into production.

I am taking the opportunity of expressing my congratulations to you in some tangible way since you have been the first person in England to use this ejection seat in an emergency, and I would like to commemorate the event by the enclosed little parcel (which has caused some little delay in replying to your letter) but which I trust will be useful to you.

'I was shocked and ashamed when I read that letter,' Lancaster recalls. 'I wished that I had written immediately, or at least sooner.' He was struck by the modest tone of the letter from the man whose engineering talents had designed the ejection seat that had saved his life, and who had thought that he would only be another in the queue waiting for Lancaster's attention. Apparently reserved and unassuming, James had not tried to seek publicity out of Lancaster's escape, as many people in his position would have done. And Lancaster was astounded by the generosity of the gift.

The 'little parcel' contained a wooden box marked 'DANGER', 'HANDLE WITH CARE', 'THIS BOX CONTAINS EXPLOSIVES'. Inside was a leather case enclosing a gold Rolex wrist-watch, engraved with his name and the date of his ejection. He was surprised and delighted to receive this watch, but felt somewhat undeserving of it. Had he had any say in the matter, it would not have been Jo Lancaster who was the first man to use a Martin-Baker ejection seat in anger. The commemorative gift was not only generous but thoughtful. James had obviously paid attention to its presentation, and his sense of fun, so clearly stamped all over the wooden box, had made a memorable gift unique.

Did James Martin, on 30 May 1949, have any idea of the true significance of the seat that he had designed and that would have such a profound effect on the lives of so many people, not just those other unfortunates who, like Lancaster, found themselves in the wrong place at the wrong time, but their friends and relatives too? What had made him turn his mind to aircraft escape systems at the age of 53, and what indeed had he been doing for the half-century before then?

As Lancaster contemplated the letter and the gift and the man who had sent them, he had no idea that 30 May 1949 had been a milestone in aviation history. He could not have known then that he would be the first of so many, and that over 40 years later he would be drinking champagne at Claridges Hotel in London, at a reception given by the Martin-Baker Aircraft Company Limited to celebrate 6,000 lives saved by the Martin-Baker ejection seat, which is now in service with 86 military forces. On that occasion he talked to the young RAF men who had been shot down by the Iraqis during the Gulf War and who had escaped with their lives, as Lancaster had done, using a Martin-Baker seat. What a different experience theirs had been, their aircraft destroyed by sophisticated, high technology weapons that had hardly been dreamed of in 1949, travelling at supersonic speeds more than twice that that Lancaster had been trying to reach, and blasted out of their aircraft on rocket packs, not the basic cartridge of Lancaster's seat. They chatted happily, different generations of pilots trained to fly different generations of aircraft, but all of them with one thing in common: because of James Martin and his ejection seat, they had all cheated death and lived to fly again.

Chapter Two

Irish Heritage

James Martin had an inauspicious start in life. He was a farmer's son, born in the Ulster province of County Down in 1893. His ancestors had been farmers in County Down for as far back as it is possible to trace, and the farm on which he was raised had been worked by the Martin family since 1738. The life was hard. Toil and trouble were to be expected but opportunities for betterment were not. Nevertheless, James's parents, Thomas and Sarah Martin, realized their good fortune in having the recognized tenure of their smallholding. They had one daughter, Jane, born on 12 March 1891, and when James was born two years later, on 11 September 1893, they were pleased to have a son who would take over their farm and continue the farming tradition.

Thomas Martin had a great talent with machinery. He had a well-equipped workshop on the farm where he would make and repair farm implements and machinery for himself and his neighbours. He was also a bit of an inventor, and among other things, he designed and built a bicycle. Who knows what Thomas himself might have achieved in life had he ever escaped the confines of his Ulster farmstead?

Unfortunately, while James no doubt inherited his father's inventive flair, Thomas died when James was only two, and James therefore never had the benefit of his father's teaching or example. Thomas, at the time of his marriage to Sarah, had been living on the farm with his widowed mother and his spinster sister Georgina, as Irish law at that time provided for widows and spinsters to be supported by their families to the extent of an interest in the property in which they all lived. Sarah did not remarry, so James was brought up in this household of women with his mother, grandmother, aunt and sister. It is hardly surprising then that, within the constraints of their simple way of life, he had a somewhat pampered and cossetted childhood.

Too young to help on the farm, James was often left to amuse himself. His elderly grandmother and his Aunty Georgina doted on him, and although he grew up with a gentlemanly respect for women, they were not safe from his mischief in those early days. Aunty Georgina was seen one day scurrying out of the outside privy in some distress shouting to the family that there were wasps in there. James was hiding behind the back wall of the privy, poking a long stem of stinging nettles in through a hole in the wall.

On Sundays they went to the local Presbyterian church at Raffrey, about 2 miles away across the fields, and the local vicar, the Reverend Legate, knew them well. James and Jane went to Sunday School too, but this does not seem to have been a chore for James. All his life he kept his copy of John Bunyan's *Pilgrim's Progress*, which was presented to him in the summer of 1905 for full attendance at Sunday School. It was a strict Presbyterian household and James was brought up to accept and obey the Ten Commandments and the teachings of the Bible. Bible reading was a part of their lives and it was in these early days that he began to acquire that prodigious knowledge of the Bible that was to surprise so many people in his later life.

James started school at the age of four and attended the local schools until he was 14. His friend and neighbour, Hugh Coulter, remembers him as being 'the liveliest little boy that ever went to school'. The lessons did not interest him, and this seems to have been reflected in his behaviour there. But he had a voracious appetite for knowledge about how things worked. He read technical books late into the night and would then be unable to get out of bed in the morning and one of the women in the household would take him breakfast in bed. He frequently played truant and could be found in the workshop on the farm, finding out how to work the lathes and other tools, experimenting and making things, or up in the engineering workshops of Belfast observing the men at work. On his own admission, he spent a considerable amount of time with the charge hands and foremen at these workshops, and there is no doubt that he acquired a lot of knowledge this way. When he was only 14 he made a kerosene lamp for the Reverend Legate which worked well for over 30 years.

In the summer of 1908, James left school with no intention of entering another educational establishment. He had no interest at all in farming, and was adamant that he would not bow to the apparent inevitability of his inheritance. His mother tried to insist that if he would not be a farmer then he must have some formal qualification, and she decided that he should go to university and study civil engineering. She arranged for a private tutor to help James study the subjects for matriculation, and in 1908 she escorted him to what was then known as Queen's College in Belfast to attend an interview with Professor FitzGerald, who was the professor of civil engineering. James remembered this interview well. He wrote to a friend many years later:

I can still remember Professor FitzGerald; he was a very nice old gentleman with a long beard, and in his little office he had a roll top desk. He asked me to unscrew the old type electric switch which was porcelain. I unscrewed it and he asked me to move the switch up and down and asked me what caused the little blue spark. I said I did not know and I asked him if he could tell me.

Professor FitzGerald did not oblige. During the discussion that followed, he quickly came to the conclusion that James was not suited to a university education or a career in civil engineering, and that he would be better off engaged in the more practical side of engineering. So the private tutor was sent home and James never sat his matriculation examinations. James's view on all this was clear. He said later: 'As far as I am concerned, if I had matriculated I would probably have got some sort of BA degree and died of boredom as some county council surveyor.' He would also sometimes remark in later years: 'Queen's University didn't want me, but I haven't done too badly have I?' And it was a source of some satisfaction when, in 1968, Queen's University invited him to accept the honorary degree of doctor of science in recognition of his services to engineering and air safety. He did, however, have the grace to write an appreciative letter of thanks to the Vice-Chancellor of the University to say: 'I have received many honours over the years but I can say, without any hesitation, that I appreciate this much more than any honour I have ever had.' His mother, Sarah, was still alive and in her 97th year. It was a pity that her mental faculties had so deteriorated that she was quite unable to appreciate this award to her son.

The industrialization of Ulster which had started in the previous century was progressing fast. Belfast was the centre of this development and engineering was now a thriving industry. No doubt James could have secured an apprenticeship at one of the many small engineering firms in the locality, but he was firmly convinced that he did not wish to work for anybody. He knew what he wanted to do and how he wanted to do it. He wrote later:

If I look back over the years from when I was a very young person until the present time, I had always got the notion that I wanted to design things and not to be employed by anyone. It was always my policy that I must have a place of my own, to be free to work on my own inventions and develop them.

James's interest at this time was in making and developing small engines and dynamos. He remembered converting a gas engine to oil for a nearby town council and riding there on his motorbike to fix it up. But he was not always so successful. One day, a local farmer asked him if he could mend his steam tractor. James was not prepared to admit to his total ignorance of steam tractors and readily agreed to see what he could do. He managed to get it working, but rather too well, and the tractor built up such a head of steam that he quickly had to cut some grass turves and put them on top of the chimney to stop it blowing up.

James was not, however, totally preoccupied with his own engineering work and there were two developments which were attracting his interest at that time. The first, of course, was the motor car. It was several years before James would acquire his first car, but he would observe the development and manufacture of cars in the Belfast factories with great interest. The other development, which was capturing the imagination of so many people during the early part of the twentieth century, was the growth of aviation. James was fascinated by aircraft at a young age and as a teenager used to make small model aeroplanes. He would visit the premises of Harry Ferguson in Belfast where he was able to watch the construction of Ferguson's aeroplane, a low wing monoplane, and he watched its first flight in 1909. James later reminisced with his (unrelated) namesake, Joe Martin, who was one of the mechanics who worked on this aeroplane:

> Indeed, I remember seeing Harry Ferguson in his aeroplane on the grounds of the Slieve Donard Hotel where he used to run it up. If my memory serves me right, it was fitted with a Clarkson propeller and the engine, I believe, suffered from overheating. In order to get over this, a ring of holes was drawn round each cylinder so that a certain proportion of exhaust could escape from these holes. The net result was the oil was thrown out through these holes and they had to be tapped and fitted with short play screws.

These were not the observations of a casual observer; rather, they reflected the interested mind of an engineer who was to go on to build his own aircraft in later years.

James's understanding of this and other early aeroplanes was, indeed, acute. He was shortly to set to work on a warning device for aeroplanes. In April 1911 he applied to the Patent Office in London to patent an invention which he called a speed alarm. Unfortunately, although the patent application was registered, the patent was never granted, presumably because James failed to produce the necessary paperwork within the prescribed time. Even then there were formalities to be observed and adhered to before a patent could be granted, which James would no doubt have found as tiresome then as he did in later life. We only have James's informal description of this invention which was designed to warn the pilot if his airspeed became dangerously high or dangerously low. It consisted of two tubes which when struck made a completely different warning sound. Two propellers, which were rotated by the airflow, operated spring-loaded weights which were arranged so that one of the tubes was struck if the airspeed became too high and the other was struck if the airspeed became too low. The device was simple and straightforward and, not having access to an aeroplane, James borrowed a car in order to test it. It worked and was subsequently tested successfully on an aeroplane by the Bristol and Colonial Aircraft Company, but James did not have the resources to manufacture and market this device, and he did nothing further about it. It is interesting, however, that one of his first designs related to pilot safety.

It was about this time that James lost the companionship of his sister Jane. She left Ireland in 1911 at the age of 18 and took a job in London. Her reasons for leaving Ireland were not new: life was difficult, opportunities for work and marriage were both limited, and economic necessity dictated that she must try and make her own way in the world.

Doubtless she and James would have discussed these issues over and over again, and it must have crystallized for James some of his own feelings of discontent. Her decision to leave left an enormous gap in James's life, but he was not yet ready to follow her.

After his unsuccessful attempt to enter the world of aviation he reverted to the more familiar field of engines. His next major project came some three years later when he built an internal combustion engine for electricity generation. James agreed to sell this engine to a Mr Perry, who lived on the Isle of Man, and on 5 August 1914, James and his engine left Belfast on the ferry to the Isle of Man. This journey was his first visit to the Isle of Man and, indeed, his first journey outside Ireland. He never forgot this trip, and often delighted in telling the story of how, with no money to buy breakfast, he picked up a bit of slate off the ground and carved it into the right size and shape in order to extract a bar of chocolate from a machine. The sale of the engine was concluded and the engine was successfully installed in Mr Perry's business premises in Douglas where it did good service for many years. Any engineering success enriched James's life, and the successful development of this engine was a source of great satisfaction to him and one which he would often refer to.

But it is clear that his limited achievements in life were not fulfilling his ambitions and aspirations. He enjoyed designing and making engines, and experimenting with other gadgets and ideas, but he could see no future in what he was doing. Perhaps he remembered his escapades with his schoolfriend Hugh Coulter. 'You're no good, Martin, and you'll never be any good', Hugh would say to James, and looking back on what he had done so far, what could James say in his own defence? He felt guilty about not helping his mother more on the farm. She was adamant that he should stay and fulfil his responsibilities, but increasingly James was frustrated by the limitations of his life, and he was not a man to give in. He had been brought up on the creed of self-help and perseverance and he firmly believed, as he explained later, that:

> We should not let circumstances rule us. So very often circumstances cause people to do things that do not produce the best results. It is absolutely vital to have enormous tenacity of purpose and not be influenced by anyone. Go it alone. It means hard work and long hours, and a person cannot work hard or long hours unless his heart and soul are in the job.

James's heart and soul were certainly in his work. He would often say that any talents that he possessed had been given to him by the Lord, and he felt that it was his duty to work hard and use those talents. He became increasingly determined to do justice to the ability bestowed on him and to persuade his mother that his future lay elsewhere. But the First World War had started and he would have to wait before leaving Ireland in search of a better life. Conscription was not introduced in Ireland and James was therefore never under threat of being called up.

The war did not particularly interest him and he did not volunteer, and the war years brought little change to his daily routine.

It is interesting that, despite his strong religious convictions and his resolute approach to life, he did not become involved in the ferment of religious and political activity in which the Irish were engaged at that time as they focused on the question of Home Rule for Ireland. James was by no means indifferent to the issues being so earnestly debated but he was not politically active. He was not a member of the Orange Order, which he could not reconcile with the teachings of God, nor of the Ulster Volunteer Force. Indeed, in correspondence with a friend in later years when he mentioned 'the insanity of Northern Ireland', the friend referred to 'all our efforts in the Boys Club and such' and concluded: 'We did try but, oh Lord, did we fail.' Perhaps, then, James tried as a young man to argue against the propaganda of the day and suggest a more peaceful and godly course of action. He was certainly appalled by the events of the sixties and seventies and greatly saddened too that his home province was so troubled and divided. Perhaps the absence of a father and the absence of uncles and brothers meant that there was little political debate in the Martin household. The issues that were to ignite such fervour in so many of James's contemporaries were probably little discussed on the farm.

One day news arrived from James's sister in London that she was going to be married. Jane returned home with her fiancé, Edwin Burrell, in May 1918 to be married at Raffrey Parish Church. Now was the time for James to give serious consideration to leaving Ireland. When the war was over, there would be opportunities in the post-war regeneration, and he had a sister in London who now had a proper home. Sarah was still determined that he should stay, but James's mind was made up. And so, in August 1919, when he was nearly 26, James set sail for England.

Chapter Three

The Acton Inventor

James liked to tell the story of how he arrived in England with £10 in his pocket, knowing no-one, and with nowhere to go; he had made his own way in the world, and anything he had achieved in life was due entirely to his own efforts. There is no denying that his early years in England were a tremendous struggle. He had very little money, and for several years he lived a hand to mouth existence, never quite knowing how long his money would last. He had no job to go to – not that he would have wanted one – no workshop, and no contacts in the engineering world to call upon. He did, however, have a good friend in his sister Jane, and he found lodgings in Acton to be near her.

Acton was fortunately an excellent place for James to be based. Situated to the west of London, it was a fast-developing suburb, and although primarily a residential area, the twenties saw increasing commercial activity there. It was the home of D. Napier & Son, the aero-engine manufacturers, and was fast establishing itself as a centre of the automotive industry.

James soon found himself a small workshop. His early years in Ireland, spent visiting factories, mixing with the men on the shop-floor, the charge hands and the foremen, and generally getting to know the local businesses and the people in them, was the best possible training he could have had for his present situation. He went out and about, meeting people, finding out what work he might be able to do, where he could buy raw materials, and where he could get specialist work done. It was very much a case of self-help and self-sufficiency. He needed a work bench and managed to buy some suitable timber very cheaply from a demolished building site. There was no question of anyone delivering it to his premises and he had no van to collect it in, so he carried the timber back to his workshop, part of the journey being made on a London bus, much to the surprise and irritation of the other passengers.

It was sometime during his first year in Acton that his money first ran out. He could no longer afford the rent for his lodgings and the rent for his workshop. Clearly he had no future if he gave up his workshop, so he gave up his lodgings instead and moved in with Jane and Edwin, where he stayed until he married over 20 years later. Their childhood years in Ireland had built a bond between James and Jane which was unaltered by the years of separation after Jane had moved to England. Jane was important because she believed in James's talents and abilities and could provide encouragement and resolve when times were hard. Fortunately for them both, her husband, Edwin, was a man of immense tolerance and patience who was prepared to accept the intrusions on his life perpetrated by his brother-in-law. Not everyone would have countenanced a brother-in-law living permanently in the house, particularly one as unconventional (to Edwin's way of thinking) as James. Invalided out of the army during the First World War because of prolonged sickness acquired during his time in the Dardanelles, Edwin had been posted to the Ministry of Pensions in East Acton. He was still working there in the twenties, a regular job with a steady income which enabled him to provide a simple but comfortable life for his wife and their daughter Joan, born at the beginning of 1920. He had not bargained for an out-of-work brother-in-law, with a head bursting full of impractical ideas that brought in very little in the way of income. It was Edwin's view that James should get a job like everyone else. He would get exasperated when he got home at the end of a long day in the office to find James in the kitchen dismantling his motorbike or some other piece of machinery. There would be arguments with James and about James. But Jane was loyal to James, and could be tough and determined too. James worked hard, he had always worked hard, and one day he would succeed. Meanwhile, Edwin would just have to put up with motorbikes in the kitchen.

For James, a young man in his late twenties, so long constrained by life at home on a small farm in a rural community, the independence and opportunity that were now a part of his daily life must at times have seemed something of a burden, and the promise of a better life a somewhat forlorn hope. But as always throughout his life, James was sustained through difficult times by his faith. Many people came to be impressed by his extraordinary knowledge of the Bible and his impromptu sermons. When expounding his belief in the sureness of God's promises, James would sometimes relate the story of when, shortly after his arrival in England, he met a South African who was engaged in evangelistic work. This man invited James round to his lodgings one Sunday evening which were in a rather poor part of London. When they were having tea, James noticed that the man was eating dry bread and that he made the tea by reusing old tea to economize. James, always inclined to be direct, asked him how he was off financially. The man replied that he could manage, but James could not reconcile eating dry bread with having enough to live on, so he pressed him further. Eventually the man explained that he owed his landlady £25 in rent and that she had his good suit and watch as security. James's total financial resources at that time were only about £30, but he remembered having read in the Bible where Jesus said: 'In as much as you do it to the least of these my brethren, you do it unto Me.' The Bible was unequivocal and it was clear to James what he should do, so he gave the man £25. As James would later explain: 'It was a test but I did not fail, and God has blessed me enormously over the years.'

Among the first people he met in Acton were Francis Snell and his son and daughter-in-law, George and Ivy. Francis Snell owned Friars Place Farm near Gipsy Corner in Acton. This had originally been a home of rest for old horses, but at that time it had 125 grass tennis courts which were let out to tennis clubs and to members of the public. It was a pleasant location: an old house (the only remaining moated house in Acton) with a garden and an apple orchard, all surrounded by a large number of attractive old barns and stables, and altogether rather more to James's taste than his existing workshop premises. Francis Snell agreed to rent him one of his large barns to use as a workshop and James moved in.

He did odd jobs, tinkered about with engines and earned what he could. He made a reputation for himself locally, and soon it was the case that if anybody wanted anything repaired they would bring it to James. He is remembered then for his great sense of humour and his gift for telling stories that kept people entertained for hours if he was in the right mood, but most of the time he just worked. The Snell family could not help feeling a little sorry for him, because they felt that he was 'such a brilliant man but so dreadfully ignored'.

Ivy's daughter, Patsy, had her own memories of James. She was told that he was an inventor and she had little understanding of what went on in the big old barn that he had taken over. Patsy used to love to visit James at work there, and he always found time for the little girl. Patsy wanted a cat, but was not allowed one, and one of the reasons that she liked to visit James was to stroke his cat. The cat always seemed to be asleep in a towel when she visited, but James would tell her stories of what it had been up to and would let her stroke the furry bundle in the towel. Recalling those visits some 70 years later, Patsy could only laugh. She never saw a face on the cat, and could never understand why everyone was so amused when she stroked it. Clearly there never was a cat; it must have been a soft brush of some sort that James kept in the towel to please her.

Money continued to be a problem for James, for he still had to pay the rent in respect of the barn, and one day he ran out of money again. He was not prepared to borrow, even assuming he could have found someone to borrow from, because that was against his principles. As he later explained: 'I have never borrowed from anyone. If I could not afford a thing I went without until I had earned enough money to buy it. It is as simple as that and this is the proper way to build up a business.' He went to see George Snell and explained his predicament. He was extremely upset to find himself in the position of being unable to honour his obligations, but he had a proposal to put to George. George had two horse-drawn grass cutters which he used regularly to cut the grass on the tennis courts. James offered to convert one of these into a motor mower in lieu of paying rent, as he felt confident that he could do a good job. He went to one of the local car dumps and bought an engine out of an old Ford car, built a gearbox for it and installed the engine and gearbox in the mower. George was delighted to accept this motorized mower in lieu of rent, and it revolutionized his life.

With his interest in engines and aeroplanes, it was not long before James became known at Napier. It was, in James's words, 'a very honest and hard-working engineering firm', and often he would call in there and have lunch with the managers. It was here that James found his first employee, Eric Stevens, who was a Napier apprentice. Eric's father had met James and was impressed by this fascinating Irishman who visited the factory and who seemed so informed about machine tools and engines and who was also so full of ideas. When Eric's apprenticeship was over, his father took him to see James. James gave Eric a bit of metal and said: 'Can you file that?' Obviously Eric could, and James decided to give him a job. This was in 1921, and it was a milestone in James's life: he had just taken on his first employee. He and Eric developed a close and harmonious relationship, and Eric worked for James for the rest of his life. He started work for 9d. an hour, but sometimes he had to wait to receive his pay when James had no money. But because of his faith in James, or perhaps simply because he liked the job, Eric was loyal to James, and few people today can remember James without Eric by his side.

James was always looking for work. He would visit the car dumps to see what he could buy or salvage. Sometimes there would be an old engine which could be repaired and sold or taken apart for spare parts for another job. He would dismantle these engines and examine them closely to see what he could learn and how they could be improved: in some cases he claims to have been able to improve the fuel consumption. During his reconnaissance trips around the neighbourhood he discovered a depot in nearby Slough which sold old army surplus Peerless lorries. James would overhaul and modify the engines, repair the bodywork and then sell them on. He was able to buy wooden frameworks locally and sometimes he would rebuild lorries with these new frameworks on the old chassis, and then sell the reconstructed lorries to a depot in Uxbridge.

Soon James began to experiment with his own frameworks for lorries, and began to build one-off, specialized road vehicles such as trailers and vans. The design of these was always straightforward and practical: simple, square boxes on wheels. With Eric's help, he did as much of the work as he could himself. James was an accomplished blacksmith and a proficient worker with a hammer and forge. He had a big engine in the corner of the barn which drove the second-hand machinery which he acquired and reconditioned when funds allowed. He and Eric made a good team and gradually James began to build up a small business.

In November 1923 James applied for a patent for a new design for a body frame for vehicles, the object of which was to provide a form of construction that would give great strength but which would at the same time be light and cheap to produce. The framework was a normal box-like framework, but James's idea was to brace each of the eight corners by members which extended across the three right-angle surfaces at each corner, and to adapt the lower horizontal girders so that they could be connected to springs which would support the wheels of the vehicle. The body frame was fitted with battens so that a covering material could be fixed to form an enclosed lorry. This time James was determined not to be defeated by the tiresome machinations of bureaucracy, and he employed a patent agent, George Raynor, to ensure that the necessary formalities were satisfied, and the patent was duly accepted in January 1925. As regards selling his idea, however, James faced the same problems as he had with his speed alarm. His patented invention might well have been successful if manufactured and sold commercially, but James did not have the capacity to manufacture it in any numbers, and it would not have suited him to persuade somebody else to do that for him.

James was working morning, noon and night. George Snell used to tease him because he was always with Eric and never out with the ladies. James took it all in good heart. He felt that in his precarious financial state he was in no position to take on the responsibility of a wife, so there was no point in going out to meet potential candidates. Eric, however, was not quite so hard on himself, and in 1924 he married a young lady called Anne. According to James, 'it was she who married Eric actually as he was too busy working for me at the time to worry about buying wedding rings, etc'.

James's tinkering with engines and lorries was not, however, always in order to earn a living. James was extremely interested in car racing, and from about 1921 onwards he spent a lot of time at Brooklands, the home of the famous car racing track and the venue for many national and international events. He liked to talk to the people who drove there and to their mechanics and to study the cars. One car that particularly interested him was the Bugatti. In his own words, he was 'fascinated by the superb design and the detailed work on this car – it was years ahead of its time. The built-up disk crankshaft was right in design, short and stiff and the weight in the right place. The whole car was a masterpiece of high grade mechanical engineering'. This was high praise indeed from a man who had such faith in his own ability that he insisted on working alone so that he could have the freedom to develop his own designs in his own way.

Inevitably, it was only a matter of time before James decided that car racing was not a spectator sport and that he must participate. Eric was ideally qualified to be his riding mechanic and second driver and he shared James's enthusiasm for this latest idea. James had acquired a yellow French Salmson motor car which he endeavoured to modify for the purposes of competitive racing. He did a lot of work on the bodywork to change the shape, and in fact rebuilt the whole of the rear end of it, and he modified the engine. No official records exist of James's racing exploits at Brooklands, but several stories have survived. He made an attempt on the 24-hour record. He and Eric managed to complete about 19 hours before problems with the car forced them to retire. On another occasion he failed to turn up at a check point. The immediate reaction was that he must have crashed and people began to panic, but James appeared a few minutes later and went racing on. Apparently he had just stopped on the track to answer a call of nature. During another race, the shock absorbers failed and that meant near disaster. According to

Eric, they attempted to continue the race with Eric trying to hold the shock absorbers together – a hopeless task.

Undaunted, the indomitable pair set off for Ulster to try their luck in the Ulster Tourist Trophy race in August 1928. This was an ambitious objective as it was an international race with entrants from seven countries. It was a Le Mans-type race, that is, a race on closed roads and not on a race track. It was the first time that the British had tried to stage their own Continental-style motor race, and it seems to have lived up to all expectations. The circuit of nearly 13 miles is widely considered to have been the best ever used in Britain. Thousands of people arrived in Belfast the night before, in steamships, trains and cars, on foot and even in donkey carts. Jane had travelled to Ireland with James for this occasion and she and James's mother, Sarah, left the farm early on the Sunday morning to travel up to Belfast.

At eleven o'clock, Lord Craigavon, the Premier of Northern Ireland, started the race. Some 88 drivers and mechanics ran to their cars and started driving. James was racing with the best, as the entrants included teams from Lagonda, Alvis, Riley and Lea-Francis. Even the famous suffered their misadventures, and of the 44 starters, only 12 passed the finish. James completed eight out of the 30 laps, but disaster struck in the ninth at Comber where the brakes failed on a corner and the car ended up in a butcher's shop. It was a bad crash which destroyed the car, but which fortunately left James and Eric unscathed save for their wounded pride and shattered hopes.

This was the end of the Salmson car and James's racing exploits. He did not, however, lose his love of driving at speed: he continued to drive as fast as he liked but just gave up doing it competitively. Judging by some of the stories that are told about his fast driving, it is surprising that the Ulster TT seems to be the only occasion on which he crashed a car at speed. In later years he would terrify employees and visitors to Martin-Baker by 'driving like a maniac' through the narrow lanes of Buckinghamshire and Oxfordshire. As Don McGovern from McDonnell said: 'A ride with him in a car was an experience that no-one should have.'

Business must have improved a little by this time to have enabled James to enter the racing world, although it was largely James's do-it-yourself approach to modifying, maintaining and racing his car that allowed him to participate. Certainly his ideas were becoming more ambitious. He had already taken on another employee, Jim Chadwin, who had been studying at Acton College, and in 1928 he took on his third employee, Philip Clampitt. James thought that Philip was a rather posh name that did not really suit the lad or the style of the establishment he had come to work in. As the other new boy was called Jim, he decided to call Philip Jim, or Jim boy, too. And so Philip was renamed and remained Jim, at least for the purposes of his working life, ever after.

James was still interested in aeroplanes, and his second patent, applied for in March 1927 and registered later that year, related to an improved method for the construction of vehicle body frames, aircraft fuselage frames and other conveyors for transporting goods. The object was to provide a strong rigid metal frame which would, again, be light and cheap to produce. The most interesting thing about this patent is that it is one of only two patents which were registered by James jointly with someone else, in this case John Campbell. James was very much a loner and he had a possessiveness about his inventions which would normally preclude any joint venture. He always liked the ideas to be his own, and he found it difficult to accept a suggestion from somebody else until he had had a little time to digest it and could re-present it in a later discussion as his own. Perhaps the realities of life had caused James to think that co-operation with someone else might be advisable. In 1927 he was 34 years old and still had no established line of business. Any knowledge that he had about aircraft construction would be only what he had gleaned from watching the construction of Harry Ferguson's monoplane and talking to the men working on it.

The partnership with John Campbell was brief, and in July 1929 James applied for another patent, again relating to the construction of body frames for vehicles, aircraft fuselage frames and other conveyors for transporting goods, and also for aeroplane wings and spars. This time the application was in his name only. It was clearly a further development of the ideas that he had worked on with John Campbell, the object being to facilitate the assembly of girders and brackets, to reduce the weight of the connecting parts without reducing the strength of the connections or of the structure as a whole, and to reduce to a minimum the extraneous projections from the completed assembly. Obviously not satisfied with the previous patent, he had continued working on the ideas in order to improve them, a trait which was to become more obvious in later years.

Private flying was becoming popular at this time, at least among the more affluent members of society, and it was as much a spectator sport as a participating activity. It was almost inevitable that James, with his interest in aeroplanes, should start to frequent the flying clubs, and in 1928 he started visiting the London Aero Club at Stag Lane on a regular basis. After his car racing aspirations had been shattered along with his car in the butcher's shop at Comber, James was looking for another interest. Flying seemed likely to provide something of the thrills and excitement of car racing, and he started taking flying lessons with Valentine Baker. His lack of financial resources meant that learning to fly was a slow process and it was not until 1934 that he gained his pilot's licence. In the days when only a few hours' solo flying and a simple flying test were required in order to obtain a licence, this indicates that his flying lessons must have been few and far between.

It seems that everyone liked Valentine Baker and that he was universally admired and respected as an instructor. James remembered him as 'a wonderful instructor; so natural, no excitement, and it was easy to understand what he wanted you to do'. He was a cheerful and engaging man who endeared himself to the flying club fraternity, not just as a pilot and teacher, but as a friend and companion too. Although very different people, he and James struck up an immediate rapport, out of which grew an extraordinary friendship.

Baker had spent most of his adult life in the Services, and had managed to serve in all three before he returned to civilian life. Born on 24 August 1888, Henry Valentine Baker was the third and youngest son of Mr and Mrs J.M. Baker of Llanfairfechan in North Wales. He was 26 when the First World War broke out, and he joined the Royal Naval Air Service (Armoured Cars Section) as a dispatch rider. He took part in the first landing at Gallipolli, and during the fighting on the beaches there he was severely wounded by a bullet in the neck. It was a lucky escape, because the bullet was lodged very close to the spinal nerve system, too close in fact for the doctors to operate to remove it without a serious risk to Baker's life. And so it stayed there, and it is a tribute to this gallant man that his legendary good humour never betrayed his discomfort. He was discharged as unfit and sent back to England, but this did not suit his nationalistic fervour and sense of duty. He volunteered for military service again and was accepted for the Royal Welch Fusiliers, becoming a Second Lieutenant in November 1915. In the spring of the next year he got the opportunity he had been hoping for: the chance to become an aviator. He was posted to the School of Aero Flying at Reading and from there to the Central Flying School where he graduated as a flying officer of the new Royal Flying Corps. A month later he joined 41 Squadron with which he served all his operational flying.

Baker completed nearly nine months' active flying in France, during which time most of his original comrades in 41 Squadron were killed or badly wounded. He crashed several times but managed to escape unhurt. He gained a reputation as a brave and successful fighter and is reputed to have shot down over 15 German aircraft. He was awarded the Military Cross and later the Air Force Cross.

In 1921 he returned to civilian life. He spent three years working for Vickers-Armstrongs Limited in the Dutch East Indies and later Chile and then returned to England and took up the appointment of flying instructor to the Lancashire Flying Club, and then of chief flying instructor at Stag Lane.

In Baker, the highly talented aviator, James found someone with whom he could share his ideas and plans. James had already given some considerable thought to the problems of constructing aeroplanes. He was learning to fly and gaining some knowledge and experience of aerodynamics, and so it was inevitable that the two would talk about aeroplanes and the ways in which they might be improved, and Baker would have been able to provide an exceptional stimulus to these discussions.

In the meantime, James got to know many of the flying 'crowd' at Stag Lane, and one of the people he came to know best was Amy Johnson, one of Baker's pupils, who had started her flying lessons in 1928, and who was always to be found at the clubhouse at weekends if she was not in the air. She was galvanized by the prejudice against women flyers; not only did she want to learn to fly, but she wanted to make a name for herself as a flyer. One day James said to her: 'Why don't you fly to Australia and make a name for yourself that way?' Was this the first time that the idea had been put into Amy's head? Perhaps it was. Certainly James was to be involved in the preparations for this epic journey which took place in 1930.

Meanwhile, it was becoming clear to James that his ideas were outgrowing his premises and that he needed more space. Engines and lorries had provided him with a small income over the last ten years, but there seemed little to be gained by continuing in this line of business. Aeroplanes had now replaced lorries as far as James's design aspirations were concerned, and a barn in Acton was not a suitable place in which to build them. He began a search for new premises and better buildings, and in April 1929 he visited the building exhibition at Olympia. He bought a pre-fabricated steel building and returned the next day to supervise its dismantling. Unfortunately, the exhibition workmen did not work fast enough for James and he climbed up onto the erection in order to help them, from where he fell backwards about 30 ft onto a concrete base. He suffered a severe blow to the head and it was felt that he should be taken to hospital. James, stunned though he was, would hear none of this, and went home on the bus. He was suffering from extreme pain in his head and blood was trickling out of his left ear. When he arrived home to his sister Jane there was no debate, and he was taken to Hammersmith Hospital where he was admitted with a fractured skull.

James was not pleased to be in hospital. He argued with the medical staff that he be allowed to go home, but they were adamant that with his head injuries he must stay in hospital and rest. But James was never one to be defeated by rules and regulations and he certainly did not like to be idle. He waited until visiting time was nearly over, and sundry visitors were making their way out of the hospital. Then he quickly dressed and sauntered out with a group of departing visitors and took the bus home again. Unfortunately, he did not get the welcome he wanted, and he was returned to hospital. The accident left him permanently deaf in one ear, but otherwise he made a complete recovery and resumed the search for new workshop accommodation as soon as he was able.

By then, Jane had moved down to Gerrards Cross in Buckinghamshire to live, and he made enquiries in that area to see what was available. He travelled down from Acton and looked down from the top of a hill. There was a garage on the side of the road, and a little further away, a disused factory. The garage looked ideal for his purposes but unfortunately it had recently changed hands and the new owner was not minded to sell, so he went on to look at the factory premises. The existing buildings were vastly more extensive than his premises in Acton and there was ample space to expand. They were also close to Denham village, which was not far from Gerrards Cross. His long-suffering brother-in-law was persuaded that this property would be a good investment, and the factory was duly purchased by Edwin and leased to James. On 3 August 1929, James left Friars Place Farm and set out for Denham.

Chapter Four

The First Aircraft

For the journey to Denham, James hired a horse and cart which was packed up with his few machine tools and other engineering equipment from the workshop in Acton. Eric and his wife and Jim Clampitt came with him. No-one had thought to bring any food with them, so when they arrived the first job was to organize a meal. James sent Eric off to the local butcher's shop to get some meat. He arrived back with the meat but nothing to go with it, so James started his life in Denham with a picnic of meat cooked on a shovel over an open fire.

The somewhat disreputable premises that James had taken over were at the end of a long, rough lane. Originally an army camp in the First World War, they had later been used as a linoleum factory. There was a long, single-storey wood and breeze block factory building, a small wooden building with offices in it and some open space. There was no water, the nearest water supply being the nearby marsh, no drainage and no telephone. Nevertheless, it had potential (Martin-Baker still occupies the site today), and there was nothing wrong with it that they could not put right. They set to work to clean up the site and set up the machine tools. Once again self-help and self-sufficiency were the order of the day, for James was in no position to hire extra workmen to help him. But at this stage in his life, there was not much in the way of general repair work that he could not do himself.

James had come to Denham with the ambition to build aeroplanes. Even in those days, when aircraft construction was a relatively simple process compared to what it is today, it was undoubtedly a formidable and probably unrealistic objective to set out to build aeroplanes with a work-force of two and no relevant experience or training, but it was typical of James to be unconcerned by the problems that he faced, at least as far as his design work was concerned. Never having built an aeroplane before, he was perhaps not sufficiently aware of the difficulties that this task would present, but being a practical and not a theoretical engineer, he felt sure that there was nothing that determination and hard work could not achieve. It is apparent from the patents that James registered in the 1920s that the hallmark of his design work was straightforward practicability, and it was the straightforward, practical approach that he wanted to introduce into aeroplane construction.

The factory was called Martin's Aircraft Works, although the notepaper at that time states that Martin's Aircraft Works were manufacturers of Martin's integral construction and Martin's patent propeller shafts. Martin's integral construction was clearly a reference to the vehicle and fuselage construction methods which he patented while working in Acton, but the reference to Martin's patent propeller shafts was a little premature. It was a month after he arrived in Denham that he and Percy Waterman Pitt lodged a joint patent application relating to a better way of arranging and constructing an aeroplane, including the positioning of the propeller shaft, and it was not until March 1931 that it was accepted. Pitt had a certain amount of money as well as a great deal of enthusiasm for his own inventive flair, and he had agreed to contribute some financial backing for the construction by James of an aeroplane incorporating these new ideas.

One of the problems of private flying at that time was the rather crude and elementary nature of the aircraft available. The pilot and any passenger sat behind the engine in an open cockpit, which meant that they sat immediately behind, and were exposed to, the heat, noise and fumes produced by the engine. There was obviously a certain amount of discomfort which had to be endured by those seeking the thrill of private flying, and James had decided, in his usual practical way, to try and do something about this.

The object of the new design was to construct an aeroplane in a way that would give particularly good visibility to the occupants and which, while retaining the tractor form of drive with the propeller at the front of the aeroplane, would allow the engine to be located behind the occupants, thus alleviating the unpleasantness experienced when sitting behind the engine.

James threw all his efforts into putting his ideas to the test, and started to build his first aeroplane immediately. It was unconventional at that time in that it was a low-wing monoplane, and the two occupants sat side by side in front of the engine, which drove a fixed pitch propeller in the nose via a 5 ft long shaft which passed between the pilot and passenger. The engine was housed in a sound-damping, fireproof compartment in the fuselage and was cooled by a large fan driven by the engine. There is some debate as to which engine was used for this aircraft, but it was probably a 120 hp Cirrus Hermes engine.

The project got off to a good start and James kept Baker appraised of progress. Baker had by this time left his job at Stag Lane and had accepted the post of chief flying instructor at the new flying school at Heston. James and Baker would often meet for dinner and discuss this new aeroplane. In addition to the new configuration, the aircraft was designed to have a low stalling speed and to be economical to operate and easy to maintain. Amy Johnson was often there and, during the course of their discussions, James decided that Amy should fly this aeroplane. The idea appealed to Amy: no longer would she be just another private flyer, she would also be a test pilot, and as far as James was concerned, a lady test pilot might be a good bit of publicity for him. Looking back, it is interesting to note that it was Amy who was intended to fly this aeroplane and not Baker, but as Baker had only recently started instructing at Heston, it was perhaps early days for him to be thinking of extra-curricular activities such as test flying.

James promised Amy that he would build her an aeroplane, and this was to be her machine. No record has survived of exactly when the construction started and when it stopped, and the best indications are those gleaned from Amy's letters. She wrote to her mother telling her about the possibility of

> a splendid job for me about Christmas . . . The job would be that of demonstrator of an entirely new machine which is being built now. All the people in the concern are friends of mine and it will be ideal if it comes off. However, one never knows with a new machine. There is such keen competition to face from the popular ones already on the market.

This letter was written on 9 September 1929 and indicates that James had wasted no time in getting to work.

Amy visited the works at Denham as often as possible to observe the progress of this new machine. She was tremendously excited about the whole project and wrote to her mother: 'It's all very secret but I am in the secret. It's a machine I hope to demonstrate some day and if everything comes off as planned it's going to make my reputation. And I'm going to make its.' This letter was written in November, but despite the previous references to Christmas, there is no mention of an imminent completion of the project.

Unfortunately, everything did not come off as planned. In March 1930, Amy wrote to her mother: 'Tomorrow I'm going to Denham to see how the machine is getting on . . . I am going to help with the wings myself.' The wings were never completed, because James ran out of money. The construction of the aeroplane was quite well advanced: the fuselage, engine mountings, tailplane and rudder were finished, and engine runs had been successfully undertaken. Pitt had agreed to provide James with the engine, but as the Depression set in, he met his own financial pressures and eventually had to ask James to return it. As James could not afford to buy a replacement engine, the construction of this first aeroplane came to an abrupt halt. It was a bitter blow to James. Again and again it was lack of money that proved to be his biggest problem. In later years he wrote to a friend in Ireland: 'If I had only a fraction of what I have now so many years ago, what a difference it would have made.' We can only guess how big a difference.

Financial difficulties were something that Amy was well acquainted with, and she must have had some sympathy for James's situation. She was disappointed when the project was finally abandoned, but she did not let this unhappy situation colour her friendship with James. By this time she was planning her solo flight to Australia, and James was involved in these preparations.

Later that year, on 4 May, she flew her aeroplane from Stag Lane to Croydon in preparation for her departure. James was there to meet her, to fuel up the aeroplane in preparation for the next morning, and to make sure that it was safely stowed away for the night. Amy was to carry a spare propeller, strapped to the fuselage of the aeroplane. They were worried that it might be sabotaged during the night so, for safe keeping, James took the propeller home and it spent the night in the front hall propped up against the staircase. History does not relate what Edwin had to say about this overnight visitor.

Early the next morning, James returned to Croydon with the spare propeller which was strapped in place. Someone noticed a smell of petrol, the cause of which was a leaking pipe connection. James set to work to remedy the problem as quickly as possible. Back in the cockpit, Amy realized that her watch was not working. James unstrapped his and handed it up to her. Her first take-off run was abortive. With the extra equipment and fuel, the aeroplane lumbered down the airfield but clearly was not going to make it over the boundary fence. James did a few quick calculations, walked to where Amy had taxied back to try another take-off run, and then paced out the required length. He told her to pull back the stick and take off when she drew level with him. She followed James's instructions and slowly the heavily laden aeroplane lifted up into the sky.

Amy had asked James to try to sell her story to one of the London newspapers. James remembered this situation well. He went up to Fleet Street on the morning of her departure and visited the offices of the *Daily Mail* and the *Daily Express* without success. He finally procured an offer of £1,000 from the *News of the World* which he did not accept because it was too low. Within a few days, however, Amy's flight was causing great interest in the newspaper world, and the *Daily Mail* finally offered him £10,000 for the story, which he accepted on her behalf.

James, however, remained in dire need of money himself. Having abandoned his aeroplane, he clearly needed a project which was cheap and quick to produce, and which would not require much testing in order to prove its worth. In short, he needed something to sell, and he set to work on an idea for a wind indicator. Aircraft need to land into the wind, and in the days when small aircraft had no ground-to-air radio facilities, pilots had to be able to work out the wind direction for themselves. Some airfields used windsocks, but these of course were no use at night or when there was very little wind.

In February 1931, James applied for a patent for a wind indicator for aerodromes. It was a light hollow body shaped to act as a pointer with an arrow head at one end which rotated on its base. It was about 30 ft long, and therefore easily visible from the sky, and had four light bulbs on the head and six on the tail so that it could be seen at night. It was an ingenious device: it contained a damping mechanism to stop it swaying with each little gust of wind, and another mechanism which caused the arrow to return to a predetermined position if there was no wind at all so that pilots could choose to land in whatever direction was most suitable to the aerodrome. It could be mounted on the ground or elsewhere, such as the top of an aircraft hanger, and was hinged in the centre so that when a light bulb had to be replaced the body could be folded round its hinges to bring the light bulb within reach. It was a typical Martin invention: simple and straightforward. It addressed all the problems that needed to be dealt with, and was easy to maintain. One of these indicators was erected at Heston Aerodrome, but despite that, no orders were forthcoming for it. James remained convinced that the idea was a good one and in February 1935 he produced a revised version. There was hope of an order from the Crown Colonies, but it never materialized, and although he managed to sell two of these indicators, James finally had to accept that there was no future for them.

By this time Baker had acquired a new pupil at the Heston flying school who was to have a dramatic impact on the lives of both James and Baker. The man was Francis Francis. Born on 28 May 1906, he was therefore quite a few years younger than them. He was an exceptional character, extremely talented and a brilliant athlete. He won the Saddle at Sandhurst which he entered in January 1925, passing out from the college in July 1926 when he was commissioned a second lieutenant in the Royal Horse Guards (The Blues). He was asked to represent Great Britain in the 1928 Olympics in three sports: riding, middle distance running and fencing, but unfortunately he contracted diphtheria shortly before the Olympics and had to withdraw. Despite his prowess at these three sports, his real passion was golf and he went on to win many international events.

Francis did not spend long in the army. The ceremonial duties did not interest him: he felt he was little more than a painted policeman. But he had an eye for the ladies, and they for him. Tall, charming and very good-looking, he was the archetypal dashing Guards officer. He fell for a popular American actress, Sonny Jarman. In those days, Guards officers were not allowed to marry actresses, and his commanding officer made it clear to him that he had to make a choice between his army career and Sonny. The choice was easy. Bored with the army, he had recently inherited a sizeable fortune from his grandparents (his grandfather was one of the founders of The Standard Oil Company) and he had no need for a mundane job and a small salary. In 1930, he resigned his commission and married Sonny.

About this time he started taking flying lessons at Heston and met Baker, and the two of them quickly became friends. Francis had a great interest in aviation, and having learned to fly, he went on to buy several private aircraft of his own. Baker, by now a close friend of James's, realized that Francis, with his love of flying and his private fortune, might be prepared to finance James's work. Baker introduced them and they took to each other immediately. They were three very different men but all with a common interest in aeroplanes, and their friendship has been described as magic. The interreaction between them could be electric. Tuned into each other, they exchanged ideas with an equal abundance of enthusiasm.

Francis was delighted to become involved in an aeroplane project, and it was soon agreed that he would fund the building by James of another aeroplane, later designated the MB1, which would be a small aeroplane for civilian use. The idea was to produce a machine which was cheap, easy and quick to manufacture and maintain, and which could be marketed to the ever-growing number of private flying enthusiasts. James obviously thought that he could build it as quickly as he had the first aircraft, for a report in the February 1931 edition of *Flight* stated that he had, in collaboration with Baker, produced a novel design of aeroplane which would make its appearance in the spring. In fact, the completion of the MB1 was still several years away.

The MB1 was a two-seater, single-engined, low-wing monoplane. James had discarded his idea for situating the engine in the centre of the fuselage, and the pilot and passenger sat one behind the other behind the engine, which was installed in the more conventional position at the front of the aeroplane, driving a fixed pitch wooden propeller. The engine was a Napier Javelin Series 3A which Napier had agreed to loan him for the purposes of producing a prototype. The aeroplane therefore looked fairly conventional, but James was determined to simplify the whole basis of aeroplane construction. He devised an ingenious method of building the fuselage out of steel tubes, a system of lattice girder construction which was both simple and economical. The fuselage was made of four tubular longerons with tubular cross bracing struts. Short sleeves were inserted into the longerons and moved to the point where the cross struts were to connect. Each sleeve had a nut brazed to the inside. With a hole in the sleeve lined up with a hole in the longeron, a stud was screwed into the nut through the longeron, thus receiving the sleeve and providing a stud for connection of the cross strut. The tubular cross struts had flattened ends through which a hole had been drilled to accept the stud, and a further nut and shaped washers completed the joint. The result was a method of attachment which was very strong and which made the construction of the aircraft and the replacement of parts straightforward.

The centre and front sections of the fuselage had short lengths of longerons terminating in machined fork ends which were bolted to fittings to which the bracing members were attached in the same way. The fuselage was shaped by using brazed, small-diameter tubes which were attached to the longerons by simple clamp fittings. Stainless steel stringers were simply clipped to these formers by springing them between small claws brazed to the formers.

The construction of the wing was similar to that of the fuselage, with the main spar consisting of three large-diameter steel tubes of constant diameter arranged as points on a triangle tapering towards each other as they approached the wing tips, and braced in the same way as the fuselage main structure. The outer wings were designed so that they could fold backwards and thus reduce the space taken up by the aeroplane when it was parked, an exercise which could be undertaken by one person alone. The windscreen was V-shaped with vertical front panes designed so that it would remain clear in rain or snow and minimize reflections. Although his main efforts were concentrated on producing a simple, efficient and practical design, James also gave considerable thought to the cockpit layout and the means of getting into it, and insisted on a high standard of finish. This was to be an aircraft for the manufacturer, the maintainer and the pilot: their different interests were all addressed.

As the MB1 progressed, so did the enthusiasm for it. Baker and Francis fell under James's spell. His irrepressible spirit, his own personal mix of imagination and determination, captivated them both. Francis, however, had inherited some of his grandfather's business acumen and realized that this *ad hoc* funding of a new aeroplane was no basis for a successful business. When it became apparent to him that James could indeed produce a worthwhile machine, he became concerned to formalize the business arrangements between the three of them. He suggested to James and Baker that they should set up a company which would take over the business of Martin's Aircraft Works and that he would finance the company. For Francis, with a private fortune and no career, the idea of setting up an aircraft company was very attractive. For Baker, with years of flying experience, the prospect of combining flying with a business that might make him some money was irresistible. And for James, at the age of 41, with a lifetime of design work behind him but little to show for it, the opportunity of having a company with the financial resources to enable him to build the superlative aircraft he believed he was capable of was the answer to his prayers.

Their objectives were not of course exactly the same. As Francis himself later remarked: 'The trouble with this company is that we all want something different. Val wants to make as much money as possible, I want to build up a successful company, and James wants to build the best aircraft.' But despite their different priorities, the company was formed.

Chapter Five

The Start of Martin-Baker

Martin-Baker Aircraft Company Limited was duly incorporated on 17 August 1934. As the financial backer with several other business interests, Francis felt that it would be inappropriate for his name to be included in the name of the company, and he was happy that the company should bear the name of the designer and the test pilot. He employed Fladgates, the solicitors who advised on his other business concerns, to form the company and prepare the necessary documents. All three men were appointed directors. James agreed to work full-time for the company and to contribute certain of his patents, and in return he received 6,500 shares in the company. Baker agreed to test fly the prototype aeroplanes manufactured by the company, in return for which he received 6,500 deferred shares. Francis purchased 3,000 shares for cash and transferred to the company certain assets that he had paid for over the previous years when he had been financing James's work, including the MB1, now in flying trim, and certain machine tools.

It was still a very small concern in 1934. Apart from James, Eric Stevens and Jim Clampitt, there were only three other workers, although quite a few more were employed over the next few years. Baker visited occasionally, and sometimes he would arrive with his friend, Mrs Packenham, to show her what progress the company was making. Throughout their extraordinarily close friendship, the only friction that anyone can remember between James and Baker was caused by Baker's relationship with Mrs Packenham. Baker had a wife and James disapproved strongly of his liaison with Mrs Packenham, not for any reason relating to the lady herself, but purely as a matter of principle. He believed that once a man had assumed the responsibility of a wife, he should honour that responsibility, and other women in his life were quite improper. He had a horror that there might be a divorce, and that somehow or other he or the company might be involved. This did not happen, but James still continued to disapprove of this state of affairs.

Francis was rarely seen in the office, and is remembered by the employees then as the man they called upon when they ran out of money, which they frequently did. James went through money easily. His approach to design work was not cost-effective as ideas were continually revised or abandoned. Money was no object, it had to be no object, because he had to get it right. It made him cross when work went on the scrap heap because he did not like to waste money, but he was not put off by it. And he was always anxious to improve and upgrade his factory by installing new machine tools. He would convince Francis of the necessity for them, and he spent a lot of money this way.

Francis suggested that the time had come for James to have a secretary. James had no idea how to find such a person, and he turned to one of his friends, Lady Gracie Drummond-Hay, who ran her own office up in London, to find one for him. She was an aviation journalist and a private flyer whom James had met at Heston. He was impressed by her judgement and abilities and would often turn to her for advice. Gracie answered an advertisement in *The Times* for a secretary seeking employment, preferably outside London, who had a knowledge of engineering terms, and arranged for the lady who had placed it, Helen Adamson, to meet James. Miss Adamson recalls this first meeting vividly. There was no interview, and no discussion about the job. Miss Adamson had worked for Harland & Wolff, the Irish shipbuilders based in Belfast, and James simply said that if she was good enough for Harland & Wolff, she was good enough for him. He announced that he would take her by car to see the factory. On the way they went over a hump-back bridge and James deliberately accelerated as they approached it. They flew over the top of the bridge, and Miss Adamson laughed. She concluded afterwards that this must have been some sort of test to see how she would react. They arrived at Denham, James showed her around and then asked her when she was going to start. Miss Adamson was rather taken aback by this somewhat unusual manner of choosing a secretary, but accepted the job nevertheless.

She found herself doing everything in the office that needed doing and not just the secretarial work, but once she had settled down and got advice when necessary, she was happy enough. There was only one small cloud on the horizon and that concerned holidays. These were frowned upon. James was not interested in holidays, and did not think that anyone else should be. He did not want people working in the factory who were not committed to their work, and if they enjoyed their work, they did not need a holiday from it.

Despite this, Miss Adamson got on well with James. She was a calm, organized lady who spoke her mind and James liked that. On one occasion, she took him to task over one of the men he employed as a panel beater. This man was good at his job, but he used to disappear from the factory during the week and go to Wembley where he would spend all his money betting on the dogs. Then he would want to work all Sunday on double pay to make up the money he had lost. Miss Adamson told James that he must not allow this sort of thing to carry on, because it was not fair to the other men. James was reluctant to remonstrate with the man because he was a good worker and James liked him, but in the end, Miss Adamson got her way, and the man in question did not get his Sunday double time unless he had put in a certain number of hours during the week.

This incident reveals quite a lot about James. One of the most important things about working for him was whether or not your face fitted. It has always been generally accepted at Martin-Baker that if James did not like someone then that person might as well find themselves another job, as they would have no future in the firm. James wanted to be surrounded by people he liked, people he thought were good at their job and who were prepared to do things his way. He was not interested in demarcation among his work-force. As long as you did what you were told and did it well, that was all that mattered. Harold Roxbee Cox (later Lord Kings Norton) visited the factory one day when he was head of the Air Defence Department at the Royal Aircraft Establishment and saw two men who he knew were machine tool operators doing some brick-laying. They did not mind: that was the sort of thing that happened when you worked for James. If something needed doing then someone had to do it. It was typical of the man.

He did not like people who took notes: they annoyed him intensely, because he felt that a person was no use to him if he needed to write things down. And there was no point in contradicting him or arguing with him, because it only made him cross. His answer was always that that was the way he wanted it, so that was that. But although he could be very hot-tempered, particularly in those early days, his anger never lasted long. It was more of an explosion, and then it was all over and he was equable again.

As a practical engineer with a love of machine tools, he was always happy in the environment of the shop-floor. The men operating the machines were important to him because as far as he was concerned, they were the only people who made him any money. It is often said that he could do the job of any man that he employed, and in these early days, this was certainly the case. If he thought that someone was not doing something quite right, he would take over operating the machine in question and show them how to do it properly, or at least the way that he would do it, which was usually, but not always, the same.

He was certainly demanding to work for, but then it was recognized that he was demanding on himself also. Second best was always totally unacceptable and compromises in design work were never contemplated. But some of his employees felt that he was perhaps deliberately very demanding, and that he had no real expectation of his demands bearing fruit. In other words, he felt that if he asked for too much, what he got would be better than what he would get if he asked for less. In any event, there was often no hope of what he asked for ever being delivered. Having issued instructions for a job which might take two or three days, he would sometimes return 20 minutes later with another idea which superseded the job in hand, or with another job which had to take priority over the job already started.

His mind was constantly active, reworking ideas, changing his designs, always trying to improve on what he had already produced. It was a trait which remained with him throughout his life. Only the best was good enough and any amount of hard work was justified and indeed required if there was still room for improvement. 'Throw it away', he would snarl when the drawings were not what he wanted. It did not matter to him how many times a man had to start again or how irritated the draughtsman got with the continued changes. Particularly in the early days, he was not good at making up his mind about designs. And many times, of course, he came back to the original idea, or something close to it. But he liked to be sure that he had exhausted every possible avenue.

Despite his perfectionist approach, he was not good at concentrating on one idea until he had developed it fully before moving on to the next. His mind jumped from one idea to another. Halfway through a conversation, the person talking to him would sometimes realize that he was no longer hearing what they were saying. He had started to think about something else and would dismiss the person on some pretext so that he could follow his thoughts.

Notwithstanding his ambition to build aeroplanes, many believe that he was an engineer before anything else. He was continually coming up with new ideas for gadgets and devices, covering a wide spectrum of uses: bicycles with hoods to protect the rider from the rain, baths with shower attachments and curtains. About this time he prepared drawings for a small three-wheeler motor car for one person, but he never followed it up. When he needed a small piece of equipment he would often design something for himself, be it a device for sharpening tools or a fish fryer for the canteen. His creative talents were manifest, but he seemed to lack the discipline to sort out the wheat from the chaff and follow through on his good ideas. It was up to Francis to harness this creative ability. As Miss Adamson said: 'If it had not been for Captain Baker introducing him to Mr Francis, I doubt if he would have got as far as he did with Martin-Baker.'

James's daily routine was unaltered by the formation of Martin-Baker and the growth of the company. He would arrive at the factory early, nobody quite knows when because he was always the first to arrive. Those who worked closely with James would gather in Eric's office at about eight o'clock and there would be a discussion of what had happened the previous day and what was going to happen that day and the next day. Then James would return to his own office with Eric and a few others and they would all have tea. During the day he would work in his own office or walk around the factory to see how everyone was doing. He walked quietly, and would come up behind people unawares. The first that they would know about it was his iron grip on their shoulder or arm, for he was an immensely strong man, and an enquiry as to how they were doing in his soft voice and unmistakable Ulster accent. Sometimes he would go home for lunch, but often, if he was particularly engrossed in thinking through an idea or a problem, he would stay on. There was no particular time for stopping work as far as James was

concerned. Sometimes his sister, Jane, would come down and insist that
he come home, sometimes he would just carry on working. It was not
unheard of for him to spend all night at the factory, and catch a few
hours' sleep on the floor, or with his head on the desk, before starting
out on a new day.

At home in the evenings, James would carry on working. He would
sit with a large pad of paper, writing down his thoughts and sketching
new ideas. These notes would be produced the next morning at the eight
o'clock meeting and he would enlarge upon his ideas or scrap them if
he had had a better idea in the meantime. Design work was not a science
that took place at the drawing board, and in fact he never used a drawing
board. Ideas spilled out of his mind onto paper. He would explain what
he meant by a series of rough drawings, and then it would be for the
drawing office staff to make what they could of it. There was a certain art
to deciphering these scribbles correctly. Even James himself did not
always know exactly what he wanted, but he would always recognize it
when he saw it. He would prowl round the drawing office at night when
everyone else had gone home, and people knew to be slightly
apprehensive when they arrived in the morning. On a good morning
there would be some complimentary remark on the side of the drawing
written in his unmistakable handwriting and thick-nibbed pen; on other
mornings there would be a thick line through the previous day's work
and some comment such as 'Rubbish' written across it. At least the
draughtsmen were never in any doubt as to how well they were
interpreting his ideas.

But despite the frustrations of working for him, the work-force were
utterly committed to their jobs and devoted to him. One of James's
attributes was an ability to instil a drive and enthusiasm into the people
working for him. In those early days the men were often working
phenomenal hours, but they were happy to do so. Although they will
admit that he was sometimes difficult to work for, no criticism of him
by anyone else is allowed. He aroused in them a quite extraordinary
degree of loyalty and affection. Those working for him, both then and in
his later life, remember particularly the fact that he always had time for
them. James wanted to understand his work-force, and he liked to talk
to them, enquiring after their families and making sure that everyone
was managing. If they needed help and he was in a position to give it,
he did. He was genuinely interested in their happiness and well-being
and this direct contact between 'the guv'nor' or 'the old man', as he was
affectionately referred to, and the workers was part of the character of
life at Martin-Baker. Even when the company expanded and, inevitably,
it became more difficult to know everyone as well as he would have liked,
James continued to take an interest whenever he could, and it is this
kindness and concern that he is best remembered for. Lord Kings Norton
summed up the situation when he said: 'The man was an autocrat, but
he was the ideal benevolent autocrat. He did everything for everybody.
He was one of the kindest men I have ever known. He ran his own show,

he ran it his way, but he ran it a way which people enjoyed.' This comment was equally true of James in later years too, for he never changed the way he worked or the way he ran his factory.

The work on the MB1 was James's major project at this time, but as Baker and Francis came to the factory infrequently, James was left to continue in his own way and the MB1 was a long time in the making. When it was nearing completion, James was approached by Mr Raoul Hafner, an Austrian who had moved to England in 1932, in connection with his latest design for a gyroplane. Mr Hafner had already built several small helicopters, and James was intrigued with these new machines. He agreed that Hafner's latest design would be built by Martin-Baker on a 'cost-plus' basis. If successful, it might provide an interesting source of income for the company while James was working on his aeroplane. It was a small, single-seat machine which was duly completed and flown by Baker at Heston in September 1935. James was singularly unimpressed by it when he saw it demonstrated, and he quickly lost interest. It was sold to Hafner for £930, which represented a negligible profit to the company, and the relationship with Hafner ended there. With the MB1 finally completed, James did not have time for other people's machines that did not work as he thought they should.

The MB1 was completed in the spring of 1935. It was painted black and registered G-ADCS. Its wings were folded backwards and it was towed along the main road to RAF Northolt for its first flight. It was sometime in March or April of that year that Baker settled himself into the cockpit, looked around at the familiar interior, started the Napier Javelin engine and began his take-off run. The flight was highly successful. It was a momentous moment for James as he watched 'his' aeroplane accelerate down the runway and up into the sky. His faith in himself and in the talents which his Lord had given him was justified. The aircraft performed well and fulfilled all expectations. There was jubilation at the factory that day. It was still early days in the life of Martin-Baker and the work-force were certainly justified in feeling a great sense of achievement, but unfortunately this did not last long. A market had to be found for the aeroplane, but the climate was not good for new ventures such as this. In the aftermath of the Depression, it was a bad time to be trying to sell a new private aeroplane. Baker flew it at Heston, where he and James had the opportunity of expounding its virtues to the flying fraternity there, but try as they might, they could find no takers for it.

A contemporary report in *Aeroplane* expressed the view that many potential purchasers would consider that the aircraft was over powered for a two-seater aeroplane, but that nevertheless there would probably be some who would be interested in 'a very finely built machine of this class, in which no expense has been spared to make every detail perfect'. The report continued:

. . . its real interest lies rather in its entirely novel construction than in the machine as a type. If it shows itself in its flying tests to have a reasonably good performance, the new type of structure will have vindicated itself and the Martin-Baker Aircraft Company will then be able to make the best use of the potentialities of this kind of construction by producing peculiarly robust high-performance machines which are cheap to build.

The novel construction had indeed been vindicated in the flight trials and James was not yet prepared to give up his ambition to bring practicality and simplicity into aircraft design. Already he was scheming other aeroplane projects, and having failed to find a market for his civilian aeroplane, he decided to build a military one. The Air Ministry had recently released a new Specification, F.5/34, for a new fighter aeroplane. There was clearly no point in this embryonic company approaching the Ministry for a contract, but Francis was sufficiently enthusiastic about the idea and well impressed by James's abilities to agree to finance the building of another prototype, this time to the Air Ministry Specification. This aeroplane became known as the MB2 and was the next aeroplane to be produced by Martin-Baker, although James did in the meantime consider some ideas for other aircraft, including in 1936 a twin-engined, single-seater fighter to be built to Specification F.33/35. This aeroplane did not get beyond the initial project stage, but with twelve .303 inch machine guns in four banks of three mounted on the fuselage, it would have been one of the most heavily armed fighters of the time. James proposed the Rolls-Royce Merlin engines for this aeroplane, fitted with two three-bladed airscrews, but it would have been impossible for Martin-Baker to have worked on more than one aircraft at a time, and the project was dropped in favour of the MB2.

In 1936, James developed appendicitis and was admitted to hospital. He was only there for a short while, but during his stay he became captivated by the nursing sister in charge of his ward, Muriel Haines. It was an acquaintance which he kept up, and over the next few years he continued to see her.

He was flying very little at this time and, unlike Baker, he rarely offered to take people up for a joy ride. Despite his love of aeroplanes and his consuming desire to build them, he never seems to have enjoyed piloting. 'You can't call the fire brigade in the sky' was one of his favourite sayings. It seems that he was conscious of the inherent dangers of flying right from the start, even though he did not seem to acknowledge the corresponding dangers in car racing. Nevertheless, piloting was still a fashionable pastime then, and he demonstrated his piloting skills to Muriel by taking her up for a ride. Why did he eventually give up flying completely? Time and expense were doubtless two of the factors involved, but as Muriel said: 'Perhaps flying just wasn't fast enough for him.'

Meanwhile, James had started work on the MB2. The design and mock-up began in 1935, but it was not until March 1936 that construction commenced. At this stage the company had little else to sell and was relying almost totally on Francis for finance. James had designed an apparatus for rotating articles whilst under treatment in an electroplating bath in order to ensure a uniform deposit of metal during the electroplating process, but like so many of his ideas, it was never produced. In such circumstances one might have supposed that James would have finished the aeroplane more quickly than he finished the MB1, but this was not the case.

The MB2 was a single-seater, eight-gun fighter. It had straight, clean lines and looked rather unusual because the fuselage was of almost constant depth, and the wheels on the fixed undercarriage were encased in 'trouser'-type fairings. The cockpit was placed well back in the fuselage to give a good view behind the wing, the length exceeded the wing span, and there was no fin.

James worked on the basis that an aeroplane was useless unless it was available to be flown. It therefore had to be easy to build and maintain and its various components had to be reliable and simple to service. James always considered the men who would have to deal with his aeroplane, whether as part of the factory force engaged in building it, as part of the maintenance team responsible for its upkeep, as the armourer required to reload the guns, or as the pilot who would fly it and who would be concerned with matters of comfort and convenience, such as the layout of the cockpit, and not just with matters of safety and manoeuvrability.

The structure was based on the simple structure employed and developed for the MB1. Steel tubing was again used, but many improvements were made which strengthened the airframe and further simplified production and, of course, maintenance. It would have been quite impossible for James to have used an old idea in a new project without finding some way of fine-tuning his original design.

The aircraft was designed so that it could be broken down into assemblies which could be produced independently of each other at small engineering factories using labour which was not experienced in aircraft construction. In this way, the aircraft could have been produced quite quickly and in large numbers had orders been forthcoming, and the company would not have been dependent on its own very small manufacturing capacity.

One interesting aspect of this aeroplane was the fact that it incorporated a crash pylon behind the cockpit which was raised during take-off and landing, the purpose of which was to protect the pilot in the event of a crash and the aircraft turning over. Pilots were at far greater risk in these circumstances when flying low-wing monoplanes than they were when flying bi-planes or high-wing monoplanes. Once again, James was considering pilot safety, and the workers from the early days of Martin-Baker remember that this was indeed always the case. The device was patented, and indeed the report on the MB2 from the Aeroplane & Armament Experimental Establishment (A&AEE) at Martlesham Heath stated that it should be considered for standardization in Service aircraft. This did not happen, however, and James dropped it from the design of his later aircraft.

James wanted his prototype to be fitted with the Rolls-Royce Merlin engine, but there was pressure at that time on the Rolls-Royce production lines, and the Ministry did not consider that this private venture warranted one of these engines. Supermarine were in a position to refuse a Napier Dagger engine for their Spitfire, but James was not, and it was the Napier Dagger III engine that he was supplied with. It had to be slightly non-standard in order to accommodate some of James's unusual design ideas, particularly in this case in relation to the engine bearer feet.

Although the MB2 was built as a private venture, the Ministry supplied him with eight .303 inch Browning machine guns for installation in the prototype, four on each wing. It was common at that time for the ammunition tanks to be set at right angles to the guns, inevitably passing through aircraft structure and thus complicating the process of rearming. James could not bear complications and his approach was always the simple one. He devised a system whereby the ammunition tank lay alongside its gun, clear of the aircraft structure. The guns and tanks were secured to the wing by quick-release pins, so that the eight guns could be rearmed in a very short time. The time taken for two men to remove all the guns from the MB2 was only three minutes, compared to 60 minutes for the Hurricane and 70 minutes for the Spitfire.

Access to the weapons bay was simple. An entire section of the wing surface above the bay could be raised simply by turning a small handle. A rubber-covered platform was attached to the wing structure which could be swung out and used as a seat or kneeling pad to enable the armourer to carry out work on the guns efficiently and comfortably. It was another feature of the aircraft which the A&AEE at Martlesham Heath considered worthy of standardization.

But, like the MB1, the MB2 was a long time in the making. James was developing some revolutionary ideas for the controls of the aircraft. He decided to dispense with a fin on the basis that the panels over the wheels would provide the necessary directional stability. He experimented too with the rudder and aileron design, both of which were unusual. Such a radical departure from the more conventional approach to aircraft design meant inevitable delays as ideas were tried out and rejected, and theories developed and disproved. The whole design concept was flexible and, with Baker and Francis still infrequently at the factory, it was nearly two years before it was finally wheeled out of the factory.

James arranged for the MB2 to be test flown at RAF Harwell. The wings and propeller were transported there first, because there was still some last-minute work to be done on the wire from the cockpit to the fin. Then the completed fuselage was towed there on its main wheels behind a truck driven by Eric Stevens. There had been a heated debate at the factory about how fast the aeroplane could safely be towed. Some were firmly of the view that it should not be towed at more than 30 mph, but James, of course, was not so cautious. In the end, Eric drove the truck at a hearty 50 mph, without mishap. They arrived in the early hours of the morning, much to the surprise of the sleeping duty officer who stumbled out of the guard house, struggling into his jacket, and shouting for them to stop. No-one took any notice: they drove on in and began reassembling the aircraft. Baker made his first flight in the MB2 on 3 August 1938.

Unfortunately, James's innovative approach to the design of the MB2 was not successful as regards its flying qualities. His theory that he could build an aeroplane that would fly successfully without a fin was ill-founded and the aircraft was very unstable. Baker took it up for several flights but it was clear to him that there was no way of avoiding the unpalatable truth that it needed a fin.

It was a disappointment to James that he had been wrong in his calculations, but he was not one to be defeated by setbacks. He immediately arranged for the use of some hangar space at the airfield and decided that the tail fin would be built there rather than back at the factory. One of the fitters had a motorbike and a side car and he was sent back to the works that afternoon to pick up steel tubing, fixing nuts, gas bottles, burner heads for welding and brazing, sheet metal and all sorts of other bits and pieces, so that the work could start as soon as possible.

It may seem strange that such a fundamental change to the design of the aircraft should be undertaken at an RAF airfield rather than at the factory, but James, as always, had faith in his own abilities, and he was anxious that the aircraft should be delayed for the minimum time possible. He did not want to give the impression that his aircraft was fundamentally flawed. He designed a small fin which was built and installed at the airfield in a very short time. This improved the performance and the Ministry agreed to carry out a test programme at Martlesham Heath.

The aircraft arrived there on 10 November 1938. The maintenance personnel were very impressed with its construction and maintainability. The report on the Ease of Maintenance Trials, dated 1 December 1938, stated that:

Many features are excellent and seem hardly capable of improvement – the accessibility of the gun installation is a notable example . . . The engine installation is excellent from the maintenance point of view, and the time taken to remove and replace an engine is the best that has been tried in recent years for an engine of this size . . . All the smaller details, such as inspection doors, accessibility of greasing points etc are exceptionally good.

Unfortunately, the small fin had not adequately solved the problem of the machine's stability in flight. Because of this, the Gunnery Trials report concluded that it would be difficult to hold an accurate aim. And the Handling and Stability Trials report, dated 1 February 1939, stated:

Owing to the peculiarities of the rudder and ailerons, the aeroplane is not pleasant to fly. It requires great concentration to fly accurately in turns and level flight. It is considered that some alteration of the aileron and rudder is necessary before the aeroplane is acceptable. The elevator control is too sensitive on the glide and should be geared lower. The longitudinal, lateral and directional stabilities are not good and should be improved.

The aircraft was returned to the factory for further modifications and the fitting of a new and more conventional fin and rudder, and a second set of Handling and Stability Trials took place in September 1939. The handling of the aircraft was much improved but was still not good enough. The report stated that 'the modification to the rudder has made this control considerably more effective and it now compares favourably with rudders of other aircraft of similar type. The heaviness and ineffectiveness of the aileron control is now very noticeable by comparison with the other controls'. Despite these criticisms, the shortcomings in the aircraft's design, which doubtless could have been solved successfully in due course, did not prevent Baker from giving several very convincing demonstrations of the MB2 in flight, including a public demonstration at a flying display at Heston in May 1939 when he is reported to have flown it with 'considerable *élan*', executing, among other manoeuvres, a 400 mph dive and several very steep turns near ground level.

But time was against James. The Performance Trials never took place. He received a letter from the Chief Technical Officer at Martlesham Heath saying that there would be no orders for it because 'it is built to a specification which is already five years old and although it was agreed that the aeroplane had good constructional points, by the time a number had been manufactured it would be out of date'. It was a bitter disappointment to James, both personally, because it was his design that had been turned down, and commercially, because the company would not receive production orders that it desperately needed. He found it difficult to accept this decision and he was not alone in questioning the wisdom of it. It scored so highly as regards ease of servicing and incorporated such unique and valuable design points that there was clearly an argument for proceeding with further modifications to solve the handling problems, particularly in view of the fact that it could have been produced quickly, by sub-contracting assemblies to factories whose work-forces were unskilled in aircraft production, thus leaving the limited aircraft production facilities then available in the country free for other projects. With a little time and money, some believe that it could have been developed and produced in time for the Battle of Britain, and that the Ministry were wrong to turn it down. An article in *Aeroplane* reported that:

In spite of its fixed undercarriage, the MB2 had a performance as good as that of contemporary eight gun fighters and a capacity for quick and cheap production by the simplicity of its structure and easy assembly. Repair and maintenance were also simple and these factors might have influenced the authorities towards putting the MB2 into production when the country's fighter strength was disproportionately low.

James would have received a sympathetic ear at Rolls-Royce, too. In March 1939, Ernest Hives (later Lord Hives), the chairman, wrote to his assistant Bill Lappin to say that while the MB2 was dead from the point of view of possible orders,

> the aircraft, however, had many excellent features and is far and away superior to any aeroplane we know of at this moment, from the point of view of serviceability with the squadrons, and the excellent manner in which Martin had anticipated the maintenance requirements although not familiar with that side of the R.A.F. In fact it is probably true to say that where other fighters will do one job, the Martin & Baker will do two.

It was little consolation that the letter from Martlesham Heath went on to say that 'the AM were keen to encourage the firm and it was probable that the firm would be asked to make a limited number of aeroplanes to a new specification'. Nor was it any consolation that in July 1939, the Ministry purchased the prototype for evaluation purposes for £13,500, which left Martin-Baker with a loss attributable to the MB2 of over £30,000, a quite considerable figure in 1939.

Why was it that the authorities showed so little interest in this aircraft? James himself believed that a great part of the problem lay in the fact that he ran a small, relatively unknown company that was not a member of the Society of British Aircraft Constructors, and that he was an outsider as far as the big aircraft manufacturers and the Establishment were concerned. He was excluded from that inner ring of companies on which the Air Ministry relied for the design and supply of new aeroplanes, and these companies would obviously exert their not inconsiderable influence to ensure that this situation did not change. It would have been difficult for a newcomer to break into that network, but particularly difficult for someone like James who was clearly not an Establishment man. An independent, outspoken Ulsterman with no qualifications, who refused to treat the Ministry men with the deference they felt was their due, was not likely to win official support. There were some people on the inside of government circles at that time who would agree that James was right. Air-Vice Marshal Tedder (later Marshal of the RAF, Lord Tedder), who first became connected with James when he was in the Air Ministry before the Second World War, believed that the MB2 was a good fighter but that the Establishment simply did not take much notice of James. Even when they did take notice of him, it was apparent that they had great difficulty in coping with his unconventional and unorthodox approach. To have accepted that a private venture from this small company with virtually no experience in aircraft design and construction should have produced a fighter aircraft that should go into production would have required a degree of enlightened initiative on the part of the Air Ministry for which it was not renowned.

James proposed a Mark 2 version of the MB2 using the Rolls-Royce Merlin engine that he had originally wanted, but he was unable to elicit any interest in this project either, and so it was dropped. The MB2 was returned to Denham and stored in one of the factory buildings, but the space was valuable and James came under increasing pressure to dismantle the aircraft. Eventually he reluctantly agreed that it should be broken up and only the propeller was kept which still hangs on the wall outside the door to his office.

There was one positive development, however, from the trials of the MB2. The Martin-Baker blast tube, which had been designed for use in the MB2, had proved to be such an advance on anything of a similar nature that James was asked to produce some for the Hurricane aircraft. The blast tube was located within the aircraft wing and around the gun barrel, sealed at one end by the gun and at the other by a fitting on the leading edge of the wing. When the gun was fired the blast tube prevented gas at high pressure from entering the wing space. Trials with the Hurricane blast tubes were carried out in March and April 1939 and the results were conclusive. James's attention to ease of maintenance had produced an outstandingly successful product. The time taken to remove the Martin-Baker blast tube was 34 seconds, as against 4 minutes 20 seconds for the type of blast tube then in use, and for replacements it was 41 seconds as against 6 minutes 25 seconds. It was decided in view of the great saving in maintenance time that the Martin-Baker blast tube should be adopted for all fixed gun installations in the future and that they should be retrofitted to existing aircraft. The orders for the blast tubes provided Martin-Baker with some much-needed profitable work during the war years, but by this time, the summer of 1939, James was already deeply engrossed in two other important projects.

Chapter Six

The End of an Era

For several years before the outbreak of the Second World War, the authorities had been devising barrage balloons which would be used to suspend heavy steel cables over important targets to guard them against low-level attack by enemy bombers. It was clear that these balloons were likely to be a hazard to British as well as enemy aircraft, and that similar obstacles would be encountered over enemy territory, so some means of severing these cables by aircraft in flight was obviously necessary. The problems were clear. The extreme hardness of the steel cable used made it difficult to cut, and the problem was compounded by the obvious difficulty of collecting and holding the cable whilst it was being cut by a device small enough not to affect the aerodynamic stability of an aircraft. James conceived the idea of gathering the cable into a cutter mounted on the leading edge of a bomber wing, and holding it there on an anvil whilst a cutter, operated by an explosive charge triggered by the entry of the cable, cut cleanly through it. It was a simple and ingenious device, smaller than a man's hand, and in September 1937 James wrote to the Ministry to ask them if they were interested in it. After some experimental activity in the workshop, the Ministry decided to test the device in the air.

In order to do this, James designed a simple form of metal glider with a wing span of about 12 ft, which was fitted with the cable cutters and flown into test cables. The Air Defence Department catapulted these gliders off the edge of a cliff at the Isle of Portland into cables suspended by barrage balloons and attached to winches on the beach below. When these tests proved successful, the cutters were installed on a Vickers-Armstrongs Wellington bomber and tested in flight. Mr Vivien Chalwin, the special Vickers representative at the Royal Aircraft Establishment (RAE) at Farnborough, recalled one test flight vividly. 'During the experimental flight which followed, we succeeded in creating havoc with the overhead electric cables supplying Exeter, and I nearly got my head chopped off when Flight Lieutenant Fulton who was flying the aircraft struck the cable with the starboard wing instead of the armoured port wing. Fortunately the airscrew severed the cable!'

James remembered other flights with Flt. Lt. Fulton, in particular the night he flew back with him from Exeter to Farnborough in a Halifax bomber. As James recalled:

> I happened to be at the back end of the aircraft and so I decided that I would move forward to the cockpit end. In the dark, as I was finding my way, I nearly stepped into an open space where the trap door had been left out and this gave me a bit of a shock. Anyhow, I decided that I wanted to have a 'pee' and this trap door opening seemed to be the obvious place. So what happened was that the 'pee' was going up into my face.

James, the practical engineer, who relied on tests and not theory, would clearly have benefited on this occasion from some prior consideration about the theory.

James decided to set up a new company, J. Martin Armaments Limited, to manufacture some of his non-aircraft inventions. This company became responsible for the manufacture of the cable cutters. About 250,000 were manufactured during the war, although only about 80,000 by J. Martin Armaments, the rest being made by the Austin Motor Company to James's drawings. Problems inevitably arose from having another company manufacturing one of James's inventions, particularly in this case because he modified the design after Austin had started manufacturing the cutters, and on one occasion J. Martin Armaments had to apologize formally for certain omissions from the drawings and information that they had supplied to Austin. James also annoyed the Director of Armament Development by writing to tell him about 'slight modifications to the firing assembly which are advantageous from several points of view and particularly as regards servicing' which he had already introduced without reference to the technical branch concerned. Nevertheless, the cable cutters became standard equipment for all aircraft in Bomber Command.

The English barrage defences were as much a threat to English bombers as the enemy defences, and of the first seven reported uses of the Martin cable cutters, six involved domestic barrage balloons and only one was used over enemy territory. That was during a daylight attack by a Blenheim on the Rotterdam Docks at 20 ft. The aircraft hit a crane cable which was successfully cut and the pilot reported feeling only a sharp crack as the cutter fired. The incident was cited as 'a striking testimonial of the efficacy of the cutters'.

It is impossible to calculate the success of the cable cutters, but on the basis of the feedback that he received, James estimated that in excess of 500 aircraft and 2,500 crew were saved by the cutters, which just as importantly helped to maintain the morale of the bomber crews, particularly when flying low-level bombing missions. One such occasion was the attack on the aqueduct of the Dortmund–Ems Canal on the night of 12/13 August 1940 by bombers from 49 and 83 Squadrons, which resulted in the canal being blocked for ten days. After this attack, S/L Thomas Murray wrote to James:

I have just completed my second tour of operations with Bomber Command and I would like if I may to express my appreciation for the good work you are doing in supplying us with the Cable Cutter.

This invention is our only safeguard against balloons not only in enemy territory but also in this country. I don't know how many crews we lost in the early days through the enemy barrages, but we undoubtedly lost some, and it was most unpleasant to have to go into targets below balloon height when you knew that if you touched one you would not have a hope in hell of getting out.

Certain operations had to be held up until we could be issued with the Cable Cutters. We had to wait until we had two aircraft in the group fitted up before we could carry out our attack on the Dortmund–Ems Canal. This was a low level attack during which Squadron Leader Learoyd won his Victoria Cross. At the beginning of the action we sent in the two Hampdens fitted with cutters and we swept the canal free of balloons. We were then able to send the main force in to bomb the aqueduct.

Since that date we have come to rely on your cutters and to us the balloon is no longer a bogey whether it be British or German. Many of us owe our lives to your work and to all of us it has made our jobs much easier.

Despite the appreciation expressed for this device, James felt that he was very harshly treated by the authorities. The cutters had involved a considerable amount of development work, all at his own expense, and he spent a lot of time visiting aerodromes to supervise the fitting of the cutters and advising armourers on how to load and service them. He was denied the right to recoup his development costs through production, and he had been compelled to assign his patents to the Secretary of State. A long and somewhat acrimonious debate ensued for several years as to what he should be paid for his invention, and it was never resolved to James's satisfaction.

Meanwhile, during the latter part of 1938, when James realized that he might not be getting any orders for the MB2, he turned his mind to the design of another fighter which he designated the MB3. Once again he wanted a Rolls-Royce engine, and he went directly to his friend Ernest Hives at Rolls-Royce to discuss possibilities with him. Rolls-Royce were themselves working on the design of a new aero-engine, the Griffon, and Hives decided to provide James with one of these for his new aeroplane.

In February 1939, James wrote to Hives:

I am sending you under separate cover, by express letter, a G.A. [General Assembly Drawing] showing the new engine installed in a single-seater fighter, MB3 and do hope and pray that you will be able to put it across with old Freeman.

With the experience we had building the MB2 it will be possible for us to turn out this machine in record time and we could incorporate all the features that have been appreciated at Martlesham as regards maintenance of the machine and armament installation. You will notice that in the drawing we have given an all-up weight of 7600 lbs, and this is for 180 gallons of petrol and twelve Browning guns. No doubt the Ministry may wish to change some of these to cannon, but that is their affair.

I have no doubt if you can put this thing across with the Air Ministry I can make a huge success of the aeroplane as regards performance, easy manufacture and all the other essentials.

The reference to 'old Freeman' was to Air Marshal Sir Wilfred Freeman at the Air Ministry. James realized that he would need help in breaking into the inner ring of established aircraft manufacturers and in procuring a contract for his new design, and his friend Hives was clearly in a position to help him. But the discussions between James and Hives ranged beyond that. In March, Hives sent a memo to his assistant, Bill Lappin, setting out his views on the MB2 which have already been quoted in Chapter Five, 'to emphasise that in spite of the limitations at Martin and Baker they have produced an excellent aircraft – a fact we should recognise, as we may be co-operating with them in the near future on some similar types'.

James, Baker and Francis met with Freeman and Tedder to discuss the new prototype, out of which came the proposal that Martin-Baker would get an order for three single-engine, single-seater aircraft with two cannon guns. James had been right in thinking that the Ministry would not accept his suggestion for 12 Browning guns. It was intended that the first of these three aircraft should be fitted with the Rolls-Royce Merlin engine, the arrangement and the centre of gravity being fixed so that the new Griffon engine would drop straight in. Rolls-Royce's interest in James's new aeroplane was that it would serve as a test machine for proving the new Griffon power plant. They arranged with James that they would supply the complete power plant, including the propeller, as a complete unit which would then be attached to the bulkhead of the prototype. They insisted that the Ministry should place a contract for the power plant with them, and that the contract with Martin-Baker should be for an aeroplane without those parts because, as Hives wrote to Freeman, their chief interest in the Martin-Baker project was that it would be their first 'opportunity of starting with a new machine to build into it the best possible power plant'.

Freeman accepted the Rolls-Royce position, and on 16 June the contract was signed with James for three prototypes. It referred to Air Ministry Specification F.18/39 for a fighter capable of a speed of at least 400 mph and a ceiling of 35,000 ft. There is no record of any other firm building a prototype to this Specification and the probability therefore is that the Specification was produced to cover the Rolls-Royce/Martin-Baker proposal for the MB3. The contract stipulated that the first aeroplane was to be completed no later than 15 December of that year for a fixed price of £28,000, and that the other two should be completed no later than 15 February 1940 for a fixed price of £18,000 each. These prices were subject to reduction if the delivery dates were not met, and the contract could be cancelled without liability by the Ministry if the first aeroplane was not finished by 15 March 1940.

It was a tough contract, and the non-delivery penalties facing the company have been described as grossly unfair. For a small work-force with limited facilities, limited financial resources, and limited experience in the design and construction of fighter aircraft, it would have been an almost impossible task to meet the contract deadlines, let alone produce an aeroplane in that time that was superior to those being built by its competitors. Indeed, to talk about competitors was perhaps presumptuous. The aircraft manufacturers already engaged in the production of fighter aircraft were established firms, with skilled workers and adequate manufacturing capacity. James Martin was simply not in the same league. It was Hives's private view that James was 'mad, promising the machine in six months' time'.

Work on the new machine got off to a good start. James wrote to Hives in the middle of August inviting him to Denham in September 'to see our new works, and three new fuselages, with all the bits and pieces on'. In early September Bill Lappin reported on 'quite a good "mock-up" in the shop of the aeroplane including a complete working model of a very simple, straightforward, electrically operated undercarriage'. James was planning to have three fuselages in the shop by the end of the month.

But despite his usual optimism, his problems were mounting. The outbreak of war on 3 September upset his plans for getting work done by sub-contractors. It also upset the machine tool market and delivery of tools to Martin-Baker practically ceased. The position as regards the supply of raw materials was equally difficult. But worse was to come.

After three months' work on the drawings and stressings, Rolls-Royce told James that they had made an error in the figures they had supplied him with in respect of their power unit, and that the weight was now 264 lb more than they had originally advised and the position of the engine 1.53 in further forward. James was very upset by this news. He estimated that this increase in weight meant that he would have to bring the installation's centre of gravity forward by 1.12 in and the wings forward by 3.1 in in order to restore the aeroplane's centre of gravity to the correct position. He wrote to Hives to tell him that he regarded the position as

> very serious indeed, as the fuselage has been stressed, all the drawings are completed and tubes delivered, and we are ready to start manufacture, and this increase in weight means that the geometry of the front fuselage has been changed, also the design of the petrol tank, consequently the drawings of these components will be scrapped. In addition to this it will be necessary to re-stress the whole of the fuselage; the estimated time for re-drawing and re-stressing is eight weeks.

At this stage, of course, he had only 12 weeks left to complete the first aeroplane.

James well understood the inevitability of making changes to designs in the search for perfection, and it was dismay rather than anger that he felt in this situation. But in view of the rigorous penalty clauses in his contract with regard to delivery of the prototypes, James wrote to Hives telling him that 'in the circumstances we feel it is up to you people to get in touch with the Contracts Department and get us an extension of time of two months for our delivery date'. A few weeks later, Ray Dorey, the manager of Rolls-Royce's Hucknell Flight Test Centre, visited Denham, and he reported back to Hives that:

> The position is that the aircraft was drawn and detailed for the old Griffon weights, and it has now been re-drawn for the new Griffon installation, moving the wings 3" further forward, and Martin does not know which set of drawings to issue to the shop to start making his parts.
>
> The forgings, etc., for his three aircraft are lying on the floor, and his machine men are standing off waiting for a reply from you regarding the weight question . . . Incidentally, the weight of the power unit is not the only cause for the forward movement of the wings: the C.G. of the power unit has also moved forward, and this contributes quite an appreciable amount towards the necessity for changing the wings on the body.

Dorey was very impressed with what he saw of the aircraft during this visit, but believed that James would require a significant extension to his contract delivery date before the machine would be complete. Hives was willing to help James and on 5 December, the month for delivery of the first aircraft, he wrote to Freeman asking for a four-month extension for the delivery of the Martin-Baker fighter.

James needed Hives's co-operation. The missed delivery date was clearly not the fault of Rolls-Royce alone, or James would have been able to meet the revised date, which he did not. Apart from the unrealistic contract deadline and the problems attributable to the outbreak of the war, James was experiencing his usual difficulty in finalizing his design.

The Ministry accepted that the delivery date should be extended for reasons not attributable to the company, but they did not see fit to increase the contract price in the light of the wasted work that the company had undertaken through no fault of its own. And when the first aircraft failed to materialize on the new delivery date, the contract lapsed. James was not deterred. Throughout his life he had demonstrated enormous reserves of resilience, determination and perseverance. They were the hallmarks of the man. In 1940 he was to celebrate his 47th birthday, and it was far too late in life for him to change. He continued with the construction of the aeroplane.

At the end of May, James heard unofficially that the new Griffon engine was not likely to be available for his aircraft, and the Ministry later advised him that they were substituting a Napier Sabre engine. James was livid. He did not trust the Napier engine and he certainly did not want it in his aeroplane. His opinion of Napier had very definitely changed since those days in the twenties when he would drop in there for lunch. But he was told that a lot of money had been spent developing the Sabre engine and the Ministry were determined that it would be used. James had no choice but to accept it if he wanted his contract to be renewed, but it was a capitulation on his part that was to haunt him in later years.

The Napier Sabre engine was heavier than the Griffon by nearly 1,000 lb, which necessitated considerable structural alterations to the fuselage and a lot of restressing and new drawings which were put in hand in early June. The change of engine also meant that Martin-Baker was now called upon to design and make the whole engine mounting and cooling system, a lot of extra work which was not catered for in the original contract.

The matter was placed before Lord Beaverbrook at the Ministry of Aircraft Production. He authorized a payment of £27,000 to be made in July, in anticipation of a new contract being entered into which would set out new payment terms. This new contract, entered into on 11 August 1940, stipulated a maximum price for the first prototype of £25,500 and £17,000 each for the other two. The actual prices were to be calculated on the basis of the cost to the company of producing the aircraft plus a profit of 5 per cent of the cost figure. No delivery date was stipulated and the contract merely specified that the delivery programme was to be satisfactory to the Director of Aircraft Production. Was this pragmatism on the part of the Ministry because they did not believe that James would meet a contractual delivery date and they did not want to be involved in another round of discussions for extension of the contract? Probably it was not. A fixed delivery date would have given them a clear right to cancel the contract had James failed to produce the aircraft on time. It seems more likely that it suited them to have the contract worded this way. James had already demonstrated his ingenious design capability with the blast tubes and the cable cutters. He was capable of producing extremely useful gadgets and solutions to problems which did not involve interrupting the work of the main aircraft suppliers, a factor which was of increasing importance as the war continued, and as more problems presented themselves. It is likely that they wished to maintain the freedom to call upon his ingenuity in the future without having to confuse the position under the contract. And it was not long before they did.

At the end of September 1940, Freeman approached James with the proposal to mount forward-firing guns in the Douglas DB-7 (Boston) light bomber aircraft so that it could be used for night fighting duties, particularly for the defence of London against the German night bombers. James pointed out that this would delay the production of the MB3 and that he would need permission to undertake this new job, which was duly given. James designed a new nose forward of the front cockpit bulkhead, which had been the bomb-aimer's position in the Boston. The new nose was equipped with twelve .303 inch Browning machine guns, the armament which James had suggested for the MB3. This fantastic fire power was made possible by the ingenious arrangement of the guns and by the use of Martin-Baker ammunition boxes which lay alongside and parallel to the guns, the arrangement that had been used on the MB2. George Edwards, later Sir George Edwards and the Chairman of British Aircraft Corporation, was at that time the Experimental

Manager at Vickers-Armstrongs Limited in charge of this conversion job, and he recalls this project vividly. He wrote:

> I was asked to go to Denham to see the great man, James Martin. He was kindness itself, and this visit began a friendship which was to last over all the years. It was immediately obvious to me, when I looked at the design of this installation and the other projects he was doing, which he showed to me with great pride, that he was an absolute genius in the art of immaculate detailed design. His thorough examination of what was really needed, be it cable cutters, blast tubes, or ammunition feeds, ended up with a concept that was simple (the hallmark of real design genius) and he finished the job with a quality which nothing less than infinite care and patience could bring about.

Tests were completed successfully in the spring of 1941 and the new nose was rapidly put into production. Almost 100 aircraft were modified and renamed the Havoc night fighter. Although it was entirely his design, and its success was largely due to the incorporation of James's patented ammunition box, the production contract was awarded to the Heston Aircraft Company. As a result, Martin-Baker made a substantial loss on the job and James was furious at being denied the opportunity to manufacture the modification. The test report from the A&AEE at Boscombe Down stated that it was an outstanding example of an efficient gun installation and that 'very few gunnery layouts which can compare with it have been seen at this Establishment since the trials of the Martin-Baker 1 fighter'. The conclusions set out in this report are worth quoting because they succinctly describe James's approach to design work:

> The efficiency of the installation can be gauged by its effortless maintenance, complete accessibility and simplicity of design . . . The great merit of the design is that the user's (i.e. the armourer's) point of view has been considered.

On 25 April, Lord Beaverbrook wrote to James:

> In designing the 12-gun nose for the Havoc, your firm has achieved an outstanding success.
> And in adding so markedly to the fighting power of this machine, you confer a real benefit upon the Royal Air Force.
> I send you my congratulations and my thanks.

In early November 1940, the Air Ministry Armament Board asked James to design a new type of gun mounting for the 0.5 inch guns in the Grumman Martlet aircraft. James responded that he would need Lord Beaverbrook's permission to undertake this work, which was given. Work commenced almost immediately and converted wings were delivered to Fairey's aerodrome in February 1941.

While this work was in progress, the next request materialized. During the Battle of Britain, when intensive fighting and a high casualty rate of fighter aircraft were common, the urgent need arose for a jettisonable canopy for the Spitfire in order to improve the chances of escape by parachute when the aircraft had to be abandoned, because the existing canopies were prone to jamming. In December 1940, Air Vice-Marshal Sholto Douglas of Fighter Command asked James if he would undertake this task. With permission from Lord Beaverbrook again, work commenced in late December and was completed in the middle of January. The requirement for safe and immediate jettisoning was coupled with the need to design a scheme capable of easy retrofit by RAF personnel under field conditions without any special equipment. James's design used unlocking pins actuated by cables which were in turn operated by the pilot pulling a small red rubber ball mounted on the hood arch. As soon as the canopy was freed it was carried away by the slipstream. It was tested successfully at varying speeds, culminating in a final test at 500 mph, and was made standard for all Spitfires. The device went into immediate production by the company, and over 60,000 were produced. Seven man hours were required for the retrofit, and in order to expedite the task of retrofitting all Spitfires, a course of instruction was set up at the company and each Spitfire squadron sent their Engineering Officer to the factory to be instructed on how to fit the jettison gear. James received a letter from the Headquarters of Fighter Command in May 1941 to 'express our thanks for all the good work you have done in connection with the clever design and rapid supply of the Jettisonable Hood for the Spitfire. There is no doubt that this effort of yours will contribute greatly to the pilot's peace of mind when fighting operations are on'.

The fact that James was almost totally engaged in military wartime projects seems to have made little difference to the way he ran his factory. James never had any time for petty bureaucracy, tiresome rules or even what some people might call ordinary discretion. The war years were full of regulations that affected James, particularly in connection with the secrecy that surrounded all military production. The employees at Martin-Baker were required to sign secrecy undertakings. James went along with this, but would often pick up the telephone to his friends and talk freely about his designs, other people's designs or anything else that was on his mind at the time. Some of his friends recall how horrified they were about these highly secret matters being discussed on the telephone, but James did not care. Lord Kings Norton remembers visiting James at Denham during the early part of the war, and having reached his office very easily, asked him what he was doing about security. James announced that he looked after security himself. He took a revolver out of the top drawer of his desk and fired two shots through the window.

In November 1940 Tedder was preparing to leave for the Far East. He had known James for several years and had a high regard for his abilities and designs. He also knew how frustrated he got in his dealings with the Ministry – men behind desks served no useful purpose as far as James was concerned and indeed were responsible for the problems that he was having in getting recognition for the merits of his aircraft –

and Tedder had therefore been taking a special interest in the MB3 in an attempt to help James in his dealings with the Ministry. He wrote to James before he left to say that 'I know it is no use asking you not to lose your temper with the Ministry, but I hope you won't lose patience with it. So much of what you have done in the past has been invaluable to the Service and I know enough of what you have in hand to know that there is a great deal more to come'. It was a pity that James lost this supporter to a posting abroad, although it is perhaps unlikely that Tedder would have been able to influence the outcome of events had he stayed in England mediating on James's behalf. But he was certainly one of the more influential men of the time who sincerely believed in the value of James's work. Many years later, at a dinner in 1965 to celebrate 500 lives saved by the Martin-Baker ejection seat, he gave an amusing after-dinner speech in which he described James as 'the bane of my life – the most indefatigable, invincible, unspeakable nuisance, because he came up with one good thing after another which I couldn't persuade anybody to follow up and take'.

It is hardly surprising that James was getting little opportunity to work on the MB3. Although the Ministry took the view that he should be able to work on more than one project at a time, and that the work on the aeroplane should not be affected by the work on the one-off designs they requested from him, this was in fact utterly disingenuous on their part, because they were giving James this work so as to avoid causing delays among their main aircraft suppliers. James's resources were very limited, and in practice it was difficult for progress to be made on more than one front at a time. James was the only designer, and although he had draughtsmen producing drawings for him, and stressmen doing calculations, the ideas were all his and he maintained absolute control over the whole design process in the same way that he had done when the company was first set up and the number of people working for him was much smaller. Also, because of his belief that only the machine operators made him any money and everybody else was just an expense, he kept the drawing office staff in particular to a minimum. As Ken Neil, a draughtsman at Martin-Baker explained: 'We were always staffed very light: he was the staff, he was the design, he was everybody'.

James would have been incensed had he known that, while he was being asked to undertake these extra development projects, the Ministry were actively considering whether or not to proceed with the MB3. At the end of 1940, consideration was being given to the various aircraft types not yet in production. In December, the Rt. Hon. Sir Archibald Sinclair, the Secretary of State for Air, wrote to Lord Beaverbrook about the MB3: 'Since this aircraft is no advance on the Tornado and Typhoon and it is unlikely to be ready until much later, we do not think there is much point in proceeding further with it unless it possesses marked production advantages over either of these two types of aircraft.' Lord Beaverbrook rather cryptically replied that: 'We have reached the stage where we would like to see the prototype anyway'. Perhaps he felt, having authorized the additional development contracts and thereby the delay to the MB3, that it would be a little awkward to cancel the MB3 contract at this stage. However, ten days later he explained that he was continuing with the MB3 as it did possess marked production advantages, although a decision as to whether or not to produce it would depend on tests of the prototype.

Apart from the gun installation for the Boston, the gun mounting for the Martlet, and the Spitfire canopy jettison, James had over the previous two years been asked to design and produce blast tubes for a number of aircraft in addition to the Hurricane, including the Typhoon, the Tornado, the Douglas DB-7, the Grumman Martlet and the de Havilland Mosquito, and the Ministry of Aircraft Production had asked him to consider a multi-action cable cutter that could be used more than once without intermediate rearming. In addition he had also designed a variety of other items for aircraft including a quick detachable, rubber-insulated engine mounting for the Sabre engine, a quick detachable bulkhead connection for all engine controls, and an anti-frothing oil tank for use with high-powered engines. James estimated in the summer of 1941 that he had lost a total of 16 months on the production of the MB3 because of the Rolls-Royce changes and the other development work, which meant that, according to his estimate, they had only spent eight months working on the MB3. Admittedly he had promised the aircraft in six months originally but that had been unrealistic, even had he been able to work without interruptions, and the delay in the production of the MB3 caused by stopping and starting the process of design and construction and the repeated rejigging of machine tools for the different jobs that the company was working on, inevitably exceeded the aggregate time spent on the other projects. As a result of this other work, the construction of the prototypes was becoming an inefficient and expensive process. 'You must take into account', James wrote to the Ministry, 'the numerous projects we were called upon to cope with simultaneously, obviously with far-reaching results to our production programme'. He pointed out that all the development work connected with these other jobs, the co-operation with and instruction to third parties, and the design and construction of the fighter, was undertaken with a drawing office staff never exceeding 25 and a works of little more than 200 people. Because the Ministry placed great value on his ability to produce these one-off designs, it was not until the summer of 1941, when they had for the time being no new additional work to give him, that the dialogue with the Ministry about the delivery of the first prototype gathered momentum.

Meanwhile, other important developments had been taking place in James's life. In October 1940, he bought a leasehold interest in a house in Denham called Southlands Manor, and his sister Jane organized the furnishing for him. James loved this house and its surroundings, and he lived there for the rest of his life. Southlands Manor is a rambling Elizabethan house set in 30 acres of farmland and bordered on one side by the River Misbourne. The house is reputed to have been a nunnery

at one time and one of the 'safe' houses used by the Jesuits to perform
the Mass when this was forbidden during the reign of Elizabeth I, but
despite various searches, a secret priest hole was never found. James was
now 48 years old and still a bachelor, but he finally decided that it was
time to get married, and he married Muriel Haines on 28 February 1942.

Muriel Mary Haines, the nursing sister who had looked after James
in 1936 during his stay in hospital for an appendectomy, was born on
24 October 1913, and was therefore 20 years James's junior. She had
an itinerant childhood, attending eight different schools before her family
finally settled in Reading and allowed her an uninterrupted few years at
her senior school where she achieved distinction in all subjects. Her
passion for gardening and flower-arranging meant that Southlands Manor
suited her well, and her deep love of literature helped to fill the evenings
when James was working. She coped with his long hours without
complaint and was always completely supportive of all that he tried to
achieve. She too had faith in his talents and was an understanding and
loyal partner.

Shortly after their marriage, she visited the factory and was helping
James sort out his office. In the top drawer of his desk she found some
loose gunpowder. James assured her that it was quite safe because small
amounts of gunpowder will smoulder but not explode. To prove his
point, he put a lighted cigarette in the top drawer. Clearly he must have
misjudged the amount of gunpowder in the drawer and the explosion
which followed singed his eyebrows away and blew out the windows to
his office. Once again, the practical approach had gone wrong! Several
of the workers at Martin-Baker remember hearing this loud bang and
seeing the comical spectacle of an angry James with a blackened face
bursting out of his office. Their immediate reaction was a desire to laugh,
but nobody dared.

Notwithstanding this incident, James was very experienced in working
with explosives. He spent a lot of time in the armoury at Martin-Baker
trying out guns and gun feeds by firing into a bank of earth and
experimenting with the explosive charges that he used in his designs. It
was work that he particularly enjoyed, and his expertise in this field was
recognized. He never wore ear defenders, however, a fact which must
have resulted in some damage to the hearing in his one good ear and
contributed to the hearing problems that he suffered from in later life.

In the summer of 1941, the Ministry began to give serious consideration
to the delivery of the MB3. They prepared a report on the financial history
of the company and its present financial condition. They pressed upon
James the need to proceed with the fighter, and he informed them that
he was confident that the aircraft would be ready for its first flight in
September. In August, the project seemed no nearer completion and the
Ministry decided to visit Denham so that they could judge the situation
for themselves. Frustrated by the unreliability of James's forecasts, and
armed with their financial reports, the discussion ranged beyond the
immediate question of when the MB3 would be ready to fly. The Ministry

felt that the future of the firm was the real subject for discussion. Despite the income arising from the blast tube contracts and contracts for the modification work, the company was relying heavily on Francis for funds, who was owed about £100,000 by the company at this stage in shares, debentures and loans. The reports make interesting reading.

> The conduct of the Company's affairs has been characterised by the usual indifference to accounting detail which is found when technical men with outstanding ideas are financed by a wealthy man, all being imbued with the following of an ideal, rather than the primary idea of profit. Nevertheless there is no evidence of slackness or extravagance, but an air of quiet efficiency about the offices and factory and all connected with them . . . Mr Martin and Captain Baker appear to be men of absolute sincerity and honesty whose chief object in life is to see their fighter aircraft go into production.

In August 1941, Linnell at the Ministry of Aircraft Production wrote to Cotton, the Director of Contracts:

> First as regards their fighter, having gone so far, I think we must certainly have the aircraft flying and that it would be very unwise to cancel the contract at this juncture. There are many ingenious devices in the design and although I fear that the performance will be badly down, there is much we can learn by flying the aircraft.
>
> Secondly, as regards their future. There is no gainsaying the fact that this little firm is extremely useful in designing and producing gadgetry. As examples of their past work, the balloon cutter, the Havoc gun noses and the fly-away hoods of the Spitfire are three which spring readily to mind. It is just this sort of modification which holds up things in the main producing factories, and it is valuable to have a firm on tap to which we can put the work without delaying production lines.

On the assumption that the performance of the first fighter would be such as to kill it from the point of view of bulk production, he suggested that the company be designated as a repair unit but with the overriding proviso that it would remain available for dealing with special modifications as and when the need for these arose.

This perhaps sums up the Ministry's appraisal of James's aircraft. Although they paid lip service to the possibility that the aircraft might be worth a production contract, in reality they seemed to be little interested in that possibility, and while they wanted to see the finished product because of the many design innovations that would be incorporated in it, their real interest in James lay in his ability in 'designing and producing gadgetry . . . without delaying production lines'. While James has received virtually no recognition in respect of his wartime inventions, there is no doubt that he made a significant contribution to the war effort. But recognition for these successes was not what James was seeking, and the suggestion that Martin-Baker become a repair unit available for modification work was totally unacceptable to him. He told the Ministry in no uncertain terms that it was his intention to build aircraft. For too long he had produced equipment whose sole purpose was to improve other people's aircraft, and now it was time for them to consider his own aircraft.

James was undoubtedly right in his fear that the reason the Ministry wanted him to finish the prototype was so that they could plagiarize his ideas. He was adamant that he was not prepared to be transferred to aircraft repair work nor to become engaged in sub-contract work for the rest of the aircraft industry, although he agreed that he would make a reasonable business out of doing this. That was not, however, the point. To do so would have been a complete anathema to him. All his life he had been determined to pioneer on his own, to invent things in the way that he thought best, without having anyone telling him how to do it. He had survived more difficult times than these, and he was certainly not going to be deflected from his purpose now. In fact, he had some difficulty in understanding why the Ministry officials thought that the future of his company was in question. When asked how he proposed that his work-force be employed, he replied that in his view he should be given a production order for the MB3 for at least 50 aircraft. The Ministry officials realized that both James and Baker were almost fanatical in the belief which they had in the new aeroplane, and agreed among themselves that James was genuinely unable to understand why the Ministry men could not see good reasons for putting his aeroplane into production.

James was prepared to have his product put to the test. He expected the MB3 to be at least 30 mph faster than a Typhoon with an equivalent engine, but it was in the maintenance sphere that he felt the aircraft would score most highly. He suggested that a stop-watch test be taken of the comparative maintenance times for the MB3 and the Typhoon. He argued for a production contract now which could be cancelled if the aircraft did not come up to expectations, on the basis that if the contract had to be cancelled, the money that had been spent in the meantime would be less than that spent on countless other abortive orders, and it would at least enable him to get on with the jigging and tooling for production and to arrange for sub-contract work to be done so that the aircraft could quickly be produced if it was accepted. James was well aware that one of the problems he faced if his aeroplane was to go into production was the logistical one of arranging for it to be manufactured elsewhere, as clearly Martin-Baker did not have adequate manufacturing capacity.

While this proposal was not altogether unreasonable, and some in the Ministry would have accepted it, others were not convinced. The delays to date, however caused, meant that the aircraft was now being built to an outdated Specification and would not reach the altitude other fighters could. James persisted that with its speed and armaments, it would still have a valuable role to play. But it was now August: only a few weeks ago James had been promising that the aircraft would be ready for flight in September, and now he was talking about December. The reason for this delay related to a changeover of the radiators into the wings, which he hoped would add 10 mph to the speed. He went on to assure the Ministry officials that the design was now complete and he had no further changes to incorporate. We shall never know whether he believed this to be the case when he said it. Probably he did, but he could not stop himself considering possible improvements.

The fate of James's prototype was debated by those officials who so infuriated him. Internal memos went from desk to desk but despite their reluctance to back him and award him a production contract, they were equally reluctant to turn him down outright. Even those who felt that Martin-Baker were entitled to as favourable treatment as it was possible to give did not think that this extended to devoting men and material to tooling up for a new machine unless it was likely to be a war winner. It was suggested, however, that if it appeared from its trials that the aircraft might be suitable, with or without modification, for a particular role, it might be worth trying to persuade the Americans to produce it, as the Martin-Baker manufacturing process seemed to be very suited to American mass production methods.

In November 1941 an internal memorandum from the Director of Technical Development stated that the MB3 could not go into production in any event because it was 'designed around the Sabre and we shall not have enough Sabres for it', and that as it used the same engine as the Typhoon, there were no grounds for considering it a competitor to the Typhoon. After three drafts of a suitably tactful letter had been discussed, James was told in December that a production contract for the MB3 would not be forthcoming until after the flight trials which James had suggested might take place in February. James replied that he would do his utmost to complete the aircraft by then, adding: 'I have no doubt that the performance figures will be a very substantial improvement on existing aircraft.'

Meanwhile, James and Baker were making enquiries about the possibility of an American engine for the second MB3, namely the Wright Aeronautical Corporation Tornado engine. In March 1942, Linnell told them it was only in the early stages of development and no production models were likely to be ready until the beginning of the next year. In view of the lack of interest being shown by the Ministry, James and Baker tried to elicit American support for the MB3 in the hope that it could be put into production there. Representatives from North American Aviation Inc. of Inglewood, California, took this proposal seriously and visited Martin-Baker in April to make their own detailed appraisal of the machine. Their Assistant Chief Designer was of the view that 'whether or not the M-B aircraft satisfies the performance predictions of its designer, the many design innovations (such as Armaments, Power Plant etc.) warrant the immediate attention and analysis of qualified personnel, and the dissemination of this design data to Aircraft Designers, both in the UK and America, for ultimate incorporation in all Service Aircraft'. But despite this report, North American concluded that the performance of the MB3 was likely to fall short of the performance that they expected from their Mustang, and they declined to take the matter any further.

Despite the pressure on James to produce the MB3, he was still considering other projects. In early 1942, he proposed a heavily armed aircraft that could be used against tanks. The Ministry were not interested, although they did arrange for him to be supplied with a field artillery gun for experimental purposes. The problem with installing such a gun in an aircraft was, of course, the immense recoil of the gun after firing. Some elementary firing tests were carried out with this gun in a field by Southlands Manor, where Eric Stevens fired the gun and was thrown off his feet by the recoil, much to James's amusement. The project never got beyond the drawing board, but it was a unique-looking aircraft: a pusher prop configured machine with a twin tail boom. It provided for a six-pounder anti-tank gun to be located in the nose of the aircraft on the horizontal axis of the centre of gravity to ensure that the aircraft would not pitch while the gun was firing. The Rolls-Royce Griffon engine was placed behind the cockpit at the rear of the fuselage, the fuselage and engine cowling being covered in half-inch armour plate. Pilot escape was considered too, and the fuselage had a trap door in the bottom to ensure that the pilot could fall clear of the propeller and the tailplane if he had to bail out.

The Ministry were still not interested. James wrote to Tedder, who at that time was at the Headquarters of the Mediterranean Air Command, in an attempt to elicit his support, but Tedder confessed that he was 'a poor market for tank busters'. James, convinced that the idea of an anti-tank machine was a good one, turned his mind back to his lorry-building days in Acton and designed an armoured vehicle with a six-pounder gun. He patented the design which he described as 'an extremely mobile, fast-moving gun on a motor vehicle of normal dimensions and not excessive weight. The load was well distributed between the wheels and good protection provided for the driver and gunner. The gun itself could swivel through a complete circle thus enabling it to be quickly brought to bear on the target'. Fast enough to overtake or outdistance tanks, with a gun big enough to destroy them, and designed in James's usual fashion with attention to detail and practicability, it was an interesting proposition, but he could not elicit any enthusiasm for this either.

The debate with the Ministry on the MB3 went rumbling on meanwhile. James promised a first flight in March 1942. By February, that was looking more like April or May. In April an internal memo at the Ministry reported that:

> The chances of bringing this new type into production are rapidly receding with the interminable delay in completing it.
>
> The lay-out and the general gadgetry of the aircraft are beyond comparison for ingenuity and when completed will undoubtedly prove of great value.
>
> This firm are doing themselves the greatest dis-service by their continued dilatoriness in getting the aircraft to its flying trials.

In April a further visit was made to the factory at Denham. The aircraft was clearly at least a month off completion. The latest change was the repositioning of the ducted radiator in order to reduce drag. The change involved a complete redesign of the ducted surfaces of the wings, and although the design of this was almost finalized, it still had to be built by the radiator manufacturers. James was also considering a similar arrangement for oil cooling which would involve another delay. Pressed for a date for the first flight, James was reluctant to commit himself, but eventually agreed to the middle of June.

The Ministry realized that James was depending on the top speed and the ease and speed of maintenance work as the selling points for the aircraft, and was therefore concerned to make it as aerodynamically clean as possible. They appreciated also that he was not going to release the aircraft for flight trials until he had incorporated all the improvements he could think of. James was determined not to give them grounds for turning down the MB3 as they had done the MB2.

The Ministry considered various courses of action in relation to the aeroplane. They could threaten to terminate the contract if the aircraft was not delivered by a certain date and make a claim for recovery of the amounts already paid to them. This of course would mean that the company would keep the aircraft, so they considered giving the firm the right to hand over the aircraft in its incomplete state, which would at least give them the opportunity to finish the aircraft and fly it if they felt that this might be worthwhile. James was eventually told that the aircraft must be finished by the end of July otherwise he would be required to deliver the aircraft in its incomplete state for a price to be agreed.

The delays crept on because of hold-ups in the delivery of the radiator and the oil piping, and the Ministry agreed extensions of time to cover these, but on 27 August, the aircraft was wheeled out of the factory and tethered to the ground just outside the factory doors for the first engine runs. The Minister was present. Everything went according to plan, and the aircraft was moved to RAF Wing for its test flights.

James had wanted the first flights to take place at RAF Harwell where the surrounding area was largely free of obstructions, but the Ministry had not agreed. A heated debate ensued, but again James was in no position to make demands and he had to accept Wing. It was another capitulation to the Ministry that he was to regret deeply.

Whatever the doubts of some members of the Ministry about the potential of the MB3, the RAF personnel in charge of security at Wing were told in their briefing session that the MB3 was likely to be a formidable competitor to the Spitfire and the Hurricane, and they were fascinated to see it in action. When it arrived they were not disappointed and many of the RAF personnel there were hugely impressed by it. The MB3 was a low-wing monoplane, with a Napier Sabre II engine driving a variable pitch, three-blade propeller. While it was based on the lessons learned in the design and construction of the MB1 and MB2, the MB3 inevitably incorporated many new features. The fuselage primary structure was still the round steel tube arrangement, but metal panels had taken the place of wood and fabric, and there were numerous access panels for maintenance purposes. The wings, of torsion box construction about a laminated steel spar, gave a remarkably strong and stiff structure in which flexing was not perceptible. James had designed and built his own pneumatically actuated and wide-tracked undercarriage which made the aircraft very stable on the ground. The main wheels were set far enough forward to allow the engine to be run up to full power without the aircraft nosing over. But perhaps the most remarkable aspect of this aircraft was the armament of six 20 mm British Hispano cannon, three in each wing, capable of firing 60 shells a second, each with 200 rounds, served by the Martin-Baker flat feed system developed for the MB2.

James himself created a lasting impression among the RAF personnel at Wing as a quiet and unassuming man, constantly active, and who seemed happiest and most at ease when working with the fitters on the aircraft. A senior official from the Ministry was there too, and the onlookers noticed that James spent quite a lot of time arguing with him.

Baker made a spectacular arrival on 31 August in a Tiger Moth. He gave a brief acrobatic display over the airfield and executed a falling leaf manoeuvre at the end before stepping out of the Tiger Moth and surprising his audience, who were expecting a young man. He was then 54 years old.

The first two flights of the MB3 were made by Baker that afternoon. On the first flight, the radiator cooling was not satisfactory and the temperature rose dramatically so that Baker could only do one circuit of the aerodrome before landing. As the aircraft had been doing fairly lengthy taxying before take-off, the Napier representative thought that the temperature had been initially high and there would be no danger in carrying out another flight trial after allowing the coolant temperature to drop. The second flight was made later that evening, but again the coolant temperature rose excessively, and Baker was forced to land the aeroplane immediately. There was nearly a disaster when Baker was temporarily blinded by the setting sun moments before he touched down, and the landing that followed was a hard one, but the undercarriage withstood the impact well. After these flights Baker reported to James that the handling characteristics seemed to be good. They discussed the coolant temperature problem and what modifications were needed to increase the air intake and, within a few days, James had rectified the problem and the test flights continued.

In the factory, Baker and James were usually closeted in James's office and the employees did not often see them together. The extent of their compatibility was judged more by the gales of laughter which would frequently emanate from James's office when Baker was there than by a first-hand observation of the two together. At Wing, however, with no office to retire to, the two were often observed together. They would stand facing each other, head to head, leaning forward. It was obvious to all who watched them that they had a marvellous working relationship and a unique rapport. They talked freely and with great informality, and they radiated the friendship that so obviously bound them together.

The test flights continued. James told Baker to take his time, and gradually Baker increased the manoeuvrability of the aircraft in flight. He reported after each flight on the excellent flying qualities of the MB3 and there was no talk of further modifications. One day he did a low-level run across the airfield just above the rooftops. He flew in from about two miles out and passed over the airfield at an impressive speed. Those watching understood that this was his way of demonstrating that this was no ordinary aircraft.

On 12 September, James and Baker travelled to Wing together in James's car. On the way they stopped at a convenient place to answer the calls of nature. While the two of them were standing behind a hedge, Baker suddenly said to James: 'I have a feeling, Jimmy, that something is not quite right, and I don't know what it is.' The conversation that followed was inconclusive, and the two men returned to the car and continued on their way.

When they arrived at Wing preparations were already underway for that day's flight. There had been problems during the previous few days with the fitting of the engine. A Napier engineer had been sent to Wing to oversee the fitting of the engine and the propeller. When he came to fix the transfer tube into the base of the propeller, before the pitch change mechanism was fitted, the tube would not bottom down properly, so consequently the pitch change mechanism would not bottom either. He had returned to the factory at Acton for extra equipment, and came back with a tap (an engineering tool that is used to cut a thread). He packed the tap with grease, put it on an extension piece, and inserted it inside the propeller and cut another thread and a half *in situ*. When he brought the tap out, the idea was that the pieces of metal resulting from that cutting of the threads would be embedded in the grease and all would be well. Some doubted the wisdom of this exercise and believe even now that it was a mistake to do this and that the engine should have been returned to the factory for the job to be done properly.

According to Baker, the engine was not running smoothly and it was shedding a lot of oil. The flight engineers had to clean the oil off the windscreen and the fuselage as part of the preparations for the flight. Eventually they decided that it was ready and Baker climbed into the cockpit and strapped himself in. He had apparently forgotten about his premonition from earlier in the morning. He was his usual cheerful self and showed no signs of worry or concern. Owen Gilbert, a Martin-Baker mechanic, climbed onto the aircraft to wipe the last of the oil off the windscreen before take-off, and Baker smiled and nodded his thanks.

Baker started the engine and taxied the aircraft down to the end of the runway. He started the take-off run and began to accelerate down the runway. James and the flight engineers were standing watching as they usually did. Suddenly the engine cut out. The onlookers tensed and became immediately alert. It looked as if Baker would have to abort the take-off run, and there was not much of the runway left for him to stop on, but almost immediately, the engine cut in again and the aircraft continued down the runway without stopping. The tension eased and as the aircraft lifted into the sky, the ground crew began to turn away and talk among themselves, the moment of danger having passed. But just then, the reassuring roar of the engine stopped and a deadly silence overtook them. Panic and disbelief gripped the onlookers. The aircraft was somewhere between 50 and 100 ft above the ground. It had already passed the end of the runway so a landing back on the runway was out of the question.

As is often the case when a disaster strikes quickly, people have difficulty in recalling exactly what happened, and in this case the aircraft disappeared out of sight behind a line of trees on the boundary of the airfield immediately before it crashed. It seems, however, that Baker tried to manoeuvre the aircraft towards a safe place to crash land, but that the wing tip hit a tree stump, causing the aircraft to cartwheel. The onlookers dropped everything and jumped onto their motorbikes or just ran. They heard the crash of the aircraft hitting the ground, an explosion, and then they saw the smoke rising into the sky. When they reached the tree line it was all over. The top of the cabin was embedded in a bank and the rest of the aircraft had cartwheeled out. It had lost the rear half, the engine section and the wings up to the stub, and the centrepiece with about 120 gallons of high octane fuel was ablaze. Steel tubes and panelling just virtually melted. There was nothing they could do. James flung himself onto a grass bank and lay there sobbing. 'My dear Val, my dear Val,' he said over and over again.

When the heat died down they were able to venture forward to the wreckage. It soon became clear that Baker must have been killed or knocked unconscious instantly and had not had to suffer the agony of burning to death as they had feared. His shoulder harness had been attached to the aircraft fuselage behind him, and it had ripped through the panelling like a knife and was hanging loose. Baker would have been thrown forward, and would have smashed his head as he hit the front of the cockpit. They got stakes of wood out of a nearby fence to try and prise his body out. His shrivelled and charred remains rolled down the wing stub and hit the ground. His body had been burned to less than half its size. Many of the men had seen crashes before, but nothing like this. It was utterly gruesome and horrific.

They all felt sick and distressed. They talked very little. Eventually they returned to the hangar as nobody knew quite what to do next. James was there, a solitary figure, walking up and down, apparently oblivious to what was going on around him. A young flight engineer nervously took him a cup of tea. 'Thanks, boy', he said as he took it from him.

Baker's death had an incalculable effect on James. The horror of the crash, the heat of the blazing aircraft, the stench of burning human flesh, were enough to make an indelible impression on those who only knew Baker as James's partner. Fifty years on, the memories of that day are still vivid enough to be upsetting. But James had lost his dearest friend. And more than that, his dear Val had been killed test flying an aeroplane that James had designed and constructed with his own hands. It was, of course, the failure of the Napier engine that had caused the crash, not any defect in the aircraft itself, but it still remained that he had died flying one of James's aeroplanes.

The personal loss was one that he lived with thereafter. Photographs of Baker still hang on the walls of James's office, years after his own death. In later years James, in his more reflective moments, would gaze at these photographs and wonder what he and Baker would have been doing had the crash not happened, whether indeed Baker would still have been alive. His loss became a yardstick for measuring other disasters in a quite simple way. James once said: 'When you have watched your best friend burn alive, nothing else really matters.'

He felt the loss so keenly that some have wondered how he ever came to terms with it sufficiently to carry on and succeed in life as he did. He believed that the accident need not have happened. If the Ministry had not forced the Napier engine on him, it would not have happened. And if the Ministry had allowed the test flights to take place at RAF Harwell, which had more open country around it, even an engine failure need not have been fatal, and Baker would not have been manoeuvring the falling aircraft in an attempt to find a safe place to land. He had always been frustrated by the Ministry men and their committee mentality, and by what he perceived as their arrogance and ignorance of the business of aircraft engineering. But Baker's unnecessary death was something he would never forget, and he vowed never to give in to the Ministry again.

But it was not just a personal loss that James had to bear. He had lost his business partner and test pilot, and the man who for 14 years had shared his enthusiasm for building a better aircraft. And he had lost the prototype. The aircraft was badly delayed as it was, and the second prototype had hardly been started and could not be finished in the foreseeable future.

Baker's body was in due course returned to Martin-Baker. His coffin was laid on a stand and a Union Jack draped over it. He lay in state in the machine shop at the factory, and his funeral service was conducted there, with the staff of Martin-Baker in attendance. A small booklet was prepared in memory of the fearless pilot whom everybody mourned, with photographs and a short biography, which was inscribed by James as follows:

This book is a tribute to one of the most kindly and lovable souls it has ever been my luck to meet with and his loss to me was a terrible blow. When I look over our partnership of the past 14 years I have nothing but happy memories of every moment of the time I spent with him – time will not cause me to forget him.

Chapter Seven

The MB5

At Martin-Baker it was definitely not business as usual. Ken Neil, who joined the company shortly after the crash to work in the drawing office, remembers that it was months before he saw his new boss. James remained closeted in his office. Occasionally his face would appear in the hatchway between his office and the drawing office, and he would exchange a few words with the chief draughtsman, but otherwise no-one saw him. It was several months before he continued his patrols of the factory, checking on progress and the well-being of his work-force. In the meantime, he bore his shock and grief alone.

The Ministry wrote to James on 3 October 1942 to clarify the contractual position *vis-à-vis* the crashed MB3. They accepted their liability to pay for the crashed prototype, but the amount that they were bound to pay was the cost to Martin-Baker of building it plus 5 per cent, up to a maximum of £25,500. The position was, however, somewhat complicated because the Ministry believed that the cost of the aircraft exceeded this figure, and the progress payments already made to the company exceeded this figure too. The Ministry thought that Martin-Baker had financed part of this excess expenditure by overcharging for sub-contract work on other items of equipment, in particular the blast tubes. They were anxious to regularize this position, particularly in view of the outstanding issues still to be addressed, namely the two remaining prototype aircraft still required under the contract. They therefore suggested that it would be necessary to segregate the cost of the aircraft from the sub-contract work so that the prices of each could be determined independently. They told James that, following agreement on the adjustment to be made to the sub-contract prices, they would seek from the Treasury a higher price for the three aircraft in substitution for the existing contract price, and James was asked to submit his proposals.

At this stage, the Ministry wanted James to complete the other two aircraft, and they stipulated 1 January 1943 as the new delivery date for the second aircraft. That gave James just three months to produce it, which he simply could not do. James had been considering a Mark II version of the MB3 with a blister-shaped canopy, but this only got as far as the drawing board. He had, however, decided to alter the layout of the aeroplane and to move the position of the cockpit forward by about 5 ft, and the drawings for this, designated the MB3A, were sent to the Ministry in October. James explained that the change would increase the pilot's view enormously as the previous position was too far back from the point of view of the gun sight's position. He went on to state that in his view the modification was 'an absolute essential and will greatly improve the fighting characteristics of the machine, without materially affecting the time of completion of the aircraft'. The next day, he wrote to the Ministry to express his full agreement to the desirability of clarifying the financial position but that he envisaged great difficulties in submitting a dissection of costs in the required form, even though he had called in a firm of London accountants to help him, and that while he was doing everything possible to complete the second aircraft by the end of the year, he could not guarantee it.

Both the desirability of this latest change to the aeroplane, and the ability to effect it without unduly delaying the aircraft, were accepted by the Ministry, and they gave James a revised delivery date of 1 February 1943. But despite an internal memorandum to the effect that James really seemed to be making every effort to get the aircraft ready by the time required, there were some at least who remained sceptical about his ability to finish the aircraft on time, however reasonable the task. In a Ministry minute dated 31 October 1942, one official summed up his view of the situation as follows:

> I must point out, however, that I saw no evidence of a change of front in Mr. Martin's attitude in regard to the relative importance of early flight trials and achieving 100% efficiency in his gadgetry. He is for example engaged on improving the engine and cannon mountings. While no-one could deny that all these designs are of very real importance, there is of course no end to them. Since it is difficult to visualise circumstances which would cause Mr. Martin to freeze his design during the next few weeks, I think it must be regarded as doubtful, as things stand at the moment, that we shall have the second aeroplane flying before the end of March.

Those working with James then remember the situation well. Baker's death made him re-evaluate each and every aspect of the aeroplane. It seems that he felt as if the aircraft was fundamentally flawed in some way and he wanted to incorporate numerous changes. Unfortunately, change for the sake of change is no basis for successful development, particularly in many cases where change was not required. But there was nothing that anyone could do to alter his approach at this stage, and the need to redesign became a self-fulfilling prophecy as he tried to mend what did not need mending.

The only happy event at this time was the birth of James's twin sons, John and James, in November 1942. James was exceptionally pleased, and wasted no time in telling his work-force about their arrival. 'It's a bloody sight easier making twins than it is making aeroplanes,' he told them. The delivery date was easier to forecast too. And James's quick grasp for the necessities of life led to a steel air-raid shelter being built over the twins' cot in a matter of days.

At the end of February 1943, the Ministry noted the disturbing reports about the slow progress of the second aircraft and the fact that they seemed to be heading for the same sort of delays as before. The Ministry estimated that they could not expect flight tests before July, and so in early May, the Director of Contracts submitted the matter for a policy decision. The Ministry had received a report from the firm of accountants that James had called in to help him. This report revealed that the state of the company books prevented a precise apportionment of costs as between aircraft and blast tubes, but they put the cost of producing the three aircraft as at 17 August 1942 (nearly nine months previously) at £97,934. The maximum payable under the contract for all three aircraft was only £59,500. The delivery date for the second aircraft had by now slipped to the end of July, which meant that the cost of another year's work had to be added to the accountants' figure. James was unable to estimate the cost of completing the aircraft. The Ministry estimated that costs would have risen to about £130,000 by the time the second aircraft was completed, but this left entirely open the question of the time and cost of producing the third.

The Ministry realized that whether they liked it or not, and they did not, they now found themselves in the position that the contract terms had been superseded by circumstances, and that payment could only be made on the basis of cost as long as the work on the aeroplanes continued with their knowledge and approval. Were the two remaining aircraft to be completed regardless of time and cost? This could only be justified on the basis that the design of the aircraft had exceptional potential value or that it was desirable to keep the company in existence, for the Ministry were then of the view that if they cancelled both aircraft, Martin-Baker would 'practically close down'.

The Ministry officials went down to see James again. They considered that it would be most undesirable if he were to be forced out of business in view of his invaluable sideline projects. In the light of the delays in producing the second aircraft, there seemed no point in continuing with the third. But they were worried that if they cancelled the third, James might refuse to co-operate with them on the *ad hoc* modification work they still wanted him to do, and would argue that he was no longer in a position to do this without prejudicing the production of the remaining aircraft.

James had been pressing for a Rolls-Royce Griffon engine, the engine that he had originally wanted for the MB3, to replace the Napier engine which had been the cause of the crash. The Ministry told James that they were prepared for him to continue with the second aircraft and complete it but not the third and, in order to soften this blow, that they would let him have a Griffon for installation in the second aircraft if he could assure them that it could be done without undue delay. As part of the deal for giving James the Griffon, he was also asked if he would undertake more modification work, and to extend that work beyond the initial design phase into a pre-production flow.

James was in no position to say no and could only argue that shortage of labour might impede his efforts. And so James was asked to design a sliding hood for the Mustang, and to take the design through the pre-production stage. In summary, the Ministry Minute recorded that: 'The Martin-Baker fighter undoubtedly has features which we would like to see put to the full flight trial stage, that we want to make the best use possible of Martin's small factory, and because of his great belief in his own design, it will be necessary for him to complete it as part of the bargain.' It would appear from this Minute that the Ministry had lost any real interest they might have had in this aircraft from a production point of view, and that their desire to see it finished was based on expediency.

In June, James was talking about having the second aircraft finished in three months' time. A month later the Director of Contracts took up the point, insisting that there must be a time limit imposed for completion and that to avoid any question of their being unreasonable, James should be asked to set his own date. James was unwilling to commit himself, and there were discussions at the Ministry as to whether James should be told, because of his failure to specify a completion date, that he should stop work immediately or, alternatively, that if the aeroplane was not finished by the end of September, no further extensions would be granted. They concluded that they could not tell him to stop work, because it had become more profitable to complete the aircraft than to discard it, and that there was no point in threatening him with cancellation at the end of September when he could so easily call their bluff. Instead, his suggestion that the second aircraft might be ready to fly at the end of September was acknowledged, he was formally told that the aircraft work took priority over the Mustang hood, and that when considering the profit to be allowed to him from the second aircraft, they would take into account the efficiency displayed in getting it finished. This last stipulation was, of course, a meaningless threat to James. It was not profit that he was looking for but orders. He had never been financially motivated except to the extent that survival demanded it, and threatening to limit his profit if the aircraft was delayed would have had no influence on him at all.

James's unconventional approach to business was apparent in other ways, too. In 1943 he was looking for a new secretary. His accountant, Ronald Ogden, put him in touch with a secretary, Miss Gladys Nicholls, who was looking for a new job. James insisted on visiting her that evening, took her out for dinner and then drove her to the factory where he made her climb up ladders and walk along planks, so that he could explain the MB5 (as the aircraft was now designated) to her. Miss Nicholls was rather perturbed by the whole situation, particularly as at no time was there an interview of any description, any discussion of the job or any mention of wages. James just asked her when she could start work, and within minutes she realized that she would be working for this extraordinary man on the next Monday. She very soon also realized that working for James successfully had nothing to do with experience and qualifications. 'Either your face fitted or it did not', she said.

He was still working very long hours, but the delays with the aeroplane continued. The Ministry continued to visit and discuss the situation. By December 1943, they were reporting 'one of the usual stir-ups with Martin, but find that he has now got into difficulty on the centre of gravity when using a Griffon engine and has to make a change to move the engine further forward'. The report continued: 'I really think that there is no good purpose served in continuing to talk about any date, because Martin being Martin, will never leave the job alone. All I can do is to push him along to the best extent possible, and hope that we shall get it into the air one of these days.' But there was a certain pragmatism in this evaluation of the situation. The report went on to say: 'I do not think any undue loss is being experienced over this delay, because it is only Martin himself and a very small number of men who are engaged, and the Fighter is not affecting the output of small parts for which we rely upon this firm to produce.'

As mentioned above, the prototype with the Griffon engine had now been designated by James the MB5. While trying to secure a different engine, James had considered the Bristol Centaurus, and drawings of an aircraft with this engine had been prepared on a preliminary basis, to be known as the MB4. But the Griffon had been the engine he had wanted from the outset of the MB3 and, when this became available, he dropped his consideration of alternatives.

Once the decision had been taken that it was now cheaper to finish the aircraft than cancel it, and that the delivery date was no longer really significant, it seems that James was less bothered by officialdom. The aircraft proceeded at his pace, until he had a machine nearing completion and could no longer proceed without a pilot. It is interesting that at this stage James did not have a test pilot for the MB5 and had made no attempt to find someone for this job, for the pilot was generally considered to be an essential part of the team required to design a new aeroplane. James had no-one in mind for the job, and it was the Ministry of Aircraft Production who suggested Bryan Greensted, the chief test pilot at Rotol Limited. James invited him to Denham. He showed him the MB5 and invited him to climb into it to have a closer look. James then asked him if he would like to test fly it. Greensted agreed, although he thought it was absolutely incredible that James should have left it so late before deciding who the pilot was going to be and that he should have invited someone whom he did not know, who was no part of his organization, and who in fact worked for someone else, to fly his aircraft.

But James had never felt constrained by what other people did and how they did it. He was an individualist and, as always, he did things his way. Surprised though Greensted was at this method of proceeding, it would have been more surprising to those who knew James at that time had he tried to replace Baker after the crash. Baker, the man, was irreplaceable and as far as James was concerned, the advice and encouragement he had provided to James over the years had been a part of their special relationship and could not be given by anyone else.

It was May 1944 when James finally decided that the aircraft should be flown. It was dismantled into its major components, loaded onto a transporter and taken to RAF Harwell. There it was reassembled, checked and flown for the first time all on the same day, 23 May, in itself a remarkable achievement.

James had by this stage designed and patented a method for tethering an aeroplane on the ground whilst the engine was being run up for testing purposes or prior to take-off. He had discovered that the usual practice of placing chocks in front of the landing wheels of an aircraft to prevent it from moving on the ground due to the thrust produced by the rotation of the airscrew was unsatisfactory with the increased thrust produced by variable pitch and contra-rotating airscrews because there was a tendency for the aircraft to jump the chocks. His simple tethering device, which provided for one or more cables to be connected to the forward parts of the aeroplane to take the forward thrust, and a further connection to the tail end of the aeroplane to restrain its tendency to lift, overcame these problems.

It is sometimes forgotten that the MB5 was in fact a rebuilt MB3 with a different engine, built to the same specification, and incorporating those design changes that James decided upon during the course of construction, and that it was not a completely new aeroplane. There were therefore some obvious similarities between the two aircraft, in the tubular steel construction, the wide-tracked, pneumatically operated undercarriage, and the torsion box construction of the wings. In the MB5, however, the cockpit was further forward (the change that James had suggested for the MB3 in the month after the crash), the armament was reduced from six to four 20 mm Hispano cannon, and the Griffon engine was installed in a slim fuselage nose with the intercooler, main coolant and oil radiators situated underneath the fuselage behind the cockpit.

Surprisingly, the MB5 suffered similar problems to those experienced with the MB2, and which James had tried so hard to rectify quickly, namely directional instability. Although there were no formal flight trials of the MB3, there are those who watched Baker fly it and who listened to his comments on landing it, to confirm that its directional stability was not a problem. Greensted however remembered very clearly his first flight in the MB5, and he recalled: 'Right from the very beginning I suppose you could say that it was a badly designed aircraft because it didn't work in the sense that it was directionally unstable. It was an absolute swine to fly because it wouldn't keep itself straight.' He was amazed that this should have been a problem. 'I still don't understand why the thing wasn't right when I first flew it. After all, the theory of design of aircraft at that stage was pretty advanced and I don't understand how he could make a mistake about the directional stability . . . I would certainly have thought that if he made a mistake at all he might have made it too straight so that it was difficult to turn the aircraft, but to have one which was turning itself all the time seemed to me to be stupid.' But then, of course, James's design of aircraft was based more on his own ideas than on any generally accepted theories.

As a result, the rear end of the aircraft had to be substantially modified and it was nearly six months before Greensted was asked to fly it again. A further problem arose out of the failure of the translational unit in the contra-rotating propeller after only a few hours of flying. After his tragic experience with the MB3, James felt that he could not take any risks with this unit and that the problems would have to be solved immediately. He found that there was no proper system of lubrication, and that lubrication was carried out in a haphazard way by hand, which caused excess oil to be flung onto the windscreen of the aircraft. He therefore designed a new translational unit with an effective system of lubrication which was undertaken as a private venture job. There were other minor things wrong with the aircraft too which had to be rectified, and it all took time. James's dream of building the best fighter aircraft was slipping through his fingers. The war was drawing to a close and with it the need for better fighter capacity.

Nevertheless, whatever the problems from the pilot's point of view, the MB5 created a good impression in other respects. Sir Stafford Cripps from the Ministry of Aircraft Production wrote to James on 31 May 1944 to say:

> I was very interested and thrilled by my visit to Harwell and the inspection of your prototype. From the constructional and accessibility point of view I have never seen anything to equal it and I do congratulate you most heartily upon the result. I think you will now have to get on with a new one looking even further ahead.

There were indeed many aspects of the MB5 which were, in their own way, exceptional. Greensted remembered some of the points that impressed Sir Stafford Cripps and others, such as the fact that the cockpit had a covered floor. He was used to flying aircraft in which the floor of the cockpit was the inside of the aircraft fuselage, which could sometimes be problematical if the pilot dropped something. He recalled:

> James was full of ingenious ideas which were good ones. One of the great things about his fighter, the MB5, was that it was very easy to take to pieces and put together again, to repair and change the engines and so forth, and the sort of thing that he had thought about was that in order to make the engine change as speedy as possible, he had on the fireproof bulkhead behind the engine, split pins that were all the right size, so that the chap who was changing the engine didn't have to go back to the stores for them, they were already

there on the fireproof bulkhead. Nobody else did it, nobody else had thought of doing it, but it was brilliant in the sense that it was an extremely good and very sensible idea.

Greensted also recalled how James was the sole designer behind the MB5. He would meet James after every test flight or series of test flights to report to him on the snags and problems. James would listen very carefully to everything he said and he knew that James would take immediate action to deal with the points he raised, but no-one else in the factory was ever invited or even allowed to listen. Indeed, no-one else in the factory appeared to be involved in the MB5. 'He was very much a one man band,' Greensted remembered.

Once again, this single-handed approach to his design work could only delay the modifications which needed to be made to the MB5 before its official trials. But the delays did not affect Greensted who only came to fly the MB5 when asked to by James, and they did not mar his enjoyment of the stimulating discussions in which he inevitably became embroiled when visiting James. Greensted's memories of him then echo the memories of those working for him in earlier days. He remembered James as:

> a remarkably ingenious sort of chap. He would think about three different things at the same time. He was very, very versatile in his thinking, brilliant, but mercurial. He was bubbling over with ideas all the time, and if you started talking on a subject with him you knew very well that within a quarter of an hour you would be just as deeply in discussion on a subject that was completely unrelated to the theme you were supposed to be discussing.

Between May 1944 and October 1945, the aircraft was flown for only 40 hours, during which time there were no mechanical problems, but in October 1945 it made a spectacular public appearance at the RAE Farnborough 'At Home' three-day event. This included flying displays by British aircraft and static exhibits, including captured German aircraft, together with displays of the work of some of the RAE departments.

The flying displays included the MB5, expertly flown by Greensted, who gave an impressive display of the aircraft's flying potential including its short take-off ability, its exceptional rate of climb, and generally excellent handling characteristics. Unfortunately, in a subsequent display flight, when those watching included the then Prime Minister, Winston Churchill, there was an engine failure. It was a quite dramatic incident because the engine seized and pushed out a lot of oil and fumes. Suddenly, Greensted found that he was unable to see out of the cockpit. There was a quick-release lever on the cockpit hood, and he elected to use this and release the top of the canopy immediately so that he could clear the air in the cockpit. Unfortunately, the jettisoned hood hit and badly damaged the new, redesigned tailplane. It was not disastrous, and Greensted successfully executed a dead-stick landing back on the runway, but the aircraft was badly damaged and took months to repair.

Apart from the damage to the aircraft, Greensted suffered a very sore shoulder, because the quick-release lever was on the hood itself, so that when he pulled it, the hood flew off and wrenched his arm badly in the process. With the benefit of experience, this was the wrong place to have positioned the lever, and it had to be redesigned and repositioned on the floor.

In the end, it was February 1946 before the aircraft was delivered to Boscombe Down and underwent its formal trials. By this time, Greensted had flown the aircraft for about 80 hours in the 21 months since its first flight. This time James did not have to endure the criticisms that had been made of the MB2 in 1938. The Engineering and Maintenance Appraisal report was clear:

> The general design and layout of this aircraft is excellent and is greatly superior from the engineering and maintenance aspect to any other similar type of aircraft.
>
> The layout of the cockpit might very well be made a standard for normal piston-engined fighters; and the engine installation might, with great advantage, be applied to other aircraft.
>
> The time necessary for a quick turn round, i.e., arming, refuelling, re-plenishing oxygen and accumulators, would appear to be very low when compared with existing types of aircraft.

The MB2 had scored well on maintenance aspects too but had fallen short on flying qualities. But with the MB5, James got it right. The report on the Handling Trials concluded that:

> the Martin-Baker MB5 was easy and pleasant to fly, and highly rated by all pilots as regards its flying qualities. Apart from minor criticisms of cockpit layout and flying controls the chief fault of the aircraft was its relatively poor performance by present standards. Its combination of steady flight behaviour, good control and excellent view should make it a very good gun platform, and from the maintenance aspect the design is excellent.

In June 1946, the MB5 made another public appearance at the four-day exhibition and flying display of British aircraft at Farnborough, this time piloted by the Polish pilot, S/L Jan Zurakowski. He was exceedingly impressed by it, and is quoted as having exclaimed to his colleagues after his first flight in it: 'What is the matter with you English? This is the best aeroplane I have ever flown. Why was it never put into production during the war?'

The MB5 is invariably highly praised. It has been described as the best piston-engined single-seater fighter built in Great Britain, ahead of its time in terms of engineering performance, handling and pilot appeal, an enigma in the annals of aviation history as it never went into production. Why then did it never go into production? Was it simply too late? In 1946, the war was over and the advent of the jet engine had removed the need for new piston-engined fighters. As Greensted said: 'It was a very, very good aeroplane, but nobody was thinking in terms of building a piston-engined fighter aircraft from scratch then; imagine the organisation necessary for putting it into quantity production.'

In considering the fate of the MB5, it is relevant to look back to the summer of 1939 and the start of the MB3. The MB3 and the MB5 were built under the same contract to Specification F.18/39. The MB5 was the second aircraft built under this contract and was, in effect, the MB3 modified to take the Rolls-Royce Griffon engine. As we know, James had intended that the MB3 should have a Griffon engine and it was the Ministry decision to substitute the Napier engine in 1940 that changed this. If the Ministry had not insisted on this engine substitution, the timing of James's Griffon-engined fighter would have been very different. The development of it from the commencement of work in 1939 would inevitably have taken a different course, and it is perhaps idle speculation to try and guess how good an aircraft it would have been. However, it is probably safe to assume that from the maintenance point of view it would have been as successful as the MB2 and the MB5: there is no reason to suppose otherwise.

It is more difficult to second guess its flying qualities, but arguably these might have been impressive too by the standards of the time. The MB3 had none of the directional instability problems of the MB2 and the MB5, and it had certainly impressed those who saw it flying during the ten flights before its crash. The directional instability problems of the MB5 had crept into the design after the complete reappraisal of the MB3 following the crash, and they were in any event completely eradicated.

There are grounds then for suggesting that this Griffon-engined fighter could have been worthy of a production order and been in time to make production of a new type from this small factory with limited manufacturing capacity a viable proposition (although recognizing, of course, that the logistical problems of producing an aircraft in these circumstances would have been enormous), particularly bearing in mind the requirement to re-engine the Spitfire with a Griffon engine. In the autumn of 1942, the Ministry recognized the need for a high performance, low altitude fighter to meet the threat of the Focke-Wulf 190, and the Spitfire was modified to take the Griffon engine to meet this requirement.

W/Cdr. M.A. Smith, who flew the MB5 in 1946, wrote:

There is no doubt that when the Martin-Baker 5 made its first flight in May, 1944, it was in many ways ahead of its time. A great deal might have been learned from such an aircraft had it been put into production and service, and if a decision had been taken without undue delay, the M-B5 could have reached the squadrons in time to do useful work against the enemy.

The problems encountered by Greensted when he first flew the MB5 were not widely known, and W/Cdr. Smith may not have been aware of them when he made his appraisal of the MB5. Greensted agreed that the MB5 probably would have gone into production, although perhaps only for a limited order, if everything had been right from the outset. But James took too long to correct the problems.

There is no doubt that James's innate inability to finalize a design without considering all the possible alternatives greatly contributed to the delay in producing the MB5. But this innate trait was greatly accentuated by what he considered to be his unfair treatment at the hands of the Ministry in connection with the MB2, and then again by the effect of Baker's crash. In 1938, when James had delivered the MB2 to Martlesham Heath, the official trials demonstrated that certain modifications were necessary. This, however, was the basis on which other aircraft designers habitually delivered their designs for trials. They gave priority to getting their aircraft into the system, and knew how best to get their aircraft through the system. But James, as a newcomer to this set-up, had not fared so happily. Thereafter he was determined that the Ministry should not be given the opportunity to turn down another of his aircraft on the basis of some deficiency which could be remedied, and so it was a long time before he was prepared to release the MB5 for its trials. As Greensted explained:

> he felt wary of the politics of the situation. He felt that as an outsider, if there was even a small problem with the aircraft, this could be seized upon as grounds for turning him down. The other thing was, of course, that companies such as Vickers, Supermarine and Hawker were in an incredibly strong position. But James had no leverage with the Ministry at all.

James's attention was also diverted from the MB5 by his work on assisted escape systems for aircraft which he had begun in the autumn of 1944. It was only five months after the MB5 was delivered to Boscombe Down for its official trials that 18 months of intensive test and development work culminated in the first live airborne test of the ejection seat, and it is undeniable that James's efforts were increasingly directed towards the development of the ejection seat during the course of 1945. James must have been torn between his great desire to build a successful aeroplane, to fulfil the dream that he and his dear Val had set out to achieve, and to acknowledge the realities of the situation that the chances of the MB5 going into production were receding day by day, but that he had a real chance of winning official support for his ejection seat. But he was not one to give up and it would have been inconceivable for him to have abandoned the MB5 at such a late stage.

Indeed, James's ambition of building a great fighter aircraft did not end with the MB5. James had commenced the design of two other aeroplanes while finalizing the design of the MB5 and of two more in 1946. The first of these, a twin-engined, twin boom pusher aircraft, was probably a sequel to the tankbuster. The next was an experimental twin-engined jet fighter with two Rolls-Royce Derwent engines. Then there was the MB6, often thought to be his Delta wing design, but which was in fact a single-engined jet fighter with four 20 mm Hispano cannons. Finally, his Delta wing jet fighter, which was designed to Specification F.43/46, with a Rolls-Royce AJ-65 engine, two 20 mm Hispano cannon, and an ejection seat in a fully pressurized cockpit which was faired into the base of the fin. None of these designs progressed further than the drawing board, but James displayed a model of his Delta wing jet at the SBAC show at Radlett in 1947 and it attracted quite a lot of interest. The periodical *Air International* expressed the view that 'Advanced aerodynamics and a jet engine thus combined with the proven engineering features of the MB5 could have produced a world beater in the late forties, when supersonic flight was still in its infancy', but the development of this project was unfortunately well beyond the resources of Martin-Baker.

Lack of resources was of course another reason for the delays in producing his aircraft. He did not have a big enough factory or work-force, nor did he have the financial resources to support his development programme adequately. He simply could not produce a new prototype as quickly as Vickers or Hawker or Supermarine, and he certainly could not produce a new prototype efficiently when heavily engaged on other projects.

Notwithstanding the development of the ejection seat and James's propensity for changing his designs, it is difficult to avoid the conclusion that the reasons why the MB5 did not go into production must lie to a large extent in James's relationship with the Ministry. Throughout the war they hampered his attempts to build aircraft by their insistence that he undertake the modification work that he did so well, so that this disruptive work could be kept away from the big aircraft manufacturers. They did not let him have the engine he wanted until too late in the day and, while they backed many other ventures which were unsuccessful or disappointing (ironically, the Napier Sabre engine was an expensive and problematical venture for the Ministry), they were unwilling to support James's aircraft work in this way, despite their reliance and outspoken praise of his other design work.

A report in the periodical *Flight International* in 1979 expressed this view:

The Air Ministry's interest in the Martin-Baker prototypes was somewhat ambivalent; it was considered that they served a useful purpose in allowing Martin to develop and prove some of his ingenious engineering ideas, but the company was not regarded as a likely source of a fighter to be built in quantity (even by licensees) for RAF service unless the established fighter design and production companies proved completely incapable of meeting the RAF's needs or had been bombed out of existence . . . as the last of the Martin-Baker aeroplanes, the MB5 remains today a monument to the designer's engineering skill and his tenacity in putting his ideas into practice in the face of adversity.

The Ministry men did not like James. They found him difficult to deal with, which of course he could be, and they had no idea how to cope with his outspoken and abrupt manner, his lack of co-operation, and his complete belief in the value of his own work. It is of course true that James did nothing to help himself in this regard, and made no attempt to hide his frustration and irritation with these people, and he was quite definitely his own worst enemy in his dealings with the Ministry. Sir George Edwards said of James: 'It was not a question of him not suffering fools gladly, he simply did not suffer them at all', and he had his own, narrow notion of who was a fool. Ministry officials habitually came within this definition: they produced nothing and so served no useful purpose. They were not aircraft designers and were in no position to tell him what to do and when to do it. He felt that he had been unfairly treated by them, and he could not forgive them for the Napier engine and the crash of the MB3. As a result of his attitude to them, they were not prepared to be sympathetic towards him or to try and accommodate him in any way. But people of extraordinary ability are not always the easiest to deal with, and it is a pity that the system could not cope with and did not support the brilliant eccentricity and undoubted ingenuity of this exceptional man for, if it had, the RAF might have benefited from some very useful aircraft.

Chapter Eight

Learning to Blast People Out of Aeroplanes

During the later years of the war, the British aviation authorities began to give serious consideration to the question of assisted escape for pilots from military aircraft. As aircraft became faster, so it became increasingly difficult for pilots to overcome the blast of the slipstream and climb out of the cockpits of their aircraft and parachute to safety. In combat conditions, where injury to the pilot, pilot disorientation and unfavourable g conditions in out-of-control aircraft were all likely to occur, escape was often impossible. The prospect of jet-engined aircraft entering service in the near future emphasized the pressing need to address the problem of emergency escape from high-speed aircraft, and the problem was brought into focus on 4 January 1944 when S/L Davie, a Royal Aircraft Establishment test pilot, was killed while test flying a Gloster F9/40, a Meteor prototype. Although he had managed to climb out of the cockpit, he had been hit by the tailplane and injured or knocked unconscious, with the result that he had been unable to deploy his parachute.

On 27 April 1944 a meeting took place at the Ministry of Aircraft Production to discuss the possible methods of emergency escape from aircraft. The meeting was reminded of the 'excessive hazards' facing pilots who attempted to escape from aircraft travelling at high speeds. Various schemes were briefly discussed whereby the pilot, with or without his seat, would be propelled clear of the aircraft, either upwards or downwards, or where part of the aircraft itself, including the cockpit, would be ejected, or where the tail of the aircraft would be blown off and the pilot thrown clear. It was clear that if the escape took place at high altitude, the pilot could be killed by exposure to the freezing cold and lack of oxygen which he would experience after leaving the aircraft, and that any ejection apparatus would have to cope with this eventuality. Here was an entirely new set of problems to be solved and there was no relevant data in Great Britain to which the Ministry could refer.

At a meeting at the RAE at Farnborough the next month, further difficulties were discussed. One of the problems to be overcome was thought to be that of avoiding the great difference in pressure that a pilot would experience on various parts of his body if he tried to climb out of the aircraft in the normal way. It was feared that these pressure differences might be enough to injure or even break off any part of a man's body which became exposed to the slipstream whilst the rest of his body was still in the aircraft. It was also thought that the blast of the slipstream might be sufficient to cause lung damage. These discussions led to some preliminary conclusions. Firstly, it might be necessary to eject the pilot at such a speed that for all practical purposes the whole of his body would enter the slipstream at the same time, although no-one knew whether a man could withstand the force necessary to do this, and it was felt that the modifications that would need to be made to aircraft to achieve this would make it an impractical solution for existing aircraft. Secondly, it might prove necessary to eject the entire cockpit and slow it down on a parachute before the pilot made his escape, a scheme which would again require considerable modifications to existing aircraft and which might impose unacceptable forces on the pilot. The third proposal was to slow the speed of the aircraft itself by using a brake parachute before the pilot escaped, which initially seemed the most feasible alternative for existing aircraft, albeit one which would be difficult to test. However, a report from the Parachute Section received the next month indicated that the idea of slowing down an aircraft in this situation was unrealistic.

By August 1944 the authorities had reached the tentative conclusion that the forced ejection of the pilot, most probably with his seat, seemed the best way forward, together with a barometrically controlled, automatically opening parachute that would open only at or below a predetermined altitude. Research began at the RAF Physiology Department on such fundamental questions as how much acceleration a man's body could withstand during this sort of ejection process. It was decided to initiate some designs for assisted escape apparatus by approaching certain identified firms. Bearing in mind the parlous state of knowledge about the subject, the design of an escape system of universal application to all aircraft seemed preferable to allowing each of the aircraft manufacturers to design their own system for their own aircraft. The first firm mentioned as a suitable candidate for the proposal was R. Malcolm Limited (later known as ML Aviation Limited), a firm run by Marcel Lobelle, a Belgian national, but a Ministry Minute of the next day mentioned a second firm, Martin-Baker. It was the end of September 1944 and the Ministry decided that these two firms should be approached for their initial reactions.

Although not strictly part of the story of James Martin and his work, it is interesting to see how far the development of an assisted escape system for pilots had progressed in the meantime in Germany and Sweden, the two countries that already had aircraft ejection seats in limited use. By the autumn of 1944, the Ministry had received a copy of a German patent for an ejection unit for a pilot. They had also received various reports of German ejection seats and sightings of pilots being fired into the sky. An unidentified German radio station in November 1944 described the assault fighter squadrons of the Luftwaffe, equipped with what were translated as 'spring' seats, operated either mechanically or by an explosive charge, which were to be used for ramming attacks against Allied bombers which, if successful, would destroy the bomber and its crew whilst the German pilot ejected to safety. But the full extent of the development of ejection seats overseas only became apparent, of course, after the end of the war when foreign research and development data became available, and foreign seats could be shipped to England for examination. Until then, the British were inevitably duplicating much of the research that had already been undertaken abroad.

The Germans began working on ejection equipment in 1939 when Junkers designed a seat which was used in prototypes of the Junkers 88 and their design was patented in Germany in 1941. The Germans used test rigs to assist their research and had allowed the different aircraft manufacturers to develop their own systems, with the result that a system using compressed air to eject the seat was used in the Heinkel 219 and the Dornier 335, and a system using explosive cartridges was used in the Focke-Wulf Ta 154 and the He 162. During the development of a rocket-propelled aircraft, the He 176, the Heinkel company had also worked on the idea of providing for the separation of the cockpit from the rest of the aircraft in an emergency, so that the cockpit capsule could be slowed down by a brake parachute, thus enabling the pilot to make an escape at a much slower speed. But with the advance of the jet engine, Heinkel favoured their compressed air-operated ejection seat which was put to the ultimate test on 13 January 1942 when their test pilot Helmut Schenk successfully ejected from an He 280 when the aircraft iced up and became uncontrollable, and so became the first person on record to save his life in an emergency situation using an ejection seat. It is believed that over 60 Luftwaffe aircrew were saved by the compressed air-operated ejection seats, the first escape during combat being by the two aircrew of an He 219 on 11 April 1944 when the British were only just beginning to address the question of escape systems.

As the war progressed, German aircraft manufacturers put several different designs of seat into service, and they eventually abandoned the compressed air-operated ejection seat and universally adopted the cartridge-operated seat. The progress of their work was however severely hampered by the demands and priorities imposed by the war, and shortly after the end of the war, when James was authorized to visit Germany to inspect some of their test facilities, it was clear that Martin-Baker was as far advanced with its work on ejection systems as any of the German companies.

Meanwhile, the Swedish company Saab was also developing its own ejection seat. Their research started in 1940 and in October 1941 they registered their first patent for an ejection seat. On 8 January 1942, they successfully ejected a dummy from an airborne Saab B17 aircraft, which was the first recorded ejection in the air. Like James a few years later, the Swedes started with a cartridge-operated seat and did not in the early stages of their work get involved in the compressed air system. Their ejection seat first went into production in 1943.

James was first approached with the problem of assisted escape from aircraft on an informal basis. In the early summer of 1944, W/Cdr. John Jewell of Fighter Command visited Denham and told James that, following the death of S/L Davie in January and the imminent introduction of Meteor aircraft to RAF squadrons, there was considerable anxiety among RAF pilots in connection with bailing out, and that some means of escape would have to be devised which would make it possible for pilots to abandon aircraft at high speed, since climbing out of the cockpit of a jet aeroplane was clearly out of the question.

When the Ministry approached James and Lobelle in October 1944, it was apparent that they had both given some thought to the problem. Notwithstanding the official preference for a forced ejection system, both James and Lobelle at this stage favoured the idea of a swinging arm apparatus. This was a sheet metal arm, lying along or recessed in the fuselage of the aircraft, with its rear end pivoted to the aircraft structure and its front end attached to the pilot's seat or to his parachute harness. The idea was simple. The pilot would jettison the cockpit canopy, the front end of the metal arm would be raised, whereupon the arm would hoist the pilot clear of the aircraft, and aerodynamic forces acting on the arm would take over and throw the pilot clear of the aircraft fin. It was a device which seemed to bear similarities to a mediaeval catapult system, but despite this, it appealed to the Ministry. One of the official concerns about an ejection system was the fear that the pilot might not be propelled high enough to clear the tailplane, and it seemed that the swinging arm device would always ensure that the pilot was thrown clear of the aircraft structure. Lobelle thought that the pilot's feet should be tucked in and the pilot thrown out in his seat, whereas James felt that the pilot should be hoisted out by his shoulder harness without his seat. His version, with the swinging arm mounted on the top of the fuselage and the rear end attached just forward of the fin, had a 'U'-shaped fixture on the front end which attached to special rings on the parachute harness and pulled the pilot into a standing position as he was extracted from the aircraft. He did not think that the absence of a seat to support the pilot's back would cause problems, but he emphasized the Martin philosophy that the only way of ascertaining this would be by progressive experiment.

James took a model of his swinging arm apparatus to Freeman at the Ministry of Aircraft Production on 11 October 1944. Freeman was very impressed by this device and immediately took James and his model to see the Minister, Sir Stafford Cripps. At this meeting they agreed that he should start his development work as soon as possible. James asked for the loan of an aeroplane in which to fit his device in order that he could fully demonstrate the principle which was, in James's words, 'like drawing a fish out of water', and it was agreed that he would receive delivery of a Defiant fuselage within two days for this purpose.

The Controller of Research and Development at the Ministry was of the view that James's idea 'appears simple and most attractive' and he asked the Director of Technical Development to arrange for 'a practical trial to be done by Martin with the aid of some old fuselage'. Years of dealing with James had taught the Ministry to be a little cautious. The Minute continues: 'When you lay this on you must watch that Martin does not claim retention of draughtsmen because of this work. I think you will agree it should not require any drawing work.' (In October 1944, the Ministry were still waiting for the MB5 to be delivered to Boscombe Down for its official trials following its first flight in May of that year.)

At this point it was not entirely clear whether the Ministry wanted an escape system that could be retrofitted to existing aircraft, or whether they required a system for installation in new aircraft types, and this was obviously a very relevant factor. The Ministry had imposed a requirement for improved emergency escape facilities in all aircraft Specifications dated after the end of October 1944 for high-speed aircraft (which, for this purpose, was an aircraft which could fly at speeds in excess of 400 mph), and, at a meeting in August 1944, the Ministry had decided to proceed with the development of forced ejection gear and, when it had been successfully developed, to consider the possibility of retrofitting it into existing types.

James at this stage was working on the assumption that his design had to be capable of retrofit, and that two of the principal aircraft involved would be the Spitfire and the Hurricane. The cockpits of these aircraft were too small to allow the pilot to be removed in the sitting position in his seat as there was insufficient clearance for the pilot's knees and feet to pass the windscreen arch, and there was very little that could be done to increase the space in the cockpit. It was these considerations that had led James to conceive his version of the swinging arm.

On 1 November 1944 the Director of Technical Development wrote to James asking him to proceed with the development of the swinging arm scheme which they had discussed the previous week at Denham. He was told to apply his ideas first to the gunner's cockpit in a Defiant, but to bear in mind that they were primarily concerned with an escape system for use with high-speed types. He stressed the fact that they were not contemplating a contract to cover this work at this stage, although they might reconsider the position when the work was more advanced. This did not bother James, however, who did not want a contract either, primarily because he was concerned that a contract might prejudice his design and patent rights in any ejection system he successfully developed.

Shortly after this, the Ministry wrote to the designers then working on high-speed aircraft, and to James and Lobelle, inviting them all to a meeting on 14 November 1944 to discuss the escape problem. Everyone attended in person or by substitute except James, who replied that the MB5 would probably be flying at Harwell that day and, accordingly, he would be unable to attend. He did not, of course, send a substitute and

the meeting took place without him. The various schemes were discussed
and it was decided that the Ministry's original idea of a forced ejection
system was the best way forward. A copy of the minutes of this meeting
was sent to James for his information. Later that month the Ministry
discussed the possibility of placing a contract with Malcolm for the
development, in conjunction with the RAE, of a suitable ejection device,
and Lobelle was asked to quote for supplying one or two ejection units.

On 6 December 1944, James wrote to Freeman on the subject of his
proposal:

> When I called on you on 11th October last I showed you a model of a scheme
> I had got out for the Forced Ejection of Pilots from Cockpits, and you kindly
> took me in to see Sir Stafford Cripps and demonstrated my design to him.
>
> Two months have nearly elapsed and as yet I have not received a fuselage
> for the fitting of one of these mechanisms.
>
> I understand that a Conference was held at MAP London on the 14th
> November, a month after I had shown you my model, to discuss this problem
> with various designers and to pool ideas. I did not attend this Conference as
> I had already thought out a scheme, but I was under the impression that
> there was some urgency about the matter.
>
> I should be glad if you would let me know if the interest in this device has
> died down.

James's letter was no doubt somewhat irritating to those trying to collect
and co-ordinate ideas from all interested parties. This irritation was
apparent in the Ministry Minute dealing with the question of why James
had not received the Defiant fuselage he had been promised by the
Minister in accordance with the delivery arrangements he had been
informed of: 'we naturally gave Martin credit for being enterprising
enough to let us know if the arrangement went wrong'. An obsolete type
of Defiant aircraft eventually arrived at Denham on 11 December 1944.

Some further consideration was given to James's swinging arm device.
The Ministry now felt that there might be some danger of the pilot being
swept back against the swinging arm on leaving the cockpit, some risk of
injury if his exit from the aircraft was not sufficiently rapid to ensure
that the whole of his body entered the slipstream quickly, and some
uncertainty as to whether and how the swinging arm would operate if
the aircraft was in a manoeuvre such as a spin. Nevertheless, they were
still happy for James to proceed with its development (with no contract
in place, the development was of course at James's expense), on the basis
that it might have some value as an interim means of escape from existing
aircraft types pending the development of an alternative system.

The Ministry meanwhile continued their discussions with Lobelle,
and arrangements were made for him to visit Gloster and to see the
Meteor development. James was undeterred. Indeed, it seems that James
was one step ahead of the others at this stage, for he had realized that
if an escape system was being considered for retrofit to existing aircraft

types, one would soon be required for new types, a point which had been confirmed in the Ministry letter of 1 November. Despite his letter of 6 November, he had already abandoned the idea of a swinging arm device and was designing his first ejection seat. With the freedom of thought that was possible on the basis of a cockpit that could be designed to suit the requirements of the escape system, he agreed that the most effective way of getting a pilot out of a cockpit in an emergency would be to eject the seat with the pilot sitting in it. He had concluded also that the power for actuating this would need to come from an explosive charge which would fire the seat and pilot out of the aircraft, leaving the pilot to disengage himself from his seat and pull the ripcord on his parachute in the normal way, and that in order to control the exit of the seat from the aircraft he would have to fit guide rails to the aircraft and rollers to the seat, to ensure that the seat would be fired out of the aircraft on the correct trajectory.

It was uncharted territory. James had known little about the theories of aerodynamics when he started building aircraft, but he had watched aircraft being built, watched aircraft flying and indeed had flown aircraft himself. But neither he nor anyone else in Britain knew anything of any significance about the problems associated with blowing people out of aircraft. However, as James had never been a man for theory, this sort of project was ideally suited to his approach to design work. Where the theory did not exist, the only way to identify the nature and extent of the problems and to solve them was by testing and more testing: the theory would come later.

The primary problem to be solved in the design of an ejection apparatus was the question of how much g force a man could withstand without physical injury, and in particular without injury to his back. G force is the measure of acceleration due to gravity, and the problem was originally thought to be simply how much acceleration could be applied to the human body for the purposes of ejecting it from an aircraft. The only data available at that time was based on the experience of horizontal thrust of 4–5 g during catapult launching from aircraft carriers, but this force was insufficient to eject a man from an aircraft and the data was, in any event, unsuitable for application to the problem of upward compressive thrust. It was necessary therefore to carry out a series of tests to see what g force the human body could withstand in the vertical position. The seat needed to have sufficient propulsion to leave the aircraft and clear the tailplane, and the effect of this exercise on the human body could only be guessed at. Fortunately for James, however, he had recently met a surgeon, Miss Peggy Loudon, who was to be of significant help to him in his quest for knowledge and understanding of these problems.

Peggy Loudon was a general surgeon heavily involved in air raid casualty work at the Elizabeth Garrett Anderson Hospital in South London. She was billeted with the mother of James's secretary then, Miss Gladys Nicholls, who soon realized that James would be interested in meeting her. James was indeed delighted to have a visiting surgeon to talk to, especially as it was rather unusual at that time to meet a lady surgeon. Miss Loudon remembers James as always very amusing and very hospitable, but more importantly, as a man who was very precise and painstaking in everything he did. She feels that his genius lay in his infinite capacity to take pains. His repeated tests, increasing the force little by little, investigating every conceivable detail of every aspect of every test, was the reason why, in her opinion, James succeeded with the ejection seat where others did not. This is an interesting observation from a professional person when one considers some of the criticisms levelled against James as his development work progressed.

Miss Loudon and James discussed the problems of James's research at great length. She explained the mechanics of the spine to him, showed him numerous x-rays demonstrating fractures of the spine, and even provided him with bones and sections of lumbar vertebrae to examine. Miss Nicholls remembers these 'ghastly bits of body' that Miss Loudon would produce and that had to be wrapped up and put in the refrigerator at the factory. On one occasion Miss Loudon provided him with a complete human spine which she had removed from one of her casualty fatalities with the permission of the relatives, and James delighted in keeping this gory specimen in his office where he could constantly refer to it. He started to attend some of the operations she undertook on air raid casualty victims, and while this would not have provided him with much insight into the problems relating to the spine, Miss Loudon remembers how he was always very anxious to acquire every bit of knowledge he could. She also undertook a lot of post mortems, and James was particularly interested to watch her at work in the post mortem room where she had more time than in the operating theatre to explain the injuries and what might have caused them. According to Miss Loudon, James would not have been able to tell how much pressure the spine of a living person could withstand by using the spine she had procured for him, but this spine and the sections of lumbar vertebrae she supplied him with helped him to understand how the spine worked, and how spinal injuries could occur.

James produced drawings for his first ejection seat in December. He realized that it would be necessary to have some means of simulating the condition of being shot out of an aircraft, and he decided to start with controlled tests on an experimental rig. He designed and built a 16 ft high tower at Denham which was in the form of a tripod. One of the legs formed an inclined track which was fitted with guide rails and ratchet stops up which a seat could be fired using a cartridge. The ratchets were fitted at 3 in intervals so that the seat could be held at the top of its travel up the tower; in this way it was possible to undertake progressive tests with very small increases in the height of the ride, and to measure the rate of acceleration and the g produced.

The first test using this tower took place on 20 January 1945 with the seat loaded with 200 lb of ballast in the form of sand bags. The seat and tower system worked as required, and James decided that the next step was to put a man in the seat. The test was undertaken by Bernard Lynch, a fitter in the experimental department at Martin-Baker. Lynch was an Irishman like James, although he came from the South and not the North, and he had worked previously as a fitter in the Irish Free State Air Force before joining Martin-Baker in 1936. He was a big, burly man with a handlebar moustache and a smile to go with it. He had a reputation of being something of a likeable rogue, a man who could lay his hands on anything, by fair means or foul, and a man who was prone to getting himself into trouble. He was devoted to James and James in turn always spoke of Lynch with affection and understanding. It is widely believed that Lynch's volunteering for the job of test ejectee had more to do with James's efforts at getting him out of trouble with the local police than with Lynch's altruistic desire to further the cause of technology. But whatever Lynch's motives, he must be given full credit for undertaking this potentially hazardous test and the other tests which followed it.

The first test was uneventful. On 24 January 1945, only four days after the first firing of a seat up the rig, Lynch was strapped into an elementary seat on the bottom of the rig, the cartridge was fired, and Lynch and the seat were propelled 4 ft 8 in off the ground. He suffered no discomfort from this short journey, and the height of the seat's trajectory was increased over the next three tests until, on a shot up 9 ft 11 in, Lynch reported that he had felt quite a considerable degree of pain.

James immediately undertook an intensive series of tests to discover how to overcome this problem, and by 3 February 1945, when the Resident Technical Officer from the Ministry of Aircraft Production visited Denham to inspect the rig and had a ride up it, he had made considerable improvements. The RTO was very impressed. In his report he stated: 'Personally, I felt no bodily discomfort which one would expect from such a violent acceleration.' He stated that James seemed to have overcome the effect of g on the body by ensuring that the subject of the test was in a knees-up position, with feet resting on foot rests, and the body well strapped in. He also reported that:

Martin has benefited considerably in this job by his experience with explosives. It appears to me that the crux of the problem is to control the explosive so that the kick is not too severe, and looking into Martin's design, he has coped with this problem very successfully by providing suitable orifices and expansion chambers. The cartridges he makes up himself and his tests have reached the point where he has settled on the size of the cartridge required and the control of the explosion to give consistent results in so far as ground tests can settle the problem.

This was an optimistic conclusion to have reached only 14 days after the first test on the rig with a ballasted seat and one which proved to be simplistic in its evaluation of the problems. Nevertheless, James was greatly encouraged by this support. He was anxious to test the seat from an aircraft in flight and asked the Ministry to let him have some dummies for use in these tests, and the loan of another aircraft from which flight tests of the ejection seat out of the Defiant could be observed. He also told the Ministry that he intended to proceed with live tests of the seat in flight as soon as possible.

There is no doubt that James's research and development work was progressing at a fantastic rate, but at this stage he encountered his first serious problem. Mr Charles Andrews, the technical representative from the periodical *Aeroplane*, visited Denham to report on James's development work. He had a ride on the rig and complained of considerable pain in the lumbar region of his back immediately afterwards. He was taken to hospital where an x-ray revealed a crushed lumbar vertebra as a result of being shot up 10 ft. James was understandably upset that he had caused Mr Andrews this injury, but it turned out to be an accident that was extraordinarily helpful to James in understanding the effect of g force on the spine. The mean acceleration experienced by Andrews on his ride was virtually the same as that experienced by Lynch on his first ride, although the peak g was reached more quickly in the Andrews test. It was obvious that much higher accelerations would have to be used to give enough velocity for the seat to clear the fin of an aircraft at high speeds, and it was apparent that the nature of the acceleration and not just its magnitude required further investigation.

James decided that future tests on the 16 ft tower should be filmed so that a cine record of the movement of the seat could be examined. For this purpose, a Kodak high-speed camera was used, running at 720 frames per second. An indicator was fitted to the seat and the guide rails were painted in black and white stripes, 1 in apart, making it possible to gauge the acceleration per inch. The photographs were analysed afterwards and a g curve obtained from them. As a result of studying the x-ray of Andrews's damaged vertebra and the high-speed film of numerous tests, James reached two important conclusions. Firstly, the intervertebral discs would not sustain compression if the vertebrae were not square to each other, as would be the case if the pilot's legs were raised above a certain point; as a result of this he realized that the foot pedals on the seat would have to be lowered. Secondly, the amount of g was not the critical factor, but rather the rate at which the maximum g force was imposed; accordingly, the explosive pressure in the ejection gun would have to come on more slowly and then be increased to its maximum value so as to eliminate the jolt that could cause spinal injuries. The seat mechanisms were therefore adjusted repeatedly and further tests undertaken as James explored these preliminary conclusions.

Although he was still working on the MB5 and had nearly completed a new tailplane of increased size, weather conditions had not been suitable for test flying and James was therefore adopting an unusually single-minded approach to the problems of ejecting a pilot from an aircraft. However, as already suggested, this work was well suited to James's trial and error approach to design, and it was Greensted's view, who was able to observe James's work on the MB5 running concurrently with his early work on the ejection seat, that the development of an ejection system, which was something that no-one else in Britain had done or knew how to do, presented James with an intriguing set of problems which he would have found more interesting and challenging than building yet another aeroplane.

Meanwhile, the official visits and the correspondence with the Ministry continued. Despite the very favourable report from the Resident Technical Officer, the Director of Technical Development and representatives from the RAE and the RAF Physiology Department who had also visited Denham were not prepared to proceed with flight tests as quickly as James was suggesting. They felt that the RAE should be fully satisfied first that no undue risks were being run, and the Ministry told James in a letter dated 5 March 1945 that it would be necessary for the Directorate of Armament Development to approve formally the explosive used in the cartridge and the arrangements for igniting it in an aircraft before any trials could be made in flight, and that, in due course, the cartridge and the ignition arrangements would have to be approved for Service use.

Despite the earlier problems with Mr Andrews, James felt that he was already well on the way to solving the problems of ejection which had been highlighted by Mr Andrews's injuries. Modifications to the seat by this stage had resulted in a marked improvement in the subjective effects of acceleration, the usual sensation being only slight discomfort in the ankles or abdomen. He accepted the requirements for approval of his cartridges set out in the Ministry letter, but pointed out that Martin-Baker had:

> carried out very lengthy and careful experiments in connection with the type of explosive used, and we have it so well under control that we can calculate with precision the precise height to which we can throw the pilot and the seat. We make the whole of the cartridges and load them up here, and we have never had a failure in some hundreds of tests carried out. The construction of the cartridge is such that it is perfectly normal and presents no manufacturing difficulties.

Although it was less than two months since James had started tests on the rig, the RAE agreed at a meeting at the factory on 12 March 1945 that his ejection seat had reached the stage where it was satisfactory for flight tests, and proposed a flight test programme with the RAE providing an observer aircraft from which to film the test ejections. On 16 March 1945, James was advised that Lynch would be allowed to receive parachute training at RAF Ringway in preparation for the first live airborne test.

It is apparent, however, that the various interested parties were not yet in agreement as to how James's work should be allowed to proceed.

There had been two minor incidents with test ejectees on the rig, both involving RAF officers, which fuelled this debate. Because of these injuries (one RAF officer had suffered pain between the shoulder blades, although an x-ray had revealed only an old compression fracture, and the other had suffered back strain), the Ministry wished to ascertain whether this was due to some weakness in the individuals or to other factors, and a notice was issued from the headquarters of the Ministry of Aircraft Production restricting 'the launching of RAF officers' in the Martin-Baker rig to those who had written authority from the Ministry. On 21 March 1945, the Director of the RAE wrote to the Secretary of the Ministry of Aircraft Production to express his view that there should be a considerable number of further tests both on the ground and in the air before there was any question of a live airborne test, because 'It would appear from what we have heard and witnessed, in tests with the firm's apparatus, that this ejection charge is somewhat variable and this may have serious consequences.' This letter, of course, contradicted the earlier proposal by the RAE that airborne tests should be allowed to proceed.

In spite of the notice restricting the launching of RAF officers up his rig, James was proceeding on the basis of the earlier decision to allow airborne tests, and he wrote to the Ministry on 28 March to set out his proposed approach to the first live test in flight. He suggested that there should be dummy tests with a rubber dummy weighing 200 lb with an observer-type parachute operated by a 15 ft static line, photographed by the RAE. There should be four or five tests starting at about 150 mph and increasing by 50 mph to about 450 mph, 'if Greensted felt like it'. If satisfactory, live tests should follow at the same range of speeds. It is interesting that the top speed of the tests was dependent on the test pilot, Greensted, and reflects the often overlooked fact that some considerable skill is required to fly and maintain control of an aeroplane when an explosive charge sufficient to eject a seat and a dummy is let off immediately behind the pilot.

Notwithstanding the official disagreements about James's work, it is clear at this stage that his work was further advanced than Lobelle's and the work being carried out by the other companies then engaged in similar projects. Despite the original decision to develop an escape system that would be capable of standardization in all aircraft, several of the aircraft manufacturers, namely Gloster, Westland, Vickers and Saunders-Roe, had been invited to consider their own schemes in conjunction with the Armament Research Department, but they were all a long way behind James. It had been proposed that the RAF Physiology Department should test these alternative systems on a specially constructed ground rig using a net or sheet to catch the seat in after each test, but once the RAE had seen James's 16 ft test rig in action, they wanted to use one similar to that, although they realized that this might be slightly awkward to arrange whilst James was still working on a private venture basis with no contract.

The Ministry broached with James the possibility of him now accepting a development contract in respect of his work on the ejection seat. With the prospect of live airborne tests taking place sooner or later, the Ministry became very concerned to be able to control James's work. They also wanted to help themselves in connection with the parallel work being undertaken by the Armament Research Department with the other firms, so they wrote to James on 30 March asking him if he would be willing to supply drawings of his 16 ft rig or to manufacture a similar rig for their use.

With the question of the contract still unresolved, the official disagreements continued and on 5 April 1945, the Head of the RAF Physiology Department joined the Director of the RAE in forcibly expressing his reservations on the subject of James's work in a letter to the Ministry in which he wrote:

> Up to the present time these launchings have been made without any record of the acceleration obtained, and there is little information of the exact nature of the damage sustained by those who have been injured during these tests.
>
> A great deal of valuable information could be obtained if Martin-Baker's hand was forced to such an extent that the fitting of adequate recording devices was made part of the requirements of the test.

It was no doubt a cause of irritation to the RAF Physiology Department and the RAE that James was working on his own without reference to them. It was also the case that not all the live shots up the rig were strictly speaking 'tests', because James was in the habit of giving all sorts of people a ride on the rig, including secretaries and unofficial visitors, and this obviously served to confuse the question of test data. But it was certainly the case that the results of each actual test were formalized and examined in detail, although not necessarily in the manner required by the authorities. James had his own reservations about some of the recording devices that the RAE suggested he should use. One example of these was the accelerometer. James, as a practical engineer, had little faith in this device because he felt that the results which it produced could be easily distorted. It was James's view that if a man sat on a table while the table was hit with a sledge-hammer, the resulting jolt would be easily absorbed by the man, whereas an accelerometer would record a huge jolt. He insisted that the results of all his tests be plotted manually on graphs, a laborious task which took at least an hour to complete, but which produced results that James was prepared to rely on.

On 6 April 1945, the Chief Superintendent of the Armament Research Department reported that James's ejection seat, as a mechanical assembly, 'is ingenious, neat and compact'. However, he did not consider the ballistic aspect of the system to be satisfactory because of the high pressure that was rapidly developed following the initiation of the firing process, and that the charge system was 'fundamentally unsuitable and would not be recommended for Service use'. The report was, however, irrelevant because James had already adopted a new cartridge. While the officials deliberated, James proceeded quickly with his work.

On 11 April 1945, the Ministry paid a further visit to Denham. The representatives from the Ministry were given a ride on the rig and were fully satisfied. They suggested that there should be a dummy ejection from the Defiant on the ground followed by flight tests, although as James had already changed the explosive in his cartridges from neonate to cordite to avoid the peak of high pressure that the previous cartridges had produced, these new cartridges would need official approval.

James was now focusing on the first airborne tests. The Defiant that had been delivered in early December of the previous year was not only an obsolete type but was also in a dilapidated condition, having been used by the US Army Air Force for target towing. It had to be completely overhauled and reconditioned before it was safe to fly, and it also required modification, including strengthening of the aircraft structure, in order for an ejection seat to be fitted and for the aircraft to accept the loads imposed by the ejection process. The ejection seat was installed in the space formerly occupied by the dorsal gun turret. Along with the modifications to the MB5 and the seat tests on the rig, the work on the Defiant took several months to complete and it was not until 14 April 1945 that a seat loaded with ballast was fired successfully from the stationary aircraft, jacked up into an in-flight position, into a specially erected catch net. The Visiting Technical Officer who watched the test recommended that the system was safe for flight tests.

In anticipation of the flight tests, a contract was issued to Martin-Baker on 17 April 1945 for the design, development, manufacture and test of two complete pilot ejection units for use in high-speed aircraft. The contract specified the installation of one or both of these units in aircraft for ground and flight tests as instructed by the Ministry of Aircraft Production, who told James that he would be given a Meteor III aircraft for this purpose. The contract price was not to exceed £10,000 without further authority. It was a pity, in their desire to exercise control over James's work, that no-one at the Ministry bothered to check that James had accepted this contract, for James was not yet minded to be constrained by contract. He felt that the Ministry were guilty of plagiarizing what they saw at Denham and giving his ideas to Lobelle. Employees at Martin-Baker can remember how exceptionally cross James became when he thought that another instance of this had taken place. Having thwarted his efforts so far to enter the aircraft production business, he was convinced that the Ministry were now trying to thwart his early successes in the development of an ejection seat by helping his competitor.

On 28 April 1945, the RAF Physiology Department reported to the Ministry on their visit to Martin-Baker four days earlier and the test ejection that had taken place. The maximum acceleration was 9–10 g, the shape of the diagram being entirely satisfactory with no excessive peak values having occurred. There was no subjective sensation of strain and it was considered that the acceleration would not cause injury to any normal member of an aircrew. Once again it was proposed that James

An extraordinary life

James with his sister and mother, about 1907.

Left *Capt. Valentine Baker, about 1919.*

Below *Trailer designed by James in the 1920s.*

Right *Amy Johnson with Capt. Valentine Baker.*

Below right *Martin's Aircraft Works and work-force about 1930. Jim Clampitt is on the left and Eric Stevens on the right.*

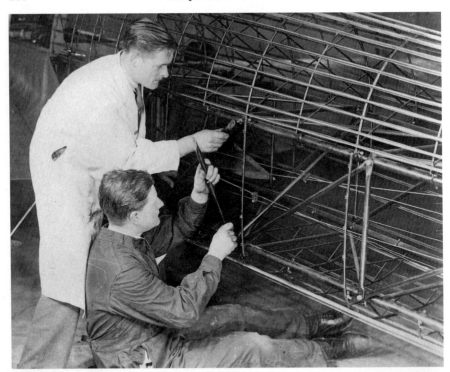

Above left *Eric Stevens and Jim Clampitt building the MB1.*

Left *The MB1 in the factory. James is standing front right.*

Above *The MB1 in flight.*

Below *The Second Wind Indicator designed by James.*

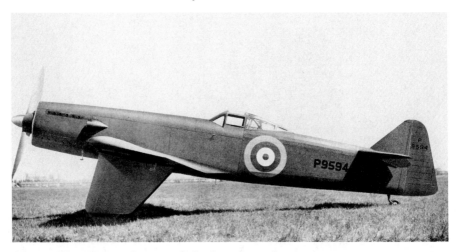

Above *The MB2 on the ground, final configuration.*

Below *Capt. Valentine Baker (left), James and Francis Francis in front of the MB2.*

Right *The MB2 with some of the men who built it. From left to right: Ted O'Connor, Jim Clampitt, Bill Piggott, Jack Eastment, Bernard Lynch, Eric Stevens, Fred Robinson, Peter Cawte, Jim Elliot and Joe Waterman.*

Below right *The MB2 in flight.* (Topical Press Agency)

Above *The shop-floor at Martin-Baker in the early 1940s, with blast tubes in the foreground.*

Left *The 12-gun nose for the Havoc night fighter.*

Above right *The MB3 on the ground.*

Right *The MB3 wing showing three of the six 20 mm cannon.*

Above *The MB3 preparing for take-off.*

Left *Capt. Valentine Baker in 1943.*

Above right *Capt. Baker's funeral in the machine shop at Martin-Baker.*

Right *The MB5, final configuration.*

The MB5 taking off.

The cockpit of the MB5.

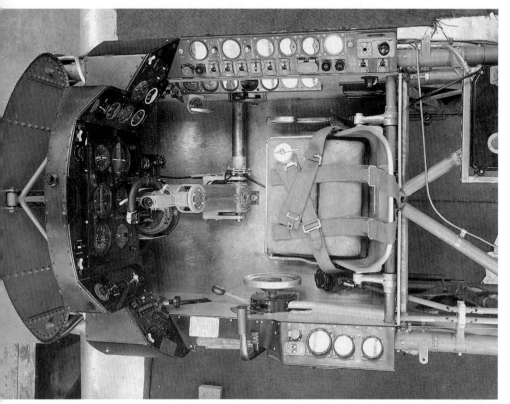

The swinging arm apparatus.

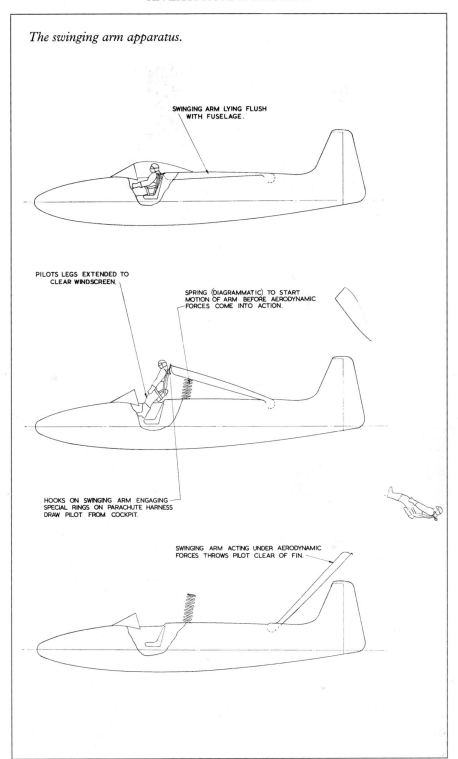

SWINGING ARM LYING FLUSH
WITH FUSELAGE.

PILOTS LEGS EXTENDED TO
CLEAR WINDSCREEN.

SPRING (DIAGRAMMATIC) TO START
MOTION OF ARM BEFORE AERODYNAMIC
FORCES COME INTO ACTION.

HOOKS ON SWINGING ARM ENGAGING
SPECIAL RINGS ON PARACHUTE HARNESS
DRAW PILOT FROM COCKPIT.

SWINGING ARM ACTING UNDER AERODYNAMIC
FORCES THROWS PILOT CLEAR OF FIN.

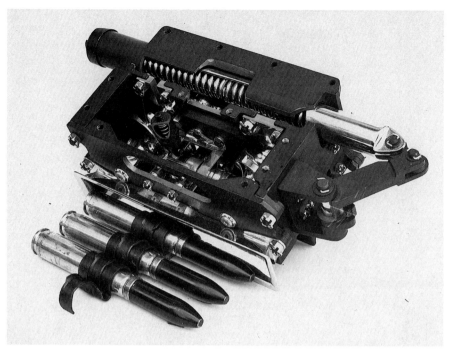

Gun feed for the British Hispano cannon.

James in the ruins of Hamburg in 1946 in the uniform of a Wing Commander.

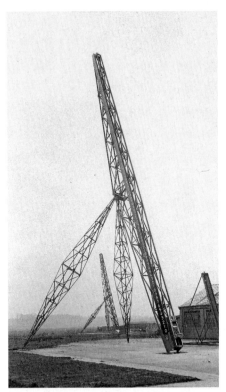

Above *The three Martin-Baker ejection seat test rigs. The original 16 ft tower is on the right, the 65 ft tower is at the back, and the 110 ft tower is in the foreground.*

Above right *Bernard Lynch with James after the first live airborne test ejection on 24 July 1946.*

Right *Cdr. D. W. Gressley of the US Navy receiving instructions from James prior to his test ejection on the rig in the Philadelphia Navy Yard in August 1946.*

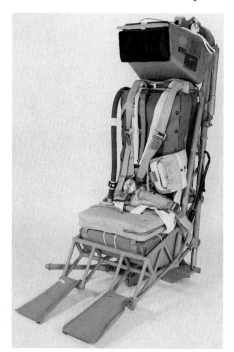

Far left *Pre-Mark 1 ejection seat as used by Jo Lancaster. The D-ring used to deploy the parachute after manual separation can be seen on the wide waist belt.*

Left *The Mark 1 ejection seat, the first production seat.*

Below left *Bernard Lynch in the rear cockpit of the Meteor preparing for a live test.*

Right *Capt. John Scott with Lt. Cartier (French test ejectee) in 1948.*

Below *Bernard Lynch (left), James, Jo Lancaster and Mr R. Walker in front of a Meteor cockpit in the Science Museum in London* (Science Museum).

Right *The world's first ejection from the runway by S/L Fifield in September 1955.*

James receiving the Royal Aeronautical Society Wakefield Gold Medal in 1952 from the President, Sir George Dowty (RAeS).

Below right *Sidney Hughes with James after his live test ejection on 28 August 1957 at Patuxent River.*

S/L 'Fifi' Fifield (test pilot and live test ejectee).

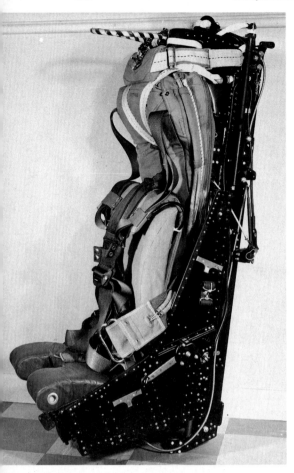

Left *The Mark 4 ejection seat.*

Below *Southlands Manor.*

Right *W. T. Hay's rearward-facing test ejection from a Valiant on 1 July 1960.*

Below right *The Martin-Baker inclined test rig.*

W. T. Hay preparing for the first live zero/zero test ejection in a rocket seat on 1 April 1961.

Emergency ejection by Lt. Kryway, US Navy, as an F8 Crusader crashes from the flight deck of the USS Franklin D. Roosevelt *on 21 October 1961.*

W/Cdr. Peter Howard with James after his airborne test of the rocket seat on 13 March 1962.

Lady Tedder, James, Lord Tedder and Lady Martin at the dinner in 1962 to celebrate the saving of 500 lives.

Left *Emergency ejection by George Aird, de Havilland test pilot, from a Lightning on 13 September 1962 (Mirror Syndication International).*

Above *James with Sir Harry Broadhurst and other ejectees at the dinner in 1965 to celebrate the saving of 1,000 lives.*

Below *James with Bill Bedford, emergency ejectee.*

Left *Cartoons featured in the menu at the dinner to celebrate the saving of 1,000 lives.*

Above *Emergency ejections by Lt. A. Gleadow and Lt. P. King RN as their Buccaneer aircraft crashes off the flight deck of HMS* Eagle *on 20 November 1965.*

Above right *Sir James and Lady Martin.*

Right *The Mark 7 ejection seat.*

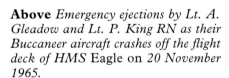

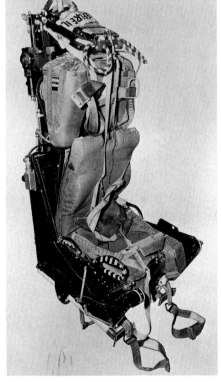

Left *Dummy test of the Mark IT10LY rocket seat from an AMTX cockpit.*

Above *The Martin-Baker rocket test track in Northern Ireland.*

Below *James receiving the Queen's Award for Industry in 1967 from the Lord Lieutenant of Buckinghamshire.*

James showing the factory to His Royal Highness the Duke of Edinburgh in 1976.

The Mark 10 ejection seat.

Jo Lancaster (first emergency ejectee) and Benn Gunn (emergency ejectee) with Gulf War ejectees after the reception to celebrate the saving of 6,000 lives. From left to right: Flt. Lt. Rupert Clark, Jo Lancaster, S/L Bob Ankerson, Flt. Lt. John Peters, Ben Gunn, Flt. Lt. John Nichol and Flt. Lt. Robbie Stewart (Times Newspapers Ltd).

Denis Burrell (Chairman) with Her Royal Highness the Princess of Wales when she visited Martin-Baker to present the ejectee ties to some of the Gulf War ejectees in 1991.

James in the 1970s.

James's children. From left to right: Anne Hess, James Martin, Jane Livesey and John Martin.

should carry out dummy airborne tests followed by a live ejection. The report concluded: 'It is the opinion of the Laboratory that the problems of sudden exposure to slipstreams at high velocity, with rotation, can only be solved by experience and that at some stage live ejections from such an aircraft would be advantageous.'

By this time, about 180 tests with both ballast and people had been carried out on the test rig, as James investigated the effect of variations in the type of explosive charge, the quantity of explosive, the expansion volume and the use of restrictor orifices within the gun. This research had enabled James to finalize his conclusions that the peak acceleration should not exceed 21 g and that this peak should not be sustained for more than one-tenth of a second; that the rate of rise of g should not be greater than 300 g/sec; and that in sustaining this acceleration, the body should be held in a position to ensure that adjacent spinal vertebrae were square to each other. This was a significant breakthrough in understanding the effect of g forces on the human spine, and in allowing James to proceed successfully with the development of an ejection system. These conclusions also became generally accepted, and have been used all over the world as the criteria for defining the limitations of human endurance in connection with ejection seats.

By this time the first two criteria had been successfully addressed by a substantial redesign of the ejection gun. The ejection gun originally consisted of two steel tubes telescoped into each other with a cartridge and a firing unit at one end. Having decided that the explosive pressure in the gun would have to increase progressively, James discovered, by trial and error, that the best results could be obtained by using a gun with two cartridges, one to start the ejection sequence and the other to continue it. When the first, or primary, cartridge was fired, the seat would start to rise smoothly. As the piston rose, the second cartridge was exposed and fired by the flame from the first cartridge, building up the pressure to the maximum required. This allowed the seat to reach the required velocity in a manner which minimized the possibility of damage to the vertebrae.

The third of these criteria had been partly met by repositioning the foot pedals, and was further addressed by the introduction of the face blind method of firing the seat. During tests on the 16 ft rig, it had become apparent that the head of the person in the seat was being forced forward during the ejection process. As the ejection velocity increased, James realized that this was likely to precipitate injuries, and he initially adopted a method of securing the head by a band around the forehead. However, as it would be impractical for a pilot to fly with his head restrained in this way, he conceived the idea of initiating ejection by the pilot reaching up and pulling a face blind down over his face. When the face blind was fully pulled down, the head was held firmly in position and the pilot was in a good position for ejecting by virtue of having straightened his back in order to reach up and pull down the blind. The first dummy test with the new design was made successfully on 20 June

1945 on the 16 ft rig. But with the new twin ejection gun, the seat was overshooting the available space on the rig, and while the g curve obtained from the shot was satisfactory, it was apparent that a much higher rig would be needed in order to check the physiological effects of the new twin cartridge by a live shot.

Meanwhile, following the successful ground test from the Defiant on 14 April 1945 and the successful demonstration to the RAF Physiology Department, the Defiant had been taken to RAF Wittering from where, on 11 May, Greensted flew the aeroplane and the first airborne dummy ejection in Great Britain took place. The test was photographed from an accompanying Firefly. It was completely satisfactory and the dummy and seat descended together on a parachute attached to the seat and operated by a static line. During this and subsequent airborne tests, the ejection of the seat from the aircraft was accomplished by means of an ejection gun in the same way as when firing a seat up a rig, and once the seat was clear of the aircraft, a small drogue parachute was deployed to stabilize the seat, after which a 24 ft parachute attached to the seat was deployed by a delayed action release, so that the seat would parachute to the ground and could be used again.

A week later, on 17 May, a further six ballasted seats were ejected at various speeds of up to 300 mph, this time at Beaulieu, the photographs of the tests being taken from a Mosquito. On the first test, the parachute failed to open, and on two other tests the parachute only opened just before the seat hit the ground. In these two cases, the dummy and seat rotated when falling freely at a rate which the official observers thought would seriously prejudice the ability of a pilot to disengage himself from the seat and deploy his parachute. Nevertheless, in all cases the seat left the aircraft successfully, and James regarded the results of the tests as encouraging.

At the end of May, representatives from the RAE visited James with their analysis of these dummy ejections, and it was at this meeting that James finally agreed to the RAE making acceleration measurements on his rig. They believed that the velocity of the seat was too low on ejection, but James was already in the process of designing a new ground rig to accommodate test ejections with larger cartridges so that he could continue his investigations into the physiological problems of ejection. This new tower was 65 ft high, and was built at the factory and erected at Denham on 17 August 1945. It was based on the same principles as the 16 ft tower, being a large tripod with ratchets on the inclined slope to stop and hold the seat. However, because of the height of this tower, James devised a trolley system to bring the seat back to ground level with the help of winching gear. A dummy ejection was tried first, and then, five days later, on 22 August 1945, Lynch carried out the first live test, being successfully fired up to a height of 26 ft 3 in by the new ejection gun with two cartridges, after which he reported that the ride had been very 'soft' and he had not experienced any discomfort.

During the tests on the 65 ft rig, the face blind method of ejection was examined more fully. Its importance was demonstrated by W/Cdr. Stewart of the RAF Institute of Aviation Medicine when he underwent a test on the rig at reduced acceleration without using the face blind. It was very clear from the extent that his head was thrown forward that a pilot would suffer critical injury at the velocity required to eject him from an aircraft if his head was not adequately restrained. The face blind also had the advantage of protecting the pilot's face from the blast of the slipstream as he left the aircraft. It was developed further and shaped to conform to the shape of the human face in order to prevent the head moving sideways during ejection.

The high-speed camera method of investigation was abandoned for tests on the 65 ft rig. Instead, James developed a method of measuring g over time by recording the gas pressures in the gun during the ejection. It was confirmed by comparison with records taken simultaneously by the RAE with accelerometers on the seat that the effect of friction was only very slight, so that the pressure diagram could be converted to values of g against time and stroke.

In October 1945, the question of payment to Martin-Baker under the contract arose. James had already spent the maximum amount of £10,000. The Director of Technical Development asked for a statement of his expenditure to date and an estimate of future expenditure, and James replied that it was impossible to estimate future expenditure because the Meteor III aircraft he had been promised for the purposes of work under the contract had not arrived, and he therefore had no means of gauging the amount of modification work that would be required. James was duly reimbursed for the £11,500 he had already spent because of the priority of the work involved. Because of the progress he had made, some were beginning to question the necessity of funding parallel development work by Malcolm. But it was not until March the next year that the Ministry realized that James had not yet accepted the contract which had been issued to him nearly a year previously.

The Meteor III that the Ministry had promised James was finally delivered to Denham on 6 November 1945. James started designing the considerable modifications which would have to be made to it to enable it to be used as a test vehicle. In January the next year, James began addressing the problems of fitting the ejection seat into the pilot's cockpit of the aircraft for the purpose of retrofit rather than testing, and another Meteor was delivered to Denham for this purpose. Although the modifications to this second aircraft were less extensive than those for the first, much more careful thought had to be given to them than to the one-off experimental job. A completely new hood had to be produced in close collaboration with the Gloster Aircraft Company who had designed the Meteor, and over 200 drawings, much restressing and a complete summary of calculations supplied to Gloster.

By March 1946 the Ministry were intending to install the Martin-Baker seat for Service use in both the Meteor and the E1/44 and possibly several other types also. Unfortunately, at this point James suffered a most unfortunate accident. In April 1946 a group of gypsies arrived in the vicinity and camped in a field close to Southlands Manor. On the night of 13 April, they were making a lot of noise and everyone at Southlands Manor was becoming angry at the disturbance. James went down to their encampment to ask them if they could be a bit quieter. The gypsies were in a rowdy mood, some were drunk, and they did not take kindly to this short, stocky Irishman telling them to be quiet. One of them attacked James with a metal bar. It was not long before the alarm was raised. James was unconscious and clearly badly injured. The police and the ambulance services were called and James was taken to Hillingdon Hospital and the gypsy to the local police station.

It was a critical night and the family feared for his life. In view of his very serious condition, the doctors did not think it was worthwhile treating James for anything other than shock, but he survived the night and during the next few days his condition became more stable. Two experienced and well-regarded doctors from University College Hospital in London were asked to examine him, the orthopaedic surgeon Watson Jones and the neuro-surgeon Wylie McKissock. As soon as James was well enough to move, he was taken to University College Hospital where the two surgeons undertook a joint operation on him. James's left leg had been badly smashed and Watson Jones found that he had to insert a metal plate into the lower part of his leg in order to hold the bone together. Wylie McKissock operated on his skull, which had also been badly smashed, and had to remove bits of bone from the left frontal region of his head. The operation was successful and, despite the fears for his life and for his mental faculties, he began to recover.

Francis, recently released from his duties in the Air Transport Auxiliary where he had served during the war, went to the factory after the accident happened to help Eric and the others close to James to try to keep the factory going in James's absence. At the factory, everyone was stunned. It was not just the boss who had been injured, it was the life-blood of the factory who was lying in hospital. James was the driving force upon whom everybody depended. Morale was very low, for inevitably rumours were spreading about James's injuries, his ability to return to work, and the future of the company. The work-force lost their drive and enthusiasm, for without him there seemed no point in doing anything.

Shortly before James was due to leave hospital, Francis came to visit him with some shattering news. In James's words: 'He expressed the desire that he would like to take his money and get out.' Francis asked James to arrange for the repayment of the loans which he had made to Martin-Baker and to buy his shares in the company. James had struggled to find the money to buy Baker's shares after his death in order that his widow might have the money. He simply did not have the funds to pay off Francis. It was up to his brother-in-law, Edwin, to save the day. Edwin took out another mortgage on his house and by various means raised the necessary money to pay off Francis. James's sister, Jane, remained unforgiving of Francis for his sudden departure from the firm at such an inopportune moment, and for the pressures and anxieties that it imposed on the family. But James harboured no ill-feelings towards Francis. He knew that without his financial support, it was unlikely that Martin-Baker would have progressed as far as it had. Francis went to live in the Bahamas, and although their paths crossed infrequently in the years ahead, they remained in contact and exchanged friendly letters.

James was a good patient while in hospital in that he did what he was told to do, but McKissock remembers that James considered it a matter of urgency that he should return to the office, and this is hardly surprising. The modification work on the Meteor was well advanced and the next step would be airborne tests out of the Meteor. He was in a critical phase of the ejection seat development, he had still to deliver the MB5 to Boscombe Down for its trials, he was out of touch with what was going on at the factory, and it was imperative that he return to the factory at the earliest possible moment.

Chapter Nine

Will the Seat Work?

Six weeks after the gypsy attack, James returned to the factory. It would be several years before he would recover fully from the injuries he had received, during which time he suffered recurrent violent headaches which inevitably reduced his capacity for work. For several months he was dependent on crutches because of his leg injury, but proper recuperation was out of the question as far as James was concerned because there was just too much work to be done.

James was right to be concerned about his absence from the office. At a meeting on 15 March 1946, the Ministry had discussed the desirability of having a standard make of ejection seat for all Service aircraft, but they were unable to choose between the Malcolm and the Martin-Baker product. High-speed flight tests of the Malcolm seat were due to start in a week, to be followed shortly by the physiological tests. The Martin-Baker seat had successfully completed the physiological tests, but the high-speed flight tests were not due to take place for a month or so. By 1 May 1946, after a period of inactivity at Martin-Baker during James's absence, the Ministry had concluded that the Martin-Baker work had fallen behind the Malcolm work.

The Ministry were concerned not only about the delay of the high-speed flight tests of the Martin-Baker seat, but also about the fact that they still had no contract with James. They had delivered the Meteor aircraft to Martin-Baker for the purposes of development work under the contract, but James's refusal to sign a contract brought into question the basis on which these aircraft were being made available to him and who was going to pay for the modifications to them. There had been considerable disagreement between James and the Ministry over the contractual terms relating to patents, but on 22 June 1946, James finally returned the signed contract to the Ministry with a covering letter saying that his acceptance of it was without prejudice to the position regarding patents. He pointed out that he had applied for nearly all the major patents relating to his ejection seat before the contract had been issued and that therefore it was only a question of clarifying the position with regard to the patents relating to the smaller, detailed improvements. The

Ministry agreed to forego any rights that they might have had to the patents taken out before the issue of the contract, and they told James that it was now satisfactory for flight tests to proceed under the terms of the contract, which they had backdated to the date of issue, 17 April 1945. They also told him that they were anxious to get ejection seats into the Meteors that were already in service as soon as possible.

By the beginning of June 1946, Martin-Baker had completed the modifications to the Meteor III aircraft, and it was delivered to Chalgrove Airfield where the airborne tests were to take place. As Greensted's test flying of the MB5 was now finished, he was no longer available to fly for James, who therefore needed to find two test pilots. He turned to his friend Roxbee Cox who was at that time the chairman of the National Gas Turbine Establishment (NGTE) which was engaged in the development of the jet engine. Roxbee Cox agreed to loan two of his pilots, Capt. John Scott and S/L Stewart (Fifi) Fifield to James as and when required.

Scott was an experienced and highly competent pilot who had flown for Imperial Airways before the war and as an RAF instructor and night fighter during the war, and he now agreed to fly the modified Meteor for the airborne tests of James's ejection seat. The test ejections were to be photographed from a second Meteor which Fifield agreed to fly. Fifield, another skilful pilot, had joined the RAF shortly before the beginning of the war and had spent the first years of the war as an instructor before flying Spitfires in combat, for which he had been awarded the DFC and the AFC. After leaving the RAF he too joined NGTE and agreed to fly for Martin-Baker. They made an interesting team of pilots: the careful airline pilot and the daredevil fighter pilot who never lost his love of making low-level passes over the airfield, but despite their differences they were able to work together successfully.

On 8 June 1946, a static dummy ejection was successfully made from the jacked-up Meteor, the seat being caught in a net suspended at the top of a specially erected 45 ft tower. On 24 June, the day on which the Ministry agreed that flight tests could proceed, an airborne dummy ejection was made from the Meteor at an altitude of 2,000 ft and a speed of 415 mph. This was a significant advance on the dummy ejections out of the Defiant, where the speed of the aircraft had never exceeded 300 mph, and demonstrated that a seat could be ejected successfully from a 'high-speed' aircraft. But although the seat left the aircraft cleanly and was fired sufficiently high to clear the tailplane, the delay action release mechanism on the parachute did not work satisfactorily, with the result that the main parachute opened too soon and burst because of the speed at which the test occurred, and the test seat was damaged beyond repair. James modified the release mechanism, but during the second test six days later, the same thing happened. James then quickly developed a hydraulic type of delay action release which was tested two days later, on 2 July 1946, at a slightly higher speed of 440 mph, but the main parachute did not deploy because the stabilizing drogue parachute, which was spring-loaded, was drawn into the wake of the seat and became entangled with it. Despite these problems with the drogue system, in each of these tests the ejected seat had cleared the fin by an ample margin, and James was able to write to the Ministry to advise them that the seat was performing well in the high-speed tests and to enquire how many tests he was to carry out in order to prove the ejection process.

After examining the films of these tests, James realized that it would be necessary to extract the drogue parachute by force, and that the drogue would have to be attached to the seat by a line of sufficient length to allow it to develop and control the seat outside the turbulence of the seat wake. He therefore designed a new device called a drogue gun, which consisted of a main body with a gun barrel containing a firing pin and a bullet. A line was attached from the top of the bullet to the drogue, so that when the gun fired, the bullet extracted the drogue at great speed from the container into the slipstream where it was instantly deployed, thus obviating any possible risk of the drogue becoming entangled with the seat.

The drogue gun was ready for testing only four days later, and at a speed of 400 mph the hydraulic release worked successfully in conjunction with the new drogue gun, but this time the cables attached to the drogue parachute broke because the loads imposed on them at this speed were considerably greater than those for which they had been designed.

Scott recalls these early tests vividly:

> We often heard the drogue break or separate from the main parachute, and we used to have terrific arguments about what we should do with this drogue. Some of us were in favour of having a smaller drogue, some of us were in favour of having a larger hole in the middle of it to reduce the pressure naturally and so on. Eventually we got it right. And then the drogue guns used to burst because we had not got the right material for the tubes and bits of them used to fly out. We even had one or two go through the fuel tank.

According to James, no reliable data existed then with regard to the high-speed opening of small parachutes, so he had once again to discover the solution through a trial and error approach to testing. Those working at the RAE would no doubt have taken issue with this viewpoint, and the Ministry were becoming increasingly frustrated by James's refusal to seek the advice of the RAE or to co-operate with them. But James was confident that he could solve the problems himself. The drogue parachute he had been using was 4 ft in diameter with a 9 in vent hole. During three tests with a smaller drogue only 3 ft in diameter, the drogue cables broke again. During five further tests with a 3 ft drogue with a larger vent of 16 in, two were satisfactory and one perfect, but in the last test the drogue broke. James then tried a specially shaped drogue parachute 2 ft in diameter with a $7^{1}/_{2}$ in vent hole and 12 nylon lines, and on 24 July 1946, this was successfully tested twice at 350 mph.

At this stage James felt that he had developed the ejection gun to the point where it would give the seat and the man in it the required velocity to clear the fin of a Meteor aircraft, and had solved the problems relating to the deployment of the main parachute. To James's practical mind there was only one further step to be taken. Dummies cannot talk and describe what it feels like to be ejected forcibly from an aircraft in flight, so if he was to develop a successful ejection system, it was essential that a man try it out.

Lynch was to be the test ejectee, having completed a Parachute Regiment training course. James decided on a speed of 320 mph for this first test ejection because he believed that the dynamic air pressure that Lynch would experience on leaving the aircraft at this speed would not be sufficient to cause any damage to his body, and at this speed he was also confident that there would be no problem with the drogue system. The last two successful tests with the new drogue had taken place earlier in the day. After watching these, James proposed that a live test should be made that evening after the wind had died down. The two Meteors, one flown by Scott with Lynch in the test seat behind him, the other fitted with a camera and flown by Fifield, took off from Chalgrove Airfield at about nine o'clock that evening. At a quarter past nine on 24 July 1946, Lynch became the first person in Great Britain to use an ejection seat in the air when he fired himself out of the Meteor at 8,000 feet, in front of representatives from the Ministry, the RAE, the US Army Air Force and the US Navy. He pulled down the face blind to initiate the ejection, the twin cartridge ejection gun fired and ejected the seat with him in it, the drogue gun fired and deployed the drogue which stabilized the seat in a horizontal position and slowed it down and, after the pre-set interval controlled by the hydraulic release, the seat parachute opened. Lynch released the seat harness, fell away from the seat, and pulled the ripcord on his own parachute to descend safely to the ground.

It is a pity that no detailed record remains of what Lynch thought about this experience. The only comment of his that is clearly remembered is his observation that ejecting from an aircraft in flight into the tremendous blast of the slipstream could only be likened to being thrown into a brick wall. However, he had no complaints about his ride in the seat, which proved to James the smoothness of the twin cartridge ejection gun, the effective protection of the face blind and the efficiency of the stabilizing drogue. Lynch was renowned for his love of beer, and he landed within easy walking distance of a pub and a welcome pint. His public demonstration of James's ejection seat proved to the RAF and the Ministry that James knew what he was doing, and that safe ejection from aircraft was now a reality.

The Ministry representative who watched this test reported the following day that

it was not possible to see the actual jump from the ground, but the main seat parachute was seen to develop at a safe distance behind the aircraft and a very short while after the observer's parachute was seen to open and to descend safely. On being interviewed afterwards, he seemed quite happy and unaffected by his descent and expressed his willingness to do it again.

The report made it clear, however, 'that although Mr. Martin had taken all possible official advice and seemed to have taken care of safety in all ways, these tests should be regarded as being made under his own responsibility and not in the nature of official trials'.

This live test was totally James's responsibility and was not made pursuant to the contract. The question of live tests had been discussed by the Ministry at a meeting on 1 July 1946. Originally, they had decided that airborne tests of ejection equipment should be undertaken with dummies only. However, it became apparent after discussions with Service personnel that a successful live test would be of enormous help in persuading Service pilots of the advantages of an ejection seat. Despite the need for some means of assisted escape from high-speed aircraft, not all pilots were convinced that the ejection seat was the right answer to the problem. Accordingly, after considerable discussions, the Ministry had concluded that official live tests of ejection seats could be made, but only when a fully automatic ejection seat had been developed providing for the automatic separation of the pilot from his seat and the automatic deployment of his parachute. James was already working on such a seat.

Shortly after Lynch's test, James was asked to visit the United States of America. On 11 October 1945, Cdr. J.J. Ides and R.B. Barnes, two officers from the US Office of Naval Research, had visited James at Denham for the purpose of seeing his ejection seat and the test tower. After considering the alternative types of apparatus, the US Navy had placed an order for a test rig 110 ft high, together with a complete ejection seat for installation in a suitable aircraft, for which purpose a Douglas A-26 Invader was eventually chosen after James had persuaded them not to conduct tests from a wireless-controlled, single-seat Hellcat fighter. The test tower had now been completed and shipped to America where it was ready to be erected.

James realized the critical importance of creating the best possible impression with the US Navy, and despite the fact that he was still using crutches to walk, he insisted on going to Philadelphia in August to supervise the tests in the Navy Yard. His doctors had tried in vain to persuade him not to go, but eventually they reached a compromise and James went, accompanied by a nurse. The first dummy test on the rig was successfully made on 14 August 1946 to a height of 93 ft 6 in, and the same day Stan Steer of Martin-Baker tested the seat successfully, being shot up 72 ft 6 in. After two further dummy tests, Cdr. D.W. Gressley of the US Navy completed two successful tests. The Americans asked James what guarantees he could give as regards the performance of his seat, and he gave a typically ebullient reply: 'I won't give you any guarantees, but if you don't like it, you can throw it in the Delaware River.'

James had also wanted to go to Philadelphia because he had been invited to be the guest of honour at a conference at the Naval Air Experimental Station at Philadelphia on the subject of Seat Ejection and Crash Hazards. At this conference he expounded his views on the necessity of a twin cartridge to give an acceptable acceleration curve and the value of the drogue in preventing the seat from tumbling after ejection. He also told the conference that he believed it was essential that goggles should be removed before ejection because in every case in which they had been worn by a dummy they had been ripped off during the ejection. This turned out to be advice that should have been heeded by Martin-Baker staff in the future.

By this time, the Martin-Baker ejection seat had been installed in the rear cockpit of a Douglas A-26 aircraft and a dummy ejection from that aircraft on the ground took place at the Navy Yard, followed, between 17 September and 7 October, by a series of successful airborne dummy ejections at speeds of up to 350 mph. Finally, on 1 November 1946, the second live test of the Martin-Baker seat took place, this time by Lt. Furtek of the US Navy, from the Douglas A-26 at a speed of 250 mph at 5,000 ft. Although the ejection itself was successful, the 28 ft diameter parachute attached to the seat unfortunately did not develop but only streamed. Nevertheless, Furtek was able to detach himself from the seat, deploy his own parachute as planned and make a safe descent.

James had by then returned to England. During development, the seat had been modified on an *ad hoc* basis, the changes being dictated by the results of the test programme. After Lynch's first successful airborne ejection, James realized that he would have to give some considerable thought to the design of the seat in order for him to produce a version capable of being put into production, and upon his return to England he set to work to do just this.

He also had to have another operation for the injuries received during the gypsy attack. His head was cut open and a titanium plate fitted, 3 in in diameter, to cover the hole in his skull where he had been hit. His leg was also cut open and the metal plate removed and replaced with steel pins, which meant that James was at last able to walk without crutches.

As soon as he was able, James returned to the factory. The Ministry were concerned that any escape equipment should work satisfactorily wherever in the world the RAF were operating, and James therefore undertook further experimental work to examine the effect on his cartridges of the extremes of temperature that might be experienced by aircraft flying in tropical or arctic conditions. For the tropical tests, the cartridges were heated to 130°F, maintained at that temperature for 24 hours, and then fired. For the arctic tests, the cartridges were kept in a refrigerator below freezing point so that ice had to be scraped off them before they could be inserted in the ejection gun. In each case the cartridges fired as they should and the pressure graphs obtained from these tests did not differ significantly from those obtained from tests at normal temperatures. The seat was also tested to see how it would work in a situation where negative and positive g forces were applied to it. James undertook tests using a bungee cord to apply the downward pressure, from which he concluded that ejection would be possible with down forces up to the structural strength of the aircraft without serious physiological effect.

At the beginning of October 1946 the Directorate of Aircraft Research and Development wrote to James to tell him that Malcolm were experiencing difficulty in devising a suitable method of firing the cartridges in their ejection seat and in providing suitable support for the pilot's head during ejection and that, accordingly, they had instructed Malcolm to develop a roller blind device similar to the device that James had developed for his own seats. The purpose of the letter was to advise James of this because, whether or not this device was the subject of a patent, he would 'wish to be informed of the present proposal'. James was incensed. This was exactly the sort of behaviour which had made him reluctant to sign a contract with the Ministry. In reply, he pointed out that the face blind was the subject of a patent application made nearly two months before he received the contract from the Ministry. He wrote:

> In the circumstances I cannot agree to the use of this patent device in a seat designed by another firm. I would, therefore, like to have your written assurance that this patent will not be infringed as I think you will agree that each firm's designs should be judged on its own merits.

The Ministry, however, had an answer. They wrote to say that 'the Department is anxious that the best devices be made available to RAF pilots, and that if it is necessary to ensure the safety of pilots that patented devices of one contractor be incorporated in equipment manufactured by other contractors then the Department will authorise other contractors to use such patented devices'.

James's concern was that the use of his patents might jeopardize his chances of getting a production contract for his seat. With his experience of being asked to design modifications for other people's machines, and in the knowledge that certain aspects of his prototype aircraft had been recommended for standardization in other aircraft, he was justifiably worried that features of his ejection seat would be incorporated in the Malcolm seat, and that his seat would be turned down in favour of the Malcolm seat. At this stage, the Ministry considered that James's contribution to the development of the ejection seat had been 'most valuable', but there seemed to be advantages to the Malcolm seat: it used a single rather than a twin cartridge, it required less space and would therefore be easier to retrofit into existing aircraft, and it was appreciably lighter.

The Ministry had now stipulated that, despite their desire for a fully automatic seat, they required first an ejection seat fitted with a standard parachute operated manually, and that work on a fully automatic seat should be deferred until a manual seat had been put into production. However for the Meteor, earmarked for the Martin-Baker seat, it was not possible to use a standard parachute because the only available space in which to put the parachute was behind the pilot's head. It had been agreed that an existing parachute should be modified for this purpose as an interim measure until a fully automatic seat was available and the Irvin Air Chute Company had been asked to do this. Irvin, however, needed co-operation from Martin-Baker, because the two firms needed to identify and agree the exact size and shape of the parachute pack. James had no intention of co-operating with anyone else in connection with the design of his ejection seat if he could possibly avoid it. He evaded all the Ministry's attempts to set up meetings between himself and the relevant people at Irvin and told them quite firmly that he had the matter in hand himself and required no help from any other firm.

After a visit to Martin-Baker in December 1946, the Ministry concluded that James seemed to be intent on proceeding with a fully automatic seat from the outset, rather than introducing a manual system first. While they conceded that there was no reason to suppose that his design would not be satisfactory, as he was following general supply-dropping parachute practice closely, it would nevertheless cause them enormous problems because of the number of tests that would have to be undertaken on each aspect of the system in order for it to be approved for Service use, which would cause delays in getting a seat into service. The official view was that James needed to use an existing parachute and harness if there was to be any hope of providing an ejection seat for the Meteor within six months. Nevertheless, it was intended that several aircraft would soon be flying with a Martin-Baker seat, including the Armstrong Whitworth E9/44, the Saunders-Roe E6/44, the Meteor, the English Electric B3/45, the second prototype of the Supermarine E10/44, the Boulton Paul E27/46 and probably the de Havilland 108. At this stage it was intended that the Malcolm seat should be installed in the Hawker N7/46 and the Westland N12/45. Both seats required further flight tests and the Ministry believed that considerable work was still required in connection with the stabilization of the seat after ejection, but they did not believe that this need hold up the installation of seats in aircraft. Their main concern in connection with the drogue system was not so much that it should be completely reliable, but rather that it should provide an arrangement for stabilizing the seat after ejection which would give pilots a better chance of escape than they currently had.

Although James was certainly scheming a fully automatic seat even in 1946, by the beginning of 1947 he was intending to produce a Mark 1 seat with a standard parachute pending approval of the automatic system by the Ministry. However, in February the Ministry were complaining that Martin-Baker were being uncooperative in their refusal to divulge information about what they were doing and their refusal to accept advice. The drogue that James had been supplied with, and which had caused the problems during the dummy tests in June and July of the previous year, had been issued to him on the understanding that it required a delay of about three seconds between the seat leaving the aircraft and the deployment of the drogue. James had ignored this and had simply told the Ministry that the drogue had failed, and they had only just found out that James was using a much smaller delay which had imposed intolerable loads on the drogue. At this stage James would only tell them that Martin-Baker were preparing their own equipment and would come to them for approval when it was completed. The Ministry's frustration was increased by the fact that nothing they had seen of James's work suggested that it would be anything other than satisfactory, although they noted that because of constant changes in the design, it was only during the last two months that there would have been any point in carrying out any work in connection with James's drogue system. In April a Minute on the Ministry file reported that:

> As you are probably aware it is most difficult to obtain reasoned statement from Mr Martin in conversation or to keep him to the point. As far as I can gather he does not appear to appreciate that his expenditure under this contract is limited; his attitude appears to be that he is merely doing what he has been requested to do, namely develop pilot ejection equipment.
>
> I endeavoured to impress on him that he must not exceed the amount allowed under a contract without prior authorisation but I doubt whether any words have had much effect. His views are unorthodox and he tends to regard contracts as so much paper work.
>
> There is, however, no doubt as to the value of the work which Martin-Bakers have done; nor do I doubt the cost figures they have submitted.

By the end of April 1947 James had completed the installation of the seat in the Meteor III, and although certain aspects of the parachute arrangements had still to be approved formally, the Ministry considered it to be 'a good example of an installation in a fighter aircraft not originally designed for pilot ejection', and that the relevant aircraft manufacturers should be encouraged to view it.

On 31 May 1947, a Ministry Minute addressed to the Director of Contracts suggested that it was now time to choose between the Martin-Baker seat and the Malcolm seat. While the existence of parallel development programmes had been helpful in the early stages, it was now becoming expensive in terms of effort and money, and increasingly difficult for design features from one system to be incorporated in the other system in an attempt to produce the best product. It seemed that in many respects it would be better to standardize on the Martin-Baker seat because it was at this stage further advanced than the Malcolm seat and because Malcolm were overloaded with other work. However, the Minute warned that 'the difficulty is that if we put all our eggs in the Martin-Baker basket he [James] may hold us up to ransom'. Once again the Ministry faced the difficult question of how best to deal with this intractable man.

On 5 May 1947, the ejection seat was given great support by W/Cdr. Bird Wilson. He had climbed out of a Meteor IV aircraft and parachuted safely to the ground when it became uncontrollable. He estimated that he was only about 1,000 ft above the ground when he deployed his parachute and that, as the aircraft had been spiralling, it would have been pure chance whether he would have survived an ejection. However, his exit from the aircraft had been successful because the aircraft had lost its tailplane, and he stated in his report: 'In conclusion, I consider that priority should be given to the fitting of the ejector seat even in the present stage of development as it might give the pilot a chance.'

By June 1947, the design of the Mark 1 Martin-Baker seat was nearing completion. James had redesigned it for production purposes and so as to reduce its weight, and flight tests with dummies began on 10 June 1947, nearly a year after Lynch's first live test. The initial tests were to prove the reliability of the drogue, and on completion of these tests, James intended to undertake a series of live test ejections at increasing speeds to demonstrate the success of the system and to explore further the problems of ejection at high speed. Notwithstanding this, the Ministry considered that the Martin-Baker seat and the Malcolm seat were sufficiently far advanced to justify their installation in aircraft, the choice of which seat to use being left to the aircraft designer.

Some 31 dummy ejections out of the Meteor were carried out using the redesigned seat while James perfected the design of the drogue and its stowage and various other teething problems which arose. Twenty-three of those 31 shots were described as perfect, including the last 11, completed during the course of July and August. James wrote later: 'In the course of these tests, seven seats were damaged beyond repair, but it is difficult to imagine any method of discovering the snags other than by practical experiment.'

One of the other problems of airborne tests, particularly those at higher speeds, was that the distances travelled by the seat could vary considerably. Scott recalls again:

Consequently, we seemed to cover most of Oxfordshire on foot in those early days, tramping across soggy farmland hunting for small components which would give us a clue as to what had gone wrong.

These excursions produced some amusing incidents. On one occasion a seat fell through the roof of a pigsty and the enraged owner complained that his sow had produced her litter ahead of schedule. He had to be soothed with soft words and have his roof repaired in the best Martin-Baker manner.

The dummy shots were made fairly low so that cameras on the ground could take photographs, but at low level it was often quite bumpy, especially during warm weather. On one occasion, when Scott was flying the Meteor at about 300 ft, the aircraft met some turbulence and the seat fired itself. They had to go and look for the seat some two miles from the aerodrome, and it was eventually found, with most of the relevant bits, having narrowly missed falling in a river.

Meanwhile, the Ministry were still concerning themselves with the problem of James's independent work on parachutes. The RAE had supplied him with six parachutes for the purpose of flight tests to prove his stabilizing parachute. These were stronger parachutes which were designed to avoid frequent wrecking of the test seat. However, on 18 June, the RAE expressed the view that these parachutes would not solve James's present problems which arose because of the unsatisfactory method of stowing the parachutes in metal containers, and that the answer to his problems was for the parachutes to be packed in a bag by skilled personnel. The next day, the Ministry wrote to James asking him to discontinue parachute development work under his contract as soon as he had completed the tests to prove his drogue system. If the tests were satisfactory, they proposed to give provisional approval to his drogue until an RAE type of parachute was available. The letter went on to explain the basis of their decision: 'The reason for this is the need for using to best advantage the specialist parachute staff and facilities available in this country. If they are used for checking and approving "private venture" designs, it will be to the detriment of developments of more general value.'

Their decision seems reasonable, but it upset James tremendously. He explained in reply that there seemed to be some confusion, as all that Martin-Baker were doing was ejecting dummies from aircraft to demonstrate the effectiveness of the drogue and gun, and the main parachute was only used to save the seat. As the Mark 1 type seat would use a conventional parachute and stowage arrangement, the question did not arise of arranging for tests of the main parachute. James was still working on the problems of automatic ejection, and he said that this directive from the Ministry was 'most unfortunate, as we had already acquired a considerable amount of experience of high-speed operation of drogues and parachute equipment which, of course, figure very prominently in the automatic seat problem'.

At a meeting on 7 July, the Ministry concluded that the Martin-Baker seat should be adopted to the exclusion of the Malcolm seat and wrote to James the next day to advise him that: 'It is probable that, if some outstanding points could be settled satisfactorily, the decision will be in favour of your firm.' The letter went on to identify the main outstanding points as being the agreement with James of the administrative machinery for stabilizing the design of his seat quickly, and the procedures for continuing the development of the seat in such a way that changes could only be introduced once they had received official approval. These points were discussed at a meeting on 18 July when it was agreed that the design should be defined by a complete set of signed and sealed working drawings, and that subsequent changes would need approval in order to be incorporated into the design. James agreed to supply the necessary drawings by the end of July and, on this basis, the Ministry decided that the Malcolm contract should be cancelled, but not until the Martin-Baker drawings had first been signed and sealed.

Meanwhile, following the series of successful dummy tests of the redesigned seat, another live test was now essential and on 11 August 1947, Lynch successfully completed his second live airborne ejection from the Meteor at 6,000 ft and a speed of 200 mph. Apart from the fact that the face blind was torn when the main parachute developed, the test was in all respects perfect. Having left the aircraft and disengaged himself from the seat, Lynch was on a fully developed parachute eight seconds after the ejection.

Apart from one dummy test ejection three days later, no further dummy airborne ejections were carried out until the end of 1948. Now that his seat was about to become standard equipment for Experimental and Service aircraft, James realized that a series of live test ejections would have to be made to convince the sceptics that the system really worked. He also realized that he should have another person in addition to Lynch ready and able to do these. With this in mind he hired Peter Page, a wartime paratrooper who, on leaving the army, was employed by Martin-Baker as a fitter and specifically as a test ejectee. The next live test ejection using a Martin-Baker seat was done by Page at the same altitude and speed as Lynch's last test. This ejection, on 12 August, went as planned, although the blind again tore when the main parachute developed, and he landed safely.

Following this, a dummy test ejection was carried out perfectly at a speed of 400 mph, and James then decided that a live test at this speed, the highest yet attempted, should be made. Page was the test ejectee and, unfortunately, serious problems arose. The ejection from the aircraft was perfect, but after the ejection Page's feet came off the foot rests on the bottom of the seat and as a result of this his body slewed sideways in the seat and the ripcord on his parachute was pulled as he slewed. The seat parachute deployed as it was supposed to, but because the main parachute had been released, fabric was billowing around Page while he was still strapped in his seat. He was faced with a dreadful dilemma. If he released himself from the seat, there was a very real possibility that his parachute would become entangled in the seat and fail to develop. As the 28 ft seat parachute was fully deployed, he decided to stay in the seat. His rate of descent with the seat parachute was obviously too fast, and landing in a slumped sitting position in the seat gave the most enormous jolt to his body. He was fortunate to survive this crash landing, which broke his neck. After several months in hospital, he eventually made a complete recovery, but it was a shock to James and those working with him.

It was 15 days before the next live shot was attempted. James needed time to analyse the distressing Page ejection and to convince himself that it was safe to proceed. On 29 August 1947, Lynch was ejected at 420 mph at 12,000 ft. He made a completely successful landing and the only problem was that the front strap of his leg guards came loose and bruised his legs below the knee.

The Ministry representative at this test interviewed Lynch afterwards and was able to report that: 'Mr. Lynch stated that no difficulty was experienced and that the ejection equipment functioned satisfactorily. No ill effects were experienced due to the air blast nor was any difficulty experienced in leaving the seat and descending on his own parachute.' The interesting point about this test is that James told the Ministry afterwards that Lynch had not, as first thought, suffered bruising to his legs. James was not averse to making slight changes to history when it suited his purpose to do so, and he obviously felt that it would be better if the Ministry thought that the test had been completely successful in all respects.

Unfortunately, it was not long before disaster struck again. On 20 September 1947, Lynch was to have done a demonstration ejection at RAF Benson out of the Meteor. The occasion was a Battle of Britain display and Benson had asked James if he could lay on an ejection as part of the display. Lynch was happy to do this and James was also happy to agree to it as it was to be at a low speed and therefore seemed to involve little risk. When the aircraft had reached the required speed and altitude, Scott gave Lynch the green light. Lynch pulled the face blind down but nothing happened. Scott looked through the window between the front and rear cockpits and signalled to Lynch that he would take the aircraft down. It was a nerve-wracking experience for both men, because neither of them knew why the ejection gun had not been activated when Lynch pulled the face blind, and they were therefore afraid that the seat could fire at any moment. As the aircraft got closer to the ground, so the level of danger increased, because an ejection at low altitude would have meant certain death for Lynch. Scott had to call on all his skill and experience to execute the smoothest landing of his life.

Once they were safely on the ground and Lynch had extricated himself from the seat, Eric Stevens ventured forward and was able to fix the problem, which was simply that a new type of sear had been fitted to an old-type firing head, which meant that it was impossible to withdraw the sear because there was not enough clearance. As several thousand people had come to watch the Benson display, Scott asked Lynch if he felt like trying it again. Not surprisingly, Lynch declined, but a Mr Keyes was among those watching, and he came forward and offered to do the test. He had made it known some three weeks previously that he would like to do a test ejection, but James had not accepted his offer because he wore glasses, and James was not prepared to accept the risk of this because of his previous experience with goggles. However, James was not at Benson that day and Eric accepted Keyes's offer. Scott briefed him about the procedure. Keyes told him that he wanted to wait a bit before pulling the ripcord on his parachute and Scott made it clear to him that on no account must he do this. However, Scott was not sure that Keyes was going to heed his instructions and gave him extra altitude just in case. He gave Keyes the green light to eject at 4,500 ft.

His premonition was correct. Scott remembers that Keyes ejected and dropped through the sky like a stone. His parachute opened just as he hit the ground, where he lay unconscious. Surprisingly enough, he did not break any bones although he was black and blue all over and unconscious for three days, during which time James was frantic. The explanation of this incident was simple. Keyes was very shortsighted and had lenses in his goggles. His goggles blew off when he ejected and he could hardly see anything. Instead of pulling the ripcord immediately as he should have done, he pulled it only when the ground began looking green.

The Ministry were not pleased by this incident. They noted that the 'incidents at Benson were deplorable particularly as they occurred in the presence of a large crowd and are likely to bring ejection equipment into disrepute'. They were annoyed that James had not sought their permission before agreeing to participate in the display, and he was told that their Meteor aircraft were not to be used for unauthorized purposes or for any further live tests without their prior approval. James, however, did not miss his opportunity to have a dig at the Ministry in return. He replied:

> I might here mention that the type of sear which was used in this last flight was a type that had been modified at the request of Wing Commander Bird; but my own private opinion is that the earlier type of sear was perfectly satisfactory. In fact, my experience is that if one has too many cooks making suggestions one gets nowhere, as a lot of suggestions come from people who sit at office desks, whereas the equipment we are working upon is the result of hard practical testing.

Meanwhile, the Martin-Baker seat had still not been approved for Service use, because the design had not yet been identified by the set of drawings that James had promised for the end of July but had failed to produce. A conference was held on 19 September to approve the seat, shortly to become the Mark 1 seat, for the Meteor, and with minor alterations it was accepted. But the Ministry were concerned that James 'had failed to deliver a seat for the Meteor which he had promised originally for 26 July, and this delay was adversely affecting the introduction of the seat into production aircraft. James then modified one of the cartridges, and whilst this was an improvement, the revised cartridge had to be approved, and the Ministry were once again exasperated that James should have made this modification without authorization. Gregory from the Ministry of Supply wrote: 'We have of course experienced this sort of thing repeatedly with the firm but short of stopping the work, we can see no method, which has not already been tried, of curing them. We are however reviewing our policy towards Martin-Baker in view of the extreme difficulty in dealing with them.' No change of policy became apparent, however.

On 11 October, the Martin-Baker seat was submitted for approval for

Service use. In November, James made another change to the cartridges when he increased the amount of propellant, a change which he had felt was necessary after watching live tests a few weeks previously. But finally, on 15 December 1947, the drawings for the Martin-Baker seat were sealed, and authority was given for cancelling the Malcolm contract. And on 2 January 1948, the Martin-Baker seat was approved for installation in production Meteor 4 aircraft.

The seat which was approved was the original version of the Mark 1 seat. It incorporated the same features as the experimental seat used by Lynch except that the 24 ft seat recovery parachute was dispensed with. In addition, these seats were provided with an adjustable seat pan which could be raised and lowered to accommodate pilots of varying height without increasing the height of the seat. It also incorporated adjustable foot rests which were hinged to the seat frame and spring-loaded downward so that they remained at floor level regardless of any adjustment to the seat pan, and thigh guards which were integral to the seat pan and which prevented the ejectee's legs being blown apart by the air blast or thrown outwards by centrifugal forces should the seat spin on the drogue after ejection. This seat also included the Martin-Baker back-type dinghy pack which incorporated a rigid tubular framework which maintained the shape of the pack to close dimensions and contained the emergency oxygen bottle in an aluminium cradle in such a way as to be readily removable for inspection. The seat was guided during ejection by four rollers on the seat structure running in a guide rail assembly bolted to the aircraft structure, the ejection gun being located within the hollow guide rail assembly. The seat structure and guide rails were constructed of light alloy, and the whole apparatus, including drogue, pilot's parachute, dinghy, emergency oxygen and water bottle, weighed only 172 lb, of which 143 lb was ejected weight.

Just over three years had elapsed since James had shown his model of the swinging arm to Sir Stafford Cripps. During that time he had made the most extraordinary progress with his escape system. James was 56. Success had come to him late in life but hard work and determination had eventually won the day. Despite his continuing desire to build aircraft, the ejection seat seems to have been ideally suited to his own individual brand of inventive talent. It was a project which can be described as the perfectionist's dream. The increasing speed and sophistication of aircraft imposed greater and different demands on the ejection seat and the circumstances in which it would be required to operate, and there was always scope for improvement. An article printed in 1965 in the periodical *Aircraft Engineering* commented on James's comprehensive approach to testing:

> Since Martin-Baker Aircraft were working in a new field with a minimum of previous experience being of direct application, it was necessary and is still necessary to pursue this trial and error technique on a comprehensive scale. This point is worth emphasising, because although it is true to say that

a large number of the features embodied in Martin-Baker ejection seats are the result of the enlightened applications of basic mechanical engineering principles (conceptions for which Martin has been principally responsible), it is also true that the standard of reliability for which these seats are renowned has only been achieved by the most rigorous proving tests and a vast amount of sheer hard work – much of it of a purely repetitive nature.

One would be forgiven for assuming that the decision to supply ejection seats to the Royal Air Force would have been a remarkably popular one among aircrew, but oddly enough, their reaction was in many cases quite the opposite. A great many pilots had a vehement objection to sitting on an explosive charge. They felt they were at greater risk from the seat firing accidentally than they would be from the remote risk of having to abandon the aircraft. Some would insist that the cartridges were removed before they would fly the aircraft, which of course rendered the seat totally inoperative. Others would leave the safety pins in the seat on the basis that if an emergency situation arose, they would remove the safety pins and then use the ejection seat. It is an interesting analogy to the suggestion in the 1930s that parachutes be issued to all aircrew, an idea which was opposed by many in the Air Ministry on the basis that it would encourage pilots to abandon their aircraft in circumstances when recovery of the aircraft was still possible.

The French were at this stage also becoming interested in equipping their aircraft with ejection seats, and they asked James if Lt. Cartier of the French Air Force could test the Martin-Baker seat. The Ministry had no objection to this provided the test was made entirely at Lt. Cartier's own risk, and on 28 February 1948, he ejected from the Meteor over Chalgrove at 350 mph from 5,400 ft. Scott was again flying the Meteor for this test. He remembers Cartier arriving for the test clutching various notepads, and Scott had gently to point out to him that he would have no time to look at them. The test was entirely successful, but the seat and the seat parachute could not be found by the evening of the next day, and this was causing some consternation at Martin-Baker as it was essential that the relevant components be found and analysed after each test. Scott had seen a man on the ground looking at the seat parachute, but when questioned, the farmer who owned the field where the seat had landed denied all knowledge of the whereabouts of the seat and its parachute. It was only two days later, when threatened with the police and search warrants, that he confessed to having put the seat and parachute in the back of one of his barns. Rationing of clothing was still in force and he thought that the fabric of the parachute could be put to good use by his wife.

Cartier returned to France to give two further live demonstrations of the seat at Bretigny and Rennes, his shot at Bretigny being at 470 mph, the fastest live ejection at that date. At Rennes, Cartier had arrived wearing a very large helmet which Scott had tried to persuade him to take off, because he thought it might cause problems when he tried to pull the face blind over it. Scott was right and the few seconds' delay while Cartier struggled with the face blind meant that he only narrowly avoided landing in a sewerage farm.

Inevitably it is often said of James that he took unnecessary risks undertaking the live test ejections. Such criticisms always come from outside Martin-Baker from those who were not close to James or the work he was doing. But those who understood what he was doing always reject any such criticism out of hand. It was a business where risks could not be avoided. Using explosives to blast a man into the sky is an inherently hazardous project, but the unanimous opinion among those involved with his test work was that James took every possible precaution, and undertook any number of tests, to ensure that no avoidable risk was taken with human life.

Despite the series of live tests, the development of the ejection seat was still progressing. While it had been adequately demonstrated that the performance of James's ejection seat under multiple g conditions was satisfactory, it was not known whether the pilot would be able to reach the face blind handle in these conditions. One further cause for concern was the possibility that after the cockpit hood had been jettisoned, the pilot's ability to operate the face blind successfully might be impeded by the turbulent air flow about the cockpit. Flight tests to check these effects were made on 11 November 1948. Recording and visual accelerometers were installed and it was found that with the aircraft in a steady 5 g turn, it was quite possible to grasp the firing handle and pull down the face blind. A second test with the cockpit hood removed from the aircraft demonstrated that at speeds of up to 420 mph, no aerodynamic interference with the operation of the face blind could be detected.

On 30 May 1949, James received the wonderful news of the first emergency use of the Martin-Baker seat by Jo Lancaster from the AW52 Flying Wing. James was enormously excited and soon word began to spread around the factory. Anne Mower, his secretary since May 1947, recalls that there was 'a frisson of excitement' in the factory that day. Basil Macnab, then an apprentice of 18, who is still employed by the company, remembers meeting James that day and recalls that James 'was very animated and out of his mind about how successful it had been'. But there were no special celebrations at the factory or at James's house that day. Any engineering success was important to James, but there was always more work to be done and another goal to strive for.

Chapter Ten

The Forbidden Test

The year of Jo Lancaster's emergency ejection (1949) saw a temporary lull in Martin-Baker's experimental activity: only two live test ejections and two dummy test ejections took place during the course of the year. There were two principal reasons for this. Firstly, of course, there was the growth of Martin-Baker's commercial work. The ejection seat had to be 'tailored' in order for it to be retrofitted into existing aircraft and installed in those new aircraft where the cockpit design was already well advanced. These modifications were relatively minor ones and did not require extensive testing, but they nevertheless occupied James's time and attention, and the manufacture of seats to meet Martin-Baker's contractual commitments was imposing an increasing strain on their manufacturing capacity. By the end of 1950, Martin-Baker had orders for ejection seats for the RAF alone worth £750,000, and they had also received orders from France, Belgium, Holland, Denmark, Canada, Australia and Argentina. This foreign interest required James to travel abroad to visit the representatives of the governments concerned and to discuss the seat with them. It also meant that he needed to start setting up the network of Martin-Baker agents in the countries buying the ejection seat which is now a major part of the Martin-Baker organization. These agents perform the essential task of liaison between Martin-Baker and the parties abroad in all matters relating to the supply and modification of the seats.

The second reason for the lack of experimental activity was the amount of design work in which James was involved which was not yet ready for testing, in particular the design of an automatic seat, which James regarded as a necessity. If a pilot was for any reason unconscious or otherwise incapacitated after initiating the ejection process, he would be unable to release himself from the seat and deploy his parachute. Even if he was able to do this, the ejection had to take place at sufficient altitude to allow the pilot time to complete the manual separation process, and to allow enough time for the main parachute to open and control the pilot's fall. It was obvious to everyone that an automatic seat separation and parachute deployment process would be quicker than a pilot trying to complete these procedures manually. The minimum height at which a successful ejection could occur was not absolute because it depended on how quickly the pilot in question could complete the necessary procedures, but the lowest level at which a successful ejection occurred with a manually operated seat was 900 ft, and some pilots were inevitably killed when the ejection took place too low.

The development of the automatic seat was a continuing process over a period of years. James's early experimental work for the RAF had been stopped in June 1947 when the Ministry told him to stop further work connected with parachutes which were an essential part of the automatic process, but, even at this stage, James was looking outside Great Britain for possible markets for his seat. Following the successful demonstration of his ejection seat at the Navy Yard at Philadelphia in the autumn of 1946, the US Navy had placed an order for a small number of ejection seats for further testing and evaluation. Shortly afterwards, the USAAF also ordered seats from Martin-Baker for evaluation purposes. The only seats then available were the manual Mark 1 seats, but James explained to the Americans the importance of an automatic system, and both authorities had agreed to take delivery of the automatic seat when it became available. The design of an automatic seat took much longer than James had anticipated, however, and he was not able to meet the delivery dates he had promised the Americans. It was not until 1950 that he had a seat ready for testing.

Although the basic construction of this seat was similar to the Mark 1 seat, James was not trying at this stage to modify the existing seat, but rather to design a new seat with automatic capability. The parachute pack and the harness arrangements in particular were completely new. James provided in this design for the pilot to sit on his dinghy and for the parachute to be packed in a specially designed back-type pack. The face blind for firing the seat was situated on the front of the parachute pack. The separate seat and parachute harnesses of the manual seats were discarded, and James designed instead a single harness which combined both functions and which was attached to the seat at six points.

The ejection process in this seat followed the same sequence as that for the Mark 1 seats up to the opening of the drogue. Thereafter, by means of a clock mechanism built into the seat, six seconds after ejection the drogue released the seat, drew the pilot's parachute out of the pack, and simultaneously released the pilot's harness from its attachment points to the seat. Thus the pilot's parachute would develop in the usual way while the seat fell away, the only action required by the pilot in this entire process being the pulling of the face blind. James built a barostat control into the clock mechanism which prevented it from functioning above 10,000 ft, so that in the case of an ejection at high altitude, an emergency oxygen supply stored in the dinghy pack would be automatically activated, and the pilot would breathe this oxygen throughout his fast descent in the seat, controlled only by the drogue, until the automatic separation from the seat and parachute deployment took place at a safe altitude.

The operation of the seat was completely straightforward for the pilot even on the ground. When leaving the aircraft, he had only to release his single harness by operating a single quick release mechanism and step out of the aircraft, leaving his parachute, dinghy and harness in place. Ejection seats at that time had to provide for the pilot to be able to override manually the automatic mechanisms, and James provided for this at two stages. If the pilot was unable to operate the ejection seat in an emergency because, for example, the seat mechanisms had been damaged in combat or because he was unable to jettison the canopy, he could, by operating a release handle, leave the seat wearing his harness with the parachute and dinghy attached and attempt an unassisted escape from the aircraft. Once out of the aircraft, the parachute could be operated manually in the usual way. If manual override was necessary after ejection because, for example, the clock barostat mechanism or drogue gun failed to operate, the pilot could still use the release handle to free himself from his seat before deploying his parachute.

James considered his design to be 'a first class job' and, in the spring of 1950, he went to America to visit the US Navy in connection with the possible introduction of his automatic seat into US Navy aircraft. He also wanted to talk to them about the infringement of his patents relating to the seats which he had demonstrated to them in 1946. The US Navy Department considered that James's automatic seat was ten years ahead of their own work. They told him that all their experimental work on ejection guns had been modelled on his conclusions about pressure curves which they did not consider could be improved on. They also freely admitted that they had infringed his patents and asked James how much money he wanted by way of compensation. This, of course, was a difficult question for James to answer. Financial compensation was unattractive to him because so much of it would disappear in high taxation. He simply wanted them to stop plagiarizing his designs and buy his seat. As a result of this visit, the US Navy ordered several seats for testing purposes and James was asked to supervise these tests and to arrange for some live test ejections. But despite their appreciation of James's work, and despite further orders for small numbers of seats for evaluation, it would be several years before they placed orders for Martin-Baker seats for operational use.

James combined the trip to America with a visit to Canada. He took the opportunity to visit Avro Canada who had placed an order for Martin-Baker seats for their new fighter, the CF100, but an important purpose of the visit to Canada was to investigate the possibility of setting up a company there which, in addition to manufacturing ejection seats, could hold his American and Canadian patents and receive the compensation in respect of their infringement. He had chosen Canada rather than America because the tax system there was more favourable.

Meanwhile, James had carried out several successful airborne tests of the automatic seat, and the Ministry of Supply requested that 50 further tests be carried out, all photographed, in order for the seat to be approved.

James had by now realized that low-level airborne testing was essential as air-to-air photography tended to miss the vital parts of the ejection sequence. In order to assist in measuring the performance of the seat by photography from the ground, a line of posts 20 ft high and 100 ft apart was set up, along which the aircraft was flown at between 50 and 80 ft above the ground. The film could then be analysed using the posts as height and distance references. In order to get good photographs, the camera was mounted on a tripod and fitted to what James described as 'a gun mounting affair which is free to swivel on two planes so all the photographer does is to look through the gun sights to follow the seat down'.

The seat was airborne tested 28 times in 1950 and worked well on each occasion. But unfortunately, because of size constraints affecting the size of the parachute pack, a 17 ft lightweight celanese parachute was used which was not accepted for Service use, with the result that the entire project was abandoned. This was unfortunate, not just for Martin-Baker, but frankly also for the Service pilots who had been destined to use it, because it represented a great deal of advanced and innovative design work. It also delayed the introduction of automatic capability for ejection seats into Service use, a delay which inevitably cost lives, because it was not until the abandonment of this new seat that James turned his mind to the design of another automatic seat based on the Mark 1 seat, so that the Mark 1 seat could be modified to have automatic capability.

Meanwhile, in the autumn of 1949, James had a visit from the Chief Medical Officer of the Swiss Air Force who was very concerned about the absence of ejection seats in the Vampire aircraft. He told James that he considered it nothing less than criminal to compel pilots to fly in aircraft like the Vampire without ejection seats, and asked James if there was anything he could do about it. James immediately telephoned the de Havilland Aircraft Company, who had designed and produced this aircraft, and asked them to let him have a damaged Vampire nose so that he could investigate the possibility of installing an ejection seat in it. De Havilland were not interested in James's proposal, and told him bluntly that it was not possible to fit an ejection seat into the Vampire. James was naturally not put off by this response. He badgered Air Chief Marshal Sir Alec Coryton to give him a Vampire fuselage so that he could consider the matter for himself. In October 1949 he wrote:

> I decided that, since de Havilland were so unco-operative, we would take the bull by the horns, and we have now designed a seat which we think will go into the Vampire without any modifications whatsoever to the aircraft structure; at least if any modifications should be necessary it would only involve a possible reduction of the length of the windscreen by about one and a half inches to cover the tallest pilots.

Having received the Vampire fuselage, James decided that the problems could be overcome by 'just a bit of Martin-Baker ingenuity'. In rather less than two weeks he had installed the seat in the aeroplane without altering the windscreen, by making only a cutaway in the bulkhead and redesigning the hydraulic tank. Martin-Baker made a complete mock-up of the installation and gave it to de Havilland who accepted the seat installation arrangements, following which the Ministry of Supply gave de Havilland a contract for the Vampire with the ejection seat.

Despite the demands of the development and manufacture of the ejection seat, James was still spending time designing other pieces of equipment. It was by no means certain what future the ejection seat would have, and during the previous few years he had been constantly considering other projects that might be commercially viable. He had a brief foray into the possibility of manufacturing refrigerators, but these got no further than the Martin-Baker canteen. He accepted a small contract for the manufacture of some photographic stands, but his more successful sideline projects were those related to aircraft.

He had designed the original test rigs for his seat development work, but he promoted the idea of mobile test rigs for training purposes, and these were soon recognized as being a valuable piece of equipment for training pilots in the new emergency escape procedures. These mobile rigs, unlike the fixed rigs, were of tubular construction and embodied an air brake to lower the seat and occupant. On the occasion of the first live test on a mobile rig, James insisted that the person responsible for the stressing should take the first ride. Many of these mobile test rigs were ordered by James's customers and provided Martin-Baker with a limited but nevertheless important ancillary business.

James designed an emergency explosive feathering device for turboprop propellers. If a propeller was allowed to overspeed due to any defects or sluggishness in the constant-speed unit, it was likely that the unit would explode and the aircraft would then crash. James's device provided for a governor to fire an explosive charge in the hub of the propeller in these circumstances which caused the propeller to feather in two seconds. The device was tested successfully by the de Havilland Aircraft Company who then paid him for his design.

He had also received a contract for the installation of a new 30 mm gun in a Beaufighter and several other small projects including a retractable fin for high-speed bombs, but his most successful sideline was the flat feed mechanism for the British Hispano 20 mm cannon. After the war, James had been asked to consider how to overcome the problems that were being experienced with the feed mechanism for this gun, particularly when g was applied during firing. James developed and perfected a flat feed system for this cannon entirely at his own expense over a period of several years. The feed mechanism was, as its name suggests, flat in shape and very compact and therefore suitable for installation on an aircraft wing. James wrote: 'I was entirely responsible for the design of every detail of it and it had the capacity to empty the ammunition containers with 5 G applied during the time of firing.' The mechanism was tested successfully at Boscombe Down in early 1950 and proved to be very reliable, and it was standardized for all new gun installations in British aircraft.

Although Martin-Baker produced a large number of these feeds, it was not a happy situation. James considered that he was 'double-crossed' by the Weapons Section of the Ministry of Supply. The Contracts Department pressed him for a complete set of manufacturing drawings for this device, which he was understandably reluctant to give them. In return, however, they offered to place an order with him for 1,000 mechanisms at a fixed price to be agreed, and to give him the orders for at least 50 per cent of their remaining requirements, subject to the price and delivery dates being acceptable. The Ministry justified their position on the basis that they did not want to create a monopoly for the supply of these feeds. James pointed out that as they had placed development contracts with four other companies, all of which had failed to produce a mechanism acceptable to them, he should not be penalized for the fact that a monopoly situation had arisen, particularly as his development work had taken several years and had cost Martin-Baker a considerable sum of money. He further pointed out that the report on his gun feed in 1949 had been so unfavourable that if Martin-Baker's work had been the subject of a development contract, the Ministry could not have justified further expenditure, and they would not, therefore, have ever had a successful flat feed system.

James eventually agreed to hand over the drawings on the understanding that the Ministry would sell him, at a fair and reasonable price, from the Ministry's strategic reserve, certain machine tools, and that the Royal Small Arms Factory would not be asked to manufacture the gun feeds if Martin-Baker could meet the Ministry's delivery requirements. James handed over the drawings, at the suggestion of an official at the Ministry of Supply, as a Christmas present, on the basis that the official letter about the gun feed would be rewritten, but there was obviously some considerable misunderstanding about the arrangement as the Ministry maintained that they simply did not have the necessary machines available to sell to him, and they gave the drawings to the Royal Small Arms Factory which made several thousands of the gun feeds. James wrote in August 1953:

> By the end of this year we shall have made about five thousand Martin patent gun feeds, and the Royal Small Arms Factory will have made the same, and they have paid nothing for the design and development work or anything else. So I have told them in no uncertain language that they are crooks etc., but they don't seem to mind this at all.

For some time James had been thinking about designing another aircraft. He had in mind 'a small kind of interceptor fighter, perhaps a little unconventional in its shape'. However, official support was, he noted, conspicuous by its absence, and he was told that there were other things the Ministry would much rather that he did. James suggested, provocatively, during a meeting with a Ministry representative, that they might like him to design a new high-velocity gun, and rockets that shot straight, and the man from the Ministry replied that they would indeed be very interested in such a thing. After his problems with the gun feed, however, James had no intention of dealing further with the Weapons Section. He wrote some years later: 'Indeed, it would be true to say that the gun mechanism is right up my street. I like that kind of work and if the Government had played the game there would have been some high class guns today.' Shortly afterwards he got involved in another argument with them about the production of his gun feeds and he reluctantly came to the conclusion that it was time to give up working on this sort of military equipment. It was merely unfortunate, as far as he was concerned, that he would still have to deal with the Ministry in connection with his ejection seats.

Working on the development of the ejection seat could sometimes be a gruesome task. Although James never experienced a fatality during his test work, fatalities involving his seat inevitably occurred in emergency situations, and many were investigated in order to ascertain not only the cause of the emergency, but also the reason for the failure of the pilot to eject successfully. In February 1950, James was asked for the first time to investigate one such incident. A de Havilland 108, a tailless, high-speed monoplane, had crashed and killed the pilot. James was asked by the Ministry to inspect the wreckage, a particularly gory and unpleasant task, to ascertain why the pilot had not ejected. Fortunately, the answer was quickly apparent and did not involve a failure of the seat. The examination revealed that the seat was still in working order, although damaged by the impact of the aircraft hitting the ground, and the pilot had not jettisoned the hood. It seemed that the wings had come off the aeroplane, and with the aeroplane falling to pieces around him, the pilot had had no chance to begin the ejection process.

This year also saw the award of the OBE to James, which he regarded with some pride and some scepticism. While it was gratifying, even to James, to be honoured in this way, it highlighted his frustrations with the machinations of the Establishment which he felt had taken far too long to recognize the merits of his work. It was, he said, 'only fit for lavatory paper', a remark which was followed by: 'they are all a lot of low grade bastards'. James was never to be won over by the Ministry, whatever compliments or congratulations they gave him, and his dislike of the Establishment and the men who worked in it remained, untempered, for the rest of his life. Some of those who worked for James will admit that they derived a certain amount of vicarious pleasure from his outspoken approach to civil servants and politicians because he would say what he thought, which in many cases was what other people thought too, although they would never have dared to say such things.

By now he was a full member of the Society of British Aircraft Constructors, that 'group of Freemasons and crooks' that he felt had excluded him and contributed to his problems during the war years. His opinion of them had not improved, and he wrote:

> Though I am a Council Member I never go to their meetings. Handley Page, Roy Dobson and a few of those who are the big shots occupy the middle places of a large oval table, whilst the microbes tend to be dispersed out of hearing range. They are lacking in fire and enthusiasm as far as I am concerned . . . They are far too wet and very timid with the Air Ministry and sort of apologising for being alive. This is not up my street at all. I like to give the bastards the works.

James's latest complaint with the Ministry concerned his treatment by them in connection with his gun feed and their decision not to make a suitable payment to him in respect of any of his wartime inventions. Discussions regarding the latter had been going on for some time. Because of the high taxation at that time, the greater part of any payment they might make to him would be recovered from James in tax. James was firmly of the view that the idea of giving him something with one hand, only to take most of it back with the other, was a backhanded way of trying to pretend that their offer to him was reasonable when clearly it was not, at least as far as James was concerned. Indeed, any mention of taxation, whether or not connected to the question of these payments, was always guaranteed to incense James. He was vehemently against high taxation because it restricted his ability to use the company's profits to build up his business, and he was equally opposed to death duties, for it seemed to him that when he died, the company would have to be sold to pay the death duties. He summed up his views in a letter to Francis when he wrote: 'So if you tear your guts out and try and build up some sort of business the net result is that your biggest problem is to know how to avoid the Cripps gang collecting the lot.'

His point was illustrated sadly on 31 August 1950, when James received some distressing news. His sister, Jane, telephoned him in the morning to tell him that her husband, Edwin, had died in his sleep. Edwin had been suffering from high blood pressure for some time but his doctor had not thought it was serious. It was a very great shock to James who had lived in Edwin's house for over 20 years before his marriage. He knew how much he owed to his brother-in-law's tolerance and understanding, and how much his business owed to the financial support that Edwin had provided. Edwin had lived long enough to see the seeds of success beginning to take root in Martin-Baker, but James would often remark in the future that it was a great pity that Edwin died before Martin-Baker became really successful. Edwin had already experienced considerable difficulty in raising the funds necessary to repay the loans made to the company by Frank Francis and to purchase his shares. The effect of Edwin's death so soon after this was almost sufficient to bankrupt the family.

In September 1949 Martin-Baker were producing five seats a week; by March 1950 this had risen to 20. By the summer, they were struggling to produce 45 or 50 a week to meet their contractual commitments. The Ministry of Supply began pressing James to open up a second factory in the United Kingdom to cope with the fast-increasing workload. With this in mind, James visited Northern Ireland and the Isle of Man. His interest in the Isle of Man was the tax position there: low income tax and no death duties. His interest in Ireland was sentimental. It would be some years before factories were opened in these two places, independent of Martin-Baker but for the purpose of supporting its manufacturing capacity, but he was also persuaded to visit France to discuss the ejection seat with the French authorities, and it was eventually agreed that the French would manufacture Martin-Baker seats under licence. In February 1950 he wrote to a childhood friend of his in Ireland: 'It is a curious thing, Teenie, that it always appears that success comes too late in life for one to appreciate it. When you get older you don't put the same value on success as you would when you are – say – twenty five to thirty years of age.' James was 57 and, as was often the case, was remembering those difficult years when he first arrived in Acton, the years that were probably the most difficult and depressing of his life. But it was his commercial success that meant less to him than it would have done in his youth, and his engineering successes continued to make the hard work worthwhile.

In March 1951, James told Francis that 'the works are now so congested with tools and workers that you can hardly move about, and we are running a night and day shift, and also Sunday mornings'. Martin-Baker was then employing about 400 people, but James would have employed twice that number if he had had the room. He realized that he would have to extend the factory and he set about building a new extension which would give him another 20,000 sq ft. James confessed to Francis:

> In point of fact I might say that this last six months I have felt for the first time in my life that I could really do with a holiday and a change. I feel quite tired at times and to work with all these low grade people who are not 'civil' or 'servants' and who are just plain low down crooks gets more than exacting.

The frustration and anger that James felt because of the dictates from the Ministry as to what would be acceptable for Service use, the cancellation of his automatic seat, the lack of payment for his wartime efforts, his treatment over his gun feeds, and unacceptably high taxation, on top of the long-term effects of the injuries he had received during the gypsy attack, and the various operations on his head that he had had as a result of those injuries, were taking their toll on James. It was fortunate that news of further successful ejections was beginning to arrive at Denham to hearten him.

Since the first emergency ejection by Jo Lancaster, the general practice has grown up worldwide of informing Martin-Baker when their seat has been used. In the early days of the ejection seat, it was obviously a

momentous achievement as far as aircrew and air forces were concerned
that there was an escape system for pilots, and the impact of a successful
ejection seems, in most cases, to have been adequate impetus for them
to take the trouble to contact the company. There are always cases where,
for one reason or another, the company is not notified of an ejection
and other cases where it is not notified until later, sometimes years after
the ejection occurred. Although there were nine ejections during the
course of 1951, James was only told about seven of them at the time,
but news of the seven successes was still very gratifying for him.

In June 1951, FO Stoney of the Royal Australian Air Force ejected
successfully from a Meteor over Japan. Sgt. Tollitt of the RAF was the
next successful ejectee that James heard about when he ejected on 3 July
1951 following a collision between two Meteors at 30,000 ft. His aircraft
got into an inverted spin at such a high rate that he became temporarily
blind due to the pressure of blood in his head. He nevertheless succeeded
in ejecting himself, and notwithstanding his inability to find the seat
harness box and release himself from his seat, he pulled the D-ring on his
parachute which successfully deployed and he made a safe landing in
his seat. The pilot of the other Meteor attempted to land his aircraft,
but at low altitude he lost control and the aircraft turned upside down.
Although he ejected from the aircraft there was insufficient time for his
parachute to deploy and he was killed.

Two weeks later, Flt. Sgt. Tickner of the RAF ejected successfully
from his Meteor at 20,000 ft following instrument failure in thick cloud.
And on 29 August, the first successful emergency ejection in combat
took place when Flt. Lt. Guthrie of the Royal Australian Air Force was
shot down by a MiG-15 over Korea. Having ejected at over 38,000 ft, it
took him 25 minutes to reach the ground. He landed safely but was
unfortunately captured by the enemy and spent some time as a prisoner
of war.

News of these successes began a gradual change in James's outlook
which would take several years to mature. When he first designed the
ejection seat, it was another engineering achievement, and the life-saving
aspect of the seat took several years to impact fully on him. He had had
to wait a long time before the first emergency ejection took place, and
after that, he had to wait another two years before the second. It was
not immediately apparent to him, therefore, that his ejection seat would
save as many lives as it has done, but after the series of ejections in 1951,
some of which were in very adverse circumstances, he gradually began
to realize the true importance of what he had produced.

Many people believe that the death of Val Baker was a tremendous
impetus to James in his ejection seat work, and the principal reason why
he became so dedicated to the job. James did not himself give Baker's
fatal crash as his reason for starting with this work, but once he came
to realize that his seat could save lives, the memory of Baker certainly
fuelled his increasing dedication to this task. And as he became more
deeply involved in his ejection seat work, so he inevitably became more

interested in the details of each emergency ejection. Although he had not thought it necessary to meet Jo Lancaster to discuss his ejection experience, by 1952 he had realized that input from the emergency ejectees could be invaluable as far as the future development of the seat was concerned, because they were the men, using the seat in the critical circumstances for which it had been designed, who could identify the problems that the ejection seat had not yet overcome, and thus influence or confirm the direction of James's design work. In January 1952, he summoned Jock Bryce, a test pilot for Vickers, to his office to discuss his ejection from the prototype Valiant on 12 January of that year.

It had become clear that pilots were sometimes experiencing difficulty in getting out of their seats after leaving the aircraft, and that there was a need for a mechanism to tip the pilot out of the seat. It had also been recognized that existing seats would not in all flight conditions clear the fins of the new high fin aircraft such as the V-bombers which were then in the design phase. Both problems were demonstrated in this accident involving the prototype Valiant when a fire broke out on the starboard wing and the aircraft was quickly, in Bryce's words, 'caught up in a catastrophic fire'. It was clear that the crew needed to escape. He gave the order for the three rear crew members with no ejection seats to abandon the aircraft, and then the co-pilot ejected, followed by Bryce. The co-pilot unfortunately was not ejected high enough to clear the high tail fin of the Valiant and he was killed. Bryce successfully cleared the fin but then experienced great difficulty in extracting himself from his seat. He looked down and saw a blue harness with a gold buckle and a white harness with a silver buckle, one being the seat harness and the other the parachute harness, and he hesitated until he was as sure as he could be which harness he should be unbuckling. Having successfully unbuckled the seat harness, he was utterly puzzled to find himself still sitting in the seat, which he had expected would fall away as soon as the harness was released. In fact, far from falling away, the seat seemed to be stuck to him and he had the greatest difficulty in pushing the seat away as he fell through the air. He finally separated from the seat just in time to pull the D-ring of his parachute and for the parachute to open before he fell through a tree and landed on his back on the ground with, surprisingly, no injuries.

James telephoned Bryce as soon as he heard about the ejection and told him that it was of the utmost importance that he should speak to him while the details of the ejection were still fresh in his mind. Bryce went to see James at the factory and spent most of a morning answering his questions and explaining the problems that he had experienced. Bryce remembers that James could not have been more impressive in the intent way he listened to everything that Bryce said, and in the way that he explained the background to the different features of the seat and why he had designed them the way he had. While Bryce was there, James showed him drawings of a canvas apron device which he had designed to solve the problem that Bryce had had in getting out of the seat, and which would clearly be an important feature of the new automatic seat that James was working on.

The question of emergency escape from V-bombers was one with which James was already very concerned. For V-bombers – the Vickers Valiant, the Handley Page Victor and the A.V. Roe Vulcan – it was originally intended that the entire pressurized compartment containing the five crew members would be separated from the aircraft in an emergency and would be provided with parachutes so that the capsule itself could parachute to the ground. The Ministry of Supply had asked James to accept a contract for the design of a jettisonable portion of the fuselage. James pointed out to them that it would be quite impractical to test this, as it would necessitate writing off the whole aircraft. He recalled that 'the alleged experts decided that all this could be done by models and scientific studies', but James's practical mind regarded this approach as 'sheer nonsense'. He also pointed out that it would not be practicable to do a safe escape at low altitude with this arrangement, and as there could be no guarantee of height, it would be quite useless. He declined to accept the contract. James did not want any more Ministry development contracts, and the development of the ejection seat continued under James's direction and not that of the Ministry. When James felt that he had produced something which the RAF should have, he would offer the completed product to the Ministry.

Following James's refusal to accept this contract, the Ministry gave it to James's old rival, M.L. Aviation. James had some satisfaction in reporting that 'when the contraption was tested it functioned just as I depicted, namely, crashed into the ground'. Martin-Baker was duly asked in 1951 to provide ejection seats for the pilot and co-pilot in the prototype V-bombers, although it was not at this stage intended that these ejection seats would be provided in the aircraft which eventually went into service. As the Mark 1 seat would not always clear the fins of these aircraft, James had to work out how to give the seat a higher trajectory on leaving the aircraft. From an engineering point of view, he could have achieved this easily by increasing the explosive charge in the ejection gun, but James well understood the physiological limitations of the human body, and an increased charge which would have produced a higher peak acceleration was clearly not an option. He solved the problem instead by increasing the stroke of the ejection gun, and this new gun produced a velocity of 80 ft/sec rather than 60 ft/sec, which sufficiently increased the height of the seat's trajectory while maintaining the low peak acceleration and low rate of rise of g of the earlier gun. This new gun was made up of three tubes telescoped into each other, powered by one primary and four secondary cartridges, arranged in pairs. When the primary cartridge was fired, the inner tubes began to rise, uncovering first one and then the other pair of secondary cartridges, which were in turn ignited by the flame from the cartridge already fired. Airborne tests of the seat with the new gun at moderate speeds produced seat trajectories of about 90 ft, which was enough for the purposes of ejecting from a V-bomber.

The development of the telescopic gun was a significant advance by James, and it resulted in a clear performance advantage for the Martin-Baker seat. At this time, the Americans were working on a downward ejection seat which was fitted in the Lockheed F-104 aircraft because they had been unable to develop an ejection catapult with sufficient velocity to ensure that the seat would clear the fin of this aircraft at the maximum aircraft speed. James thought that the idea of downward ejection was utterly ludicrous. Events proved him right and the downward ejection seat was replaced.

It was eventually decided that the ejection seats developed for the pilot and co-pilot in the prototype V-bombers would be fitted in operational aircraft also, but that seats would not be provided for the rear crew members. James told the Ministry that this was criminal. He felt vehemently that all aircrew deserved an equal chance of escape, but with the design of the aircraft finalized, he was firmly told that it was not now possible to fit ejection seats for the rear crew members.

James had already been upset that the two seats with the new ejection gun, which he had delivered to Vickers some time before the crash involving Bryce, had not been fitted. According to James, at that point there had been 'no interest' in the improved version of the seat. James was becoming increasingly preoccupied with the job of saving aircrew, and he was not happy that the British authorities were allowing test pilots and RAF crews to fly with no ejection seats or inadequate ejection seats. In January 1952 he wrote: 'British pilots are, without any doubt whatsoever, the "salt of the earth", and the present day planes, and armament fitted, are tragically below what England should be producing.' Later that year he employed W/Cdr. John Jewell, formerly of the RAF, to be his Service Liaison Representative, as he believed that he would be 'of great value to this company in our many contacts with the RAF, and in our efforts to study the exact needs and reactions of the RAF'.

James was now beginning to end his letters, business and personal, with news of the latest escapes. He was particularly interested in the ejection by Cdr. V. Cuss on 10 April 1952 from the prototype Fiat G80 after the aircraft went into a dive and disintegrated, and the escape by S/L P.D. Thompson on 5 May 1952 after the tail of his Meteor was knocked off following a mid-air collision with another aircraft. Then, in September of that year, he received a letter from PO Poppe of the RAF who had ejected in the Canal Zone. He had been diving vertically at a speed of nearly 600 mph when the wings and tail of his Meteor came off. James invited him to the factory and Poppe gave a talk over the loudspeaker to the workers to say how grateful he was for having a Martin-Baker ejection seat. James was working harder than he had ever worked in his life, but he was beginning to receive a steady trickle of letters from pilots who had used his seat, which pleased him immensely. He wrote to a friend in September 1952 to say: 'There is nothing fresh here at the Works – just hard grind and a lot of worry. All what for I don't know except that there is a certain amount of satisfaction in reading about people saving their lives with our equipment.'

During 1952 another dramatic ejection occurred, a near fatality, which again illustrated the shortcomings of the Mark 1 seat. It took place on 29 August, when A.E. (Ben) Gunn, the chief test pilot at Boulton Paul Aircraft Limited, was test flying a high-speed research aircraft known as the Boulton Paul P120 Delta research aircraft. He was flying at 5,000 ft when suddenly, as Gunn recalls, 'there was a high-pitched buzz, instantly followed by the loudest bang I have ever heard in the air'. He became disorientated as the aircraft executed a series of rapid rolls to port. Instinctively, he rammed the control column towards the starboard wall of the cockpit, but this only reduced the rate of roll. He then applied full starboard rudder, the rolling stopped, and he found himself diving towards the ground with a set of controls which were clearly not working as they should. He gingerly adjusted the trim setting and to his relief the nose slowly came up. But his problems had only just started.

He continued descending and at 3,000 ft the aircraft hit bumpy conditions and became uncontrollable. It started an inexorable bank to port and Gunn realized that the aircraft would shortly roll, so he decided to eject. By the time he had pulled the face blind, the aircraft was inverted and Gunn was ejected downwards. The drogue could not cope with this situation and was unable to stabilize the seat, which was spiralling and twisting wildly downwards. The Mark 1 seat had only basic leg restraint, and Gunn's arms and legs were flailing so badly that he experienced extreme difficulty in reaching anything. He knew that he had to release himself from the seat and then deploy the parachute, but he could not reach the seat buckle. He found the ripcord, but realized that he should not pull it until he had left the seat. He finally located the seat strap on his right leg and gradually worked his hand up that strap until he got to the seat buckle and released it. As the seat fell away, the main parachute roman candled and jerked him up just as his feet crashed through the upper branches of a tree. The ripcord caught in a sapling some 20 ft off the ground. The parachute canopy, the seat and the drogue were all caught up in the branches of the tree that he had fallen through, and Gunn landed on the ground at the bottom of the tree, no longer in his parachute harness although it was still buckled, which indicates that he must have turned upside down during his fall through the tree and somehow fallen out of it. He had a cracked wrist and ankle and was very shaken, but well enough to stagger through the trees to a nearby cottage where he found a man on the telephone already reporting the crash and recognized a Boulton Paul calendar on the wall: he was in the house of a retired Boulton Paul test pilot, Pinky Stark.

James contacted Gunn and asked him to visit him at Denham to talk about his experience. James was very interested to hear about the problems with the drogue and more particularly the great difficulties that Gunn had experienced in releasing himself from his seat. As with Bryce, James listened intently to what Gunn had to tell him. The story confirmed James's fears, and he asked Gunn to tell the Ministry that they should place orders with him for his new automatic ejection seat.

During 1952, James completed the design of a conversion set for the Mark 1 seat to make it fully automatic once the pilot had pulled the ejection handle. On the Mark 1 seats, the drogue was attached to the top of the seat by a solid shackle, because it was never necessary to disconnect the drogue from the seat. In order for automatic capability to be introduced to the Mark 1 seat, the drogue had to be used not just for stabilizing the seat after ejection but also for deploying the main parachute, and it was necessary therefore to provide for the drogue to disconnect from the seat and transfer its pull to the parachute whilst simultaneously providing for the separation of the pilot, with parachute and dinghy pack attached, from the seat. James designed a scissor shackle, capable of being opened automatically at a predetermined time, to replace the solid shackle. He designed a clockwork time release unit which was bolted to the top of one of the side beams of the seat and was activated by a static line as the seat rose on ejection. The time release mechanism was set for a five-second delay, after which a plunger in the mechanism opened the scissor shackle, releasing the seat from the drogue and releasing the face blind. Simultaneously, the mechanism unlocked the seat harness attaching the pilot to the seat by pulling on a cable which rotated the face plate of a modified harness release box. The seat was now free of drogue and pilot and as the drogue pulled away from the seat its pull was transferred to a canvas apron, positioned between the back-type parachute and its container, which then tautened and tipped the pilot out of the seat. This apron was attached to the parachute withdrawal line which then released the closure pins on the parachute pack and pulled out the apex of the parachute, which then deployed with the drogue and apron still attached to its apex. The time release mechanism was fitted with a barostat to prevent it from running above 10,000 ft, and an emergency oxygen supply was turned on automatically during ejection.

To allow for manual separation in the event of the failure of the time release unit, it was necessary to enable the pilot to disconnect the parachute withdrawal line which was connected to the drogue via the apron before he undid his seat harness to separate from the seat. James designed a slide disconnect pin in the parachute withdrawal line which was situated inside the parachute pack and operated by an additional D-ring on the parachute harness similar to the parachute ripcord D-ring. The parachute ripcord D-ring was covered by a canvas flap which was removed as the other D-ring was pulled, in order to prevent the wrong D-ring from being pulled first. Along with these modifications, James also introduced an improved version of the drogue gun. The gun had previously been fired by a 24 ft static line, but the redesigned version was operated by a one-second clockwork time delay and tripped by a short static line attached to the aircraft.

This new automatic seat became known as the Mark 2 seat, and all versions of the Mark 1 seat were eventually modified to this standard. The seat was tested extensively in 1952, and Lynch undertook two live tests. James was extremely pleased with the results of the tests. He wrote in the summer of 1952: 'Our tests would indicate that it is possible to be ejected as low as 450 feet and have 200 feet to spare when the main chute is fully developed. This refers to level flight, and at speeds up to 600 m.p.h. This is a very great improvement on the manually operated seat.' It was an achievement that was duly recognized by the Royal Aeronautical Society that year when they awarded him their Wakefield Gold Medal for his research and development work on ejection seats. This caused James to remark, with a twinkle in his eye, that the medal 'is supposed to be pure gold, so if I get hard up I can always melt it down'. The modifications to the Mark 1 seats were started in August 1953. Martin-Baker modified the RAF seats at the factory in Denham, and the Royal Navy seats were modified on site by Navy personnel trained by Martin-Baker.

Despite the obvious advantages of the Mark 2 seat, there was still a great deal of scope for further improvement in its performance. The 80 ft/sec ejection gun designed for the V-bombers was introduced in the Mark 3 version of the ejection seat, and although it was discovered that this increased the trajectory height at low speeds too, James realized that further improvements were necessary to facilitate successful ejections at low altitudes and at very high speeds.

The existing drogue arrangements provided for the drogue to stream the main parachute five seconds after ejection. This time delay was to allow the seat to slow down from the highest speed likely at the time of ejection to one at which the main parachute could be safely deployed. This system was obviously only efficient at a certain combination of speed and altitude and was unnecessary at slower speeds and counter-productive when a slow-speed ejection took place at low altitude. In order to improve the chances of escape at low level, it was necessary to speed up the deployment of the main parachute, but when tests were conducted at high speeds with a three-second delay, the 2 ft drogue was unable to slow the speed down sufficiently to allow the main parachute to develop without bursting.

High-speed tests were undertaken with a 5 ft drogue, but this was totally unsuccessful because the loads produced by the larger drogue at high speed were sufficient to tear the face blind and break the seat harness before bursting the drogue itself. This was a classic example of James's trial and error method of design where tests were conducted over and over again until an answer was eventually found. James considered using a rocket to slow the seat down, but eventually the solution turned out to be the use of two drogues instead of one. A smaller drogue of 22 in diameter, known as the controller drogue, was deployed by the drogue gun on ejection, and this operated by bringing the seat into the horizontal position then extracting the main 5 ft drogue from its container. The main drogue streamed the pilot's parachute after he separated from the seat which in turn lifted the pilot clear of the seat. The purpose of the controller drogue was to put the seat into the horizontal position so that the subsequent deceleration of the seat by the main drogue would be linear and consequently more tolerable, and secondly to prevent the main drogue from bursting. In its turn, the main drogue prevented the main parachute from bursting and the system therefore reduced the time delay between ejection and deployment of the main parachute from five to three seconds. With the duplex drogue system it was also possible to reduce the delay in firing the drogue gun from one second to half a second, and the system was also introduced in the Mark 3 seat.

James also investigated further the question of leg restraint, because experience of emergency ejections was proving that the thigh guards of the Mark 1 and Mark 2 seats were not always fully effective. At higher speeds, the blast of the airstream could lift the feet off the foot rests and the legs over the top of the thigh guards, and in these cases the ejectee could easily sustain severe injuries to his knee and hip joints. James investigated several different ways of securing the pilot's legs during ejection, and eventually decided on a simple system whereby the legs were secured to the front of the seat by nylon cords. The cords could be loosened to allow free movement of the pilot's legs during flight, but they were automatically tightened on ejection, and were released when the time release mechanism released the seat harness.

Although the automatic seats were fitted with barostatic mechanisms, nobody knew what effect a free fall at high altitude would have on the human body, even if the person had an adequate supply of oxygen. Once again, with no experience to call upon and no theory that could be relied upon, James decided that the only way to proceed was with another live test, and Lynch was again the test ejectee. On 17 March 1954, Scott took off in the Meteor with Lynch in the open cockpit behind him and climbed to 30,000 ft. He gave Lynch the green light and he ejected. For this test Lynch had an altimeter and a stop-watch strapped to the inside of his wrist and he watched these instruments as he descended. At 6,000 ft he was still in the seat and the automatic separation had not taken place. Clearly it had not worked for some reason and he had to go through the manual emergency procedures before deploying his chest-mounted emergency parachute.

Unfortunately, Lynch's problems were not quite over. As he neared the ground and looked down, he realized that he was likely to land on a wire fence. He landed while still trying to slip sideways to avoid the fence and badly fractured his ankle. The injury did not mend well, and this incident marked the end of Lynch's career as a test ejectee. That test had been his 17th live airborne test, an incredible record, during which this fractured ankle was his only injury. James would frequently pay tribute to Lynch and his immense contribution to the development of a successful ejection seat, as James believed that the input from men like Lynch, who could tell him what the ejection felt like, was worth more to him than any amount of data and hypothesis. Lynch was awarded the British Empire Medal in recognition of his work.

The cause of the failure of the time release mechanism was simple. On ejection, a plunger on the mechanism moved outwards to trigger the mechanism which could not run at 30,000 ft because it was held by the barostat. Lynch had lost his grip on the face blind handle shortly after ejecting, and the blind was consequently blowing about violently. The end of the face blind handle knocked the plunger back into the cocked position where consequently it would not operate. The required modification was straightforward: the plunger was modified so that it had to be turned before it could be pressed back into the cocked position. A simple solution to a simple problem, but a problem which the theorists would not have foreseen. It was the practical demonstration that caused it to happen.

With this problem resolved, the testing of the modified seat continued and further problems came to light. It was found that it was possible for the separated seat to end up above the pilot, so that when the main parachute developed, there was a danger that the seat might hit the pilot or damage the parachute. James thought of an ingenious scheme to overcome this problem whereby the seat itself was clipped to the parachute harness so that the seat remained with the harness until the parachute developed, at which point the deceleration of the pilot caused by the parachute opening caused the spring-loaded clips to release, thus releasing the seat which would then fall away.

The continuous testing of seats that James insisted on is undoubtedly one of the major factors that has contributed to the success of the Martin-Baker seats. The philosophy of continuous testing was, of course, innate in James. He could acknowledge no other way of developing a concept to a successful conclusion. A good design was not enough and he believed that only by endless testing was it possible to produce a product with the high reliability that is necessary for an ejection seat which is only ever used once. Experience proved again and again that while several tests of identical seats could be successful, the next repeat test might demonstrate a problem. During the early fifties Martin-Baker was sometimes conducting four or five tests a day. James did not personally witness many of these tests as he begrudged the time taken in travelling to and from Chalgrove Airfield and, in any event, more was revealed by the cine films of the tests. Overnight processing was arranged at local laboratories and James was frequently to be found in the factory the next morning impatiently awaiting the arrival of these films. He reviewed each film in slow motion, frame by frame, and had the process repeated until either he was satisfied with the test or he had a solution to any problem. A very large part of the factory was geared to providing test seats and to carrying out the tests and analysing the results, and the development costs relating to the seats, borne entirely by the company, were and still are considerable.

Although the seat mechanisms were being improved to reduce the time from ejection to parachute deployment, James had not yet addressed the question of the canopy jettison. At this stage, the pilot had to jettison the cockpit canopy manually before pulling the face blind, a process which could take valuable seconds. If the aircraft had been damaged, or if the emergency occurred in adverse aerodynamic conditions, the canopy might not leave the aircraft cleanly, and cases had occurred where in these circumstances the seat had collided with the canopy on ejection, with fatal results. In some instances, the pilot simply forgot to try and jettison the canopy before ejection, in which cases the seat was ejected through the canopy, a process which could injure the pilot and damage the seat. With ejections at higher speeds, pilots were also experiencing difficulty in reaching the face blind after the canopy had been jettisoned because the slipstream entered the cockpit and caused buffeting which became more severe the higher the speed of the aircraft. James therefore designed an automatic canopy jettison triggered by the pilot pulling the face blind, which initiated a one-second delay on a time delay mechanism. During this delay, a cartridge was fired which unlocked the canopy and explosively extended two jacks which forced the canopy off the aircraft. When the one-second delay ran out the primary cartridge in the ejection gun was fired and the seat ejection commenced. The canopy jettison was extensively tested in early 1955 for the Gloster Javelin night fighter and the three V-bomber types. James succeeded in achieving successful canopy jettison from the static case, where the hood had to be thrown clear of the cockpit, up to the high-speed case with the fuselage at an angle of 45°.

Despite the introduction of the Mark 3 seats, and the modification of earlier seats to Mark 3 capability, the casualty rate was still too high. Fatalities were occurring during or shortly after take-off and there was an obvious need for an ejection seat with ground-level capability. It was necessary to reduce further the timing for the opening of the main parachute and James began to experiment with further reductions in the delay on the time release mechanism. James believed that if this could be successfully reduced from three seconds to one and a half seconds and still cope with the exigencies of a high-speed ejection, then it would be possible for pilots to eject at ground level provided that they had sufficient forward speed, probably not less than 90 knots. This would make escape possible for pilots who encountered problems on landing and take-off.

It was a challenge for James's inventive mind, but one he did not fail. His solution was a simple weight and spring governor which was attached to the time release mechanism and prevented it from operating when a force greater than 4 g was applied downwards on the seat. If an ejection occurred at low speed, the governor only came into operation during the period of the stroke of the ejection gun, approximately a quarter of a second. During a high-speed ejection, the deceleration load applied by the drogue would be more than 4 g, and the governor would continue to operate until the seat slowed down. Using a time release mechanism set at 1¼ seconds, during a low-speed ejection, the time between ejection and release of the parachute was 1½ seconds, but during high-speed ejections, the time was greater, depending on the aircraft speed when the seat ejected. In this way, both high- and low-speed ejections were safe and the performance envelope was increased.

Meanwhile, the Meteor III used by Martin-Baker for seat testing was reaching the end of its useful life, and the Ministry offered to replace it with a Meteor 4. This aircraft, although faster, was found to have poor flying characteristics at high speed in rough weather and was therefore unsuitable. Eventually a Meteor T7 was provided, having the advantage of already having two cockpits, but this aircraft showed a marked tendency to 'snake' at speeds above about Mach 0.76. This problem was cured by replacing the tail with one from a Meteor F8 and, after panels above the rear cockpit were removed from the canopy, the aircraft became a suitable platform for launching ejection seats.

James was now, for the first time in his life, beginning to earn some money. He had always loved motor cars, and in 1952 he bought himself a Bentley. He exchanged it two years later for an automatic version which he kept for the rest of his life. It was very fast and very comfortable and therefore suited him well. It was also reliable, which was something of a necessity, as James was quickly annoyed by other people's machines that did not work as they should.

Shortly after he took delivery of the automatic Bentley, Fifield decided to tease him about it and accused him of buying a car with a 'woman's' gearbox. James just smiled. He took Fifield for a drive in the car, demonstrating to him how he could get the car to change gears with the accelerator, and then he put his foot down. Fifield was petrified as James drove along the Buckinghamshire roads at 100 mph. He then stopped the car and told Fifield that he could drive it. Fifield was relieved to be behind the wheel and in control of the car, but not for long. James leaned across and put his hand on Fifield's right leg, forcing him to accelerate, and there was nothing Fifield could do, for James was a very strong man. Fifield remembers the cold sweat on the back of his neck as he became more terrified than he had been when James was driving, and the twinkle in James's eye afterwards. He was more careful about what he said to him after that.

On 13 October 1954, there was an extraordinary success with a Martin-Baker ejection seat when Lt. B.D. Macfarlane of the Royal Navy ejected from a Wyvern aircraft following an engine failure immediately after a catapult launch from the escort carrier HMS *Albion*. It was a Mark 2 seat and witnesses estimated that it fired at about 25 ft below sea level when the aircraft was in a 30° nose-down attitude. There was some entanglement of the seat with the parachute and MacFarlane had to undo the harness and inflate his life jacket, but although he was suffering from the preliminary stages of drowning by the time he was rescued, he made a complete recovery. It would be several years before James designed a seat which was specifically intended to cope with ejections underwater, and this lucky escape, the first underwater ejection, was exciting news.

In the spring of the next year, James was asked by Avro Canada if he would arrange for a live ejection from the rear seat of a CF100. He agreed to do this and Fifield volunteered to be the test ejectee. James decided, however, to make a few enquiries first to find out why they wanted the test, and discovered that there had been several emergencies with this aircraft and in each case the pilot had ejected successfully but the navigator had not. There were some CF100s in England at that time at the Central Fighter Establishment at West Raynham, and the CO agreed to let Fifield fly in the rear seat of one of these aircraft with the hood removed. This flight disclosed the fact that there was very severe air turbulence in the rear seat due to the close proximity of the engines to the sides of the fuselage, and to the fact that the small sections of the wings that joined the engines to the fuselage were very thick. This meant that when the canopy had been jettisoned, the navigator would have severe difficulties in raising his hands to pull the face blind handle. As the seats in this aircraft were not fitted with a canopy jettison, Avro Canada made and fitted a small perspex windshield to the rear seat which improved the situation.

James also discovered that the dinghy pack, which was a special Canadian pack, was far too high, which meant that the face blind handle was, in some cases, at the back of the navigator's head and very difficult to reach. This problem was compounded by the very large helmets that the Canadian crews wore. James advised Avro to use another type of seat pan and a lower type of dinghy pack to give a sitting position $3^1/2$ in lower, or, in James's words, he gave Avro a report on his findings 'just telling them what they would have to do if they want their navigators to live. It was a pretty blunt and crude document, with some drawings, which they cannot easily ignore'. The episode caused James to remark rather crossly that 'it is quite amazing how casual people can be in connection with safety equipment'. Shortly afterwards there was another emergency involving a CF100, and both pilot and navigator ejected successfully.

Meanwhile, the live test by Fifield took place on 9 March 1955 at Camp Borden, near Toronto, and was, as James described, 'completely satisfactory and uneventful'. An ambulance was standing by at the side of the aerodrome and James went over to see them before the test and pointed out that, if the seat did not work, it was not an ambulance that would be required but an undertaker. Despite the apparent flippancy of his remark, James was anything but flippant about these live test ejections. Fifield's live test in Canada was the 27th live test, but live testing was not something that James would ever get used to. He was, if anything, more relaxed about the early live tests than he was about the later ones. As we have seen, he regarded his early successes with the ejection seat more as engineering achievements than as milestones in the development of life-saving equipment, and as his awareness of the life-saving potential of the seat grew, so did his concerns about the live tests. He would later explain:

This ejection seat business is a most exhausting job, in the sense one is dealing with human lives and thank God, over the years, we have been most fortunate

in no fatal accidents in tests. You just can't believe what a nervous strain these
live tests can cause – when it is all over I could lie down and sleep for a week.

Shortly after that test, the first supersonic emergency ejection occurred,
which James was particularly pleased to hear about. It took place on 3
August 1955 when FO H. Molland ejected from a Hunter F5 from a
height of approximately 25,000 ft after he had lost control of the aircraft.
In James's view, 'this escape was special in the sense that it was at a
speed of Mach 1.1 – in other words about 800 miles per hour, or, in an
easily understood way, 1100 feet per second!'

Low-level rather than high-speed escape was still, however, his main
concern at that time and preparations were already well in hand for the
first runway test which was one of James's most important achievements
in the development of the ejection seat. Arguably, with automatic ejection
seats a live test is not necessary because the result of the test can be
observed and the effect on the dummy examined afterwards. But dummy
ejections had no power to convince those who did not want to believe
that ground-level ejection was safe and realistic, and there were indeed
some who were not convinced that a man could survive the forces
imposed by such an ejection. Nobody, however, could argue with a man
who had done it, and Fifield agreed to do the test. This was the first
ejection anywhere in the world from ground level, and its significance
for the future business of Martin-Baker was obvious.

Although Fifield had already done three live tests, they did not fully
prepare him for this one. There was no margin for error when one started
on the ground. It had been a dry August and the ground was very hard.
Fifield asked James if they could work out where he was likely to land
and have the ground there ploughed in order to make it softer. James
happily agreed. There were some bolts protruding out of the back of the
cockpit, and Fifield was worried that he might catch his boots on these
as he ejected, so James arranged for the bolts to be reversed.

Many weeks of testing had already taken place, and James was as sure
as he could be that the seat would work. But nevertheless, the
responsibility for Fifield's life was his, and it was not going to be an easy
day. The test was scheduled for 5 September 1955. The day started
badly when a telegram arrived from the Air Ministry stating: 'You must
not, repeat must not, under any circumstances, use the Meteor aircraft
for such a hazardous test.'

It was an interesting message. There was far less risk of damage to the
Meteor during this runway test than there was during airborne tests when
a malfunction of the seat could cause damage to the aircraft and precipitate
a crash. The Ministry had no power to stop James conducting tests
because he did not have a development contract. All they could do was
forbid the use of their aircraft which, if James had heeded the instruction,
would have stopped the test proceeding. The Meteor had been modified
to make it suitable as a test vehicle and there was no other aircraft available
into which the seat could be fitted for the purposes of this test.

The telegram definitely disturbed James. Everybody's nerves were on edge as it was. A good luck message might have been appreciated, silence would have gone unnoticed, but a message purporting to forbid the test, within hours of the scheduled time for it, after weeks of preparation and mounting tension for all concerned, but particularly for James and Fifield, was, to say the least, unhelpful.

There were those who thought that the Ministry should be obeyed and a heated debate in James's office ensued. But James's unflinching determination won the day. He would not be deflected from doing what he had decided to do, and the test went ahead. Fifield and James drove to Chalgrove together. Scott climbed into the front seat of the Meteor and Fifield was strapped into the back in a Mark 3 seat. Eric Stevens was there, as he always was on a live test, puffing on his pipe and quietly checking that everything was in order. Some of the Martin-Baker employees were watching, although others were so concerned about the outcome of this test that they had decided to stay away rather than risk seeing Fifield killed, and representatives from the Air Ministry and the press were also there.

Scott began the take-off run down the runway. It was apparent to him that Fifield's idea of having the ground ploughed had been a bad one, because the ground was so dry that he now had hard ridged ground to land on rather than hard flat ground. He endeavoured to reach 145 knots, the ejection speed, at a point on the runway where he felt that Fifield would have the best chance of avoiding the ploughed furrows. At 145 knots he gave Fifield the green light, Fifield pulled the face blind handle and six seconds later landed safely on the ground. To a casual bystander the test would have been unspectacular, but to each person in that tense gathering who had come to Chalgrove to watch this test, it was six very long seconds before they saw Fifield stand up and signal that all was well.

But the man who above all others should have been there to see that safe landing had disappeared. James did not see the world's first ever ground-level ejection. He had been upset by the telegram from the Ministry and the debate that followed it. He understood the risks involved and knew that the responsibility was his and his alone. During the last-minute preparations he had slipped away unnoticed to the far side of the aircraft hangar, away from the eyes of the world. There he had dropped to his knees and prayed.

His prayers were answered, his faith rewarded. The test was a complete success. Fifield got into the car with him to drive back to the factory and tell him about the test. James stopped the car beside the man from the Ministry and wound down the window. 'Not bad, was it!' he said and drove off.

Chapter Eleven

Rocket Propulsion

The runway ejection was followed shortly by another live test at 40,000 ft, to demonstrate, as James put it, 'the long and short of it'. Fifield was again the test ejectee for this high-level test, which took place on 25 October 1955. There was some concern about whether the barostat would function at this altitude, which was significantly greater than the altitude of Lynch's high-level test the previous year. The barostat was put in a refrigerator on the day before the test to simulate the temperature at 40,000 ft and to see whether the barostat would freeze, which it did. Fifield therefore had a stop-watch sewn onto his sleeve and was told how long to wait for the barostat to work before beginning the manual override procedures. The test was completely successful, however, and all the components functioned as they should at high altitude. For the first 15 seconds of his descent after ejection the seat was fully stabilized. Thereafter it developed a slow spin of between 15 and 20 rpm around the longitudinal axis before disappearing into the clouds. When Fifield reappeared, the parachute was fully deployed and he landed safely. He reported that the spinning of the seat had not been uncomfortable, and his only problem was slight frostbite to the cheeks which he suffered during his climb to altitude in an open cockpit and his free fall through the freezing atmosphere at 40,000 ft.

James had certainly made remarkable progress in his ejection seat work. Paradoxically, he was both ruthless and meticulously careful in his determination to advance the development of his seat, and that determination, combined with his innate flair for this type of design work, had enabled him to produce a product which was arguably the best of its kind in the world. Roxbee Cox wrote to him to say: 'You have brought escaping from high speed aircraft in flight to a pitch of reliability and automaticity inconceivable a few years ago. This you have done not only by imaginative thinking, but by bold experiment.'

There is no doubt that Martin-Baker's commercial success was strengthening, and the quieter years of retirement that most of James's contemporaries were already enjoying or looking forward to were something that James would never know. He wrote at the beginning of 1956:

I am working seven days a week trying to meet the ever pressing demands of the Royal Air Force . . . This last year has been the most hectic one in my lifetime – everyone wants something yesterday, and we are only too anxious to give it if possible as I want the Royal Air Force to have the best possible escape facilities.

Despite the successes that he had achieved, however, there were still problems to be addressed.

One aircraft that was causing him particular problems was the Canberra. The success rate for ejections from Canberras was not good and in early 1956 James was trying to rectify this. On 8 February 1956, a successful dummy test took place at RAF Wittering and James felt confident that the introduction of fully automatic seats, which would blast through the penetrable fibreglass hatches recommended by him, would make an enormous difference. James wrote to Gp. Capt. Clayton (later Air Vice-Marshal Clayton) to tell him about the latest development:

This 'plane is certainly one of the black spots in our list of escapes and we are making every endeavour to get conversion sets into production so that safe escape will be possible. If you knew all the facts in connection with this fibreglass hatch you simply wouldn't believe it – nothing but opposition from the Ministry of Supply, English Electric not interested, and any success we have had entirely due to the people at Bomber Command being enthusiastic.

It will be a memorable day for the RAF when they can get a divorce from the Ministry of Supply. The whole lot of them are fast asleep and couldn't care less, and that is very depressing.

For quite a long time it has been our policy here to press on regardless of everything. At times of course you can well realise that the name of J.M. stinks, due entirely to the fact that some people are incapable themselves and object to anyone who takes the initiative.

James's proclivity for taking the initiative resulted in an *ad hoc* approach to the development of the ejection seat. As each particular problem presented itself, he addressed it by a modification to the relevant version of the seat, and these changes were often retrofitted to other existing versions of the seat. Although different seat types were known by different Mark numbers, in practice there were various versions of each Mark, depending on which aircraft the seat was fitted in and which modifications had been retrofitted to that seat. By the spring of 1957 James estimated that Martin-Baker was producing about 30 different types of seat, a fact which he regarded as 'an absolute curse'.

However, the introduction of a new class of aircraft known as the 'light fighter' in the mid-fifties, which required a correspondingly lightweight seat, presented James with the opportunity to design a new ejection seat, although retaining the essential components of previous designs. While he retained the 80 ft/sec ejection gun and the duplex drogue system, many of the other components of the seat were redesigned to reduce their weight. He replaced the large box section guide rails with small rails which were attached to the sides of the ejection gun which was bolted to the aircraft structure. The solid seat beams were replaced by beams made from light alloy sheets. The seat structure consisted of a framework of two side beams, on which the drogue gun and the time release unit were mounted, bridged by three cross members, and this framework supported the seat pan and the drogue container. The top cross beam took the full thrust of the ejection gun and contained the seat latch mechanism for locking the seat to the ejection gun. The centre cross member was the attachment part for the shoulder harness and the lower cross member provided an anchorage for the seat height adjusting mechanism. The face blind method of firing the seat was also retained but for the first time James incorporated an alternative firing handle fitted to the front of the seat pan which allowed a pilot to reach down and pull a handle between his legs in order to initiate the ejection in circumstances where he was unable, through injury or aerodynamic forces, to reach up and pull the firing handle located above his head.

James also redesigned the harness, the parachute pack and the dinghy pack. He produced a new single combined parachute and safety harness, with only one quick-release fitting. The harness was attached to the seat by two locks in the rear of the seat pan and another lock in the back of the seat at shoulder height, and he installed a redesigned time release unit on the seat which released the harness locks after ejection by a linkage system. A manual separation lever was provided in case of failure of the time release unit, and in order to reduce the number of actions which had to be completed to effect a manual separation after ejection, James designed a guillotine system for disconnecting the parachute withdrawal line from the drogue. This involved mounting a small guillotine unit, usually on the side of the drogue container, with the parachute withdrawal line positioned in a spring-loaded guard immediately above the cutter of the guillotine. The cutter was operated by a cartridge fired by a short static cable between the back of the parachute case and the sear of the guillotine firing unit. As the ejectee moved forward on separation, taking his parachute pack with him, the cable removed the sear to fire the guillotine and cut the withdrawal line. This arrangement meant that it was no longer necessary to have two D-rings on the parachute harness. All that was now necessary was for the ejectee to use the harness release lever on the seat and then pull the ripcord D-ring to deploy the parachute. This series of seat was known as the Mark 4, and whereas the earlier seats had been fitted only into British-designed aircraft, the Mark 4 seat was also fitted into foreign aircraft types.

Later Mark 4 seats were fitted with a snubbing unit in the top lock and a release lever which permitted the occupant to lean forward in the seat whilst also providing for him to be secured firmly in the event of an ejection or crash landing. Various survival packs were designed for this seat according to the requirements of the air forces concerned, but all incorporated a seat cushion and a container for the dinghy and survival equipment. The cushion, designed to make the seat more comfortable, was filled with a resilient type of padding which was slow to return to its original shape after compression and which therefore helped to absorb the acceleration forces imposed during ejections. The first emergency ejection using a Mark 4 seat was in March 1957 when Mr R. Bignamini, a test pilot for Fiat, ejected from a Fiat G91 following an explosion on an experimental flight. The aircraft lost its tail and wings, but Mr Bignamini ejected successfully at 1,000 ft at 520 knots.

The Canadians asked James to consider installing automatic ejection seats and hood jettison gear in the T-33, the Lockheed two-seater trainer jet, of which the Royal Canadian Air Force had about 600, because the casualty rate had been quite high. They arrived at a meeting with him with a large parcel of drawings for him to consider. James was in a typically ebullient mood. He told them that he did not understand drawings very well: 'it was like looking at a good-looking woman in a photograph, the photo was alright but you want to see them in the flesh'. He asked to see 'the old crate', but the men from Canadair, who were making the T-33 in Canada under licence from Lockheed, were very concerned about the security aspects of this. James told them that security did not interest him and, in any event, they had nothing to be secure about as what they were making was obsolescent. The result, as usual, was that James saw the aircraft, was confident that he could fit proper hood jettison gear and an automatic seat, but said he would need an airframe to be delivered to him in England as 'we were not magicians – just ordinary low grade blacksmiths'. His attitude and approach surprised the Canadians who believed that the drawings of the aircraft should have been sufficient for James's purposes. But, as always, the paperwork did not interest James: he was interested only in the nuts and bolts and metal of an actual airframe.

In the spring of 1956, the news of successful ejections was interrupted by the disturbing news that a man had been injured on one of the Martin-Baker ejection towers. James went to investigate the accident. The man concerned had sustained two cracked vertebrae and James was very upset by the incident because his test rigs had by then been in use for over ten years and thousands of people had been shot up them with no problems. James quickly discovered the reason for the accident. On the top cross-shaft of the seat on which there was a sliding plunger, the part which should have been only slightly greased had been pumped full with a grease gun until it was like a cylinder shock absorber, and it was not free to act due to the heavily viscous grease preventing travel of the plunger. As a result of this, the ratchet stops on the rig had not been able to engage, and the seat had fallen about 24 ft. James redesigned the top sliding plunger so that it was chrome-plated and would need no lubrication at all. He believed that designs should be easy to maintain without the need for highly qualified technicians, and it was accidents such as this one, caused by incorrect servicing, that he endeavoured to eliminate through straightforward design.

This incident was shortly followed by a much more serious accident with the ejection seat, when a pilot ejected from a Meteor and was found dead in his seat. The RAF Station concerned had no idea why he had ejected, but the investigation revealed that on ejection he had released the face screen which had flipped over the back of the seat. As a result, the bullet of the drogue gun had gone through the handle of the face screen and effectively trapped the drogue so that it could not develop. James believed that if proper hood jettison gear had been fitted to the Meteor this incident could not have happened, but, as the Meteor was unlikely to be fitted with such gear for some time, he devised a scheme to ensure that it could not happen again. The new scheme provided for two bungee cord tie-lines to pick up on the face screen, and while they did not interfere with the normal use of the face screen, they effectively prevented the handle from overreaching the drogue gun area. He invited Fighter Command and the Institute of Aviation Medicine to have a look at it, but typically he did not inform the Ministry of Supply.

The pressures of James's work were still increasing. He wrote in May 1956:

> At the moment I am overwhelmed with technical design problems, not only for the RAF here, but for the Air Forces of countries like Switzerland, France, and Italy, all of whom buy our equipment, and of course they want delivery at once – before the order is placed. In almost every case the orders are such that modifications have to be carried out to the seats to suit the particular aircraft and this is all time consuming.

He went on to explain:

> The fact of the matter is that I am a self-employed slave, and often times I feel that I am quite daft to work the hours that I do for, as far as my personal income is concerned, it seems to be that I am working for the Income Tax people. If it were not for the fact that I am interested in this kind of work I would have packed up long ago and sold out.

Although he complained constantly about the taxes he paid, the accumulation of personal wealth was of no interest to him and, in fact, he rarely spent any money. He never moved house or took holidays abroad, and as his only interest outside his home was his work, there was indeed very little for him to spend his money on. Frank Francis remarked one Christmas that it was difficult enough to buy a present for the man who has everything, but even more difficult to buy presents for James, the man who did not want anything. His lack of interest in money is illustrated by the fact that he never carried any. If he needed some, someone with him would pay for whatever needed paying for, and those travelling with him knew to be prepared to pay for cigarettes, snacks, drinks, taxis and anything else he might want. One day in the factory at Denham, he got into a debate with Clifford Gaskell who had joined Martin-Baker in the drawing office in 1939 and worked there until his death in 1993. Gaskell worked closely with James, for he was good at interpreting James's sketches and understanding what it was that he wanted drawn. During a light-hearted exchange between the two, Gaskell bet him a sum of money that he was right on a particular point, and James accepted. When James was proved wrong, he turned to Eric Stevens and said: 'Pay him, Eric.'

By the end of 1956 James was employing about 900 people. Although James felt that he was losing the personal touch in dealing with his work-force, this did not appear to be the case to outsiders visiting the factory, and Air Marshal Sir Harry Broadhurst commented on 'the obvious keenness and enthusiasm of the chaps in your factory' following his visit there after his ejection from a Vulcan B1 in October of that year. Inevitably, James would never get to know many of the newcomers as well as he would have liked, but his attitude to his work-force never changed.

By this time, two new factories had been set up to support Martin-Baker. In 1954, his sister had opened a factory in the Isle of Man for the purpose of doing sub-contract work for Martin-Baker. James had visited the Isle of Man several times to assist in the choice of a site for this new factory. His nephew, Denis Burrell, had fortuitously graduated from Cambridge University in 1953 with a double first in engineering, and after spending two years on the shop-floor at Denham learning about the practical side of engineering, he went to the Isle of Man to supervise the building and setting up of the factory there. By 1956 the factory was established and was employing about 100 people.

Meanwhile, James had made several visits to Ontario in Canada with Brian Holt, the husband of his niece Joan, who had been persuaded to leave the legal profession and set up a subsidiary of Martin-Baker in Canada to make seats for Avro Canada. Suitable premises were eventually found on the shores of Georgian Bay in a town called Collingwood, and by the end of 1956 this factory was also well established.

For some time James had wanted a factory in Northern Ireland, and in 1957 he and his sister began actively looking for premises as the volume of business justified another manufacturing plant. In 1958 a company owned by his sister succeeded in buying a disused US Air Force Station at Langford Lodge on the shores of Loch Neagh which had a runway, 11 large hangars, and an enormous area of smaller buildings, as well as about 1,000 acres of land. Much of this land had become wild and overgrown, and James decided that it should be cleared. Faced with the problem of how to get rid of some tree stumps, he decided to blow them up using gelignite and made a guess as to how much to use. He used far too much, there was a huge explosion, the tree stumps were obliterated, and a man sitting on the roof of a nearby building, fortunately a low one, was blown off the roof and broke his leg. It was an unfortunate accident but a typical one. A machine shop and a sewing room for the parachute packs and harnesses was set up there and, as the factory in the Isle of Man was by then running well, Denis Burrell moved to Ireland to set up and run this new operation.

James's twin sons were teenagers by this time and recall what a delight
it was to help their father with exciting activities such as blowing up tree
stumps. James also had two young daughters by then, Jane and Anne,
born in 1945 and 1949 respectively. Inevitably his commitment to his
work meant that Muriel had to bring up the children virtually on her
own, and James took no part in family outings and holidays. This on
occasions laid a heavy burden on Muriel's shoulders, but she had a deep
understanding of James's passionate involvement with his work, and
knew that she could always rely on his wisdom and support. He did tear
himself away for one holiday on the Isle of Wight, but only lasted two
days before deciding that the factory needed him!

Southlands Manor was a superb place to bring up young children,
with its river and large garden. James built an island on the river to
encourage the ducks to breed there, so that he and the children could
feed them regularly. He allowed his daughter Jane to keep a large number
of donkeys, animals he particularly liked and which he would occasionally
allow into the house, and brought a donkey cart back from Ireland so
that the children could ride in it. He encouraged other interests too, and
taught all his children to shoot with rifles. Muriel was therefore used to
the sound of gunshot, and while the children will forever recall the day
James ripped up the lawn when demonstrating an old Sten gun which
they had found in a shed, they were more impressed that their mother did
not bother to come to the window to see what they were all up to. He
derived an enormous amount of pleasure from his children, but he was
a private man who preferred to keep his family life to himself.

In the autumn of 1956 the Royal Navy were preparing to send an
aircraft carrier to sea with a number of Sea Venom aircraft on board.
James had already designed the seat installation for this aircraft, but he
had discovered, during extensive testing of the seat, that there were one
or two problems which occurred at very high speeds which needed
rectification. On hearing about the imminent departure of the aircraft
carrier, James sent a working party down to the Royal Navy base to
complete the modifications. As he said: 'This has necessitated some
quick thinking and action; but I could not tolerate the idea of our seats
going as far away as Malta and Suez and not being 100% right.'

This was typical of James. The fact that he had sold a seat did not
mean that it was no longer his concern, for James never understood the
concept of having a customer. While he would be the first to insist that
a shop should sell him what he asked for rather than what the shop
wanted to sell, he never accepted that governments and air forces were
his customers who were entitled to buy what they had ordered. As far
as James was concerned, the ejection seat was his design and only he
could tell them what they needed. To James, contractual specifications
were irrelevant and procedures for changing the specification a complete
waste of time. If he conceived an improvement in the design, then it had
to be incorporated immediately and the required paperwork was best
ignored. Don McGovern, who got to know James well during the years

he worked at the McDonnell Aircraft Company, remembers this aspect of James well. As McGovern explains:

> He may sell you an ejection seat, and you may pay him for it, but the seat still belonged to him as far as he was concerned. He would proceed to make changes to the seat, and some of these changes were pretty damned significant and they would affect spare parts, they would affect handbooks, all sorts of logistics elements, and he didn't care about following all the standard bureaucratic practices that one should follow in these things, he would just make the change. And we at McDonnell Aircraft Company kept nagging him about that and telling him that there were certain change control procedures that he had to follow and that sort of thing. Nevertheless, he persisted. One time we finally said to him: 'You will either cease and desist or we will consider stopping taking delivery.' He sent us a message back saying: 'Not to worry, I've stopped delivering.' But you can't deliver an aeroplane without an ejection seat, and we soon came to see things his way.

The Sea Venom seats represented the latest design of ejection seat which made it possible for pilots to do ejections on the runway taking off with a 40 ft clear drop on their parachute after it had deployed fully. These seats were obviously a great improvement on earlier seats for aircraft operating from aircraft carriers and, in the event of an engine failure just after take-off, gave the pilot the chance, if he acted quickly enough, to eject and land in the sea with a fully developed parachute and thus avoid the danger of being submerged with the aircraft.

Although Navy pilots had ejected successfully from aircraft underwater, it was a hazardous operation. The ejection gun was too powerful for use underwater, and there was always the danger that the seat might become entangled with the drogue or the parachute in these circumstances. There had been fatalities with attempted ejections in these circumstances and James therefore turned his mind to the problems of underwater escape. He devised a gas-operated propulsion system for the seat (the concept the Germans had worked on during the war) which incorporated an air cylinder mounted on the seat itself, or on the aircraft bulkhead, charged to 3,000 lb/sq in. This cylinder was opened by a hydrostatic valve which operated when a pressure equivalent to 10 ft of water was exerted, whereupon air was released under pressure into the ejection gun cylinder, causing the extension of the ejection gun tubes and thus the ejection of the seat. This also disconnected the trip rod which prevented the drogue gun from firing and fired the guillotine to prevent the deployment of the parachute. The time release mechanism operated in the usual way to effect seat separation, and bladders positioned behind the parachute pack and beneath the survival pack inflated during separation to push the pilot out of the seat. The pilot's life-jacket automatically inflated and the pilot would therefore rise to the surface.

This was a truly automatic seat, because the pilot was not required to initiate the ejection process, and it was not long before James became deeply embroiled in arguments for an automatic seat to deal with other circumstances too. The modifications required to give a seat underwater capability were in addition to the existing seat mechanisms, and could therefore be fitted to seats without limiting their ability to eject a pilot in the air. The system was tested in tanks by volunteers drawn mostly from the ranks of Navy divers, and having been proved effective, was installed by way of modification to Mark 4 seats in Royal Navy Buccaneer aircraft. It never saw emergency use, however, because other developments of the ejection seat soon rendered this special underwater capability unnecessary.

In 1956 the authorities in the United States became increasingly aware of the outstanding performance of the latest Martin-Baker seats. The Americans were using only American-designed and -manufactured seats but were experiencing problems, particularly with ejections at low level. According to the information made available to Martin-Baker, the survival rate in the US Navy for ejections below 1,000 ft was only 4 per cent, between 1,000 and 2,000 ft it was less than 50 per cent, and between 2,000 and 3,000 ft it was 66 per cent.

Martin-Baker of course had seats with runway capability, a factor that the Navy's Bureau of Aeronautics felt it could no longer ignore. Despite the lobbying within America for American aircraft to be fitted with American seats, they ordered 70 Mark 4 seats for flight test and evaluation in conjunction with the US Air Force. The Bureau of Aeronautics asked James to give a live demonstration in America of his latest seat, but they laid down strict criteria for this test. They insisted that it should take place at the US Navy test facility at Patuxent River, Maryland, from a Grumman F9F-8T Cougar aircraft flown by a Grumman test pilot and not a Martin-Baker test pilot. Martin-Baker were to supply the ejectee, but he had to be someone who was not a professional parachutist and who had not ejected before, and the test was to take place at runway level at a speed of 90 knots.

Fortunately, people would often write to Martin-Baker at that time offering to undertake test ejections for the company, so it was not difficult to find someone to do this test. James selected a young RAF officer, FO Sidney Hughes, who was flying Hunters in 66 Squadron. Following several successful tests with dummies, on 28 August 1957, Hughes ejected successfully as the Grumman fighter trainer began to take off, in front of a large crowd of officials, Servicemen and pressmen. Hughes is reported to have said: 'You feel a terrific crash on your rump, and the next thing, you are out on the end of your 'chute.'

Afterwards, James was guest of honour at a fairly large luncheon party at the Naval base at which the Secretary of the US Navy gave a speech in which he noted how much the United States owed to Great Britain for inventions, including their ejection seat. He quoted figures relating to the casualty rate experienced with American ejection seats, and that of the 276 men killed during the previous year, most would probably still have been alive if Martin-Baker seats had been installed. Following this live demonstration, the US Navy finally decided to standardize Martin-Baker seats for all US Navy jet fighters and trainers, and thereby became Martin-Baker's biggest customer. The success of this single test was therefore immensely important to the future business of Martin-Baker, for had the test not taken place, or had there been a failure, it is doubtful whether the US Navy would have made the decision to buy Martin-Baker seats. This one live test was sufficient to overcome the significant American opposition to a British ejection seat. James's achievements were recognized in 1958 when he became the first non-American to receive the Laura Taber Barbour Air Safety Award.

The US Navy had greater strength requirements for the ejection seat than the RAF, and required a seat for a 40 g crash situation rather than the 25 g requirement of the RAF. The seat structure and harness were strengthened accordingly to withstand these increased loads and a new seat to meet these special requirements, the Mark 5 seat, was introduced in 1957. In most other respects the Mark 5 seat was similar to the Mark 4 seat, although the Mark 5 seats were provided with special canopy-breaker peaks on the head box to cope with the eventuality of having to eject through the canopy, which was standard practice on the seat installed in the Grumman Cougar. On the majority of the other Mark 5 seats, the American system of jettisoning the canopy was linked up with the face blind firing handle.

The American order meant an enormous amount of work for Martin-Baker, as seats had to be retrofitted to all the US Navy aircraft then flying. But it was an immediate increase in workload which was not expected to continue once the retrofit programme had been completed. James therefore decided to engage a considerable number of sub-contractors to cover the immediate problem, as he did not want to find himself with a largely redundant work-force in a few years' time. The US Navy order also covered the McDonnell Phantom, then in the development phase, which was the biggest order for one aircraft that Martin-Baker had ever had to cope with. When it was decided that the US Air Force should take delivery of Phantoms too, an attempt was made to install American seats, but the Martin-Baker seat remained, and was only slightly changed from the US Navy version to suit the different harness and survival kit used by the US Air Force. James reported in October 1958:

> This last month or so I am just about driven crazy with trying to cope with engineers or designers or whatever they call themselves, from Lockheeds, McDonnell, Douglas, Grummans and Chance Vought. We have at the moment six of their aeroplanes here for the fitting of seats to them. They all arrived here within a few days as though it were a kind of Charing Cross station.

After the introduction of the Mark 5 seats, James designed a new device which became known as the Personal Equipment Connector. The purpose of this was to simplify the connection of the various vital services from the aircraft to the pilot, which was achieved by combining all the aircraft service lines at one point with the connector so that everything was connected by one action rather than several. When the seat ejects, the supplies of anti-g, oxygen and air ventilation, as well as the telephone/microphone (tel/mic) communication system, are automatically disconnected and sealed whilst the emergency oxygen supply is turned on and supplied via the main oxygen supply line. Because the Personal Equipment Connector connects all services at the same time, the aircrew can check that their oxygen and other supplies are correctly connected simply by checking the use of the tel/mic system.

In 1957, James was appointed a Commander of the British Empire. He was pleased by the award but still claimed that he got 'far more pleasure out of getting letters from pilots who have had occasion to use our seats'. James always replied to every letter personally. Typically, he would write: 'I can assure you that nothing in the world causes me more pleasure than to hear from people like yourself who have had reason to use our equipment. As the person responsible for the design of ejection seats it is a source of some satisfaction to know that the seat seems to do what it is intended to do.' He would also extend an invitation for the ejectee and his family to visit the factory, and when such invitations were taken up, took the greatest pleasure in meeting them and showing them around.

Some ejectees did not write to him at all and some wrote factual and business-like letters of thanks. Many, however, believed that they owed their lives to James and their letters were often emotive and contained sincere messages of gratitude. One ejectee, David Nightingale, ejected from a Blackburn NA39 prototype on 5 October 1960, after the aircraft went out of control and commenced rolling and yawing. Nightingale was the flight observer, and when the pilot jettisoned the canopy, Nightingale's right arm was held alongside his head by the air blast. The pilot ejected and for 22 long and lonely seconds Nightingale struggled to reach the seat pan handle and eject. He escaped successfully, but the incident had such a profound effect on him that he sent James a message on every anniversary of his ejection, thanking him for another year of life.

Some ejections were obviously more interesting to James than others, and two which particularly interested him took place in 1958 and 1959. On 9 April 1958, two RAF crew, Flt. Lt. J.P.F. de Salis, the pilot, and FO P.H.G. Lowe, the navigator, ejected from a Canberra in Mark 1 seats following a severe explosion which caused loss of control. This ejection was particularly significant in that it took place at approximately 56,000 ft and is today still the highest successful ejection with a Martin-Baker seat on record. Then, in October 1959, Johnny Squier ejected from a P1 Lightning at a speed of 1,200 mph at 40,000 ft. He was lost for about 30 hours and was eventually washed up on the Scottish coast in his dinghy, none the worse for his experience except that he was a bit stiff as a result of lying for 30 hours in the water-soaked dinghy. He had been flying at Mach 1.7 when quite suddenly there was a nasty crunch, the aeroplane yawed badly and he realized that he had lost control. James was very pleased to hear about this escape. The Americans had sometimes criticized his seat on the basis that it was good for low-altitude escapes but not for high-speed ones, and he remarked: 'They cannot really call 1200 m.p.h going slow.'

As his business became more successful, so James found himself invited to more official functions which he tended to avoid when he could. With hearing in only one ear, and the hearing in that ear damaged by years of working with explosives, he found it difficult to hear what people were saying in a crowded environment. As a non-drinker who liked plain, home cooking, cocktail receptions and fancy dinners were a chore. As far as he was concerned, these functions meant a lot of bother dressing up and getting home afterwards, and at the end of a busy day at the factory, he rarely felt like it. Despite his great interest in people, he had never been a man who enjoyed going out and meeting new people and making conversation with them. He chose his friends carefully from among those who interested him, and enjoyed the opportunity for lengthy discussions with them, but he was not a socializer.

James still had an active interest in the current design of aircraft, and it is apparent from his remarks about other people's aircraft that he still believed in the merits of his own designs. In January 1947 he had written: 'I have come to the conclusion that design in this country has almost reached stagnation, as far as fast aeroplanes are concerned. If they go fast enough through the air it is only due to enormous horse power and not due to low drag.' Exactly ten years later his advice to Sir Sydney Camm of Hawker Aircraft Limited in connection with the Hawker Hunter was based on the same theme. He wrote to Sir Sydney to tell him:

> The fact of the matter, of course, is that it is simply not fast enough, and I feel that there is something like 50–60 m.p.h. unnecessary drag on it in its present form. I should think the cabin top would represent as much as 25 m.p.h.; and an extended nose (about 6 ft. forward) to a sharp spike, would represent probably another 12 to 15 m.p.h.; then there is the wing root. It is no use your aerodynamicist saying how efficient the air intake is: I have no doubt it is efficient looked at as an air intake – but it is equally efficient as a drag producer too. I am quite certain that if your wing came into the side of the fuselage, and the maximum thickness here was 6%, and the air intake arranged somewhere else, say at each side of the nose, with the fuselage well thinned away, this, with the changes mentioned above, would make your aeroplane equal to the fastest in the United States.

His advice was well-intentioned (although history does not relate how well Sir Sydney received it) in that James wanted 'to see the Hawker name established as one of the best in the world'. Nevertheless, it was unusual advice for a man who had not designed a production aircraft to give to a man who had, and it reflected James's growing concern about the decline of the aircraft industry in Britain.

In 1959, John Scott retired as Martin-Baker's chief test pilot. Scott

had made an enormous contribution to James's development work, for
he had ejected over 700 test seats from airborne aircraft. Fifield took
over as the chief test pilot, and the Air Ministry tried to insist that he be
given formal training in flying their Meteor, but James was not interested.
As far as he was concerned, Fifield flew the Meteor quite competently,
had years of flying experience behind him, and certainly did not need
to waste time having flying lessons at this stage in his career. He avoided
attempts by the Ministry to discuss the question and refused to release
Fifield from his flying duties and eventually the Ministry gave up.

Fifield still enjoyed making low-level passes over the airfield when he
had ejected the test seat, his aim being to fly low enough to make people
duck when he flew over their heads. James did not mind this, even when
there were important visitors who had come to watch the test. On one
occasion, when it was rather wet, James had some high-ranking German
officials with him. As Fifield approached over the runway at his customary
low level to fly over their heads, James's sense of humour got the better
of him. Knowing what Fifield was going to do, he threw himself to the
ground as he approached. The high-ranking officials followed suit, and
were more than a little upset by having to lie in the mud in their smart
uniforms because of Fifield's low-level attack, but James was delighted.

Meanwhile, James had not given up his crusade to get ejection seats
fitted for rear crew members in the V-bombers. Since Bryce's ejection
in 1952, four aircrew had been killed in a crash of a Valiant in May 1956,
four more in a crash of a Vulcan in October 1956 when Air Marshal Sir
Harry Broadhurst had been one of the ejectees, and five more in a crash
of another Vulcan in October 1958. The rear crew members sat in
rearward-facing seats, so James had to satisfy himself and others that a
man could eject safely when facing backwards. At his own expense he
designed a special version of the Mark 4 seat for this purpose which was
installed in a Valiant aircraft. After a series of static tests, a programme
of three dummy ejections was carried out, one on the runway during
the take-off run which was completely satisfactory, the parachute being
fully developed 4.3 seconds after ejection providing a controlled drop
of 38 ft, and two at an altitude of 200 ft. These tests culminated in a
live test by W.T. (Doddy) Hay on 1 July 1960 at a height of 1,000 ft
and a speed of 250 knots. This test was witnessed by several Air Force
officers and Ministry officials and was completely successful. Martin-
Baker believe that this was the first rearward-facing live ejection in the
world, but unfortunately no interest was shown in this development.

Another version of the Mark 4 seat was that designed to cover the
unusual requirements of the VTOL (vertical take-off and landing) aircraft
and those aircraft which could fly very slowly. Instead of the normal
drogue gun, the seat had a very powerful parachute gun which used a
heavy projectile to deploy both the drogue and the main parachute,
which, coupled with the 80 ft/sec ejection gun, made it possible to fire the
seat whilst the aircraft was stationary on the ground and still enable the
pilot to land safely with a fully developed parachute. This was the

beginning of what became known as the 'zero/zero' seat, i.e. the seat which is designed to provide a safe ejection at zero altitude and zero speed. This form of seat was only suitable for comparatively slow aircraft, as at high speed the early development of the main parachute would have led to its destruction. This type of seat was fitted into the P1127, which led to the prototype Harrier VTOL aircraft.

James never liked the Harrier. He considered its potential as a military aircraft to be severely limited, and he wrote several times to the designer, Sir Sydney Camm, to tell him that he was wasting his time with it, because the aircraft lacked both speed and military load-carrying capacity. He also thought the aircraft was exceedingly dangerous. He would explain again and again that if the engine failed while the aircraft was in the hover at low level, gravity certainly would not, and the aircraft would be destroyed and the pilot dead before he had time to eject.

During the development of the Harrier, he proposed that it should have automatic ejection seats which would fire immediately if the engine failed. He would explain:

Suppose that at a height of, say, sixty feet you are hovering and the engine cut suddenly. You would be on the ground in less than two seconds and it would be quite unreasonable to expect a pilot to get out in under two seconds – he would have to be a very quick worker. That is the reason why I say that if a pilot wants to live in a V.T.O. aeroplane, he must have automatic ejection in the case of engine failure.

It was an interesting proposition and one which exercised a lot of minds while the possibilities and problems were considered. No-one else, however, was convinced that he was right. The combined brain power of the engine and airframe designers, the Air Ministry and the test pilots, could not agree what device would be used to trigger the ejection. The only consensus they could reach was that the risk of a malfunction, which could lead to a pilot being ejected from a perfectly serviceable aircraft, outweighed the risk of an engine failure at low level which could result in the death of the pilot. James considered this conclusion to be both ridiculous and indefensible. He was now totally engrossed in his work on life-saving equipment and could not accept that the risk of losing a serviceable aircraft was greater than the risk of losing a life.

Even Bill Bedford, the Hawker chief test pilot, was more pragmatic than James. He believes that flying is an inherently dangerous occupation and that the risks can never be totally eliminated by any escape system. James, however, never missed an opportunity to give instructions on how to fly the VTOL aircraft safely in order to increase the probability of escape if this proved necessary. Flying safely meant flying conventionally whenever possible as far as James was concerned, despite the fact, as Bedford would point out to him, that this would defeat some of the main advantages of a VTOL aircraft, and it was at one of these meetings, when James was expounding his views on the VTOL aircraft, that he gave Bedford the piece of advice which probably saved his life: 'Bill, if you are ever short of time, don't use the handle above your head, use the handle between your legs.'

On 14 December 1961, Bedford set out to do some high-speed flutter tests in a P1127. The aircraft was responding well and Bedford had been flying for about 20 minutes. Suddenly there was a shattering bang and a tremendous roaring noise. Bedford felt a rapid deceleration which might have been due to a partial engine failure, but the aircraft was still flying normally and the instruments were still showing normal readings. He thought it must be some sort of engine problem so he elected to make a conventional landing at the Royal Naval air base at Yeovilton, which he had just flown over.

He went through the routine pre-landing checks and everything seemed fine. But then, in the final stages of the approach, the aircraft began to roll to port, for no apparent reason. He tried to level the aircraft but nothing happened as the aircraft was not responding to the controls. He tried again, kicking the rudder pedals and moving the control column with increasing force as he tried to elicit some response from the aircraft. He recalls: 'I finished with the stick in one corner and the rudder in the other to try and stop it rolling. It was only going very slowly and I thought I must regain speed to regain control, and fed on the power, but as I did so the aeroplane continued rolling and I knew that I'd had it.'

Bedford felt what he described as 'a phenomenal surge of adrenalin which sharpens you mentally and physically, and makes you think very quickly'. In that microsecond, when he realized that he had lost control and must eject, James's words flashed through his mind. He grabbed the secondary ejection seat firing handle between his legs and pulled hard. There was a terrific bang as the cartridge fired and his ejection seat blasted its way through the cockpit canopy, a tug as the parachute deployed and then, almost immediately, he was safely on the ground in a ploughed field, thinking, 'Thank God for James Martin.' The second, or fraction of a second, saved by pulling the handle between his legs, rather than reaching up for the one above his head, was enough to make the difference between life and death. As James would often say: 'There are two sorts of pilots, the quick and the dead.'

At this stage of their development, about 93 per cent of ejections in Martin-Baker seats were successful in saving the life of the ejectee. Approximately 60 per cent of the unsuccessful ejections occurred at low altitude with the aircraft descending at a high sink rate, and in most cases the pilot had successfully ejected from the aircraft but hit the ground before his parachute had deployed fully. James realized that it was still necessary to increase the height of the seat's trajectory on ejection, but he concluded that because of physiological constraints, he had now developed the ejection gun to its full potential, and that he would have to solve this problem by other means. The Americans were already experimenting with rocket-powered seats, and clearly Martin-Baker would be considered to have fallen behind in their ejection seat development if they did not also produce a rocket-powered seat. And so, in the late fifties, James began this work.

He was reluctant to dispense with the ejection gun. It had performed very efficiently since the first ejection seat went into service, and he therefore decided not to interfere with its design but to add a rocket motor to the existing seat in order to increase its trajectory height. The rocket would fire as the ejection gun tubes separated, and would continue the thrust applied to the seat.

The first question he had to answer was whether the rocket power would pull the seat or push it. It was still the case that the tests established the theory rather than tested it. He decided that a rocket stowed on the side of the seat and attached to the top of the seat by a chain would pull it out. Seat tests with dummies were going ahead at the rate of about 300 a year, often at weekends, and it was one Sunday morning at Chalgrove Airfield that James conducted a test to see whether his idea would work. It did not. The chain broke immediately, and the rocket motor, from a 2 in air-launched missile, flew off into the sky to a great height and landed in a field about a mile away.

James then designed a system whereby two solid fuel rockets were mounted on the rear of the seat pan, one on each side, leading into an efflux chamber which discharged downwards below the seat providing the required thrust. James took care to ensure that the line of thrust passed through the centre of gravity of the seat/man mass in order to ensure as near vertical a trajectory as possible, and that the seat did not cartwheel. Unlike the American rocket seats which fired upwards and forwards, which could be disastrous where the aircraft was in a severe nose-down attitude at low level because the trajectory of the seat would be horizontal, James's design fired the seat upwards and backwards to achieve the maximum vertical trajectory. To ensure seat stability, the rocket motor was arranged to have a very short burning time so that there was little time for the seat to become unstable before rocket burn-out, while the thrust was kept high in order to attain the desired velocity and therefore the required high trajectory.

The test programme for the first rocket seats was extensive. The first tests were done on ground rigs. Other test vehicles used were a launching stand for the zero-zero ejections, a specially adapted motor vehicle for the low-speed runs, a Meteor T7 aircraft for the medium-speed tests and a Hunter T7 for the high-speed runs. The tests covered a wide range of speeds, from 0–600 knots, and a wide range of body weights to cover the likely variations in body weights of different size pilots that the seat would have to cope with, as changes in the size of the pilot result in changes in the position of the centre of gravity of the ejected mass.

For the first time, James encountered problems with the dummies when testing the rocket seat. He discovered that the centre of gravity of a dummy bears little relationship to the centre of gravity of a human being. James said:

We had to learn that the hard way from some hundreds of tests. We wondered why in some cases the seat did not perform according to calculations, and when we checked the CG of the dummy it was three or four inches out. The dummy was all right as a space model, but all wrong from the point of view of reproducing a man from the rocket seat point of view.

Finally, on 1 April 1961, a live test was carried out, again by Hay, which was the first ever live zero speed, zero altitude ejection. The seat was fired from a ground-level static rig. All went well, the seat reaching a height of more than 300 ft with the parachute almost completely developed by the time the seat reached the top of the trajectory. Hay quickly carried out the post-ejection action and had discarded the face blind, released his survival kit and had the parachute under control by the time he landed.

The Ministry representative had arrived late and missed seeing the ejection. He approached James to apologize for his late arrival and to offer his congratulations on the success of the test. James, with a mischievous twinkle in his eyes, barked in reply: 'That's the trouble with you chaps from the Ministry – you spend far too much time on your backsides – I'll have to write to your wife and tell her to kick you out of bed in the morning.'

Hay reported that the ride was smooth and comfortable, and James was relieved that he had successfully mastered the fundamental problems relating to rocket-powered ejection. He wrote: 'I was much relieved to see the chute fully developed at nearly 300 feet and also I gave a sigh of relief when he told me it was a beautiful ride. There is no substitute for a live test. Better than all the graphs and curves in the world!' James had been worried about the effect of the kick of the rocket coming on just as the end of the gun stroke was finishing. He went on to say:

In point of fact my nervous system has been strained to the limit for these past few months. As you know it is a strain to put a human being in a seat, and if things do not work that is the end of the man. However, I am relieved now that the first difficult job is well under control now, and I have no qualms whatsoever.

It had been agreed that Hay would give a public demonstration of the rocket seat at the Paris Air Show that year, but before this demonstration could take place, James found himself faced with what he regarded as a very serious tax problem for the company. Because of the American orders, in the previous two years Martin-Baker had been producing about 250 seats per month for export to the USA, and with the increased efficiency in manufacturing, the company's profits had risen quite steeply. The company accountant came to see James one morning in the middle of March to advise him of the profit for the current financial year, and that distribution of profits in private companies could be subject to a direction from the Special Commissioners of the Inland Revenue. It was explained to James that the Inland Revenue would probably direct that the profits remaining in the company after he had paid tax be distributed to the shareholders (James and his family), who would then each have to pay tax on the distribution received by them. James was outraged, for in his view it was double taxation, but he was utterly dismayed as well, because whatever the company would be allowed to retain for trading purposes would be insufficient. His decision to refuse Ministry development contracts meant that he expended very substantial sums of money on research and development, and with the amount of work he was involved in, he simply could not afford to run out of money to support his test programme. He remarked: 'So the net result would have been that we were no better off than we were – say – seven years ago when we never had the bother of making American seats.'

Once again he was reminded of the Isle of Man with its low income tax and no death duties and, in the heat of the moment of anger and despair, he decided to move himself and his family to the Isle of Man before the beginning of the next financial year on 6 April. His house was packed up in its entirety and the contents shipped and flown to the Isle of Man where he moved in once again with his sister, Jane, to start his new life.

This new life lasted two weeks: two weeks of mental anguish and trauma, after which he decided to return to England. Fifield arrived in the Martin-Baker DC-3 to bring them back. James was desperately upset by the conflicting issues he had to face, and uncertain whether he had made the correct decision. On the return journey his doubts overcame him and he told Fifield to turn back to the Isle of Man. Fifield told him they had insufficient fuel. James tried to persuade him to divert to Southern Ireland, but there was insufficient fuel for that journey too. As James recalled: 'So I came back with a heavy heart in the sense that for a life-time I had next to nothing – only a hand-to-mouth existence and only in the last two years have I been able to build up any kind of reserve.'

The reasons for his return were a complex mix of domestic and commercial issues which could not otherwise be resolved. Suitable schooling for his daughter, the prospect of being unable to see his aged mother, now living in England, for at least a year, assuming that she did not die in the meantime, and the fact that he felt isolated from Denham and out of touch with the people he wanted to see. The factory at Denham was the centre of his activities. He was conscious that he had not yet finalized the design of the rocket seat, and clearly his work would be very disrupted if he stayed on the Island. He wrote: 'I have returned to Denham as I feel it is necessary to be here all the time and press on with the job to its proper conclusion.' Martin-Baker was his life and nothing could replace that.

When he left the factory, the workers were stunned. They had heard rumours about this precipitous departure but they refused to believe that 'the old man' would really leave them. Two weeks later, when the bush telegraph in the factory told them that Fifield was on his way back to Chalgrove with James on board, they all relaxed. As Arthur Bates, who had been working at Martin-Baker since 1947, said: 'we all said that he would never stay in the Isle of Man. His home was here, that office was his home, and he didn't want anything else except that.'

The next year, on 26 January 1962, James hosted a dinner at the Dorchester Hotel in London to celebrate the saving of 500 lives with his ejection seat. It was a unique occasion and James was delighted that 115 ejectees, many with their wives, were able to attend. It was an opportunity to look back over 17 years of development work and remember the time when 12–15 ft was the limit to which they could fire a man up. As he looked around the room, he realized that he was looking at approximately the same number of people as the number whose lives had been saved with his ejection seat. He remarked afterwards:

> In the ordinary course of events, when you read about someone bailing out there does not seem much to it, but the end result is rather different. There are now 515 ejectees, and if one saw them all together with their wives and children, it would make a fairly large assembly. It is one part of the ejection seat business that a person like myself does not think about as we are hard pressed to try to make the seat better and better. All we want to read about is successful escapes, and apart from that it is just an ordinary job with lots of problems. However, when you see the end product it makes you think that after all it has been worth it.

Bill Bedford, whose recent escape was still fresh in his mind, and who spoke on behalf of the ejectees, could not resist giving the assembled company a hint of the pleasure he derived from James's involvement in the sometimes interminable discussions on the development of the ejection seat for installation in the Harrier. He said:

> He can demolish the most serious minded committee meeting in minutes and bring it down to earth; he enters the meeting towards its close like a breath of fresh air, turns a deaf ear to irrelevance, murmurs something about it all being like a comic opera or a pantomime – then proceeds ruthlessly to sift the wheat from the chaff, brings everyone to their senses, wraps the meeting up and leaves members in no doubt that decisions and future actions are in his capable hands whether they like it or not – regardless of what the learned committee think!

Since his return from the Isle of Man, James had been working continuously on the development of the rocket seat. Although the dual rocket system tested by Hay had worked well, it was not adopted largely due to difficulties in finding the necessary space in which to install the rockets in the close confines of the various cockpits. The design was ultimately changed to a multi-tube rocket pack which could be fitted underneath the seat. This consists of a number of combustion tubes containing the solid fuel propellant which are screwed into a central gallery mounted transversely across the bottom of the seat pan. The gallery also accommodates the efflux nozzles which point downwards. The pack is attached to the seat pan in a manner which facilitates quick and simple removal and replacement without the use of special tools, and this, combined with the fact that James designed the rocket propulsion to take over from the cartridge rather than to replace it, meant that only minimal modification work was required to retrofit these rocket packs to ejection seats already in service. It was this form of rocket that was installed on some of the existing Mark 4 seats turning them into Mark 6 seats, while Mark 5 seats became Mark 7 seats.

James asked W/Cdr. Peter Howard, an RAF doctor at the Institute of Aviation Medicine who was a specialist in aviation physiology (he later became an Air Vice-Marshal and Commandant of the Institute), to test the new multi-pack rocket seat for him. James still placed his faith in the spoken word of the ejectee rather than on instrumentation. The test department at Martin-Baker made a number of attempts to instrument test seats and dummies, and James was unforgiving if any of this instrumentation affected the performance of the test seat in any way.

Howard completed a parachute training course and made about 20 trips to Chalgrove to prepare for the test. He recalls that James 'was so meticulous about getting things right'. Howard climbed in and out of the Meteor a large number of times while James addressed various details that he was not satisfied with, and there was a great deal of discussion with James and the others involved with the test. Finally, on 13 March 1962 the test took place. Howard remembers that despite the careful preparations, James was nevertheless nervous. Always a little irascible, he was decidedly pushy and ill at ease that day. The test, which took place at 250 knots at 250 ft, was completely successful, and Howard remembers that it was James himself who was the greatest hazard as he came careering across the airfield in his Bentley to meet Howard as he landed and at the last minute had to swerve to avoid running into him.

Howard duly wrote a report of his test ejection which was precise and factual. James was not very pleased with it because he wanted Howard to include all sorts of personal and unscientific observations such as 'I was surprised by the gentleness of the ride'. Howard and James had become friends by this stage and Howard did not want to upset him, so he agreed to rewrite his report and incorporate James's suggestions, and James was able to report happily: 'I expect Peter Howard's report has served some useful purpose in connection with those people who were trying to lay down what rate of rise of "g" is acceptable.'

Howard continued to visit Denham regularly after the test although it was rarely connected with James's work. Age was catching up with James at last, and he was taking more time to talk to people whom he liked and who interested him. Howard describes James as 'one of the most infuriating, honest and lovable men I've ever met. I really was so fond of that man and yet he was a rogue really in all sorts of ways'. James had not mellowed over the years and the reasons why Howard found James so infuriating were not new. As Howard explains, what made him infuriating was

the fact that he always had to be right. He knew damn well he wasn't and the

next time you met him he put the opposite view. He was infuriating in that he
didn't really listen, or seemed not to listen, he'd just pick on something you
said and worry away at that and not let the argument develop. He'd make up
his mind just there and then. Either you got on well with James or you didn't.

Notwithstanding the success of Peter Howard's live test, the development
of the rocket-assisted seat continued. James was faced with the problem
of how to get two aircrew out of the same aircraft in rocket seats,
particularly with a two-seater side-by-side seating arrangement. If one
aircrew ejected before the other, there was the possibility that the flames
from the rocket on the first seat would burn the person left behind. The
solution seemed to be to delay the firing of the rocket until the first seat
was up and back far enough to ensure that no flames got into the cockpit.
James therefore modified the seat so that the firing of the rocket was
delayed for 54 in, that is until separation from the ejection gun, which
equated to a time interval of only one-sixteenth of a second, and during
the course of tests this arrangement worked well.

Hay agreed to test the modified system, and on 6 December 1963,
he ejected himself over Chalgrove at a speed of 200 knots, but received
an unusually large jolt from the ejection and arrived back on the ground
with a very sore back. X-rays confirmed that the injury was muscular
only, but the fact remained that the seat was unacceptable. James wrote
to Hay shortly afterwards and said:

> The time interval was only 1/16 of a second and I assumed that such a small
> element of time would not make any serious difference, with the result –
> enough said. When I saw you at the moment of landing I knew instantly that
> this was no use. That is why I wanted to be there at the moment of touch
> down. I know you have immense courage and I felt that you might want to
> conceal how bad the jolt was. I did not need any convincing.

The dummy tests had not revealed the problem, but the live test could not
conceal it. As a result, James designed another rocket motor in which the
centre body was much further back and the nozzles were set at a tangent
so that the rocket could be fired at the instant of gun separation. He
mounted wood around the stand from which the test seat was fired, which
was the same size as a two-seater cockpit, and no flames singed the wood.
Stationary tests gave a good trajectory and a clean separation of the
dummy from the seat. He considered doing a further live test to prove
the effectiveness of his latest modifications to remove the jolt, but decided
against it. Hay's test on 6 December 1963 was the last live test ejection
that Martin-Baker made. Having been abruptly reminded of the results
of his own development work, James would not again depart from his
own parameters. The modifications complied with his own ejection
criteria, the rocket seat had been proved by live test, live tests were no
longer necessary to demonstrate that ejection was possible, and the testing
of seats since then has been done with fully instrumented dummies only.

Chapter Twelve

The V-Bomber Debate

In 1963, James turned 70. Inevitably he lacked the vigour of his youth, but he had lost none of his commitment. He would arrive at the office at seven thirty or eight o'clock in the morning and would stay there until eight o'clock in the evening. It often suited him to have supper at the office, and he had by this time initiated the practice of having supper there with those who worked closely with him, which was served in the boardroom promptly at six o'clock. Usually this was a time to recap on the events of the day and to plan the next day, but there was a certain protocol which those attending felt compelled to observe, which included everyone finishing their meal – unfortunate for those who wanted to go home for dinner, and of course, no-one was expected to leave until James had decided that the discussions were concluded. Although some found this supper club rather inconvenient, all agreed that it was a unique and effective way of running a business.

James was no longer always totally involved in his design work, for he was beginning to allow himself more time for debate and discussion, sometimes with the various visitors to his factory, but also by letter with friends, customers and even complete strangers. The decade beginning in the early sixties was very definitely the letter-writing phase of James's life. In his younger days, letters were a chore. Miss Nicholls, his secretary during much of the forties, remembers how he would creep past her office to avoid being seen by her and made to deal with the post. She would have to corner him somewhere with a cup of tea, ignore his protestations, and sit him down. He rarely dictated a letter, but would tell her the sort of thing he wanted to say and leave it to her to concoct something suitable. In these later years, however, James opened all the post that arrived at the factory, and if a letter addressed to someone else interested him, he would often keep it and the addressee would receive only the empty envelope. Letter-writing was now a hobby, and a means of airing his still uncompromising views. He would hold forth at great length on the political and military issues of the day, but he was also becoming more vociferous on theological subjects.

James did not give the impression of being a religious man. He was not a churchgoer, nor was he a pious follower of any particular faith. Having been brought up in a strict Presbyterian household, he had been introduced at an early age to the teachings of the Bible which had stimulated his curiosity. This interest had grown with him, and throughout his life he had conducted a detailed study of the Scriptures and had developed his own brand of evangelical faith which, while sometimes unorthodox, he held to with a stubborn and steadfast conviction.

During the sixties, the Ulster community from which he had come came to realize that he had done well for himself. He received an increasing number of letters from Protestant ministers in Ireland requesting financial support for their churches. James gave money to several hundred churches in Northern Ireland. Some were lucky and received only a two-line reply to their letters, enclosing a cheque which James hoped 'would serve some useful purpose'. Others would receive a sermon on the failings of themselves and their congregations, sometimes running to several pages, for James firmly believed that the reason why so many churches were short of funds was due entirely to the fact that the parishioners did not give a full and honest tithe, that is, one-tenth of their income, to support the Church and God's work as the Bible clearly stated that they should. He felt that to raise money by means of fetes and other such events was an abomination and an insult to God. He believed that if a person's faith did not cause them to fulfil the demands set out in the Bible, then it was not a faith at all, and he would exhort these ministers to set the right example to their congregations, and then to tell them a few home truths with regard to how they had been cheating the Creator. James certainly gave an honest tithe himself, and felt certain that his successes had been largely due to the sure promise that the Creator had made to bless those who did this.

He did not need to refer to a Bible when giving these homilies, for he could quote at length from the Bible from memory and give chapter and verse for the quotations. Inevitably he became drawn into exchanges of correspondence with some ministers who did not remain silent in the face of his criticisms. He would point out the gross error they were preaching in certain areas and refer them to the relevant part of the Bible. He felt that there were a large number of very sincere religious people in the world, but that what they had been taught to believe was not in accordance with the simple messages of Jesus Christ as set out in the Bible. He made a point of studying all the different religions in order to be acquainted with what they taught and believed, but all of them, it seemed, had their failings, for most of what they preached was 'blasphemous error'. Like his knowledge of engineering, his religious knowledge was self-taught and he had developed it in his own way without the influence and discipline of a conventional education.

He felt particularly strongly on the subject of man's immortal soul and death. He would write: 'If man was born with an immortal soul, then those who had never repented of their sins would be kept alive for millions of years in some awful state of torment . . . Of course, such teaching is only of Satanic origin – it would make the Creator into a great monster.' He would continue: 'the dead know nothing and the idea that when we are dead we go to Heaven, of course, is nonsense. We will go after we have accepted Christ, at the last trump . . . Only then do we become immortal.' He regarded the Bible as a book of prophecy and his sermons would often conclude with the statement that the end of the world must surely be approaching. He would often say: 'I am quite clear in my own mind that we are living in the last days. All the evidence is there to prove it. You have only to look at the newspapers to see that this state of affairs is now happening . . . The whole earth today is full of upheaval and this will continue to increase at a great rate because people are no longer interested in the Commandments of God.'

He firmly believed that Freemasonry, to which so many people in industry seemed to belong, was 'only of the Devil', and indeed that any secret society, such as the Orange Order, was irreconcilable with the teachings of Jesus Christ. And such was his acceptance of what the Bible said that there was no room in his perception of life for ancient history, for as far as he was concerned there was nothing before Jesus Christ other than as told in the Bible. James would justify his beliefs by the assertion: 'This is not my opinion, it is all there to read in the Bible and the Bible's word is sure.' But for a practical engineer, who would accept nothing that he could not test by practical experiment, his own brand of the Christian faith, which accepted without any question what is written in the Bible, was in many ways extraordinary.

As in all other matters, James liked to be right in his interpretation of the Bible, and it was during these later years of his life that he took the time to expand and explore his already extensive knowledge of the Scriptures through detailed debate with others. One man whom he came to like and respect in particular was Pastor George Keough, a Seventh Day Adventist, who was a teacher at the Newbold College of Theology. In Pastor Keough he discovered a kindred spirit and someone whose knowledge of the Bible he came to value, and he would often send him letters from clergymen with whom he was corresponding to seek his views on how best to counter their apostate preachings.

He was still deeply interested in people, and it was not unusual for him to start corresponding with a total stranger if they had expressed some views that he wished to endorse or had done something that he approved of, and in some cases the correspondence would continue. He responded to a request for financial assistance from Miss Mathers, a lady who ran an orphanage in Southern Ireland. Although they never met, they kept in touch over the years, and the children in the orphanage would write to him with their news and thank him for his latest donation for their home. Another example was Miss Sally Alexander, a nurse from Ballymena, who wrote to him asking for a donation towards the cost of building the nurses a recreation hall. He sent her £200 but shortly afterwards the committee that had been set up to consider the building

of the recreation hall decided to abandon the idea. Miss Alexander wrote
to tell James this and offered to return his donation, but the mention of
a committee saying no was enough to settle the matter for James. He
told her to take no notice of the committee for they were always useless,
and to keep the money for he was sure that the nurses would get their hall
eventually. In due course it was built and James went to Ireland to open
it. In the meantime, James wrote frequently to check on progress, and
after their first meeting they kept in touch, and Miss Alexander would
sometimes visit England to stay with James and his wife.

James's generosity was by no means directed only at the Irish and he
was a regular contributor to a host of different British charities. When
approached for a contribution towards the cost of a new church hall for
the local church at Denham, he decided to take over the whole project.
He invited the architect to come and see him so that he could tell the
architect the kind of building he had in mind, and so that the architect
could amend his plans accordingly. He got involved in discussions on
all aspects of the job: drainage for the toilets, the number of windows
and the materials to be used, and the entire project was completed by
Martin-Baker men, sometimes to the detriment of other projects. He
was obviously concerned that there should be firm foundations, and it was
clear that some of the graves would have to be moved in order for the
hall to be built. Some people would have been somewhat disconcerted
by this prospect, but James was pragmatic. He told the vicar, the Reverend
Corr: 'we could very quickly dig these out, and the bones could be put
in sacks with a label on them so that these could be appropriated to the
particular headstones in another part of the churchyard'. When the time
came to excavate the graves, he was delighted by what he found. He
reported: 'the bones were in marvellous condition and, of course, due
to the work that I have done on ejection seats, I made a close examination
of their spines. It is simply fantastic that these bones, after 200 years,
have shown no signs of decay'. He took it upon himself to provide 20
tons of crazy paving for the paths leading to the hall because 'it is
imperative that there is no grit on any of the paths which lead into the hall
so that people's feet are clean when they get inside. I am having a sunken
mat placed inside the door as this will be useful'. As in all things that
James became involved in, if the job was worth doing, it had to be done
properly.

But interested though he was in religious debate, he would now also
take the time to write long letters on other matters which he considered
important, his favourite themes being the failings of politicians and the
wickedness of the taxation which they imposed, and the demise of
Britain's aircraft industry. The first was, of course, an old hobby horse
which still incensed him, and the second an increasing concern.

In general, he had no time for politicians, whom he put in a similar
category to civil servants. As he explained: 'Parliament seems to be
composed of two groups of people whose sole purpose is to try to belittle
each other, each side promising something which it knows full well it

cannot possibly do. Just vote catching of a pretty lousy low grade.' He denigrated the 'old school tie' system of education and the leaders that it purported to produce. 'But what sort of leader?' he would ask. 'Political leaders, Parliamentary leaders, not the ones that really want to do any hard graft, only the ones that have very little original thinking.' One notable exception was Margaret Thatcher.

He deplored high taxation, and regarded the surtax imposed by the Labour government in the sixties as nothing short of robbery, legalized by Act of Parliament, and indefensible on any grounds, socialist or otherwise. Such wanton behaviour could only be another indication that the end of the world was approaching. Estate duty also remained a major complaint. He wrote to many politicians, journalists and industrialists on this subject. As far as James was concerned, estate duty demonstrated the stupidity of politicians in failing to understand the debilitating effect of this tax which discouraged private companies from expanding their business and which, in many cases, resulted in private companies going bankrupt or being sold when estate duty became payable. He could not see the point of the government spending monies in the so-called distressed areas to create industry, only to single out private, profit-making companies for this penal taxation which could bankrupt them.

He regarded the rate of decline of the British aircraft industry as nothing less than tragic. He would reminisce about the days of the Spitfire and the Hurricane, when in his opinion Britain produced the best aeroplanes in the world, and would deplore the fact that by the mid-sixties, the country had nothing that could compete with the Phantom in terms of speed, range and weight-carrying capacity. He concluded that: 'due to a combination of gross muddling by M.O.A. and the firms themselves there will continue to be a further decline in the military field'.

James, of course, had close contacts with the aircraft firms because of the fitting of ejection seats to their aircraft, so his comments, although subjective, were not ill-informed. He castigated the aircraft firms for paying too much attention to the Ministry and thereby contributing to the decline of the British aircraft industry. Instead of keeping control of their companies and the aircraft they were designing, they looked to the government for free finance and therefore had to accept government specifications. He wrote:

> In point of fact they were indolent and they were milking an old cow called M.O.A. for years. Now the cow has decided there is no more milk, and they hold up their hands in horror! Over the years the firms collected enormous sums for so-called development work and built up grand palaces to live in and held conferences and talked about aeroplanes, but the goods never arrived – that is, goods better than anybody else's in the world.

He still believed in the merits of his MB5, and felt that if the Ministry had ordered only a few of these, Britain would not be buying American aircraft. He was critical of the design of many of the new generation of jet aircraft because they were so far removed from his ideas of simplicity and reliability. He wrote in the summer of 1968:

> This war in Vietnam has highlighted one feature of jet aircraft and that is they are extraordinarily vulnerable to small arms fire. The Viet Cong simply fill the air with machine gun bullets and let the 'planes fly through it. This is lethal due to the fact the whole aeroplane is a mass of wires, pipes, hydraulics and in their present form they cannot take much punishment from small arms fire.

The MB5 had only one small hydraulic operation and was what he called 'a good blacksmith job'. He added:

> the fact is that there are very few what I would call 'competent designers', that is a mixture of mechanical engineering and enough horse-sense with regard to aerodynamics. All this fatigue business that we read about is proof that the people on the design side are all amateurs. Who would think of making the front axle of a car or the springs out of light alloy! . . . The majority of designers today are not capable. They live in a world of computers and decimal points. They know everything except how to design aeroplanes.

James was still toying with the idea of designing a new aircraft. He had been very critical of the development of the TFX swing wing aircraft, a design concept which he had already considered and rejected. His latest idea, however, which demonstrated his desire to abandon the generally accepted laws of aerodynamics in the quest for some new, simpler design, as he had already demonstrated in the design of the MB2, would have attracted criticism itself, as he was the first to admit. When describing it he wrote:

> I am certain that the aerodynamic experts would laugh at my scheme. This would have a low aspect ratio, something like 35 foot chord by 8 foot span and a TC ratio of about three and a half per cent with the man and the cockpit in the fin and it would have three small engines with 4,500 lbs. of thrust each. Such a shape would, no doubt, have an exceedingly low drag and it would be possible to get a terrific performance. The problem would be, of course, that I would have to do a lot of experimental work in order to cope with low speed, that is landing, so you would not have to land with the nose cocked up in the air at about 30 degrees. This would necessitate some unusual changes in the wing shape to get air circulation to cope with landing.

Perhaps fortunately, this aircraft never got as far as the drawing board. He had also taken out a patent for a scheme whereby a rocket would be fitted to the rear portion of an aircraft which could, in the event of the aircraft getting into a stall condition, lift the tail up so that the aircraft could be brought under control again, but the authorities were not interested, even though James felt that it could have application for commercial airliners.

In 1963, James's attention turned to Chalgrove Airfield. Martin-Baker had been using the aerodrome intensively over the last 20 years. The surface of the runway was deteriorating quite quickly and needed resurfacing, but the Ministry refused to do this on the grounds that the airfield was redundant. James then asked them if they would sell it to him, and after a lot of bargaining about the price, a sale was agreed. At this point, James went ahead and got the runways reconditioned, several miles of 6 ft high chain-link perimeter fencing put up, the hangar reroofed and various other repairs done. Unfortunately, at that point Fifield flew too low over the house of one of the local residents in the Hunter, and upset the lady concerned quite considerably. She claimed to know a lot of people in government circles and said she would make sure that the aerodrome was not sold to Martin-Baker. She certainly did her best to carry out her threat and James was asked if he would accept a long lease at a low rental. James had several acrimonious meetings with government officials, threatened to have questions raised in the Houses of Parliament about it, and finally ended up with an audience with the Prime Minister, Sir Alec Douglas-Home. A secretary was in attendance with her shorthand notebook, and James told her that if she proposed to take down what he was going to say, her notebook would catch fire. He told her to put it away, which she did. In the 45 minutes that followed, James left Sir Alec in no doubt as to what he thought about the situation.

The matter seemed to have been satisfactorily resolved by the end of the meeting, but shortly afterwards, James received a polite and charming letter from Sir Alec setting out the terms of sale, which included the stipulation that Martin-Baker would sell the aerodrome back to the Air Ministry at the price of agricultural land prevailing at the time when they no longer required it for testing ejection seats. That was not part of the original agreement, and James wrote a forthright letter in reply saying that he would agree to sell it back only when they no longer required it, for the then prevailing price. James was upset and enraged by the government's handling of this matter, and wrote: 'I think it is fair to say that there are very few aircraft firms in England today who have given such long and faithful service to the R.A.F. and to be treated in this way, to say the least of it, causes one to lose confidence in anything to do with the Government.'

This year also saw a downturn in Martin-Baker's business by about 50 per cent. James was concerned about how to deal with this. It was difficult for him to cut back completely on the overtime being worked, because so many of his work-force had got used to spending the extra money they earned by the continual overtime of previous years and would have experienced financial difficulties if it had suddenly been stopped completely. But less work did not mean fewer problems.

His relationship with the Americans, while vital to the continued commercial success of Martin-Baker, was one which he found tiring.

They talked too much and carried around far too much paperwork. It seemed that he was always fighting with them about some issue or other, and that even after the major orders that were received by Martin-Baker in 1957, many Americans would still go to enormous pains to ensure that Martin-Baker equipment would not be installed in American aircraft.

In July 1964, when corresponding with Grumman Aircraft Engineering Corporation about modifications to the escape system for the Mohawk, he pointed out that

> no matter what we put up in the way of a modification or change, it is hardly ever accepted . . . It would appear to me that as far as any changes to our seat are concerned, it seems to be your policy to see if you can buy accessories from an outside firm and adapt them. Such a system, of course, is only a very amateurish way of trying to do the job.

He went on to cite various examples where his changes had only been accepted after an accident which would otherwise have been avoided, and other cases involving patent infringement. 'I would fall over backwards to give the US Navy any help in any way,' he said, 'but as things are at the moment it is impossible to give technical help because it is not wanted.'

His problems with the Ministry of Aviation were similar. He wrote:

> I only wish the powers that be would take my advice. I can remember a few years ago saying that our new visual top lock should be fitted. Nothing happened and they had to lose a few aeroplanes before the penny dropped. Over the years it has never been my policy to recommend any changes unless I have been absolutely certain that they will be effective.

The trouble of course was that James had no understanding of how other companies and government departments ran their business, and he would never accept that commercial considerations should play a part in deciding what changes to make to seats which were already in service. For James, the efficiency of the seat was not a commercial matter, and his customers continued to be frustrated by his changes to the seat, while he continued to be frustrated by their commercial approach to the job of saving lives.

In the summer of 1964, James went through what he described as 'one of the most trying ordeals I have ever had'. The situation arose from the sudden and unexpected demands of the US General Accounting Office. When Martin-Baker received the large orders for ejection seats in 1957, these orders were made by standardized official order contracts which included some stipulations that James would not accept, in particular a clause which empowered the US General Accounting Office to examine Martin-Baker's books. Following James's objections, he had received a written explanation from the Navy Purchasing Office in London to the effect that this clause would be invoked only if fraudulent or improper conduct was suspected, and on this basis, James accepted the clause.

He was greatly agitated, therefore, to receive a letter from the General Accounting Office informing him that unless he opened his books for them and allowed them to make a full inspection of all Martin-Baker's records, they would have no option but to instruct the US Navy to withhold payment of any outstanding accounts. James quickly drew their attention to the letter of 1957 and the General Accounting Office agreed that they would have to allow payment for the seats and parts delivered under the contracts which had already been placed. However, it still left James with the problem of accepting the clause in any future orders placed by the US Navy. The problem was succinctly described by James in a letter to Admiral Schoech of the Navy Department in Washington when he wrote:

> I think it is necessary for me to explain here that over all the years we have been making seats, or indeed any other equipment, no proper record has been kept of the cost of any particular item as such. We take an overall picture of the whole set-up. Some might make a loss and some make a substantial profit, but due to the enormous variety of bits and pieces, to set up a system which could identify the man hours and so forth would require an enormous staff and computing machines and goodness knows what. It is my policy to run the place economically with the minimum staff, and as long as the end product is satisfactory, this is all I care about.

James realized that he would have to agree to the establishment of a system which would make it possible to identify the production of US Navy seats and spares, and to isolate this from his other work, but it would obviously take some time to set up this system and, in the meantime, the Navy Purchasing Office in London had orders for spares and seats which were urgently required. James was frantic trying to think of a way around the problem in the short term and it was fortunate for all concerned that a US Navy representative, Spencer Robbins, thought up the idea of going to the British Ministry of Defence and operating through them until the proper systems could be established. James told Admiral Schoech that 'I feel so relieved that words fail to express how grateful I am to him for how efficiently he has been able to carry out this solution to what appeared to be an almost insolvable bottle-neck'. It had been made abundantly clear to James that the General Accounting Office would do absolutely nothing to help him in this situation. At this time, the orders from the US Navy accounted for over half of Martin-Baker's order book, and it would have been very damaging to its business if the US Navy order had been prejudiced. James was once again facing the dictates of an organization which had the power to thwart him. After so many years struggling against the British Establishment and securing for himself a virtually unassailable position in the British market, it would have been a cruel blow if his success had been largely wiped out by a foreign governmental agency.

James's position as a defence contractor within the United Kingdom was in many ways unique. Because he was the only British supplier of ejection seats, and because there was no alternative foreign supplier, the Ministry was stuck with James, his refusal to accept development contracts, his refusal to co-operate with them, and indeed his total independence as regards the development of the ejection seat. James was only too well aware of this, for in his own words: 'We just ignore the MOA as if they have never existed. We do not take the slightest notice of them in any shape or form, and as the result, we are free to do what we like and carry out all sorts of tests.' When commenting on the fact that he did not accept development contracts, he would explain that if he did, 'a lot of amateurs would come down from MOA to advise us what to do and write out specifications of something which they know nothing about'.

In the early summer of 1964, questions were asked in the House of Lords about ejection seats for V-bombers. The debate suggested that the cost of a seat for each man would be between £20,000 and £50,000 and the retrofit programme would take from three to five years. When Sir Sydney Camm raised the question with James, James was typically forthright in his response. He said:

> The only idea of quoting these times and prices is to once and for all get rid of any further questions being asked. It is more expedient to kill crew members than it is to become involved in saving their lives. If a determined effort were made by your people to make a hole in the roof and put a strengthening ring around it, I should think you could do three or four fuselages a week. You have plenty of surplus capacity and supplying the seats would be no problem to us. The price then would be only about £2000 per seat.

The debate in the House of Lords, instigated by James, followed the crash of a Vulcan B2 which became uncontrollable while coming in to land and went into a spin. The pilot and co-pilot, Mr Hawkins and Flt. Lt. Beeson, ejected at very low altitude and survived, but the rear crew members had no chance. Since Hay's rearward-facing test ejection in July 1960, James's information indicated that 14 rear crew members had lost their lives in V-bomber crashes. On 22 March 1962, control of a Victor B2 was lost during a stall investigation, and the aircraft entered a spin at 14,000 ft from which it would not recover. The pilots, Mr P. (Spud) Murphy and Flt. Lt. J. Waterton, ejected at below 1,000 ft but two of the three rear crew members failed to leave the aircraft and were killed. Three further crashes that year claimed the lives of another six rear crew members, and another tragedy occurred on 20 March 1963 when control of a Victor B2 was lost and the aircraft entered a spin at between 4,000 and 5,000 ft. The rear crew members were unable to open the escape hatch. The pilot could hear them shouting over the intercom that they could not get out. He ordered the co-pilot, Flt. Lt. Jackson, to eject so that one of them at least would survive to tell the world what had happened, and the pilot continued battling with the aircraft and died with the rear crew members. James was still convinced that it was possible to provide ejection seats for rear crew members, but he was unfortunately too heavily involved with other projects then, including the escape system for the TSR2, to develop his ideas any further.

It was 1968, following another crash, when the problem once more became the focus of James's attention. On 30 January 1968, a Vulcan B2 aircraft crashed near the end of the runway during circuit and bump trials, killing four crew members in the back who were burnt to death. James felt that this time he would have to take some action, and he telephoned Air Chief Marshal Sir Wallace Kyle to tell him, in his usual blunt fashion, that he was rather disturbed to hear that the RAF were flying portable crematoriums. Air Chief Marshal Kyle asked if he could meet with him, and at the meeting the next day James told him that he thought it would be possible to retrofit ejection seats for rear crew members. James asked to see a Vulcan in operational condition with all the equipment inside, to check up on the space available, and he was taken to RAF Finningley to see one. James then told Kyle that if he was given a Vulcan fuselage he would fit an escape system for the rear crew members free and for nothing, and a damaged Vulcan fuselage was duly delivered to Denham. James made it quite clear that as he would be making no charge for producing a retrofit system for demonstration, he did not want any interference from the Ministry or anybody else and that if they did not like it, that would be their concern, but he would guarantee that it would work.

He was therefore rather irritated when, two days after the fuselage arrived, he was being asked how the job was progressing, an enquiry which he received regularly throughout the course of the work. Having ignored the issue for some 11 years, the Ministry of Technology now regarded the matter as one of some urgency if they were to be able to obtain the most useful advantage from this retrofit in the course of the remainder of the Vulcan's life.

Some months later James received a letter from the Chief Security Officer at Hawker Siddeley Aviation Limited, who were involved with James's retrofit plans as the manufacturer of the Vulcan, telling him that they were treating the matter as 'Company Confidential' and no doubt he would wish to do likewise, and that the Ministry of Technology had classified the work as 'Restricted'. As James had taken the initiative in suggesting that he undertake this work, and had agreed do it free of charge, he was more than a little irritated by the letter. He replied:

I have no contract for the job, either from the Ministry of Technology or from your Company, so I am afraid that under the circumstances it is rather absurd to ask us to treat this as "Restricted" and "Company Confidential". I can assure you, however, that we shall not disclose to the Press any work that we are doing on it. We have never sought newspaper publicity with regard to our work. All I am concerned about is providing a practical system which can be fitted to the Vulcan at a reasonable price.

James faced significant problems in completing this task. He himself said that it would tax his ingenuity to the utmost. The problem was not the fitting of the seats, but the fact that there was no hole in the top of the pressurized fuselage for the seats to eject through. He had to cut a hole in the top of the fuselage and then restore the fuselage strength to what it was prior to the change. The ejection process was not straightforward either. Firstly, the main canopy was jettisoned, which automatically jettisoned the hatch, and when that was clear of the ejection path of the seat, the centre seat ejected, followed by one side seat and then the second side seat, both of which had to tilt so that they could eject through the hatch opening above the centre seat. The sequence of ejections had to be automatically controlled so as to avoid the seats colliding with each other, and James also provided for the shoulder harnesses to be pulled back automatically by power reels so that the occupant of each seat was held back before ejection.

In September 1969 the seats were ready. James gave a demonstration of the system at Chalgrove Airfield. A crowd of RAF officers and Ministry officials were taken out to the middle of the airfield and the three seats were ejected in three seconds, and all came down on fully developed parachutes. As James recalled: 'There was a great silence from all concerned because they were the people who said it was not possible for ejection seats to be fitted for the other crew members in this aircraft . . . It will be interesting to see the outcome.' The outcome was very disappointing. Although James was told that his private venture effort was very much appreciated, the decision was made not to accept James's scheme, and the Vulcan flew for the rest of its operational life with only two ejection seats, a state of affairs which James continued to regard as criminal. There was, however, nothing further that he could do about it.

Meanwhile, the main work at Martin-Baker was progressing well. By the end of 1964, the company had completed nearly 500 rocket tests under all conceivable conditions. James felt that his rocket seat was 'the biggest step forward we have made in the escape system for a long time'. As well as increasing the escape envelope, the rocket seats also led to a dramatic decrease in the number of back injuries among ejectees, for it was possible, with the rocket pack fitted, to reduce the thrust from the ejection gun.

The first emergency use of a Martin-Baker rocket-assisted seat came on 14 September 1964 when George Bright, an American test pilot employed by EWR-Süd in Germany, ejected from a VJ-101C aircraft. He began a conventional take-off but lost control as soon as the aircraft left the ground when it began a violent left-hand roll. After rolling through 320°, he ejected by using the seat pan handle. This ejection took place in extreme conditions. The aircraft's nose was elevated 18°, it was yawing

17° and the starboard wing tip was only 10 ft above the runway. Nevertheless, the ejection was successful and Mr Bright survived with only minor injuries.

In 1964 James was awarded the Royal Aero Club Gold Medal for his work on ejection seats, and the next year, Martin-Baker held their second large celebration, another dinner dance at the Dorchester Hotel, to celebrate 1,000 lives saved by the Martin-Baker ejection seat. The ejectees presented James with a portrait of himself in oils painted by Mr Howard Barron. The portrait is a very good one, but had to be painted largely from photographs as James's ability to sit still for the artist was limited to periods of a few minutes.

The following year, James was made a Knight Batchelor. He was delighted to receive this honour. He said very little about it, but as his son John remarked, that was a sure sign that he was pleased, because he never wasted any time in making his views known when he was not pleased! He received many letters of congratulations which he collected together in two albums. For a farmer's son from County Down, it was enormously satisfying that the powers-that-be, against whom he had battled so often, considered that his successes deserved a knighthood, although it took him some time to accept that his employees were not poking fun at him when they addressed him as 'Sir James'.

By this time, James was appearing in publications such as *Who's Who*. When advising them of his knighthood, he also requested them to omit his date of birth from his entry. Most people would have been proud to have his energy and output at 73, but James did not want to admit to that age.

In early 1965 news arrived from Australia of a fast escape out of a Mirage by S/L I.A.G. Svensson, an RAF pilot on exchange with the Royal Australian Air Force. He had been completing some engine performance trials when the aircraft inadvertently entered a descending spin, and his recovery attempts were unsuccessful. With the nose down and spinning, he ejected at 720 knots, the fastest speed on record for an ejection with a Martin-Baker seat. He unfortunately fractured both his legs and suffered pelvic and groin dislocations, but this was due to the fact that the RAAF had not followed Martin-Baker instructions about crossing the leg lines. James was delighted by this fast escape and particularly interested by the fact that the pilot did not suffer body injuries due to blast on leaving the aircraft. James calculated that he would have been travelling at about 1,120 ft/sec and that the blast pressure would have been about 1,640 lb/sq ft, and he wrote to Svensson to say: 'In the past I have read many reports by so called medical experts limiting the speed at which it would be possible to eject and live and so you are living testimony to the fact that all their estimates are sheer nonsense.'

In 1965 a large programme of evaluation and testing of the Martin-Baker rocket seat was undertaken in America, in particular using the high-speed rocket sled track at China Lake, following which the US Navy decided to fit Martin-Baker rocket seats in their Crusader, Intruder and

Phantom aircraft by modifying the Mark 5 seats already in service and ordering rocket seats for new aircraft. Another large order followed when the US Air Force decided to modify the seats in their Phantoms as well.

That year too, the German Air Ministry asked James if he could supply a rocket seat which could cope with zero/zero conditions, on the level and at an angle of 30°. The Germans had already acquired some Lockheed F-104s fitted with rockets with sufficient power to lift them into the air and keep them there until they reached flying speed. James completed some successful tests in England using an F-104 fuselage, but the Germans asked for a demonstration in Germany. James wrote: 'the first shot was perfect, but the second shot was a flop and the cause was so ridiculous that I was most upset'. The rocket was supposed to be fired by a static line just before the end of the gun stroke. The static line had a fitting which attached to the rocket motor by a rivet which sheared at about 200 lb. As James explained: 'some fool in the Experimental Shop put in a high-tensile steel rivet which has a shear value of about 800 lbs. The net result was that the cable was not designed for taking this load and the cable broke and the rocket motor did not fire'.

The Germans accepted that it was an unfortunate mistake and not a design fault, and James arranged a repeat shot. Unfortunately, on that occasion the override handle on the right-hand side of the seat pan fouled the canopy lever handle on the side of the cockpit, damaged the side of the seat pan, and pitched the seat in the wrong direction so that it hit the ground just as the parachute was opening. In a letter to Bill Bedford, James wrote:

I only mention this to tell you what a tiresome business some of these rocket tests can be – not due to any fault of the rocket motor, but a combination of circumstances. It was lack of supervision, I suppose, and also we ought to have checked the clearance on the handle to see that there was adequate clearance, but like all these one-off jobs you have to learn the hard way – I can assure you I was most upset.

Although often criticized for his perfectionist approach and the constant changes that he made, these tests demonstrated how inattention to detail could be disastrous, and how even the smallest oversight would mean death if the seat ever had to be used in an emergency.

Despite these unfortunate incidents, the series of tests completed later successfully demonstrated the superiority of the Martin-Baker seat, and the Germans specified the Mark 7 seat for retrofit in their Lockheed F-104s. This marked the culmination of a protracted and often acrimonious debate, much of it conducted publicly, about the respective merits of the Martin-Baker seat and the Lockheed C-2 seat already installed in the German F-104s. In the summer of 1959, the German Ministry of Defence had stated their preference for a Martin-Baker seat for their new F-104s rather than the Lockheed seat, and James had agreed to develop a version of the Mark 5 seat, which the Germans had already accepted for retrofit in the F84F, RF84F, T-33, Sabre 6 and F86K, for the F-104. Lockheed were understandably hostile to this suggestion and made great efforts to persuade the Germans to accept their C-2 seat and to promote the problems, which they maintained were insurmountable, of installing a Martin-Baker seat into an aircraft which had not been designed to take it. Lockheed, however, were forced to place a development order with Martin-Baker and the prototype seat was successfully tested by Lockheed up to a speed of 700 knots on their sled test facility. An order for production seats was placed but, during the flight trials of the aircraft, the Lockheed pilots made complaints about the Martin-Baker seat in relation to the sitting position, proximity to the instrument panel and the accessibility of certain instruments. Martin-Baker presented proposals to overcome these problems which Lockheed confirmed in February 1961 would remedy the complaints, but at a further meeting in March of that year to discuss the Martin-Baker proposals and the alternative Lockheed proposal to reinstall the Lockheed seat which they had originally offered for this aircraft, the committee expressed no interest in seeing the modified Martin-Baker seat. The C-2 seat was installed instead and the order with Martin-Baker was cancelled even though delivery of seats had already commenced.

A very public debate about this decision took place over the ensuing years, fuelled by inaccurate and derogatory comments about the Martin-Baker seat which outraged James and which he insisted should be corrected, and by the number of fatalities arising from the use of the C-2 seat. With the introduction of rocket motors, the Mark 5 seat could now be upgraded. By that time the performance of the Martin-Baker rocket seats had been verified by their extensive test programme and by the first emergency ejections using them, and the decision to retrofit the German F-104s was announced in March 1967. It was another notable success for Martin-Baker, but its importance to James lay in the fact that attempts by third parties to denigrate his escape system and thereby prejudice the reputation of his company had failed, and had failed in a public and spectacular fashion.

His problems with the Germans were not quite over, however. In 1968, the German authorities complained that Martin-Baker had removed the g switch from a test seat without prior consultation with them. It was explained to them that this action was based on sound technical considerations and on an adequate background of previous research and test, and James wrote to them to say:

As the Managing Director and Chief Designer of my Company I do not exercise nominal functions but personally and constantly initiate, control and supervise all design work. So far as escape systems are concerned I have been doing this for twenty-five years during which time the sole criteria I have applied has been not commercial advantage or production gain but the improvement of the escape envelope.

His attitude in this respect was exceptional.

An examination of the circumstances surrounding unsuccessful ejections indicated quite clearly to James the area in which even the rocket seat could be improved, and that was where the aircraft was nose-down at low altitude. Notwithstanding the fact that the rocket seat had zero/zero capability, this was not always sufficient where an aircraft was in a high-speed dive at low altitude, for in these circumstances, the ejected seat follows the same glide path as the aeroplane. No test on a sled running horizontally could reproduce those conditions and it was obviously not possible to conduct airborne tests in these circumstances.

James therefore designed an inclined rocket track, the first of its kind in the world. This rig consisted of a 200 ft long track, supported at one end by an 80 ft high tower so that it was inclined at an angle of approximately 20°. The total assembly was welded together *in situ* on a concrete base and levelled up accurately for straightness in two planes. High-tensile flexible cables were attached from the top of the tower to blocks of concrete in the ground, and stressed to allow for a wind load of up to 100 mph. The ground portion of the track rested on a special fitting which allowed for expansion of the ramp from below freezing up to 100°F in order that the vertical portion of the tower was not subject to bending loads due to expansion or contraction of the main track. A small sled with a rocket was mounted on the track, and the seat to be tested was installed on this sled which was then winched to the top of the tower. The sled was then propelled by its rocket down the sled and the seat ejected from it at a predetermined point. This enabled Martin-Baker to conduct very realistic tests for the nose-down, low-altitude situation for a speed of about 100 mph and a sink rate of 60 ft/sec.

With the rocket seat, James soon realized that where there was more than one member of the aircrew, it would be necessary for the pilot to be able to initiate the ejection of all of them if the advantages of the rocket seat were to be realized fully. The usual procedure was for the pilot to order his crew member to eject before ejecting himself, a procedure which wasted valuable seconds and which could in some cases cost the life of one or both of the crew. James therefore designed a command control system operated by the pilot pulling a lever, whereupon the aircrew were ejected in a predetermined sequence.

James began developing this command control system when he was designing a special seat for the TSR2, a new aircraft being developed by the British Aircraft Corporation, which became known as the Mark 8 seat. James applied a lot of new thinking to the design of this seat which incorporated not only the command system of ejection and an arm restraint system, but also a new power retraction system for tightening up the top harness and restraining the head immediately prior to ejection. The optimum position for ejection remained the upright position with the back straight and the vertebrae square to each other, and James decided when designing the Mark 8 seat to introduce a mechanical means of ensuring that the ejectee was in the correct position prior to ejection. This was worth a great deal, in particular when the aircraft was spinning, as there had been cases where the pilot had been forward of the axis of the spin and had been unable to sit back in the seat. James's power retraction system consisted of two straps attached to the shoulder straps of the harness, each strap being wound round a reel capable of being rotated under power in order to pull back the shoulders of the seat occupant. The power for the retraction system was a cartridge, the firing of which was linked to the seat firing handle. The system allowed the seat occupant complete freedom of movement, the straps pulling out of the unit as he moved forward and retracting on the spring-loaded reels as he moved back, unless high g forces were applied, in which case the system locked until the g forces were reduced. The Mark 8 seat, with these new features, was the most advanced ejection seat available at that time, and James was disappointed when the TSR2 was cancelled in 1965 because he had spent an enormous amount of time and money in designing the seat, and his contract covered only the supply of a certain number of seats and left him completely uncovered for the cost of the design and development work. This development work was not however wasted, for some of the new design features were later incorporated in other seats.

One of the problems that James still faced was the fitting of pieces of equipment made by other companies to his seat. It was a practice which upset James greatly because, while he could not be held responsible for someone else's equipment, these additional items in some cases adversely affected the performance of the seat for which, of course, he was solely responsible. One example of this was the pararaft. For some time RAF Buccaneer crews sat on a soft pararaft pack which was not of Martin-Baker design. This could result in back injuries for ejectees because the soft pararaft pack was compressed by the thrust of the ejection gun, which had the effect of slackening the pilot's lap belt, which in turn could cause the pilot to slide forward in the seat at the critical moment of ejection and to have a curved spine as he ejected. These pararaft packs were eventually replaced by the Martin-Baker hard-shell type pararaft.

Another example was the fitting by McDonnell of an American-designed, ballistically controlled shoulder harness reel instead of James's design. The American-designed reel was not always satisfactory, and of course if the seat occupant was not properly restrained, the rocket seat would spin as his movement changed the centre of gravity of the ejected mass, sometimes with disastrous results. The incorporation of a new reel amounted to a change in the seat as far as James was concerned, and any change needed to be thoroughly tested. It was still the case that Martin-Baker's insistence on comprehensive and repeated testing was a crucial element in their ability to produce a reliable ejection seat. In writing to the US Navy on the subject of this reel, James said:

I am most cautious about making any changes to the seat except those that have been well tested out and I feel these changes are a hazard. To assume that a couple more high speed tests would prove a system is, of course, nonsense when one considers the very large number of tests that we do over a wide range to test repeatability.

He pointed out that to fit other equipment to the Martin-Baker seat was like asking McDonnell to fit another manufacturer's tailplane to one of their aircraft. In 1968 he was invited to attend a meeting in America to discuss the shortcomings of the American system. James felt sure that he had been invited to this conference by the US Navy because they had no-one who had the necessary technical knowledge to criticize the American reel. James was quickly bored in large meetings, and thought that the discussion process was a waste of time, particularly as he usually felt that he knew the answer. Eventually he was asked to say his piece and as he reported:

> Normally I hate to be involved in acrimonious and useless discussions but when one is very familiar with the set up one can say an awful lot with a few carefully chosen words. Well, there was a great silence after I had said my piece and everyone just sat there and looked at each other so I said, "is this a prayer meeting?" and I just got up and walked out so that was the end of the meeting.

He then took the next available flight back to England. The Martin-Baker reel subsequently replaced the American reel.

James had never enjoyed travelling and being away from home. He found it very tiring, and he disliked staying in hotels which he found depressing and extremely inconvenient as he was not able to eat what he wanted at the times that he wanted. He was a difficult person to travel with because he was never satisfied with the hotel he was in. If it was too comfortable then he felt ill at ease in the plush surroundings and irritated at the amount of money it was costing, but on the other hand, if it was not comfortable enough, he would refuse to stay there. He never slept well abroad, particularly when a time change was involved, and got bored with nothing to do when he was unable to sleep. Those travelling with him knew that they would probably be awakened at some uncivilized hour in the morning and summoned to his room because he wanted someone to talk to. At the end of a long day, or on the flight home, the trick was making sure that someone else sat next to him, because James would always order Coca-Cola to drink, and insist that whoever was sitting next to him had one too. If you wanted something stronger, you had to sit out of earshot.

He added to his discomfort abroad by refusing to make any concessions about what he wore. Winter and summer, and wherever in the world he happened to be, he wore a thick suit and waistcoat. On one of the very rare occasions when he took a few days' holiday and visited his old friend Frank Francis in the Bahamas on his way back from one of his trips to America, he caused much amusement to Francis and his family by his insistence on wearing this formal attire when everyone else was in shorts and T-shirts. But this habit of his would sometimes worry those he was with, and on exacting business trips in hot weather, they would have to think of excuses to divert him from wherever he was to somewhere where it was air-conditioned.

Much of the travelling, particularly in the early days of the ejection seat, he did himself because the ejection seat was his design and he did not want anyone to think otherwise. Never good at delegating, he did not readily delegate the visits to his customers. But it was a double-edged sword, for if he visited his foreign customers and satisfied himself that he was in full control of that relationship, he had inevitably to be away from Denham, which he hated.

It was now some ten years since James had had the opportunity to reconsider the general design of the seat as he had done with the Mark 4 seat, and it had now become quite complex. Following the cancellation of the TSR2, James decided to draw on the experience he had gained in designing the Mark 8 seat and design a new, less complicated but more efficient rocket seat. He retained many of the features of earlier seats such as the ejection gun and guide rail, the barostat time release unit, the drogue gun and the personal equipment connector, but he made considerable changes to the general seat structure, the drogue container, the parachute and the seat pan. This new seat became known as the Mark 9 seat and was fitted in the Harrier and the Jaguar. This approach was typical of James. While he would incorporate endless modifications to existing seats in his quest for perfection, he did not believe in change for change's sake, and saw no need to redesign successful components. He wrote:

> It would be fair to say that we do more genuine research and development work than anybody in the world today. People may say our seats are old-fashioned, they are this and that, but the only thing that matters is how many lives do they save. If you introduce a completely new seat, it will take some years to get all the bugs out of it and any malfunction means a fatality, so I feel that it is sometimes better to stick to a well tried piece of mechanism that has proved reliable over a long period of time.

James was still concerned about the dangers of VTOL aircraft and during 1966 was developing a new rocket motor to cater for the potential of a high sink rate and no forward speed. The existing rocket motor could only cope with a sink rate of about 30 ft/sec. If engine failure occurred while hovering at low level then the pilot had hardly any time to eject. James decided therefore that the seat must be able to cope with a sink rate of 100 ft/sec to give pilots a more realistic chance of survival. The existing motor for conventional aircraft gave a thrust of about 6,000 lb for 0.24 of a second, and had an explosive charge of $1\frac{1}{8}$ in diameter. The rocket motor which he developed for the Harrier had an explosive charge which was 2 in in diameter and this gave a thrust of 6,000 lb for half a second.

But increasing the burning time of the motor had other implications, namely coping with changes in the centre of gravity of the seat and its occupant caused by differences in the weights of pilots and the height of the seat pan. For the smaller rocket motor, James had designed a scheme whereby the centre of gravity changes consequent upon the seat pan being moved up or down were dealt with automatically on the basis of a light, medium and heavy man. But this basic scheme did not work with the larger rocket motor and the longer burning time, and it proved quite impossible to control the trajectory of the seat with it in tests. He therefore devised a pitch control device consisting of a knob on the side of the seat pan which, when revolved, turned a screw which rocked the rocket motor about its axis. When the knob was turned, different weights appeared on an indicator and the pilot merely selected the weight corresponding to his own weight in flying gear.

Even with this new rocket motor, James considered VTOL aircraft to be 'extraordinarily lethal'. Hawker Siddeley had complained that the bigger rocket motor was compromising the space available for the pararaft to take the full desert survival pack. James delivered his usual homily on the inherent dangers of VTOL aircraft and concluded that: 'it does not seem to have dawned on the Air Force, or anyone else, how lethal these aeroplanes can be in the event of loss of engine power at an awkward height. So therefore it is far more important to have an escape system that can cope with the most difficult conditions than to be able to carry full desert survival packs'.

James also introduced in the Mark 9 seat an improved method of firing the rockets. In previous designs, the rocket had been fired by a static line withdrawing a sear from a sear-operated firing unit on the rocket, a method which had not been totally satisfactory because of the possibility of the static line being damaged. James introduced a remote firing system, consisting of a firing unit mounted high up on the seat in which the static line is contained and protected. As the seat leaves the aircraft, the static line is withdrawn, pulls taut and removes the sear to fire the cartridge in the remote firing unit. The gas pressure produced is delivered to a gas-operated firing unit in the rocket which fires and ignites the rocket propellant.

During the course of 1967, tests with the new rocket motor were proving successful. They were spectacular, too, as the seat was climbing at over 200 mph by the time the rocket motor had burned out, and it could propel the seat up to about 450 ft with the parachute fully developed at that point. James had to redesign the seat pan, however, as it became clear that stiffness rather than strength was the requirement for the rocket seat. With the high thrust of the bigger rocket motor, it was possible to distort the seat pan 2° or 3°, which had a serious effect on the trajectory of the ejecting seat.

The design of the Mark 9 seat for the Harrier was often problematical and the completion of the design took several years and sometimes strained the relationship between James and Hawker Siddeley. On one occasion, Mr John Fozard, the chief designer of the Harrier, wrote to James to say that he was pleased that James was working to eliminate the severe criticisms made by the US Marine Corps Evaluation Team of the seat harnessing arrangements. James replied bluntly: 'the fact is we are not working on it'. James had intended to fit the Mark 9 seat with a torso harness and a mock-up and prototype seats had been supplied to Hawker in 1966, but as James pointed out:

> We were overruled by all sorts of people and we reluctantly fitted the combined parachute and seat harness, which I think is simply awful but you were advised by the experts. It is cumbersome, unnecessarily complicated and just a mess. So the present situation falls entirely in the lap of Hawkers and Co. through being forced by various so-called experts to fit the harness which we were opposed to.

The seat had to be modified to take a revised harness arrangement, which was quite a major job.

Time, however, was slipping by, and whatever the reasons for the delay, the Mark 9 seat was still not available. By the end of 1967 Hawker were becoming extremely concerned, particularly after they missed flying their first production Harrier on time on account of the seat which at that time suffered from two problems, namely the candling of the parachute and the shape of the seat back. They felt it might take some time to get the Mark 9 seat to a satisfactory standard and in the meantime they were trying to produce production aircraft with the wrong seat fitted.

James understood that they were 'tearing their hair out' at not being able to get their hands on a Mark 9 seat but, as ever, the seat was not going to leave Denham until he was happy with it, particularly as no-one had asked him to improve the performance of the Mark 6 seat or to design the Mark 9 seat. In early 1968 he changed from straight to angled jets so that in the case of the two-seater version, if the pilot ejected first the back-seater would be protected from the jets. He wrote to Bill Bedford: 'Your people at Kingston just have no idea the enormous thrust there is from these rocket motors and I certainly take jolly good care that we do not kill anyone.'

By the middle of 1968, Hawker Siddeley felt that their flight programme would inevitably be delayed unless Martin-Baker could lend them some Mark 6 seats pending availability of the Mark 9 seats. But by March 1969, James had carried out 150 tests on the Mark 9 seat, proving the seat to be reliable and very consistent in its performance, and the seat was eventually made available.

Chapter Thirteen

The Best Seat

In the summer of 1968, news arrived of another successful ejection in Vietnam. On this occasion, 28 April 1968, an F-4 Phantom piloted by Lt. Cdr. Duke Hernandez, with Lt. David Lortscher in the back seat, was on a strike mission in North Vietnam. The aircraft was hit by anti-aircraft fire while in a dive-bombing attack. The pilot secured the port engine immediately but a fire persisted. He used the remaining engine to climb to 9,000 ft, but by that stage they had also lost the utility hydraulics, the generators and had a fire warning on the remaining engine. They were now several miles out to sea and elected to eject. The ejection was successful and they were not long in the water before being rescued by helicopter. James was always pleased to hear about another successful escape, but there was no reason to suppose that this one was in any way significant.

Two years later, however, on 14 September 1970, Lt. Lortscher had to eject again. This time he ejected at 1,500 ft and 250 knots, west of San Diego from an F-4J, following an engine flame-out due to lack of fuel. The ejection was uneventful and he received no injuries.

Almost exactly a year later, on 22 September 1971, he ejected for the third time, again west of San Diego, from 23,000 ft and approximately 400 knots after the pilot's canopy had inadvertently separated from the aircraft. Lortscher looked up both sides of the front cockpit but could not see the pilot and, assuming that the pilot had ejected, he ejected himself. Again, the ejection was uneventful and he received no injuries, but he became only the third man to have ejected in a Martin-Baker seat three times.

However, on 15 October 1973, he created a new record. He ejected at between 300 and 500 feet and approximately 250 knots, three miles north of RAF Leuchars, following a double engine flame-out. He landed hard in the middle of a dried-up loch, and blacked out momentarily from the pain of the impact. He was somewhat dazed and disorientated, a state of mind which was not helped by two woodcutters who ran up and insisted on trying to help him, but he shortly regained his faculties, stood up and was able to walk to the rescue helicopter. His was an extraordinary experience that has not since been equalled.

The American involvement in the Vietnam conflict had, of course, resulted in a huge increase in the use of the seat, and James received a continual flow of letters from the ejectees, sometimes after several years of captivity. There were many spectacular ejections, but one that particularly interested James was the escape by Lt. Col. Harry Hagaman and his navigator of the US Marine Corps from a Phantom. The aircraft was carrying napalm bombs, and when it was struck by anti-aircraft fire, the bombs blew up, blowing off the wings, engines and tail of the aircraft and leaving the two aircrew falling through the sky in the front part of the fuselage only. In spite of this, the two men ejected successfully with no injuries and were picked up by helicopter shortly afterwards. Some years later, when Hagaman had a two-year tour of duty in England, he came to meet James and was invited to Southlands Manor for dinner. He had been warned that James had the unusual habit of writing his guest's name on the back of his hand with a felt-tip pen and was not, therefore, surprised to be met by James with his head down trying to decipher his own handwriting.

The Vietnam War had identified several unforeseen problems for aircrew, one being the danger of the parachute becoming entangled in tree branches following an ejection over the jungle, leaving the ejectee dangling helplessly in the treetops. James designed a simple system, worn as part of the aircrew equipment and requiring no modification to standard flying clothing, which incorporated a friction device with five rollers and a length of nylon tape which can be wrapped round the branch of a tree, enabling the ejectee to make a controlled descent to the ground. The war also brought to James's attention the need for an escape system for helicopters, and in 1966 he started work on a new type of ejection seat for helicopters. It was a new and intriguing problem for James. As he said: 'It is quite a tricky business on account of the fact that the blades are flying around above your head so I propose to shoot the seat out at right angles, that is sideways, and then a rocket motor tips the seat round and it will climb vertically.' His ideas never got beyond the drawing board, however, even when he considered blowing off the rotor blades to facilitate a normal upward ejection, because no-one was particularly interested. He even offered to design a seat and demonstrate it for no charge, but still no interest was shown.

In September 1970, His Royal Highness the Prince of Wales visited James at the Martin-Baker stand at the Farnborough Air Show and spent some time discussing the ejection seat with him. The Prince was shortly to start training with the RAF in a Jet Provost, and James told him that his seat would be fitted with a rocket motor with the dial control and explained to him how this would work. The Prince replied that he hoped he would not have to use it, and James was quick to respond: 'I hope you do. It will work O.K.' James, however, had no authority to tell him that his seat would have a rocket motor as Jet Provosts were fitted with cartridge seats. According to the information given to Martin-Baker, there had been a total of 57 ejections out of Jet Provosts, of which 54 had been successful and the remaining three had ended in fatalities. Of these three, James believed that a rocket motor would have saved two of them. In the third case the aircraft was nearly upside down and near the ground at the time of ejection so the rocket motor would have made no difference. But he considered it imperative that the heir to the throne be given the best possible escape system, and that a rocket seat, which greatly reduced the chances of back injury, was essential.

In 1965, James had been asked to put up a proposal for a rocket motor for the Jet Provost seat, but the Ministry had subsequently decided that, due to the high success rate of the existing cartridge seat, the addition of a rocket motor was unnecessary. James had received that decision with his usual contempt. He often remarked that if those people who made the decisions had to ride the seat, then they would come to some very different conclusions about what modifications were worth paying for. However, when James realized that the Prince of Wales would be flying a Jet Provost he decided, on his own initiative and at his own expense, to fit a rocket motor to this seat, and then conducted 20 tests of the modified seat, all of which were very satisfactory. These tests were witnessed by representatives of Boscombe Down, but nevertheless the Ministry decided against the modifications. James was astounded.

It was becoming difficult for Martin-Baker to conduct the increasing number of high-speed tests of the rocket seat that James felt were necessary as his development work progressed. James disliked high-speed airborne tests because of the dangers to the test pilot flying the aircraft, and the top speed for tests out of the Hunter was in any event only 600 mph. There was a small test track at Pendine in Wales, and two larger and faster test tracks in America, but it was costly and inconvenient to take seats to these tracks for testing, and it also prevented James from following his usual policy of secrecy about what he was doing. James realized that the time had come for him to have his own test track. He said:

> By having our own track we can do our own development work and no-one knows what our problems have been and how we overcome them . . . These tests that we did at Pendine and elsewhere were put on record for the world to read at a later date and so over the years I have found that it pays to spend one's own money and then no-one has any idea of what we have been doing.

The track was constructed at Langford Lodge in Northern Ireland. It was 6,000 ft long, and its construction was as exacting as the building of an ejection seat, for the tracks had to be dead straight in two planes so that they did not vary more than one-sixteenth of an inch in the 6,000 ft. Typically, this job was carried out by Martin-Baker and not by outside contractors. It took nearly two and a half years to build and was completed in 1970. The foundation was made of thousands of tons of quarried stones which were rolled in, and then a concrete base was cast the full length of the track with expansion joints.

For the track itself, the rails were welded together and stretched by hydraulic jacks so that they are always in a state of tension and machined off at the welds. The track is held down by thousands of steel sleepers which had to be skimmed to make the track exceedingly level, and James designed a special machine for grinding the rails *in situ*. Markers were fitted every 50 ft which send out electronic signals to a receiving station some distance away which record precisely the speed of the sled as it travels down the track. James designed various sleds which are mounted on the rails and then propelled by rockets down the track, and stopped by a water brake which throws up a spout of water some 150 ft into the air. Depending on the speed required, a number of rockets are used, each giving a thrust of 7,500 lb for two seconds. Then sustaining rockets take over to keep the sled going at a steady speed for a fraction of a second during the ejection of the seat. It is a spectacular piece of equipment and as a private test facility it is unique. James was thrilled to watch the first demonstration run on the new track. He wrote to Francis to tell him: 'It is an alarming sight to see the sled go up to 1,000 feet per second in two seconds and then stop it.'

Meanwhile, James was still embroiled in patent disputes with the American authorities. He fully appreciated the large body of opinion in America which was hostile to the fitting of British ejection seats to American aircraft. But as James pointed out, he never advertised his seat or sent out brochures to potential customers, but left it to the success of the seat to sell itself. He did, however, object to the Americans borrowing his ideas for their own seats.

In the early sixties, the US Navy had asked him if he could improve the performance of the Mark 5 seat on the runway to get more parachute height without any increase in the thrust from the ejection gun. James had embarked on an intensive programme of tests involving 61 ejections over a period of ten weeks, during which he tried all the conventional and known methods of causing a parachute to open faster, but they had all had some serious technical difficulties, because any device that would make the parachute open faster would also cause explosive opening at high speed which would wreck the parachute. James then designed his own scheme, which he called the Martin Patent Anti-Squid Line, which is a line which goes down from the crown of the parachute to the shoulder harness. The drogue, which pulls the parachute out, is connected to this line so that when the drogue is pulling on the parachute the canopy lines are not subject to tension. The line pulls the crown of the parachute down about 2 ft and, as air flows inside the parachute, the inverted conical crown produced by pulling the line down causes the parachute to fill up quickly, one second faster than normal, a time difference which can be critical. He designed the line to be frangible so that at high speeds it would break and not cause explosive opening of the parachute.

In 1970 he received another request from the US Navy to reduce the timing on the seat. This necessitated certain changes to the anti-squid line, but James was able to achieve a significant reduction. However, he had an outstanding claim against the US Air Force in connection with the original anti-squid line which he told the US Navy would have to be cleared up before he would talk to them about his latest modifications. He became increasingly annoyed by this situation and on 26 June 1970, he wrote to President Nixon, setting out the situation as he saw it.

> As the person solely responsible for the design, development and introduction into service of this anti-squid line, I record my strong objection to the U.S.A.F. copying our drawing and changing the title of my patented feature from Martin Patent Anti-Squid Line to Pull Down Vent Line (PDVL) without making any reference whatsoever to the source of origin.

He regarded the attitude of the US Air Force as 'unacceptable' and considered it quite unfair and unjust for them to invite competitive tenders for an article which was cheap to manufacture when the high cost of development and testing was disregarded. In due course, he received an unsatisfactory reply to his letter to President Nixon from the US Air Force. James reported:

> They propose to carry on as they are doing and made some comment to the effect that they will make some sort of payment which, of course, will be quite trifling in relation to the amount that we have spent on developing this scheme. I do feel most upset because I put a lot of work into this patent device which works extraordinarily well.

For a short while there was a drop in orders for new seats. James was getting ejection seats back for repair, some of which had been made up to 19 years earlier. He did not agree with this practice, because it meant that aircrew were not being given the benefit of the great improvements which had been made to his ejection seat in that period, which would not only increase the circumstances in which safe escape was possible, but which would also significantly reduce the chances of back injury. In the spring of 1971, James reported that since the fitting of his rocket motor to ejection seats in America, the back injury rate had dropped from about 32 per cent to about 3 per cent. On 6 September 1972, he received news of another ejection when S/L Tim Gauvain and his co-pilot, a Belgian officer on a NATO exchange visit, ejected from a Lightning T5. Gauvain received back injuries, which upset James because he had already put up a proposal to fit a rocket motor to the Lightning seat. It had been turned down on the basis that the Lightning had comparatively few years left in service. James wrote to Gauvain: 'In the meantime, people like yourself pay the price which, to my mind, is quite wrong.'

Despite the increasing success rate achieved with the seat, there were still fatalities. Many of course were not the fault of the seat. Aircrew landing in the sea often drowned before they could be rescued, and there were even reports of pilots being lost in shark-infested waters. Occasionally aircrew would land in the fireball of their aircraft, which was again no fault of the seat. On many occasions, particularly with the older seats, the seat was used outside the performance envelope for which it had been designed, and in these cases, although the seat had failed to save the occupant, it had never been intended that it would save the occupant in those circumstances. James would point this out to people whenever he could, because he did not like anyone to conclude that the seat was at fault.

Feedback from ejectees often highlighted problems which even the latest design of seat did not cope with. In 1970, James received a report from the US Navy of two ejections from a Phantom. The aircraft had been taking off from an aircraft carrier when the catapult towbar broke and the aeroplane careered along the deck and went into the sea. Both aircrew ejected and landed safely back on the deck, which would have been an impressive escape had they not both been blown overboard and only one recovered. James studied the ejection report and realized that if it had been possible for the airmen to have effected an instant release of their parachutes they would both have remained safely on deck. He remarked sadly: 'It is certainly a problem today to cope with all the things that can happen when an emergency arises.' But accidents such as this were not lost on him, and he designed a new harness quick release fitting which enables the pilot to jettison the parachute very quickly.

Another example was the arm restraint. It became apparent to James from the injuries appearing on the accident reports that at speeds in excess of 400 knots there was a great risk of arm and leg damage. He had developed an arm restraint system for the Mark 8 seat for the cancelled TSR2 and in 1970 he resurrected the idea and designed a simplified version. The use of arm restraints meant that the seat pan firing handle would always have to be used, and that the face blind firing handle, an important part of his ejection system since the pre-Mark 1 seats, would finally be abandoned. James was pleased about this because he was convinced that it must take a pilot longer to reach over his head for the firing handle than to reach down for a handle on the seat pan. Another persuasive reason for adopting the seat pan handle method of firing the seat became apparent to James after he had talked to several American pilots who had been flying in Vietnam. They all told him that they flew with their seats raised so high that their bonedome helmets touched the canopy in order that they could see behind them in case they had a MiG on their tail. With the seat in such a high position, it was extremely difficult to locate the face screen handle, and it also made them lean forward in order to be able to pull it out.

The problems that James faced, however, did not always relate to the seat itself, and one of his biggest problems concerned aircraft canopies which either had to be jettisoned before the pilot could escape or had to be such that the seat could safely blast through them. In July 1970, when discussing the escape system for the proposed Multi-Role Combat Aircraft (which became the Tornado) with British Aircraft Corporation, he wrote:

'I would like to point out that in our experience more lives seem to be lost in emergencies through malfunction of the canopy unlocking or jettison systems than from any other cause.'

BAC were currently rescheming the canopy mechanisms and hinge positions for this aircraft and did not think it was necessary to decide upon the release angle for the canopy at that stage but wanted to develop the canopy jettison arrangements on test. While James would be the first person to agree that designs could be developed and finalized only through extensive testing, he did not accept that approach by other people when he felt that the necessary testing had already been satisfactorily completed by himself. He pointed out that his specification of a release angle of 65° gave the best performance, as indicated on the film of the test which he had already shown them, and that 'merely hoping for something to happen during subsequent tests seems to be a poor policy'.

In 1969, Grumman approached James for a proposal for an escape system for the EA-6B Prowler. James quoted a price and told them that he could get the four occupants out in just under two seconds. Grumman got a better proposal from an American firm who quoted a total escape time of one second, which they accepted. Some two and a half years later, however, Grumman came back to James and asked him if he would, after all, accept the job. James, as usual, asked for a fuselage. He fitted it with special slippers so that it could be installed on the test track at Langford Lodge and shipped it to Ireland. James arranged for two test ejections to be witnessed by Grumman and the US Navy. The tests were completely successful and Grumman were pleased when two occupants were fired out in half a second. They did not ask for a test to fire all four occupants out, but James decided to go ahead at his own expense and fired four occupants out, zero/zero, in 0.93 seconds, and achieved four fully deployed parachutes before the dummies hit the ground. James wrote: 'it certainly was a most spectacular sight and quite a big distance between all the seats'. The two back-seaters left first, followed by the two front-seaters. He sent a film of this test to Grumman and consequently received an order for all the EA-6B aircraft to be fitted with this system. The four-man sequenced ejection was a good example of the need to shoot seats out at different angles to ensure, in this case, that the seats did not collide with each other or the parachutes become entangled. Divergent ejection also reduces the chances of ejectees at low altitude losing their parachutes in the fireball, a danger which had by then manifested itself several times after ejections with rocket seats.

In 1970 the Germans asked to see a series of tests with the Phantom seat, which were all successful. They then asked for a test out of the VAK 191, a VTOL aircraft, at a bank of 45°, with the nose 10° down. James realized that the Phantom seat could not successfully meet these requirements and the test proved him right. It set him thinking again and he converted the ejection gun on the Harrier Mark 9 seat to a two-piece gun which enabled him to get nearly 200 ft with an open parachute in these circumstances due to the fact that the two-piece gun is much stiffer and there is little deflection due to the bending of the gun. The ejection velocity lost from the lack of the third tube was regained by a slight increase in the diameter of the rocket charges. He felt that the modification would also get over the problems he had been having with the seat spinning and he intended to modify the seat for the F-14 Tomcat. He told the Martin-Baker technical representative in America about his latest ideas, but not his customer. He wrote: 'We have not told Grumman about this. If we did they would tear their hair out. What I intend to do is to test it and if it works O.K. then show Grumman a film of the difference between the two schemes.'

In 1971, a successful year for James, it appeared from the Martin-Baker records that the success rate of their seat for the US Air Force was 100 per cent, less one pilot who was not rescued from the sea. The success rate for the RAF was also 100 per cent that year, less one American pilot flying a Harrier who forgot to remove the safety pin from the rocket motor prior to flight, with the result that it did not fire when he ejected. The Americans made up a very large part of James's market. By the end of 1971, Martin-Baker records showed a total of 3,100 lives saved, of which nearly 2,000 were American aircrew.

By this time James was designing a series of modifications to the seat which were eventually embodied in a new seat known as the Mark 10 seat. The new seat combined a reduction in weight with improved performance and was designed to provide a safe escape in the zero/zero situation and at speeds of up to 630 knots. By the summer of 1971, James had completed three Mark 10 seats and was confident that they would successfully out-perform the American seats.

The Americans often complained that the Martin-Baker seat was too heavy. James had no patience with complaints about such matters: the only thing that mattered was whether it worked effectively, and he believed his seat to be more effective than the lighter American versions. The new Mark 10 seat, however, was 50 lb lighter than the Martin-Baker seat in the Phantom or the F-14, so he was satisfied that he had at last answered his critics in this respect.

One of the main developments embodied in the Mark 10 seat was the extension of the gas-operated firing system which James had introduced on the Mark 9 seat to include not only the actual firing of the seat and the operation of the harness power retraction unit, but also the release of the drogue and the operation of the harness release system. The seat also incorporated a gas-operated manual separation system in the event of the failure of either or both the drogue gun and the time release unit.

The ejection process on the Mark 10 seat is initiated by pulling the seat firing handle which withdraws the sear from the seat firing unit under the seat pan and fires the initiator cartridge. Gas from this cartridge fires the cartridge in the harness power retraction unit breech to operate the harness retraction system and, via a piston, fires the ejection gun firing unit. The pilot is thus pulled into an upright position and the seat begins to eject. As the seat rises, the sears of the drogue gun and time release unit are withdrawn and the remote rocket initiator cartridge is fired by its static cable, which fires another cartridge which in turn ignites the rocket fuel. The drogue gun primary cartridge fires half a second after ejection and deploys the drogue. Subject to the barostat mechanism, the time release unit fires one and a half seconds after ejection and releases the drogue shackle, operates the harness locks and releases the leg restraints and also the man portion of the personal equipment connector and arm restraints if fitted.

The barostatic time release unit and the drogue gun had to be redesigned for incorporation in the gas-operated system, and James introduced a twin cartridge drogue gun. The drogue and parachute were combined as a complete assembly and packed in one quickly detachable container at the top of the seat structure to form a headrest. This did away with the need for a separate parachute pack, simplified the harness arrangements, and permitted both drogue and parachute to stream quickly and clear of the seat structure.

The new manual separation system was designed to cover failure of the barostatic time release unit and failure of the drogue gun. The seat occupant has only to pull the manual separation handle which fires a cartridge to deliver gas pressure to operate the drogue gun, time release unit and harness release mechanism. The drogue gun deploys the drogue, which in turn streams the main parachute without the ejectee having to pull a ripcord.

The Mark 10 system also incorporated the command ejection system and arm restraints. A great deal of testing was undertaken to prove and improve the performance of this new seat. In April 1971 James reported that he had been testing the new seat to cut down the timing of the drogue gun to one-quarter of a second and the time release to about a second and a half, and at 540 mph this saved about 200 ft. But he still needed to test the zero/zero case and the 600 knots case.

Some quite major changes were made to the Mark 10 seat during the course of testing but by the end of 1972 James was hopeful that it was now in its final form. Unfortunately, improvements and modifications were still necessary and it was not until the end of 1973 that he finalized the design. One of the problems he had faced concerned the parachute and he eventually decided that he would have to give up using Irvin parachutes, which he had been using since the forties, and use instead a GQ parachute. The reason for this was that with the GQ aeroconical parachute he was able to cut down the timing on the time release mechanism from two and a quarter seconds to one and a half seconds. When this shorter timing was used with the Irvin 1.24 parachute, the canopy lines and panels in the canopy burst. Also, the maximum g did not exceed 20 with the GQ parachute during a test at 700 mph and the one and a half second timing, whereas with the Irvin parachute, the g went up to 27 and the parachute became inverted for a fraction of a second after opening. The qualification tests for the Mark 10 seat were completed in the autumn of 1974 and confirmed its performance. At a speed of 700 mph, or 1,000 ft/sec, it took just two and a half seconds from the moment the seat was fired until the parachute was fully developed.

That year James had been discussing the Mark 10 seat with the Germans who had recently complained that Martin-Baker was not adequately responding to their requirements or replying with sufficient promptness. James could only say that if such complaints were justified it was only because of his recent heavy preoccupation with the Mark 10 seat. He wrote:

> As Chief Designer, my aim, throughout the life of my Company, has been to give aircrew the best equipment of which I am capable. As an engineer, you will know that it is seldom possible to achieve the ultimate design aim at the first attempt and that, in most cases, a really sound and reliable piece of equipment evolves from a series of prototypes with searching examination and testing at each stage. This is why our new Mark 10 seat has undergone several configuration changes. I am convinced that ultimately this process will be justified by the operational record of the Mark 10 seat, which I am convinced is the best seat we have ever made.

In 1973, James came up against a new problem. He had been testing a seat for Northrop and completed ten shots in a row which were all successful. Northrop wanted the tests repeated at the Holloman Air Force Base in New Mexico. James was somewhat mystified when some of these shots were not successful. He then realized that the humidity in that area was very low, about 3 per cent, the temperature was about 90°, and the test track was at an altitude of about 4,000 ft, representing a 15 per cent change in atmospheric pressure. He realized that this combination had quite a drastic effect on the pull produced by the drogues. He carried out some modifications to the anti-squid line to address the problem but he confessed to several people, including the Vice-President of Northrop, that this was the first time in his life he had had such trouble in getting seats to work according to requirements.

But it was not just the Northrop seat that was causing him problems. At the end of 1973 he had representatives from two other aircraft manufacturers at the factory, 'all clamouring for seats'. On top of that, British Aircraft Corporation were asking for the seat for the MRCA to be tested with a 98 percentile dummy, approximating to a man weighing about 240 lb. James reported: 'The fact is, with our Meteor aircraft there is not the room or depth to accommodate such an enormous dummy and we are having a bit of a problem to cope with this.' In addition, at the end of 1973, Britain was in the throes of the three-day week. Typically, James thought that the arrangement was 'simply mad' and that it would be quite impossible to meet the demands of his customers. Due to labour shortages he was already behind on his delivery schedules. He had recently purchased some very expensive new machine tools to cope with the labour problem but even these could not totally solve the problem because there was such a variety of seats being made and many still had to be made by the old methods as they did not have the jigs and tools to suit the older seats. The power cuts in 1972 had cost him a lot of money in paying wages to people who were standing around idle. In 1973 he had purchased a diesel generator so that he could keep the factory working through any further power cuts. Although it was against the law to use this generator during the three-day week, he was quite prepared to take the risk of a fine and imprisonment in order to keep the factory working. He wrote: 'The fact is that I have never had so much worry in my life all in one heap. However, I try never to let circumstances rule me and so I will do my best.'

Old age and hard work were clearly beginning to take their toll on James. In 1973 he had turned 80 and he was still at the office every day. By now his nephew, Denis Burrell, had assumed much of the responsibility for the day-to-day running of the factory, and his two sons, John and James, also worked there, but even so, James had no intention of letting them take over yet. He wrote: 'I cannot understand why people should want to retire. When Jesus Christ was on earth he worked hard and long hours.' It was a common theme for James who did not approve of retirement any more than he approved of holidays. He wrote: 'There is no doubt, whatsoever, that it is a frightful mistake to retire. Once people retire then they are only waiting to die.'

On 8 March 1973, he received a spectacular ejection report, news that made his worries worthwhile. Four members of the American 'Blue Angels' display team were practising a four-plane tail loop. After 200° of loop, the second aircraft either collided with the first, or the first aircraft suffered a catastrophic explosion. Then the second aircraft struck the tailplane of the third aircraft. The fourth aircraft managed to avoid this mid-air débâcle, and the three pilots of the first three aircraft all ejected successfully.

James was undoubtedly still bullish. In 1973, when the company was having some engine problems with its Hawker Siddeley 125 jet, James got into a spat with Rolls-Royce. He made it very clear that he was not flying in the aeroplane until the problem engine had been removed as he did not want to become a part of the Experimental Department of Rolls-Royce. The Rolls-Royce representative was left in no doubt as to what James thought, both of the situation and the length of his hair.

James had always kept a gun, for he enjoyed shooting and was, indeed, a very fine shot. As a child, his mother had repeatedly confiscated his airgun because of his habit of amusing himself by shooting at cows in the fields and watching them jump. His airgun had long since been replaced by a pistol which he used to shoot fish and water rats in the river which ran through his garden at Southlands Manor. While the Thames Valley Constabulary did not dispute that he was a fit person to possess a firearm, they needed convincing that he had an indisputable reason for having a .22 Colt semi-automatic pistol. James told them first of all that he needed it for the destruction of vermin on his property, but that was not accepted as a good reason. James then replied: 'You might be interested to know that apart from shooting at water rats which infest my place I use this pistol to test the vulnerability of our seat from bullets fired at close range. In point of fact, this is a requirement for American seats fitted with rocket motors.' The Constabulary felt that a .22 rifle would be more accurate for killing vermin and equally appropriate for shooting at the seat, but James was determined not to relinquish his pistol. He then told them that he was required to carry out tests on life-saving equipment, namely the Mae West, which carried, among other items, a pistol. As James explained: 'these have to be tested at high speeds to see whether the means of retaining the pistol are adequate and in a recent test the pistol and the cartridges were torn away from the Mae West and it took us about a day to find the pistol at the aerodrome'.

James kept his pistol, but some time later had an unfortunate accident with his son John's shotgun. In 1974, James was finally persuaded by his two sons that it was time to buy a new car. His beloved Bentley was now 20 years old and James finally agreed to buy a new Rolls-Royce. He was, in fact, very pleased with it. The power steering and the smooth ride impressed him. One day, however, a pigeon left its calling card on his new Rolls while it was parked outside his office. The pigeon, a fairly friendly one, had been making a nuisance of itself for some time and had on occasions got into the factory. It was generally known that 'the old man' liked pigeons and so nobody dared to do anything about it. But James was not going to let the pigeon sully his Rolls and he borrowed the shotgun and went outside to sort the pigeon out. Unfortunately, the gun had a very light trigger and he fired it prematurely. He shot a hole in the Rolls and the pigeon flew away never to return.

James was still as disparaging about British politicians and the fact that Martin-Baker had appeared in the list drawn up for the Labour Party of those companies which were candidates for nationalization only served to fuel the fire of his discontent. It is unlikely that the Labour Party had any idea what they were contemplating taking over, as James made it quite clear that he would refuse to co-operate with them on any level, and would simply refuse to deliver the seats. Happily, the threatened take-over never materialized. But when, in March 1976, James met Harold Wilson at a reception in Buckingham Palace, he told him: 'Mr Prime Minister, you know that our line of business is ejection seats. Now, if you bought a large number of these seats and fitted them to some of the useless people you have at No. 10 and the building next door and fired them out through the roof, you could then make a clean start.'

If anything, James had become more entrenched in his unorthodox views as the years went by. When some theories were advanced on the subject of how old planet Earth might be, he had this to say:

With regard to what scientists (so-called) have to say in connection with the age of the earth, of course, they talk sheer nonsense. In point of fact, who are scientists anyway? They are not really scientists, they are only people who have acquired a little elementary knowledge with regard to how the Creator makes all things work. They are under satanic control, they imagine they are clever but for years I have written off all such people. It is a waste of time talking to them.

He did not, of course, necessarily believe everything he said. He liked to shock and surprise people and often said things which were designed to produce a reaction. While he certainly did not always accept the scientific approach, he did accept that there should be some balance between creative and qualified people and he had insisted that his two sons complete degrees in engineering at Dublin University before joining the company.

In 1974, he became embroiled in a debate with the Ministry about leg garters. The Ministry told him that they would not accept the new double leg garters. James was frustrated by this approach and replied that he would demonstrate to them that the double leg garters worked efficiently and that if their pilots wanted to fly with single leg garters and get dislocated legs and thighs, then that was their responsibility. The Ministry however were not prepared to accept that responsibility and instead agreed to accept the double garters. The debate caused James to conclude: 'In the past I was not tough enough with the RAF and others', a conclusion which would, perhaps, have surprised the RAF and others.

There were of course occasions when the boot was on the other foot. With the Tornado, because of the material used to make the cockpit canopy it is not possible to eject through the canopy and the canopy must be jettisoned first. James designed the canopy jettison system as part of the job of installing the seat in this aircraft but the Institute of Aviation Medicine had doubts about the rocket motors that he proposed to use for the canopy jettison. They were concerned that the efflux from the rocket motors might burn the second pilot and that the noise of these rocket motors might damage the hearing of the Tornado aircrew. James did not agree. As regards the level of noise, James felt that the Tornado was a very noisy aeroplane anyway and that the ears of the crew were adequately protected by their helmets. In the final analysis, did the Ministry want to get the men out quickly and alive or not? James told the Ministry that he would lay on a live demonstration for them. He invited them to the factory at Denham, issued them all with ear defenders, and then produced a volunteer from the shop-floor, George Howe, who agreed to sit in the Tornado fuselage wearing protective clothing fitted with heat sensors while the canopy was blasted off. This was duly done, the heat sensors did not record unacceptable levels and Howe told the Ministry men that the noise level of the rocket motors was not a problem. James liked to tell this story with some embellishment, to the effect that the volunteer for the test was carefully chosen in that he was stone deaf but a good lip reader. This, of course, was not the case, but James never liked to miss an opportunity to score, or at least to appear to score, against officialdom.

At the beginning of 1975 James took his Mark 10 seat to America to demonstrate it. James was very pleased with this design. He wrote:

> Here is a seat that actually exists and has been fully tested from zero/zero up to 650 knots with a 99 percentile dummy. It is quite impressive to see the actual shot from the sled. 610 knots is about 700 mph, or 1,000 feet per second and from the moment the seat is shot out until the parachute is fully developed the time is $2^1/2$ seconds. There is no sign of any damage to the drogues or parachute and I have no doubt that this speed can be greatly exceeded.

The seat was presented to Grumman, Chance Vought, General Dynamics and McDonnell. James felt that the seat had been well received, as he expected, for he believed that the Mark 10 was more advanced than any of the American seats. Although he had to wait quite a long time for an order, he was not disappointed, and in 1976 Martin-Baker was awarded the contract for the Mark 10 seat to be fitted in the McDonnell Douglas F-18 Hornet.

This was an important order, because although the Mark 10 seat was already flying in the Tornado and the Hawk, and Martin-Baker had received several other orders for it, at the beginning of 1976 the factory was short of work. For over 12 years, Martin-Baker had been producing about 260 seats per month, but orders had dropped off enormously, due, James felt, to the fact that new aircraft had become so costly and that delivery was spread over a very long period. Once again he found himself employing too many people but felt that it was too expensive to pay them off because of the redundancy payments he would be obliged to make.

James was, however, delighted that year when His Royal Highness the Duke of Edinburgh agreed to visit the factory at Denham. James was always pleased to have an opportunity to show his factory to visitors, and could now be justifiably proud of the enterprise he had built up. But the visit by His Royal Highness was a very special occasion for James. He had great respect for the Royal Family and some say that they were the only people to whom he ever showed any deference. He had always considered himself a loyal subject, and the Royal visit meant a great deal to him.

But the year did not continue happily and March 1976 found him a patient in the RAF Hospital at Halton. He had fallen on the newly polished linoleum in the corridor in the main office block and had hurt his shoulder which was very painful. He went to the RAF Medical Centre in London for treatment and while he was there asked them to look at his leg, which he had scratched and which had become infected. This turned out to be a deep-seated infection and he was immediately admitted to the RAF Hospital for treatment. He was there for three weeks, during which time they did an unsuccessful skin graft, and when discharged he was told that it was likely to take at least another six months for his leg to heal completely.

Despite the constant treatment on his leg, by the beginning of 1977 it had still not healed. The doctors at RAF Halton advised him to keep his leg up at more than right angles, but James found this impossible because he was constantly on the move around the factory. In desperation he wrote to his old friend Peggy Loudon who had helped him in the mid-forties with his early pioneering work. Peggy was unable to offer a miracle cure and the infection lingered on.

In the early summer of 1979 James had an unfortunate fall in his garden and fractured his hip. His infected leg had never healed completely but now he had to undergo a hip replacement operation after which he found it painful to walk and he needed two sticks to get about. It was clear that his activities at the office would now be seriously curtailed and in the autumn of 1979 his two sons, John and James, were made directors of Martin-Baker. He never fully recovered his mobility and never returned to the office on a full-time basis, although he insisted on going there as often as he could. On 5 January 1981, at the age of 87, he died peacefully at his home. To that date, 4,788 lives had been saved by his ejection seat.

James had not mellowed over the years, had not compromised his beliefs or his principles, and had remained a benevolent autocrat. He had achieved extraordinary success in his lifetime, and left behind him a company with an international reputation for the excellence and reliability of its product. He had been asked many times over the years for the secret of Martin-Baker's success, and on one occasion he gave his answer. He wrote:

> The person concerned, that is me, has always been interested in design work, even as a child. I have taken out some 150 patents all over the world for various things. I am also capable of doing any kind of machine work in any works – milling, grinding, drilling, tool making and so on – anything to do with mechanical engineering. The result was that those who came here to be trained became infected with the same idea, and as the people grew up so also grew a sort of religion for perfection of workmanship.
>
> Another point which very few people realise is that when you have people working for you you must realise that they are human beings. They also have problems and I take a personal interest in their troubles. If they want financial assistance I help them out. We do not sack people at five minutes notice and their jobs are safe and secure; it is vital that men are sure of their jobs. Our workers are allowed to earn the maximum amount of money and work overtime so that they can maintain a high standard of living and run motor cars and so on. Some people call this public relationship. You can call it what you like, but if big public companies only realised that those employed by them are human beings, there would not be so much friction.
>
> Another angle of successful business is that the person in charge must be

above average in his knowledge of the subject he is dealing with. If he is not this is reflected in the product he makes and the result is that the article manufactured is not high grade. There are far too many businesses today where all they are concerned about is getting an easy buck as you say in America. It has never been my ambition to acquire large sums of money. I always try to give the highest possible standard of design married to the best workmanship.

We now come to another stage which is vital to a successful business; that is there should be adequate finances to buy the very best kind of equipment. Only a small proportion of the population is highly skilled so the high standard of workmanship must be got by mechanical means, therefore high class machines capable of working to fine limits are required.

You will see therefore, that to be successful in business you must ask yourself how can you maintain a high standard of workmanship. This is a combination of good management, the right tools capable of reproducing parts accurately to close limits, good personnel who are loyal and want to maintain the high standard, plus the treatment of employees as human beings instead of disposable stores to be thrown on the scrap heap when a difficult period arises.

There is far too much emphasis put on college degrees. Everywhere in the papers people are asking for people with degrees. Here at these Works there are only a couple of people with any degrees, but the rest have got something which cannot be got at Universities – they have know how which has been developed over a period of years. When I look at the firms here in England who employ large numbers of graduates they do not seem to get far. The thing is they are not creative designers. I suppose it is fair to say that a certain amount of people are born into the world that can create something out of nothing – new ideas, new schemes and so on. Why have those people got that particular ability? There is only one answer – the Creator. The Creator made everything out of nothing, and for some reason which we cannot understand He has given the ability to paint to some and to others wonderful voices and so on. Special qualities cannot be man produced.

The nations of the world have got to the stage where they think each one can rule the world. They each threaten the other with big sticks and have got Atom and Hydrogen bombs for frightening each other. This can only lead to bankruptcy. Where does the desire to destroy each other come from? From Satan, the Great Deceiver. Few people recognise this potent and lethal power which is hidden away but is working every moment of the day.

I am smart enough to realise that I know very little. I oftentimes think if you could take someone up into the sky to a height of say 500 miles and the atmosphere was clean enough to see the earth, the first thing that would cross the person's mind was that the earth was sitting in space. The same force that supports the earth keeps the sun and stars in their place.

Therefore, my philosophy of life, apart from the burning desire to create, is much wider. I can see the relationship of man in time and space. Human beings are trying to buy pleasure over the counter – pictures and so forth. None of these things give any satisfaction. They only last for a few minutes and are a waste of time. Few people realise that they are nothing. As the Prophet Isaiah said '. . . Nations are as drops in the bucket and sand on the shore', and yet the rulers of the nations during their brief stay here on earth think they are immortal. If you go into a churchyard of a big town there are lots of notice boards telling you all about those buried there, but they cannot talk. They are only clay. However, we read in the Bible that at the sound of the last trumpet the dead in Christ shall rise, together with those Christians on earth, and be caught up to meet the Lord in the air. These shall then live and reign with Him for a thousand years. This is Revelation. The wicked that are left on the earth at the return of Christ will be destroyed by the brightness of His coming and there will be no inhabitants on the earth for a thousand years. The principle thing in my life is to try and serve the Creator with all my heart and soul. Few people realise this.

The factory was inundated with thousands of messages of condolence from all over the world, from corporate executives who had learned to respect James, and ejectees who owed their life to him. His funeral service took place at the local church at Denham. It was a private affair, attended only by the family, close friends and employees – too many, indeed, to fit in the church, so many stood respectfully outside in the churchyard which was smothered under hundreds of floral tributes.

Lord Kings Norton wrote an obituary letter to *The Times* a few days after James's death in which he paid great tribute to James and his achievements. He concluded by saying:

James Martin was one of the great engineers of his generation. He did not have to learn the laws of motion, he knew them intuitively. He thought three-dimensionally and his designs had the natural artistry of genius – and that is what he had . . . Those that knew him considered it a privilege that they did.

A memorial service was held at St Clement Danes, the central church of the RAF, in London. Bill Bedford, ejectee number 511, who had escaped from the P1127 in 1961, gave a short address. He concluded this with these words:

I stand here today paying tribute to Sir James Martin because of James Martin. As one of the five thousand whose lives have been saved because of his genius, I can say from my very heart: never in the history of aviation has the safety of aircrew and happiness of their families owed so much to one man. Thank you, Jimmy.

Epilogue

At the end of 1990, preparations were well advanced for the joint American and European invasion of Kuwait to liberate the country from the Iraqi forces of Saddam Hussein. An American aircraft carrier was on its way to join the liberation forces already amassed in the Middle East, and was 200 miles east of Bermuda. The aircraft on board were making training flights on and off the carrier during the journey. On 31 December, an EA-6B Prowler piloted by Lt. J. Meier of the US Navy came in to land back on the carrier. Meier recalls: 'The arrestment felt normal (to a point).' Then:

> we felt a "bang" and a release of tension. (The bang was later learned to be the broken arresting gear cable hitting the aircraft.) At that time ECMO 1 and I both pulled the ejection handle, initiating the command ejection sequence. After I pulled the ejection handle I felt the effects of time compression. The 1.2 second delay in the pilot's ejection seat seemed like a lifetime. I pulled the handle while still on the flight deck, and did not "go up the rails" until the aircraft was 30° nose down and approximately 40 ft above the water. After the ejection, I realized that I had heard the other seats leaving the cockpit, but at the time, I didn't think my ejection seat was working.

Lt. Meier remembers the ejection as a loud bang and a big flash of light as the rocket motor started to fire. Because of the forces imposed during landing, he was leaning forward, which was, he later remarked, 'poor for ejection, but great for a bird's-eye view of leaving the cockpit'. All four aircrew were successfully ejected in their Martin-Baker GRUEA7 ejection seats before the aircraft hit the water. They were quickly recovered and brought back on board the ship.

James had spent 35 years trying to improve the performance of the seat and to minimize the time lapse between the firing of the seat and the full deployment of the parachute. The tests for the first four-man sequenced ejection had been completed at his own expense and the GRUEA7 seat had been designed by James. It was a spectacular sight to watch four men eject from an aircraft rolling off a carrier before the aircraft hit the water, and James would have been pleased and proud to have achieved this successful ejection in such exacting circumstances.

On 11 February 1991, Lt. Cdr. Stan Parsons of the US Navy was flying an A-6E Intruder off the coast of Florida on a practice electronics warfare flight. Lt. Linda Hyde, an electronics counter-measures officer, was in the other seat. Suddenly, the aircraft suffered a serious hydraulic failure. Parsons and Hyde went through their emergency procedure. At this point, Hyde recalls that they were both calm and indeed quite complacent about a single hydraulic failure, for as she said, 'no-one believes that they're going to eject'. Two and a half minutes later, having failed to solve the hydraulics problem, the pilot declared an emergency. At this stage, he was still in control of the aircraft, but suddenly it shuddered and Parsons reported that they had lost the other hydraulic system. The aircraft began rolling to the left and he ordered Hyde to leave the aircraft. The aircraft was flying at about 15,000 ft, and travelling at 270 knots, and in a 60° left bank. She recalls: 'I pulled the upper ejection handle. There was a bright flash of light as the seat went through the canopy.' She blacked out and came round to find herself hanging on the end of her parachute. 'It felt like forever on the 'chute . . . It was probably only about a minute, but it felt like ten. I was really angry too. I remember thinking that this ruins my whole day. I had dinner plans for later.'

She landed in the ocean, which was very cold, and climbed into her raft. 'The waves were pretty huge and it was pretty scary,' she recalls, as she waited for rescue and hoped that she would not become another statistic, one of those aircrew who eject successfully but are not picked up or not picked up in time. It was half an hour before she was sighted by a P-3 overhead which rocked its wings to indicate she had been seen and shot off flares to mark where she was. She then had a further cold wait before the rescue helicopters arrived. The rescuer who came down on the cable to pick her up was 'somewhat surprised to find me a woman'. Lt. Hyde was the first woman to have used a Martin-Baker ejection seat.

James would have had mixed feelings if he had heard about this ejection. He would have preferred women not to fly aeroplanes. His friends Amy Johnson and Valentine Baker had been killed in flying accidents and, after years of developing ejection seats, his view was that aeroplanes were 'nasty dangerous things'. During the war he had stopped his niece, Joan Holt, from joining the Air Transport Auxiliary, and he would certainly have been most concerned at the thought of women flying modern military aircraft. He had a delightful, if now old-fashioned, view of women that they should let the men do the dangerous things in life. However, once women had won the opportunity to fly in military machines, he would have regarded it as absolutely essential that they be provided with the best possible escape system, and he would have been relieved to hear that his seat had saved Lt. Hyde.

On 15 May 1992, Lt. Cdr. J.R. Muir of the US Navy was piloting an F18 Hornet off the coast of Florida. He recalls:

> During an overhead evasive manoeuvre an unexplained failure of the flight control system momentarily diverted my attention away from the task at hand. The aircraft entered what is referred to as a Falling Leaf Mode in which the nose slices back and forth from right to left as well as oscillating from 70° left wing down to 60° right wing down. Couple this with pitch oscillation of 10–60° nose down and a 22,000 foot per minute rate of descent and you have a rather wild ride.

At 10,000 ft there was still no response from the controls. As he was over water and did not have to worry about rising terrain, he decided to go through the recovery procedures again to try and save the aircraft. At 7,500 ft he reached for the ejection handle. He recalls:

> It was just a blur at the time . . . all I remember was the brown smoke from the canopy thrusters as it left the aircraft milliseconds before me. The NACES seat must have worked flawlessly because the next cognizant thought I had was how absolutely quiet it was hanging in a parachute a mile above the Atlantic Ocean . . . Not realizing that I had ejected with my visor up, I reached up and removed my sunglasses and stowed them in my G-suit pocket. This should be some indicator as to how smooth the SJU-14 ejection seat actually is.

James had always tried to ensure that the ride in the seat was as smooth as possible. It was his early research and development work in the forties that had established the necessity for controlling the rate of rise of g, and his brutal determination to produce the best system possible that had made him undertake live test ejections so that he could be told what the ejection felt like. He would have been truly delighted to hear about this ejection that saved Lt. Cdr. Muir and his sunglasses.

Fifteen years after his death, Martin-Baker remains as James would have wanted: a totally family owned and directed business. His nephew, Denis Burrell, is the Chairman, his sons, John and James Martin, are joint Managing-Directors, and his great nephew, Richard Holt, is the Production Director. Looking to the future, John's son Robert has been working in the design office since 1993 and James expects his son, Andrew, to join the company in a few years' time. James instilled in his family his belief that their job is to save pilots' lives, that time wasting is life wasting, and that the seat can always be improved. The next generation has succeeded in meeting the challenges of a fast-changing world, has addressed issues such as cost controls that James would have ignored, and has invested in modern technology to ensure that the company remains a centre of excellence. Martin-Baker today is more competitive and more responsive to customer requirements, and the number of military forces using the Martin-Baker seat has increased.

While James would not now recognize his beloved machine shop, and would have some difficulty in accepting some of the new design innovations such as the microprocessor, he would nevertheless be pleased with progress, and with the development of the Mark 11, 12, 14, 15 and 16 seats. In 1985, the US Navy selected the Mark 14 seat as its Navy Aircrew Common Ejection Seat which will remain in production into the 21st century, as will the Mark 16 seat for the Rafale and the European Fighter Aircraft, and the Mark 16LA lightweight seat for the Beech Mk II turbo-prop trainer chosen by the US Department of Defense for the Joint Primary Aircraft Training System Programme for the US Navy and Air Force. While James did not succeed in eliciting interest for an ejection seat for helicopters, Martin-Baker has since produced a crashworthy seat for helicopters which is installed in the Augusta 129, and has significant orders for crashworthy crew and troop seats for other helicopters.

The number of lives saved by his seats rather than the number of customers and orders was, however, what mattered most to James, and he can rest assured that this priority remains. The latest designs of the Martin-Baker seats now save an even higher percentage of the aircrew who use them, and the number of successful ejections is increasing by approximately two each week. So strong was his influence while he lived, he was able to bequeath an enduring legacy: a work-force still loyal to his family and the ideals he espoused, and a company that remains committed to saving the lives of aircrew all over the world, and dedicated to the task of making the Martin-Baker ejection seat even better.

Martin-Baker Prototype Aircraft

MB1: *G-ADCS*

Type Two-seat light touring aircraft.

Wings Low-wing cantilever unbraced monoplane.

Fuselage Round-section, thin-gauge steel tubing with fabric covering.

Tail unit Sweptback fin and rudder with non-swept fixed incidence tailplane and elevators.

Landing gear Fixed main wheels and castoring tail wheel. Tubular construction undercarriage incorporating simple shock absorbers.

Power plant One 160 hp Napier Javelin Series 3A, six-cylinder inverted air-cooled engine with electric starter and dual fuel pumps, installed in a tubular engine mounting with all parts accessible for easy servicing and driving a fixed-pitch wooden propeller. The engine cowlings could be hinged upward and held by a strut providing protection for engine and engineer when working on the engine in the open.

Accommodation Two seats in tandem within enclosed cabin with access via a side-hinging canopy. 'V'-shaped windscreen with vertical front panels.

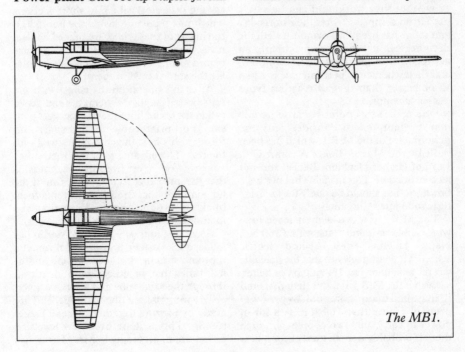

The MB1.

Dimensions

Wing span 37 ft 0 in

Length overall 28 ft 10$^{1}/_{2}$ in

Span (with wings folded) 13 ft 2 in

Tailplane span 10 ft 0 in

Wing area 206 sq ft

Wheel track 7 ft 0 in

Weight Fully loaded (including pilot, passenger and 70 lb of luggage): 2,350 lb

Performance

Cruising speed 160 mph

Stalling speed 50 mph

The aircraft had very pleasant and safe handling characteristics.

The following is the text of an article entitled 'A New Way of Building Aeroplanes' which appeared in the 19 December 1934 edition of *The Aeroplane*:

The worth of a new aeroplane is generally assessed by its performance in the air considered in relation to the pay-load it carries and the power of its motor. But sometimes features which are incorporated in the design of the machine are more interesting, and possibly more important, than the actual performance of the machine. There may, for instance, be in the design certain novel features which are so unorthodox that the first thing to do is to prove that they work, and can be safely used in an aeroplane. After their suitability and safety has been thus demonstrated, the designer can get down to producing an aeroplane in which those ideas are used, and then whether its performance is equal to or better than that of existing types begins to count.

One makes this point because people may be tempted to consider only the performance of the M.B.1, which has been built by the Martin-Baker Aircraft Co., Ltd., of Higher Denham, Bucks, and not its construction. This machine has not been flown yet, but should be ready for its flying tests soon after Christmas . . .

The M.B.1 is a two-seat enclosed low-wing cantilever mono-plane with a 160 h.p. Napier Javelin Series 3A, and electric starter. Mr Martin guesses that the machine will do something like 150 m.p.h., or better.

Even if the M.B.1 is faster than that, and it may be, many potential buyers will probably think that 160 h.p. is a lot of power to carry only two people, although there is probably a small market for a very finely built machine of this class, in which no expense has been spared to make every detail perfect.

From a personal inspection of the machine, the writer considers that its real interest lies rather in its entirely novel construction than in the machine as a type. If it shows itself in its flying tests to have a reasonably good performance, the new type of structure will have vindicated itself and the Martin-Baker Aircraft Company will then be able to make the best use of the potentialities of this kind of construction by producing peculiarly robust high-performance machines which are cheap to build.

One of the special features of the machine is the triangulated single spar, which for this particular job has proved on static test to have a factor of 9. It consists of three tubular booms of the same diameter from root to tip, although the spacing between the three is greater at the inner end than at the outer, as one would expect.

Steel tubes with flattened and brazed-up ends are used to brace the booms together. These are fixed to the spars by studs. These studs pass through holes in the flattened ends which rest on saddle-washers, into the spars where they are fixed very ingeniously.

A number of narrow rings are made by sawing up a steel tube into short sections which just telescope inside the boom. To the inside of these rings are brazed conical nuts. The tubular booms of the spar are placed in a jig and have the necessary holes for the studs bored in them.

After this operation the rings, with the nuts brazed on inside them, are slid down inside the boom until the nut registers with the appropriate hole in the spar, and through this hole the stud is screwed into the nut. The advantage of this method of construction, apart from its cheapness, is that the inner ring stabilizes the rim of the hole in the boom itself and prevents local buckling aroung the stud, so that the material there develops its full strength.

According to tests which Mr. Martin has made, a load can be transmitted through a tube and stud fixed in this way one-and-a-half times that which can be transmitted through the same tube and a tubular rivet.

The wing ribs are of girder type, and are made by brazing together pieces of steel tubing. This is done by a new Swedish process, and, according to Mr. Martin, has a less deleterious effect than welding. A standard rib made up in this way was attached to a rigidly held section of the spar and vibrated a million or so times to see how it stood the strain – and it did so quite satisfactorily.

The ribs are made in two sections, and are held by 2 B.A. bolts through a lug to clips on one of the spar-booms. These clips are split and are also held in position by bolts. The idea of this method of fixing is to make possible the replacing of any rib without trouble, as each can be separately detached from the spar. Moreover, skilled, or specially experienced, labour is not needed, as the method of removing the damaged rib and replacing a new one is obvious to any mechanic as soon as he looks inside the wing.

The formers which carry the fairing on the fuselage are clipped to the main longerons in the same sort of way. The longitudinal stringers are drawn sections of very thin stainless-steel strip, which is merely sprung into place between small claws brazed into the formers.

A form of construction similar to that of the wing is used for the fuselage, except that four longerons are used. These are braced longitudinally and transversely by rigid bracing-tubes attached in exactly the same way as they are to the booms of the spar.

As an engineering job, the M.B.1 is most impressive. For instance, when the wing is folded, a suitably strengthened stud on it comes up against a stop in the fuselage, which stop is carried by a light girder clipped to the upper and lower longerons. There is thus no chance of the fairing or the formers or the trailing-edge of the wing being damaged by careless folding. The spring-loaded plungers which hold the folding flaps down in place are likewise well made and work smoothly. They are released from the trailing-edge.

Another example of the painstaking design of details is the locking-pin which fastens the front boom. The spar folds about hinges in the upper and lower spar-booms. The locking pin is worked in and out by turning from the leading-edge a screw with a two-start thread. To this screw the pin is attached by a universal joint, so that there is no tendency for the pin to bind anywhere, and it is quite free to enter the holes in the ends of the spars.

The structure looks heavy, but Mr. Martin told the writer that the wing uncovered weighs 164 lb., which compares favourably with other machines in the same class, particularly when one remembers that the spar has a factor of safety of nine.

This form of single spar is especially interesting because it makes possible the production of a wing the incidence of which, relative to the fuselage, can be controlled from the cockpit . . .

If produced in quantities, machines built according to the Martin method of construction should be cheap to make.

There is a neat point about the cowling of the motor. Not only are the various panels strongly stiffened and securely fastened so that they shall not give trouble in the air after a few hours' flying, but, when lifted up and supported by their struts, they form a protection against the weather for a man working on the motor, and keep the rain off both. When the panel is down the strut is not clipped to it, but to part of the motor-mounting.

Altogether the machine is peculiarly interesting, because it is a genuine attempt to make progress in the construction of aeroplanes. We have often pointed out in this paper that designing for cheap construction is far more important than designing for mass production with the idea that only mass production can make aeroplanes cheaper.

Until aeroplanes are cheaper flying cannot become as popular as it should, and anything which will, or even may, make construction cheaper is a step in the right direction. Mr. Martin's method may turn out to be a long jump rather than a mere step. So we await the flying-trials of the machine with much interest.

MB2: *G-AEZD*, later *P9594*

Type Single-seat, low-wing cantilever monoplane fighter to Specification F.5/34 (private venture).

Wings Tubular steel construction, similar to MB1. Wing main spar constructed from three tubes with cross-bracing and attached directly to fuselage structure. The wing was duralumin-skinned, the ailerons being fabric covered.

Fuselage Tubular steel construction. Forward of the wing trailing edge, the fuselage was metal covered with large detachable panels to simplify access for

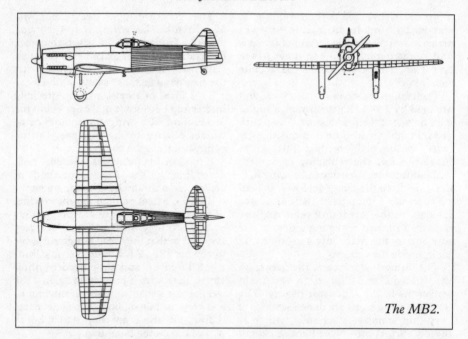

The MB2.

servicing. Crash pylon behind cockpit interconnected with flaps which raised it on take-off and landing.

Tail unit Initial version was finless but a conventional fin and rudder were added. The tailplane was positioned on the fuselage top surface. Construction was entirely metal tube. The fin and tailplane were metal covered with the control services being fabric covered.

Landing gear Fixed undercarriage with an oil cooler built into the port leg fairing. Two compressed air oleo shock absorbers were incorporated in each leg which was aerodynamically trousered. Wheel brakes operated by a low-pressure (60 lb/sq in) compressed air system, as were the flaps and roll-over pylon.

Power plant Napier-Halford Dagger III (serial no. 77101), 24-cylinder air-cooled upright 'H', rated at 1,020 hp with a boost pressure of 13 lb/sq in, giving 798 hp unboosted at 5,500 ft, and driving 10 ft 6 in diameter two-bladed fixed-pitch wooden airscrew. Fuel capacity: 83 Imp gal in two equal tanks in the fuselage. Oil: 3½ gal.

Accommodation Single-seat cockpit enclosed by a 'tear drop'-shaped canopy, entered by raising the canopy and part of the fuselage hinged on the starboard side.

Armament Eight Browning .303 in machine guns, four in each wing, 300 rounds per gun (approx. 30 seconds' firing). Simple weapons bay access, a small handle raising the entire section of wing surface exposing guns and tanks. The armourer was provided with a special seat or kneeling pad.

Dimensions
Wing span 34 ft
Length (final configuration) 34 ft 9 in
Wing area 212 sq ft
Wing loading 26 lb/sq ft
Track 9 ft 8 in
Tailplane span 11 ft
Weight 5,400 lb
Performance
Max level speed at ground level: 265 mph
Max level speed at 9,250 ft: 305 mph
Stalling speed at ground level, flaps down: 73 mph, flaps up: 85 mph
Max rate of climb at ground level: 2,200 ft/min
Max rate of climb at 9,250 ft: 2,360 ft/min
Service ceiling: 29,000 ft
Time to service ceiling: 32 min

MB3: *R.2492*

Type Single-seat, low-wing cantilever monoplane fighter to Specification F.18/39.

Wings 'D'-shaped torsion box made up of plate ribs, light alloy main spar, high-

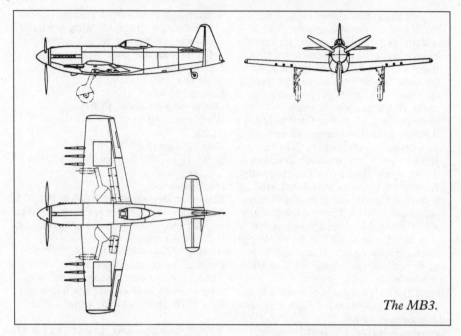

The MB3.

tensile steel strips laminated to form the upper and lower spar booms, the whole wing being covered with a thick, flush-riveted stressed skin. Low-pressure, pneumatic flaps which could be positioned fully up or fully down only.

Fuselage Simple tubular steel construction skinned with stressed light alloy with numerous access panels.

Tail unit Conventional all-metal single fin and rudder. The tailplane and elevator were positioned on the top of the aft fuselage.

Landing gear Fully inward retractable main legs and rearward retractable tail wheel using a low-pressure pneumatic system. Main wheels with low-pressure tyres had a wide track and were set far enough forward to permit full-power ground running without nosing over.

Power plant Napier Sabre II, 24-cylinder flat 'H' type, rated at 2,020 hp and driving a three-bladed variable pitch de Havilland propeller. A shallow Delaney Galley radiator was positioned beneath the starboard wing and the oil cooler beneath the port wing.

Accommodation Single-seat cockpit enclosed by aft-sliding canopy.

Armament Six 20 mm British Hispano cannon, three in each wing. 220 rounds ammunition per gun (approx. 20 seconds' firing) fed parallel to the gun via a Martin-Baker flat feed mechanism. Easy access to each gun and ammunition bay provided by raising one large panel.

Dimensions

Wing span 35 ft
Length 35 ft 4 in
Standing height over airscrew: 15 ft 6 in
Standing height minus airscrew: 10 ft 1 in
Tailplane span: 13 ft 8 in
Wing area: 262.5 sq ft
Undercarriage track: 15 ft 5 in

Performance No performance figures verified due to the early loss of the prototype but specification called for a level speed in excess of 400 mph and ceiling of 35,000 ft. There is every indication that this requirement would have been met.

MB5: *R.2496*

Type Single-seat low-wing monoplane fighter to Specification F.18/39.

Wings MB3 type, simplified and strengthened by laminated high-tensile steel spar booms. All-metal stressed skin with low-pressure pneumatic flaps which could be positioned fully up or fully down and large access panels.

Fuselage Tubular steel construction skinned with stressed light alloy and large access panels.

Tail unit Single, fabric-covered fin. Tailplane positioned on top of the aft fuselage.

Landing gear Fully inward retractable main and rearward retractable tail wheels using a low-pressure pneumatic system. All three wheels were raised very quickly together and the high-pressure tyred main wheels had a wide track.

Power plant Rolls-Royce Griffon Mk 83 liquid-cooled 12-cylinder 60 vee, with two-stage supercharger, driving two three-bladed contra-rotating airscrews of 12 ft 6 in diameter. The propeller translation bearings were lubricated by a special Martin automatic centrifugal oiling unit. Take-off power 1,900 bhp at +8 lb boost. Maximum power at 500 ft was 2,305 bhp at +25 lb boost. Large radiator located in the fuselage below and behind the wing with airflow controlled by a rear scoop.

Capacity Fuel: 200 gal in two tanks in the fuselage: forward tank 70 gal, rear tank 130 gal; oil: 14 gal.

Accommodation Enclosed single-seat cockpit with floor and a clear view 'bubble' canopy fitted with a Martin canopy jettison. All instrument panels were hinged to allow access for maintenance and the control column and rudder bar could be removed as one unit for servicing or repair.

Armament Four British Hispano 20 mm cannon, two in each wing with 200 rounds per gun fed via a Martin-Baker flat feed mechanism.

Dimensions

Wing span: 35 ft
Length: 37 ft 9 1/8 in
Height over airscrew: 15 ft
Wing area: 263 sq ft
Track: 15 ft
Tailplane span: 15 ft 6 in
Weight: 11,000 lb (normal), 12,090 lb (maximum)

Performance

Maximum level speed: 460 mph at 20,000 ft
Maximum level speed at sea level: 395 mph
Stalling speed with flaps and undercarriage down: 95 mph
Service ceiling: 40,000 ft
Operational ceiling: 35,000 ft
Time to operational ceiling: 15 minutes
Rate of climb at sea level: 3,800 ft/min
Rate of climb at 7,000 ft: 4,000 ft/min

The following assessment by R.G. Worcester is taken from *The Aeroplane* of 9 January 1948:

Taken by and large, the Martin Baker M.B.5, with its top speed of 460 m.p.h, will be remembered as the piston-engined fighter pushed to the extreme limit of

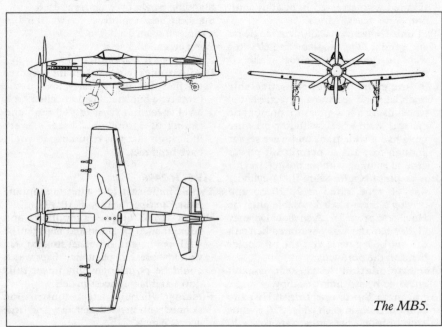

The MB5.

technical achievement, although a few miles per hour might be gained here and there by small developments and refinements, such as a two-speed reduction gear. And flying the machine recently at R.A.F. Chalgrove, showed that this performance was in no way gained at the expense of other essential characteristics of a modern fighter.

Primarily, the flight was made to get a picture of the war-potential of the machine and to assess the relationship between its capabilities in 1948 and its performance in May 1944, when it first flew in the hands of Mr. L.B. Greensted at R.A.F. Harwell. But a second aspect of this fighter arises from the first, which is to discover the extent to which the pilot is affected by the design innovations. It will always remain a milestone marking the end of an era – this basic fighter formula which has carried us successfully through World War II.

The M.B.5 is an all-metal low-wing single-seat fighter powered by a 2,340 h.p. Rolls-Royce Griffon 83, driving a D.H. six-bladed, dural, contra-prop through a 0.4423 reduction gear. The aircraft has a novel construction – the emphasis being placed on maintenance and simplicity – and was designed by Mr. James Martin and his associates at this Denham factory.

FIGHTER QUALITIES

The M.B.5 has a number of outstanding qualities, of which the first is its excellent visibility forward over the nose despite the length of 139 inches from the cockpit to the front of the contra-prop. The 8-degrees angle of depression must be admirable for gun-firing and would be ample for the firing of rockets.

The windscreen has a Martin patent three-piece suspension, and, clamped in the centre and at each side, it is easily detachable. The glass is not thick enough to meet current protection requirements, but this is only a minor detail. The view sideways and downwards is good; the pilot sits on about the mid-chord point of the wing (area, with ailerons and C/S, 263 sq.ft.) and as the root chord is 120 ins., vertical view downwards is not possible. The rear view fuselage allows an uninterrupted view aft and is the best in this respect of all the fighters that I can remember.

In the cockpit the instruments are placed rather low and remind one of the layout of the Skua. They are all easily readable, which is the main requirement of a good instrument panel. The panel, in three pieces, is held by hinges and each section will fold, thus making accessible the back of the individual instruments.

In front are the blind-flying instruments and a vacant space is left for a gyro gunsight. In the place previously occupied by the gunsight is an inter-cooler coolant-temperature indicator provided as a temporary lash-up. The right-hand side of the front panel contains the engine instruments and the left-hand side the flaps control lever and supercharger selector – which can be manually selected M or S gear, or operated automatically.

The brake-pressure indicator and a few other instruments are placed at one's elbow. All the instruments should really be located on the front panel somehow – it is not altogether satisfactory to tuck them away in odd corners because the pilot does not need frequently to refer to them. Pilots sympathize with the harassed designer in this universal problem, not peculiar to the M.B.5, but it must be underlined once again that the front panel is the proper place for all instruments.

The elevator trimmer is on the left and is worked easily by a wheel which moves rotating rods; the rudder trimmer is low on the left. The throttle (about 12-in. movement) and pitch lever (about 3-in. movement) are adjacently located slightly under the side coaming of the cockpit. The throttle lever is a little too far back for comfort and it lacks a positive rear stop. It moves in a gated quadrant in which the forward section is available for the application of up to +24 lb. of boost. This manifold pressure is disallowed since only 100-octane fuel is used now.

On the right-hand side is a comprehensive series of "prototype-only" instruments which include the fuel pressure at the pump inlet; fuel temperature at the outlet; radiator coolant temperature outlet; header tank temperature; oil cooler pressure inlet; oil pressure outlet; fuel pressure at the carburetter; engine cowling temperature; outside-air temperature indicator and the venturi differential pressure. It is worth noting that practically all of this test equipment relates to the engine. There is no provision for a set of strain-gauges leading from points all over the structure.

Taxi-ing is easy; the Dunlop pneumatic differential brakes are worked from a standard spade-grip, complete with "press to speak" and the gun-firing/safety-switch button.

It will perhaps be evident from the foregoing that the M.B.5 has many qualities of a Naval aircraft. It has an excellent forward visibility; the contra-props ensure that there is no swing on take-off, a strong undercarriage (12-ft.5-in. vertical velocity) and it has a useful internal tankage in two fuselage tanks of 70 and 130 gallons – the last fitted under the pilot's seat.

FLYING CHARACTERISTICS

With the booster and magneto switches on, first the starter must be pressed, second the fuel feed to the Bendix carburetter must be turned on, and third the engine given one pump with the primer (three simultaneous operations – two hands).

The cockpit drill before take-off includes a glance at the pneumatic pressure which should be about 350 lb./sq.in.; elevator and rudder trims should be placed neutral; the mixture is automatic; airscrew control lever in max.-rpm.; flaps up (there is no intermediate position for maximum lift); radiator shutters and supercharger control to "automatic". Take-off should not be attempted until the oil temperature is over 15 degrees C. and the coolant temperature above about 60 degrees C.

The throttle can be opened to +12 lb., which is ample, although +18 lb. would shorten the run; the airscrew control should be in the maximum r.p.m. position at 2,750 r.p.m. Initial acceleration (in comparison with jet types) is tremendous and, as noted, there is no tendency to swing. The take-off was somewhat out of wind, but the side wind had no effect whatever. The stick was held a shade back during the take-off run (the wing, incidentally, has +1½ deg. of positive incidence) and the M.B.5 flew itself off at 102 m.p.h. IAS. In the air the slight nose-up attitude when the undercarriage is raised can be trimmed out by a little forward application of the elevator trimmer. The climb is made at + 9 lb. manifold pressure and 2,600 r.p.m. (max. coolant-outlet temperature, 125 degrees C.; oil inlet, 90 degrees C.).

Unfortunately, the day I flew was so miserable that no real flying assessment could be made – other than a brief handling trial. The visibility was not more than a mile or two and I was reduced to flying in the vicinity of the airfield. The cruising speed in M or S gear is with +7 lb. of boost and 2,400 r.p.m. (max. coolant-outlet temperature 105 deg.C.; max. oil inlet 90 deg. C.). The IAS under these conditions was 290 m.p.h., but as I was going round a corner all the time and (despite the under-wing pitot head) there was some positive position error, this spot-reading inevitably will not mean very much. At 20,000 ft., using 2,750 r.p.m. and +25 lb. boost in M or S gear, the maximum speed was 460 m.p.h. TAS (max. coolant outlet, 135 deg.C.; oil inlet, 105 deg.C.).

Lateral stability is good – which is not surprising, considering the 4½ deg. of dihedral. Both the ailerons (area 15.1 sq.ft.) and rudder (area 17.2 sq.ft.) are responsive and there is no tendency to tighten up when turning.

There was no clue anywhere as to the maximum speeds for undercarriage and flap operation, but at 190 m.p.h. I put the wheels down. They go down by gravity plus spring with a characteristic hissing noise (like the Seafire's flaps) from the pneumatic system being released. The gravity plus spring is an inherent safey device requiring no emergency lowering gear. At 150 m.p.h. IAS the flaps were depressed to their 60-degree position (area 28 sq.ft. each side) and a green light below the flap-selector lever showed when they were fully extended. The resulting nose-down attitude is so slight that it can be taken up by an unusually small aft elevator-trimming.

Even with the contra-prop in fine pitch – the vibration is much less than usual with fighters built to this general formula. The positive nature of the hood-locking gear must contribute to the welcome absence of vibration in all conditions of flight. Forward view is so good that the impression of an unusually steep nose-down attitude is formed on the approach for a normal landing. Crossing the hedge at 115 m.p.h. IAS I went through the motions of flattening out. In fact the tail was already down and the machine simply flopped on to the runway. (It is worth noting that the tailplane incidence is +1½ deg.). This was, unwittingly, an aerodrome dummy deck-landing (ADDL). Even during the ADDL, the runway can be seen over the nose – this is remarkable and, with the exception of possibly the Wyvern and Sea Fury XI, is unique. The braking effect of the contra-prop is most marked when the throttle is closed and this, when deck landing, is a good feature.

Taken all round, this is a highly manoeuvrable aircraft; the controls respond finely like those of the Spitfire family. No aerobatics in the looping plane or even a check-stall was possible owing to Chalgrove's low cloud base, but the machine, at about 350 m.p.h. IAS, rolls in the same way as a Spitfire and the feel throughout this manoeuvre seemed very similar. The elevators (area 25.64 sq. ft.) if anything were a shade heavier, but this is a good fault because the Spitfire was sensitive fore and aft. Raising the flaps produces a Spitfire-like hissing from the pneumatics. Taxi-ing back to the hangar, the thermostatic control managed to keep the coolant temperature steady at about 120 degrees C. The margin below the 135-degree maximum would, of course, be smaller in summer. Area of the Morris "intercooler coolant-oil cooler" radiator is not large (entry area 175.5 sq.in.); probably it is just right.

The atmosphere in this aircraft was thoroughly "likeable" and there was a feeling of security in the knowledge that it has an enormously strong structure. Construction follows the Martin principle of interchangeable tubular-steel units bolted to each other and secured to the longitudinal members by fork ends, taper pinned. The tubular-steel engine mounting allows the maximum space for maintenance. The spars are made of 14 s.w.g. laminated steel and form a D with the leading edge to take wing-bending loads. The light-alloy ribs are covered with an Alclad sheet skin, pop-riveted, shaped into an R.A.F. 34 aerofoil section, which defiantly preserves its large thickness/chord ratio to the tip; Mr Martin doesn't believe in low-drag wings under 500 m.p.h. and we may look back and realise he was right.

Drawn but Unbuilt Martin-Baker Aircraft

TWIN-ENGINED FIGHTER

Type Single-seat twin-engine fighter to Specification F.35/35 (private venture).

Wings Low-wing cantilever monoplane of all-metal tube construction. The wing main spar was triangular with wing tip ailerons.

Fuselage Simple tubular steel construction similar to wings.

Tail unit No fin, and rudder formed by an extension of the slab-sided fuselage. Crash pylon behind the cockpit similar to MB2.

Landing gear Retractable main and tail wheels. Both main wheels retracting into each engine nacelle directly behind the engine.

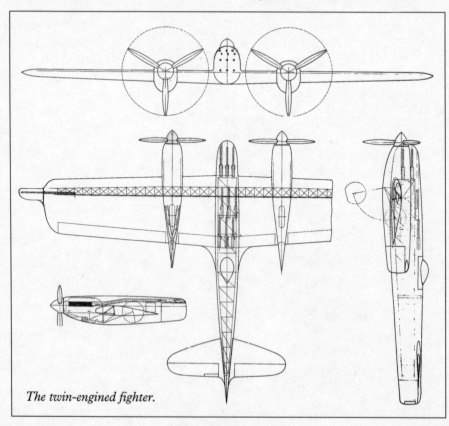

The twin-engined fighter.

Power plant Twin Rolls-Royce Merlin engines driving two three-bladed airscrews. Exhaust manifolds fitted flush with cowlings and finned to assist heat dispersion. Three 56 gal tanks.

Accommodation Single-seat cockpit enclosed with a clear view bubble canopy.

Armament 12 Browning machine guns in four banks of three mounted in fuselage.

Dimensions

Wing span: 50 ft
Length: 36 ft
Wing loading: 25.7 lb/sq ft
Weight: 8,500 lb

TANKBUSTER

Type Single-engine fighter for ground attack tank busting.

Wings Low-wing monoplane with parallel loading and trailing edges and square wing tips.

Fuselage All-metal, housing engine, nose gun, ammunition and fuel tanks, covered in $1/2$ in armour plate weighing approximately 4,900 lb. Radiator and oil tanks were installed inside fuselage in front of the engine and covered by off-set ducts, armour-plated internally to prevent bullets from being deflected inside duct.

Tail unit All-metal, twin booms with fixed incidence tailplane and elevator.

Landing gear Fixed tricycle undercarriage, each leg and wheel covered with aerodynamic fairing.

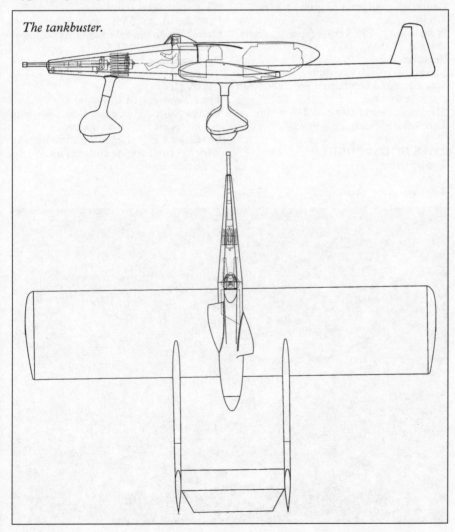

The tankbuster.

Power plant Rear-mounted Rolls-Royce
  Griffon II engine producing 1,760 hp
  and 10ft 6in airscrew.
Accommodation Single-seat cockpit with
  tear drop-shaped canopy, with trap door
  in bottom of fuselage to ensure pilot fell
  clear of airscrew and tailplane during
  emergency bail-out.
Armament Six-pounder anti-tank gun
  with a 30 shell automatic feed in the
  nose. Gun installation was arranged on
  horizontal axis of centre of gravity to
  ensure aircraft would not pitch during
  firing.

Dimensions
Wing span: 48 ft 0in
Length: 40 ft 10 in
Centre of gun barrel to ground level: 7 ft
  6 in
Wing loading: 25.5lb/sq ft (approximately)
Weight 12,000lb
Performance
Maximum speed: 270 mph
Stalling speed (no flaps): 85 mph; (with
  flaps): 76 mph
Maximum rate of climb: 2,250 ft/min
Take-off run (still air): 360 yd

TWIN BOOM PUSHER
Type Fighter.

The twin boom pusher.

Wings Low-wing monoplane with twin
  booms.
Fuselage Simple tubular steel structure
  skinned with stressed light alloy.
Tail unit All-metal twin booms with fixed
  incidence tailplane and elevator.
Landing gear Fully retractable, wide-
  tracked undercarriage. Main wheels
  housed in wing booms.
Power plant Twin Rolls-Royce Griffon
  liquid-cooled engines each driving two
  three-bladed contra-rotating airscrews.
Accommodation Enclosed side-by-side
  seating in cockpit with clear view bubble
  canopy.
Armament Unspecified.
Dimensions
Wing span: 53 ft 0 in
Fuselage length: 33 ft 2 in
Overall length (including booms): 51 ft 8 in
Main wheel track: 20 ft 0 in
Performance Unspecified.

TWIN JET
Type Twin-engine jet fighter.
Wings All-metal stressed skin, low-wing
  monoplane with twin booms.
Fuselage Cigar-shaped with nose intake
  for the front engine and side intakes for
  the rear-mounted engine.

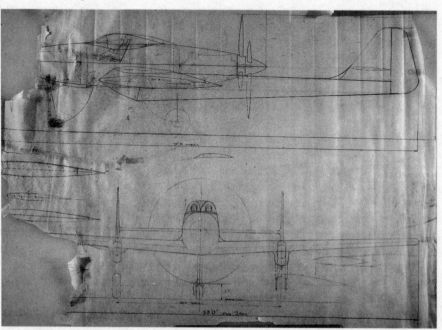

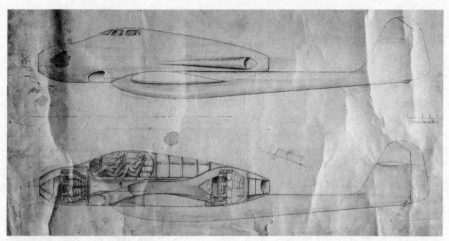

The twin jet.

Tail unit All-metal twin fins and rudders joining the wing booms.
Landing gear Retractable tricycle undercarriage.
Power plant Two Rolls-Royce Derwent engines, mounted in the nose and fuselage.
Accommodation Enclosed cockpit housing two seats in tandem.
Armament Unspecified.

Dimensions
Fuselage length: 30 ft 0 in
Overall length (including boom): 51 ft 0 in
Performance Unspecified.

MB6
Type Single-engine jet fighter.
Wings All-metal stressed-skin low-wing monoplane.
Fuselage Cigar-shaped with nose intake

The MB6.

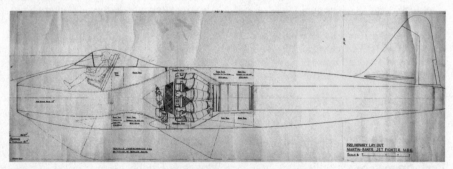

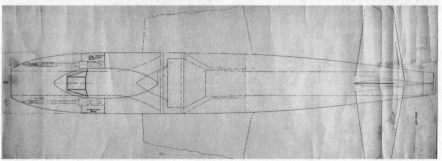

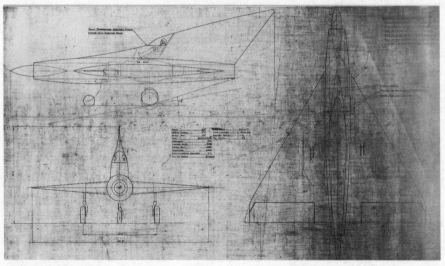

The delta jet fighter.

with unspecified engine mounted within the fuselage directly above the wing mountings.

Tail unit Conventional all-metal single fin and rudder. Tailplane and elevator positioned on top of the aft fuselage.

Landing gear Two skids with option to fit tricycle undercarriage.

Power plant Unspecified. Two forward fuselage fuel tanks of 330 and 200 gal, and two rear fuselage fuel tanks of 200 and 370 gal.

Accommodation Enclosed single-seat cockpit with clear view bubble canopy.

Armament Four 20 mm Hispano cannon with 200 rounds of ammunition per gun.

Dimensions
Tailplane span: 13 ft 4 in
Length: 36 ft 3 in
Wing area: 263 sq ft
Height of fin/rudder from ground: 12 ft 0 in
Area of fin/rudder above fuselage: 21 sq ft
Performance Not specified.

DELTA JET FIGHTER

Type Single-seat jet fighter to Specification F.43/46.

Wings Delta shaped.

Fuselage Unspecified.

Tail unit A delta-shaped fin commencing flush with the cockpit section and extending upwards and along the remaining fuselage length.

Landing gear Tricycle undercarriage retracting upwards and stowed to the rear in line with the fuselage.

Power plant One Rolls-Royce AJ-65 engine with nose intake and fuel capacity of 300 gal contained in two fuel tanks mounted in the wings.

Accommodation Single ejection seat immediately above the engine enclosed in a fully pressurized cockpit.

Armament Two 20 mm Hispano cannon fitted in wing section, one each side, adjacent to fuselage attachment points, with 200 rounds per gun.

Dimensions
Span: 36 ft 0 in
Length overall: 39 ft 6 in
Height: 14 ft 0 in
Wing area: 360 sq ft
Wheel track: 11 ft 0 in
Weight: 8,710 lb
Preliminary performance estimates
Maximum speed at ground level: 640 mph
Maximum speed at 45,000 ft: 600 mph
Time to 45,000 ft: 6 minutes
Rate of climb: 500 ft/min
Take-off run to clear 50 ft screen: 350 yds
Landing run over 50 ft screen (half fuel): 800 yds

Appendix Three

Live Test Ejections

This list does not include the volunteers who tested the ejection seat underwater.

Date	Place	Speed	Altitude (ft)	Ejectee
24.07.46	Chalgrove	320 mph	8,000	B. Lynch
01.11.46	Philadelphia	250 mph	5,000	Lt. Furtek
11.08.47	Chalgrove	200 mph	6,000	B. Lynch
12.08.47	Chalgrove	200 mph	6,000	P. Page
14.08.47	Chalgrove	400 mph	6,000	P. Page
29.08.47	Chalgrove	505 mph	12,000	B. Lynch
20.09.47	Benson	200 mph	4,500	Mr Keyes
29.02.48	Chalgrove	350 mph	5,400	Lt. Cartier, FAF
25.05.48	West Raynham	300 mph	4,000	B. Lynch
09.06.48	Bretigny	470 mph	6,000	Lt. Cartier, FAF
10.07.48	Gatwick	320 mph	2,500	B. Lynch
17.07.48	West Raynham	300 mph	3,000	B. Lynch
05.09.48	Rennes	300 mph	4,000	Lt. Cartier, FAF
11.09.48	Belfast	300 mph	3,000	B. Lynch
18.09.48	Benson	250 mph	3,000	B. Lynch
11.11.48	Chalgrove	300 mph	4,000	S/L Fifield
23.07.49	Gatwick	300 mph	3,000	B. Lynch
17.09.49	Benson	275 mph	2,500	B. Lynch
06.06.50	West Raynham	300 mph	2,500	B. Lynch
11.06.50	Orly, France	300 mph	2,570	B. Lynch
23.08.50	Chalgrove	300 mph	3,000	M. Allemand, FAF
26.08.50	Belfast	300 mph	2,400	B. Lynch
16.09.50	Benson	280 mph	2,200	B. Lynch
27.06.52	Chalgrove	245 mph	8,040	B. Lynch
01.07.52	West Raynham	250 mph	4,000	B. Lynch
17.03.53	Chalgrove	180 mph	30,000	B. Lynch
09.03.55	Canada	300 mph	3,000	S/L Fifield
22.06.55	Benson	230 mph	2,000	S/L Fifield
03.09.55	Chalgrove	145 knots	runway	S/L Fifield
25.10.55	Chalgrove	222 knots	40,500	S/L Fifield
19.10.56	Chalgrove	420 knots	1,800	M. Tournier
19.07.57	Chalgrove	250 knots	1,200	S/L Fifield
28.08.57	Patuxent Md, USA	130 knots	runway	PO S. Hughes, RAF
05.05.58	Germany	120 knots	runway	Mr R. Bulwinkel (Autoflug)
01.07.60	Chalgrove	250 knots	1,000	Mr Hay
01.04.61	Chalgrove	zero/zero		Mr Hay
03.06.61	Le Bourget	zero/zero		Mr Hay
13.03.62	Chalgrove	250 knots	250	W/Cdr. P. Howard
06.12.63	Chalgrove	200 knots	300	Mr Hay

Emergency Ejections

Since Martin-Baker ejection seats first went into service, the practice has grown up of notifying the company when a life has been saved by the seat. This practice is not, however, universal and Martin-Baker believe that there are probably several hundred successful ejections of which they have never been officially notified and ejections are sometimes reported several years after their occurrence. The amount of information given to Martin-Baker in respect of each ejection also varies considerably. The data set out in this Appendix has been supplied by Martin-Baker in good faith, but has been supplied, and is reproduced here, in the full knowledge that it may be incorrect, for it represents only the information which Martin-Baker has received from third parties and which the company has no means of verifying.

Martin-Baker has been notified of 6502 successful emergency ejections with the Martin-Baker seat. Three of these ejectees were women, and 86 were civilians. 155 men have ejected successfully twice, 4 men have ejected successfully three times, and one man has ejected successfully four times.

It is sometimes impossible to identify the reason for an ejection, and sometimes there is more than one contributing factor, but based on the information given to the company, the reasons for ejection are:

engine failure	1336
loss of control	986
enemy action	820
collision	490
landing	253
fire	227
spin	176
fuel	117
take-off	109
bird strike	97
undercarriage failure	73
explosion	53
weather	41
hydraulic failure	34
electrical failure	27
instrument failure	14
air show accident	4
unknown	1645

Following is a list of those whose lives have been saved by the Martin-Baker ejection seat. Classified entries are in groups where actual dates are not known. In this list, the following abbreviations have been used:

CAUSE OF EJECTION

EA	enemy action
OC	other cause
NK	not known

AIRCRAFT TYPES

AJEET	Ajeet
ALPHAJET	Alpha
AMX	AMX
ATTACKER	Att
BUCCANEER	Bucc
CANBERRA	Canb
CASA 101	C.101
CF100	CF100
CHEETAH	Cheet
CHENGDU F7	Ch.F7
COUGAR	Coug
CRUSADER	Crus
DAGGER	Dag
DEMON	Demon
DOUGLAS F4	D.F4

ETENDARD	Etend	**FORCE**	
F100	F100	Abu Dhabi	Abu D
F14	F14	Argentine AF	ArgAF
F18	F18	Argentine Navy	Arg N
F5	F5	Australian AF	AusAF
F84	F84	Australian Navy	Aus N
F86	F86	Belgium	Belg
FIAT G91	F.G91	Botswana	Bots
FURY	Fury	Brazil	Braz
GRIPEN	Grip	Canada	Can
HARRIER	Harr	Chile	Chile
HAWK	Hawk	Civilian	Civ
HUNTER	Hunt	Colombia	Col
IMPALA	Imp	Denmark	Den
INTRUDER	Int	Dubai	Dubai
JET PROVOST	J.Pro	Ecuador	Ecuad
JAGUAR	Jag	Finland	Finl
JAVELIN	Jav	French AF	Fr AF
KIRAN	Kiran	French Navy	Fr N
LOCKHEED F104	L.F104	German AF	GerAF
LOCKHEED T1A	L.T1A	German Navy	Ger N
LOCKHEED T33	L.T33	Ghana	Ghana
LIGHTNING	Light	Greece	Gree
MARUT	Marut	Honduras	Hond
MB326	MB326	Indian AF	IndAF
MB339	MB339	Indian Navy	Ind N
METEOR	Met	Iran	Iran
MIRAGE	Mir	Iraq	Iraq
MOHAWK	Moh	Italian AF	Italy
MYSTERE	Myst	Japan	Japan
NANCHANG A5	N.A5	Jordan	Jord
ORAO	Orao	Kenya	Kenya
PC9	PC9	Kuwait	Kuw
PHANTOM	Phant	Lebanon	Leb
PROTOTYPE	P	Libya	Libya
PROWLER	Prowl	Morocco	Mor
PUCARA	Puc	Netherlands	Neth
SEA HARRIER	S.Har	New Zealand	NZ
STRIKEMASTER	S.Mas	Norway	Nor
SHENYANG F6	SY.F6	Oman	Oman
S211	S211	Pakistan	Pak
SCIMITAR	Scim	Paraguay	Parag
SEA HAWK	S.Hk	Peru	Peru
SEA VENOM	S.Ven	Portugal	Port
SEA VIXEN	S.Vix	Qatar	Qatar
SKYRAY	Skyr.	Royal Air Force	RAF
SWIFT	Swift	Romania	Rom
TORNADO	Torn	Royal Navy	RN
TUCANO	Tuc	Singapore	Sing
VALIANT	Val	Somalia	Somal
VAMPIRE	Vamp	South Africa	SA
VENOM	Venom	Spain	Spain
VICTOR	Vict	Sri Lanka	Sri L
VULCAN	Vulc	Sweden	Swed
WYVERN	Wyv	Switzerland	Switz
		Thailand	Thail
		Togo	Togo

US Army   USA   Venezuela   Venez
US Air Force   USAF Zaire   Zaire
US Marine Corps   USMC Zimbabwe   Zimb
US Navy   USN

No.	Date	Name	Force	Type	Cause	No.	Date	Name	Force	Type	Cause
1	30.05.49	MR J.O.Lancaster	Civ	P	OC	67	19.10.54	F/O P.G.Cook	RAF	Venom	OC
2	20.03.51	LT P.L.McDermot	RN	Att	OC	68	20.10.54	MR M.C.Muir	Civ	Venom	NK
3	14.06.51	F/O A.T.Stoney	AusAF	Met	NK	69	16.11.54	SGT W.A.Wilding	RAF	Hunt	OC
4	03.07.51	SGT W.T.Tollitt	RAF	Met	OC	70	05.12.54	F/O B.Cross	RAF	Met	OC
5	17.07.51	F/SGT H.A.Tickner	RAF	Met	OC	71	20.12.54	F/O C.B.Crombie	RAF	Canb	OC
6	29.08.51	FL/LT R.Guthrie	AusAF	Met	EA	72	21.12.54	FL/LT J.G.H.Carter	RAF	Met	OC
7	15.09.51	F/O L.J.B.Smith	RAF	Met	OC	73	23.12.54	F/O D.J.Wyborn	RAF	Venom	OC
8	11.11.51	F/O K.Blight	AusAF	Met	OC	74	23.12.54	F/O G.Taylor	RAF	Venom	OC
9	01.12.51	FL/LT V.Drummond	AusAF	Met	EA	75	23.12.54	F/O J.M.P.Annand	RAF	Venom	OC
10	21.12.51	MAJ H.N.Lester	USAF	Canb	NK	76	23.12.54	F/O J.S.Crane	RAF	Venom	OC
11	12.01.52	MR J.Bryce	Civ	Val	OC	77	31.12.54	F/O F.Pickles	Can	CF100	OC
12	20.01.52	FL/LT G.M.Smith	RAF	Met	OC	78	26.02.55	F/O K.N.Carpenter	RAF	Met	OC
13	18.02.52	SGT A.Verrico	RAF	Met	OC	79	13.03.55	S/LT M.Cahill	RN	S.Hk	NK
14	10.04.52	CDR V.Cuss	Italy	P	OC	80	12.04.55	F/O L.E.Sparrow	Can	CF100	OC
15	12.04.52	S/L J.Miller	RAF	Met	OC	81	19.04.55	CAPT C.G.Gillespie	RAF	Met	OC
16	05.05.52	S/L P.D.Thompson	RAF	Met	OC	82	19.04.55	S/L G.J.Storey	RAF	Met	OC
17	13.05.52	LT T.F.B.Young	RN	Att	OC	83	21.04.55	F/O D.A.Kestrup	RAF	Venom	NK
18	06.06.52	F/O R.J.Davies	RAF	Met	OC	84	13.05.55	F/O R.C.K.Alcock	RAF	Venom	OC
19	17.06.52	P/O P.J.Poppe	RAF	Met	NK	85	02.06.55	SGT S.G.Snip	Neth	Met	OC
20	10.07.52	SGT C.Groenendijk	Neth	Met	OC	86	28.06.55	F/O J.Flury	Can	CF100	OC
21	10.07.52	SGT J.De Nijs	Neth	Met	OC	87	28.06.55	F/O C.S.Forest	Can	CF100	OC
22	31.07.52	FL/LT B.A.W.Stobart	RAF	Met	OC	88	19.07.55	F/O J.D.H.Price	RAF	Venom	OC
23	19.08.52	S/L G.M.Hermitage	RAF	Met	OC	89	19.07.55	F/O G.H.Winspear	RAF	Venom	OC
24	29.08.52	MR A.E.Gunn	Civ	P	OC	90	03.08.55	F/O H.Molland	RAF	Hunt	NK
25	04.12.52	2/LT J.V.Kemenade	Neth	Met	OC	91	12.08.55	FL/LT D.R.Mair	Can	CF100	OC
26	05.02.53	FL/LT P.G.Greensmith	RAF	Met	NK	92	12.08.55	F/O J.L.C.Filiatrault	Can	CF100	OC
27	27.02.53	FL/LT S.A.E.Newton	RAF	Met	OC	93	12.08.55	LT A.M.Steers	RN	Wyv	OC
28	28.05.53	P/O G.M.E.Pullen	RAF	Met	OC	94	17.08.55	SGT P.M.Stone	RAF	Hunt	OC
29	15.06.53	F/O D.W.Pinkstone	AusAF	Met	EA	95	17.08.55	MR G.J.Horne	Civ	P	NK
30	22.06.53	F/O J.R.Coleman	RAF	Met	OC	96	19.08.55	F/O J.A.Gulyes	Can	CF100	OC
31	15.07.53	LT C.R.Bushe	RN	Att	OC	97	19.08.55	F/O A.J.Legg	Can	CF100	OC
32	30.07.53	F/O G.W.Hunter	Can	CF100	OC	98	14.09.55	MR H.Haflinger	Switz		OC
33	27.08.53	FL/LT M.O.Bergh	RAF	Met	EA	99	14.09.55	LT L.R.Bushe	RN	Wyv	NK
34	05.10.53	F/O R.A.Locke	RAF	Met	OC	100	26.09.55	F/O D.E.Taylor	RAF	Canb	OC
35	07.11.53	P/O P.C.S.Cockell	RAF	Met	OC	101	26.09.55	S/L S.G.Hewitt	RAF	Canb	OC
36	30.11.53	P/O W.D.E.Eggleton	RAF	Met	OC	102	27.09.55	SGT A.Durieux	Neth	Met	OC
37	30.11.53	FL/LT R.C.Wood	RAF	Met	OC	103	01.11.55	P/O R.H.Jago	RAF	Vamp	OC
38	15.12.53		Belg	Met	NK	104	01.11.55	M/PIL F.J.Evans	RAF	Vamp	OC
39	16.12.53	FL/LT G.Hoppitt	RAF	Met	OC	105	03.11.55	P/O K.R.Curtis	RAF	Hunt	OC
40	16.12.53	F/O A.Martin	RAF	Met	OC	106	03.11.55	F/O W.L.Donald	Can	CF100	OC
41	16.12.53	F/O R.Rimmington	RAF	Met	OC	107	05.12.55	LT J.P.Smith	RN	Wyv	OC
42	20.01.54	K.Gregson	RN	S.Hk	NK	108	05.12.55	F/O A.Ginn	RAF	Hunt	OC
43	07.02.54	LT Monsell	RN	S.Hk	OC	109	08.12.55	S/L A.D.Dick	RAF	Jav	OC
44	23.03.54	F/O S.H.D'Arcy	RAF	Venom	NK	110	16.12.55	F/O R.P.Duplessis	RAF	Venom	OC
45	03.04.54	SGT J.Vegtel	Neth	Met	OC	111	01.01.56	P/O C.H.Smith	RAF	Met	OC
46	03.04.54	P/O W.J.Ellis-Hill	RAF	Met	OC	112	13.01.56	F/O J.Wood	Can	CF100	OC
47	07.04.54	LT J.D.Newman	RN	Wyv	OC	113	13.01.56	FL/LT J.M.Sorfleat	Can	CF100	OC
48	07.05.54	S/L G.J.Storey	RAF	Swift	OC	114	13.01.56	F/O J.W.Delorey	Can	CF100	OC
49	31.05.54	SGT D.A.Oswald	AusAF	Met	OC	115	13.01.56	FL/LT J.C.Kitchen	Can	CF100	OC
50	03.06.54	G.K.Gorton	RN	Att	OC	116	25.01.56	FL/LT H.A.Merriman	RAF	Hunt	OC
51	10.06.54	F/O D.J.R.Beard	RAF	Met	OC	117	27.01.56	LT A.R.Campbell	RN	S.Hk	OC
52	15.07.54	SGT M.Forster	RAF	Met	OC	118	08.02.56	FL/LT M.J.Norman	RAF	Hunt	OC
53	15.07.54	F/O R.T.Stock	RAF	Venom	OC	119	08.02.56	S/L W.Ives	RAF	Hunt	OC
54	22.07.54	S/LT G.Foster	RN	S.Hk	OC	120	08.02.56	LT/CDR N.R.Williams	RAF	Hunt	OC
55	26.07.54	F/O F.R.Bennett	RAF	Met	OC	121	08.02.56	FL/LT J.A.Macpherson	RAF	Hunt	OC
56	14.08.54	S/L M.Walton	Civ	Hunt	OC	122	09.02.56	LT G.J.Sherman	RN	S.Hk	OC
57	23.08.54	MR J.Zurakowski	Civ	CF100	OC	123	09.02.56	M.W.Hadcock	RN	S.Hk	OC
58	25.08.54	F/O J.Hobbs	RAF	Swift	OC	124	25.02.56	F/O D.T.Bryant	RAF	Hunt	OC
59	09.09.54	F/O R.P.Deas	RAF	Met	OC	125	05.03.56	FL/LT C.P.Francis	RAF	Vamp	OC
60	09.09.54	F/O J.N.M.Pickersgill	RAF	Met	OC	126	22.03.56	P/O S.O.Loefdahl	Swed	Hunt	OC
61	14.09.54	F/O E.J.Cross	RAF	Venom	NK	127	23.03.56	FL/LT R.Watson	RAF	Hunt	NK
62	28.09.54	LT/CDR N.J.P.Mills	RN	S.Hk	OC	128	03.04.56	F/O D.D.Reeves	RAF	Met	OC
63	04.10.54	P/O D.P.J.Melaniphy	RAF	Met	OC	129	17.04.56	F/O J.A.H.Anderson	RAF	Hunt	OC
64	04.10.54	P/O B.W.Buchanan	RAF	Met	OC	130	26.04.56	F/O W.E.Pierce	Can	CF100	OC
65	12.10.54	LT Mills	RN	S.Hk	OC	131	26.04.56	F/O W.C.Kornyk	Can	CF100	OC
66	13.10.54	LT B.D.Macfarlane	RN	Wyv	OC	132	28.04.56	S/LT D.E.Ferne	RN	S.Hk	NK

No.	Date	Name	Force	Type	Cause	No.	Date	Name	Force	Type	Cause
133	01.05.56	F/O T.J.D.Price	RAF	Hunt	OC	204	17.09.57	S/LT G.W.Smith	RN	Wyv	OC
134	05.05.56	S/L C.C.Povey	RAF	Vamp	OC	205	17.09.57	S/LT R.W.Edward	RN	Wyv	OC
135	11.05.56	FL/LT C.D.Preece	RAF	Val	OC	206	20.09.57	LT J.L.Williams	RN	Vamp	OC
136	17.05.56	LT R.King	RN	Wyv	OC	207	20.09.57	FL/LT M.A.R.Heald	RAF	Vamp	OC
137	22.05.56	F/O K.B.Parker	Can	CF100	OC	208	24.09.57	LT M.J.Doust	RN	Wyv	NK
138	11.06.56	F/O T.L.Lecky-Thompson	RAF	Venom	OC	209	25.09.57	LT S.Idiens	RN	S.Hk	OC
						210	03.10.57	F/O A.S.Brown	RAF	Canb	OC
139	25.06.56	CDR K.A.Leppard	RN	S.Hk	OC	211	10.11.57	W/C D.Dennis	RAF	Hunt	OC
140	25.06.56	MR G.J.Horne	Civ	Swift	OC	212	06.12.57	LT/CDR W.G.B.Black	RN	S.Ven	OC
141	30.06.56	P/O J.E.Hutchinson	RAF	Met	OC	213	09.12.57	F/O G.D.Andrews	RAF	Vamp	OC
142	06.07.56	J.F.Yeates	RN	Att	OC	214	09.12.57	FL/LT G.Willis	RAF	Vamp	OC
143	13.07.56	FL/LT G.McBacon	RAF	Vamp	OC	215	09.12.57	B.P.Marindin	RN	S.Hk	OC
144	13.07.56	AVM C.D.C.Boyce	RAF	Vamp	OC	216	13.12.57	FL/LT J.C.Bryce	RAF	Hunt	OC
145	13.07.56	LT L.E.Middleton	RN	S.Hk	OC	217	13.12.57	F/O F.N.Buchan	RAF	Canb	OC
146	17.07.56	F/O N.R.Williams	RAF	Hunt	OC	218	13.12.57	S/L C.C.Blount	RAF	Canb	OC
147	23.07.56	F/O G.A.Larkin	Can	CF100	OC	219	13.01.58	CAPT P.Krikken	Neth	Met	OC
148	23.07.56	FL/LT G.Murray	Can	CF100	OC	220	11.02.58	F/O P.Baigent	RAF	Jav	OC
149	07.08.56	F/O R.J.Smith	RAF	Venom	OC	221	11.02.58	F/O F.H.B.Stark	RAF	Jav	OC
150	10.08.56	LT M.McCook Weir	RN	S.Hk	OC	222	15.03.58	FL/LT J.C.Newby	RAF	Hunt	OC
151	13.08.56	S/L W.Edwards	RAF	Hunt	OC	223	25.03.58	MR J.Brunner	Civ	P	OC
152	14.08.56	LT M.V.Maina	RAF	Hunt	OC	224	27.03.58	LT J.W.Moore	RN	Vamp	OC
153	24.08.56	FL/LT P.K.V.Hicks	RAF	Hunt	OC	225	27.03.58	S/LT B.A.Waters	RN	Vamp	OC
154	24.08.56	FL/LT R.E.Jefferies	RAF	Jav	OC	226	29.03.58		IndAF	Hunt	OC
155	02.09.56	F/O A.C.Preston	RAF	Hunt	OC	227	29.03.58		IndAF	Hunt	OC
156	13.09.56	FL/LT K.A.Williamson	RAF	Hunt	OC	228	09.04.58	FL/LT J.P.F.De Salis	RAF	Canb	OC
157	27.09.56	SGT A.Durieux	Neth	Met	OC	229	09.04.58	F/O P.H.G.Lowe	RAF	Canb	OC
158	01.10.56	AM SIR H.Broadhurst	RAF	Vulc	OC	230	15.04.58	LT D.J.Schofield	RN	S.Ven	OC
159	01.10.56	S/L D.R.Howard	RAF	Vulc	OC	231	15.04.58	LT J.Webster	RN	S.Ven	OC
160	04.10.56	LT J.D.Bridel	RN	S.Hk	OC	232	18.04.58	FL/LT H.O.Hood	RAF	Hunt	OC
161	15.10.56	LT P.Cardew	RN	S.Hk	OC	233	21.04.58	LT C.Buisseret	Belg	Hunt	NK
162	20.10.56		Belg	Met	OC	234	22.04.58	R.A.Chandler	RN	S.Hk	OC
163	03.11.56	LT D.F.McCarthy	RN	Wyv	EA	235	07.05.58		Can	CF100	OC
164	04.11.56	FL/LT J.B.Flannigan	Can	CF100	OC	236	13.05.58	F/O N.H.Hjelm	Swed	Hunt	OC
165	04.11.56	LT D.F.Mills	RN	S.Hk	EA	237	13.05.58		Can	CF100	OC
166	04.11.56	F/O H.S.Marlin	Can	CF100	OC	238	13.05.58		Can	CF100	OC
167	06.11.56	LT/CDR W.H.Cowling	RN	Wyv	EA	239	19.05.58	FL/LT G.G.Lee	RAF	Swift	OC
168	06.11.56	LT J.H.Stuart-Jervis	RN	S.Hk	OC	240	25.05.58	F/O Petrie	Can	CF100	NK
169	11.11.56	FL/LT M.M.Foster	RAF	Hunt	OC	241	05.06.58	F/O J.J.Jackson	RAF	Jav	OC
170	18.11.56	2/LT A.R.Alizzy	Iraq	Venom	OC	242	11.07.58	FL/LT B.Bedford	RAF	Jav	OC
171	20.11.56	F/O P.A.Marsh	RAF	Hunt	OC	243	16.07.58	ADJ L.Hanson	Belg	Hunt	OC
172	05.12.56	FL/LT W.L.Pigden	Can	CF100	OC	244	16.07.58	SGT G.Cornette	Belg	Hunt	OC
173	05.12.56	F/O A.W.Hanson	Can	CF100	OC	245	29.07.58	CAPT O.Halminen	Finl	Vamp	OC
174	07.12.56	P/O J.Attenborough	RAF	Vamp	NK	246	25.08.58	F/O B.T.Pharoah	Can	CF100	OC
175	10.12.56	F/O D.F.Reid	Can	CF100	OC	247	01.09.58	LT R.C.Dimmock	RN	S.Hk	OC
176	10.12.56	F/O J.J.Paskaruk	Can	CF100	OC	248	02.09.58	SGT E.Sjamaar	Neth	Hunt	OC
177	08.01.57	R.J.Gaunt	Zimb	Vamp	OC	249	08.09.58	LT D.W.Ashby	RN	S.Ven	OC
178	08.01.57	F/O B.N.Horney	Zimb	Vamp	OC	250	08.09.58	LT T.M.Tuke	RN	S.Hk	OC
179	10.01.57	U/OFF M.A.Hicks	RAF	Vamp	OC	251	08.09.58	LT/CDR A.A.Knight	RN	S.Ven	OC
180	04.02.57	SGT J.H.Witman	Neth	Met	NK	252	17.09.58		Belg	Hunt	NK
181	14.02.57	LT B.B.Hartwell	RN	Wyv	OC	253	20.09.58	S/L G.P.Kingston	RAF	Jav	NK
182	15.03.57	MR R.Bignamimi	Civ	F.G91	NK	254	25.09.58	F/O Wilhawk	Can	CF100	NK
183	25.03.57	CADET R.L.Thomas	RAF	Vamp	NK	255	25.09.58	2/LT W.J.O'Connor	USN	Coug	OC
184	25.03.57	F/O G.N.Lewis	RAF	Vamp	NK	256	01.10.58	FL/LT K.A.Small	RAF	Met	OC
185	25.04.57	F/O C.Combes	RAF	Venom	OC	257	08.10.58	MR H.U.Weber	Civ	Hunt	OC
186	25.04.57	F/O R.Joel	RAF	Venom	OC	258	09.10.58	MR D.M.Knight	Civ	Canb	OC
187		B.O.F.Axelsson	Swed	Hunt	OC	259	28.10.58	LT Neilson	RN	S.Vix	OC
188	28.04.57	F/O R.Wellington	RAF	Vamp	OC	260	28.10.58	LT Stewart-Jervis	RN	S.Vix	OC
189	28.04.57	F/O D.J.Joce	RAF	Vamp	OC	261	07.11.58	LT/CDR G.A.Rowan-Thomson	RN	S.Hk	OC
190	29.04.57	FL/LT C.M.F.Mc D Palmer	NZ	Venom	OC						
191	30.04.57	F/O M.Thurley	RAF	Hunt	OC	262	25.11.58	C.C.Cromer	USN	Coug	OC
192	25.05.57	F/O A.P.Hilton	RAF	Hunt	OC	263	27.11.58		Belg	Hunt	NK
193	07.06.57	F/O C.W.G.Young	RAF	Hunt	OC	264	08.12.58	S/L R.J.Burnett	Can	CF100	OC
194	13.06.57	LT G.A.M.Van Wermeskerken	Neth	Met	OC	265	08.12.58	F/O L.Back	Den	Hunt	OC
						266	16.12.58	CAPT J.O.Callahan	Can	CF100	NK
195	03.07.57	FL/LT G.C.Hubbard	NZ	Venom	OC	267	19.12.58	C.M.Schalks	Neth	Met	NK
196	09.07.57	M.Van Ingen-Schenau	Neth	Met	OC	268	22.12.58	FL/LT A.T.Morgan	RAF	Jav	OC
197	09.07.57	P.G.Van Sprundel	Neth	Met	OC	269	12.01.59		Neth	Met	OC
198	22.07.57	F/O J.M.Davies	RAF	Swift	OC	270	12.01.59	LT M.Ralli	Italy	Vamp	OC
199	26.07.57	LT G.W.Barras	RN	Vamp	OC	271	14.01.59	LT/CDR R.H.Fielding	USN	Coug	NK
200	26.07.57	FL/LT R.M.Agate	Can	Vamp	OC	272	22.01.59	MR N.Hancock	Civ	CF100	OC
201	02.08.57	F/O C.G.Reith	RAF	Hunt	OC	273	02.02.59	S/LT N.K.Lover	RN	S.Ven	NK
202	15.08.57	FL/LT G.M.Collins	AusAF	Vamp	OC	274	18.02.59	FL/LT R.A.V.Carrey	RAF	Jav	NK
203	10.09.57	F/O B.J.Stephens	RAF	Hunt	OC	275	26.02.59	SGT D.Hogenbirk	Neth	Hunt	OC
						276	18.03.59	SGT J.G.Demey	Belg	Hunt	OC

No.	Date	Name	Force	Type	Cause	No.	Date	Name	Force	Type	Cause
277	24.03.59	FL/LT R.V.Boult	RAF	Hunt	OC	351	18.03.60		USN	Coug	OC
278	07.04.59	CAPT J.A.Smitherman	RAF	Vamp	OC	352	18.03.60		USN	Coug	OC
279	07.04.59	FL/LT D.Allison	RAF	Vamp	OC	353	28.03.60	LT J.Etter	Switz	Venom	OC
280	09.04.59	FL/LT B.J.St. Aubyn	RAF	Swift	OC	354	30.03.60		USN	Coug	OC
281	10.04.59	FL/LT S.N.Rampal	IndAF	Canb	OC	355	06.04.60		USN	Coug	OC
282	10.04.59	FL/LT B.A.Lewis	RAF	Vamp	OC	356	06.04.60		USN	Coug	OC
283	10.04.59	F/O P.M.Dickenson	RAF	Vamp	OC	357	09.04.60	F/O J.Cleaver	RAF	Hunt	OC
284	13.04.59	F/O G.A.Larkin	Can	CF100	OC	358	14.04.60	F/O Clark	Can	CF100	NK
285	13.04.59	FL/LT G.K.Murray	Can	CF100	OC	359	14.04.60	F/O Saulinier	Can	CF100	NK
286	14.04.59	SGT G.Grifani	Italy	Vamp	OC	360	15.04.60	MAJ J.Lauwers	Belg	Hunt	OC
287	14.04.59	SGT M.Luccioli	Italy	Vamp	OC	361	05.05.60	LT/JG R.M.Byrne	USN	Coug	OC
288	15.04.59	S/L C.J.S.Wood	RAF	Jav	OC	362	21.05.60	FL/LT D.J.Wyborn	RAF	Jav	OC
289	21.04.59	G.Wery	Belg	Hunt	NK	363	21.05.60	FL/LT J.S.Wilson	RAF	Jav	OC
290	06.05.59	F/O N.H.J.Ferguson	RAF	Hunt	OC	364	21.05.60	F/O E.Wood	RAF	Jav	OC
291	30.05.59	CAPT J.S.Ratzlaff	USN	Coug	OC	365	21.05.60	FL/LT D.J.S.Clark	RAF	Jav	OC
292	30.05.59	LT/JG B.B.Woodworth	USN	Coug	OC	366	24.05.60	CADET K.J.Williams	AusAF	Vamp	OC
293	10.06.59	L.L.Lindgren	Swed	Hunt	OC	367	07.06.60		USN	Crus	OC
294	25.06.59	S/LT A.R.Bradshaw	RN	S.Ven	OC	368	15.06.60	LT E.D.Sandberg	Aus N	S.Ven	OC
295	25.06.59	LT P.J.Dale	RN	S.Ven	OC	369	15.06.60	S/LT B.A.Dutch	Aus N	S.Ven	OC
296	01.07.59		USN	Coug	OC	370	16.06.60	SGT J.P.Vleeming	Neth	Hunt	OC
297	09.07.59	FL/LT J.Buckley	RAF	Jav	OC	371	17.06.60	AP/O O.M.J.Kendrick	RAF	J.Pro	OC
298	09.07.59	SGT D.U.Epe	RAF	Jav	OC	372	29.06.60	2/LT E.M.Ten Honten	Neth	Hunt	OC
299	13.07.59	LT/CDR R.P.Taylor	USN	Coug	OC	373	06.07.60	LT/JG C.D.Metzler	USN	Crus	OC
300	13.07.59	1/LT J.J.Klinges	USN	Coug	OC	374	06.07.60	1/LT H.G.Haffner	USMC	Coug	OC
301	17.07.59	FL/LT J.H.Turner	RAF	Swift	NK	375	06.07.60	1/LT D.B.Grimes	USMC	Coug	OC
302	21.07.59		Neth	Hunt	OC	376	14.07.60	SGT G.Tresoldi	Switz	Venom	OC
303	21.07.59		Neth	Hunt	OC	377	19.07.60	FL/LT J.J.Mudford	RAF	Vict	OC
304	24.07.59	MR R.G.Proudlove	Civ	Vulc	OC	378	01.08.60	2/LT T.I.Laache	Nor	F86	OC
305	24.07.59	MR J.G.Harrison	Civ	Vulc	OC	379	02.08.60	Riddell	USN	Coug	OC
306	04.08.59	FL/LT R.S.McCarty	RAF	Met	OC	380	02.08.60	Jacobs	USN	Coug	OC
307	07.08.59	F/O A.J.B.Barnetson	RAF	Hunt	OC	381	04.08.60	F/O E.J.Shere	RAF	Vamp	OC
308	10.08.59		Neth	Hunt	OC	382	14.08.60	CAPT C.C.Chisholm	USMC	Coug	OC
309	25.08.59	FL/LT P.R.Rayner	RAF	Hunt	OC	383	16.08.60	P/O V.Faulkner	RAF	Vamp	OC
310	27.08.59	FL/LT R.Rimmington	RAF	Swift	OC	384	16.08.60	F/O F.W.Mitchell	RAF	Vamp	OC
311	01.09.59	FL/LT F.H.B.Stark	RAF	Jav	OC	385	01.09.60		Peru	Hunt	OC
312	01.09.59	F/O P.Baigent	RAF	Jav	OC	386	06.09.60	LT M.T.H.Styles	RN	S.Hk	OC
313	04.09.59	W/C J.R.D.Braham	Can	CF100	OC	387	24.09.60	LT E.J.Thaubald	USN	Demon	OC
314	04.09.59	S/L J.H.C.Boby	Can	CF100	OC	388	28.09.60	CAPT G.C.Pipornetti	Italy	F.G91	OC
315	15.09.59	G.W.Konijnenburg	Neth	Hunt	OC	389	05.10.60	MR D.Nightingale	Civ	Bucc	OC
316	19.09.59	LT G.P.Carne	RN	S.Ven	OC	390	05.10.60	MR G.R.I.Parker	Civ	Bucc	OC
317	19.09.59	LT L.F.Hilditch	RN	S.Ven	OC	391	10.10.60	CDR C.E.Rich	USN	Crus	OC
318	23.09.59	LT/JG D.G.Macintyre	USN	Coug	NK	392	19.10.60	F/O K.M.Rasmussen	Den	Hunt	OC
319	23.09.59	FL/LT A.K.Ghosh	IndAF	Hunt	OC	393	21.10.60	CDR E.W.Holloway	USN	Demon	OC
320	28.09.59	LT/JG B.J.Smith	USN	Demon	OC	394	24.10.60	FL/LT J.P.Wighton	RAF	Canb	OC
321	29.09.59	F/O C.P.Cowper	RAF	Jav	OC	395	24.10.60	F/O R.G.Braithwaite	RAF	Canb	OC
322	29.09.59	CAPT R.E.Nietz	RAF	Jav	OC	396	25.10.60	CADET P.J.Headley	RAF	Vamp	OC
323	30.09.59	SGT L.M.Cramer	Neth	Hunt	OC	397	25.10.60	FL/LT J.W.Badham	RAF	Vamp	OC
324	01.10.59	MR J.Squier	Civ	Light	OC	398	27.10.60	CAPT C.C.Snow	USN	Demon	OC
325	16.10.59	J.G.Wood	RN	S.Hk	OC	399	16.11.60		USMC	Coug	OC
326	26.10.59	FL/LT A.Martin	RAF	Swift	OC	400	16.11.60	LT/COL K.E.Huntington	USMC	Coug	OC
327	10.11.59	LT N.Grier-Rees	RN	Scim	OC						
328	28.11.59	S/LT P.M.Walker	RAF	Canb	OC	401	24.11.60	S/LT G.Dobbie	RN	S.Hk	OC
329	28.11.59	W/C C.E.W.Ness	RAF	Canb	OC	402	24.11.60	S/LT N.Soper	RN	S.Hk	OC
330	08.01.60	S/L D.S.White	RAF	Hunt	OC	403	28.11.60	LT B.P.Marindin	RN	S.Hk	OC
331	19.01.60	1/LT K.Rasmussen	Den	Hunt	OC	404	09.12.60	LT J.W.H.Purvis	RN	Scim	OC
332	01.02.60	P/O N.H.Lokuge	Sri L	J.Pro	OC	405	19.12.60	F/O P.Jarnum	Den	F86	OC
333	02.02.60	MR G.W.Stinnett	Civ	P	NK	406	11.01.61		USN	Crus	OC
334	02.02.60	J.A.Osbourne	USN	Coug	OC	407	23.01.61	FL/LT G.Richards	RAF	Vamp	OC
335	02.02.60	LT A.L.Alexander	USN	Coug	OC	408	23.01.61	LT M.J.M.Wilkin	RAF	Vamp	OC
336	05.02.60	FL/LT E.J.E.Smith	RAF	Swift	OC	409	01.02.61	LT/CDR A.C.O'Neal	USN	Crus	OC
337	06.02.60	LT/CDR Davies	RN	Scim	OC	410	01.02.61	P/O I.F.Mitchinson	RAF	J.Pro	OC
338	09.02.60		USN	Demon	OC	411	08.02.61	LT G.W.G.Hunt	RN	S.Vix	OC
339	10.02.60	LT G.Stanley	RN	S.Ven	OC	412	08.02.61	LT J.S.Morris	RN	S.Vix	OC
340	10.02.60	LT S.J.Sturgeon	RN	S.Ven	OC	413	24.02.61	1/LT T.De Jager	Neth	Hunt	OC
341	24.02.60	S/LT James	RN	S.Ven	OC	414	24.02.61	LT F.A.Grant Jr.	USN	Demon	OC
342	24.02.60	LT Wilkinson	RN	S.Ven	OC	415	01.03.61	F/O B.I.Berglund	Swed	Hunt	OC
343	05.03.60	S/L R.Harding	RAF	Light	OC	416	10.03.61	F/O J.O.Bergman	Swed	Hunt	OC
344	07.03.60	FL/LT J.E.Nevill	RAF	Swift	OC	417	23.03.61	P/O J.B.Fardell	RAF	J.Pro	OC
345	09.03.60	SGT R.Lydall	RAF	Jav	OC	418	24.03.61	S/L L.A.Boyer	RAF	Vamp	OC
346	09.03.60	FL/LT M.Gill	RAF	Jav	OC	419	28.03.61	MID/SHP M.Dugan	RAF	J.Pro	OC
347	11.03.60	LT C.L.Cliff	USN	Coug	OC	420	28.03.61	F/O A.F.Marshall	RAF	J.Pro	OC
348	11.03.60	CDR R.P.Coogan	USN	Coug	OC	421	17.04.61	2/LT F.P.T.Horne	Den	F86	OC
349	15.03.60	LT R.W.N.Riley	RN	S.Ven	OC	422	17.04.61	2/LT P.Schever-Larsen	Den	F86	OC
350	15.03.60	S/LT J.D.Brown	RN	S.Ven	OC	423	24.04.61	FL/LT Winspear	RAF	Vamp	OC

No.	Date	Name	Force	Type	Cause	No.	Date	Name	Force	Type	Cause
424	24.04.61	P/O Greenland	RAF	Vamp	OC	496	04.11.61		USN	Fury	OC
425	01.05.61	Hamilton	USN	Demon	OC	497	10.11.61	1/LT R.C.Deyo	USMC	Skyr.	OC
426	02.05.61	1/LT R.S.Moore	USN	Coug	OC	498	12.11.61	LT/JG J.J.James	USN	Crus	OC
427	02.05.61	LT W.S.Kelly	USN	Coug	OC	499	15.11.61	1/LT C.W.Vogt	USMC	Crus	OC
428	03.05.61	CAPT J.A.Rogers	USMC	Coug	OC	500	17.11.61		USN	Demon	OC
429	03.05.61	LT W.J.Smith	USMC	Coug	OC	501	22.11.61	LT C.E.Campbell	USN	Coug	OC
430	05.05.61	CADET R.McPartland	Civ	Vamp	OC	502	22.11.61	K.R.Toby	USN	Demon	OC
431	05.05.61	MID/SHP C.A.Skillett	RAF	J.Pro	OC	503	25.11.61	LT/JG W.Logan	USN	Demon	OC
432	05.05.61	FL/LT	RAF	J.Pro	OC	504	27.11.61	S/L Saunders-Davies	RAF	Jav	OC
		W.A.Langworthy				505	27.11.61	FL/LT P.Doughterty	RAF	Jav	OC
433	06.05.61	ENS R.D.Farley	USN	Crus	OC	506	30.11.61	LT/JG G.O.Lundeen	USN	Coug	OC
434	08.05.61	LT/CDR P.Mongilardi	USN	Crus	OC	507	30.11.61	L.K.Dalrymple	USN	Crus	NK
435	09.05.61	SGT P.Ruggaber	Switz	Venom	OC	508	02.12.61	CDR T.M.Smyer	USN	Fury	NK
436	12.05.61	FL/LT O.M.Nielsen	Den	F84	OC	509	04.12.61	CAPT A.L.Frucci	USMC	Crus	OC
437	15.05.61	F/O P.A.Bacon	RAF	Hunt	OC	510	10.12.61	2/LT H.Lowberg	Nor	F86	OC
438	18.05.61	P/O P.G.Nordgren	Swed	Hunt	OC	511	14.12.61	MR A.W.Bedford	Civ	P	OC
439	19.05.61	P/O K.G.Smith	AusAF	Vamp	OC	512	15.12.61		Belg	Hunt	OC
440	30.05.61	SGT K.Tungesvik	Nor	F86	OC	513	15.12.61		Belg	Hunt	OC
441	05.06.61	1/LT D.E.Auten	USMC	Skyr.	OC	514	18.12.61	CAPT Brisset	Fr AF	Mir	OC
442	14.06.61		USN	Skyr.	OC	515	26.12.61		USMC	Demon	OC
443	16.06.61	LT/CDR C.E.Dorris	USN	Demon	OC	516	09.01.62	LT/CDR Sabin	USN	Demon	OC
444	17.06.61	FL/LT S.B.Henriksen	Den	F84	OC	517	15.01.62	F/O M.F.Whittingham	RAF	Canb	OC
445	22.06.61		USN	Crus	OC	518	15.01.62	FL/LT G.Willis	RAF	Canb	OC
446	28.06.61	F/O P.J.Ginger	RAF	Light	OC	519	17.01.62		USMC	Skyr.	OC
447	29.06.61	CDR C.M.Cruse	USN	Phant	OC	520	20.01.62	LT B.Vollstad	Nor	F86	OC
448	06.07.61	LT/JG J.D.Bishop	USN	Demon	OC	521	22.01.62	2/LT F.P.T.Horne	Den	F86	OC
449	11.07.61	LT R.Meylan	Switz	Venom	OC	522	25.01.62	1/LT H.M.Spann	USMC	Crus	OC
450	12.07.61	TEN B.Giuliani	Italy	F.G91	OC	523	02.02.62	MR Stockwell	USA	Moh	NK
451	15.07.61	LT F.J.Almberg	USN	Coug	NK	524	06.02.62	LT K.Weber	GerAF	F.G91	OC
452	15.07.61		USN	Coug	OC	525	08.02.62	1/LT D.G.Doherty	USMC	Crus	OC
453	20.07.61	LT/CDR J.E.Kelly	RN	S.Vix	OC	526	09.02.62	CAPT T.Abelgaard	Nor	F86	OC
454	20.07.61	LT D.Ashby	RN	S.Vix	OC	527	15.02.62	LT M.W.Wakeland	USN	Demon	OC
455	21.07.61	LT/CDR D.Norman	RN	Scim	OC	528	16.02.62	LT H.H.Love	USN	Crus	OC
456	24.07.61		USN	Coug	OC	529	23.02.62	LT J.T.Kneeshaw	USN	Demon	OC
457	24.07.61		USN	Coug	OC	530	27.02.62	LT/JG R.G.Bengston	USN	Crus	OC
458	29.07.61	M.Sarrail	Fr AF	Mir	OC	531	27.02.62	1/LT C.A.Jackson	USMC	Crus	OC
459	04.08.61	FL/LT R.S.Rana	IndAF	Hunt	OC	532	01.03.62	P/O R.E.Turner	RAF	Vamp	OC
460	05.08.61	FL/LT E.Owens	RAF	Jav	NK	533	03.03.62	LT H.V.Spade	USN	Demon	OC
461	05.08.61	M/NAV A.Melton	RAF	Jav	NK	534	05.03.62	LT/JG T.H.Godber	USN	Crus	OC
462	10.08.61	LT/CDR	USN	Demon	OC	535	07.03.62	LT/JG D.G.Klein	USN	Demon	OC
		H.L.Halleland				536	08.03.62	CDR	USN	Crus	OC
463	11.08.61		Can	CF100	OC			A.E.Westmoreland			
464	11.08.61		Can	CF100	OC	537	09.03.62	LT/CDR J.L.Snyder	USN	Crus	NK
465	16.08.61	LT/CDR S.G.Cooper	USN	Demon	OC	538	09.03.62	S/L D.S.Burrows	RAF	Jav	OC
466	17.08.61	LT K.J.Corica	USN	Crus	OC	539	15.03.62	FL/LT K.A.Hariharan	IndAF	Hunt	NK
467	23.08.61	CAPT Rousiers	Fr AF	Mir	OC	540	15.03.62	FL/LT K.S.Vohra	IndAF	Hunt	OC
468	23.08.61	LT Adams	RN	Hunt	OC	541	19.03.62	SGT W.Artmann	GerAF	F84	OC
469	29.08.61		USN	Coug	OC	542	22.03.62	ENS I.G.Lane	USN	Demon	OC
470	29.08.61		USN	Coug	OC	543	23.03.62	MR P.Murphy	RAF	Vict	OC
471	30.08.61	LT/JG G.L.Coffee	USN	Crus	OC	544	23.03.62	FL/LT J.W.Waterton	RAF	Vict	OC
472	30.08.61	P/O J.Armstrong	RAF	J.Pro	OC	545	26.03.62	LT B.J.Bertram	USMC	Crus	OC
473	30.08.61	FL/LT I.K.McKee	RAF	J.Pro	OC	546	27.03.62	LT R.Westby	Nor	F86	NK
474	04.09.61	MID/SHP J.M.Heath	RAF	Vamp	OC	547	28.03.62		USMC	Crus	OC
475	04.09.61	FL/LT G.D.Lambert	RAF	Vamp	OC	548	02.04.62	LT/JG S.W.Betts	USN	Crus	OC
476	06.09.61	HPT W.Kruse	GerAF	F.G91	OC	549	03.04.62	SGT G.Joos	GerAF	F.G91	OC
477	09.09.61	LT W.H.Juvonen	USN	Crus	OC	550	05.04.62	CADET P.R.C.Jones	RAF	J.Pro	OC
478	10.09.61	LT/JG J.M.Walker	USN	Fury	OC	551	11.04.62	LT F.Conrad	GerAF	F84	OC
479	17.09.61	LT W.L.Cain	USN	Fury	OC	552	13.04.62	COL H.Williams	USMC	Crus	OC
480	20.09.61	CAPT L.H.Holmes	USMC	Crus	OC	553	13.04.62	LT/CDR J.M.Dowling	USN	Demon	OC
481	23.09.61	2/LT J.P.Ungar	Den	F86	NK	554	24.04.62		USN	Crus	OC
482	28.09.61		USMC	Coug	OC	555	28.04.62	LT/JG G.H.Freeborn	USN	Demon	OC
483	09.10.61	G.Meelbergs	Belg	Hunt	OC	556	30.04.62	CDR G.C.Watkins	USN	Phant	OC
484	09.10.61	Roelands	Belg	Hunt	OC	557	01.05.62	LT D.H.Ross	RN	S.Vix	OC
485	12.10.61	CDR W.F.McCullough	USN	Demon	OC	558	01.05.62	LT R.H.Burn	RN	S.Vix	OC
486	13.10.61	FL/LT G.G.Davies	RAF	Hunt	OC	559	03.05.62	CDR M.M.Casey Jnr.	USN	Phant	OC
487	16.10.61	LT/JG W.M.Boardman	USN	Crus	NK	560	03.05.62	LT/CDR	USN	Phant	OC
488	16.10.61	1/LT J.E.Strawn	USMC	Crus	NK			E.G.Montmarquet			
489	17.10.61	MAJ R.B.Haines	USMC	Crus	OC	561	07.05.62	LT/JG O.Burgdorf	USN	Crus	OC
490	21.10.61	LT/JG J.Kryway	USN	Crus	OC	562	08.05.62	LT/JG B.E.Kunkel	USN	Crus	OC
491	23.10.61	LT C.D.Metzler	USN	Crus	OC	563	09.05.62	FL/LT	RAF	J.Pro	OC
492	26.10.61	FL/LT P.G.Bevan	NZ	Canb	OC			W.D.E.Eggleton			
493	26.10.61	F/O R.H.Lloyd	RAF	Jav	OC	564	09.05.62	AP/O M.Hyland	RAF	J.Pro	OC
494	02.11.61	LT/JG R.L.Martin	USN	Crus	NK	565	10.05.62	LT D.H.Portch	USN	Coug	OC
495	02.11.61	1/LT J.F.McDonald	USMC	Crus	OC	566	14.05.62	P/O U.E.S.Jaeberg	Swed	Hunt	OC

No.	Date	Name	Force	Type	Cause
567	15.05.62	Classified			
568	16.05.62	O/LT R.Mazander	GerAF	F84	OC
569	18.05.62	M/PIL J.E.Crowther	RAF	Jav	OC
570	22.05.62		USN	Crus	OC
571	29.05.62	1/LT H.Albright	USMC	Phant	OC
572	07.06.62	FL/LT J.H.Adam	RAF	Jav	OC
573	07.06.62	FL/LT C.M.Pinker	RAF	Jav	OC
574	14.06.62	F/O Lowther	RAF	Vict	OC
575	14.06.62	W/C J.G.Matthews	RAF	Vict	OC
576	22.06.62	MAJ L.A.Seipp	USMC	Crus	OC
577	26.06.62	LT G.E.Custer	USN	Crus	OC
578	28.06.62	MAJ P.B.Montague	USMC	Coug	OC
579	28.06.62	LT/JG A.L.Hall	USN	Crus	OC
580	04.07.62	CAPT U.Musicanti	Italy	F.G91	OC
581	04.07.62	LT/JG R.N.Super	USN	Crus	OC
582	10.07.62	LT/JG G.B.Greagh	USN	Skyr.	OC
583	11.07.62	1/LT N.R.Driscoll	USMC	Crus	OC
584	11.07.62	1/LT M.M.Bomis	USMC	Crus	OC
585	13.07.62	LT N.R.Dahlstrom	USN	Coug	OC
586	13.07.62	LT/CDR W.H.Blackwood	USN	Coug	OC
587	16.07.62	CAPT J.C.Coffin	USMC	Coug	OC
588	17.07.62	LT J.E.Bangert	USN	Phant	OC
589	17.07.62	ENS K.F.Morrison	USN	Phant	OC
590	19.07.62	LT/JG J.Connor	USN	Demon	OC
591	22.07.62	CDR J.F.Bolgar	USN	Demon	OC
592	24.07.62	CAPT R.D'Andretta	Italy	F.G91	OC
593	24.07.62	MR A.Rhodes	Civ	S.Hk	OC
594	09.08.62	O/LT F.W.Heidkamp	GerAF	F84	OC
595	13.08.62	LT/CDR B.Willson	RN	Scim	OC
596	14.08.62	LT/JG H.E.Shephard	USN	Crus	OC
597	15.08.62	LT J.A.Smith	USN	Coug	OC
598	15.08.62	LT L.L.Herzog	USN	Coug	OC
599	17.08.62	LT D.B.Williams	USN	Demon	NK
600	17.08.62	2/LT R.J.Newman	USMC	Coug	OC
601	22.08.62	S/L R.A.Lees	RAF	J.Pro	OC
602	22.08.62	S/L J.D.Barwell	RAF	J.Pro	OC
603	25.08.62	CDR J.G.Brozo	USN	Crus	OC
604	13.09.62	MR G.P.Aird	Civ	Light	OC
605	20.09.62	LT G.K.Webb	USN	Crus	OC
606	02.10.62	FL/LT B.C.Gwinnell	RAF	Vict	OC
607	02.10.62	LT A.L.Riley	Aus N	S.Ven	OC
608	04.10.62	1/LT N.A.Babilla	Iraq	Hunt	OC
609	15.10.62	2/LT T.D.Carroll	USMC	Crus	OC
610	16.10.62	LT W.N.Kelt	USN	Crus	OC
611	17.10.62	LT J.F.Ruchala	USN	Crus	OC
612	17.10.62	LT/JG C.K.Dosch	USN	Crus	OC
613	27.10.62	LT W.C.Meintzer	USN	Phant	OC
614	28.10.62	FL/LT B.L.Scotford	RAF	Hunt	OC
615	30.10.62	LT Baldy	Fr AF	Mir	OC
616	31.10.62	LT G.Omland	Nor	F86	OC
617	02.11.62	SGT/CH Joulia	Fr AF	Mir	OC
618	02.11.62	LT/COL R.F.Foxworth	USMC	Phant	OC
619	02.11.62	CAPT D.T.Benn	USMC	Phant	OC
620	07.11.62	LT McDonell	USN	Crus	OC
621	07.11.62		Can	CF100	NK
622	12.11.62	LT C.H.Eley	USN	Demon	OC
623	15.11.62	LT/CDR J.F.Sullivan	USN	Crus	OC
624	15.11.62	LT/CDR J.Kennet	RN	Scim	OC
625	17.11.62	FL1R S.B.Kanne	Den	F86	OC
626	23.11.62	S/LT C.Legg	RN	Scim	OC
627	29.11.62	S/LT R.M.Gravestock	RN	S.Vix	OC
628	29.11.62	LT G.F.Dobbie	RN	S.Vix	OC
629	03.12.62	S/L F.Jolliffe	RAF	Jav	OC
630	03.12.62	W/C P.Smith	RAF	Jav	OC
631	04.12.62	LT/COL W.Panchison	USMC	Crus	OC
632	04.12.62	F/O G.Zieglansberger	Can	CF100	OC
633	04.12.62	F/O R.V.Finch	Can	CF100	OC
634	11.12.62	LT/CDR F.G.Fellowes	USN	Crus	OC
635	14.12.62	1/LT G.Scrensen	Den	F86	OC
636	05.01.63	1/LT W.D.Bethea	USMC	Crus	NK
637	05.01.63	MONS L.Bernard	Civ	Etend	NK
638	14.01.63	LT/JG W.E.Handley	USN	Skyr.	OC
639	19.01.63	2/LT F.K.Nielson	Den	F86	OC
640	19.01.63	CAPT C.V.V.Smillie	USMC	Skyr.	OC
641	24.01.63	MAJ K.C.Palmer	USMC	Crus	OC
642	25.01.63	LT W.S.Fields	USN	Crus	OC
643	02.02.63	CDR L.A.Cole	USN	Skyr.	OC
644	05.02.63	LT/CDR S.T.Zink	USN	Demon	OC
645	07.02.63	2/LT K.E.Heibek	Nor	F86	OC
646	13.02.63	CAPT Barbe	Fr AF	Mir	OC
647	13.02.63	CMDT J.Jean	Fr AF	Mir	OC
648	16.02.63	LT W.A.Everett	USN	Phant	OC
649	16.02.63	LT/CDR D.L.Varner	USN	Phant	OC
650	18.02.63	LT C.J.Herda	USN	Fury	OC
651	19.02.63	F/O W.G.Gambold	RAF	J.Pro	OC
652	07.03.63	FL/LT P.Tate	RAF	Hunt	OC
653	07.03.63	FL/LT C.J.Strong	RAF	Hunt	OC
654	08.03.63	SGT Ledoux	Fr AF	Mir	OC
655	09.03.63	CDR G.G.O'Rourke	USN	Phant	OC
656	09.03.63	1/LT E.B.Cribb	USA	Moh	EA
657	14.03.63	LT R.E.Ward	RAF	J.Pro	OC
658	14.03.63	LT A.T.Pinney	RAF	J.Pro	NK
659	19.03.63	R.Anderson	Den	F100	OC
660	19.03.63	2/LT C.Skytt	Den	F100	OC
661	20.03.63	FL/LT B.J.Jackson	RAF	Vict	OC
662	23.03.63	Classified			
663	23.03.63	LT/CDR W.L.Powers	USN	Fury	OC
664	25.03.63	CAPT D.E.Cathcart	USMC	Crus	OC
665	26.03.63	P.G.Ekstroem	Swed	Hunt	OC
666	26.03.63	LT W.L.Taylor	USN	Crus	OC
667	30.03.63	O/LT H.Adam	GerAF	F84	OC
668	01.04.63	ENG J.M.Cowart	USN	Coug	OC
669	01.04.63	LT R.K.Miklas	USN	Coug	OC
670	16.04.63	FL P.Schever-Larsen	Den	F86	OC
671	16.04.63	LT/CDR J.Wagner	USN	Phant	OC
672	16.04.63	LT/CDR W.N.Kelt	USN	Crus	OC
673	17.04.63	P/O L.Boqvist	Swed	Hunt	OC
674	17.04.63	Ungar	Den	F86	NK
675	18.04.63	P/O A.Gladwin	RAF	J.Pro	OC
676	18.04.63	FL/LT D.Shadbolt	RAF	J.Pro	OC
677	19.04.63	AP/O N.J.Tillotson	RAF	J.Pro	OC
678	22.04.63	MAJ E.D.Bernhard	GerAF	F86	OC
679	26.04.63	FL/LT T.J.Burns	RAF	Light	OC
680	30.04.63	AP/O M.Waterson	RAF	J.Pro	OC
681	30.04.63	FL/LT L.Chalmers	RAF	J.Pro	OC
682	01.05.63	LT/JG I.G.Lane	USN	Demon	OC
683	02.05.63	FL/LT G.Sturt	RAF	J.Pro	OC
684	06.05.63	F/O A.Evans	RAF	Jav	OC
685	08.05.63	FW K.Stoeber	GerAF	F84	OC
686	13.05.63	LT/CDR J.F.Nichols	USN	Phant	OC
687	15.05.63	P.S.H.Olsen	Den	F86	NK
688	17.05.63	LT/JG B.N.Walker	USN	Crus	OC
689	21.05.63	LT/JG J.S.Emerson	USN	Crus	OC
690	22.05.63	S/LT C.D.Legg	RN	Scim	OC
691	28.05.63	LT/JG J.Boyd	USN	Phant	OC
692	06.06.63	FL/LT M.Cooke	RAF	Light	OC
693	11.06.63	LT/JG F.H.Harrington	USN	Crus	OC
694	11.06.63	CAPT W.H.Ridings	USMC	Coug	OC
695	11.06.63	2/LT P.B.Wyrick	USMC	Coug	OC
696	11.06.63	CAPT R.M.Hoff	USMC	Coug	OC
697	15.06.63	LT D.R.Morris	USN	Crus	OC
698	18.06.63	MAJ D.K.Tooker	USMC	Crus	OC
699	20.06.63	ENS J.P.Robillard	Fr N	Crus	OC
700	22.06.63	1/LT A.Nersis	Iraq	Hunt	OC
701	22.06.63	O/LT C.Haesler	GerAF	F.G91	OC
702	26.06.63	LT P.Tidman	Den	F100	NK
703	03.07.63	MAJ B.E.Pedersen	Den	F100	OC
704	07.07.63	CAPT J.W.Butler	USMC	Fury	OC
705	09.07.63	LT R.T.Brinkhurst	RAF	Canb	NK
706	15.07.63	ENS W.T.Callaway	USN	Coug	OC
707	16.07.63	2/LT F.K.Nielsen	Den	F86	OC
708	19.07.63	HPT K.J.Mahncks	GerAF	F84	OC
709	24.07.63	LT L.O.Rogers	USN	Phant	OC
710	24.07.63	LT/JG R.C.Stearne	USN	Phant	OC
711	29.07.63	M/PIL A.Naismith	RAF	J.Pro	OC
712	29.07.63	AP/O P.Fisher	RAF	J.Pro	OC
713	30.07.63	CAPT D.F.Horton	USA	Moh	OC

No.	Date	Name	Force	Type	Cause
714	30.07.63	LT/CDR D.L.Whitman	USN	Crus	OC
715	31.07.63	MR D.M.Knight	Civ	Light	OC
716	31.07.63	LT C.H.Guernsey	USN	Phant	OC
717	01.08.63	LT P.Dannay	Fr AF	Mir	OC
718	02.08.63	LT J.L.Spear	RN	S.Vix	OC
719	02.08.63	LT G.F.Talken	USN	Crus	OC
720	03.08.63	LT R.D.G.Gray	Fr N	Etend	OC
721	05.08.63	LT T.R.Swartz	USN	Crus	OC
722	09.08.63	CAPT R.E.Harris	USA	Moh	OC
723	18.08.63	CAPT J.Rigault	Fr AF	Mir	OC
724	26.08.63	2/LT Dao Dac Dao	USA	Moh	OC
725	26.08.63	LT/JG D.H.Beyer	USN	Crus	OC
726	27.08.63	MR J.T.Judkins	Civ	Moh	OC
727	27.08.63	MAJ J.A.Barrett	Civ	Moh	OC
728	28.08.63	LT/JG T.V.Hillcom	USN	Crus	OC
729	29.08.63	LT D.J.Dunbar Dempsey	RN	S.Vix	OC
730	29.08.63	S/LT W.Hart	RN	S.Vix	OC
731	03.09.63	CAPT M.J.Hanley	USMC	Crus	OC
732	05.09.63	LT D.J.Mellem	USN	Fury	OC
733	05.09.63	1/LT J.B.Bisbey	USA	Moh	OC
734	05.09.63	Nguyen Hoy Binh	USA	Moh	OC
735	11.09.63	Classified			
736	18.09.63	LT J.W.Ryan	USN	Phant	OC
737	18.09.63	LT/JG B.R.Scott	USN	Phant	OC
738	19.09.63	LT R.G.Fortin	USN	Phant	OC
739	19.09.63	LT/CDR W.B.Hoskovec	USN	Phant	OC
740	20.09.63	S/LT A.J.Middleton	RN	Scim	OC
741	20.09.63	LT Kiper	USN	Crus	OC
742	22.09.63	LT J.M.Hendricks	USN	Fury	OC
743	23.09.63	LT M.Walker	RN	S.Ven	OC
744	23.09.63	LT K.R.Alderson	RN	S.Ven	OC
745	27.09.63	1/MTR Bonderf	Fr N	Etend	OC
746	28.09.63	LT/JG A.L.Uner	USN	Demon	OC
747	29.09.63	2/LT H.A.Zapf	USMC	Coug	OC
748	30.09.63	P/O D.Aylward	RAF	Vamp	OC
749	30.09.63	FL/LT P.Callaghan	RAF	Vamp	OC
750	09.10.63	LT/CDR A.D.Williams	USN	Crus	OC
751	10.10.63	LT/CDR H.L.Terry	USN	Crus	OC
752	14.10.63	SGT R.Oelmann	GerAF	F84	OC
753	15.10.63	LT D.D.Timm	USN	L.T33	OC
754	15.10.63	LT/CDR G.Augustine	USN	L.T33	OC
755	16.10.63		RAF	J.Pro	OC
756	16.10.63	O/LT Altherr	Switz	Hunt	NK
757	16.10.63		RAF	J.Pro	OC
758	17.10.63	FL/LT R.Boulton	RAF	Jav	OC
759	17.10.63	FL/LT P.Morley	RAF	Jav	OC
760	17.10.63	LT/JG J.P.Humbert	USN	Crus	OC
761	20.10.63	S/L Karmik	IndAF	Vamp	NK
762	21.10.63	LT J.J.Adams	USN	Crus	OC
763	21.10.63	LT D.P.Mears	RN	Bucc	OC
764	21.10.63	LT/CDR J.White	RN	Bucc	OC
765	22.10.63	O/LT G.Jaron	GerAF	F.G91	NK
766	29.10.63	LT D.B.Fickenscher	USN	Crus	OC
767	05.11.63	FL/LT C.Holman	RAF	Jav	OC
768	05.11.63	FL/LT D.E.Berks	RAF	Jav	OC
769	06.11.63	LT K.J.Jackson	USN	Crus	OC
770	07.11.63	ENS J.R.Andrews	USN	Crus	OC
771	07.11.63	CAPT E.F.Murray	RAF	Jav	OC
772	08.11.63	LT J.Pitaluga	Peru	Hunt	OC
773	08.11.63	LT H.E.Nelson	USN	Coug	OC
774	08.11.63	LT J.Wirthgen	GerAF	F84	OC
775	11.11.63	Classified			
776	13.11.63	LT/JG J.M.Baucom	USN	Crus	OC
777	13.11.63	LT G.De Suduiraut	Fr AF	Mir	OC
778	26.11.63	1/LT W.A.James	USMC	Crus	OC
779	27.11.63	O/LT Lusher	Switz	Hunt	OC
780	29.11.63	1/LT A.Abdullah	Iraq	Hunt	OC
781	07.12.63	LT/CDR R.R.King	USN	L.T33	OC
782	07.12.63	O/LT E.Paasch	GerAF	F84	OC
783	11.12.63	Classified			
784	11.12.63	WO N.D.Thai	USA	Moh	NK
785	11.12.63	CAPT M.F.Menefee	USA	Moh	NK
786	13.12.63	AP/O T.Michaels	RAF	J.Pro	OC
787	13.12.63	LT/JG E.J.Chancy	USN	Crus	OC
788	31.12.63	2/LT H.E.Rasch	Nor	F86	OC
789	06.01.64	LT D.K.Yadav	Ind N	S.Hk	OC
790	10.01.64	2/LT M.Freitag	USA	Moh	NK
791	10.01.64	2/LT Dao Dac Dao	USA	Moh	NK
792	24.01.64	LT A.J.Goodenough	RN	Bucc	OC
793	24.01.64	LT M.J.Howitt	RN	Bucc	OC
794	28.01.64	LT P.E.H.Banfield	RN	Scim	OC
795	29.01.64	1/LT R.M.Pennell	USMC	Phant	OC
796	29.01.64	1/LT K.F.Grennan	USMC	Phant	OC
797	10.02.64	FL/LT G.Sykes	RAF	Jav	OC
798	10.02.64	FL/LT T.P.Burns	RAF	Jav	OC
799	12.02.64	2/LT J.R.Glasscock	USA	Moh	NK
800	12.02.64	CAPT D.B.Gray	USA	Moh	NK
801	12.02.64	LT R.W.Butner	USN	Phant	OC
802	19.02.64	LT O.Johannessen	Nor	F84	OC
803	19.02.64	LT/JG D.G.Critchfield	USN	Phant	OC
804	20.02.64	LT F.O.Boone	USN	Phant	OC
805	20.02.64	LT D.V.Hanna	USN	Phant	OC
806	25.02.64	LT Roux De Besieux	Fr AF	Mir	OC
807	26.02.64	2/LT D.L.Dumond	USMC	Crus	OC
808	27.02.64	MR C.P.Garrison	Civ	Phant	NK
809	27.02.64	MR B.A.McIntyre M	Civ	Phant	OC
810	27.02.64	J.L.Svanstrom	Swed	Hunt	OC
811	03.03.64	LT B.H.McCart	USN	Phant	OC
812	03.03.64	CAPT R.E.Kemble	USMC	Phant	OC
813	04.03.64	CPL Imhof	Switz	Vamp	OC
814	04.03.64	LT J.T.Gunn	USMC	Crus	OC
815	04.03.64	O/LT P.Eichorn	GerAF	F84	OC
816	08.03.64	CAPT J.H.Ditto	USMC	Coug	OC
817	12.03.64	FT/LT R.S.S.Cox	RAF	J.Pro	OC
818	15.03.64	LT/CDR J.L.Berry	USN	Crus	OC
819	17.03.64	LT S.J.Thomas	USN	Crus	OC
820	18.03.64	LT E.Aase	Nor	F86	OC
821	19.03.64	FW J.Kammann	GerAF	F86	OC
822	25.03.64	MR D.Whitham	Civ	Light	OC
823	25.03.64	LT E.K.Somerville-Jones	RN	Bucc	OC
824	25.03.64	LT R.G.Richens	RN	Bucc	OC
825	26.03.64	LT/CDR J.R.Moore	USN	Phant	OC
826	01.04.64	LT/JG A.D.Jenkins	USN	Crus	OC
827	05.04.64	CAPT R.L.Bown	USMC	Crus	OC
828	11.04.64	MR R.E.Rostine	Civ	Crus	OC
829	21.04.64	FL/LT P.S.Martin	RAF	Hunt	OC
830	21.04.64	LT C.W.Kerber		L.T1A	OC
831	22.04.64	LT/JG H.E.Henning	USN	Demon	OC
832	23.04.64	ENS P.V.Vampatella	USN	Crus	OC
833	05.05.64	SGT J.Pedersen	Den	L.T33	OC
834	05.05.64	FL/LT B.Nielsen	Den	L.T33	OC
835	08.05.64	O/LT J.Lemm	GerAF	F84	OC
836	11.05.64	MR O.J.Hawkins	Civ	Vulc	NK
837	11.05.64	FL/LT R.L.Beeson	Civ	Vulc	NK
838	12.05.64	CAPT Breived	Nor	L.T33	OC
839	17.05.64	CAPT A.J.Ortner	USA	Moh	NK
840	17.05.64	CAPT H.L.Woodard	USA	Moh	NK
841	21.05.64	2/LT F.C.Gardner	USMC	Crus	OC
842	21.05.64	LT W.M.Tschudy	USN	Int	OC
843	21.05.64	LT/JG J.D.Harden	USN	Int	OC
844	26.05.64	ENS R.E.Plues	USN	Phant	OC
845	26.05.64	LT/JG C.W.Bennett	USN	Phant	OC
846	27.05.64	WO B.Perry	USMC	L.T1A	OC
847	29.05.64	HERR Isermann	GerAF	F84	OC
848	06.06.64	LT C.F.Klushman	USN	Crus	EA
849	07.06.64	CDR D.W.Lynn	USN	Crus	EA
850	08.06.64	LT R.H.Brown	USN	Crus	OC
851	10.06.64	LT/JG L.M.Nelson	USN	Crus	OC
852	12.06.64	CAPT R.Marozzi	Italy	F.G91	OC
853	14.06.64	LT T.R.O'Brien	USMC	Phant	OC
854	14.06.64	2/LT M.Musafer	Iraq	Hunt	OC
855	14.06.64	LT/COL R.J.Barbour	USMC	Phant	OC
856	15.06.64	FL/LT G.A.Etches	RAF	J.Pro	OC
857	15.06.64	FL/LT Denham	RAF	J.Pro	OC
858	19.06.64	LT B.C.Morehouse	USN	Crus	OC

No.	Date	Name	Force	Type	Cause	No.	Date	Name	Force	Type	Cause
859	22.06.64	LT/JG D.L.Bourland	USN	Crus	NK	932	16.10.64	LT/JG L.K.Clark	USN	Crus	OC
860	30.06.64	FL/LT M.J.Gibson	RAF	Hunt	OC	933	19.10.64	F/O H.E.Frick	RAF	Hunt	OC
861	02.07.64	HERR B.Engelien	GerAF	F.G91	OC	934	24.10.64	LT/JG R.C.Rawlings	USN	Phant	OC
862	02.07.64	CDR W.R.O'Connell	USN	Phant	OC	935	24.10.64	LT/JG R.L.McFillan	USN	Phant	OC
863	05.07.64	1/LT S.Yussef	Iraq	Hunt	OC	936	26.10.64	LT D.F.Callahan	USN	Coug	OC
864	06.07.64	SGT E.Giebelhaussen	GerAF	F84	OC	937	12.11.64	LT R.D.Marshall	USMC	Crus	OC
865	06.07.64	CAPT J.Hubner	USMC	Phant	OC	938	13.11.64	LT W.R.Moore	USN	Phant	OC
866	07.07.64	CDR A.J.Adams	USN	L.T1A	OC	939	13.11.64	LT/JG W.M.Myers	USN	Phant	OC
867	15.07.64	LT R.F.Weller	USN	Phant	OC	940	15.11.64	FL/LT P.I.Mathews	RN	Bucc	OC
868	15.07.64	LT/CDR A.L.Alexander	USN	Crus	OC	941	15.11.64	LT N.Tristram	RN	Bucc	OC
						942	19.11.64	FW W.Ottawa	GerAF	L.T33	OC
869	16.07.64	F/O C.Woods	RAF	Vulc	OC	943	26.11.64	LT/CDR A.J.White	RN	Bucc	OC
870	16.07.64	FL/LT M.H.Smith	RAF	Vulc	OC	944	04.12.64	1/LT V.W.Hansen	Den	F100	OC
871	16.07.64	FL/LT Gartner	Civ	Scim	OC	945	07.12.64	S/L I.A.G.Svensson	AusAF	Mir	OC
872	17.07.64	WO J.W.Frederick	USMC	Phant	NK	946	08.12.64	LT/JG W.C.C.Clark	USN	Crus	OC
873	20.07.64	LT J.Bordt	GerAF	F84	OC	947	30.12.64	LT A.R.Atkinson	USMC	Crus	OC
874	24.07.64	LT W.Vickers	USN	Skyr.	OC	948	31.12.64	Classified			
875	24.07.64	LT/JG G.L.Lawrence	USN	Crus	OC	949	02.01.65	S/LT A.D.Bansod	Ind N	S.Hk	OC
876	28.07.64	LT J.R.Baker	USN	Coug	OC	950	05.01.65	WO D.D.Fuller	USMC	Phant	OC
877	28.07.64	PH2 E.H.Muzylowski	USN	Coug	OC	951	06.01.65	M.Falgarone	Fr N	Etend	OC
878	29.07.64	FL/LT H.Brimer	Den	F100	OC	952	07.01.65	J.C.Doggette	USAF	Crus	OC
879	29.07.64	FL/LT Lilley	Can	CF100	OC	953	07.01.65	LT D.E.V.Unguran	Fr N	Etend	OC
880	29.07.64	FL/LT Connally	Can	CF100	OC	954	09.01.65	LT T.D.Johnson	USN	Crus	OC
881	29.07.64	FL/LT P.Holm	Den	F86	OC	955	11.01.65	S/L J.Whittaker	RAF	Light	OC
882	31.07.64	1/LT G.F.Hanke	USMC	Phant	OC	956	12.01.65	LT C.Blot	Fr AF	Mir	OC
883	31.07.64	CWO2 F.H.Schwarz	USMC	Phant	OC	957	13.01.65	2/LT D.R.Slayden	USMC	Crus	OC
884	03.08.64	J.L.Svanstrom	Swed	Hunt	OC	958	14.01.65	ODE Lorho	Fr N	Etend	OC
885	05.08.64	LT W.D.Storey	USN	Crus	OC	959	18.01.65	LT R.G.Snow	USN	Crus	OC
886	05.08.64	LT B.Skrude	GerAF	F.G91	OC	960	20.01.65	LT/JG C.Brokaw	USN	Phant	OC
887	05.08.64	O/LT S.Thormann	GerAF	F.G91	OC	961	20.01.65	LT V.L.Knaus	USN	Phant	OC
888	06.08.64	FW G.Scheurmeir	GerAF	F84	OC	962	25.01.65	CAPT W.E.Morgan	USMC	Phant	NK
889	10.08.64	LT J.E.Martin	USMC	Phant	OC	963	25.01.65	CWO2 K.Moffitt	USMC	Phant	NK
890	10.08.64	CAPT J.W.Black	USMC	Phant	OC	964	26.01.65	LT/JG L.E.Oakes	USN	Coug	OC
891	11.08.64	F/O R.S.Burrows	RAF	Hunt	OC	965	29.01.65	LT D.C.Farrell	USN	Skyr.	OC
892	13.08.64	CAPT J.M.Moriarty	USMC	Crus	OC	966	01.02.65	SGT Vuitton	Fr AF	Mir	OC
893	18.08.64	CAPT D.E.Auten	USMC	Coug	OC	967	02.02.65	CAPT A.Tveit	Nor	F84	OC
894	18.08.64	CAPT D.F.Newton	USMC	Coug	OC	968	09.02.65	ENS M.Ulrich	USN	Phant	OC
895	19.08.64	LT R.G.Evans	RN	Bucc	OC	969	10.02.65	S/LT B.Friend	RN	S.Vix	OC
896	19.08.64	LT I.M.B.Aichison	RN	Bucc	OC	970	11.02.65	LT R.H.Shumaker	USN	Crus	EA
897	24.08.64	ENS S.W.Hauck	USN	Crus	OC	971	15.02.65	SGT D.Lagnese	Italy	F.G91	OC
898	27.08.64	HERR H.J.Detzer	GerAF	F86	OC	972	15.02.65	LT Richens	RN	Hunt	OC
899	27.08.64	F/O R.Sellappa	IndAF	Hunt	OC	973	15.02.65	S/LT G.J.Broadwater	RN	Hunt	OC
900	28.08.64	CAPT A.M.Fleetwood	USMC	Fury	OC	974	18.02.65	CAPT S.N.Frost	USMC	Crus	OC
901	28.08.64	1/LT R.L.Sprinfield	USMC	Int	OC	975	18.02.65	S/SGT J.R.McFadden	USA	Moh	OC
902	28.08.64	LT/JG B.E.Allen	USN	Int	OC	976	18.02.65	CAPT R.S.Stebbins	USA	Moh	OC
903	31.08.64	CAPT D.E.Downing	USMC	Crus	OC	977	21.02.65	LT/JG R.N.Smith	USN	Crus	OC
904	31.08.64	FL/LT T.G.Gilroy	RN	Hunt	OC	978	23.02.65	CADET W.W.Buckle	Zimb	Vamp	OC
905	03.09.64	FW R.Glaser	GerAF	F.G91	OC	979	23.02.65	F/O F.D.Janeke	Zimb	Vamp	OC
906	08.09.64	O/LT Niehaus	GerAF	F84	OC	980	23.02.65	CAPT E.S.Kowalczyk	USMC	Crus	OC
907	08.09.64	LT R.C.Schroeder	USN	Crus	OC	981	02.03.65	LT/JG R.A.Bengston	USN	Crus	OC
908	09.09.64	LT O.Sandvik	Nor	F84	OC	982	04.03.65	1/LT L.R.Wilson	USAF	Phant	OC
909	11.09.64	FL/LT T.Bond	RAF	Light	OC	983	04.03.65	1/LT R.E.Goodenough	USAF	Phant	OC
910	14.09.64	MR G.Bright	Civ	P	OC	984	08.03.65	CAPT G.A.Davis	USMC	Crus	OC
911	15.09.64	MAJ W.Sutterlin	GerAF	L.T33	OC	985	08.03.65	1/LT J.W.Maples	USMC	Crus	OC
912	15.09.64	FL/LT N.K.Pathak	RAF	Hunt	NK	986	09.03.65	LT S.O.Carter	USN	Fury	OC
913	17.09.64	LT De Vaisseau Wallet	Fr N	Etend	OC	987	17.03.65	LT B.R.Scott	USN	Phant	OC
914	18.09.64	FL/LT S.Sawhney	IndAF	Hunt	OC	988	17.03.65	LT/CDR J.W.Ryan	USN	Phant	OC
915	21.09.64	LT/JG R.A.Bengston	USN	Crus	OC	989	19.03.65	LT Vermesch	Fr AF	Mir	NK
916	24.09.64		USN	Crus	OC	990	22.03.65	CAPT B.Ortensi	Italy	F.G91	OC
917	26.09.64	CAPT J.T.Smith	USMC	Crus	OC	991	26.03.65	P.J.Searle	RN	Hunt	OC
918	27.09.64		IndAF	Hunt	OC	992	26.03.65	LT/CDR M.W.Hadcock	RN	Hunt	OC
919	28.09.64	CAPT R.H.Fobair	USAF	Phant	OC						
920	28.09.64	S/LT P.J.McManus	RN	Scim	OC	993	26.03.65	LT C.F.Wangeman	USN	Crus	EA
921	28.09.64	CAPT B.R.Adams	USAF	Phant	OC	994	29.03.65	CDR Donnelly	USN	Crus	EA
922	30.09.64	P/O J.R.Brown	RAF	J.Pro	OC	995	08.04.65	LT/CDR M.W.M.Barron	RN	S.Hk	OC
923	30.09.64	FL/LT D.J.Phillips	RAF	J.Pro	OC						
924	05.10.64	FL2 R.E.Pederson	Den	F86	OC	996	09.04.65	MAJ D.G.Keast	USMC	Crus	OC
925	07.10.64	CAPT J.M.Jones	USA	Moh	NK	997	09.04.65	LT/CDR W.E.Greer	USN	Phant	OC
926	07.10.64	1/LT Bui Van Lang	USA	Moh	EA	998	09.04.65	LT/JG R.Bruning	USN	Phant	OC
927	09.10.64	LT R.N.Fitzgerald	USN	Crus	OC	999	16.04.65	ENS W.E.Walthall	USN	Phant	OC
928	12.10.64	LT J.N.Berry	USN	Phant	NK	1000	16.04.65	LT/JG B.H.Thompson	USN	Phant	OC
929	13.10.64	LT D.V.Giraud	Fr N	Etend	OC	1001	17.04.65	CAPT Suquet	Fr AF	Mir	OC
930	14.10.64	ENS C.W.Glasscock	USN	Crus	OC	1002	20.04.65	P/O Sharples	RAF	J.Pro	OC
931	16.10.64	LT D.V.D.Muizon	Fr N	Etend	OC	1003	20.04.65	FL/LT Swaine	RAF	J.Pro	OC

No.	Date	Name	Force	Type	Cause
1004	20.04.65	F/O Pack	RAF	J.Pro	OC
1005	21.04.65	LT K.R.Alderson	RN	S.Vix	OC
1006	24.04.65	LT R.Boni	Italy	MB326	NK
1007	27.04.65	LT I.P.F.Meiklejohn	RN	Scim	OC
1008	03.05.65	F/O J.Cooke	RAF	Jav	NK
1009	03.05.65	CAPT R.B.Goodman	USMC	Crus	OC
1010	04.05.65	CAPT J.H.Vandever	USMC	Phant	OC
1011	04.05.65	CAPT J.P.Dawson	USMC	Phant	OC
1012	06.05.65	CAPT J.Crown	USAF	Phant	OC
1013	08.05.65	LT/JG W.B.Wilson	USN	Crus	OC
1014	12.05.65	STDT C.Schmid	Switz	Venom	OC
1015	13.05.65	LT/CDR P.Millet	Civ	Bucc	OC
1016	13.05.65	MR J.R.Harris	Civ	Bucc	OC
1017	17.05.65	LT J.B.Best	USN	Crus	OC
1018	18.05.65	S/TEN A.Dalmas	Italy	MB326	OC
1019	18.05.65	S/TEN R.Corda	Italy	MB326	OC
1020	25.05.65	FL/LT V.Pais	IndAF	Hunt	OC
1021	28.05.65	CDR H.J.Post	USN	Crus	OC
1022	30.05.65	S/LT Kenward	RN	S.Vix	OC
1023	30.05.65	S/LT Cotterill	RN	S.Vix	OC
1024	01.06.65	LT M.R.Fields	USN	Crus	EA
1025	04.06.65	CAPT P.L.James	USMC	Coug	OC
1026	07.06.65	1/LT M.H.Rose	USMC	Coug	OC
1027	09.06.65	CAPT C.D.Keeter	USAF	Phant	OC
1028	09.06.65	CAPT G.L.Getman	USAF	Phant	OC
1029	16.06.65	CAPT W.J.Smith	USAF	Phant	OC
1030	16.06.65	LT M.R.Syptak	USAF	Phant	OC
1031	20.06.65	CAPT C.H.Briggs	USAF	Phant	EA
1032	20.06.65	Kari	USAF	Phant	EA
1033	22.06.65	ENS J.S.Ballard	USN	Crus	OC
1034	22.06.65	LT/CDR R.E.Weedon	USN	Crus	EA
1035	22.06.65	FL/LT P.J.Hart	RAF	Jav	OC
1036	22.06.65	FL/LT P.E.Dell	RAF	Jav	OC
1037	26.06.65	FL/LT A.Doyle	RAF	Light	OC
1038	29.06.65	Classified			
1039	29.06.65	Classified			
1040	01.07.65	CAPT E.S.Kowalcsyk	USN	Crus	OC
1041	06.07.65	CDR R.D.Pollard	USN	Crus	OC
1042	14.07.65	O/LT H.Escher	GerAF	F84	OC
1043	14.07.65	LT D.R.Eaton	USN	Int	EA
1044	14.07.65	LT D.V.Boecker	USN	Int	EA
1045	15.07.65		Venez	J.Pro	OC
1046	15.07.65	A.C.Hill	RN	Scim	OC
1047	15.07.65		Venez	J.Pro	OC
1048	16.07.65	ENS D.K.Johnson	USN	Crus	OC
1049	18.07.65	LT/JG W.M.Tschudy	USN	Int	EA
1050	18.07.65	CDR J.A.Denton	USN	Int	EA
1051	22.07.65	MR G.Elkington	Civ	Light	OC
1052	22.07.65	MR J.Dell	Civ	Light	OC
1053	23.07.65	CAPT Fobair	USAF	Phant	EA
1054	23.07.65	Kieren	USAF	Phant	NK
1055	24.07.65	LT Moffett	USN	Int	EA
1056	24.07.65	LT Bordone	USN	Int	EA
1057	27.07.65	LT/CDR G.B.Ball	USN	Int	OC
1058	27.07.65	LT/JG G.F.Wagner	USN	Int	OC
1059	27.07.65	LT/CDR J.N.Spartz	USN	Int	OC
1060	27.07.65	LT/CDR W.Fitzsimmons	USN	Phant	OC
1061	27.07.65	LT/JG R.L.Griffiths	USN	Phant	OC
1062	27.07.65	MAJ P.Jensen	Den	F100	OC
1063	27.07.65	2/LT R.Folven	Nor	F86	OC
1064	28.07.65	O/LT B.Bernhardi	GerAF	F.G91	OC
1065	29.07.65	AP/O S.J.Roncoroni	RAF	J.Pro	OC
1066	29.07.65	FL/LT J.J.Walker	RAF	J.Pro	OC
1067	02.08.65	MAJ S.J.Dolan	USMC	Crus	OC
1068	09.08.65	LT/CDR J.F.Dorsey	USN	Phant	OC
1069	09.08.65	LT F.G.Staudenmayer	USN	Phant	OC
1070	11.08.65	LT/CDR T.B.Green	USN	Coug	OC
1071	13.08.65	MAJ P.A.Manning	USMC	Crus	EA
1072	16.08.65	Classified			
1073	16.08.65	MR R.J.Anderson	USA	Moh	OC
1074	16.08.65	CWO P.L.Kelly	USA	Moh	OC
1075	17.08.65	LT/COL R.N.Smith	USMC	Crus	OC
1076	22.08.65	1/LT J.Dodson	USMC	Crus	NK
1077	24.08.65		USN	Phant	NK
1078	24.08.65	1/LT M.J.Phillips	USAF	Phant	NK
1079	24.08.65	F.A.W.Franke	USN	Phant	NK
1080	27.08.65	LT C.Roffignac	Fr AF	Mir	OC
1081	27.08.65	CAPT D.Saget	Fr AF	Mir	OC
1082	01.09.65	LT/JG C.Stark	USN	Phant	OC
1083	01.09.65	LT/JG J.S.Reed	USN	Phant	OC
1084	02.09.65	FW M.Straber	GerAF	F.G91	OC
1085	02.09.65	O/LT P.Lemke	GerAF	F.G91	OC
1086	07.09.65	S/L Kackar	IndAF	Hunt	EA
1087	07.09.65	F/O Gandhi	IndAF	Hunt	EA
1088	07.09.65	F/O Pingale	IndAF	Hunt	EA
1089	08.09.65	F/O M.V.Singh	IndAF	Hunt	EA
1090	08.09.65		IndAF	Hunt	EA
1091	09.09.65	LT Gmunder	Switz	Venom	OC
1092	14.09.65	SGT/MAJ Schneeberger	Switz	Venom	OC
1093	18.09.65	CDR J.R.Foster	USN	Crus	NK
1094	19.09.65	LT/JG P.S.Anselmo	USN	Phant	OC
1095	20.09.65	LT P.A.Waring	RN	Scim	OC
1096	20.09.65	S/L S.K.Sharma	IndAF	Hunt	EA
1097	21.09.65	F/O M.M.Lowe	IndAF	Canb	EA
1098	22.09.65	SGT K.H.Warzok	GerAF	F86	OC
1099	22.09.65	FL/LT K.C.Cariappa	IndAF	Hunt	OC
1100	24.09.65	1/LT W.E.Nolen	USAF	Phant	EA
1101	24.09.65	CAPT J.D.Gravis	USAF	Phant	EA
1102	25.09.65	LT/JG D.C.Duffy	USN	Crus	OC
1103	25.09.65	MAJ G.Wergeland	Nor	F86	OC
1104	29.09.65	LT V.Imbert	Fr N	Crus	NK
1105	29.09.65	FL/LT M.Molland	RAF	Light	OC
1106	05.10.65	1/LT T.J.Barrett	USAF	Phant	OC
1107	05.10.65	LT/COL J.O.Hivner	USAF	Phant	EA
1108	05.10.65	LT/JG R.F.Adams	USN	Crus	EA
1109	07.10.65	2/MTR G.Hautot	Fr N	Etend	OC
1110	08.10.65	LT M.E.Dunne	USN	Crus	OC
1111	09.10.65	LT W.E.Markley	RN	Bucc	OC
1112	09.10.65	LT/CDR H.B.Chase	RN	Bucc	OC
1113	11.10.65	SGT V.Marze	Fr AF	Mir	OC
1114	13.10.65	SGT W.Bruhns	GerAF	F.G91	OC
1115	14.10.65	LT J.Terhune	USN	Crus	OC
1116	15.10.65	2/LT S.Hernes	Nor	F86	OC
1117	16.10.65	LT E.A.Brundo	USAF	Phant	EA
1118	16.10.65	CAPT T.E.Collins	USAF	Phant	EA
1119	17.10.65	ENS R.A.Knutson	USN	Phant	EA
1120	17.10.65	ENS R.E.Gaither	USN	Phant	EA
1121	17.10.65	LT/CDR E.Stanley	USN	Phant	EA
1122	17.10.65	LT/JG A.Porter	USN	Phant	EA
1123	19.10.65	Classified			
1124	19.10.65	Classified			
1125	22.10.65	LT T.D.Wilburn	USN	Coug	OC
1126	25.10.65	LT S.Varma	RN	Hunt	OC
1127	25.10.65	LT J.Tod	RN	Hunt	OC
1128	26.10.65	LT/JG J.L.Perry	USN	Phant	EA
1129	26.10.65	LT G.G.Ericksen	USN	Phant	EA
1130	26.10.65	ENS E.T.Saucier	USN	Coug	OC
1131	26.10.65	CAPT J.Aarsheim	Nor	F84	OC
1132	27.10.65	ENS J.R.Greeve	USN	Coug	OC
1133	27.10.65	LT D.A.Moore	USN	Crus	EA
1134	27.10.65	LT/CDR A.M.Lindsey	USN	Phant	EA
1135	28.10.65		USN	Phant	EA
1136	29.10.65	LT R.W.Cooper	USN	Phant	EA
1137	30.10.65	LT J.J.De Klerk	SA	Bucc	NK
1138	30.10.65	CAPT C.M.Jooste	SA	Bucc	NK
1139	02.11.65	LT F.Huggler	Switz	Venom	OC
1140	02.11.65		USN	Crus	OC
1141	02.11.65	CAPT Fille-Lambie	Fr AF	Mir	OC
1142	04.11.65	ENS P.R.Laberge	USN	Crus	OC
1143	05.11.65	CAPT H.P.Chapman	USMC	Crus	EA
1144	07.11.65	LT Nease	USN	Crus	OC
1145	07.11.65	LT Rothgaber	USN	Crus	OC
1146	08.11.65	FL/LT P.G.W.Unsted	RAF	Jav	NK
1147	08.11.65	FL/LT Evans	RAF	Jav	OC
1148	08.11.65	FL/LT K.E.Fitchew	RAF	Jav	OC
1149	08.11.65	1/LT W.Schunemann	GerAF	L.T33	OC

No.	Date	Name	Force	Type	Cause	No.	Date	Name	Force	Type	Cause
1150	12.11.65	MR J.Mullins	Civ	S.Hk	OC	1224	24.02.66	2/LT B.R.Ellis	USMC	Phant	EA
1151	12.11.65	P/O I.G.Parfitt	RAF	J.Pro	OC	1225	24.02.66	1/LT J.W.Pierce	USMC	Phant	EA
1152	15.11.65	P/O G.Wheeler	RAF	J.Pro	OC	1226	25.02.66	ENS R.L.Forshey	USN	Phant	OC
1153	15.11.65	FL/LT J.Dearden	RAF	J.Pro	OC	1227	25.02.66	LT/JG R.G.Miller	USN	Phant	OC
1154	16.11.65	1/LT R.C.Martinsen	USMC	Phant	OC	1228	25.02.66	1/LT J.R.Coleman	USMC	Phant	EA
1155	17.11.65			Crus	EA	1229	25.02.66	1/LT R.L.Pappus	USMC	Phant	EA
1156	17.11.65	CDR R.S.Chew	USN	Crus	EA	1230	28.02.66	CAPT J.C.Kahl	USAF	Phant	NK
1157	17.11.65	1/LT G.E.Peil	USMC	Crus	OC	1231	28.02.66		USN	Coug	OC
1158	18.11.65	LT/JG W.D.Sharp	USN	Crus	EA	1232	28.02.66	LT G.H.Hall	USAF	Phant	NK
1159	20.11.65	LT P.J.King	RN	Bucc	OC	1233	01.03.66	Classified			
1160	20.11.65	LT A.R.Gleadow	RN	Bucc	OC	1234	02.03.66	LT J.W.Febel	USN	Int	OC
1161	22.11.65	LT J.R.Glasgow	USAF	Phant	OC	1235	03.03.66	M.Biraud	Fr N	Etend	OC
1162	22.11.65	CAPT J.A.Giglio	USAF	Phant	OC	1236	03.03.66	S/TEN C.Martinelli	Italy	MB326	OC
1163	23.11.65	LT R.G.Rance	RN	Hunt	OC	1237	04.03.66	CAPT C.R.Fairchild	USMC	Phant	EA
1164	25.11.65	LT H.J.Knoch	USAF	Phant	EA	1238	04.03.66	1/LT T.P.Keenan	USMC	Phant	EA
1165	25.11.65		USAF	Phant	EA	1239	05.03.66	LT R.E.Pile	USN	Phant	EA
1166	28.11.65	CDR H.E.Rutledge	USN	Crus	EA	1240	05.03.66	LT/CDR M.M.Guess	USN	Phant	EA
1167	28.11.65	LT/JG F.H.Harrington	USN	Crus	EA	1241	11.03.66	LT/CDR R.W.Moore	USN	Crus	OC
1168	01.12.65	LT R.S.McAfee	USN	Skyr.	OC	1242	14.03.66	WO1 D.D.Redmond	USMC	Phant	OC
1169	02.12.65	LT/JG R.J.Miller	USN	Phant	OC	1243	14.03.66	MAJ E.C.Paige	USMC	Phant	OC
1170	02.12.65	LT/JG G.F.Martin	USN	Phant	OC	1244	15.03.66	CAPT A.C.Peterson	RAF	Light	OC
1171	02.12.65	LT/JG Potter	USN	Phant	OC	1245	17.03.66	Classified			
1172	02.12.65	LT/JG W.Schmidt	USN	Phant	OC	1246	20.03.66	LT/JG R.R.Ratkliff	USN	Phant	EA
1173	07.12.65	F/O A.J.Perry	AusAF	Vamp	OC	1247	20.03.66	LT J.S.Greenwood	USN	Phant	EA
1174	07.12.65		USAF	Phant	NK	1248	24.03.66	S/LT E.Hughes	RN	S.Vix	OC
1175	08.12.65	CWO2 W.D.Carr	USMC	Int	OC	1249	24.03.66	S/LT I.McKechnie	RN	S.Vix	OC
1176	08.12.65	1/LT J.H.Bentley	USMC	Int	OC	1250	25.03.66	LT N.F.Rawbone	RN	Bucc	OC
1177	10.12.65	Classified				1251	25.03.66	FL/LT G.A.Smart	RN	Bucc	OC
1178	12.12.65	LT/JG W.A.Cote	USN	Phant	OC	1252	28.03.66	LT D.Brearly	RN	Bucc	OC
1179	19.12.65	LT J.Moran	USAF	Phant	OC	1253	28.03.66	CAPT L.C.Bryant	USAF	Phant	NK
1180	19.12.65	CAPT R.S.Kan	USAF	Phant	OC	1254	28.03.66	MAJ J.Peerson	USAF	Phant	NK
1181	20.12.65	LT G.Mimms	USAF	Phant	EA	1255	29.03.66	LT Y.M.Bhide	Ind N	S.Hk	OC
1182	20.12.65	CAPT R.Jeffrey	USAF	Phant	EA	1256	30.03.66	MAJ M.Turchi	Italy	F.G91	OC
1183	21.12.65	ENS E.K.Andrews	USN	Crus	OC	1257	30.03.66	LT E.W.Clexton	USN	Crus	OC
1184	22.12.65	CAPT A.B.Woodward	USA	Moh	OC	1258	30.03.66	CAPT G.Darsi	Italy	F.G91	OC
1185	22.12.65	1/LT N.P.Jenne	USA	Moh	OC	1259	04.04.66	LT/JG W.Kocar	USN	Crus	OC
1186	24.12.65	CDR P.H.Spear	USN	Crus	OC	1260	04.04.66	FL/LT A.L.Vasloo	RAF	Jav	OC
1187	26.12.65	LT/JG W.S.Brougher	USN	Crus	OC	1261	04.04.66	FL/LT Rawcliffe	RAF	Jav	OC
1188	28.12.65	LT/JG R.M.Jewell	USN	Phant	OC	1262	05.04.66	FL/LT P.G.Cowen	RAF	J.Pro	NK
1189	28.12.65	LT D.H.Forsgren	USN	Phant	OC	1263	05.04.66	FL/LT P.Goodman	RAF	J.Pro	NK
1190	31.12.65	LT M.J.Williams	RN	Scim	OC	1264	05.04.66	LT/CDR M.R.Defeo	USN	Crus	OC
1191	10.01.66	1/LT R.T.Morrisey	USMC	Phant	EA	1265	06.04.66	SP4 L.Johnson	USA	Moh	OC
1192	10.01.66	1/LT G.E.Perry	USMC	Phant	EA	1266	06.04.66	MAJ L.Duensing	USA	Moh	EA
1193	11.01.66		USN	Coug	OC	1267	06.04.66	CAPT J.Lafayettes	USA	Moh	EA
1194	11.01.66	CAPT E.D.Long	USMC	Coug	OC	1268	06.04.66	CAPT J.Gates	USA	Moh	EA
1195	16.01.66	CAPT J.A.Gagen	USAF	Phant	EA	1269	06.04.66	LT/CDR N.S.Levy	USN	Crus	OC
1196	16.01.66	1/LT F.M.Malagarie	USAF	Phant	EA	1270	06.04.66	LT P.De Souza	RN	Scim	OC
1197	18.01.66	1/LT G.J.Carpenter	USMC	Phant	OC	1271	08.04.66	LT/CDR W.S.Sams	USAF	Phant	NK
1198	22.01.66	LT/JG R.M.Brent	USN	Phant	OC	1272	08.04.66	MAJ R.E.Schreiber	USAF	Phant	NK
1199	22.01.66	ENS J.D.Kramar	USN	Phant	OC	1273	14.04.66	ENS G.W.Riese	USN	Crus	OC
1200	22.01.66	LT/JG R.C.Atkins	USN	Phant	OC	1274	16.04.66	LT Chesley	USAF	Phant	EA
1201	24.01.66	MAJ H.E.Ramsay	USAF	Phant	NK	1275	16.04.66	MAJ Johnson	USAF	Phant	EA
1202	24.01.66	CAPT Kinser	USAF	Phant	NK	1276	17.04.66	LT/CDR C.D.Hawkins	USN	Int	EA
1203	28.01.66	LT/CDR J.Riendeau	USN	Phant	OC	1277	17.04.66	LT/CDR S.L.Sayers	USN	Int	EA
1204	28.01.66	1/LT H.K.Sieglinger	USMC	Int	OC	1278	19.04.66	CDR R.F.Mohrhardt	USN	Crus	EA
1205	28.01.66	1/LT J.E.Spear	USMC	Int	OC	1279	19.04.66	LT R.F.Ball	USN	Crus	EA
1206	28.01.66	S/LT Z.K.Skrodzki	RN	Scim	OC	1280	21.04.66	1/LT R.E.Goodenough	USAF	Phant	EA
1207	28.01.66	LT/CDR J.S.Bertrand	USN	Phant	OC	1281	21.04.66	1/LT P.A.Busch	USAF	Phant	EA
1208	31.01.66	LT/JG J.N.Stineman	USN	Phant	EA	1282	22.04.66	2/LT J.L.Arendale	USMC	Phant	NK
1209	31.01.66	LT W.F.Klumpp	USN	Phant	EA	1283	22.04.66	CAPT F.A.Huey	USMC	Phant	NK
1210	02.02.66	CAPT R.Harris	USMC	Crus	EA	1284	23.04.66	LT/JG H.E.Vaughan	USN	Phant	OC
1211	02.02.66	LT E.E.Weller	USN	Phant	OC	1285	23.04.66	CAPT J.M.Davey	USN	Phant	OC
1212	02.02.66	LT W.H.Brinks	USN	Phant	OC	1286	26.04.66	LT/JG R.N.Blake	USN	Phant	OC
1213	04.02.66	PF/C J.E.Corkill	USA	Moh	OC	1287	26.04.66	LT N.W.Smith	USN	Phant	OC
1214	04.02.66	1/LT M.L.Bellamy	USA	Moh	EA	1288	27.04.66	LT W.R.Westerman	USN	Int	EA
1215	09.02.66	S/LT P.Latham	RN	S.Vix	OC	1289	27.04.66	2/LT R.L.Robinson	USMC	Phant	OC
1216	10.02.66	LT/JG J.H.Morgan	USN	Crus	OC	1290	27.04.66	CAPT H.F.Stroma	USMC	Phant	OC
1217	14.02.66	CAPT Brechet	Fr AF	Mir	OC	1291	27.04.66	LT/JG B.E.Westin	USN	Int	EA
1218	14.02.66	CAPT Guichemere	Fr AF	Mir	OC	1292	28.04.66	LT/JG D.C.Lewis	USN	Phant	OC
1219	16.02.66	S/LT Z.K.Skrodzki	RN	Scim	OC	1293	28.04.66	LT/JG R.A.Schiltz	USN	Phant	OC
1220	18.02.66	LT L.M.Spencer	USN	Phant	NK	1294	29.04.66	CAPT W.Abbott	USN	Crus	OC
1221	18.02.66	LT Ruffin	USN	Phant	NK	1295	02.05.66	LT E.J.Chancy	USN	Crus	EA
1222	21.02.66	M.J.Peters	USAF	Phant	EA	1296	03.05.66	F/O T.K.Topaz	RAF	Canb	NK
1223	21.02.66	CAPT J.L.Moore	USAF	Phant	EA	1297	04.05.66	CAPT M.A.Illiou	Fr AF	Mir	OC

No.	Date	Name	Force	Type	Cause	No.	Date	Name	Force	Type	Cause
1298	04.05.66	CAPT Masson	Fr AF	Mir	OC	1369	19.07.66	LT T.A.Dennison	USN	Crus	EA
1299	05.05.66	LT J.Heilig	USN	Crus	EA	1370	27.07.66	LT R.D.Clark	USAF	Phant	EA
1300	06.05.66	S/SGT R.H.Huebner	USMC	Phant	OC	1371	27.07.66	CAPT M.C.Mayfield	USAF	Phant	EA
1301	06.05.66	1/LT J.F.Longo	USMC	Phant	OC	1372	27.07.66	FL/LT R.B.Myles	RAF	J.Pro	OC
1302	08.05.66	LT Marro	Fr AF	Mir	OC	1373	29.07.66	S/L D.Johnson	AusAF	Mir	OC
1303	10.05.66	LT A.L.Tarver	RN	S.Vix	OC	1374	02.08.66	1/LT F.H.B.Nielsen	Den	F100	OC
1304	13.05.66	LT B.L.Christiansen	Den	F84	OC	1375	02.08.66	ENS Wenzle	USN	Crus	OC
1305	15.05.66	LT/COL R.G.Blackwood	USN	Int	OC	1376	02.08.66	2/LT J.Sorensen	Den	F100	OC
						1377	03.08.66	1/LT J.C.Lesieur	USMC	Phant	OC
1306	15.05.66	LT/COL J.C.Ellison	USN	Int	OC	1378	03.08.66	SGT R.Vincent	Fr AF	Mir	OC
1307	17.05.66	LT/JG E.S.S.Osbolt	USAF	Phant	OC	1379	03.08.66	LT/JG F.D.Litvin	USN	Crus	OC
1308	17.05.66	CAPT D.G.Rokes	USAF	Phant	OC	1380	03.08.66	CAPT R.C.Johnson	USMC	Phant	OC
1309	18.05.66	LT/COL W.K.Sullivan	USN	Phant	EA	1381	05.08.66	LT C.R.Hunneyball	RN	S.Vix	OC
1310	18.05.66	LT/COL C.W.Summers	USN	Phant	EA	1382	05.08.66	LT W.Heart	RN	S.Vix	OC
						1383	06.08.66	LT Tarre	USAF	Phant	EA
1311	21.05.66	LT R.A.Nester	USAF	Phant	OC	1384	06.08.66	CAPT Bavousett	USAF	Phant	EA
1312	23.05.66	LT L.S.Miller	USN	Crus	EA	1385	08.08.66	LT J.Eatwell	RN	Bucc	NK
1313	26.05.66	1/LT F.T.King	USAF	Phant	OC	1386	08.08.66	LT G.Heron	RN	Bucc	OC
1314	26.05.66	CAPT D.D.Friesen	USAF	Phant	OC	1387	10.08.66	ENS D.W.Garwood	USN	Coug	NK
1315	26.05.66	F/O T.G.Thome	RAF	J.Pro	OC	1388	11.08.66	LT/JG C.A.Balisteri	USN	Crus	EA
1316	26.05.66	P/O D.Sedman	RAF	J.Pro	OC	1389	13.08.66	LT/CDR N.S.Levy	USN	Crus	EA
1317	26.05.66	FL/LT D.Henderson	RAF	J.Pro	OC	1390	14.08.66	CAPT E.S.Kowalczyk	USMC	Crus	OC
1318	27.05.66	1/LT A.G.Graham	USMC	Crus	OC	1391	17.08.66	1/LT W.J.Doherty	USMC	Crus	OC
1319	31.05.66	LT C.Geiger	USMC	Phant	OC	1392	17.08.66	LT/CDR D.A.Verich	USN	Crus	EA
1320	31.05.66	LT M.L.Crabb	USMC	Phant	OC	1393	17.08.66	CAPT T.W.Baxter	USMC	Crus	OC
1321	01.06.66	ENS J.D.Baker	USN	Coug	OC	1394	18.08.66	LT Jacquot	Fr AF	Mir	NK
1322	01.06.66	CAPT Meyers	USAF	Phant	EA	1395	18.08.66	LT Baudevin	Fr AF	Mir	NK
1323	01.06.66	CAPT J.Borling	USAF	Phant	EA	1396	18.08.66	ADJ M.Herve	Fr AF	Mir	NK
1324	02.06.66	LT Ogle	USAF	Phant	EA	1397	19.08.66	LT Milikin	USAF	Phant	EA
1325	02.06.66	CAPT W.S.Laushlin	USMC	Coug	OC	1398	19.08.66	Hatch	USAF	Phant	EA
1326	06.06.66	F/O T.D.Taylor	RAF	Canb	NK	1399	21.08.66	CAPT E.T.Hawks	USAF	Phant	NK
1327	07.06.66	MAJ C.F.Frost	USAF	Phant	OC	1400	23.08.66	LT/JG H.J.Meadows	USN	Crus	OC
1328	07.06.66	MAJ R.M.Keith	USAF	Phant	OC	1401	24.08.66	FL/LT A.Turley	RAF	Light	OC
1329	09.06.66	LT H.P.Ellis	RN	Bucc	NK	1402	25.08.66	FL/LT J.J.Jackson	RAF	Jav	OC
1330	09.06.66	LT A.R.Gemley	RN	Bucc	NK	1403	25.08.66	FL/LT P.J.Hart	RAF	Jav	OC
1331	11.06.66	LT K.M.Hannon	USN	Phant	NK	1404	27.08.66	LT T.H.Walsh	USAF	Phant	EA
1332	13.06.66	Pyle	USAF	Phant	EA	1405	27.08.66	MAJ J.E.Barrow	USAF	Phant	EA
1333	13.06.66	Laurie	USAF	Phant	EA	1406	27.08.66	LT/JG G.T.Coker	USN	Int	EA
1334	14.06.66	F/O South	RAF	Jav	NK	1407	27.08.66	LT/CDR J.H.Fellowes	USN	Int	EA
1335	14.06.66	FL/LT A.Johnson	RAF	Jav	NK	1408	30.08.66	CAPT R.L.Penn	USAF	Phant	OC
1336	14.06.66	2/LT J.Madsen	Den	Hunt	OC	1409	30.08.66	Finser	USAF	Phant	OC
1337	15.06.66	ENS D.W.Vemilyea	USN	Phant	OC	1410	31.08.66	LT/CDR T.Tucker	USN	Crus	EA
1338	15.06.66	LT W.Bennett	USN	Phant	OC	1411	13.09.66	CAPT P.H.Patterson	USAF	Phant	OC
1339	17.06.66	LT/JG H.E.Bines	USN	Phant	OC	1412	13.09.66	CAPT J.H.Crietzberger	USAF	Phant	OC
1340	17.06.66	LT/CDR D.R.Patterson	USN	Phant	OC	1413	13.09.66	LT R.W.Thomas	USAF	Phant	OC
						1414	15.09.66	Classified			
1341	20.06.66	CAPT J.L.Anderst	USMC	Int	OC	1415	15.09.66	S/LT W.W.Burgher	RN	S.Vix	OC
1342	20.06.66	1/LT J.K.Engstrom	USMC	Int	OC	1416	15.09.66	LT/CDR D.B.Knowles	RN	S.Vix	OC
1343	20.06.66	LT C.A.Clark	USMC	Int	OC	1417	16.09.66	Geire	USAF	Phant	NK
1344	20.06.66	2/LT W.Llewellyn	USMC	Int	OC	1418	16.09.66	LT H.J.Knoch	USAF	Phant	NK
1345	21.06.66	LT/CDR C.Black	USN	Crus	EA	1419	16.09.66	Buchanen	USAF	Phant	EA
1346	21.06.66	FL/LT F.E.Zerlaut	USN	Crus	OC	1420	16.09.66	Robertson	USAF	Phant	EA
1347	21.06.66	1/LT D.Lehmann	GerAF	F.G91	NK	1421	17.09.66	D.G.Browning	USAF	Phant	OC
1348	21.06.66	LT L.C.Eastman	USN	Crus	OC	1422	20.09.66	MR P.G.Hay	Civ	Light	OC
1349	22.06.66	FL/LT J.Mason	RAF	Canb	OC	1423	21.09.66	CAPT R.C.Kellems	USAF	Phant	EA
1350	22.06.66	FL/LT P.Holme	RAF	Canb	OC	1424	21.09.66	1/LT J.W.Thomas	USAF	Phant	EA
1351	25.06.66	CAPT R.C.Lawe	USMC	Coug	OC	1425	22.09.66	1/LT K.H.Burhop	GerAF	F.G91	OC
1352	25.06.66	LT/CDR R.M.Weber	USN	Int	EA	1426	22.09.66	OBT FW H.Lipprasch	GerAF	L.T33	OC
1353	28.06.66	LT J.R.Dobbins	USN	Crus	OC	1427	23.09.66	CAPT D.Bartsch	GerAF	F84	NK
1354	30.06.66	2/LT A.E.Wehn	Nor	F86	OC	1428	24.09.66	CAPT T.P.O'Mahoney	USMC	Crus	OC
1355	01.07.66	F/O G.Fish	RAF	Light	OC	1429	27.09.66	LT A.Sinha	Ind N	S.Hk	OC
1356	06.07.66	Classified				1430	29.09.66	S/LT P.Lewis	RN	Hunt	OC
1357	10.07.66	CAPT Weeks	USAF	Phant	EA	1431	29.09.66	LT Glover	USAF	Phant	NK
1358	10.07.66	CAPT Lennon	USAF	Phant	EA	1432	30.09.66	1/LT E.Knets	USAF	Phant	OC
1359	11.07.66	LT/JG M.McCarthy	USN	Phant	OC	1433	02.10.66	1/LT L.Workman	USAF	Phant	EA
1360	11.07.66	LT/JG D.F.Granitto	USN	Phant	OC	1434	02.10.66	CAPT J.Lacassee	USAF	Phant	EA
1361	12.07.66	LT/JG R.F.Adams	USN	Crus	EA	1435	03.10.66	CAPT P.J.Gros	USAF	Phant	OC
1362	14.07.66	SGT K.Schneider	GerAF	F.G91	OC	1436	03.10.66	SER/AIR B.D.G.Albinson	Swed	Hunt	OC
1363	14.07.66	CDR R.M.Bellinger	USN	Crus	OC						
1364	15.07.66	1/LT C.D.Smith	USMC	Phant	NK	1437	04.10.66	CAPT W.Andrews	USAF	Phant	EA
1365	15.07.66	SGT R.R.Bischoff	GerAF	F84	OC	1438	04.10.66	LT/CDR P.E.Eriksen	USN	Int	NK
1366	15.07.66	MAJ B.D.Pritch	USMC	Phant	NK	1439	04.10.66	LT E.W.Garland	USAF	Phant	EA
1367	18.07.66	CAPT J.F.Preston	USAF	Phant	EA	1440	04.10.66	LT/CDR D.R.Vandermolen	USN	Int	NK
1368	18.07.66	CAPT F.D.Moruzzi	USAF	Phant	EA						

No.	Date	Name	Force	Type	Cause	No.	Date	Name	Force	Type	Cause
1441	05.10.66	LT/JG J.J.Cunningham	USN	Phant	OC	1515	16.01.67	Mastin	USAF	Phant	EA
1442	05.10.66	LT/CDR R.A.Fyles	USN	Phant	OC	1516	19.01.67	LT G.Kramer	USAF	Phant	EA
1443	06.10.66	LT R.D.Leach	USN	Crus	OC	1517	19.01.67	CAPT J.S.Jayroe	USAF	Phant	EA
1444	06.10.66	FL/LT C.C.Scriven	RN	Bucc	OC	1518	21.01.67	LT J.T.English	USAF	Phant	OC
1445	06.10.66	LT/CDR J.D.Eagles	RN	Bucc	OC	1519	21.01.67	CAPT W.T.Saylor	USAF	Phant	OC
1446	08.10.66	LT/JG F.D.Lituin	USN	Crus	OC	1520	22.01.67	1/LT D.R.Spoon	USAF	Phant	NK
1447	09.10.66	LT R.R.Terry	USN	Phant	EA	1521	22.01.67	Baugh	USAF	Phant	EA
1448	09.10.66	LT/CDR C.N.Tanner	USN	Phant	OC	1522	23.01.67	LT P.J.Love	RN	S.Vix	NK
1449	10.10.66	MAJ B.L.Talley	USAF	Phant	EA	1523	24.01.67	LT H.Khidhir	Iraq	Hunt	OC
1450	11.10.66	LT S.Pirali	Italy	MB326	OC	1524	27.01.67	LT L.D.Peterson	USAF	Phant	NK
1451	13.10.66	FL/LT N.K.Bhasin	IndAF	Hunt	OC	1525	27.01.67	MAJ J.A.Hargrove	USAF	Phant	NK
1452	13.10.66	FL/LT Y.S.Rao	IndAF	Vamp	NK	1526	30.01.67	LT A.C.Selman	RN	S.Vix	OC
1453	14.10.66	1/LT M.V.Marlowe	USAF	Phant	OC	1527	30.01.67	LT/JG S.R.Farrow	USN	Coug	OC
1454	14.10.66	1/LT F.E.Hawley	USAF	Phant	OC	1528	30.01.67	CDR L.C.O'Neil	USN	Coug	OC
1455	19.10.66	LT G.L.Anderson	USN	Phant	OC	1529	31.01.67	LT Meneir	Switz	Venom	OC
1456	19.10.66	LT H.D.Wisely	USN	Phant	OC	1530	01.02.67	ENS D.Manlove	USN	Phant	NK
1457	20.10.66	1/LT J.Merrick	USAF	Phant	EA	1531	01.02.67	LT/CDR J.C.Barenti	USN	Phant	OC
1458	20.10.66	MAJ L.Breckonridge	USAF	Phant	OC	1532	03.02.67	CAPT B.Downing	USMC	Coug	NK
1459	22.10.66	LT E.Turner	USN	Phant	EA	1533	03.02.67	LT/CDR T.Schaaf	USN	L.T1A	OC
1460	03.11.66	LT J.P.Picolli	USN	Phant	EA	1534	03.02.67	LT/CDR T.T.Riley	USN	L.T1A	OC
1461	03.11.66	LT/CDR R.Schaffer	USN	Phant	EA	1535	03.02.67	CAPT Gauthier	Fr AF	Mir	OC
1462	03.11.66	LT W.A.Wood	USN	Phant	OC	1536	03.02.67	CAPT H.G.Brodsky	USAF	Phant	OC
1463	03.11.66	LT E.J.Ducharme	USN	Phant	OC	1537	03.02.67	CAPT R.L.Clamme	USAF	Phant	OC
1464	09.11.66	CDR P.T.Gilchrist	USN	Crus	OC	1538	09.02.67	ENS L.P.Amborn	USN	Coug	OC
1465	10.11.66	LT F.M.Hammond	USN	Int	OC	1539	10.02.67	SGT E.Schwilgin	GerAF	F.G91	OC
1466	11.11.66	CAPT R.Biss	USAF	Phant	EA	1540	11.02.67	LT/JG T.F.Carrier	USN	Crus	OC
1467	11.11.66	LT/COL O.G.Swindle	USMC	Crus	EA	1541	20.02.67	2/LT G.A.Thornton	USN	Phant	EA
1468	11.11.66	1/LT R.L.Butt	USAF	Phant	EA	1542	20.02.67	FL/LT W.D.Thomson	RAF	Hunt	OC
1469	11.11.66	Monlux	USAF	Phant	EA	1543	20.02.67	F/O D.Sowler	RAF	Hunt	OC
1470	11.11.66	CAPT Ringsdorf	USAF	Phant	EA	1544	21.02.67	LT/JG M.Larry	USN	Phant	OC
1471	21.11.66	ENS B.S.Foster	USN	Crus	OC	1545	21.02.67	CDR A.R.Burt	USN	Phant	OC
1472	22.11.66	MAJ Crecca	USAF	Phant	OC	1546	22.02.67	MAJ A.A.S.Moreira	Port	F.G91	OC
1473	22.11.66	LT G.S.Wilson	USAF	Phant	OC	1547	24.02.67	1/LT H.G.Floyd	USN	Phant	OC
1474	28.11.66	1/LT W.W.Detki	USMC	Phant	OC	1548	24.02.67	CAPT S.B.Hudson	USAF	Phant	OC
1475	28.11.66	MAJ M.Jarriges	Civ	Mir	OC	1549	25.02.67	LT/JG R.C.Ewing	USN	Phant	OC
1476	29.11.66	CAPT J.D.Weides	USAF	Phant	OC	1550	25.02.67	LT D.W.Hoffman	USN	Phant	OC
1477	29.11.66	1/LT L.Liebe	USMC	Phant	OC	1551	27.02.67	LT/JG J.D.Orsburn	USN	Phant	OC
1478	02.12.66	Burns	USAF	Phant	EA	1552	27.02.67	FL/LT Kilzul	Can	Canb	OC
1479	02.12.66	Flescher	USAF	Phant	EA	1553	28.02.67	1/LT K.C.Simonin	USAF	Phant	EA
1480	02.12.66	ENS D.G.Rehmann	USN	Phant	EA	1554	28.02.67	MAJ J.F.Clayton	USAF	Phant	EA
1481	02.12.66	Ducat	USAF	Phant	EA	1555	28.02.67	CAPT R.I.Harris	USMC	Crus	OC
1482	02.12.66	COL K.W.Cordier	USAF	Phant	EA	1556	01.03.67	CADET	USN	Coug	OC
1483	02.12.66	Classified						M.B.Bartholomew			
1484	02.12.66	LT/COL M.Lane	USAF	Phant	EA	1557	01.03.67	CAPT E.W.Kimmel	USMC	Coug	OC
1485	06.12.66	CAPT W.R.Fannemal	USAF	Phant	EA	1558	02.03.67	1/MTR Robert	Fr N	Etend	OC
1486	06.12.66	LT/COL T.W.Dyke	USAF	Phant	EA	1559	03.03.67	Richardson	USAF	Phant	EA
1487	07.12.66	E4 K.G.Bakos	USA	Moh	OC	1560	03.03.67	F/O S.Pearse	RAF	Light	OC
1488	07.12.66	CAPT W.T.Ebert	USA	Moh	OC	1561	03.03.67	LT/JG D.D.Johnson	USN	Crus	OC
1489	08.12.66	LT F.H.Porter	USAF	Phant	EA	1562	06.03.67	SGT Paille	Fr AF	Mir	OC
1490	08.12.66	MAJ J.K.Young	USAF	Phant	EA	1563	07.03.67	CAPT W.C.Stewart	USMC	Phant	OC
1491	11.12.66		USAF	Phant	EA	1564	07.03.67	1/LT T.L.Jones	USMC	Phant	OC
1492	11.12.66	MAJ G.Woodcock	USAF	Phant	NK	1565	08.03.67	MR Garrison	USN	Phant	OC
1493	14.12.66	FL/LT T.P.Burns	RAF	Jav	OC	1566	10.03.67	LT R.Houghton	USAF	Phant	EA
1494	14.12.66	F/O J.W.Pierce	RAF	Jav	OC	1567	10.03.67	CAPT E.D.Aman	USAF	Phant	EA
1495	20.12.66	LT/JG B.L.Donglow	USN	Phant	OC	1568	10.03.67	LT S.A.Wayne	USAF	Phant	EA
1496	20.12.66	CAPT J.L.Kulmayer	USA	Moh	OC	1569	10.03.67	CAPT R.Pardo	USAF	Phant	EA
1497	20.12.66		USAF	Phant	EA	1570	15.03.67	LT/JG J.W.Duffy	USN	Phant	OC
1498	26.12.66	FL/LT Abbas	Pak	F86	NK	1571	17.03.67	CAPT W.O.Keneipp	USMC	Crus	OC
1499	27.12.66	LT G.D.Shepard	USAF	Phant	OC	1572	17.03.67	LT/CDR J.P.Viniti	USN	Crus	OC
1500	27.12.66	MAJ R.E.Gust	USAF	Phant	OC	1573	17.03.67	LT/JG E.E.Davis	USN	Crus	OC
1501	30.12.66	FL/LT P.P.Curtin	RAF	Hunt	OC	1574	18.03.67	LT C.W.Clarke	USN	Crus	OC
1502	02.01.67	FL/LT Gross	RAF	Light	OC	1575	19.03.67	1/LT R.G.Lathorp	USMC	Coug	OC
1503	02.01.67	S/L Carlton	RAF	Light	OC	1576	19.03.67	CAPT F.F.Harshbarger	USMC	Coug	NK
1504	04.01.67	LT A.M.Vanpelt	USN	Phant	OC	1577	21.03.67	LT L.R.Egea	USAF	Phant	OC
1505	04.01.67	LT/JG R.A.Morris	USN	Phant	OC	1578	21.03.67	MAJ C.W.Hetherington	USAF	Phant	OC
1506	05.01.67	CAPT P.H.Albrecht	USAF	Phant	OC	1579	24.03.67	LT K.B.Wagner	USN	Crus	OC
1507	06.01.67	ENS J.E.Esco	USN	Coug	OC	1580	26.03.67	Crow	USAF	Phant	EA
1508	06.01.67	CPT W.J.Groves	USAF	Phant	EA	1581	28.03.67	LT N.R.Czuchra	USN	Int	OC
1509	06.01.67	LT L.N.Martin	USAF	Phant	EA	1582	28.03.67	CDR R.Bristol	USN	Int	OC
1510	06.01.67	LT/CDR R.D.Mullen	USN	Crus	OC	1583	29.03.67	FL/LT L.A.Reynolds	Can	Canb	OC
1511	09.01.67	LT J.A.Anderson	USAF	Phant	OC	1584	30.03.67	1/LT J.B.Geller	USMC	Phant	NK
1512	09.01.67	LT/COL R.L.Larsh	USAF	Phant	OC	1585	31.03.67	MAJ Cobb	USAF	Phant	EA
1513	16.01.67	CAPT M.S.Kerr	USAF	Phant	EA	1586	31.03.67	LT L.D.Peterson	USAF	Phant	EA
1514	16.01.67	Storey	USAF	Phant	EA	1587	03.04.67	FL/LT J.L.Ellis	AusAF	Mir	OC

No.	Date	Name	Force	Type	Cause
1588	04.04.67	CDR J.L.Rough	USN	Phant	OC
1589	04.04.67	CAPT D.W.Crowe	USA	Moh	OC
1590	04.04.67	CAPT E.D.Marshall	USA	Moh	OC
1591	04.04.67	LT/JG C.R.Jones	USN	Phant	OC
1592	06.04.67	LT/JG F.A.Nutting	USN	Phant	OC
1593	06.04.67	LT/JG M.L.Tuft	USN	Phant	OC
1594	07.04.67	1/LT D.M.Melson	USAF	Phant	OC
1595	07.04.67	MAJ R.E.Ross	USAF	Phant	OC
1596	08.04.67	ENS F.A.Schumaker	USN	Phant	EA
1597	08.04.67	LT J.R.Ritchie	USN	Phant	OC
1598	11.04.67	LT M.Swanik	USAF	Phant	OC
1599	11.04.67	CAPT B.L.Henderson	USAF	Phant	OC
1600	12.04.67	CAPT J.R.Childers	USAF	Phant	OC
1601	12.04.67	LT/CDR R.Donnelly	USN	Crus	OC
1602	12.04.67	2/LT M.C.Deerr	USAF	Phant	OC
1603	12.04.67	ALT L.Walter	USN	Crus	OC
1604	14.04.67	AN T.C.Sweeney	USN	Phant	OC
1605	14.04.67	LT R.F.Herzog	USN	Phant	OC
1606	14.04.67	ENS DV F.Bourgeois	Fr N	Crus	OC
1607	18.04.67	F/O S.Creak	RAF	Hunt	OC
1608	18.04.67	CADET U.A.Ostman	Swed	Hunt	OC
1609	21.04.67	1/LT S.D.Gulbrandson	USAF	Phant	OC
1610	21.04.67	CAPT L.A.Showalter	USAF	Phant	OC
1611	23.04.67	Mekkers	USAF	Phant	NK
1612	23.04.67	M.Holland	USAF	Phant	NK
1613	24.04.67	ENS J.W.Laing	USN	Phant	OC
1614	24.04.67	LT/CDR C.Southwick	USN	Phant	OC
1615	24.04.67	LT/CDR E.B.Tucker	USN	Crus	EA
1616	25.04.67	LT/JG L.I.Williams	USN	Int	EA
1617	25.04.67	LT/JG M.D.Christian	USN	Int	EA
1618	29.04.67	Torkelson	USAF	Phant	EA
1619	01.05.67	LT/JG C.R.Ramskill	USN	Crus	OC
1620	01.05.67	1/LT E.M.Gibbons	USAF	Phant	OC
1621	01.05.67	CAPT R.F.Rader	USAF	Phant	OC
1622	03.05.67	LT/JG J.L.K.Corcoran	USN	Phant	OC
1623	06.05.67	ENS P.N.Halverson	USN	Coug	OC
1624	08.05.67	LT/JG M.L.Tuft	USN	Phant	OC
1625	09.05.67	FL/LT R.Ledwidge	RAF	Canb	OC
1626	10.05.67	LT/CDR R.B.Rebber	USN	Coug	OC
1627	10.05.67	A/MAN C.B.Howard	USN	Coug	OC
1628	11.05.67	LT R.S.Sodhi	Ind N	Vamp	OC
1629	11.05.67	LT A.Carlier	Ind N	Vamp	OC
1630	12.05.67	Jefferson	USAF	Phant	EA
1631	12.05.67	COL Gaddis	USAF	Phant	EA
1632	14.05.67	LT/CDR C.E.Southwick	USN	Phant	EA
1633	14.05.67	LT D.J.Rollins	USN	Phant	OC
1634	15.05.67	FL/LT I.Ord	RAF	Hunt	OC
1635	16.05.67	CAPT O.E.Hay	USMC	Phant	EA
1636	16.05.67	1/LT M.Carson	USMC	Phant	OC
1637	17.05.67	LT R.W.Dodge	USN	Crus	EA
1638	18.05.67	LT K.Cummings	USAF	Phant	NK
1639	19.05.67	LT J.K.Patterson	USN	Int	EA
1640	19.05.67	LT/JG G.L.Anderson	USN	Phant	EA
1641	19.05.67	LT/JG W.R.Metzger	USN	Crus	EA
1642	19.05.67	LT/CDR W.R.Stark	USN	Phant	OC
1643	19.05.67	LT/CDR E.B.McDaniel	USN	Int	EA
1644	19.05.67	LT/JG J.C.Plumb	USN	Phant	OC
1645	19.05.67	LT/CDR K.Russell	USN	Crus	EA
1646	20.05.67	MAJ Vanloan	USAF	Phant	EA
1647	20.05.67	1/LT Milligan	USAF	Phant	EA
1648	20.05.67	1/LT J.E.Hill	USMC	Phant	OC
1649	20.05.67	1/LT D.W.Gregory	USMC	Phant	OC
1650	21.05.67	LT/CDR R.G.Hubbard	USN	Crus	OC
1651	21.05.67	ENS J.W.Laing	USN	Phant	EA
1652	21.05.67	LT H.D.Wisely	USN	Phant	EA
1653	23.05.67	T.H.Normile	USAF	Phant	NK
1654	24.05.67	ENS C.R.Golden	USN	Phant	OC
1655	24.05.67	LT/JG J.A.Hawley III	USAF	Phant	OC
1656	25.05.67	MAJ C.C.Rhymes	USAF	Phant	EA
1657	25.05.67	LT J.T.McLaughlin	USN	Crus	OC
1658	25.05.67	LT R.E.Randolph	USAF	Phant	EA
1659	30.05.67	F/O P.McKellar	RAF	Jav	OC
1660	30.05.67	Macdougall	USAF	Phant	EA
1661	30.05.67	SAC M.Lokanadan	RAF	Jav	OC
1662	30.05.67	Schrupp	USAF	Phant	EA
1663	31.05.67	CAPT Wolff	USAF	Phant	EA
1664	31.05.67	MAJ Fulcher	USAF	Phant	EA
1665	01.06.67	1/LT D.H.Clarke	USMC	Crus	OC
1666	02.06.67	LT D.E.Cowles	USN	Crus	OC
1667	03.06.67	CAPT S.Harb	Leb	Hunt	EA
1668	04.06.67	LT/COL L.P.Bates	USMC	Crus	OC
1669	05.06.67	LT J.R.Forshey	USAF	Phant	OC
1670	05.06.67	Classified			
1671	05.06.67	LT/CDR C.H.Haines	USN	Crus	EA
1672	06.06.67	LT/JG T.R.Hall	USN	Crus	EA
1673	07.06.67	ENS H.M.Austin	USN	Phant	OC
1674	07.06.67	LT/JG W.C.Vaughn	USN	Phant	OC
1675	07.06.67	LT J.C.Postlewaite	USN	Phant	OC
1676	07.06.67	LT W.M.McGuigan	USN	Phant	OC
1677	07.06.67	Classified			
1678	08.06.67	CAPT Apodaca	USAF	Phant	EA
1679	08.06.67	1/LT Busch	USAF	Phant	EA
1680	09.06.67	1/LT R.Frank	USAF	Phant	EA
1681	09.06.67	MAJ C.A.Colton	USAF	Phant	EA
1682	10.06.67	LT/JG T.R.Hall	USN	Crus	EA
1683	10.06.67	LT B.Becker	USAF	Phant	OC
1684	10.06.67	MAJ C.Allen	USAF	Phant	OC
1685	11.06.67	CAPT R.J.Webb	USAF	Phant	OC
1686	11.06.67	LT/JG J.R.Miller	USN	Crus	OC
1687	11.06.67	1/LT Pearson	USAF	Phant	EA
1688	11.06.67	M.A.J.Klemm	USAF	Phant	EA
1689	11.06.67	LT/COL H.S.Stockman	USAF	Phant	OC
1690	12.06.67	MAJ M.G.Slapikas	USAF	Phant	EA
1691	12.06.67	MAJ Fulgram	USAF	Phant	EA
1692	12.06.67	CAPT W.K.Harding	USAF	Phant	EA
1693	12.06.67	LT J.N.Fendley	USN	Phant	OC
1694	12.06.67	LT T.E.Bougartz	USN	Phant	OC
1695	14.06.67	1/LT McManus	USAF	Phant	EA
1696	14.06.67	1/LT Mechenbier	USAF	Phant	EA
1697	16.06.67	MAJ D.Mitchell	USMC	Crus	OC
1698	16.06.67	FL/LT Naqvi	Pak	F86	NK
1699	19.06.67	ENS C.Lewnes	USN	Phant	OC
1700	19.06.67	LT/CDR F.L.Raines	USN	Phant	OC
1701	22.06.67	1/LT A.J.Lundell	USAF	Phant	OC
1702	22.06.67	CAPT A.T.Dardeau	USAF	Phant	OC
1703	23.06.67	SGT Fenech	Fr AF	Mir	OC
1704	25.06.67	LT R.F.Pepra	USN	Crus	NK
1705	26.06.67	EWS P.A.Svare	USN	Crus	OC
1706	26.06.67	1/LT J.M.Jarvis	USAF	Phant	EA
1707	26.06.67	MAJ J.C.Blandford	USAF	Phant	EA
1708	27.06.67	1/LT R.J.McDonald	USAF	Phant	OC
1709	27.06.67	MAJ G.W.Deavers	USAF	Phant	OC
1710	28.06.67	CDR W.P.Lawrence	USN	Phant	OC
1711	28.06.67	LT/JG J.W.Bailey	USN	Phant	EA
1712	29.06.67	F/O Hudson	RAF	Canb	OC
1713	29.06.67	F/O Hill	RAF	Canb	OC
1714	29.06.67	EL/SGT Pulver	Switz	Venom	OC
1715	30.06.67	Classified			
1716	30.06.67	Classified			
1717	30.06.67	Classified			
1718	30.06.67	Classified			
1719	30.06.67	Classified			
1720	30.06.67	Classified			
1721	30.06.67	Classified			
1722	30.06.67	Classified			
1723	30.06.67	Classified			
1724	30.06.67	Classified			
1725	01.07.67	2/LT H.A.Hill	USMC	Phant	OC
1726	01.07.67	CAPT S.P.Huey	USMC	Phant	OC
1727	02.07.67	MAJ B.A.Martin	USMC	Crus	EA
1728	06.07.67	Pollock	USAF	Phant	EA
1729	06.07.67	Hughey	USAF	Phant	EA
1730	06.07.67	LT W.R.Moore	USN	Phant	OC
1731	06.07.67	LT/JG J.C.Tanner	USN	Phant	OC
1732	10.07.67	LT G.Kuehner	USAF	Phant	NK

No.	Date	Name	Force	Type	Cause	No.	Date	Name	Force	Type	Cause
1733	10.07.67	CAPT R.Headley	USAF	Phant	NK	1806	12.09.67	LT R.A.Kopp	USAF	Phant	EA
1734	10.07.67	MAJ J.D.Underwood	USAF	Phant	OC	1807	12.09.67	1/LT J.F.Pierce	USAF	Phant	OC
1735	10.07.67	LT R.B.Jones	RN	Phant	NK	1808	12.09.67	CAPT J.T.Kirkby	USAF	Phant	OC
1736	10.07.67	Classified				1809	13.09.67	FL/LT J.Sneddon	RAF	Light	OC
1737	10.07.67	1/LT J.R.Drake	USAF	Phant	OC	1810	13.09.67	LT J.E.Shaw	USN	Crus	OC
1738	12.07.67	1/LT T.H.Plank	USAF	Phant	EA	1811	13.09.67		USAF	Phant	EA
1739	13.07.67	T/SGT M.Eriksen	Den	L.T33	OC	1812	16.09.67	LT G.H.McKinney	USAF	Phant	EA
1740	16.07.67	CAPT H.E.Pyle	USMC	Phant	OC	1813	16.09.67	MAJ L.Boothby	USAF	Phant	EA
1741	16.07.67	LT/CDR D.A.Verich	USN	Crus	EA	1814	16.09.67		USAF	Phant	EA
1742	16.07.67	CAPT J.A.Gordon	USMC	Phant	OC	1815	16.09.67		USAF	Phant	EA
1743	17.07.67	LT G.Persson	Swed	Hunt	OC	1816	17.09.67	LT G.S.Venanzi	USAF	Phant	EA
1744	19.07.67	LT A.McMeekan	RN	Hunt	OC	1817	17.09.67	Stavast	USAF	Phant	EA
1745	19.07.67	LT/CDR R.N.Blair	RN	Hunt	OC	1818	20.09.67	ENS R.K.Hill	USN	Coug	OC
1746	20.07.67	LT J.W.Nunn	USN	Crus	OC	1819	21.09.67	ENS D.L.Boulluec	Fr N	Etend	OC
1747	20.07.67	2/LT R.J.Therriault	USMC	Phant	OC	1820	21.09.67	LT/CDR M.J.Vescelius	USN	Crus	OC
1748	20.07.67	MAJ W.P.Hutchins	USMC	Phant	NK	1821	21.09.67	S/L H.W.J.Rigg	RAF	P	OC
1749	20.07.67	ENS D.J.Loest	USN	Phant	OC	1822	25.09.67		USMC	Phant	EA
1750	20.07.67	CAPT J.W.Manz	USMC	Phant	OC	1823	25.09.67	Classified			
1751	21.07.67	CAPT J.S.Sinclair	USAF	Phant	EA	1824	25.09.67		USMC	Phant	EA
1752	21.07.67	CAPT D.M.O'Hara	USAF	Phant	EA	1825	25.09.67	F/O M.Susans	AusAF	Mir	OC
1753	31.07.67	MAJ J.M.Foley	USAF	Phant	OC	1826	26.09.67	CAPT D.J.Ankeny	USAF	Phant	EA
1754	31.07.67	LT/COL M.Encinias	USAF	Phant	OC	1827	26.09.67	LT J.D.Mynar	USAF	Phant	EA
1755	31.07.67	C.P.Zuhoski	USN	Crus	NK	1828	26.09.67	CAPT L.Perillo	Italy	F.G91	OC
1756	31.07.67	Classified				1829	26.09.67	1/LT J.W.Beasley	USAF	Phant	OC
1757	01.08.67	ENS J.R.Naye	USN	Coug	OC	1830	26.09.67	MAJ R.L.Lewis	USAF	Phant	OC
1758	01.08.67	LT D.J.Patz	USN	Coug	OC	1831	26.09.67	2/LT O.Ingvaldsen	Nor	F84	OC
1759	03.08.67	F/O D.Roome	RAF	Hunt	OC	1832	26.09.67	MAJ P.M.Cole	USMC	Phant	OC
1760	06.08.67	Page	USAF	Phant	EA	1833	29.09.67		USMC	Phant	EA
1761	06.08.67	Kemmerer	USAF	Phant	EA	1834	29.09.67		USMC	Phant	EA
1762	07.08.67	CAPT B.J.Beets	USAF	Phant	OC	1835	01.10.67	PF/C A.W.Banks	USA	Moh	EA
1763	07.08.67	MAJ J.Otto	USAF	Phant	EA	1836	01.10.67	CAPT J.P.Ratcliff	USA	Moh	EA
1764	07.08.67	L.E.Meeks	USAF	Phant	EA	1837	02.10.67	MAJ L.Browne	USAF	Phant	EA
1765	11.08.67	1/LT H.B.Cox	USAF	Phant	OC	1838	02.10.67	MAJ D.M.Miller	USAF	Phant	EA
1766	11.08.67	CADET T.W.Gizesky	USN	Coug	OC	1839	03.10.67	LT Gulbandson	USAF	Phant	EA
1767	12.08.67	MAJ R.Dilger	USAF	Phant	EA	1840	03.10.67	MAJ J.D.Moore	USAF	Phant	EA
1768	12.08.67	LT/CDR F.S.Teague	USN	Crus	OC	1841	04.10.67	HFW P.Boeckelmann	GerAF	F.G91	OC
1769	12.08.67	LT G.L.Rawlings	USAF	Phant	EA	1842	05.10.67	F/O R.M.S.Datta	IndAF	Hunt	OC
1770	17.08.67	CAPT Conley	USMC	Coug	OC	1843	05.10.67	LT E.T.Leech	USN	Crus	OC
1771	21.08.67	LT/JG J.M.McIlrath	USN	Phant	OC	1844	05.10.67	ENS D.P.Matheny	USN	Crus	EA
1772	21.08.67	CDR R.H.McGlohn	USN	Phant	OC	1845	06.10.67	1/LT J.L.Fuller	USAF	Phant	OC
1773	21.08.67	LT/CDR W.M.Hardman	USN	Int	EA	1846	06.10.67	1/LT J.E.Nicholson	USAF	Phant	OC
						1847	07.10.67	MAJ Appleby	USAF	Phant	EA
1774	21.08.67	CDR L.T.Profilet	USN	Int	EA	1848	08.10.67	LT/JG J.J.Dantone	USN	Phant	OC
1775	21.08.67	LT R.J.Flynn	USN	Int	EA	1849	08.10.67	LT/COL E.G.Weaver	USAF	Phant	OC
1776	21.08.67		USN	Int	EA	1850	09.10.67	CAPT D.R.Calvert	USAF	Phant	OC
1777	22.08.67		USAF	Phant	EA	1851	09.10.67	LT J.V.Macnab	USAF	Phant	OC
1778	22.08.67	1/LT A.M.Silva	USAF	Phant	EA	1852	13.10.67	1/LT J.H.Warner	USMC	Phant	EA
1779	22.08.67	CAPT W.P.Samora	USMC	Phant	OC	1853	13.10.67	LT/COL E.W.Miller	USMC	Phant	EA
1780	23.08.67	FLT S.E.J.Jensen	Den	F100	OC	1854	15.10.67	CAPT W.S.Paul	USAF	Phant	EA
1781	23.08.67	MAJ C.B.Demarque	USAF	Phant	OC	1855	15.10.67	COL R.W.Maloy	USAF	Phant	EA
1782	23.08.67	MAJ C.R.Tyler	USAF	Phant	EA	1856	16.10.67	MAJ W.E.Hitchcock	USAF	Phant	OC
1783	23.08.67	CAPT Gerndt	USAF	Phant	OC	1857	16.10.67	LT/COL J.P.Mullins	USAF	Phant	OC
1784	23.08.67	LT J.M.Piet	USAF	Phant	OC	1858	19.10.67	Classified			
1785	23.08.67	CAPT L.E.Carrigan	USAF	Phant	EA	1859	22.10.67	T.E.Cote	USA	Moh	OC
1786	25.08.67	1/LT R.W.Wade	USAF	Phant	OC	1860	23.10.67	CAPT W.F.Tremper	USMC	Phant	OC
1787	25.08.67	MAJ G.L.Henry	USAF	Phant	OC	1861	23.10.67	MAJ J.L.Eddy	USMC	Phant	OC
1788	27.08.67	CAPT Boggs	USMC	Int	EA	1862	24.10.67	LT/JG R.F.Frishman	USN	Phant	OC
1789	27.08.67	MAJ V.H.Bacik	USMC	Int	EA	1863	24.10.67	LT/JG R.C.Clark	USN	Phant	OC
1790	05.09.67	LT/JG J.D.Hunt	USN	Int	OC	1864	24.10.67	CDR C.R.Gillespie	USN	Phant	OC
1791	05.09.67	LT/JG D.W.Driver	USN	Int	OC	1865	24.10.67	LT/JG E.G.Lewis	USN	Phant	EA
1792	05.09.67	MAJ D.K.Wolf	USAF	Phant	OC	1866	26.10.67	G.Mori	Italy	F.G91	OC
1793	07.09.67	1/LT F.N.R.Espina	Venez	Venom	OC	1867	26.10.67	G.Pirzio	Italy	F.G91	OC
1794	07.09.67	COL J.E.Clarke	USAF	Phant	OC	1868	26.10.67	LT/JG C.D.Rice	USN	Crus	EA
1795	07.09.67	MAJ H.H.Andrews	USAF	Phant	OC	1869	27.10.67	CAPT Black	USAF	Phant	EA
1796	07.09.67	MAJ O.P.Gilly	Venez	Venom	OC	1870	29.10.67	CAPT J.J.Hare	USMC	Phant	EA
1797	07.09.67	S/L R.Blackburn	RAF	Light	OC	1871	29.10.67	MAJ D.I.Carroll	USMC	Phant	EA
1798	07.09.67	LT E.W.Clexton	USN	Phant	OC	1872	30.10.67	LT/JG J.R.Borst	USN	Phant	OC
1799	08.09.67	CAPT R.L.Drage	USMC	Phant	OC	1873	30.10.67	LT/CDR E.P.Lund	USN	Phant	OC
1800	08.09.67	CAPT J.B.Caskey	USMC	Phant	OC	1874	31.10.67	CAPT S.J.Kott	USMC	Int	EA
1801	08.09.67	LT/CDR D.Baker	USN	Crus	NK	1875	31.10.67	CAPT H.N.Fanning	USMC	Int	EA
1802	08.09.67	LT T.R.Kniffen	USN	Crus	OC	1876	02.11.67	LT P.R.Gallagher	USN	Coug	OC
1803	09.09.67	LT J.Silliman	USAF	Phant	EA	1877	04.11.67	LT G.L.Rawlings	USAF	Phant	OC
1804	09.09.67	MAJ L.D.Appleby	USAF	Phant	EA	1878	04.11.67	MAJ R.R.Lester	USAF	Phant	OC
1805	12.09.67	CAPT J.E.Birmingham	USAF	Phant	EA	1879	04.11.67	CAPT J.J.Quaid	USMC	Int	OC

No.	Date	Name	Force	Type	Cause
1880	04.11.67	1/LT R.J.Suter	USMC	Int	OC
1881	07.11.67	CAPT K.Fisher	USAF	Phant	EA
1882	07.11.67	1/LT L.F.Ellis	USAF	Phant	EA
1883	07.11.67	CAPT F.L.Barrett	USAF	Phant	OC
1884	08.11.67	LT R.Brenneman	USAF	Phant	EA
1885	08.11.67	CAPT Gordon	USAF	Phant	EA
1886	09.11.67	1/LT L.P.Sijan	USAF	Phant	EA
1887	09.11.67	LT/COL J.W.Armstrong	USAF	Phant	EA
1888	11.11.67	LT J.L.Unruh	USN	Crus	OC
1889	15.11.67	MAJ R.E.Ross	USAF	Phant	EA
1890	15.11.67	CAPT Hobbs	USAF	Phant	EA
1891	16.11.67	LT/CDR P.H.Schulz	USN	Phant	EA
1892	16.11.67	LT/JG T.B.Sullivan	USN	Phant	EA
1893	18.11.67	LT/JG J.D.Clark	USN	Crus	OC
1894	19.11.67	LT/COL Ligon	USAF	Phant	EA
1895	19.11.67	LT/JG W.O.Estes	USAF	Phant	EA
1896	19.11.67	LT/CDR C.D.Clower	USN	Phant	EA
1897	19.11.67	LT/JG T.G.Stier	USN	Phant	EA
1898	19.11.67	LT/JG J.E.Teague	USN	Phant	EA
1899	19.11.67	CAPT Ford	USAF	Phant	EA
1900	20.11.67	CAPT J.Ciminero	USAF	Phant	EA
1901	20.11.67	LT/COM J.C.Scholtz	USAF	Phant	EA
1902	20.11.67	1/LT J.L.Badley	USAF	Phant	EA
1903	20.11.67	1/LT S.Marenka	USAF	Phant	OC
1904	21.11.67	LT G.R.Adams	USN	Crus	OC
1905	29.11.67	LJ L.Lemoine	USAF	Phant	OC
1906	30.11.67	CAPT O.Cuminato	Italy	F.G91	OC
1907	30.11.67	1/LT G.A.Olney	USMC	Coug	OC
1908	01.12.67	T.H.Normile	USAF	Phant	NK
1909	05.12.67	LT H.J.Meadows	USN	Crus	OC
1910	06.12.67	CAPT J.T.Taylor	USAF	Phant	OC
1911	06.12.67	MAJ J.T.Cornelius	USAF	Phant	OC
1912	07.12.67	MAJ R.B.Ray	USAF	Phant	OC
1913	07.12.67	1/LT F.M.Cerrato	USAF	Phant	OC
1914	10.12.67	1/LT R.Riddick	USAF	Phant	EA
1915	10.12.67	MAJ G.L.Nordin	USAF	Phant	EA
1916	12.12.67	1/LT R.W.Johnson	USAF	Phant	OC
1917	12.12.67	CAPT R.A.Bedarf	USAF	Phant	OC
1918	12.12.67	CAPT J.E.Witzel	USAF	Phant	OC
1919	12.12.67	1/LT J.M.Wertz	USAF	Phant	OC
1920	13.12.67	CAPT W.T.Sakahara	USAF	Phant	OC
1921	15.12.67	CAPT F.A.McCaugham	USMC	Coug	OC
1922	15.12.67	ENS W.L.Taylor	USN	Coug	OC
1923	15.12.67	LT/JG G.Cook	USN	Phant	OC
1924	15.12.67	LT R.J.Laib	USN	Phant	OC
1925	15.12.67	LT R.H.Crowther	RN	Hunt	OC
1926	15.12.67	LT A.G.Naylor	RN	Hunt	OC
1927	16.12.67	MAJ K.R.Fleenor	USAF	Phant	EA
1928	16.12.67	1/LT T.L.Boyer	USAF	Phant	EA
1929	16.12.67	LT/JG S.L.Van Horn	USN	Phant	EA
1930	16.12.67	LT/CDR D.E.Hernandez	USN	Phant	EA
1931	17.12.67	COL D.Brett	USAF	Phant	EA
1932	17.12.67	MAJ L.Guttersen	USAF	Phant	EA
1933	17.12.67	LT B.Smith	USAF	Phant	EA
1934	17.12.67	LT S.P.Sox	USAF	Phant	EA
1935	18.12.67	FL/LT J.R.Hamilton	USAF	Phant	OC
1936	18.12.67	CAPT G.L.Hughes	USAF	Phant	OC
1937	20.12.67	CADET S.Gery	Kuw	J.Pro	OC
1938	20.12.67	FL/LT C.P.J.Coulcher	USAF	Phant	OC
1939	20.12.67	1/LT R.D.Massari	USAF	Phant	NK
1940	22.12.67		USMC	Phant	EA
1941	22.12.67	CAPT G.H.Fors	USMC	Phant	EA
1942	25.12.67	MAJ G.W.Fritchi	USMC	Coug	EA
1943	25.12.67	MAJ D.Escalera	USMC	Phant	OC
1944	25.12.67	CAPT A.D.Smiley	USMC	Coug	EA
1945	27.12.67	1/LT S.A.Martin	USAF	Phant	NK
1946	27.12.67	CAPT R.W.Coburn	USAF	Phant	NK
1947	27.12.67	Classified			
1948	27.12.67	MAJ H.W.Miller	USAF	Phant	EA
1949	27.12.67	CAPT H.Altman	USAF	Phant	EA
1950	28.12.67		USAF	Phant	OC
1951	28.12.67		USAF	Phant	OC
1952	28.12.67	1/LT J.Wadsworth	USAF	Phant	OC
1953	28.12.67	1/LT R.E.Geiger	USAF	Phant	OC
1954	29.12.67	LT/JG G.K.Flint	USN	Phant	EA
1955	29.12.67	LT J.F.Dowd	USN	Phant	EA
1956	31.12.67	Classified			
1957	31.12.67	Classified			
1958	31.12.67	Classified			
1959	31.12.67	Classified			
1960	31.12.67	Classified			
1961	31.12.67	Classified			
1962	31.12.67	Classified			
1963	31.12.67	Classified			
1964	31.12.67	Classified			
1965	31.12.67	MAJ J.I.Sorensen	USAF	Phant	OC
1966	31.12.67	1/LT J.C.Aarni	USAF	Phant	OC
1967	31.12.67	Classified			
1968	02.01.68	LT/JG C.M.Taylor	USN	Crus	OC
1969	02.01.68	2/LT S.D.Adams	USAF	Phant	OC
1970	02.01.68	MAJ G.H.West	USAF	Phant	OC
1971	05.01.68	LT J.N.Tilko	USN	L.T1A	OC
1972	05.01.68	LT/COL W.T.Rhodenbach	USAF	Phant	OC
1973	05.01.68	LT H.E.Higgingbotham	USN	L.T1A	OC
1974	05.01.68	CAPT E.T.Pizzo	USAF	Phant	NK
1975	09.01.68	HFW E.Mangels	GerAF	F86	OC
1976	09.01.68	CAPT D.W.Lorenzo	USMC	Crus	OC
1977	10.01.68	LT/JG T.Beckwith	USN	Phant	OC
1978	10.01.68	CAPT K.Hall	USAF	Phant	EA
1979	10.01.68	1/LT Hopper	USAF	Phant	EA
1980	10.01.68	LT/JG J.A.Thorn	USN	Phant	OC
1981	10.01.68	LT/JG D.A.Yost	USN	Phant	OC
1982	10.01.68	LT R.T.Fleming	USN	Phant	OC
1983	10.01.68	LT/CDR L.N.Mitchell	USN	Phant	OC
1984	10.01.68	LT/JG T.L.Hart	USN	Phant	OC
1985	14.01.68	LT G.P.Kroyer	USN	Coug	OC
1986	16.01.68	MAJ C.E.Lewis	USAF	Phant	EA
1987	16.01.68	2/LT T.A.Bannon	USAF	Phant	NK
1988	16.01.68	CAPT A.L.Lacey	USAF	Phant	NK
1989	16.01.68	1/LT T.N.Moe	USAF	Phant	EA
1990	16.01.68	CAPT S.B.Stovin	USAF	Phant	EA
1991	16.01.68	1/LT J.L.Kelly	USAF	Phant	EA
1992	17.01.68		USAF	Phant	EA
1993	17.01.68		USAF	Phant	EA
1994	19.01.68	CAPT F.G.Stone	USAF	Phant	EA
1995	19.01.68	CAPT W.B.Fredenberger	USAF	Phant	OC
1996	19.01.68	SGT/CH P.Cavalin	Fr AF	Mir	NK
1997	20.01.68		USAF	Phant	EA
1998	22.01.68	CAPT D.F.Brandon	USMC	Phant	EA
1999	22.01.68	LT/COL H.T.Hagaman	USMC	Phant	EA
2000	22.01.68	S/L M.K.Jain	IndAF	Vamp	NK
2001	23.01.68	CDR L.S.Kollmorgen	USN	Int	EA
2002	24.01.68	FL/LT S.Miller	RAF	Light	OC
2003	26.01.68	LT R.F.Shercliff	RN	Hunt	OC
2004	26.01.68	LT/CDR P.R.Sheppard	RN	Hunt	OC
2005	27.01.68	MAJ R.W.Phillips	USAF	Phant	EA
2006	27.01.68	1/LT B.C.Core	USAF	Phant	EA
2007	29.01.68	1/LT W.J.Grimm	USMC	Phant	OC
2008	29.01.68	MAJ H.D.Fagerskog	USMC	Phant	OC
2009	31.01.68	F/O M.Gillett	RAF	Vulc	OC
2010	31.01.68	FL/LT P.Tait	RAF	Vulc	OC
2011	02.02.68	LT R.A.Rau	USAF	Phant	NK
2012	02.02.68	CAPT R.D.Breslin	USAF	Phant	NK
2013	02.02.68	CAPT A.L.Turrin	USAF	Phant	OC
2014	02.02.68	CAPT W.E.Coker	USAF	Phant	OC
2015	05.02.68	CAPT J.E.Rodwell	USAF	Phant	NK
2016	08.02.68	CDR D.L.Varner	USN	Phant	OC
2017	08.02.68	CAPT T.K.Dorsett	USAF	Phant	OC
2018	08.02.68	CAPT J.Corder	USAF	Phant	OC
2019	08.02.68	LT W.A.Wood	USN	Phant	OC
2020	13.02.68	CADET P.Jabornicky	AusAF	Vamp	OC

No.	Date	Name	Force	Type	Cause
2021	14.02.68	1/LT T.J.Powers	USAF	Phant	NK
2022	14.02.68	CAPT D.L.Smith	USAF	Phant	NK
2023	14.02.68	HFW H.Corsmeyer	GerAF	F.G91	OC
2024	14.02.68	CAPT E.H.Menzer	USMC	Coug	NK
2025	14.02.68	1/LT G.H.Cramer	USMC	Coug	NK
2026	15.02.68	LT/CDR L.A.Henke	USN	Crus	OC
2027	15.02.68	CAPT L.D.Writer	USAF	Phant	EA
2028	15.02.68	CAPT J.V.Carpenter	USAF	Phant	EA
2029	16.02.68	LT C.E.Beilby	RN	S.Vix	OC
2030	16.02.68	S/LT J.S.M.Chandler	RN	S.Vix	OC
2031	19.02.68	CAPT P.J.Seiler	USAF	Phant	OC
2032	19.02.68	CAPT P.Brandt	USAF	Phant	OC
2033	21.02.68	S/LT G.F.Harris	RN	J.Pro	NK
2034	22.02.68	MAJ L.Guttersen	USAF	Phant	EA
2035	22.02.68	1/LT M.Donald	USAF	Phant	EA
2036	23.02.68	1/LT R.V.Smith	USMC	Int	OC
2037	23.02.68		USMC	Int	NK
2038	25.02.68	LT/JG W.E.Brown	USN	Crus	OC
2039	25.02.68	ENS R.E.Houser	USN	Coug	OC
2040	25.02.68	LT/CDR J.R.O'Kelly	USN	Coug	OC
2041	26.02.68	F/O J.Tye	RAF	J.Pro	OC
2042	26.02.68	FL/LT D.J.Smith	RAF	J.Pro	OC
2043	26.02.68	CAPT W.S.Paul	USAF	Phant	OC
2044	26.02.68	MAJ R.P.Bateman	USAF	Phant	OC
2045	29.02.68	LT/COL C.D.Smith Jnr	USAF	Phant	OC
2046	29.02.68		USAF	Phant	EA
2047	02.03.68	CAPT D.C.Richards	USMC	Phant	OC
2048	02.03.68	MAJ R.J.Morley	USMC	Phant	OC
2049	07.03.68	FL/LT W.Rayner	AusAF	MB326	NK
2050	09.03.68		USA	Moh	NK
2051	12.03.68	LT/JG J.A.Weber	USN	Crus	OC
2052	12.03.68	CAPT J.Reich	GerAF	F.G91	OC
2053	14.03.68	CAPT S.C.Puma	USAF	Phant	OC
2054	14.03.68	MAJ W.J.Swaney	USAF	Phant	OC
2055	14.03.68	1/LT J.E.Hamm	USAF	Phant	EA
2056	14.03.68	MAJ G.Tressemar	USAF	Phant	EA
2057	15.03.68	1/LT P.E.Huber	USAF	Phant	OC
2058	15.03.68	CAPT R.C.Fairlamb	USAF	Phant	OC
2059	16.03.68	CAPT G.L.Post	USMC	Crus	OC
2060	17.03.68	MAJ P.D.Lambridges	USAF	Phant	EA
2061	17.03.68	1/LT J.L.Tavenner	USAF	Phant	EA
2062	17.03.68	LT/CDR D.W.Doss	USN	Int	NK
2063	17.03.68	LT/CDR E.A.Shuman III	USN	Int	NK
2064	18.03.68	SGT/CH Flasseur	Fr AF	Mir	NK
2065	20.03.68	C.D.Pilcher	Civ	Phant	NK
2066	20.03.68	MR H.A.Begay	Civ	Phant	OC
2067	22.03.68		USAF	Phant	EA
2068	23.03.68	LT/JG D.B.Norem	USN	Phant	OC
2069	24.03.68	LT Ottawa	GerAF	F.G91	OC
2070	29.03.68	SGT E.Henninger	GerAF	L.T33	OC
2071	29.03.68	SP4 S.Fletcher	USA	Moh	NK
2072	04.04.68	CAPT C.Madsen	USMC	Coug	OC
2073	05.04.68	CAPT G.L.Butler	USAF	Phant	OC
2074	05.04.68	MAJ J.G.Kondracki	USAF	Phant	OC
2075	05.04.68	LT/JG P.R.Harrison	USN	Crus	NK
2076	05.04.68	ENS S.D.Graber	USN	Phant	OC
2077	05.04.68	LT C.J.Schwarze	USN	Phant	OC
2078	07.04.68	SP5 Slatt	USA	Moh	EA
2079	09.04.68	Classified			
2080	12.04.68	LT R.B.Vongrote	USN	Crus	OC
2081	13.04.68	MAJ Stischer	USAF	Phant	OC
2082	13.04.68	CAPT D.L.Verhees	USAF	Phant	EA
2083	14.04.68	LT/JG G.E.Rose	USN	Phant	OC
2084	14.04.68	CDR D.Pringle	USN	Phant	OC
2085	14.04.68	LT G.Olson	USN	Int	OC
2086	15.04.68	LT/CDR J.F.Farnsworth	USN	Phant	EA
2087	15.04.68	LT/JG R.L.McCready	USN	Phant	EA
2088	15.04.68	LT/JG G.K.Baer	USN	Phant	EA
2089	15.04.68	LT/JG J.Sarnecky	USN	Phant	OC
2090	16.04.68	P/O N.Ahmed	IndAF	Vamp	OC
2091	16.04.68	FL/LT J.Singh	IndAF	Vamp	OC
2092	19.04.68	CAPT R.E.McKenzie	USAF	Phant	OC
2093	19.04.68	MAJ L.E.Lewis	USAF	Phant	OC
2094	19.04.68	LT/CDR W.L.Hill	USN	Crus	OC
2095	20.04.68	P/O M.Dubrulle	Fr N	Etend	NK
2096	21.04.68	1/LT W.C.Vasser	USAF	Phant	OC
2097	21.04.68	MAJ C.R.Webster	USAF	Phant	OC
2098	23.04.68	MAJ/GEN H.A.Davis	USAF	Phant	OC
2099	23.04.68	MAJ B.D.Patton	USAF	Phant	OC
2100	24.04.68	M.Hall	USA	Moh	NK
2101	24.04.68	PF/C J.G.Sparks	USA	Moh	NK
2102	24.04.68	LT/CDR R.P.Lester	USN	Coug	NK
2103	24.04.68	ENS T.N.Gommer	USN	Coug	NK
2104	25.04.68	S/LT Renandin	Fr AF	Mir	OC
2105	27.04.68	1/LT W.L.Rumble	USAF	Phant	EA
2106	27.04.68	LT/COL J.S.Findlay	USAF	Phant	EA
2107	27.04.68	LT W.J.Mayhew	USN	Phant	OC
2108	28.04.68	LT/JG D.J.Lortscher	USN	Phant	EA
2109	28.04.68	LT/CDR D.E.Hernandez	USN	Phant	EA
2110	29.04.68	1/LT R.P.Tignitor	USAF	Phant	OC
2111	30.04.68	ENS P.F.Schmid	USN	Coug	NK
2112	30.04.68	LT/CDR C.C.Hoffner	USN	Phant	NK
2113	01.05.68	CAPT G.H.Christensend	USMC	Int	OC
2114	01.05.68		USMC	Int	OC
2115	01.05.68	1/LT I.F.Hunsaker	USMC	Phant	EA
2116	01.05.68	CAPT D.Evans	USMC	Phant	EA
2117	06.05.68	LT A.J.Nargi	USN	Crus	OC
2118	06.05.68	FL/LT W.Taylor	RAF	Hunt	OC
2119	07.05.68	LT/JG W.A.Kramer	USN	Phant	EA
2120	07.05.68	LT/CDR E.Christensen	USN	Phant	EA
2121	13.05.68	LT J.T.Fardy	USN	Int	EA
2122	13.05.68	LT B.B.Bremner	USN	Int	EA
2123	14.05.68	1/LT Watson	USMC	Phant	EA
2124	15.05.68	MAJ D.F.Crowe	USMC	Int	OC
2125	15.05.68	CAPT J.C.Clingerman	USMC	Int	OC
2126	18.05.68	1/LT G.McCubbin	USAF	Phant	EA
2127	18.05.68	CAPT J.Davies	USAF	Phant	EA
2128	20.05.68	F/O N.J.Roberson	RN	Bucc	OC
2129	20.05.68	S/LT A.C.A.Moore	RN	Bucc	OC
2130	22.05.68	LT/JG E.Miller	USN	Crus	EA
2131	22.05.68	CAPT R.Cox	USMC	Phant	NK
2132	22.05.68	W.S.Poole	USMC	Phant	NK
2133	25.05.68	LT A.Turner	USAF	Phant	EA
2134	25.05.68	CPT D.Ankeny	USAF	Phant	EA
2135	29.05.68	LT G.Brown	USN	Fury	OC
2136	01.06.68	CAPT E.H.Dorsett	USMC	Fury	OC
2137	01.06.68	CAPT M.P.Rhodes	USAF	Phant	EA
2138	02.06.68	LT/CDR P.A.Carroll	USN	Phant	OC
2139	02.06.68	LT/CDR E.P.Sierra	USN	Phant	OC
2140	02.06.68	MAJ E.E.Johnson	USAF	Phant	OC
2141	02.06.68	LT/COL R.F.Crutchlow	USAF	Phant	OC
2142	04.06.68	LT/JG W.H.Simmons	USN	Phant	EA
2143	07.06.68	LT/JG W.R.McClendon	USN	Phant	OC
2144	07.06.68	LT/JG R.J.Edens	USN	Phant	OC
2145	08.06.68	SP4 J.H.Baird	USA	Moh	EA
2146	08.06.68	MAJ H.F.Benton	USA	Moh	EA
2147	09.06.68	1/LT D.A.Willett	USAF	Phant	EA
2148	09.06.68	MAJ W.B.Bergman	USAF	Phant	EA
2149	11.06.68	FL/LT G.N.Morris	RAF	Canb	OC
2150	15.06.68	S/L Rehman	Pak	F86	NK
2151	15.06.68	LT J.R.Miller	USN	Crus	OC
2152	15.06.68	MAJ C.W.Redfearn	USAF	Phant	OC
2153	15.06.68	FL/LT C.P.J.Coulcher	RAF	Phant	OC
2154	15.06.68	F/O Mehdi	Pak	F86	NK
2155	16.06.68	CDR G.Wilbur	USN	Phant	EA
2156	19.06.68	LT/CDR J.A.Burns	USN	Phant	EA
2157	19.06.68	LT/CDR J.W.Holtzclaw	USN	Phant	EA
2158	21.06.68	CAPT W.B.Deacon	USAF	Phant	OC
2159	22.06.68	1/LT J.B.Penn	USMC	Phant	OC
2160	24.06.68	LT/JG J.S.Mobley	USN	Int	EA

No.	Date	Name	Force	Type	Cause
2161	25.06.68	LT/JG J.A.Weber	USN	Crus	OC
2162	26.06.68	MAJ F.McKenna	USAF	Phant	OC
2163	26.06.68	CAPT M.Jones	USAF	Phant	OC
2164	26.06.68	F/O V.W.Yates	RAF	Hunt	OC
2165	26.06.68	FL/LT Pym	RAF	Hunt	OC
2166	01.07.68	LT A.F.Hutchison	RN	Bucc	OC
2167	01.07.68	LT R.P.Turnbull	RN	Bucc	OC
2168	04.07.68	1/LT J.B.Jaeger	USAF	Phant	EA
2169	04.07.68	CAPT D.J.Coonon	USMC	Phant	OC
2170	04.07.68	CAPT F.Sundblad	Swed	Hunt	NK
2171	04.07.68	LT/JG J.F.Strahm	USN	Crus	OC
2172	04.07.68	MAJ D.A.Hamilton	USAF	Phant	EA
2173	04.07.68	MAJ J.Bibler	USMC	Phant	OC
2174	05.07.68	LT G.L.Moore	USN	Phant	OC
2175	05.07.68	LT/JG R.A.Prince	USN	Phant	OC
2176	05.07.68	LT/COL C.B.Crumpler	USAF	Phant	NK
2177	05.07.68	1/LT M.T.Burns	USAF	Phant	NK
2178	08.07.68	LT/COL Howard	USMC	Phant	EA
2179	08.07.68	1/LT D.M.Hollenback	USAF	Phant	OC
2180	08.07.68	LT Raynaud	Fr AF	Mir	OC
2181	08.07.68	CAPT R.D.Hess	USMC	Phant	EA
2182	08.07.68	1/LT C.W.Mosley	USAF	Phant	OC
2183	13.07.68	MAJ S.O.Bakke	USAF	Phant	OC
2184	15.07.68	CAPT N.F.J.Ostgaard	USA	Moh	NK
2185	15.07.68	LT C.Wheel	RN	Hunt	NK
2186	15.07.68	R.F.Green	USA	Moh	NK
2187	16.07.68	LT F.Mustaf	Iraq	Hunt	OC
2188	17.07.68	CAPT Ballhorn	GerAF	F.G91	OC
2189	18.07.68	CAPT T.C.Skanchy	USAF	Phant	OC
2190	21.07.68	LT F.W.Pfluger	USN	Crus	OC
2191	22.07.68	FL/LT C.J.Pinder	RAF	Hunt	OC
2192	22.07.68	LT T.D.Stuart	USN	Int	OC
2193	22.07.68	LT J.R.Suckow	USN	Int	OC
2194	23.07.68	MAJ R.F.Brodman	USAF	Phant	EA
2195	23.07.68	LT/JG K.C.Burgess	USN	Coug	OC
2196	23.07.68	CAPT E.H.Menzer	USMC	Coug	OC
2197	24.07.68	LT/JG Dambekaln	USN	Phant	EA
2198	24.07.68	CAPT T.D.Gill	USAF	Phant	EA
2199	24.07.68	1/LT R.G.Pierce	USAF	Phant	EA
2200	24.07.68	CDR O.Elliot	USN	Phant	EA
2201	25.07.68	MAJ C.Lawson	USMC	Int	EA
2202	25.07.68	LT/CDR N.Donovan	USN	Crus	NK
2203	28.07.68	COL F.D.C.Gomes	Port	F.G91	NK
2204	29.07.68	LT/JG P.L.Adamcin	USN	Coug	OC
2205	29.07.68	MAJ E.E.Johnson	USAF	Phant	OC
2206	02.08.68	SGT P.Sola	Italy	F.G91	OC
2207	02.08.68	R.C.Brown	USMC	D.F4	OC
2208	02.08.68	TEN G.P.Roverato	Italy	F.G91	OC
2209	04.08.68	1/LT R.C.Reese	USA	Moh	NK
2210	04.08.68	PF/C J.W.Hoffman	USA	Moh	EA
2211	04.08.68	CAPT C.D.Jensen	Den	L.T33	NK
2212	04.08.68	LT C.D.Rottgering	USN	Crus	OC
2213	05.08.68	LT D.W.Cable	USN	Int	OC
2214	06.08.68	1/LT R.J.Therriault	USMC	Phant	OC
2215	06.08.68	1/LT T.H.Tanguay	USMC	Phant	OC
2216	07.08.68	CAPT J.Denton	USN	Phant	EA
2217	08.08.68	LT D.W.Brearly	RN	Bucc	OC
2218	08.08.68	CAPT S.M.Creal	USMC	Phant	OC
2219	08.08.68	CAPT C.R.Cusack	USMC	Phant	OC
2220	09.08.68	CAPT A.J.Vognsen	Den	L.T33	OC
2221	10.08.68	1/LT R.J.Eisenlohr	USMC	Coug	OC
2222	16.08.68	MAJ L.N.Cain	USAF	Phant	NK
2223	16.08.68	LT M.Metcalfe	USAF	Phant	NK
2224	17.08.68	LT K.A.McClusky	USN	Coug	OC
2225	19.08.68	LT/JG L.R.Plotz	USN	Crus	OC
2226	19.08.68	CAPT A.R.Thomas	USAF	Phant	EA
2227	19.08.68	LT G.M.Greene	USAF	Phant	EA
2228	20.08.68	LT/JG D.C.Brandenstein	USN	Int	OC
2229	20.08.68	CAPT R.J.McPherson	Can	CF100	OC
2230	20.08.68	LT F.L.Senechal	Can	CF100	OC
2231	20.08.68	LT W.A.Neal	USN	Int	OC
2232	24.08.68	LT/JG T.L.McPherson	USN	Phant	OC

No.	Date	Name	Force	Type	Cause
2233	24.08.68	LT/JG B.S.Foster	USN	Crus	OC
2234	27.08.68	LT/CDR Hower	USN	Int	NK
2235	27.08.68	LT/JG L.T.Lockwood	USN	Int	NK
2236	27.08.68	1/LT S.F.Wilborn	USAF	Phant	EA
2237	29.08.68	LT/CDR G.G.Zimmer	USN	L.T1A	OC
2238	29.08.68	LT J.L.Seltzer	USN	L.T1A	OC
2239	31.08.68	CAPT T.G.Dorsett	USAF	Phant	EA
2240	31.08.68	CAPT D.G.Kenny	USAF	Phant	EA
2241	31.08.68	1/LT G.A.D'Angelo	USAF	Phant	NK
2242	31.08.68	LT/COL P.A.Kauttu	USAF	Phant	NK
2243	31.08.68	CAPT J.R.Wilson	USAF	Phant	EA
2244	02.09.68	MAJ M.L.Bellamy	USA	Moh	OC
2245	03.09.68	1/LT Parlatore	USAF	Phant	NK
2246	03.09.68	MAJ T.E.Assalone	USAF	Phant	NK
2247	04.09.68	MR J.Cockburn	Civ	Light	NK
2248	06.09.68	CDR K.L.Coskey	USN	Int	OC
2249	06.09.68	LT/CDR R.G.McKee	USN	Int	OC
2250	07.09.68	1/LT J.C.Church	USN	Phant	EA
2251	08.09.68	CAPT M.H.Branum	USMC	Phant	OC
2252	08.09.68	1/LT H.W.Hibbs	USMC	Phant	OC
2253	10.09.68	LT J.N.Quisenberry	USN	Crus	OC
2254	10.09.68	SP5 P.L.Fvnari	USA	Moh	OC
2255	11.09.68	1/LT R.H.Vandyke	USAF	Phant	EA
2256	11.09.68	MAJ L.E.Bustle	USAF	Phant	EA
2257	13.09.68	C.D.Pilcher	Civ	Phant	OC
2258	13.09.68	CAPT D.G.Whitney	USAF	Phant	OC
2259	13.09.68	MAJ R.G.Dilger	USAF	Phant	OC
2260	16.09.68	LT/CDR W.R.Lambertson	USN	Phant	OC
2261	16.09.68	LT/JG T.L.McPherson	USN	Phant	OC
2262	17.09.68	LT/JG P.E.Swingart	USN	Crus	OC
2263	17.09.68	LT/JG D.J.Wilcox	USN	Crus	OC
2264	17.09.68	CAPT L.L.Paul	USAF	Phant	EA
2265	18.09.68	CMDT Autret	Fr AF	Mir	OC
2266	18.09.68	SGT P.Mueller	Switz	Venom	OC
2267	19.09.68	1/LT P.Nash	USAF	Phant	EA
2268	23.09.68	LT/JG W.G.Ellis	USN	Coug	OC
2269	24.09.68	LT M.T.Najarian	USN	Crus	OC
2270	24.09.68	CAPT P.Cronauer	GerAF	L.F104	OC
2271	24.09.68	MAJ R.Prinz	GerAF	L.F104	OC
2272	26.09.68	LT B.B.Byers	USN	Phant	OC
2273	26.09.68	LT L.W.Nordstrom	USN	Phant	OC
2274	03.10.68	LT/JG G.M.Wright	USN	Crus	NK
2275	03.10.68	1/LT B.M.Kennedy	USAF	Phant	OC
2276	04.10.68	H.Bruckner	AusAF	Vamp	OC
2277	04.10.68	H.Witeschnik	AusAF	Vamp	OC
2278	04.10.68	CAPT R.W.Ruark	USAF	Phant	OC
2279	05.10.68	1/LT R.E.Walkup	USAF	Phant	OC
2280	05.10.68	CAPT S.L.Lustfield	USAF	Phant	EA
2281	18.10.68	MAJ J.W.Quist	USMC	Phant	OC
2282	18.10.68	1/LT D.T.Schanzenbach	USMC	Phant	OC
2283	20.10.68	1/LT S.Wilburn	USAF	Phant	OC
2284	20.10.68	LT D.K.Maskell	USN	Coug	OC
2285	20.10.68	LT/COL Damico	USAF	Phant	OC
2286	21.10.68	LT H.L.Karr	USN	Phant	OC
2287	22.10.68	MAJ T.A.Talbot	USA	Moh	NK
2288	22.10.68	SP4 S.C.Fletcher	USA	Moh	NK
2289	23.10.68	P.Caneil	Civ	Mir	OC
2290	23.10.68	P.Dudal	Civ	Mir	OC
2291	25.10.68	1/LT D.L.Richardson	USAF	Phant	NK
2292	28.10.68	LT/JG D.M.Hendrickson	USN	Coug	OC
2293	28.10.68	CMDT A.Brossier	Fr AF	Mir	NK
2294	29.10.68	LT J.Williamson	USN	Coug	OC
2295	30.10.68	F/O B.Roberts	AusAF	Mir	OC
2296	30.10.68	MAJ R.E.Boucher	USAF	Phant	OC
2297	30.10.68	CAPT R.D.Smith	USAF	Phant	OC
2298	01.11.68	CAPT G.S.Libey	USMC	Phant	EA
2299	01.11.68	1/LT W.H.Frizell	USMC	Phant	EA
2300	03.11.68	LT N.McCoy	USN	Coug	OC
2301	07.11.68	LT J.R.Musitano	USN	Crus	OC
2302	09.11.68	1/LT J.Gough	USAF	Phant	OC
2303	15.11.68	LT P.R.Scott	USN	Crus	NK

No.	Date	Name	Force	Type	Cause
2304	18.11.68	1/LT R.K.Boone	USAF	Phant	NK
2305	18.11.68	CAPT L.A.Stults	USMC	Coug	OC
2306	18.11.68	ENS C.F.Moon	USN	Coug	OC
2307	19.11.68	ENS J.Barber	USN	Coug	OC
2308	19.11.68	LT/JG H.L.Kendall	USN	Coug	OC
2309	21.11.68	CAPT P.N.Shiraishi	USAF	Phant	OC
2310	21.11.68	CAPT E.U.Larue	USAF	Phant	OC
2311	21.11.68	LT W.R.Logue	USN	Phant	NK
2312	23.11.68	T.C.Wright	RAF	J.Pro	NK
2313	25.11.68	F/O G.Munton-Jackson	Zimb	Vamp	OC
2314	25.11.68	FL/LT J.F.Barnes	Zimb	Vamp	OC
2315	29.11.68	FL/LT E.Rawcliffe	RAF	Light	NK
2316	29.11.68	LT/CDR W.L.Dwyer	USN	Phant	OC
2317	29.11.68	LT/CDR M.J.Ettel	USN	Phant	OC
2318	03.12.68	MAJ C.L.Gallanger	USAF	Phant	OC
2319	03.12.68	LT/JG W.Font	USN	Phant	OC
2320	03.12.68	CAPT N.H.Svarrer	USA	Moh	EA
2321	03.12.68	SGT R.W.Christiansen	USA	Moh	EA
2322	03.12.68	1/LT D.K.Chastain	USAF	Phant	OC
2323	09.12.68	CAPT J.B.Koebberling	USAF	Phant	EA
2324	09.12.68	MAJ R.I.McCann	USAF	Phant	EA
2325	11.12.68	CAPT H.J.Drewry	USAF	Phant	NK
2326	12.12.68	Classified			
2327	16.12.68	SGT Marion	Fr AF	Mir	OC
2328	20.12.68	LT R.W.Colyar	USN	Int	OC
2329	22.12.68	LT R.E.Hoffman	USAF	Phant	OC
2330	31.12.68	Classified			
2331	31.12.68	Classified			
2332	31.12.68	Classified			
2333	01.01.69	Classified			
2334	01.01.69	Classified			
2335	06.01.69	1/LT J.A.Wilkins	USAF	Phant	OC
2336	06.01.69	CAPT R.B.Meyers	USAF	Phant	OC
2337	06.01.69	CAPT S.Faulkner	USAF	Phant	EA
2338	07.01.69	P/O M.Howes	RAF	Canb	OC
2339	07.01.69	1/LT Trimble	USMC	Phant	OC
2340	07.01.69	1/LT J.A.Varni	USMC	Phant	OC
2341	07.01.69	CAPT W.F.Needham	USAF	Phant	EA
2342	07.01.69	1/LT S.D.Adams	USAF	Phant	EA
2343	09.01.69	LT M.J.Granger-Holcombe	RN	S.Vix	OC
2344	09.01.69	AS/LT D.J.Hansom	RN	S.Vix	OC
2345	12.01.69	1/LT W.C.Ryan	USMC	Phant	OC
2346	12.01.69	1/LT G.L.Bain	USMC	Phant	OC
2347	14.01.69	LT/JG P.Ringwood	USMC	Crus	OC
2348	17.01.69	CAPT J.Fegan	USAF	Phant	EA
2349	17.01.69	CAPT V.A.Smith	USAF	Phant	EA
2350	20.01.69	LT W.J.Pellegrini	USN	Phant	OC
2351	20.01.69	LT/CDR J.T.Ginn	USN	Phant	OC
2352	22.01.69	W.E.Collins	USMC	Phant	EA
2353	22.01.69		USMC	Phant	EA
2354	24.01.69	CAPT J.Nash	USAF	Phant	NK
2355	24.01.69	LT/COL R.W.Clement	USAF	Phant	NK
2356	24.01.69	1/LT R.J.Rybak	USAF	Phant	OC
2357	24.01.69	MAJ R.D.Russ	USAF	Phant	OC
2358	25.01.69	1/LT W.J.Arland	USAF	Phant	EA
2359	25.01.69	MAJ R.P.Cushwa	USAF	Phant	EA
2360	28.01.69	1/LT H.R.Dobbs	USAF	Phant	EA
2361	28.01.69	CAPT G.M.Smith	USAF	Phant	EA
2362	30.01.69	LT/CDR D.A.Pickles	RN	Hunt	OC
2363	30.01.69	LT/CDR R.J.Northard	RN	Hunt	OC
2364	31.01.69	FL/LT W.S.McAlister	AusAF	MB326	OC
2365	31.01.69	CADET R.G.Heideman	AusAF	MB326	OC
2366	03.02.69	LT P.Barber	USMC	Phant	OC
2367	03.02.69	FL/LT B.Hamilton	RAF	Hunt	OC
2368	03.02.69	CAPT W.S.Simone	USMC	Phant	OC
2369	05.02.69	CAPT D.C.Petty	USAF	Phant	OC
2370	05.02.69	CAPT A.E.Sultan	USAF	Phant	OC
2371	05.02.69	LT/COL D.T.Lynch	USAF	Phant	OC
2372	07.02.69	1/LT J.W.Maxwell	USMC	Phant	OC
2373	10.02.69	LT E.G.Sliney	USN	Phant	OC
2374	10.02.69	LT/CDR D.A.Peperson	USN	Phant	OC

No.	Date	Name	Force	Type	Cause
2375	10.02.69	LT/JG R.J.Speersschneider	USN	Phant	OC
2376	10.02.69	LT J.G.Hohlstein	USN	Phant	OC
2377	12.02.69	1/LT W.R.Teglia	USMC	Int	OC
2378	12.02.69	1/LT J.H.Schiek	USMC	Int	OC
2379	13.02.69	LT/CDR P.H.Cummuskey	RN	Bucc	OC
2380	13.02.69	S/LT J.Kershaw	RN	Bucc	OC
2381	14.02.69	1/LT G.K.Breault	USAF	Phant	OC
2382	17.02.69	LT/JG J.H.Akin	USN	Phant	OC
2383	17.02.69	LT/CDR D.J.Weaver	USN	Phant	OC
2384	20.02.69	LT/JG R.D.Work	USN	Phant	OC
2385	20.02.69	LT/JG F.H.Lloyd	USN	Phant	OC
2386	20.02.69	LT/JG D.L.Granger	USN	Phant	NK
2387	22.02.69	R.C.Roth	USAF	Phant	EA
2388	22.02.69	C.H.Gray	USAF	Phant	EA
2389	22.02.69	1/LT M.E.Hennan	USAF	Phant	EA
2390	26.02.69	LT D.Dalmas	Fr AF	Mir	OC
2391	01.03.69	CAPT W.S.Reeder	USA	Moh	EA
2392	01.03.69	SP5 D.R.Armstrong	USA	Moh	EA
2393	02.03.69	1/LT P.E.Daly	USMC	Phant	EA
2394	02.03.69	LT/COL S.E.D'Angelo III	USMC	Phant	EA
2395	03.03.69	LT A.Park	RN	Bucc	NK
2396	03.03.69	S/LT W.A.Craig	RN	Bucc	OC
2397	03.03.69	F/O B.A.J.Chown	RN	Bucc	OC
2398	03.03.69	FL/LT J.M.Yates	RN	Bucc	OC
2399	04.03.69	S/LT Agnard	Fr AF	Mir	OC
2400	05.03.69	MAJ M.G.Owens	USAF	Phant	OC
2401	05.03.69	CAPT E.A.Davis	USAF	Phant	OC
2402	05.03.69	CAPT G.Lindner	GerAF	L.F104	OC
2403	05.03.69	1/LT C.J.Wiles	USAF	Phant	EA
2404	06.03.69	LT/JG A.J.Notis	USN	Coug	NK
2405	07.03.69	1/LT E.B.Nuttall	USAF	Phant	OC
2406	07.03.69	CAPT F.P.Barrios	USAF	Phant	OC
2407	07.03.69	LT/JG R.P.Wiegand	USN	Int	OC
2408	10.03.69	CAPT Rutyna	USAF	Phant	EA
2409	10.03.69	LT/COL Luna	USAF	Phant	EA
2410	12.03.69	CAPT Dejean	Fr AF	Mir	OC
2411	12.03.69	LT D.M.Content	USN	Coug	OC
2412	12.03.69	LT/JG G.J.Carloni	USN	Coug	OC
2413	13.03.69	LT/JG E.L.Brazil	USN	Phant	OC
2414	13.03.69	LT/JG K.J.Oden	USN	Phant	OC
2415	14.03.69	LT T.N.Baggett	USN	Coug	OC
2416	15.03.69	FL/LT R.W.Colyn	SA	Mir	OC
2417	15.03.69		Switz	Mir	OC
2418	21.03.69	LT/JG B.Guthrie	USN	Phant	NK
2419	21.03.69	SP5 N.McCauley	USA	Moh	EA
2420	21.03.69	CAPT D.Peterson	USA	Moh	EA
2421	25.03.69	CAPT M.L.Hinnebusch	USAF	Phant	OC
2422	25.03.69	CAPT K.M.Mineau	USAF	Phant	OC
2423	26.03.69	LT/JG J.G.James	USN	Phant	OC
2424	26.03.69	LT P.G.Gilleece	USN	Phant	OC
2425	26.03.69	LT R.E.McKeown	USN	Phant	OC
2426	26.03.69	LT/JG R.L.Test	USN	Phant	OC
2427	29.03.69	CAPT B.L.Huff	USAF	Phant	OC
2428	29.03.69	CAPT Papendorf	USAF	Phant	EA
2429	31.03.69	S/LT O.Barwood	RN	Hunt	OC
2430	31.03.69	LT K.A.Harris	RN	Hunt	OC
2431	02.04.69	LT/COL C.G.Foster	USAF	Phant	NK
2432	02.04.69	F/O K.R.Barley	RAF	Hunt	OC
2433	02.04.69	LT A.Mencarelli	Italy	MB326	OC
2434	02.04.69	STDT A.Scolto	Italy	MB326	OC
2435	02.04.69	1/LT J.P.McMahon	USAF	Phant	NK
2436	03.04.69	LT/JG J.F.Ricci	USN	Int	EA
2437	03.04.69	LT/CDR E.G.Redden	USN	Int	EA
2438	06.04.69	1/LT D.Harlow	USMC	Phant	OC
2439	06.04.69	CAPT C.L.Lowry	USMC	Phant	OC
2440	06.04.69	1/LT C.R.Koster	USAF	Phant	OC
2441	06.04.69	CAPT R.Brandt	USAF	Phant	OC
2442	08.04.69	LT J.Garuba	USN	Crus	OC
2443	09.04.69	MAJ W.O.Armstrong	USAF	Phant	NK
2444	09.04.69	W/C J.L.Bhargava	IndAF	Myst	OC

No.	Date	Name	Force	Type	Cause
2445	09.04.69	COL W.D.Drven	USAF	Phant	NK
2446	12.04.69	CAPT C.E.Mattern	USAF	Phant	OC
2447	16.04.69	R.P.Anderson	USAF	Phant	NK
2448	16.04.69	MAJ D.Winkles	USAF	Phant	NK
2449	17.04.69	CAPT R.Bartholomew	USAF	Phant	EA
2450	17.04.69	CAPT B.F.Doyle	USAF	Phant	EA
2451	17.04.69	1/LT G.K.Muellner	USAF	Phant	NK
2452	17.04.69	1/LT J.L.Beavers	USAF	Phant	NK
2453	19.04.69	CAPT L.O'Keefe	USMC	Crus	OC
2454	22.04.69	CDTAC I.E.Watson	AusAF	Vamp	OC
2455	23.04.69	S/L M.A.Chaudhry	Pak	F86	OC
2456	27.04.69	LT/JG J.G.McGarvie	USN	Crus	OC
2457	28.04.69	CAPT F.L.Massey	USMC	Phant	OC
2458	28.04.69	CAPT J.S.Garzio	USMC	Phant	OC
2459	28.04.69	LT/JG M.E.Mansell	USN	Crus	OC
2460	29.04.69	LT/JG R.E.Treis	USN	Coug	OC
2461	29.04.69	LT/JG W.C.Houston	USN	Coug	OC
2462	07.05.69	MAJ Brasher	USAF	Phant	EA
2463	08.05.69	1/LT Mundt	USAF	Phant	EA
2464	08.05.69	CAPT H.P.Rusch	GerAF	F.G91	OC
2465	09.05.69	LT/CDR R.G.Snow	USN	Crus	OC
2466	10.05.69	1/LT C.W.Dearmond	USAF	Phant	OC
2467	11.05.69		USMC	Phant	EA
2468	12.05.69	1/LT P.Daly	USMC	Phant	EA
2469	12.05.69	1/LT D.Matzko	USMC	Phant	EA
2470	14.05.69	LT/JG R.Little	USN	Int	OC
2471	16.05.69	MAJ P.L.Noggle	USMC	Phant	OC
2472	16.05.69	LT T.R.Johnson	USMC	Phant	OC
2473	17.05.69	MAJ J.R.Rothenburger	USMC	Crus	OC
2474	18.05.69	1/LT Griffiths	USMC	Phant	OC
2475	18.05.69	MAJ Moody	USMC	Phant	OC
2476	21.05.69	LT Obar	USN	Crus	NK
2477	24.05.69	LT/JG S.L.Ritchey	USN	Crus	OC
2478	28.05.69	LT/COL J.S.Brandt	USAF	Phant	OC
2479	28.05.69	CAPT J.B.Lofgreen	USAF	Phant	OC
2480	03.06.69	LT Harkin	USN	Crus	OC
2481	04.06.69	MR D.Simpson	Civ	Harr	OC
2482	05.06.69	CAPT D.Moy (May)	USAF	Phant	EA
2483	05.06.69	COL R.F.Findlay	USAF	Phant	EA
2484	08.06.69	CAPT P.T.Gillespie	USAF	Phant	NK
2485	09.06.69	LT/JG G.R.Wimbush	USN	Coug	OC
2486	10.06.69	MAJ C.Thomas	USAF	Phant	EA
2487	10.06.69	MAJ W.R.Deans	USAF	Phant	EA
2488	14.06.69	CAPT J.W.Grace	USAF	Phant	EA
2489	14.06.69	1/LT W.J.Karas	USAF	Phant	EA
2490	16.06.69	1/LT Polster	USAF	Phant	EA
2491	16.06.69	MAJ G.Fulghum	USAF	Phant	EA
2492	18.06.69	1/LT P.D.Howman	USAF	Phant	NK
2493	23.06.69	LT/JG G.M.Watts	USN	Crus	OC
2494	25.06.69	1/LT S.S.Talbot	USMC	Phant	OC
2495	25.06.69	1/LT A.Vadyak	USMC	Phant	OC
2496	28.06.69	CAPT R.Morrison	USAF	Phant	OC
2497	28.06.69	CAPT Jones	USAF	Phant	OC
2498	02.07.69	CAPT R.Sheppard	USAF	Phant	OC
2499	02.07.69	COL Fallon	USAF	Phant	NK
2500	03.07.69	LT/JG S.G.Bambauer	USN	Phant	OC
2501	03.07.69	LT/JG K.C.Cutter	USN	Phant	OC
2502	03.07.69	LT T.R.Weinal	USN	Crus	OC
2503	03.07.69	LT/JG R.G.Benn	USN	Phant	NK
2504	03.07.69	LT/JG S.J.Shield	USN	Phant	NK
2505	06.07.69	G.P.Hahn	USN	Crus	OC
2506	07.07.69	1/LT J.L.Hiersche	USMC	Phant	OC
2507	07.07.69	MAJ C.C.McClennan	USMC	Phant	OC
2508	07.07.69	LT/CDR D.R.Herman	USN	Int	OC
2509	07.07.69	LT P.M.Soucek	USN	Int	OC
2510	09.07.69	FL/LT F.M.Pearson	RAF	Phant	OC
2511	09.07.69	FL/LT J.E.Rooum	RAF	Phant	OC
2512	11.07.69	LT/JG T.E.Albus	USN	Crus	OC
2513	17.07.69	S/TEN D.Guastamacchia	Italy	MB326	OC
2514	17.07.69	S/TEN M.Moret	Italy	MB326	OC
2515	19.07.69	MAJ R.N.Bacon	USMC	Crus	NK
2516	22.07.69	LT/FLT B.C.Newman	AusAF	MB326	NK
2517	23.07.69	S/LT Vassal	Fr AF	Mir	NK
2518	24.07.69	CDR Langlois	Fr AF	Mir	NK
2519	24.07.69	LT Lang	Fr AF	Mir	NK
2520	25.07.69			USMC	Phant	EA
2521	25.07.69			USMC	Phant	EA
2522	30.07.69	MAJ F.Gromoll	GerAF	L.T33	OC
2523	30.07.69	WO N.Nipprashk	GerAF	L.T33	OC
2524	30.07.69	CAPT A.Baumgart	GerAF	L.F104	NK
2525	30.07.69	MAJ H.Eberhard	GerAF	L.T33	OC
2526	30.07.69	SGT A.Voges	GerAF	L.T33	OC
2527	31.07.69	LT Menessier	Fr AF	Myst	OC
2528	02.08.69	MAJ J.R.Frola	USMC	Crus	OC
2529	02.08.69	LT G.Wells	USN	Crus	OC
2530	03.08.69	1/LT A.Hendrick	USAF	Phant	OC
2531	04.08.69	CAPT M.Allen	USAF	Phant	OC
2532	04.08.69	LT/COL E.Anderson	USAF	Phant	OC
2533	05.08.69	MAJ J.M.Huebel	USMC	Crus	OC
2534	05.08.69	LT/JG D.M.McCloskey	USN	Coug	OC
2535	09.08.69	CAPT P.Lang	USAF	Phant	EA
2536	09.08.69	CAPT S.Magsig	USAF	Phant	EA
2537	09.08.69	CAPT H.K.Kriegeskotten-Bartsc	GerAF	F.G91	OC
2538	12.08.69	LT/JG B.Walker	USN	Phant	OC
2539	12.08.69	LT D.Manlove	USN	Crus	OC
2540	12.08.69	LT/JG C.Brion	USN	Phant	OC
2541	12.08.69	LT J.Scales	USN	Phant	OC
2542	13.08.69	LT/CDR J.McCarthy	USN	Crus	OC
2543	18.08.69	CAPT R.Richardson	USAF	Phant	OC
2544	18.08.69	MAJ Wolf	USAF	Phant	OC
2545	19.08.69		USAF	Phant	NK
2546	21.08.69	LT S.Kanjilal	Ind N	S.Hk	OC
2547	25.08.69	LT J.Ruliffson	USN	Phant	OC
2548	26.08.69	1/LT R.W.Albright	USMC	Int	OC
2549	27.08.69	CAPT C.Wigert	USAF	Phant	EA
2550	27.08.69	MAJ J.Back	USAF	Phant	EA
2551	29.08.69	CWO L.Anderson	USA	Moh	EA
2552	01.09.69	Classified			
2553	01.09.69	Classified			
2554	04.09.69	FL/LT Foster	RAF	J.Pro	OC
2555	04.09.69	FL/LT Francis	RAF	J.Pro	OC
2556	07.09.69	CAPT D.Rietz	USA	Moh	EA
2557	07.09.69	SP4 E.McAuley	USA	Moh	EA
2558	09.09.69	1/LT Niederauer	USAF	Phant	OC
2559	11.09.69	Classified			
2560	12.09.69	LT C.Riddle	USN	Crus	NK
2561	15.09.69	1/LT Lookingland	USAF	Phant	NK
2562	15.09.69	CAPT D.C.Shultis	USAF	Phant	NK
2563	16.09.69	MAJ Neel	RAF	Light	OC
2564	16.09.69	S/LT R.S.G.Kent	RN	Bucc	OC
2565	16.09.69	S/LT R.Croston	RN	Bucc	OC
2566	19.09.69	CAPT V.D.Donile	USMC	Phant	OC
2567	19.09.69	1/LT D.Dziedzic	USMC	Phant	OC
2568	20.09.69	MAJ C.A.Thomas	USAF	Phant	OC
2569	21.09.69	1/LT R.Hargrave	USMC	Int	EA
2570	21.09.69	MAJ P.Busch	USMC	Int	EA
2571	26.09.69	LT/JG W.Bovitz	USN	Int	OC
2572	26.09.69	LT/JG G.Ganson	USN	Int	OC
2573	27.09.69	LT/CDR J.Taylor	USN	Crus	OC
2574	28.09.69	S/TEN G.Mauro	Italy	MB326	OC
2575	28.09.69	S/TEN F.Faber	Italy	MB326	OC
2576	28.09.69	S/TEN A.Gagliardi	Italy	MB326	OC
2577	28.09.69	S/TEN C.Royagnoli	Italy	MB326	OC
2578	29.09.69		Iran	Phant	OC
2579	29.09.69	G.Sarkhail	Iran	Phant	OC
2580	30.09.69	LT/JG Maxwell	USN	Coug	OC
2581	30.09.69	LT/JG G.Stubbs	USN	Coug	OC
2582	30.09.69	Classified			
2583	01.10.69	F/O H.J.Badower	AusAF	MB326	OC
2584	01.10.69	FL/LT J.A.Pedrina	AusAF	MB326	OC
2585	01.10.69	LT R.G.Zeisinger	USAF	Phant	OC
2586	01.10.69	R.A.Gieleghem	USAF	Phant	OC
2587	01.10.69	CDR Foltzer	Fr AF	Mir	NK
2588	02.10.69	LT D.Breton	Fr AF	Myst	NK
2589	02.10.69	CAPT P.Rider	USAF	Phant	OC

No.	Date	Name	Force	Type	Cause	No.	Date	Name	Force	Type	Cause
2590	08.10.69	CAPT N.Jacobs	USAF	Phant	OC	2664	19.12.69	CAPT T.A.Webb Jr	USAF	Phant	OC
2591	08.10.69	CAPT Stevenson	USAF	Phant	OC	2665	20.12.69	1/LT W.F.Daley	USAF	Phant	NK
2592	09.10.69	LT W.Ribble	USN	Crus	OC	2666	20.12.69	MAJ F.N.Brent Jr	USAF	Phant	NK
2593	13.10.69	WO M.Ambs	GerAF	L.F104	OC	2667	20.12.69	CAPT D.S.Catchings	USAF	Phant	EA
2594	14.10.69	LT R.Rusconi	Italy	MB326	NK	2668	21.12.69	CAPT C.Sloan	USAF	Phant	EA
2595	14.10.69	LT F.Crucito	Italy	MB326	NK	2669	21.12.69	1/LT A.L.Guise	USAF	Phant	EA
2596	15.10.69	1/LT White	USA	Moh	NK	2670	22.12.69	LT C.M.Riddle	USN	Crus	OC
2597	15.10.69	LT/CDR Graff	USA	Moh	NK	2671	28.12.69	1/LT E.M.Franger	USMC	Phant	EA
2598	19.10.69	LT H.Austin	USN	Phant	OC	2672	28.12.69	1/LT D.K.McClennan	USMC	Phant	EA
2599	26.10.69	LT T.L.Letter	USN	Crus	OC	2673	31.12.69	Classified			
2600	27.10.69	LT Convers	Fr N	Etend	OC	2674	31.12.69	Classified			
2601	28.10.69	LT A.Kent	USN	Phant	OC	2675	31.12.69	Classified			
2602	28.10.69	LT/JG T.Dater	USN	Phant	OC	2676	01.01.70	Classified			
2603	29.10.69	ALT D.Postance	Zimb	Canb	OC	2677	01.01.70	Classified			
2604	29.10.69	S/LT J.Stagman	Zimb	Canb	OC	2678	01.01.70	Classified			
2605	31.10.69	SGT K.Mildenburger	GerAF	L.F104	NK	2679	01.01.70	Classified			
2606	02.11.69	LT/JG E.J.Simmons	USN	Coug	OC	2680	04.01.70	LT/CDR J.W.Boyd	USN	Crus	OC
2607	06.11.69	CAPT K.O'Mara	USMC	Phant	OC	2681	04.01.70	LT/CDR W.F.Wagner	USN	Int	OC
2608	06.11.69	CAPT V.Donile	USMC	Phant	OC	2682	04.01.70	LT/CDR W.R.Westerman	USN	Int	OC
2609	10.11.69	LT/JG Sneddon	USN	Phant	OC						
2610	10.11.69	LT R.Moody	USN	Phant	OC	2683	06.01.70		USAF	Phant	NK
2611	11.11.69	LT J.G.Hoyler	USAF	Phant	NK	2684	07.01.70	1/LT Cambell	USAF	Phant	OC
2612	11.11.69	MAJ C.W.Killen	USAF	Phant	OC	2685	09.01.70	LT E.Tarr	USN	Crus	OC
2613	11.11.69	CAPT J.Boyce	USAF	Phant	EA	2686	11.01.70	LT/JG K.D.Forbes	USN	Phant	OC
2614	13.11.69	MAJ G.Lindgren	USMC	Phant	OC	2687	14.01.70	CAPT W.H.Rath	USAF	Phant	OC
2615	13.11.69	MAJ T.Leach	USMC	Phant	OC	2688	14.01.70	F.Hutto	USAF	Phant	OC
2616	15.11.69	S/TEN M.Russolillo	Italy	F.G91	OC	2689	15.01.70	LT R.D.Leblank	USAF	Phant	EA
2617	15.11.69	CAPT G.Micale	Italy	F.G91	OC	2690	20.01.70		USAF		OC
2618	15.11.69	LT/CDR J.Graf	USA	Moh	NK	2691	20.01.70		USAF	Phant	OC
2619	15.11.69	CAPT R.T.White	USA	Moh	NK	2692	20.01.70	LT/CDR R.W.Leeds	USN	Phant	OC
2620	16.11.69	1/LT A.Guise	USAF	Phant	EA	2693	20.01.70	LT A.L.Johnson	USN	Phant	OC
2621	16.11.69	MAJ E.P.Morphew	USAF	Phant	EA	2694	21.01.70	CAPT P.Comitini	Italy	F.G91	OC
2622	16.11.69	CAPT C.Sloan	USAF	Phant	NK	2695	21.01.70	S/TEN R.Biancuzzi	Italy	F.G91	OC
2623	16.11.69	1/LT D.Jessen	USMC	Int	OC	2696	22.01.70	FW G.Wegmann	GerAF	L.F104	OC
2624	16.11.69	1/LT R.Tutor	USMC	Int	OC	2697	30.01.70	LT M.J.Cummingham	RN	Bucc	OC
2625	16.11.69	MAJ Davis	USAF	Phant	EA	2698	30.01.70	LT A.C.A.Moore	RN	Bucc	OC
2626	16.11.69	LT Ernst	USAF	Phant	EA	2699	02.02.70	LT C.M.Riddle	USN	Crus	OC
2627	16.11.69	CAPT R.C.Cotten	USAF	Phant	EA	2700	02.02.70	LT G.Crowell	USN	Crus	OC
2628	17.11.69	LT Rion	Fr AF	Myst	OC	2701	06.02.70	LT/JG L.E.Smith	USN	Phant	OC
2629	17.11.69	CAPT J.J.Rabeni Jr	USAF	Phant	OC	2702	06.02.70	LT/JG Queen	USN	Phant	OC
2630	17.11.69	MAJ D.A.Bowie	USAF	Phant	OC	2703	06.02.70	LT/CDR E.P.Reese	USN	Int	EA
2631	19.11.69	CAPT J.Austin	USA	Moh	EA	2704	06.02.70	LT/JG D.R.Frazer	USN	Int	OC
2632	19.11.69	SP4 J.S.McIntosh	USA	Moh	EA	2705	06.02.70	MAJ J.K.Roschlau	USMC	Crus	NK
2633	20.11.69	FL/LT A.Irfan	Pak	F86	OC	2706	07.02.70	CAPT J.E.Sharkey	USMC	Phant	OC
2634	22.11.69	1/LT Paige	USAF	Phant	OC	2707	07.02.70	1/LT C.E.Stewart	USMC	Phant	OC
2635	22.11.69	CAPT C.Williams	USAF	Phant	OC	2708	08.02.70	1/LT J.C.Coon	USMC	Phant	EA
2636	22.11.69	LT/JG H.J.Bedinger	USN	Phant	OC	2709	09.02.70	MAJ J.B.Leonard	USMC	Phant	EA
2637	22.11.69	CAPT L.Wright	USAF	Phant	OC	2710	16.02.70	LT/JG J.H.Hickok	USN	Int	OC
2638	22.11.69	LT C.Bove	Fr AF	Myst	NK	2711	16.02.70	LT/CDR Cole	RN	Bucc	OC
2639	22.11.69	CDR Richards	USN	Int	NK	2712	18.02.70	CAPT Dotson	USAF	Phant	EA
2640	22.11.69	LT/JG Deuter	USN	Int	NK	2713	19.02.70	LT/JG L.L.Morris	USN	Crus	OC
2641	22.11.69	LT/CDR J.S.Hellman	USN	Crus	OC	2714	24.02.70	MAJ R.J.McEwan	USAF	Phant	OC
2642	22.11.69	1/LT W.Wilkening	USMC	Phant	OC	2715	24.02.70	CAPT McClenathen	USA	Moh	NK
2643	22.11.69	LT H.C.Wheeler	USN	Phant	OC	2716	25.02.70	LT A.Gilchrist	USN	Phant	OC
2644	22.11.69	CAPT I.Harrison	USAF	Phant	OC	2717	25.02.70	LT/JG T.Young	USN	Phant	OC
2645	24.11.69	LT M.J.Madden	USN	L.T1A	OC	2718	26.02.70	Classified			
2646	24.11.69	LT D.Bell	USN	L.T1A	OC	2719	28.02.70	LT R.R.Wittenberg	USN	Int	OC
2647	25.11.69	1/LT D.Tye	USAF	Phant	EA	2720	28.02.70	LT H.W.Paul	USN	Int	OC
2648	25.11.69	CAPT G.Skaret	USAF	Phant	EA	2721	04.03.70	1/LT W.Cooper	USMC	Int	NK
2649	28.11.69	LT G.W.Warrell	USN	Crus	OC	2722	04.03.70	1/LT P.Horner	USMC	Int	NK
2650	01.12.69	LT/JG J.W.Alderink	USN	Crus	OC	2723	05.03.70	WO3 E.Bustamante	USA	Moh	OC
2651	03.12.69	MAJ B.Sharp	USAF	Phant	NK	2724	05.03.70	SP5 D.Avey	USA	Moh	OC
2652	03.12.69	1/LT J.Mangels	USAF	Phant	NK	2725	06.03.70	CAPT A.Sant'Ambrogio	Italy	F.G91	NK
2653	04.12.69	1/LT J.Busse	GerAF	F.G91	NK						
2654	04.12.69	LT R.R.Marshall	USN	Coug	OC	2726	09.03.70	LT M.L.Meier	USN	Phant	OC
2655	05.12.69		USAF	Phant	EA	2727	09.03.70	CDR W.A.Lott	USN	Phant	OC
2656	05.12.69	LT J.Bergeron	USAF	Phant	EA	2728	09.03.70	MAJ C.S.McLeran	USMC	Crus	OC
2657	12.12.69	S/TEN G.Bonollo	Italy	F.G91	OC	2729	10.03.70	LT S.Ritchey	USN	Crus	NK
2658	13.12.69	1/LT X.Lizee	Fr N	Etend	OC	2730	12.03.70	LT/JG D.Erickson	USN	Coug	OC
2659	15.12.69	LT/JG R.O.Amber	USN	Crus	OC	2731	15.03.70	Classified			
2660	17.12.69	CDR R.A.Peters	USN	Crus	OC	2732	15.03.70	Classified			
2661	19.12.69	LT/JG D.L.Pitzer	USN	Phant	OC	2733	15.03.70	Classified			
2662	19.12.69	LT/JG M.D.Dewitt	USN	Phant	OC	2734	15.03.70	Classified			
2663	19.12.69	CAPT L.M.Bonner	USAF	Phant	OC	2735	16.03.70	LT F.G.Hills	USN	Coug	OC

No.	Date	Name	Force	Type	Cause	No.	Date	Name	Force	Type	Cause
2736	16.03.70	P/O R.W.Exler	RAF	J.Pro	OC	2810	08.06.70	LT/JG T.O'Connor	USN	Phant	OC
2737	18.03.70	LT D.N.Eggert	USN	Crus	OC	2811	09.06.70	CAPT C.Ripple	USAF	Phant	OC
2738	19.03.70	CAPT R.A.Rash	USAF	Phant	EA	2812	09.06.70	CAPT R.Clingaman	USAF	Phant	NK
2739	19.03.70	1/LT Frey	GerAF	L.F104	OC	2813	10.06.70	LT B.Jenkins	USN	Crus	OC
2740	19.03.70	LT Pugu	USAF	Phant	EA	2814	11.06.70	R.C.Blakely	USMC	Phant	NK
2741	20.03.70	LT/COL L.J.Shipman	USAF	Phant	OC	2815	11.06.70	CAPT Rindt	USMC	Phant	EA
2742	20.03.70	LT J.E.Overbye	Den	F100	OC	2816	12.06.70	CAPT C.Hattingh	SA	Imp	OC
2743	21.03.70	LT/JG F.W.Conroy	USN	Phant	OC	2817	12.06.70	1/LT E.Payne	USAF	Phant	OC
2744	21.03.70	LT/CDR W.J.Davis	USN	Phant	OC	2818	12.06.70	LT J.Maynard	USN	Int	NK
2745	21.03.70		USAF	Phant	EA	2819	12.06.70	CAPT Massy	USMC	Phant	OC
2746	27.03.70	CDR A.Brossier	Civ	Jag	OC	2820	17.06.70	LT W.Meldrum	USN	Coug	OC
2747	30.03.70	LT/COL W.Brown	USAF	Phant	OC	2821	19.06.70	1/LT F.Hall	USMC	Phant	OC
2748	30.03.70	LT/COL L.Melton	USAF	Phant	OC	2822	19.06.70	1/LT G.Mitchell	USMC	Phant	OC
2749	02.04.70	CAPT Gueniot	Fr AF	Mir	OC	2823	22.06.70	MAJ J.R.Gentry	USAF	Phant	OC
2750	04.04.70	1/LT G.K.Bruce	USMC	Phant	OC	2824	22.06.70	1/LT C.E.McElroy	USAF	Phant	OC
2751	04.04.70	1/LT R.J.Cecka	USMC	Phant	OC	2825	30.06.70	CDR F.B.Winton	USN	Phant	OC
2752	05.04.70	LT T.J.Terril	USN	Phant	OC	2826	09.07.70	S/L M.Akbar	Pak	F86	NK
2753	06.04.70	MAJ R.Van Brunt	USAF	Phant	EA	2827	13.07.70	CAPT J.Wilson	USAF	Phant	OC
2754	06.04.70	1/LT O.Lloyd	USAF	Phant	EA	2828	13.07.70	COL R.Campbell	USAF	Phant	OC
2755	06.04.70	SGT G.Klenz	GerAF	F.G91	OC	2829	20.07.70	1/LT A.Guise	USAF	Phant	OC
2756	07.04.70	CAPT G.Lindlar	GerAF	F.G91	OC	2830	21.07.70	LT/JG D.Russell	USN	Coug	OC
2757	08.04.70	CAPT N.Henkel	GerAF	F.G91	NK	2831	24.07.70	CAPT P.Lang	USAF	Phant	OC
2758	10.04.70	MAJ J.Leaphart	USAF	Phant	EA	2832	24.07.70	CAPT R.Mazet	USAF	Phant	OC
2759	10.04.70	CAPT J.Burnholtz	USAF	Phant	EA	2833	25.07.70	LT/JG W.Harding	USN	Phant	NK
2760	11.04.70	LT/JG O.Harris	USN	Int	OC	2834	25.07.70	CAPT R.Rigel	USAF	Phant	NK
2761	11.04.70	LT B.Bruce	USN	Int	OC	2835	25.07.70	LT R.H.Clime	USN	Phant	OC
2762	15.04.70	Classified				2836	28.07.70	LT/CDR P.Gilleece	USN	Phant	OC
2763	15.04.70	Classified				2837	31.07.70	LT/CDR R.L.White	USN	Crus	OC
2764	18.04.70	CAPT J.McCarren	USAF	Phant	OC	2838	01.08.70		USN	Crus	NK
2765	19.04.70	LT J.Laughter	USN	Crus	OC	2839	03.08.70	Classified			
2766	21.04.70	CAPT B.Smith	USAF	Phant	NK	2840	10.08.70	CAPT J.Dalton	USAF	Phant	NK
2767	22.04.70	SGT K.H.Aschenberg	GerAF	L.F104	OC	2841	10.08.70		USAF	Phant	NK
2768	22.04.70	MAJ J.Rush	USAF	Phant	EA	2842	10.08.70		USAF	Phant	NK
2769	22.04.70	CAPT B.Foster	USAF	Phant	EA	2843	10.08.70	CAPT Flynn	USAF	Phant	NK
2770	23.04.70	CAPT M.Nelson	USAF	Phant	NK	2844	11.08.70		USAF	Phant	NK
2771	23.04.70	1/LT J.Holmquist	USAF	Phant	NK	2845	11.08.70		USAF	Phant	NK
2772	25.04.70	LT S.Hancock	USAF	Phant	EA	2846	11.08.70	CAPT I.Iverson	USAF	Phant	NK
2773	28.04.70	CAPT D.Heitz	USAF	Phant	NK	2847	11.08.70	MAJ G.Thompson	USAF	Phant	NK
2774	28.04.70	1/LT Macweston	USAF	Phant	NK	2848	11.08.70	PR/LT M.Brinbo	Den	F100	OC
2775	29.04.70		USAF	Phant	OC	2849	12.08.70	Classified			
2776	29.04.70		USAF	Phant	OC	2850	12.08.70	CDR M.Wright	USN	Crus	OC
2777	30.04.70	LT J.Jackson	USN	Crus	OC	2851	12.08.70	F/O M.Rigg	RAF	Light	OC
2778	01.05.70	FL/LT J.F.Nicol	Civ	Canb	OC	2852	20.08.70	MAJ C.Fairchild	USMC	Phant	OC
2779	02.05.70	1/LT G.Jackman	USAF	Phant	NK	2853	20.08.70	CAPT D.Flynn	USAF	Phant	EA
2780	02.05.70	CAPT B.Bodenneim	USAF	Phant	NK	2854	21.08.70	LT A.Prydybasz	USN	Int	OC
2781	02.05.70	Classified				2855	21.08.70	LT L.Roberts	USN	Int	OC
2782	04.05.70	Classified				2856	25.08.70	O/LT G.Grosklos	Ger N	L.F104	OC
2783	05.05.70	LT/COL D.A.Kellum	USAF	Phant	NK	2857	25.08.70	O/LT U.Otto	Ger N	L.F104	OC
2784	05.05.70	MAJ R.E.Moffitt	USAF	Phant	EA	2858	26.08.70	FL/LT R.Statham	Civ	S.Vix	OC
2785	06.05.70	MAJ P.Dunn	USAF	Phant	NK	2859	26.08.70	FL/LT D.Allardyce	Civ	S.Vix	OC
2786	06.05.70	MAJ D.Tokar	USAF	Phant	NK	2860	30.08.70	LT E.Christensen	USN	Phant	OC
2787	07.05.70	CAPT T.Sweeting	USAF	Phant	EA	2861	31.08.70	S/LT A.Leeming	RN	Bucc	OC
2788	07.05.70	CAPT D.Yates	USAF	Phant	EA	2862	31.08.70	F/O J.Walmesley	RN	Bucc	OC
2789	07.05.70	FL/LT S.R.Tulloch	RAF	Light	OC	2863	04.09.70	LT S.Lambert	USN	Crus	OC
2790	08.05.70	S/LT B.Hothi	Ind N	Vamp	OC	2864	08.09.70	1/LT P.Farmer	USMC	Coug	OC
2791	08.05.70	CDR S.Chopra	Ind N	Vamp	OC	2865	10.09.70	CAPT J.McElroy	USMC	Coug	NK
2792	12.05.70	CAPT P.Harbison	USAF	Phant	NK	2866	14.09.70	LT C.Bertele	Italy	L.F104	OC
2793	12.05.70		USAF	Phant	NK	2867	14.09.70	LT D.J.Lortscher	USN	Phant	OC
2794	15.05.70	1/LT J.Fitzmaurice	USMC	Phant	NK	2868	14.09.70	LT/JG J.Anderson	USN	Phant	OC
2795	15.05.70	1/LT R.Rissell	USMC	Phant	EA	2869	15.09.70	1/LT E.F.Mares	USMC	Phant	OC
2796	17.05.70	LT J.Kane	USN	Phant	OC	2870	17.09.70	F/O Wilkins	RAF	J.Pro	OC
2797	19.05.70	MAJ C.Crawford	USAF	Phant	NK	2871	19.09.70	FL/LT A.Fuller	RAF	Light	OC
2798	19.05.70	CAPT F.Norton	USAF	Phant	NK	2872	19.09.70	FL/LT Simms	RAF	Light	OC
2799	20.05.70	LT/JG J.Hapgood	USN	Phant	OC	2873	20.09.70	LT/JG T.Connelly	USN	Int	OC
2800	20.05.70	LT/JG R.Williamson	USN	Phant	OC	2874	20.09.70	LT L.Boaz	USN	Int	OC
2801	22.05.70	CAPT R.Kosch	GerAF	L.F104	NK	2875	22.09.70	1/LT W.Isbell	USMC	Phant	OC
2802	23.05.70	1/LT J.D.Brewer	USMC	Phant	OC	2876	22.09.70	CAPT M.Pierson	USMC	Phant	OC
2803	23.05.70	1/LT J.Nelson	USMC	Phant	OC	2877	06.10.70	OE2 J.Perron	Fr N	Crus	OC
2804	26.05.70	LT G.Clark	USAF	Phant	OC	2878	06.10.70	FL/LT N.Wharton	RAF	Harr	OC
2805	26.05.70	CAPT L.Alford	USAF	Phant	OC	2879	08.10.70	Baty	Fr AF	Mir	NK
2806	27.05.70	R.C.Blakely	USMC	Phant	OC	2880	12.10.70	MAJ W.A.Fall	USAF	Phant	OC
2807	27.05.70	R.E.Dahart	USMC	Phant	OC	2881	12.10.70	MR M.Quarantelli	Civ	L.F104	OC
2808	01.06.70	CAPT Leisering	GerAF	F.G91	OC	2882	14.10.70	CAPT G.Joubert	SA	Bucc	OC
2809	08.06.70	LT/JG C.Buchanan	USN	Phant	OC	2883	15.10.70	Classified			

No.	Date	Name	Force	Type	Cause
2884	21.10.70	LT H.Kesler	USN	Crus	OC
2885	21.10.70	LT/CDR J.Berry	USN	Phant	OC
2886	21.10.70	LT/JG C.White	USN	Phant	OC
2887	22.10.70	LT Loiseleux	Fr N	Crus	OC
2888	22.10.70	LT/COL D.Smith	USAF	Phant	OC
2889	22.10.70	LT Hansen	USAF	Phant	OC
2890	22.10.70	MAJ S.M.Shurafa	Jord	Hunt	NK
2891	28.10.70	ALT A.Bruce	Zimb	Hunt	OC
2892	29.10.70		USAF	Phant	OC
2893	30.10.70	MAJ Weidemann	GerAF	L.F104	OC
2894	02.11.70	S/LT Marchi	Fr AF	Mir	OC
2895	04.11.70	LT L.G.Lewis	USN	Coug	OC
2896	04.11.70	LT/JG Phelps	USN	Coug	OC
2897	05.11.70		Iran		OC
2898	05.11.70	M.Amiri	Iran	Phant	NK
2899	09.11.70	F/O M.R.Lythgoe	RN	Bucc	OC
2900	11.11.70	CAPT J.M.Jones	USAF	Phant	OC
2901	11.11.70	CAPT D.C.Allen	USAF	Phant	OC
2902	13.11.70	F/O G.M.Hamlyn	RN	S.Vix	OC
2903	14.11.70	LT G.Geigel	USN	Phant	OC
2904	14.11.70	LT J.Hummell	USN	Phant	OC
2905	16.11.70	LT L.Milam	USN	Phant	OC
2906	16.11.70	LT R.Griesser	USN	Phant	OC
2907	18.11.70	LT D.G.Matthews	USN	Phant	OC
2908	18.11.70	LT J.Kerr	USN	Phant	OC
2909	20.11.70	LT/JG Rasmussen	USN	Coug	OC
2910	25.11.70	LT S.T.Nolen	USMC	Phant	OC
2911	25.11.70	1/LT R.Reid	USMC	Phant	OC
2912	26.11.70	CMDT Phelut	Fr AF	Mir	OC
2913	26.11.70	SGT Desborde	Fr AF	Mir	OC
2914	29.11.70	CDR J.O'Kelley	USN	L.T1A	OC
2915	29.11.70	CDR F.Dunbar	USN	L.T1A	OC
2916	01.12.70	M.S.Linn	USN	Phant	NK
2917	01.12.70	F/O Evans	RAF	Bucc	OC
2918	01.12.70	FL/LT Eeles	RAF	Bucc	OC
2919	02.12.70	CAPT D.Boulet	USAF	Phant	NK
2920	02.12.70	CAPT Robinson	USAF	Phant	NK
2921	08.12.70	F/O Warren	RAF	Bucc	OC
2922	08.12.70	Classified			
2923	08.12.70	Classified			
2924	11.12.70	MAJ Nevens	USAF	Phant	OC
2925	11.12.70	MAJ W.Ford	USAF	Phant	OC
2926	12.12.70	1/LT R.Kelsey	USAF	Phant	EA
2927	16.12.70	CAPT J.P.G.Pizjuan	Spain	Mir	OC
2928	16.12.70	CAPT D.A.G.Lozano	Spain	Mir	OC
2929	17.12.70	MAJ N.E.Douglas	USMC	Phant	OC
2930	17.12.70	COL Pommerenk	USMC	Phant	OC
2931	19.12.70	CAPT W.K.Louis	USAF	Phant	EA
2932	19.12.70	CAPT D.Rotz	USAF	Phant	EA
2933	19.12.70	F/O S.Bakshi	IndAF	Hunt	OC
2934	19.12.70	S/L F.Mehta	IndAF	Hunt	OC
2935	21.12.70	MAJ A.Rush	USAF	Phant	EA
2936	21.12.70	1/LT Reinhart	USAF	Phant	NK
2937	21.12.70	CAPT D.Wright	USAF	Phant	NK
2938	21.12.70	CAPT Mullis	USAF	Phant	EA
2939	30.12.70	MR W.Miller	Civ	F14	OC
2940	30.12.70	MR R.Smyth	Civ	F14	OC
2941	01.01.71	S/L S.K.Gupta	IndAF	Hunt	EA
2942	01.01.71	Classified			
2943	01.01.71	Classified			
2944	02.01.71	CAPT H.Weir	USAF	Phant	NK
2945	02.01.71	LT R.Brown	USAF	Phant	NK
2946	06.01.71	LT L.Rinne	USN	Phant	NK
2947	08.01.71	LT/CDR G.Smith	USN	Int	NK
2948	08.01.71	FL/LT Alcock	RAF	Vulc	OC
2949	08.01.71	F/O Hoskins	RAF	Vulc	OC
2950	13.01.71	MR M.Coureau	Civ	Mir	OC
2951	17.01.71	MAJ J.D.Siderius	USAF	Phant	OC
2952	18.01.71	LT S.T.Turner	USMC	Phant	OC
2953	18.01.71	1/LT W.Pickerell	USMC	Phant	OC
2954	19.01.71	O/LT P.Buendgen	GerAF	L.F104	OC
2955	19.01.71	1/LT Salewski	USMC	Int	OC
2956	19.01.71	1/LT F.J.Gose	USMC	Int	NK
2957	19.01.71	CAPT L.Gregory	USAF	Phant	OC
2958	19.01.71	CAPT A.A.Salge	USAF	Phant	OC
2959	20.01.71	CAPT D.Warner	USAF	Phant	NK
2960	20.01.71	MAJ Kiefer	USAF	Phant	EA
2961	22.01.71	LT/COL R.G.Davis	USMC	Crus	OC
2962	25.01.71	CAPT W.Povilus	RAF	Light	NK
2963	28.01.71	F/O Hitchcock	RAF	Light	OC
2964	29.01.71	F/O J.W.Pearson	RAF	Canb	OC
2965	29.01.71	F/O D.Irwin	RAF	Canb	OC
2966	29.01.71	F/O A.Threadgold	RAF	Canb	OC
2967	29.01.71	F/O C.R.Pitt	RAF	Canb	OC
2968	29.01.71	F/O P.T.Jennings	RAF	Canb	OC
2969	02.02.71	O/SFW K.Boehm	GerAF	F.G91	NK
2970	03.02.71	MAJ N.A.Gotner	USAF	Phant	EA
2971	04.02.71	LT M.Bhada	Ind N	S.Hk	OC
2972	05.02.71	LT J.Bodanske	USN	Crus	OC
2973	05.02.71	M.Ibrahim	Leb	Myst	NK
2974	06.02.71	LT/JG C.D.Boyer	USN	Phant	OC
2975	06.02.71	LT J.S.Payne	USN	Phant	NK
2976	09.02.71		Iran	Phant	OC
2977	09.02.71	M.Zarrabi	Iran	Phant	OC
2978	11.02.71	CAPT M.Ford	USAF	Phant	NK
2979	11.02.71	CAPT Vericen	Fr AF	Mir	NK
2980	15.02.71	HPT N.Henkel	GerAF	F.G91	NK
2981	15.02.71	WO1 Dover	USA	Moh	NK
2982	15.02.71	SP4 Calloway	USA	Moh	NK
2983	16.02.71	CAPT D.Warner	USAF	Phant	NK
2984	16.02.71	LT/COL W.Cox	USAF	Phant	NK
2985	18.02.71	CAPT C.Ferrell	USAF	Phant	OC
2986	18.02.71	1/LT T.Propeck	USAF	Phant	OC
2987	22.02.71	SKLT P.E.R.Anthonsen	Den	L.F104	OC
2988	24.02.71	P/O Spears	RAF	J.Pro	OC
2989	24.02.71	FL/LT F.Morrison	RAF	J.Pro	OC
2990	25.02.71	LT T.McLaughlin	USAF	Phant	OC
2991	25.02.71	CAPT J.Talley	USAF	Phant	EA
2992	25.02.71	CAPT Hedditch	USAF	Phant	OC
2993	25.02.71	LT/CDR W.Galbraith	USN	Int	OC
2994	25.02.71	LT D.D.Waters	USN	Int	OC
2995	26.02.71	MAJ Schebiella	GerAF	L.F104	OC
2996	26.02.71	CAPT Marion	Fr AF	Myst	OC
2997	26.02.71	ADJ/CH Mandon	Fr AF	Myst	OC
2998	26.02.71	LT/JG Larson	USN	Crus	OC
2999	27.02.71	1/LT E.Payne	USAF	Phant	NK
3000	27.02.71	LT/JG J.Carroll	USN	Phant	OC
3001	01.03.71	LT Druau	Fr AF	Myst	NK
3002	03.03.71	CAPT Virotte	Fr AF	Mir	OC
3003	03.03.71	LT Inge	Fr AF	Mir	OC
3004	04.03.71	FL/LT S.Agnihotri	IndAF	Marut	NK
3005	04.03.71	SPE3 Martin	USA	Moh	EA
3006	04.03.71	O/LT D.Nickolai	GerAF	L.F104	OC
3007	09.03.71	LT H.Gebhardt	GerAF	L.F104	OC
3008	12.03.71	O/LT J.Wagner	GerAF	L.F104	NK
3009	15.03.71	W/C J.Downing	AusAF	Canb	NK
3010	15.03.71	FL/LT A.Pinches	AusAF	Canb	NK
3011	15.03.71		Peru	Mir	OC
3012	16.03.71	LT R.Amber	USN	Crus	OC
3013	17.03.71	P/O A.R.Ghanam	Kuw	J.Pro	OC
3014	17.03.71	P/O J.P.S.Talwar	IndAF	Hunt	NK
3015	22.03.71	MAJ Cubberley	USAF	Phant	NK
3016	22.03.71	MAJ R.Priest	USAF	Phant	OC
3017	23.03.71	K.K.Gladziejewski	Ger N	L.F104	NK
3018	23.03.71	LT T.A.Pearl	USN	Crus	OC
3019	26.03.71	SGT A.Berg	Den	L.T33	OC
3020	26.03.71	FL/LT G.Houlind	Den	L.T33	OC
3021	30.03.71	LT W.Lawrence	USN	Prowl	OC
3022	04.04.71	LT D.R.Woltz	USN	Crus	OC
3023	07.04.71	LT/JG R.Lifer	USN	Phant	OC
3024	07.04.71	LT G.W.Kraus	USN	Phant	OC
3025	07.04.71	LT W.Meingast	GerAF	F.G91	OC
3026	08.04.71	TEN P.Mossenta	Italy	F.G91	OC
3027	15.04.71	ADJ/CH G.Cornil	Fr AF	Mir	OC
3028	16.04.71	HPT J.H.Heinrich	GerAF	L.F104	OC
3029	19.04.71	MAJ Guidotti	Italy	L.F104	OC
3030	19.04.71	LT J.R.Mac Donald	USN	Int	OC

No.	Date	Name	Force	Type	Cause
3031	19.04.71	LT/CDR B.Bremner	USN	Int	OC
3032	22.04.71	CAPT R.S.Dotson	USAF	Phant	EA
3033	22.04.71	CAPT B.D.Smith	USAF	Phant	EA
3034	23.04.71	LT F.L.T.Middleton	RAF	Harr	OC
3035	23.04.71	LT K.D.Welch	USN	Crus	OC
3036	28.04.71	LT P.Clarke	Aus N	MB326	OC
3037	28.04.71	F/O S.McClean	RAF	Light	NK
3038	28.04.71	LT E.Kavanagh	Aus N	MB326	OC
3039	30.04.71	S/M/SGT S.Liebold	GerAF	L.F104	NK
3040	05.05.71	LT/CDR J.Allen	USN	Phant	OC
3041	05.05.71	LT/JG Lehman	USN	Phant	OC
3042	06.05.71	CAPT J.E.Seaton	USAF	Phant	NK
3043	06.05.71	MAJ A.S.Blisset	USAF	Phant	NK
3044	08.05.71	CAPT R.McKendry	Can	CF100	OC
3045	08.05.71	CAPT G.E.Benson	Can	CF100	OC
3046	10.05.71	FL/LT R.D.Cole	RAF	Light	OC
3047	11.05.71	CAPT J.Nader	Leb	Mir	OC
3048	11.05.71	CAPT H.Daher	Leb	Mir	OC
3049	12.05.71	MAJ W.Rowley	USAF	Phant	NK
3050	12.05.71	FL/LT R.Holland	RAF	Bucc	NK
3051	12.05.71		USAF	Phant	NK
3052	17.05.71	1/LT L.D.Cohen	USMC	Coug	OC
3053	18.05.71	2/MTR Daumic	Fr N	Etend	OC
3054	19.05.71	LT P.Love	RN	Phant	OC
3055	19.05.71	CDR W.Hawley	RN	Phant	OC
3056	20.05.71	Classified			
3057	21.05.71	1/LT T.H.Valerga	USMC	Phant	OC
3058	21.05.71	1/LT E.Hamamoto	USMC	Phant	OC
3059	26.05.71	FL/LT A.McKay	RAF	Light	NK
3060	27.05.71	1/LT G.Kohlke	Ger N	L.F104	OC
3061	04.06.71	CDR H.H.Hall	USN	Phant	OC
3062	04.06.71	CAPT E.Zepponi	Italy	MB326	OC
3063	04.06.71	TEN R.Fabbiani	Italy	MB326	OC
3064	05.06.71	F/O R.G.Kemp	RAF	Bucc	OC
3065	05.06.71	FL/LT A.W.Marrs	RAF	Bucc	OC
3066	06.06.71	1/LT C.E.Schiess	USMC	Phant	OC
3067	07.06.71	LT K.A.Strauss	USN	Phant	OC
3068	07.06.71	LT D.McDonald	USN	Phant	OC
3069	08.06.71	SP4 R.Bailey	USA	Moh	NK
3070	08.06.71	MAJ J.Collamore	USA	Moh	NK
3071	10.06.71	CAPT J.R.Dempsey	USMC	Phant	OC
3072	10.06.71	CAPT Daubas	Fr AF	Myst	NK
3073	15.06.71	CAPT L.Catanzaro	USMC	Phant	OC
3074	15.06.71	LT H.S.Conrad	USN	Phant	OC
3075	16.06.71	LT D.Hausmanns	GerAF	F.G91	OC
3076	18.06.71	FL/LT Orak Zai	Pak	F86	NK
3077	22.06.71	SFC Hinners	USA	Moh	NK
3078	28.06.71	LT M.J.Granger-Holcombe	RN	Phant	OC
3079	28.06.71	LT D.A.Hill	RN	Phant	OC
3080	29.06.71	FL/LT C.S.Hall	RAF	J.Pro	OC
3081	29.06.71	CAPT W.Ricks	USAF	Phant	NK
3082	29.06.71	FL/LT C.J.Thompson	RAF	J.Pro	OC
3083	29.06.71	LT B.D.Buffkin	USAF	Phant	NK
3084	05.07.71	MAJ A.Politis	Gree	L.F104	NK
3085	06.07.71	LT N.E.Todd	RN	S.Vix	OC
3086	06.07.71	F/O Hamlyn	RN	S.Vix	OC
3087	07.07.71	F.R.Spraul	USAF	Phant	NK
3088	07.07.71	1/LT M.J.Lotti	USAF	Phant	NK
3089	08.07.71	FL/LT Clarke	RAF	Light	OC
3090	10.07.71	LT J.C.Bates	USN	Phant	OC
3091	10.07.71	1/LT J.F.Stermer	USAF	Phant	EA
3092	10.07.71	CAPT R.C.Wheeler	USAF	Phant	EA
3093	10.07.71	LT N.D.Hudnall	USN	Phant	OC
3094	10.07.71	LT C.M.Rubel	USN	Phant	OC
3095	10.07.71	LT/JG A.T.Beck	USN	Phant	NK
3096	21.07.71	LT T.K.Pal	Ind N	S.Hk	OC
3097	22.07.71	LT/COL Musgrove	USAF	Phant	EA
3098	22.07.71	1/LT J.F.Stuermer	USAF	Phant	EA
3099	26.07.71	FL/LT I.U.H.Siddui	Pak	Mir	OC
3100	27.07.71	CADET A.N.Mazook	Kuw	S.Mas	OC
3101	27.07.71	S/L M.Haleen	Kuw	S.Mas	OC
3102	28.07.71	LT A.T.Nilsen	USN	Int	OC
3103	28.07.71	LT/CDR G.O'Brian	USN	Int	OC
3104	02.08.71	CAPT Y.P.Yong	Sing	S.Mas	OC
3105	02.08.71	CADET N.K.Ngen	Sing	S.Mas	OC
3106	12.08.71	LT J.S.McMahon	USN	Int	OC
3107	12.08.71	LT/CDR B.S.Wade	USN	Int	OC
3108	20.08.71	CAPT G.Baxter	USA	Moh	OC
3109	20.08.71	1/LT J.Killackey	USA	Moh	OC
3110	25.08.71	LT/JG Swearingen	USN	Crus	OC
3111	27.08.71	LT M.R.Bolier	USN	Phant	OC
3112	27.08.71	F/O Scoffham	RAF	Hunt	OC
3113	27.08.71	LT/JG M.J.Stancel	USN	Phant	OC
3114	02.09.71	MAJ J.B.Compton	USAF	Phant	EA
3115	02.09.71	CAPT R.Fitzgerald	USAF	Phant	EA
3116	04.09.71	WO G.C.Cecconi	Italy	F.G91	OC
3117	06.09.71	Classified			
3118	07.09.71	HPT H.Kretschmar	GerAF	F.G91	OC
3119	07.09.71	CAPT E.C.Hebner	USAF	Phant	OC
3120	07.09.71	MAJ R.B.Reed	USAF	Phant	OC
3121	08.09.71	CAPT A.Bosi	Italy	L.F104	OC
3122	09.09.71	F.Frutschi	Switz	Vamp	OC
3123	15.09.71	FL/LT J.B.Williams	Oman	S.Mas	OC
3124	17.09.71	CDR L.T.Logue	USN	Phant	OC
3125	17.09.71	LT J.Sumnick	USN	Phant	OC
3126	21.09.71	SGT W.Oppl	GerAF	L.F104	NK
3127	22.09.71	LT D.J.Lortscher	USN	Phant	NK
3128	22.09.71	CAPT Watkins	USAF	Phant	NK
3129	22.09.71	MAJ C.J.Jeffries	USAF	Phant	NK
3130	27.09.71	CAPT J.P.Daniel	USAF	Phant	OC
3131	27.09.71	CAPT R.Hand	USAF	Phant	OC
3132	30.09.71	FL/LT R.Bealer	RAF	Light	OC
3133	30.09.71	MAJ E.C.Hebner	USAF	Phant	OC
3134	30.09.71		USAF	Phant	OC
3135	01.10.71	CMDT V.Sanserevino	Civ	L.F104	OC
3136	01.10.71	CAPT J.Sigler	USAF		EA
3137	04.10.71	1/LT Erickson	USMC	Phant	OC
3138	04.10.71	F/O K.Woolford	RAF	Canb	OC
3139	04.10.71	FL/LT W.Woolley	RAF	Canb	OC
3140	04.10.71	CAPT R.J.Dugal	USMC	Phant	OC
3141	04.10.71	F/O G.C.Edwards	RAF	Canb	OC
3142	09.10.71	LT/JG J.A.Dickey	USN	Int	OC
3143	09.10.71	LT C.J.Taylor	USN	Int	OC
3144	12.10.71	FL/LT S.B.Cox	RAF	Phant	OC
3145	12.10.71	FL/LT R.Northcote	RAF	Phant	OC
3146	15.10.71	FL/LT Miles	RAF	Phant	OC
3147	15.10.71	LT J.W.Adair	USN	Int	OC
3148	15.10.71	LT D.C.Wright	USN	Int	NK
3149	15.10.71	S/L J.D.Armstrong	RAF	Phant	OC
3150	28.10.71	LT J.M.Perry II	USN	Int	OC
3151	28.10.71	LT R.E.Klemm	USN	Int	OC
3152	28.10.71	LT/JG T.Muschlitz	USN	Coug	OC
3153	07.11.71	MAJ J.A.Robertson	USAF	Phant	OC
3154	07.11.71	MAJ H.J.Viccellio	USAF	Phant	OC
3155	08.11.71	LT/COL F.M.Totten	GerAF	L.F104	OC
3156	17.11.71	LT/JG M.A.Allen	USN	Prowl	OC
3157	17.11.71	AOAN D.R.Lavean	USN	Prowl	OC
3158	17.11.71	CDR J.O'Harmon	USN	Prowl	OC
3159	17.11.71	LT/CDR W.A.Martin	USN	Prowl	OC
3160	20.11.71	CAPT R.Bugin	Fr AF	Mir	OC
3161	20.11.71	CNE Hervouet	Fr AF	Mir	OC
3162	04.12.71	FL/LT S.Sajjadnoor	Pak	F86	EA
3163	04.12.71	FL/LT V.S.Chati	IndAF	Hunt	EA
3164	05.12.71	W/C J.L.Bhargava	IndAF	Marut	OC
3165	16.12.71	MAJ K.S.Morris	USAF	Phant	OC
3166	16.12.71	1/LT W.J.King	USAF	Phant	OC
3167	17.12.71	LT M.Murray	USAF	Phant	EA
3168	17.12.71	LT/COL A.S.Blissett	USAF	Phant	OC
3169	18.12.71	LT S.R.Vaughan	USAF	Phant	OC
3170	18.12.71	MAJ W.T.Stanley	USAF	Phant	EA
3171	18.12.71	CAPT L.O'Brian	USAF	Phant	EA
3172	18.12.71	MAJ L.L.Hildebrand	USAF	Phant	NK
3173	18.12.71	MAJ K.R.Johnson	USAF	Phant	OC
3174	18.12.71	1/LT M.H.Murray	USAF	Phant	OC
3175	18.12.71	LT K.R.Wells	USAF	Phant	NK
3176	30.12.71	LT M.Charrin	Fr AF	Mir	NK
3177	30.12.71	S/LT Paolini	Fr AF	Mir	NK

No.	Date	Name	Force	Type	Cause	No.	Date	Name	Force	Type	Cause
3178	30.12.71	LT/CDR D.W.Hoffman	USN	Phant	EA	3250	03.05.72	1/LT Sienicki	USAF	Phant	EA
3179	30.12.71	LT/JG N.A.Charles	USN	Phant	EA	3251	03.05.72	CAPT T.Ayres	USAF	Phant	EA
3180	01.01.72	Classified				3252	04.05.72	S/L P.P.W.Taylor	RAF	Harr	OC
3181	01.01.72	Classified				3253	05.05.72	Comstock	USAF	Phant	EA
3182	01.01.72	Classified				3254	05.05.72	Kulzar	USAF	Phant	EA
3183	03.01.72	CAPT R.R.Nevitte	USMC	Crus	OC	3255	07.05.72	CWO3 J.Castonguay	USN	Phant	OC
3184	10.01.72	LT C.O'Connor	RN	Phant	OC	3256	08.05.72	CAPT T.A.Webb	USAF	Phant	OC
3185	20.01.72	MAJ R.K.Mock	USAF	Phant	EA	3257	08.05.72	CAPT N.N.Nassick	USAF	Phant	OC
3186	20.01.72	1/LT J.L.Stiles	USAF	Phant	EA	3258	10.05.72	LT/JG W.Driscoll	USN	Phant	EA
3187	24.01.72	LT/JG S.Davis	USN	Phant	OC	3259	10.05.72	CAPT R.L.Locher	USAF	Phant	EA
3188	24.01.72	LT C.A.Clabaugh	USN	Phant	OC	3260	10.05.72	LT S.Rudloff	USN	Phant	EA
3189	31.01.72	CAPT O.J.Davis	USAF	Phant	EA	3261	10.05.72	LT R.Cunningham	USN	Phant	EA
3190	31.01.72	CAPT R.K.Venables	USAF	Phant	EA	3262	10.05.72	CDR H.Blackburn	USN	Phant	NK
3191	01.02.72	CAPT L.O'Brian	USAF	Phant	OC	3263	11.05.72	CAPT T.W.Reynolds	USAF	Phant	OC
3192	10.02.72	CAPT J.S.Murphy	USAF	Phant	NK	3264	11.05.72	CAPT W.K.Mathews	USAF	Phant	NK
3193	10.02.72	1/LT T.W.Dobson	USAF	Phant	NK	3265	13.05.72	1/LT W.Reich	USAF	Phant	EA
3194	11.02.72	O/LT R.Diederichs	GerAF	L.F104	OC	3266	13.05.72	LT/COL J.W.Kittinger	USAF	Phant	EA
3195	14.02.72	F/O J.Stone	RAF	Phant	OC	3267	14.05.72	Classified			
3196	14.02.72	FL/LT P.L.Preston	RAF	Phant	NK	3268	20.05.72	CAPT J.W.Williams	USAF	Phant	EA
3197	14.02.72	1/LT J.F.McCarthy	USAF	Phant	OC	3269	20.05.72	1/LT J.L.Markle	USAF	Phant	EA
3198	14.02.72	CAPT G.Profitt	USAF	Phant	NK	3270	21.05.72	LT/COL R.E.Ross	USAF	Phant	EA
3199	16.02.72	1/LT R.Galati	USAF	Phant	EA	3271	21.05.72	LT W.Key	USAF	Phant	EA
3200	16.02.72	CAPT W.R.Schwertfeger	USAF	Phant	EA	3272	21.05.72	1/LT Doyle	USAF	Phant	EA
3201	16.02.72	FL/LT P.Reynolds	RAF	Light	OC	3273	21.05.72	LT/CDR H.Sampson	USN	Phant	OC
3202	17.02.72	O/LT W.Boehm	GerAF	L.F104	NK	3274	21.05.72	LT/JG R.G.Draggett	USN	Phant	OC
3203	17.02.72	CAPT E.Hawley	USAF	Phant	EA	3275	21.05.72	1/LT D.Van Liere	USAF	Phant	EA
3204	18.02.72	LT/JG D.L.Spence	USN	Phant	OC	3276	22.05.72	CAPT W.G.Byrns	USAF	Phant	EA
3205	21.02.72	Classified				3277	22.05.72	CAPT W.R.Bean	USAF	Phant	EA
3206	03.03.72		Can	CF100	OC	3278	22.05.72	LT/COL R.Tonini	Italy	L.F104	NK
3207	03.03.72		Can	CF100	NK	3279	24.05.72	LT R.C.Beeler	USN	Crus	EA
3208	03.03.72	LT K.T.Moore	USN	Phant	OC	3280	24.05.72	LT/JG W.R.Olson	USN	Phant	OC
3209	03.03.72	LT G.H.Westfall	USN	Phant	OC	3281	24.05.72	LT T.H.Beard	USN	Phant	OC
3210	03.03.72	MAJ W.E.Conder	USMC	Crus	OC	3282	25.05.72	1/LT J.D.Buchanan	USMC	Int	OC
3211	08.03.72	HPT K.Kegel	GerAF	L.F104	OC	3283	25.05.72	1/LT J.W.Pitz	USMC	Int	OC
3212	11.03.72	CAPT D.D.Thomssen	USAF	Phant	NK	3284	26.05.72	CAPT T.E.Kincaid	USAF	Phant	EA
3213	11.03.72	CAPT R.L.Privett	USAF	Phant	OC	3285	26.05.72	CAPT A.N.Arnold	USAF	Phant	EA
3214	16.03.72	HPT W.Seifert	GerAF	L.F104	NK	3286	27.05.72	LT Kern	USN	Int	OC
3215	23.03.72	LT/JG D.P.Curry	USN	Phant	NK	3287	29.05.72	LT/CDR P.Schuyler	USMC	Int	EA
3216	23.03.72	CDR E.J.Hickey	USN	Phant	NK	3288	29.05.72	CAPT L.J.Ferracane	USMC	Int	EA
3217	28.03.72	LT G.Fonteyne	Belg	Mir	OC	3289	01.06.72	LT/COL Roga	GerAF	L.F104	OC
3218	30.03.72	1/LT J.W.Vandervolt	USMC	Phant	NK	3290	02.06.72	LT Baum	Belg	Mir	OC
3219	08.04.72	LT/JG H.Wurtzbacher	USN	Int	NK	3291	13.06.72	LT Solehgo	Iran	Phant	OC
3220	08.04.72	LT J.A.Kelly	USN	Int	OC	3292	13.06.72	LT Farahnak	Iran	Phant	OC
3221	09.04.72	MAJ C.Smith	USMC	Int	OC	3293	13.06.72	1/LT G.O'Hanson	USAF	Phant	EA
3222	09.04.72	CAPT W.Banks	USAF	Phant	EA	3294	13.06.72	1/LT R.Fulton	USAF	Phant	EA
3223	09.04.72	CAPT M.Jacobs	USAF	Phant	EA	3295	14.06.72	MAJ J.A.Fowler	USAF	Phant	EA
3224	14.04.72	LT/JG D.E.Koerner	USN	Coug	NK	3296	14.06.72	CAPT J.W.Seuell	USAF	Phant	EA
3225	16.04.72	1/LT V.Parkhurst	USAF	Phant	EA	3297	15.06.72	CAPT G.A.Rose	USAF	Phant	EA
3226	16.04.72	1/LT M.De-Long	USAF	Phant	EA	3298	15.06.72	1/LT L.Calaghan	USAF	Phant	EA
3227	18.04.72	SGT Scherrer	Fr AF	Mir	NK	3299	16.06.72	LT P.Ringwood	USN	Crus	EA
3228	18.04.72	LT R.P.McKinster	USN	Crus	OC	3300	19.06.72	LT R.Laib	USN	Phant	EA
3229	18.04.72	ENS M.Granberry	USN	Coug	OC	3301	19.06.72	LT/CDR R.Cash	USN	Phant	EA
3230	19.04.72	LT/JG Timmester	USN	Phant	NK	3302	20.06.72	CDR Davis	USN	Crus	EA
3231	19.04.72	LT B.L.Cooper	USN	Phant	NK	3303	20.06.72	CAPT W.E.Bolton	USAF	Phant	OC
3232	20.04.72	MAJ E.K.Elias	USAF	Phant	EA	3304	20.06.72	COL J.M.Potts	USAF	Phant	OC
3233	20.04.72	1/LT E.S.Clark	USAF	Phant	EA	3305	20.06.72	FL/LT J.Downey	RAF	Harr	OC
3234	21.04.72		USAF	Phant	EA	3306	24.06.72		USAF	Phant	EA
3235	21.04.72		USAF	Phant	EA	3307	24.06.72		USAF	Phant	EA
3236	23.04.72	LT L.R.Boughner	USAF	Phant	EA	3308	26.06.72	MAJ R.C.Miller	USAF	Phant	EA
3237	23.04.72	MAJ C.E.Hall	USAF	Phant	EA	3309	26.06.72	LT B.L.Cooper	USN	Phant	OC
3238	24.04.72	2/LT S.W.Hall	USAF	Phant	OC	3310	26.06.72	ENS J.L.Heitmanek	USN	Phant	OC
3239	26.04.72	FL/LT J.Marshall	RAF	Harr	OC	3311	26.06.72	LT J.C.Chehansky	USN	Phant	OC
3240	27.04.72	CAPT D.Dziedzic	USMC	Phant	OC	3312	26.06.72	CAPT L.K.Aikman	USAF	Phant	EA
3241	27.04.72	LT A.R.Molinare	USN	Phant	EA	3313	26.06.72		USAF	Phant	EA
3242	27.04.72	CDR L.T.Souder	USN	Phant	EA	3314	26.06.72		USAF	Phant	EA
3243	28.04.72	CAPT A.S.Arthur	USAF	Phant	EA	3315	27.06.72	CAPT R.L.Francis	USAF	Phant	EA
3244	28.04.72	CAPT M.C.Francisco	USAF	Phant	EA	3316	27.06.72	CAPT J.P.Cerak	USAF	Phant	EA
3245	28.04.72	LT V.K.Bhatnagar	Ind N	S.Hk	OC	3317	27.06.72	W/C McKee	RAF	Harr	OC
3246	30.04.72	FL/LT R.L.Perry	AusAF	Mir	NK	3318	27.06.72	CAPT D.Dingee	USAF	Phant	EA
3247	01.05.72	F/O C.J.E.Adams	RAF	Harr	OC	3319	30.06.72	CDR P.Varela	Peru	Canb	OC
3248	02.05.72	LT R.J.A.Bendel	USN	Int	OC	3320	01.07.72	MAJ P.K.Robinson	USAF	Phant	EA
3249	02.05.72	LT J.G.Houser	USN	Int	OC	3321	01.07.72		USAF	Phant	EA
						3322	02.07.72	LT R.Y.Jorden	USN	Phant	OC
						3323	02.07.72	LT R.Reinheimer	USN	Phant	OC

No.	Date	Name	Force	Type	Cause	No.	Date	Name	Force	Type	Cause
3324	03.07.72	CAPT A.Marshall	USAF	Phant	EA	3398	02.09.72	MAJ R.R.Greenwood	USAF	Phant	OC
3325	03.07.72	CAPT R.P.Cuthbert	USAF	Phant	EA	3399	02.09.72	CAPT W.C.Woods	USAF	Phant	OC
3326	04.07.72	MAJ W.J.Elander	USAF	Phant	NK	3400	05.09.72	CDR R.Harrison	USN	Crus	OC
3327	04.07.72	CAPT W.A.Spencer	USAF	Phant	EA	3401	05.09.72	LT J.Schultz	USN	Crus	OC
3328	04.07.72		USAF	Phant	EA	3402	06.09.72	LT/CDR D.F.Lindland	USN	Int	EA
3329	04.07.72		USAF	Phant	EA	3403	06.09.72	LT R.J.Lerseth	USN	Int	EA
3330	05.07.72	MAJ H.U.Junke	GerAF	F.G91	OC	3404	06.09.72	1/LT R.Verbist	RAF	Light	OC
3331	05.07.72	CAPT D.K.Logan	USAF	Phant	EA	3405	06.09.72	S/L Gauvain	RAF	Light	OC
3332	05.07.72	CAPT M.D.Vanwagen	USAF	Phant	EA	3406	07.09.72	L/TEN P.Cagnatel	Italy	F.G91	OC
3333	05.07.72	HPT K.A.Barenyi	GerAF	F.G91	OC	3407	08.09.72	CDR R.Bordone	USN	Phant	OC
3334	06.07.72	F/O J.W.Kindler	AusAF	Mir	OC	3408	08.09.72	CAPT P.Poppe	USAF	Phant	OC
3335	07.07.72	LT/CDR S.Hallmark	USN	Phant	OC	3409	08.09.72	LT J.H.Findley	USN	Phant	EA
3336	08.07.72		USAF	Phant	EA	3410	08.09.72	LT D.H.Johnson	USAF	Phant	OC
3337	08.07.72		USAF	Phant	EA	3411	09.09.72	CAPT T.M.Murphy	USAF	Phant	EA
3338	10.07.72	LT/COL R.E.Ross	USAF	Phant	EA	3412	09.09.72	CAPT W.J.Dalecky	USAF	Phant	EA
3339	10.07.72		USAF	Phant	EA	3413	11.09.72	CAPT G.D.Heeren	USAF	Phant	EA
3340	11.07.72	R.I.Randall	USN	Phant	NK	3414	11.09.72	A.J.Dudley	USMC	Phant	EA
3341	12.07.72	LT/JG H.W.Brooks	USN	Crus	OC	3415	11.09.72	J.W.Brady	USMC	Phant	EA
3342	12.07.72	CAPT R.E.Holt	USMC	Phant	OC	3416	11.09.72	CAPT J.D.Cummings	USMC	Phant	EA
3343	12.07.72	1/LT J.F.Amos	USMC	Phant	OC	3417	11.09.72	MAJ L.T.Lasseter	USMC	Phant	EA
3344	13.07.72	LT/JG G.T.Wierzbicki	USN	Coug	OC	3418	11.09.72	CAPT B.M.Ratzlaff	USAF	Phant	EA
3345	13.07.72	LT/JG J.J.Manis	USN	Coug	OC	3419	12.09.72	P/O Kemp	RAF	J.Pro	NK
3346	17.07.72		USAF	Phant	EA	3420	12.09.72	CAPT	USAF	Phant	EA
3347	17.07.72		USAF	Phant	EA			R.U.Zuberbuhler			
3348	18.07.72	Classified				3421	12.09.72	CAPT F.C.McMurray	USAF	Phant	EA
3349	18.07.72	HPT E.Henninger	GerAF	F.G91	OC	3422	14.09.72	LT/JG R.B.Kummer	USN	Phant	NK
3350	19.07.72	CAPT H.D.Weir	USAF	Phant	EA	3423	16.09.72	CAPT F.Cunliffe	USAF	Phant	EA
3351	19.07.72	1/LT K.Edwards	USAF	Phant	EA	3424	16.09.72	CAPT W.A.Kangas	USAF	Phant	EA
3352	20.07.72	CAPT J.L.Burns	USAF	Phant	EA	3425	17.09.72	CAPT E.B.Dyer	USAF	Phant	OC
3353	20.07.72	1/LT Nelson	USAF	Phant	EA	3426	17.09.72	CAPT D.E.Henneman	USAF	Phant	OC
3354	22.07.72	LT G.C.Paige	USN	Crus	EA	3427	18.09.72	LT/CDR	USN	Phant	OC
3355	24.07.72	CAPT S.A.Hodnett	USAF	Phant	EA			W.C.Ackerman			
3356	24.07.72	1/LT D.Fallert	USAF	Phant	EA	3428	18.09.72	LT/JG P.E.Kane	USN	Phant	OC
3357	29.07.72	CAPT M.K.Matsui	USAF	Phant	EA	3429	22.09.72	1/LT J.H.Pomery	USAF	Phant	EA
3358	29.07.72	CAPT J.D.Kula	USAF	Phant	EA	3430	22.09.72	CAPT J.W.Watts	USAF	Phant	EA
3359	30.07.72	1/LT D.W.Petkunas	USAF	Phant	EA	3431	22.09.72	1/LT N.J.Holoviak	USAF	Phant	OC
3360	30.07.72	LT/CDR D.K.Bentley	USN	Phant	OC	3432	22.09.72	CAPT G.A.Lentz	USAF	Phant	OC
3361	30.07.72	CAPT D.A.Crane	USAF	Phant	EA	3433	23.09.72	LT S.Mehta	Ind N	S.Hk	OC
3362	30.07.72	CAPT J.M.McAdams	USAF	Phant	EA	3434	25.09.72	CADET V.C.Manjappa	IndAF	Vamp	OC
3363	30.07.72	CAPT G.B.Brooks	USAF	Phant	EA	3435	25.09.72	S/L S.S.Kaushik	IndAF	Vamp	OC
3364	30.07.72	1/LT L.D.Price	USAF	Phant	EA	3436	29.09.72	LT J.T.Christian	USN	Crus	OC
3365	30.07.72	LT/COL W.J.Breckner	USAF	Phant	NK	3437	05.10.72	CAPT K.H.Lewis	USAF	Phant	EA
3366	30.07.72	LT/CDR R.A.Toft	USN	Int	OC	3438	05.10.72	CAPT J.H.Alpers	USAF	Phant	EA
3367	30.07.72	LT/JG J.D.Austin	USN	Int	OC	3439	05.10.72	R.Bates	USAF	Phant	EA
3368	01.08.72	HPT A.Brait	GerAF	F.G91	OC	3440	05.10.72	J.Latham	USAF	Phant	EA
3369	01.08.72	MAJ H.Neugebauer	GerAF	F.G91	OC	3441	06.10.72	LT/CDR G.Blundell	RN	Bucc	OC
3370	01.08.72	LT W.R.Hanley	USN	Crus	OC	3442	06.10.72	CAPT J.P.White	USAF	Phant	EA
3371	02.08.72	1/LT R.O.Lamers	USMC	Phant	OC	3443	06.10.72	CAPT A.G.Egge	USAF	Phant	EA
3372	02.08.72	1/LT S.G.Cordova	USMC	Phant	OC	3444	06.10.72	1/LT G.F.Latella	USAF	Phant	EA
3373	03.08.72	FL/LT R.V.Richardson	AusAF	Mir	OC	3445	06.10.72	LT/COL R.D.Anderson	USAF	Phant	EA
3374	07.08.72	FL/LT G.N.Fenton	RAF	Light	OC	3446	06.10.72	LT R.J.Allan	RN	Bucc	OC
3375	09.08.72	1/LT A.Haskell	USAF	Phant	EA	3447	10.10.72	CAPT L.C.Leonor	USAF	Phant	EA
3376	09.08.72	CAPT J.Beavers	USAF	Phant	EA	3448	10.10.72	CAPT P.M.Cleary	USAF	Phant	EA
3377	13.08.72	1/LT F.W.Townsend	USAF	Phant	EA	3449	11.10.72	CAPT M.A.Young	USAF	Phant	EA
3378	13.08.72	CAPT W.A.Gauntt	USAF	Phant	EA	3450	11.10.72	1/LT C.H.Brunson	USAF	Phant	EA
3379	14.08.72	LT J.E.Arbini	USN	Phant	OC	3451	12.10.72	ENS M.R.Sivers	USN	Phant	OC
3380	14.08.72	LT/JG W.A.Scott	USN	Phant	OC	3452	12.10.72		USMC	Int	EA
3381	17.08.72	ENS J.R.Owens	USN	Coug	NK	3453	12.10.72	LT R.D.Gary	USN	Phant	OC
3382	18.08.72	LT J.B.Inman	USN	Phant	OC	3454	20.10.72	SGT Ruckauf	GerAF	L.F104	NK
3383	18.08.72	LT T.E.Lecours	USN	Phant	OC	3455	24.10.72		USAF	Phant	OC
3384	19.08.72	CAPT R.E.Behnfeldt	USAF	Phant	EA	3456	24.10.72		USAF	Phant	OC
3385	19.08.72	MAJ T.Shingaki	USAF	Phant	EA	3457	27.10.72	CAPT E.L.Bleak	USAF	Phant	EA
3386	21.08.72	LT/COL W.J.Breckner	USAF	Phant	EA	3458	27.10.72	CAPT R.B.Jones	USAF	Phant	EA
3387	21.08.72	1/LT H.D.Price	USAF	Phant	EA	3459	01.11.72	LT M.Sharp	RN	Hunt	NK
3388	24.08.72	1/LT M.J.Allen	USMC	Phant	NK	3460	15.11.72	LT W.Gouslin	USN	Int	OC
3389	25.08.72	OTL D.Paque	GerAF	L.F104	OC	3461	17.11.72	FL/LT D.M.Subaiva	IndAF	Vamp	NK
3390	26.08.72		USMC	Phant	EA	3462	17.11.72	S/L C.Boyack	RAF	Hunt	OC
3391	26.08.72	1/LT D.L.Borders	USMC	Phant	EA	3463	17.11.72	CADET	IndAF	Vamp	NK
3392	27.08.72	LT D.Everett	USN	Phant	EA			Chandrashekhar			
3393	28.08.72	LT/CDR T.W.Triebel	USN	Phant	EA	3464	20.11.72	LT/CDR V.E.Lesh	USN	Phant	EA
3394	29.08.72	CAPT G.Feinstein	USAF	Phant	EA	3465	20.11.72		USMC	Phant	EA
3395	29.08.72	LT/COL C.Bailey	USAF	Phant	EA	3466	20.11.72	LT/JG D.L.Cordes	USN	Phant	EA
3396	01.09.72	1/LT J.W.Brady	USMC	Phant	EA	3467	20.11.72	CAPT W.D.Anderson	USMC	Phant	OC
3397	01.09.72	CAPT A.S.Dudley	USMC	Phant	EA	3468	20.11.72		USAF	Phant	EA

No.	Date	Name	Force	Type	Cause
3469	20.11.72		USAF	Phant	EA
3470	20.11.72		USMC	Phant	EA
3471	25.11.72	CAPT B.W.Steclein	USAF	Phant	OC
3472	25.11.72	CAPT R.L.Jaeger	USAF	Phant	OC
3473	26.11.72	LT/JG G.E.Weller	USN	Crus	OC
3474	27.11.72	LT/CDR G.L.Jackson	USN	Int	OC
3475	01.12.72	LT D.L.Thurman	USN	Phant	OC
3476	01.12.72	LT R.L.Moeller	USN	Phant	OC
3477	07.12.72	P/O G.Burns	RAF	Canb	OC
3478	07.12.72	CAPT P.P.Hayes	USMC	Phant	OC
3479	07.12.72	LT M.J.Smythe	Aus N	MB326	OC
3480	07.12.72	1/LT M.A.Hough	USMC	Phant	OC
3481	09.12.72	MAJ B.J.Williams	USAF	Phant	NK
3482	09.12.72	1/LT H.M.Acosta	USAF	Phant	NK
3483	09.12.72	LT J.R.Brooke	USN	Phant	OC
3484	09.12.72	LT G.B.Bastin	USN	Phant	OC
3485	10.12.72	LT R.A.Morris	USN	Phant	NK
3486	10.12.72	LT/JG K.C.Cooper	USN	Phant	OC
3487	14.12.72	F/O Evans	RAF	Light	OC
3488	14.12.72	S/L Spencer	RAF	Light	OC
3489	21.12.72	CDR Nakagawa	USN	Int	EA
3490	21.12.72	LT Higdon	USN	Int	EA
3491	23.12.72	J.D.Everitt	USN	Phant	NK
3492	23.12.72	MAJ H.S.Carr	USMC	Phant	EA
3493	23.12.72	LT/COL J.K.Cockran	USN	Phant	EA
3494	23.12.72	LT J.C.Ensch	USN	Phant	NK
3495	27.12.72	B.H.Ward	USAF	Phant	NK
3496	27.12.72	CAPT C.H.Jeffcoat	USAF	Phant	EA
3497	27.12.72	1/LT J.R.Trimble	USAF	Phant	EA
3498	30.12.72	CAPT H.L.Baker	USMC	Int	OC
3499	30.12.72	M/SGT F.E.Killebrew	USMC	Int	OC
3500	01.01.73	Classified			
3501	01.01.73	Classified			
3502	01.01.73	Classified			
3503	01.01.73	Classified			
3504	01.01.73	Classified			
3505	01.01.73	Classified			
3506	01.01.73	Classified			
3507	01.01.73	Classified			
3508	01.01.73	Classified			
3509	01.01.73	Classified			
3510	01.01.73	Classified			
3511	01.01.73	Classified			
3512	01.01.73	Classified			
3513	01.01.73	Classified			
3514	01.01.73	Classified			
3515	01.01.73	Classified			
3516	01.01.73	Classified			
3517	01.01.73	Classified			
3518	01.01.73	Classified			
3519	01.01.73	Classified			
3520	01.01.73	Classified			
3521	01.01.73	Classified			
3522	01.01.73	Classified			
3523	01.01.73	Classified			
3524	01.01.73	Classified			
3525	01.01.73	Classified			
3526	01.01.73	Classified			
3527	01.01.73	Classified			
3528	01.01.73	Classified			
3529	01.01.73	Classified			
3530	01.01.73	Classified			
3531	01.01.73	Classified			
3532	01.01.73	Classified			
3533	01.01.73	Classified			
3534	01.01.73	Classified			
3535	01.01.73	Classified			
3536	01.01.73	Classified			
3537	01.01.73	Classified			
3538	01.01.73	Classified			
3539	01.01.73	Classified			
3540	01.01.73	Classified			
3541	01.01.73	Classified			
3542	01.01.73	Classified			
3543	01.01.73	Classified			
3544	04.01.73	CAPT J.R.Wallerstedt	USAF	Phant	EA
3545	04.01.73	LT R.I.Roy	SA	Bucc	OC
3546	04.01.73	LT T.J.Schroeder	SA	Bucc	NK
3547	07.01.73	CAPT T.Wiles	USAF	Phant	NK
3548	07.01.73	MAJ G.B.Nunez	USAF	Phant	NK
3549	12.01.73	CAPT D.J.Russell	USAF	Phant	NK
3550	12.01.73	CAPT R.L.Heiser	USAF	Phant	NK
3551	14.01.73	LT V.T.Kouvaleski	USN	Phant	EA
3552	14.01.73	ENS D.H.Plautz	USN	Phant	EA
3553	15.01.73	CAPT E.Skliris	Gree	L.F104	NK
3554	16.01.73	LT A.Z.Kratz	USN	Phant	OC
3555	24.01.73	CAPT B.L.Madden	USAF	Phant	NK
3556	24.01.73	FL/LT McEvoy	RAF	Bucc	OC
3557	24.01.73	LT S.H.Hatfield	USN	Int	EA
3558	24.01.73	LT C.M.Graf	USN	Int	NK
3559	24.01.73	F/O Wood	RAF	Bucc	OC
3560	27.01.73	LT/CDR P.A.Kientzler	USN	Phant	EA
3561	29.01.73	LT/JG J.E.Reid	USN	Phant	NK
3562	29.01.73	LT E.A.Beaver	USN	Phant	NK
3563	14.02.73	LT Befombes	Fr AF	Mir	OC
3564	21.02.73	S/LT S.Donby	Den	F100	OC
3565	21.02.73	LT R.Rasmussen	Den	F100	OC
3566	22.02.73	O/LT W.Wohligenagen	GerAF	L.F104	OC
3567	27.02.73	F/O K.Singh	IndAF	Hunt	NK
3568	01.03.73	S/TEN G.Vuanello	Italy	L.F104	OC
3569	04.03.73	CAPT R.G.Holman	USMC	Crus	OC
3570	08.03.73	CAPT J.R.Fogg	USN	Phant	OC
3571	08.03.73	2/LT J.From	Den	Hunt	OC
3572	08.03.73	LT/CDR D.K.Bently	USN	Phant	NK
3573	08.03.73	LT M.D.Wiita	USN	Phant	NK
3574	12.03.73	A/COM A.R.Yousefzai	Pak	F86	NK
3575	13.03.73	FL/LT R.E.Pocock	RAF	Canb	OC
3576	16.03.73	CAPT Sivot	Fr AF	Myst	NK
3577	16.03.73	O/LT F.Beumler	GerAF	L.T33	OC
3578	17.03.73	CAPT R.Blaisdell	USAF	Phant	OC
3579	20.03.73	LT M.Rizzo	Italy	F.G91	OC
3580	21.03.73	MAJ R.E.O'Dare	USMC	Harr	OC
3581	22.03.73	J.E.Bradford	USN	Phant	NK
3582	22.03.73	L.B.Griffin	USN	Phant	NK
3583	23.03.73	1/LT M.R.Price	USAF	Phant	NK
3584	25.03.73	TEN M.F.C.Pessoa	Port	F.G91	NK
3585	27.03.73	F/O R.Pearson	RAF	Hunt	OC
3586	27.03.73	FL/LT S.K.Chopra	IndAF	Hunt	OC
3587	30.03.73	LT Ciros	Fr AF	Mir	NK
3588	03.04.73	FL/LT F.A.Greer	RAF	Light	OC
3589	06.04.73	FL/LT G.McLeod	RAF	Hunt	OC
3590	07.04.73	S/L J.A.Carrapeitt	Pak	F86	NK
3591	08.04.73	1/LT J.D.Chesney	USMC	Phant	OC
3592	08.04.73	CAPT R.E.McLane	USMC	Phant	NK
3593	10.04.73	LT/COL H.Stauffer	Civ	Harr	OC
3594	10.04.73	LT D.S.Nimmer	USN	Phant	NK
3595	10.04.73	LT P.T.Arenskov	USN	Phant	NK
3596	10.04.73	MAJ E.R.Bailey	USMC	Phant	NK
3597	10.04.73	1/LT W.G.Duncan	USMC	Phant	OC
3598	12.04.73	LT/CDR A.M.D.De'Labilliere	RAF	Bucc	OC
3599	12.04.73	LT W.Buehl	GerAF	L.F104	OC
3600	19.04.73	CAPT D.W.Gould	USMC	Crus	OC
3601	26.04.73	1/LT D.H.Dougherty	USMC	Phant	OC
3602	26.04.73	LT J.W.Combs	USN	Phant	NK
3603	29.04.73	CAPT R.C.Kindsfater	USMC	Phant	OC
3604	29.04.73	1/LT G.G.Stuart	USMC	Phant	OC
3605	02.05.73	1/LT J.M.Windle	USMC	Phant	OC
3606	02.05.73	1/LT J.M.Hinkle	USMC	Phant	OC
3607	03.05.73	LT/CDR J.H.Holds	USN	Phant	NK
3608	03.05.73	CDR D.E.Riggs	USN	Phant	NK
3609	07.05.73	FL/LT M.Saunders	RAF	J.Pro	NK
3610	07.05.73	FL/LT W.Durham	RAF	J.Pro	OC
3611	08.05.73	CAPT E.L.Rooth	USMC	Crus	OC
3612	09.05.73	LT P.R.V.Madsen	Den	F100	OC
3613	15.05.73	LT J.S.Payne	USN	Phant	OC
3614	15.05.73		Libya	Mir	NK
3615	15.05.73		Libya	Mir	NK

No.	Date	Name	Force	Type	Cause
3616	15.05.73	LT R.E.Forster	USN	Int	OC
3617	15.05.73	ENS M.J.McCamish	USN	Int	OC
3618	15.05.73	Classified			
3619	15.05.73	LT/JG G.L.Emigh	USN	Phant	OC
3620	16.05.73	LT F.Faberi	Italy	F.G91	OC
3621	16.05.73	LT G.Salmucci	Italy	F.G91	OC
3622	26.05.73	MAJ G.Cox	USAF	Phant	NK
3623	26.05.73	CAPT W.A.Hubbard	USAF	Phant	EA
3624	30.05.73	LT/JG M.B.Martella	USN	Int	NK
3625	30.05.73	LT E.Hall	USN	Int	NK
3626	31.05.73	LT L.G.Pearson	USN	Crus	OC
3627	01.06.73	O/LT D.Kannitz	GerAF	L.F104	OC
3628	01.06.73	S/L G.Roberts	RAF	Phant	NK
3629	02.06.73	CAPT A.Gallus	Italy	F.G91	OC
3630	05.06.73	CAPT Hansen	RAF	Hunt	OC
3631	06.06.73	W/C C.Bruce	RAF	Light	OC
3632	07.06.73	LT/COL R.K.Mock	USAF	Phant	OC
3633	07.06.73	J.B.Williams	USAF	Phant	OC
3634	07.06.73	Classified			
3635	07.06.73	Classified			
3636	08.06.73	1/LT J.R.Hansen	Den	L.F104	OC
3637	10.06.73	LT/CDR T.B.Applegate	USN	Crus	OC
3638	15.06.73	LT R.Laboureur	Belg	Mir	OC
3639	18.06.73	LT C.Desmiez	Fr AF	Mir	OC
3640	18.06.73	CAPT Reynaud	Fr AF	Mir	OC
3641	20.06.73	MR W.G.Sherman	Civ	F14	NK
3642	20.06.73	MR S.M.Purvis	Civ	F14	OC
3643	25.06.73	LT Allier	Fr AF	Myst	NK
3644	26.06.73	LT U.Centazzo	Italy	L.F104	OC
3645	26.06.73	1/LT S.H.Sandro	USAF	Phant	OC
3646	26.06.73	1/LT R.J.Snyder	USAF	Phant	OC
3647	28.06.73	M.Roussin	Fr N	Etend	NK
3648	03.07.73	LT/CDR G.D.O'Brien	USN	Int	NK
3649	03.07.73	LT B.B.Betz	USN	Int	OC
3650	03.07.73	MAJ J.L.Adkinson	USMC	Crus	OC
3651	08.07.73	LT S.D.Lambert	USN	Phant	OC
3652	09.07.73	S/L P.G.Sturt	RAF	Harr	OC
3653	10.07.73	ENS P.G.Vander Shuur	USN	Crus	OC
3654	11.07.73	CAPT Keys	USAF	Phant	NK
3655	11.07.73	COL Wimberley	USAF	Phant	NK
3656	15.07.73	LT/CDR R.G.Hoch	USN	Crus	OC
3657	17.07.73	LT J.C.Gunning	RN	Phant	OC
3658	17.07.73	LT R.C.O'Conner	RN	Phant	NK
3659	17.07.73	LT De Foucaud	Fr AF	Myst	NK
3660	19.07.73	MR A.Krauthann	GerAF	L.F104	OC
3661	20.07.73	Classified			
3662	23.07.73	F/O K.K.Sofah	IndAF	Hunt	OC
3663	26.07.73	ADJ/1C G.Harvey	USN	Phant	OC
3664	26.07.73	LT/JG G.M.Brotherton	USN	Crus	OC
3665	27.07.73	G/CAPT Pedder	RAF	Hunt	OC
3666	30.07.73	MAJ J.Gibson	RAF	Harr	OC
3667	30.07.73	ENS R.F.Schaver	USN	Coug	OC
3668	01.08.73	Classified			
3669	01.08.73	Classified			
3670	01.08.73	CAPT S.T.Palmason	USMC	Crus	OC
3671	02.08.73	FL/LT T.M.Murray	RAF	Canb	OC
3672	02.08.73	LT G.Transon	Belg	Mir	OC
3673	03.08.73	CAPT Wauber	Fr AF	Mir	OC
3674	04.08.73	2/LT M.J.De Kok	SA	Imp	NK
3675	14.08.73	LT/JG R.S.Enzinger	USN	Phant	OC
3676	14.08.73	LT S.P.Leiter	USN	Phant	OC
3677	17.08.73	Classified			
3678	18.08.73	LT/CDR J.R.Miller	USN	Crus	OC
3679	21.08.73	1/LT R.D.Alley	USAF	Phant	NK
3680	21.08.73	CAPT G.D.Crawley	USAF	Phant	NK
3681	23.08.73	FL/LT A.B.Kadam	IndAF	Vamp	NK
3682	29.08.73	FL/LT J.S.Kahlon	IndAF	Vamp	OC
3683	29.08.73	F/O S.Ghosh	IndAF	Vamp	OC
3684	01.09.73	CAPT C.A.Wanzeller	Port	F.G91	NK
3685	03.09.73	CAPT M.Cerretto	Italy	F.G91	OC
3686	03.09.73	CAPT S.Pirali	Italy	F.G91	OC
3687	04.09.73	S/LT P.M.Bate	Zimb	Vamp	NK
3688	06.09.73	S/L Edmondston	RAF	Harr	OC
3689	14.09.73	Classified			
3690	18.09.73	CAPT G.Girelli	Italy	L.F104	OC
3691	22.09.73		USAF	Phant	NK
3692	22.09.73		USAF	Phant	NK
3693	23.09.73	LT R.P.Boennighausen	USN	Crus	OC
3694	24.09.73	FL/LT Hulley	RAF	Harr	OC
3695	25.09.73	CAPT Mocaer	Fr AF	Mir	NK
3696	25.09.73	ADJ Gonneau	Fr AF	Mir	NK
3697	26.09.73	LT Lagoutiere	Fr AF	Mir	NK
3698	26.09.73	LT J.Coppenex	Fr AF	Mir	NK
3699	02.10.73	1/LT W.Ayres	USMC	Phant	NK
3700	02.10.73	1/LT R.Lamers	USMC	Phant	OC
3701	04.10.73	CAPT A.R.Cruz	Port	F.G91	NK
3702	07.10.73	Classified			
3703	07.10.73	Classified			
3704	08.10.73	Classified			
3705	09.10.73	Classified			
3706	09.10.73	Classified			
3707	10.10.73	LT/JG K.W.Chambers	USN	Crus	OC
3708	11.10.73	Classified			
3709	11.10.73	Classified			
3710	11.10.73	Classified			
3711	11.10.73	COL E.J.Campbell	USAF	Phant	NK
3712	11.10.73	Classified			
3713	11.10.73	CAPT D.M.McAuliffe	USAF	Phant	NK
3714	15.10.73	Classified			
3715	15.10.73	LT J.Hooton	RN	Phant	NK
3716	15.10.73	Classified			
3717	15.10.73	LT D.J.Lortscher	RN	Phant	OC
3718	16.10.73	R.H.Watson	USAF	Phant	NK
3719	16.10.73	W.L.Stout	USAF	Phant	NK
3720	18.10.73	LT L.E.Dawson	USN	Crus	OC
3721	18.10.73	CAPT J.R.English	USMC	Crus	OC
3722	18.10.73	Classified			
3723	18.10.73	Classified			
3724	18.10.73	Classified			
3725	18.10.73	Classified			
3726	18.10.73	FL/LT Jawad	Iraq	Hunt	NK
3727	19.10.73	LT R.D.Gray	USN	Phant	NK
3728	20.10.73	Classified			
3729	20.10.73	Classified			
3730	21.10.73	Classified			
3731	21.10.73	Classified			
3732	24.10.73	LT/CDR K.A.Rohdenburg	USN	Crus	OC
3733	24.10.73	CAPT J.J.Britz	SA	Imp	OC
3734	26.10.73	CAPT L.L.Burrill	USAF	Phant	NK
3735	02.11.73	1/LT W.Stanley	USMC	Phant	OC
3736	06.11.73	MR I.Kilgour	Civ	S.Vix	OC
3737	06.11.73	MR Welch	Civ	S.Vix	OC
3738	12.11.73	LT/JG D.J.Steffen	USN	Int	OC
3739	12.11.73	LT/CDR H.G.Sprouse	USN	Int	OC
3740	14.11.73	LT Garcin	Fr AF	Mir	OC
3741	22.11.73	MAJ W.Sadrina	GerAF	L.F104	OC
3742	22.11.73	MAJ P.Vogler	GerAF	L.F104	OC
3743	26.11.73	1/LT Snakenburg	USMC	Phant	OC
3744	26.11.73	CAPT Singleton	USMC	Phant	OC
3745	29.11.73	LT/COL B.Fredricks	USAF	Phant	OC
3746	30.11.73	1/LT D.R.Harman	USMC	Phant	NK
3747	30.11.73	1/LT D.R.Mattson	USMC	Phant	OC
3748	30.11.73	CAPT J.R.Hannemann	USMC	Phant	OC
3749	13.12.73	LT Al-Faris	Kuw	Hunt	OC
3750	19.12.73	LT R.E.Drum	USN	Phant	OC
3751	19.12.73	LT/JG C.F.Newton	USN	Phant	OC
3752	20.12.73	SGT Demarco	Fr AF	Mir	OC
3753	01.01.74	O/LT H.Genditzki	USAF	Phant	OC
3754	01.01.74	Classified			
3755	01.01.74	Classified			
3756	01.01.74	Classified			
3757	01.01.74	Classified			
3758	01.01.74	Classified			
3759	01.01.74	Classified			
3760	01.01.74	Classified			
3761	01.01.74	Classified			

No.	Date	Name	Force	Type	Cause	No.	Date	Name	Force	Type	Cause
3762	01.01.74	Classified				3836	13.08.74	LT X.Lizee	Fr AF	Etend	OC
3763	09.01.74	LT M.Tio	Sing	S.Mas	OC	3837	18.08.74	1/LT J.Smolak	USMC	Phant	OC
3764	09.01.74	CAPT T.P.Mahan	USAF	Phant	OC	3838	18.08.74	CAPT W.Lounsbury	USMC	Phant	OC
3765	09.01.74	CAPT W.A.Hill	USAF	Phant	OC	3839	20.08.74	LT/CDR T.H.Chowfin	Ind N	Kiran	OC
3766	18.01.74		USAF	Phant	OC	3840	20.08.74	S/LT Y.Choudhri	Ind N	Kiran	OC
3767	18.01.74		USAF	Phant	OC	3841	05.09.74	FL/LT N.M.Gupte	IndAF	Kiran	NK
3768	22.01.74	CAPT W.Spencer	USA	Moh	OC	3842	05.09.74	A.Raha	IndAF	Kiran	NK
3769	22.01.74	SP4 G.Phillips	USA	Moh	OC	3843	05.09.74		Braz	Mir	NK
3770	22.01.74	1/LT D.Mozingo	USMC	Phant	OC	3844	09.09.74	HPT J.Imhof	GerAF	L.F104	OC
3771	28.01.74	MAJ D.M.Stewart	USAF	Phant	OC	3845	19.09.74	CAPT L.Abbate	Italy	L.F104	NK
3772	28.01.74	CAPT L.B.Speckman	USAF	Phant	OC	3846	20.09.74	MAJ J.D.Cutter	USAF	Phant	OC
3773	31.01.74	TEN PIL V.M.F.Gil	Port	F.G91	NK	3847	20.09.74	CAPT R.F.Henley	USAF	Phant	OC
3774	01.02.74	CAPT B.Shaw	USAF	Phant	OC	3848	02.10.74	FL/LT J.E.Downey	RAF	Harr	OC
3775	13.02.74	FL/LT T.Butcher	RAF	Light	OC	3849	07.10.74	1/LT R.H.Oelfke	USAF	Phant	OC
3776	13.02.74	CAPT R.Santamaria	Col		NK	3850	07.10.74	MAJ R.A.Zang	USAF	Phant	OC
3777	15.02.74	Childress	USAF	Phant	OC	3851	09.10.74	LT D.L.Boyle	USN	Int	OC
3778	15.02.74	Christenberry	USAF	Phant	OC	3852	11.10.74	FL/LT Pilley	RAF	Phant	OC
3779	19.02.74	KAP B.Tengler	Ger N	L.F104	OC	3853	11.10.74	FL/LT Toal	RAF	Phant	OC
3780	27.02.74	CAPT Pettit	USAF	Phant	OC	3854	19.10.74	CAPT R.R.Faucher	USMC	Phant	NK
3781	27.02.74	1/LT Bradley	USAF	Phant	OC	3855	19.10.74	MAJ J.E.May	USMC	Phant	OC
3782	05.03.74	MAJ D.C.Cartwright	USAF	Phant	OC	3856	22.10.74	CAPT P.Hulliger	Switz	Mir	OC
3783	05.03.74	2/LT R.L.Westfall	USAF	Phant	OC	3857	23.10.74	LT/JG J.Turnbull	USN	Phant	OC
3784	05.03.74	MAJ G.E.Kreig	USAF	Phant	OC	3858	23.10.74	ENS G.Wilkinson	USN	Phant	OC
3785	08.03.74	LT D.A.Babboni	USN	Int	OC	3859	23.10.74	LT R.Plutt	USN	Phant	OC
3786	08.03.74	LT D.A.Woxland	USN	Int	OC	3860	23.10.74	LT J.Saumdres	USN	Phant	OC
3787	11.03.74	HPT H.Bohnke	GerAF	L.F104	OC	3861	28.10.74	F/O U.N.Ganguly	IndAF	Marut	OC
3788	12.03.74	O/LT H.Martin	GerAF	L.F104	OC	3862	29.10.74	FL/LT T.W.Jones	RAF	Light	OC
3789	12.03.74	O/LT W.Baltes	GerAF	L.F104	OC	3863	03.11.74	1/LT R.W.Reno	USMC	Phant	OC
3790	13.03.74	LT Lafferre	Fr AF	Myst	OC	3864	09.11.74	LT R.A.Smith	USN	Crus	NK
3791	21.03.74	LT Porchier	Fr AF	Mir	NK	3865	11.11.74	LT D.Thomson	RN	Bucc	NK
3792	01.04.74	2/LT P.Vantieghem	Belg	Mir	OC	3866	12.11.74	LT T.Albin	USAF	Phant	OC
3793	01.04.74	SGT N.Costa	Italy	F.G91	OC	3867	12.11.74	P.Tzouros	Gree	L.F104	NK
3794	01.04.74	FL/LT L.D.Boyd	AusAF	Mir	OC	3868	19.11.74	CWO2 R.E.Staples	USN	Phant	OC
3795	08.04.74	Classified				3869	19.11.74	LT R.C.Olson	USN	Phant	OC
3796	08.04.74	Classified				3870	21.11.74	FL/LT I.D.Vacha	RAF	Phant	OC
3797	16.04.74	ASP/AV X.A.Eder	Braz	MB326	OC	3871	21.11.74	FL/LT A.M.Keane	RAF	Phant	OC
3798	17.04.74	HPT V.Ding	GerAF	L.F104	OC	3872	22.11.74	W/C C.C.Rustin	RAF	Jag	OC
3799	23.04.74	O/LT M.Murmurachi	GerAF	L.F104	OC	3873	22.11.74	FL/LT C.J.Cruikshank	RAF	Jag	OC
3800	27.04.74	CAPT C.Livoni	Italy	F.G91	OC	3874	04.12.74	OTL H.Merkel	GerAF	L.T33	OC
3801	01.05.74	CAPT Miller	USAF	Phant	OC	3875	10.12.74	O/LT R.Chur	GerAF	L.F104	OC
3802	04.05.74	LT P.Tsolis	Gree	L.F104	NK	3876	17.12.74	LT S.Singh	Ind N	S.Hk	OC
3803	06.05.74	CAPT F.N.Markette	USAF	Phant	OC	3877	21.12.74	FL/LT S.Arshad	Pak	Mir	OC
3804	06.05.74	CAPT J.T.Sornberger	USAF	Phant	OC	3878	28.12.74	MAJ C.F.Jewett	USAF	Phant	OC
3805	07.05.74	F/O Sikandar	Pak	F86	NK	3879	28.12.74	1/LT D.L.Poling	USAF	Phant	OC
3806	10.05.74	LT T.J.Terrill	USN	Phant	OC	3880	28.12.74	1/LT M.J.Govednik	USAF	Phant	OC
3807	10.05.74	ENS J.A.Wilcox	USN	Phant	OC	3881	28.12.74	CAPT J.P.Fair	USAF	Phant	OC
3808	12.05.74	LT R.L.Lyman	USN	Phant	OC	3882	01.01.75	Classified			
3809	12.05.74	ENS R.G.Armisted	USN	Phant	OC	3883	01.01.75	Classified			
3810	12.05.74	LT J.H.Adams	USN	Int	OC	3884	01.01.75	Classified			
3811	12.05.74	LT/JG R.V.McHale	USN	Int	OC	3885	01.01.75	Classified			
3812	13.05.74	CAPT R.Favaro	Italy	L.F104	OC	3886	01.01.75	Classified			
3813	13.05.74		Iran	Phant	OC	3887	02.01.75	LT/CDR G.S.Giles	USN	F14	NK
3814	23.05.74	FL/LT L.Hurst	RN	Phant	OC	3888	02.01.75	LT/CDR R.McFillin	USN	F14	NK
3815	02.06.74	CAPT Saboonchi	Iran	Phant	OC	3889	13.01.75	LT/CDR R.Newman	USN	Prowl	NK
3816	04.06.74	CAPT L.J.Bucko	USMC	Phant	NK	3890	13.01.75	LT R.A.Kraft	USN	Prowl	NK
3817	04.06.74	1/LT R.L.Stockus	USMC	Phant	NK	3891	13.01.75	LT/CDR B.G.Swanson	USN	Prowl	OC
3818	05.06.74	A.Lely	Fr AF	Mir	OC	3892	14.01.75	LT G.W.Kowlok	USN	F14	OC
3819	16.06.74	FL/LT Jawad	Iraq	Hunt	OC	3893	14.01.75	LT/CDR D.G.Bjerke	USN	F14	NK
3820	17.06.74	FL/LT I.Firth	RAF	Hunt	OC	3894	15.01.75	CAPT M.Pirou	Fr AF	Myst	NK
3821	17.06.74	SGT Bonin	Fr AF	Myst	OC	3895	16.01.75	SGT F.Delauney	Fr AF	Mir	OC
3822	23.06.74	GEN F.Ristory	Italy	F.G91	OC	3896	16.01.75	CAPT R.M.Osborn	USAF	Phant	NK
3823	24.06.74	MAJ Afshar	Iran	Phant	NK	3897	23.01.75	SGT Vaganay	Fr AF	Mir	NK
3824	24.06.74	CAPT Seyedreza	Iran	Phant	OC	3898	25.01.75	FL/LT V.Vasudevan	IndAF	Hunt	OC
3825	24.06.74	F/O K.Mason	RAF	Light	OC	3899	29.01.75	LT/CDR M.Bickley	RAF	Bucc	OC
3826	24.06.74	LT Werne	Fr AF	Mir	OC	3900	30.01.75	CAPT D.L.Thrasher	USAF	Phant	NK
3827	28.06.74	CAPT J.W.Cizek	USAF	Phant	OC	3901	30.01.75	1/LT B.J.Smith	USAF	Phant	OC
3828	28.06.74	CAPT D.E.Healy	USAF	Phant	OC	3902	15.02.75	MAJ G.Gerelli	Italy	L.F104	NK
3829	01.07.74	LT F.Bourdin	Fr AF	Mir	NK	3903	03.03.75	F/O P.Tolman	RAF	Phant	OC
3830	22.07.74	LT K.Papadoulis	Gree	Phant	NK	3904	03.03.75	FL/LT P.Trotter	RAF	Phant	OC
3831	22.07.74	CAPT E.Papadopoulos	Gree	Phant	NK	3905	15.03.75		Zamb	MB326	NK
3832	22.07.74	MAJ B.Williginann	GerAF	F.G91	OC	3906	24.03.75	FL/LT	RAF	Vict	NK
3833	27.07.74	CAPT S.C.Torrent	USMC	Harr	OC			K.L.Handscomb			
3834	27.07.74	G/CAPT W.Azim	Pak	Mir	NK	3907	24.03.75	LT J.R.Batman	USN	Crus	OC
3835	10.08.74	CAPT Toussi	Iran	F5	OC	3908	31.03.75	ASP/AV C.Neto	Braz	MB326	NK

No.	Date	Name	Force	Type	Cause
3909	08.04.75	LT W.G.Hester	USN	Crus	OC
3910	09.04.75	FL/LT J.Buckler	RAF	Harr	OC
3911	09.04.75	LT/JG W.G.Kerr	USN	Phant	OC
3912	09.04.75	LT E.T.Dailey	USN	Phant	NK
3913	10.04.75	J.C.Cunat	Fr AF	Mir	NK
3914	14.04.75	LT/CDR D.Wright	USN	Int	OC
3915	14.04.75	LT J.Miller	USN	Int	NK
3916	14.04.75	LT A.K.Twijry	Kuw	S.Mas	OC
3917	16.04.75	S/SGT M.Yarnell	USAF	Phant	NK
3918	16.04.75	LT/COL E.McDowell	USAF	Phant	OC
3919	17.04.75	CAPT G.Neyrinckx	Belg	Mir	OC
3920	21.04.75	LT E.G.Marits	USN	Int	OC
3921	21.04.75	LT/JG M.H.Paul	USN	Int	NK
3922	22.04.75	FL/LT N.K.Bhasin	IndAF	Hunt	OC
3923	25.04.75	LT/JG B.Kociemba	USN	Int	NK
3924	27.04.75	CAPT J.M.Cluelow	USMC	Phant	OC
3925	27.04.75	MAJ M.M.Hynes	USMC	Phant	NK
3926	30.04.75	FL/LT W.Griffiths	RAF	Jag	NK
3927	10.05.75	LT R.R.Ayres	USN	Int	OC
3928	10.05.75	LT/JG R.D.Treanor	USN	Int	OC
3929	15.05.75	CAPT M.G.F.Morton	SA	Bucc	NK
3930	15.05.75	1/LT G.L.Hoffman	USAF	Phant	OC
3931	15.05.75	2/LT T.G.Kinney	USAF	Phant	NK
3932	15.05.75	2/LT A.P.Rousseau	SA	Bucc	OC
3933	16.05.75	FL/LT Lowton	RAF	Harr	OC
3934	16.05.75	FL/LT R.M.Moore	RAF	Harr	OC
3935	20.05.75	LT/COL B.Chianese	Italy	L.F104	NK
3936	20.05.75	CAPT C.Balducci	Italy	L.F104	NK
3937	29.05.75	LT G.A.Reynolds	USN	Phant	OC
3938	29.05.75	LT J.Kumpan	USN	Phant	NK
3939	06.06.75	WO R.Van Bever	Belg	Mir	OC
3940	12.06.75	LT J.A.Wagoner	USN	Crus	OC
3941	13.06.75	2/LT B.H.Johansen	Den	L.F104	NK
3942	13.06.75	2/LT J.T.Stentoft	Den	L.F104	OC
3943	16.06.75	FL/LT R.G.Haynes	RAF	Bucc	OC
3944	16.06.75	FL/LT A.Shaw	RAF	Bucc	NK
3945	17.06.75	Saint Lanne	Fr AF	Mir	OC
3946	22.06.75		Iran	Phant	NK
3947	22.06.75		Iran	Phant	NK
3948	24.06.75	M.Cornus	Fr AF	Mir	NK
3949	26.06.75	LT W.B.Bierbower	USN	Prowl	OC
3950	26.06.75	LT/JG L.T.Hunt	USN	Int	OC
3951	26.06.75	LT/CDR J.R.Capute	USN	Prowl	NK
3952	26.06.75	LT/JG R.W.McConchie	USN	Prowl	NK
3953	29.06.75	2/LT Garanpayeh	Iran	F5	OC
3954	03.07.75	MAJ W.F.Gilliland	USMC	Harr	NK
3955	07.07.75	LT/COL R.E.Lawyer	USAF	Phant	NK
3956	07.07.75	MAJ R.L.Hager	USAF	Phant	NK
3957	08.07.75	CAPT E.C.Denkwalter	USMC	Phant	NK
3958	09.07.75	CAPT H.Gommel	GerAF	L.F104	OC
3959	10.07.75	FL/LT L.A.Fernandes	IndAF	Marut	NK
3960	11.07.75	Taverier	Fr AF	Mir	OC
3961	14.07.75	LT P.Lemmens	Belg	Mir	OC
3962	14.07.75	CDT A.Bertram	Belg	Mir	OC
3963	17.07.75	A.Bonneau	Fr AF	Myst	NK
3964	17.07.75	Fremaut	Fr AF	Mir	NK
3965	20.07.75	MAJ E.R.Lindley	Peru	Mir	OC
3966	23.07.75	LT G.Eich	GerAF	L.F104	OC
3967	29.07.75	LT J.R.Batman	USN	Crus	OC
3968	29.07.75	LT F.L.T.Lillis	RAF	Bucc	OC
3969	29.07.75	FL/LT Patterson	RAF	Bucc	OC
3970	30.07.75	LT R.R.Albertson	USN	Crus	OC
3971	31.07.75	ASP G.D.Arboes	Braz	MB326	OC
3972	31.07.75	TEN AV J.S.Tsuji	Braz	MB326	NK
3973	05.08.75	LT B.J.Recame	USN	F14	OC
3974	05.08.75	CDR C.L.Lavinder	USN	F14	NK
3975	12.08.75		Fr N	Etend	NK
3976	12.08.75	Classified			
3977	16.08.75	LT S.S.Graham	USN	Crus	NK
3978	19.08.75	FL/LT R.Furlong	Oman	S.Mas	EA
3979	20.08.75	LT G.T.Wyckoff	USN	Int	NK
3980	22.08.75	O/LT S.H.J.Beyer	Ger N	L.F104	OC
3981	23.08.75	LT/COL C.W.Heinzerling	USMC	Phant	OC
3982	23.08.75	1/LT P.J.McNeela	USMC	Phant	NK
3983	02.09.75		Braz	Mir	NK
3984	03.09.75	ASP/AV Ribeiro	Braz	MB326	NK
3985	04.09.75	HPT H.Jung	GerAF	L.F104	OC
3986	09.09.75	LT F.Milana	Italy	L.F104	OC
3987	10.09.75	TEN Silva	Braz	MB326	OC
3988	15.09.75	J.Bisthoven	Belg	Mir	NK
3989	15.09.75	CAPT R.Mandernack	USAF	Phant	NK
3990	15.09.75	LT T.E.Lorincz	USAF	Phant	NK
3991	16.09.75	CAPT R.G.Dwyer	USMC	Phant	OC
3992	16.09.75	CAPT R.A.Cote	USMC	Phant	NK
3993	18.09.75	F/O Wright	RAF	Phant	OC
3994	18.09.75	FL/LT Hammil	RAF	Phant	OC
3995	19.09.75	MAJ H.Dombrowe	GerAF	Phant	OC
3996	20.09.75	KPT/LT G.Pape	Ger N	L.F104	OC
3997	23.09.75	CAPT J.L.Cross	USMC	Phant	OC
3998	23.09.75	2/LT A.E.Rogers	USMC	Phant	NK
3999	24.09.75	LT/JG D.L.Hayes	USN	Crus	OC
4000	26.09.75	HPT G.Meyer	GerAF	F.G91	OC
4001	02.10.75	HPT R.Lieke	GerAF	Phant	NK
4002	02.10.75	1/LT K.P.Judy	USAF	Phant	OC
4003	02.10.75	HPT W.D.Von Scheliha	GerAF	Phant	OC
4004	02.10.75	1/LT R.H.McCarty	USAF	Phant	OC
4005	08.10.75	CAPT Mocaert	Fr AF	Mir	NK
4006	10.10.75	LT C.Montefori	Italy	F.G91	OC
4007	14.10.75	FL/LT Alcock	RAF	Vulc	NK
4008	14.10.75	FL/LT E.C.Alexander	RAF	Vulc	OC
4009	22.10.75	CAPT R.D.Anderson	USMC	Phant	OC
4010	23.10.75	PN-1 G.Feeback	USN	Phant	OC
4011	23.10.75	LT R.Scott	USN	Phant	NK
4012	29.10.75	FL/LT B.J.Sweeney	AusAF	MB326	NK
4013	29.10.75	F/O L.G.Clayton	AusAF	MB326	NK
4014	29.10.75	LT/JG Buckley	USN	F14	OC
4015	29.10.75	LT Gastrell	USN	F14	OC
4016	31.10.75	S/L R.A.Renton	Oman	Hunt	OC
4017	05.11.75	ADJ C.Delhaye	Belg	Mir	OC
4018	10.11.75	HPT W.Plosser	GerAF	Phant	OC
4019	10.11.75	HPT P.Schunke	GerAF	Phant	NK
4020	22.11.75	1/LT G.Kuprian	USAF	Phant	OC
4021	22.11.75	CAPT J.C.Evans	USAF	Phant	OC
4022	24.11.75	FL/LT Smith	RAF	Phant	NK
4023	24.11.75	FL/LT Lunn	RAF	Phant	OC
4024	01.12.75	F/O B.C.Scott	RAF	Harr	OC
4025	22.12.75	LT J.F.Morlaix	Fr AF	Mir	OC
4026	03.01.76	MAJ G.Lindgren	USMC	Phant	OC
4027	03.01.76	1/LT E.J.Bozarth	USMC	Phant	OC
4028	07.01.76	CAPT T.R.Brady	USAF	Phant	OC
4029	07.01.76	1/LT R.M.Feeley	USAF	Phant	OC
4030	07.01.76	F.C.Richardson	USAF	Phant	OC
4031	07.01.76	2/LT C.T.Bradley	USAF	Phant	OC
4032	10.01.76	CAPT R.B.Pevey	USMC	Harr	OC
4033	22.01.76	CDR D.Kemp	Civ	Hunt	OC
4034	22.01.76	LT/CDR W.Honour	Civ	Hunt	OC
4035	26.01.76	T.M.Antonio	Braz	MB326	NK
4036	28.01.76	MAJ V.Koo	Sing	S.Mas	NK
4037	30.01.76	2/LT P.Hartmann	GerAF	L.F104	NK
4038	03.02.76	LT T.Johannesen	Den	F100	NK
4039	05.02.76	CADET M.G.Russell	SA	Imp	NK
4040	05.02.76	LT M.Silberbauer	SA	Imp	NK
4041	05.02.76	FL/LT A.I.Aitken	RAF	Jag	NK
4042	05.02.76	FL/LT R.K.Jackson	RAF	Jag	NK
4043	06.02.76	MAJ H.Fisch	GerAF	L.F104	NK
4044	06.02.76	1/LT H.Lebegern	GerAF	L.F104	NK
4045	13.02.76	FL/LT Scott	RAF	J.Pro	NK
4046	13.02.76	FL/LT J.Hall	RAF	J.Pro	NK
4047	13.02.76	2/LT R.G.Richardella	USMC	Phant	NK
4048	13.02.76	CAPT G.D.Peterson	USMC	Phant	NK
4049	15.02.76	Classified			
4050	15.02.76	Classified			
4051	15.02.76		Sing	S.Mas	NK
4052	17.02.76	CAPT L.S.Strickland	USMC	Phant	NK
4053	19.02.76	ENS G.E.Crawford	USN	Phant	NK
4054	19.02.76	LT/JG J.P.Perkins	USN	Phant	NK

No.	Date	Name	Force	Type	Cause
4055	25.02.76	SGT R.W.Minkus	GerAF	F.G91	NK
4056	25.02.76	LT P.Schive	Den	F100	NK
4057	25.02.76	LT N.Fredskild	Den	F100	NK
4058	25.02.76	CAPT H.Vinnemeier	GerAF	F.G91	NK
4059	01.03.76	MAJ B.Underwood	USAF	Phant	NK
4060	03.03.76	F/O G.Bowerman	RAF	Bucc	NK
4061	03.03.76	FL/LT C.Davies	RAF	Bucc	NK
4062	04.03.76	CDR P.A.Debrass	Ind N	S.Hk	NK
4063	05.03.76	LT/CDR P.G.Angelina	USN	F14	NK
4064	05.03.76	CDR D.D.Smith	USN	F14	NK
4065	10.03.76	CAPT D.Scharf	GerAF	L.F104	NK
4066	12.03.76	F/O Z.H.Malik	Pak	SY.F6	OC
4067	13.03.76		Venez	Canb	NK
4068	15.03.76	E.Hahn	Ger N	L.F104	OC
4069	16.03.76	LT T.Johanneson	Den	F100	NK
4070	16.03.76	LT N.G.W.Sorensen	Den	F100	NK
4071	16.03.76	FL/LT G.A.Kubank	AusAF	Mir	NK
4072	20.03.76	LT G.Caswell	USN	Phant	NK
4073	20.03.76	LT H.L.Jones	USN	Phant	NK
4074	20.03.76	FL/LT T.C.Hewlett	Oman	S.Mas	OC
4075	23.03.76	MAJ H.P.Bader	GerAF	Phant	NK
4076	24.03.76	LT/CDR C.F.Irvin	USN	F14	NK
4077	24.03.76	LT/JG S.C.Sabin	USN	F14	NK
4078	24.03.76	MAJ Garcia	ArgAF	Mir	NK
4079	25.03.76	FL/LT A.K.Joshi	IndAF	Kiran	NK
4080	30.03.76		USAF	Phant	NK
4081	03.04.76		Pak	Mir	NK
4082	07.04.76	P/O S.K.Sinha	IndAF	Hunt	NK
4083	07.04.76	FL/LT K.A.Ally	IndAF	Hunt	NK
4084	21.04.76	FL/LT W.R.Lewis	RAF	Hunt	NK
4085	21.04.76	LT V.Ahooja	Ind N	Vamp	NK
4086	21.04.76	S/LT J.Singh	Ind N	Vamp	NK
4087	01.05.76	ASP A.Muhl	Braz	MB326	NK
4088	04.05.76	LT B.W.Buckley	USN	F14	NK
4089	04.05.76	LT N.I.Arden	USN	F14	NK
4090	15.05.76	Classified			
4091	16.05.76	R.Muller	GerAF	Phant	OC
4092	16.05.76	MAJ S.Zimprich	GerAF	Phant	NK
4093	25.05.76		USAF	Phant	NK
4094	25.05.76		USAF	Phant	NK
4095	01.06.76	LT D.Graves	USN	Crus	NK
4096	08.06.76		USAF	Phant	NK
4097	08.06.76	F/O M.H.Hurman	AusAF	Mir	NK
4098	09.06.76	LT H.G.Clausen	Den	F100	OC
4099	09.06.76	LT P.V.Jensen	Den	F100	NK
4100	15.06.76	CAPT E.B.Cummings	USMC	Harr	OC
4101	15.06.76	FL/LT T.M.Thomas	Zimb	Hunt	NK
4102	16.06.76	R.Schniecke	GerAF	L.F104	NK
4103	16.06.76	CAPT H.Amirian	Iran	F5	NK
4104	19.06.76	CDR R.K.Kauber	USN	Phant	OC
4105	19.06.76	LT/JG E.E.Mercker	USN	Phant	OC
4106	23.06.76	M.Masoud	Iran	Phant	NK
4107	23.06.76	1/LT A.S.Azar	Iran	Phant	NK
4108	28.06.76	C.Vermeulen	Belg	Mir	OC
4109	06.07.76	FL/LT Kirton	RAF	Harr	NK
4110	13.07.76	CAPT V.Maddux	USMC	Phant	OC
4111	13.07.76	CAPT D.Farmer	USMC	Phant	NK
4112	15.07.76	LT/JG D.Hayes	USN	Crus	NK
4113	15.07.76	ASP A.A.Ribeiro	Braz	MB326	NK
4114	20.07.76	TEN R.V.Goltz	Braz	MB326	NK
4115	20.07.76	TEN M.L.Muller	Braz	MB326	NK
4116	20.07.76	TEN P.V.Rocha	Braz	MB326	NK
4117	20.07.76	TEN M.L.S.Rossi	Braz	MB326	NK
4118	23.07.76	FL/LT J.W.Jackson	RAF	Phant	NK
4119	23.07.76	CAPT B.A.Newberry	RAF	Phant	NK
4120	23.07.76	F/O U.Shankar	IndAF	Marut	NK
4121	29.07.76	CAPT F.J.Donnelly	USMC	Harr	NK
4122	30.07.76	F/O Manning	RAF	Light	NK
4123	09.08.76	HPT K.H.Rahn	GerAF	F.G91	NK
4124	10.08.76	F/O G.D.Shepherd	AusAF	Mir	NK
4125	10.08.76	FL/LT B.R.Wood	AusAF	Mir	NK
4126	10.08.76	O/LT H.Loffler	GerAF	L.F104	NK
4127	11.08.76	LT D.E.Foster	USN	Prowl	OC
4128	11.08.76	CDR J.F.Smith	USN	Prowl	OC
4129	11.08.76	LT/JG W.Rodman	USN	Prowl	OC
4130	13.08.76	LT J.Brown	USN	Crus	NK
4131	13.08.76		Sing	S.Mas	NK
4132	14.08.76	LT M.Postai	USAF	Phant	NK
4133	15.08.76		IndAF	Marut	NK
4134	17.08.76		USAF	Phant	NK
4135	17.08.76		USAF	Phant	NK
4136	24.08.76	O/LT Leuthner	GerAF	L.F104	NK
4137	24.08.76	CAPT M.Krenek	USAF	Phant	NK
4138	27.08.76	CAPT J.W.Cox	USMC	Harr	NK
4139	30.08.76	LT/CDR D.A.Erskine	USN	Int	NK
4140	30.08.76	LT/CDR R.A.Bankson	USN	Int	NK
4141	30.08.76	HPT R.Schnegraf	GerAF	L.F104	OC
4142	30.08.76	O/LT Waldow	GerAF	L.F104	OC
4143	31.08.76	CAPT A.A.Decandia	USMC	Harr	NK
4144	07.09.76		USAF	Phant	NK
4145	07.09.76		USAF	Phant	NK
4146	11.09.76	Classified			
4147	13.09.76	T.W.Mehlhaff	USAF	Phant	OC
4148	14.09.76	LT/JG L.E.Seymour	USN	F14	NK
4149	14.09.76	LT J.L.Kosich	USN	F14	NK
4150	20.09.76	O/LT P.Jantos	GerAF	L.F104	NK
4151	21.09.76	MR P.Millard	RN	Hunt	NK
4152	21.09.76		Fr N	Etend	NK
4153	22.09.76	LT G.F.Decker	USN	Int	NK
4154	22.09.76		Venez	Mir	NK
4155	22.09.76	LT J.G.Major	USN	Int	NK
4156	22.09.76		Venez	Mir	NK
4157	23.09.76	CADET R.H.Thomas	SA	Imp	NK
4158	03.10.76	F/O Hifazat	Pak	SY.F6	NK
4159	06.10.76	FL/LT S.V.R.Sekhar	IndAF	Marut	NK
4160	06.10.76	TEN L.Bittesini	Italy	L.F104	NK
4161	07.10.76	CAPT C.Dorance	Fr AF	Mir	NK
4162	18.10.76	Classified			
4163	18.10.76	Classified			
4164	20.10.76	LT G.Moyencourt	Fr AF	Mir	NK
4165	20.10.76	ADJ Franzoia	Fr AF	Mir	NK
4166	25.10.76	LT G.Lorenzo	Italy	MB326	NK
4167	25.10.76	CAPT A.Rossi	Italy	MB326	NK
4168	25.10.76	FL/LT E.Hunkin	RAF	Hunt	NK
4169	27.10.76	TEN M.S.O.Lima	Braz	MB326	NK
4170	27.10.76	TEN H.J.T.Moura	Braz	MB326	NK
4171	28.10.76	1/LT G.W.Luck	USMC	Int	NK
4172	29.10.76	FL/LT Parkinson	RAF	Bucc	NK
4173	29.10.76	FL/LT Easterbrook	RAF	Bucc	NK
4174	02.11.76	LT/CDR L.E.McKay	USN	Phant	OC
4175	02.11.76	LT/CDR C.B.Scott	USN	Phant	OC
4176	10.11.76	LTA C.A.Francis	Sing	Hunt	OC
4177	10.11.76	2/LT C.K.Sun	Sing	Hunt	OC
4178	14.11.76	LT/JG C.F.Bednash	USN	Phant	OC
4179	14.11.76	CDR D.A.Moore	USN	Phant	OC
4180	17.11.76	CAPT T.Kuge	Japan	Phant	OC
4181	19.11.76	2/LT D.Briel	Belg	Mir	NK
4182	22.11.76	O/LT K.Lubben	GerAF	F.G91	NK
4183	22.11.76	HPT B.Schirmer	GerAF	F.G91	NK
4184	24.11.76	1/LT S.J.Misiuk	USMC	Int	NK
4185	24.11.76	1/LT A.Kowalski	USMC	Int	NK
4186	24.11.76	Y.Asefi	Iran	Phant	NK
4187	24.11.76	MAJ D.Jalali	Iran	Phant	NK
4188	01.12.76	LT J.Wagoner	USN	Crus	NK
4189	07.12.76	LT/JG M.Checchio	USN	Phant	NK
4190	13.12.76	S/TEN F.Belisario	Italy	F.G91	NK
4191	14.12.76	CAPT A.Montalbetti	Italy	L.F104	NK
4192	14.12.76	FL/LT W.A.Langworthy	RAF	Jag	NK
4193	19.12.76	LT/JG D.J.Law	USN	F14	NK
4194	19.12.76	LT/CDR J.B.Yakeley	USN	F14	NK
4195	21.12.76	SGT/CH Mainier	Fr AF	Mir	NK
4196	23.12.76	FL/LT S.H.Ashfaq	Pak	SY.F6	NK
4197	25.12.76	FL/LT R.C.Sharma	IndAF	Kiran	NK
4198	01.01.77	Classified			
4199	01.01.77	Classified			
4200	01.01.77	Classified			
4201	01.01.77	Classified			

No.	Date	Name	Force	Type	Cause
4202	01.01.77	Classified			
4203	01.01.77	Classified			
4204	01.01.77	Classified			
4205	01.01.77	Classified			
4206	04.01.77	M.Bergasse	Fr AF	Mir	NK
4207	14.01.77	CAPT Amarger	Fr AF	Jag	NK
4208	17.01.77	FL/LT R.M.Aspinall	RAF	Vulc	NK
4209	17.01.77	S/L R.L.Hollett	RAF	Bucc	NK
4210	17.01.77	FL/LT A.Ryder	RAF	Vulc	NK
4211	19.01.77	1/LT J.J.Dicks	USMC	Phant	NK
4212	19.01.77	CAPT J.E.Beery	USMC	Phant	NK
4213	28.01.77	P.M.Degletagne	Fr N	Crus	NK
4214	01.02.77	W.Bold	GerAF	F.G91	NK
4215	01.02.77	ASP Guillot	Fr N	Crus	NK
4216	03.02.77	FL/LT M.W.Brown	RAF	Bucc	NK
4217	03.02.77	FL/LT R.P.Kemp	RAF	Bucc	NK
4218	04.02.77	LT Saissy	Fr AF	Mir	NK
4219	05.02.77	1/LT D.E.Olsen	USAF	Phant	NK
4220	05.02.77	1/LT F.Himstedt	USAF	Phant	NK
4221	09.02.77	LT T.G.Dobrovolny	USN	Phant	NK
4222	09.02.77	LT/JG E.E.Mercker	USN	Phant	NK
4223	16.02.77	SGT P.Didier	Fr AF	Myst	NK
4224	21.02.77	LT Leheup	Fr AF	Mir	OC
4225	22.02.77	LT J.O.Ellis	USN	F14	OC
4226	23.02.77	LT F.Casadio	Italy	F.G91	OC
4227	24.02.77	S/L Lawrence	RAF	Light	OC
4228	24.02.77	S/L G.Granville-White	RAF	Light	OC
4229	01.03.77	CAPT G.L.Haseloh	USAF	Phant	NK
4230	01.03.77	CAPT D.L.Heiman	USAF	Phant	NK
4231	03.03.77	O/LT P.Kornemann	GerAF	L.F104	NK
4232	22.03.77	CAPT Vargas	Peru	Mir	NK
4233	23.03.77		USAF	Phant	NK
4234	23.03.77		USAF	Phant	NK
4235	24.03.77	CAPT C.Keckeis	Switz	Mir	NK
4236	24.03.77	LT D.Trosch	Switz	Mir	NK
4237	24.03.77	CAPT D.Girardet	Switz	Mir	NK
4238	28.03.77	LT G.A.Stevens	USN	F14	NK
4239	28.03.77	LT G.A.Quist	USN	F14	NK
4240	30.03.77	S/LT Martin	Fr AF	Mir	NK
4241	04.04.77	FL/LT Summers	RAF	Bucc	NK
4242	04.04.77	FL/LT P.J.R.Hill	RAF	Bucc	NK
4243	07.04.77	LT/CDR G.P.Stone	USN	Int	NK
4244	07.04.77	LT T.L.Thorson	USN	Int	NK
4245	19.04.77	LT/CPT E.Stiemerling	Ger N	L.F104	NK
4246	19.04.77	ENS N.F.Carlock	USN	F14	NK
4247	19.04.77	LT G.A.Barrett	USN	F14	NK
4248	20.04.77	MAJ P.B.Field	USMC	Phant	NK
4249	20.04.77	CAPT C.D.Nelson	USAF	Phant	NK
4250	20.04.77	CAPT M.I.Mott	USMC	Phant	OC
4251	25.04.77	MAJ Seeger	USAF	Phant	NK
4252	25.04.77	MAJ Danborn	USAF	Phant	NK
4253	29.04.77	M.A.Peinemann	Iran	F14	NK
4254	04.05.77	MAJ A.M.Stroop	GerAF	F.G91	NK
4255	11.05.77	LT/CDR J.S.Ozbirn	USN	Crus	OC
4256	13.05.77	F/O Ruddock	RAF	Hunt	OC
4257	13.05.77	MAJ J.F.Lauritsen	Den	F100	NK
4258	16.05.77	CAPT E.D.Stites	USAF	Phant	NK
4259	16.05.77	S/L Maqsood	Pak	SY.F6	NK
4260	16.05.77	1/LT R.J.Schade	USAF	Phant	NK
4261	17.05.77	F/O T.Newby	RN	Phant	OC
4262	17.05.77	FL/LT S.Riley	RN	Phant	OC
4263	18.05.77	FL/LT R.K.Poonia	IndAF	Kiran	NK
4264	18.05.77	ENS R.B.Platt	USN	Crus	NK
4265	18.05.77	FL/LT R.Bakshi	IndAF	Kiran	NK
4266	23.05.77	CAPT R.Ponzanelli	Italy	L.F104	OC
4267	24.05.77	F/O Masroor	Pak	SY.F6	OC
4268	06.06.77	MAJ J.Sauer	GerAF	Phant	OC
4269	06.06.77	HPT U.Scholz	GerAF	Phant	OC
4270	15.06.77	CAPT L.M.Tichetti	Braz	MB326	OC
4271	15.06.77	T.Mayo	Braz	MB326	OC
4272	21.06.77	LT/CDR D.F.Green	USN	F14	OC
4273	21.06.77	1/LT D.L.Smith	USMC	Phant	OC
4274	21.06.77	MAJ R.C.Frantz	USMC	Phant	OC
4275	21.06.77	LT S.C.Miller	USN	F14	OC
4276	22.06.77	CAPT A.J.Spring	USMC	Phant	OC
4277	28.06.77	LT/JG K.L.Dilley	USN	F14	OC
4278	28.06.77	LT/JG W.R.Kirkpatrick	USN	F14	OC
4279	28.06.77	LT S.Smith	USN	F14	OC
4280	28.06.77	LT R.Keever	USN	F14	OC
4281	05.07.77	LT M.A.C.Azevedo	Braz	MB326	OC
4282	05.07.77	SGT J.A.P.Filho	Braz	MB326	OC
4283	06.07.77	CAPT R.Logan	USAF	Phant	OC
4284	08.07.77	TEN A.M.G.Filho	Braz	MB326	OC
4285	11.07.77	MAJ W.Rauch	GerAF	Phant	OC
4286	11.07.77	MAJ M.Wassel	GerAF	Phant	OC
4287	11.07.77	MAJ D.A.Fisher	GerAF	L.F104	NK
4288	14.07.77		Iran	Phant	OC
4289	14.07.77	MAJ/GEN M.Mehrmand	Iran	Phant	OC
4290	19.07.77	LT E.S.Gregory	USN	Crus	OC
4291	02.08.77	O/LT A.Sindelar	GerAF	L.F104	OC
4292	04.08.77	TEN A.I.Bittencourt	Braz	MB326	OC
4293	04.08.77	ASP A.F.C.Kanffmann	Braz	MB326	OC
4294	15.08.77	S/L Gordon	RAF	Canb	OC
4295	15.08.77	FL/LT Smith	RAF	Canb	OC
4296	16.08.77	LT/JG M.L.Clark	USN	Int	OC
4297	17.08.77	CAPT R.A.Cote	USMC	Phant	OC
4298	17.08.77	CAPT D.J.Dannewitz	USMC	Phant	OC
4299	18.08.77	FL/LT K.I.Mackenzie	RAF	Bucc	OC
4300	18.08.77	FL/LT R.A.Pittaway	RAF	Bucc	OC
4301	23.08.77	LT G.M.Jack	USN	Phant	OC
4302	23.08.77	ENS R.A.Ladd	USN	Phant	OC
4303	26.08.77	ASP P.R.Pertusi	Braz	MB326	OC
4304	29.08.77	CAPT A.Benfatto	Italy	L.F104	OC
4305	29.08.77	CAPT A.J.Spring	USMC	Phant	OC
4306	30.08.77	LT/CDR D.M.Beam	USN	Crus	OC
4307	08.09.77		Pak	Mir	NK
4308	08.09.77	FL/LT H.E.Spirit	RAF	Hunt	OC
4309	08.09.77	FL/LT S.Parfitt	RAF	Hunt	OC
4310	20.09.77	CAPT Carlton	USAF	Phant	OC
4311	20.09.77	LT Pacella	USAF	Phant	OC
4312	20.09.77	CAPT Zarras	USAF	Phant	OC
4313	25.09.77	CAPT M.Maugeri	Italy	L.F104	OC
4314	26.09.77	CAPT H.Troupin	Belg	Mir	OC
4315	27.09.77	CAPT J.E.Miler	USMC	Phant	OC
4316	27.09.77	1/LT P.D.Durbin	USMC	Phant	OC
4317	03.10.77	LT/JG B.L.Devane	USN	F14	OC
4318	03.10.77	LT W.M.Anderson	USN	F14	OC
4319	07.10.77	HPT R.Doniat	GerAF	L.F104	OC
4320	07.10.77	HPT G.Lohde	GerAF	L.F104	OC
4321	11.10.77		Pak	Mir	OC
4322	27.10.77	P/O M.M.Ayub	Pak	SY.F6	OC
4323	27.10.77	MAJ D.R.Jacobs	SA	Mir	NK
4324	31.10.77	FL/LT P.D.Locke	RAF	Bucc	NK
4325	07.11.77	1/LT J.Ulatowski	USMC	Phant	NK
4326	07.11.77	MAJ J.Cummings	USMC	Phant	NK
4327	08.11.77	CAPT Yasini	Iran	Phant	NK
4328	08.11.77	CAPT Labibi	Iran	Phant	NK
4329	10.11.77	LT/CDR J.A.Cook	USN	F14	OC
4330	10.11.77	LT L.E.Stampe	USN	F14	OC
4331	11.11.77	LT F.C.Philipsen	USN	Prowl	OC
4332	11.11.77	LT/JG T.C.Gardner	USN	Prowl	OC
4333	11.11.77	LT/CDR J.Kennedy	USN	Prowl	OC
4334	14.11.77		Iran	F14	OC
4335	14.11.77		Iran	F14	OC
4336	15.11.77	S/L T.Knight	RAF	Jag	OC
4337	15.11.77	FL/LT W.A.Langworthy	RAF	Jag	OC
4338	21.11.77	FL/LT S.W.Gyles	RAF	Phant	OC
4339	21.11.77	FL/LT A.D.Moir	RAF	Phant	OC
4340	27.11.77	G.D.Stanica	Rom	Orao	NK
4341	29.11.77	LT S.Vitaliano	Italy	L.F104	OC
4342	06.12.77	F/O B.P.Crowhurst	AusAF	Mir	OC
4343	07.12.77	LT Turner	USN	Int	NK
4344	07.12.77	LT Burbrink	USN	Int	NK
4345	08.12.77	LT V.Bourdiniere	Fr N	Crus	OC
4346	21.12.77	1/LT S.L.Smith	USMC	Phant	NK
4347	21.12.77	1/LT K.E.Cook	USMC	Phant	NK

No.	Date	Name	Force	Type	Cause
4348	03.01.78	CAPT Botte	Fr N	Crus	NK
4349	04.01.78	P/O S.Ashraf	Pak	SY.F6	OC
4350	06.01.78	CAPT J.A.Fernandez	USAF	Phant	NK
4351	06.01.78	1/LT M.B.Rogers	USAF	Phant	NK
4352	15.01.78	L.Kazoleas	Gree	L.F104	NK
4353	18.01.78	AT-1 J.Hansen	USN	Int	NK
4354	18.01.78	LT/CDR Moore	USN	Int	NK
4355	23.01.78	FL/LT D.Bowring	RAF	J.Pro	NK
4356	23.01.78	FL/LT J.Hughes	RAF	J.Pro	NK
4357	30.01.78	MAJ D.E.Benson	USAF	Phant	NK
4358	30.01.78	1/LT R.L.Barnes	USAF	Phant	NK
4359	01.02.78	1/LT Farsibi	Iran	Phant	NK
4360	01.02.78	CAPT Rezvami	Iran	Phant	NK
4361	02.02.78	CAPT R.E.Braithwaite	USMC	Int	NK
4362	07.02.78	J.A.Humenik	USMC	Phant	NK
4363	07.02.78	T.J.Lyman	USMC	Phant	NK
4364	08.02.78	LT T.E.Dewald	USN	Phant	NK
4365	01.03.78	MAJ J.J.Botha	SA	Bucc	NK
4366	01.03.78	MAJ A.J.Grobelaar	SA	Bucc	NK
4367	03.03.78	O/LT P.Hartmann	GerAF	L.F104	NK
4368	07.03.78	1/LT R.E.Garmeson	USMC	Phant	NK
4369	07.03.78	MAJ P.E.Davis	USMC	Phant	NK
4370	07.03.78	F/O Obaid	Pak	SY.F6	OC
4371	09.03.78	MAJ Filipi	ArgAF	Puc	NK
4372	20.03.78	LT S.B.Edens	USN	F14	NK
4373	20.03.78	LT/JG T.A.Cavanaugh	USN	F14	NK
4374	21.03.78	CDR E.K.Andrews	USN	F14	NK
4375	21.03.78	FL/LT P.A.New	RAF	Jag	NK
4376	25.03.78	LT/JG J.W.Lane	USN	F14	NK
4377	25.03.78	LT/CDR J.N.Punches	USN	F14	NK
4378	27.03.78	LT/JG B.D.Shaw	USN	F14	NK
4379	27.03.78	CAPT L.Wismar	USMC	Phant	NK
4380	27.03.78	1/LT R.K.Tucker	USMC	Phant	NK
4381	28.03.78	1/LT Razavi	Iran	Phant	NK
4382	28.03.78	2/LT Sedaghat	Iran	Phant	NK
4383	06.04.78	HPT A.Ewald	GerAF	L.F104	NK
4384	07.04.78	CAPT H.Yazdanshenass	Iran	F5	NK
4385	10.04.78	LT Saghir	Libya	Mir	NK
4386	10.04.78	LT/COL Khadiki	Libya	Mir	NK
4387	10.04.78		Pak	Mir	NK
4388	13.04.78	CAPT B.W.Cobb	USAF	Phant	NK
4389	13.04.78	CAPT G.P.Rice	USAF	Phant	NK
4390	13.04.78	CAPT D.J.Lacayo	USAF	Phant	OC
4391	14.04.78	2/LT R.Fathi	Iran	F5	NK
4392	14.04.78	CAPT G.H.Yazd	Iran	F5	NK
4393	29.04.78	LT/CDR D.P.Ohnemus	USN	Int	NK
4394	29.04.78	LT/JG R.N.Cassano	USN	Int	NK
4395	05.05.78	CAPT W.W.Moore	USMC	Phant	NK
4396	05.05.78	CAPT M.R.Mohr	USMC	Phant	NK
4397	08.05.78	COM E.S.Apodaca	Spain	Mir	NK
4398	12.05.78	CDR C.C.N.Davies	RN	Phant	NK
4399	18.05.78	1/LT L.S.Utterback	USAF	Phant	NK
4400	18.05.78	CAPT R.L.Gilchrist	USAF	Phant	NK
4401	24.05.78	S/LT A.S.Brooks	RN	Hunt	NK
4402	24.05.78	MR R.Statham	RN	Hunt	NK
4403	25.05.78	MAJ C.H.Nelson	USAF	Phant	NK
4404	25.05.78	S/L A.A.McDicken	RAF	Canb	NK
4405	25.05.78	CAPT K.J.Stromquist	USAF	Phant	NK
4406	30.05.78		Fr AF	Jag	EA
4407	30.05.78	CAPT Villa	Fr AF	Mir	OC
4408	30.05.78	CAPT J.P.Brunet	Fr AF	Mir	OC
4409	30.05.78	LT R.Bouquet	Fr AF	Mir	OC
4410	08.06.78	S/L Farooq	Pak	SY.F6	NK
4411	12.06.78	F/O Naeem	Pak	SY.F6	OC
4412	14.06.78	S/L T.Adcock	RAF	Bucc	OC
4413	14.06.78	FL/LT Hammond	RAF	Bucc	NK
4414	20.06.78	O/LT E.Wutke	GerAF	L.F104	NK
4415	20.06.78	CAPT J.E.Sandstrom	GerAF	L.F104	NK
4416	21.06.78	O/LT Boettcher	GerAF	L.F104	NK
4417	28.06.78	LT L.Merenda	Italy	L.F104	NK
4418	28.06.78		RAF	J.Pro	NK
4419	29.06.78	LT Vimeney	Fr AF	Mir	NK
4420	29.06.78	ASP Duclos	Fr AF	Mir	NK
4421	29.06.78	Classified			
4422	11.07.78	P/O Arshad	Pak	SY.F6	OC
4423	12.07.78	CAPT A.Pauli	Italy	F.G91	NK
4424	20.07.78	CAPT Ilcinkas	Fr AF	Myst	NK
4425	21.07.78	LT Sable	Fr AF	Jag	NK
4426	21.07.78	ADJ Grandclement	Fr AF	Jag	NK
4427	25.07.78	MAJ Robert	Fr AF	Mir	NK
4428	28.07.78	MR K.Fox	Civ	Crus	NK
4429	28.07.78	1/LT P.R.Ramos	Civ	Crus	NK
4430	30.07.78	LT/CDR D.E.Church	USN	Prowl	NK
4431	30.07.78	LT/JG J.W.Knight	USN	Prowl	NK
4432	30.07.78	LT C.R.Sharratt	USN	Prowl	NK
4433	03.08.78	OF/HR R.Sommer	GerAF	F.G91	OC
4434	03.08.78	HPT K.Hoffmann	GerAF	F.G91	OC
4435	09.08.78	CAPT A.Marais	SA	Bucc	NK
4436	17.08.78	LT/JG D.J.Svajda	USN	Phant	NK
4437	17.08.78	LT/JG S.J.Bonanno	USN	Phant	NK
4438	18.08.78	KPT/LT M.Hartmann	Ger N	L.F104	NK
4439	23.08.78	LT J.Canto	Port	F.G91	NK
4440	24.08.78	LT J.Francois	Fr AF	Jag	NK
4441	24.08.78		Japan	Phant	NK
4442	24.08.78		Japan	Phant	NK
4443	25.08.78	O/LT R.Stoll	GerAF	L.F104	NK
4444	25.08.78	LT P.G.Boughton	USN	F14	NK
4445	25.08.78	LT/JG W.E.Hafner	USN	F14	NK
4446	30.08.78	LT Palayret	Fr AF	Myst	NK
4447	05.09.78	LT P.E.Hansen	Den	L.F104	NK
4448	11.09.78	CAPT J.M.Abellan	Fr AF	Mir	NK
4449	13.09.78	LT/CDR M.A.Ostertag	USN	F14	NK
4450	13.09.78	LT T.E.Prendergast	USN	F14	NK
4451	15.09.78	Classified			
4452	15.09.78	Classified			
4453	15.09.78	Classified			
4454	16.09.78	CAPT F.Bressan	Italy	F.G91	NK
4455	19.09.78	LT W.Powelson	USN	Int	NK
4456	19.09.78	ENS V.Henley	USN	Int	NK
4457	19.09.78	O/LT Mollenhauer	GerAF	L.F104	NK
4458	28.09.78	LT/CDR W.L.Waterman	USN	Prowl	NK
4459	05.10.78	LT L.L.Kraker	USN	F14	NK
4460	05.10.78	LT D.N.Bostitch	USN	F14	NK
4461	06.10.78	J.M.Guesdon	Fr AF	Mir	NK
4462	10.10.78	HPT H.Kaiser	GerAF	L.F104	NK
4463	17.10.78	CAPT R.A.Cote	USMC	Phant	NK
4464	17.10.78	CAPT D.J.Dannewitz	USMC	Phant	NK
4465	03.11.78	P/O P.Kumar	IndAF	Hunt	NK
4466	08.11.78	CAPT Amini	Iran	Phant	NK
4467	14.11.78	MAJ Culbert	USAF	Phant	NK
4468	14.11.78	CAPT Cossalter	USAF	Phant	NK
4469	17.11.78	MAJ R.J.Micek	USAF	Phant	NK
4470	20.11.78	LT D.T.Beaver	USN	Phant	NK
4471	20.11.78	LT D.L.Davies	USN	Phant	NK
4472	24.11.78	LT R.Zappa	Italy	L.F104	NK
4473	26.11.78	LT G.J.Farrell	USN	F14	NK
4474	26.11.78	CDR D.E.Cowles	USN	F14	NK
4475	30.11.78	LT G.M.Jack	USN	Phant	NK
4476	30.11.78	LT/JG S.D.Inglis	USN	Phant	NK
4477	01.12.78	CAPT D.Anderegg	USAF	Phant	OC
4478	01.12.78	MAJ M.Nelson	USAF	Phant	OC
4479	01.12.78		Iran	F5	NK
4480	05.12.78	LT J.H.Koelling	USAF	Phant	NK
4481	07.12.78	CAPT N.Stilwell	USAF	Phant	NK
4482	07.12.78	CAPT R.Garhart	USAF	Phant	NK
4483	07.12.78	KK P.Peterson	Ger N	L.F104	NK
4484	07.12.78		Japan	Phant	NK
4485	07.12.78		Japan	Phant	NK
4486	07.12.78	FL/LT G.Morgan	RAF	Canb	NK
4487	07.12.78	FL/LT V.A.Mee	RAF	Canb	NK
4488	08.12.78		Zaire	Mir	NK
4489	08.12.78		Zaire	Mir	NK
4490	08.12.78		Zaire	Mir	NK
4491	16.12.78	F/O Javed	Pak	SY.F6	OC
4492	19.12.78	LT/COL Aluce	Fr AF	Mir	NK

No.	Date	Name	Force	Type	Cause	No.	Date	Name	Force	Type	Cause
4493	31.12.78		ArgAF	Puc	NK	4566	28.06.79		Braz	Mir	OC
4494	01.01.79	Classified				4567	02.07.79	1/LT H.S.Ruth	USAF	Phant	OC
4495	01.01.79	Classified				4568	02.07.79	CAPT G.McConnell	USAF	Phant	OC
4496	01.01.79	Classified				4569	03.07.79	CAPT Checa	RAF	Hunt	OC
4497	13.01.79	CAPT R.Sims	USAF	Phant	NK	4570	06.07.79	FL/LT Nicholson	RAF	Hunt	OC
4498	19.01.79	Huth	Fr AF	Mir	NK	4571	06.07.79	MAJ O.A.Shur	SA	Mir	NK
4499	19.01.79	LT Helies	Fr AF	Mir	NK	4572	06.07.79	1/LT U.Wagner	GerAF	L.F104	OC
4500	25.01.79		USAF	Phant	NK	4573	17.07.79	LT Roux	Fr AF	Jag	NK
4501	25.01.79		USAF	Phant	NK	4574	18.07.79	P/O Shahid	Pak	SY.F6	OC
4502	26.01.79	CAPT S.F.Hammons	USA	Moh	NK	4575	18.07.79	FL/LT G.A.Wardell	RAF	Jag	NK
4503	26.01.79	S/SGT P.H.Pheigh	USA	Moh	NK	4576	19.07.79	CDTAC R.Allan	AusAF	MB326	NK
4504	26.01.79	CAPT S.L.Elder	USA	Moh	NK	4577	26.07.79	MR M.E.Meyer	USMC	Phant	OC
4505	26.01.79	SP4 G.Lara	USA	Moh	NK	4578	26.07.79	LT/COL F.H.Menning	USMC	Phant	OC
4506	27.01.79	MAJ M.P.Larrea	Ecuad	S.Mas	OC	4579	26.07.79	CAPT R.M.Loibl	USMC	Phant	NK
4507	27.01.79	SBTE E.Merizalde	Ecuad	S.Mas	OC	4580	26.07.79	CWO4 R.A.Waltzer	USMC	Phant	NK
4508	31.01.79	LT T.E.Dewald	USN	Phant	NK	4581	07.08.79	CDR E.P.G.Sancho	Spain	Mir	OC
4509	31.01.79	LT/CDR J.E.McNair	USN	Phant	NK	4582	07.08.79	FL/LT G.Lee	AusAF	Mir	OC
4510	31.01.79	LT A.Jassim	Kuw	Mir	NK	4583	09.08.79	CAPT A.R.Poulin	USAF	Phant	OC
4511	01.02.79	LT P.Magro	Italy	L.F104	NK	4584	09.08.79	CAPT J.M.Sciacca	USAF	Phant	OC
4512	01.02.79	HPT F.Achner	GerAF	L.F104	NK	4585	09.08.79	CDR C.Afonso	Port	F.G91	NK
4513	01.02.79	F/O Younas	Pak	SY.F6	NK	4586	14.08.79	CADET A.White	SA	MB326	OC
4514	05.02.79	LT J.W.White	USN	F14	OC	4587	14.08.79	CAPT J.P.Beer	SA	MB326	NK
4515	05.02.79	OLT/Z/S W.R.Grosse-Freese	Ger N	L.F104	NK	4588	17.08.79	1/LT T.J.Newsom	USAF	Phant	NK
4516	07.02.79	F/O K.Reynolds	SA	MB326	OC	4589	17.08.79	CAPT L.J.Alley	USAF	Phant	NK
4517	07.02.79	2/LT S.Cernio	SA	MB326	OC	4590	17.08.79	F/O R.T.Knowles	RAF	Light	NK
4518	12.02.79	LT Y.Cabolet	Belg	Mir	OC	4591	18.08.79	FL/LT Rizvi	Pak	SY.F6	OC
4519	15.02.79	CAPT A.Wasserman	SA	Mir	OC	4592	20.08.79	CAPT Guerin	Fr AF	Mir	NK
4520	26.02.79	FL/LT R.Lea	Oman	Jag	NK	4593	22.08.79	LT J.M.Guesdon	Fr AF	Mir	OC
4521	28.02.79	S/L M.Gleave	RAF	Phant	OC	4594	28.08.79	CAPT R.W.Newman	USAF	Phant	NK
4522	28.02.79	F/O A.Lewery	RAF	Phant	OC	4595	28.08.79	CAPT P.Nakagawa	USAF	Phant	NK
4523	07.03.79	CWO M.M.Wagner	USA	Moh	OC	4596	06.09.79	KPT/LT U.Korst	Ger N	L.F104	OC
4524	07.03.79	CWL M.L.Grant	USA	Moh	OC	4597	06.09.79	KPT/LT H.Resch	Ger N	L.F104	OC
4525	13.03.79	A.Hatzipouflis	Gree	Phant	NK	4598	08.09.79	LT/JG R.Cummings	USN	F14	NK
4526	13.03.79	V.Hiras	Gree	Phant	NK	4599	08.09.79	S/L H.A.Khawaja	Pak	SY.F6	OC
4527	14.03.79	FL/LT I.M.Hunter	RAF	Hunt	OC	4600	08.09.79	LT L.D.Abel	USN	F14	NK
4528	14.03.79	O/LT A.Sindelar	GerAF	L.F104	OC	4601	10.09.79	LT D.W.Williams	USN	F14	NK
4529	14.03.79	CDT Metz	Fr AF	Mir	OC	4602	10.09.79	LT/CDR C.C.Farris	USN	F14	NK
4530	19.03.79	LT/CDR H.J.Bedinger	USN	F14	OC	4603	13.09.79	HPT H.Stadler	GerAF	Phant	NK
4531	19.03.79	LT C.W.Nesby	USN	F14	OC	4604	14.09.79	MAJ T.A.Galayda	USAF	Phant	NK
4532	26.03.79	FL/LT M.Brooks	RAF	Jag	OC	4605	14.09.79	CAPT A.K.Sheppard	USAF	Phant	NK
4533	26.03.79	FL/LT W.Kirkpatrick	RAF	Jag	OC	4606	16.09.79		Braz	MB326	NK
4534	28.03.79	FL/LT J.M.Doggart	RAF	J.Pro	NK	4607	17.09.79		Venez	Mir	NK
4535	28.03.79	P/O C.D.Tingay	RAF	J.Pro	NK	4608	18.09.79	G/CAPT P.Carter	RAF	Light	NK
4536	30.03.79	MAJ Viola	ArgAF	Mir	OC	4609	20.09.79	I.P.Botea	Rom	Orao	NK
4537	30.03.79		ArgAF	Mir	OC	4610	21.09.79	LT/JG J.M.Forster	USN	Phant	NK
4538	04.04.79	LT C.Norlain	Fr AF	Mir	OC	4611	21.09.79	W/C R.B.Duckett	RAF	Harr	OC
4539	10.04.79	TEN I.A.P.Xavier	Braz	MB326	NK	4612	21.09.79	FL/LT C.J.Gowers	RAF	Harr	OC
4540	17.04.79	M.Kowalewski	Ger N	L.F104	OC	4613	21.09.79	LT/CDR C.M.Lawler	USN	Phant	NK
4541	18.04.79	CAPT A.R.Poulin	USAF	Phant	OC	4614	22.09.79	S/L S.C.Batra	IndAF	Marut	NK
4542	21.04.79	Classified				4615	01.10.79	O/LT H.Hoffman	GerAF	L.F104	NK
4543	21.04.79	Classified				4616	01.10.79	O/LT K.Konietzka	GerAF	L.F104	NK
4544	26.04.79	2/LT P.Glineur	Belg	Mir	OC	4617	04.10.79	FL/LT C.C.N.Burwell	RAF	Harr	OC
4545	30.04.79	2/LT F.J.Sevenster	SA	MB326	NK	4618	12.10.79	ENS T.F.Streeter	USN	F14	NK
4546	02.05.79	LT A.Denis	Belg	Mir	OC	4619	12.10.79	1/LT J.P.Parnell	USN	F14	NK
4547	10.05.79	CAPT Webb	USAF	Phant	OC	4620	12.10.79	LT/CDR D.E.Torcy	Fr N	Etend	NK
4548	16.05.79		USAF	Phant	OC	4621	15.10.79	Classified			
4549	16.05.79	2/LT L.Beeck	Belg	Mir	OC	4622	17.10.79	Classified			
4550	16.05.79		USAF	Phant	OC	4623	22.10.79	LT C.S.K.Rodnick	SA	Imp	NK
4551	17.05.79	CAPT J.P.Notte	Belg	Mir	OC	4624	25.10.79	SGT Houben	Fr AF	Mir	NK
4552	17.05.79	2/LT R.Declercq	Belg	Mir	OC	4625	29.10.79	CWO4 E.Serna	USA	Moh	NK
4553	21.05.79	LT/CDR J.C.Trevathan	USN	F14	OC	4626	29.10.79	CAPT D.Bailey	USA	Moh	NK
4554	21.05.79	CDR G.L.Moore	USN	F14	OC	4627	29.10.79		USAF	Phant	NK
4555	25.05.79	F/O P.Coker	RAF	Light	OC	4628	29.10.79		USAF	Phant	NK
4556	01.06.79	LT/JG R.H.Gallacher	USN	Phant	OC	4629	07.11.79	CAPT Lavergne	Fr AF	Mir	NK
4557	01.06.79	1/LT J.J.Hill	USMC	Phant	OC	4630	08.11.79	FL/LT Boyens	RAF	Harr	NK
4558	01.06.79	LT/JG C.B.Campell	USN	Phant	OC	4631	09.11.79	KPT/LT L.Stryi	GerAF	L.F104	NK
4559	06.06.79		SA	Mir	NK	4632	13.11.79	O/LT R.Friedrich	GerAF	L.F104	NK
4560	07.06.79	LT/CDR S.P.Singh	Ind N	Kiran	NK	4633	13.11.79	HPT K.Braun	GerAF	L.F104	NK
4561	07.06.79	LT M.S.Mamik	Ind N	Kiran	NK	4634	15.11.79	CDR Cimati	ArgAF	Dag	NK
4562	11.06.79	G.Gerard	Fr N	Etend	OC	4635	15.11.79	Classified			
4563	12.06.79	FL/LT T.R.Watts	RAF	Harr	OC	4636	19.11.79		Mor	Mir	EA
4564	14.06.79	Classified				4637	03.12.79	S/L Nazar	Pak	SY.F6	NK
4565	14.06.79	CAPT A.Rocchelli	Italy	L.F104	OC	4638	04.12.79		ArgAF	Canb	NK
						4639	10.12.79	L.Ioannis	Gree	Phant	NK

No.	Date	Name	Force	Type	Cause
4640	10.12.79	J.Ganias	Gree	Phant	NK
4641	10.12.79	LT/CDR G.L.Emigh	USN	Phant	NK
4642	10.12.79	FL/LT C.Watson	RAF	Jag	OC
4643	10.12.79	LT/JG J.T.Weber	USN	Phant	NK
4644	16.12.79	LT P.B.Holtzbaur	USN	Prowl	NK
4645	16.12.79	LT/JG R.Handricks	USN	Prowl	NK
4646	16.12.79	LT/JG J.Mackins	USN	Prowl	NK
4647	18.12.79	CAPT R.W.Elflein	USMC	Phant	NK
4648	18.12.79	1/LT D.Harrell	USMC	Phant	NK
4649	02.01.80	LT K.Chiou	Gree	Mir	OC
4650	06.01.80	F/O A.Mazhar	Pak	SY.F6	OC
4651	07.01.80	LT/JG F.I.McClennan	USN	Phant	OC
4652	07.01.80	LT T.R.Brown	USN	Phant	OC
4653	08.01.80	LT/JG D.Butler	USN	Int	OC
4654	08.01.80	LT/JG F.Giblin	USN	Int	OC
4655	14.01.80	LT/JG M.J.Himer	USN	Int	OC
4656	14.01.80	LT B.T.Stuckert	USN	Int	OC
4657	18.01.80	CAPT A.Mazzotti	Italy	L.F104	OC
4658	23.01.80	CAPT L.Burger	SA	Imp	NK
4659	15.02.80	FL/LT G.A.Cashmere	AusAF	MB326	NK
4660	15.02.80	CADET P.J.Craven	AusAF	MB326	NK
4661	15.02.80		Rom		NK
4662	16.02.80	TEN AV G.D.Arboes	Braz	MB326	OC
4663	18.02.80	FL/LT J.Carr	AusAF	Mir	OC
4664	19.02.80		USAF	Phant	NK
4665	19.02.80		USAF	Phant	NK
4666	27.02.80	LT Houari	Mor	Mir	NK
4667	03.03.80	LT/CDR J.Kumpan	USN	F14	NK
4668	03.03.80	LT/JG B.W.Clingan	USN	F14	NK
4669	05.03.80	F/O A.C.Cairncross	RAF	Phant	NK
4670	05.03.80	FL/LT N.B.Randall	RAF	Phant	NK
4671	06.03.80	CADET A.K.Singh	IndAF	Kiran	NK
4672	06.03.80	S/L A.K.Dasgupta	IndAF	Kiran	NK
4673	06.03.80	LT/JG T.W.Trotter	USN	F14	NK
4674	06.03.80	LT/CDR L.E.Stampe	USN	F14	NK
4675	12.03.80	FL/LT P.Barton	RAF	Harr	OC
4676	16.03.80	F/O Z.I.Haider	Pak	SY.F6	OC
4677	21.03.80	TEN AV E.A.Furujawa	Braz	MB326	NK
4678	22.03.80	CAPT C.A.Small	SA	Imp	NK
4679	26.03.80	LT D.Holst	GerAF	Phant	NK
4680	26.03.80	O/LT H.J.Behrens	GerAF	Phant	NK
4681	29.03.80		USAF	Phant	NK
4682	01.04.80	LT/JG W.C.Zobel	USN	F14	NK
4683	01.04.80	LT/JG M.Chabal	USN	F14	NK
4684	04.04.80	O/LT W.Schreiber	GerAF	L.F104	NK
4685	04.04.80	TEN M.Ibarra	Ecuad	S.Mas	NK
4686	05.04.80	LT/JG K.B.Fischer	USN	Phant	NK
4687	05.04.80	LT/JG A.R.Clever	USN	Phant	NK
4688	13.04.80	LT J.G.Carlton	USN	Phant	NK
4689	13.04.80	LT/JG R.Ritorto	USN	Phant	NK
4690	15.04.80	Classified			
4691	15.04.80	Classified			
4692	26.04.80	CAPT M.S.Fagan	USMC	Phant	NK
4693	26.04.80	LT/COL B.B.Sperry	USMC	Phant	NK
4694	03.05.80	P/O G.Butterworth	AusAF	Mir	OC
4695	06.05.80	2/LT E.Christensen	Den	F100	NK
4696	08.05.80	FL/LT C.Massey	RAF	J.Pro	NK
4697	08.05.80	FL/LT P.Jones	RAF	J.Pro	NK
4698	11.05.80	F/O A.Najamul	Pak	SY.F6	OC
4699	14.05.80		Switz	Venom	NK
4700	14.05.80	LT V.P.Cambot	Fr N	Crus	OC
4701	15.05.80		USAF	Phant	OC
4702	15.05.80		USAF	Phant	NK
4703	15.05.80		SA	Imp	NK
4704	17.05.80	S/L S.Johnson	RAF	Hawk	OC
4705	20.05.80	LT/JG D.T.Hanaoka	USN	Prowl	OC
4706	20.05.80	LT/CDR D.A.Larsen	USN	Prowl	OC
4707	20.05.80	LT L.J.Stack	USN	Prowl	OC
4708	27.05.80	FL/LT Robertson	RAF	Hawk	OC
4709	27.05.80	FL/LT Butler	RAF	Hawk	OC
4710	28.05.80	F/O M.C.Longstaff	RAF	Hunt	NK
4711	28.05.80	FL/LT W.Kirkpatrick	RAF	Jag	OC
4712	29.05.80	S/L J.R.McEvoy	RAF	Hunt	OC
4713	29.05.80	S/L B.F.Mahaffey	RAF	Hunt	OC

No.	Date	Name	Force	Type	Cause
4714	31.05.80	S/L P.K.Mokharjee	IndAF	Hunt	OC
4715	02.06.80		USAF	Phant	OC
4716	02.06.80	MR M.Kolly	Peru	Mir	OC
4717	02.06.80	Classified			
4718	02.06.80	EL/TNT L.Viale	Peru	Mir	OC
4719	03.06.80	FL/LT P.R.Watling	RAF	Phant	OC
4720	03.06.80	FL/LT S.L.James	RAF	Phant	OC
4721	10.06.80	LT S.R.Perco	USN	Phant	OC
4722	10.06.80	LT J.L.Schram	USN	Phant	OC
4723	12.06.80	ASP/AV C.F.P.Santos	Braz	MB326	OC
4724	15.06.80	Classified			
4725	15.06.80	Classified			
4726	22.06.80	LT N.G.Thomas	SA	Imp	NK
4727	11.07.80	CAPT G.Barale	Italy	L.F104	OC
4728	16.07.80		USAF	Phant	NK
4729	16.07.80		USAF	Phant	NK
4730	17.07.80	FL/LT J.Wittingham	RAF	Jag	OC
4731	23.07.80		USAF	Phant	NK
4732	23.07.80		USAF	Phant	NK
4733	23.07.80	LT F.C.Cook	USN	Int	NK
4734	23.07.80	LT J.E.Nortz	USN	Int	NK
4735	31.07.80	FL/LT D.R.Chapman	RAF	J.Pro	NK
4736	31.07.80	MAJ J.A.Mitchell	USMC	Phant	NK
4737	31.07.80	1/LT H.D.Vaught	USMC	Phant	NK
4738	12.08.80	LT J.P.Hampton	USN	Phant	NK
4739	12.08.80	LT/JG W.E.Tillerson	USN	Phant	NK
4740	18.08.80	F/O S.Raza	Pak	SY.F6	OC
4741	25.08.80	CAPT S.N.Muhammad	Abu D	Mir	NK
4742	03.09.80	1/LT Bernard	Fr AF	Myst	NK
4743	08.09.80	LT/COL Post	Civ	F18	OC
4744	08.09.80	MR J.E.Krings	Civ	F18	OC
4745	13.09.80	LT/JG S.C.Schlientz	USN	F14	OC
4746	13.09.80	LT/JG C.W.Hallford	USN	F14	OC
4747	17.09.80	MAJ H.Brieger	GerAF	Phant	NK
4748	17.09.80	OF/HR R.Sattler	GerAF	Phant	NK
4749	19.09.80	CAPT Pele	Fr AF	Myst	NK
4750	22.09.80	S/SGT Plancher	Fr AF	Mir	NK
4751	22.09.80	Classified			
4752	22.09.80	Classified			
4753	02.10.80	LT W.E.McCole	USN	Int	NK
4754	02.10.80	LT/JG M.D.Anderson	USN	Int	NK
4755	08.10.80	T.Antonios	Gree	L.T33	NK
4756	10.10.80	CAPT S.Volkersz	SA	Imp	EA
4757	13.10.80	G.Tsakonas	Gree	Phant	NK
4758	13.10.80	K.Papachiliou	Gree	Phant	NK
4759	14.10.80	1/LT S.Tejsner	Den	L.F104	NK
4760	17.10.80	O/LT A.Heuser	GerAF	L.F104	NK
4761	24.10.80	S/SGT Plaste	Fr AF	Mir	NK
4762	28.10.80	FL/LT M.J.Phillips	RAF	Harr	NK
4763	29.10.80		USAF	Phant	OC
4764	29.10.80		USAF	Phant	OC
4765	29.10.80	W/C K.Khanna	IndAF	Ajeet	NK
4766	04.11.80	CAPT L.M.Bennett	SA	Mir	NK
4767	05.11.80	LT/CDR R.T.Knowles	USN	Int	NK
4768	05.11.80	LT J.A.Wieringa	USN	Int	NK
4769	12.11.80	CAPT J.H.McCormick	USAF	Phant	NK
4770	12.11.80	CAPT M.A.Beason	USAF	Phant	NK
4771	13.11.80	CAPT T.Poole	USAF	Phant	NK
4772	14.11.80	LT/CDR C.T.Brannon	USN	F18	OC
4773	20.11.80	Lanzzarini	Braz	Mir	NK
4774	21.11.80		USAF	Phant	OC
4775	21.11.80	L.Black	USAF	Phant	OC
4776	01.12.80	CADET Balut	Fr AF	Mir	OC
4777	01.12.80	LT/CDR M.Blisset	RN	S.Har	OC
4778	04.12.80	HPT G.Ruge	GerAF	L.F104	OC
4779	08.12.80	1/LT C.Johnson	USMC	Phant	OC
4780	08.12.80	CAPT J.Casey	USMC	Phant	OC
4781	09.12.80	FL/LT S.J.Martin	RAF	Phant	OC
4782	09.12.80	FL/LT N.Morgan	RAF	Phant	OC
4783	10.12.80		USAF	Phant	OC
4784	10.12.80		USAF	Phant	OC
4785	17.12.80	LT/COL R.Ayres	USAF	Phant	OC
4786	17.12.80	CAPT J.Jordan	USAF	Phant	OC
4787	29.12.80	FL/LT Gunashekhar	IndAF	Ajeet	OC

No.	Date	Name	Force	Type	Cause	No.	Date	Name	Force	Type	Cause
4788	04.01.81	LT M.W.Posthuma	USN	Prowl	OC	4862	27.06.81	LT D.Pittman	USN	F14	NK
4789	08.01.81	CAPT P.Correia	USAF	Phant	OC	4863	27.06.81	LT/CDR D.McCort	USN	F14	NK
4790	08.01.81	MAJ G.D.Haines	USAF	Phant	OC	4864	03.07.81	LT/COL C.Martina	Italy	MB339	OC
4791	12.01.81	CAPT G.R.Barnett	USAF	Phant	OC	4865	03.07.81	S/M S.Copriglione	Italy	MB339	OC
4792	12.01.81	CAPT E.S.Ford	USAF	Phant	OC	4866	06.07.81	CDR D.A.Wright	USN	Int	NK
4793	12.01.81	CAPT C.F.Toler	USMC	Phant	OC	4867	06.07.81	MR C.Sewell	Civ	F14	NK
4794	12.01.81	F/O Marwat	Pak	SY.F6	OC	4868	06.07.81	MR P.Merana	Civ	F14	NK
4795	15.01.81	MAJ P.Michelis	Gree	F5	OC	4869	06.07.81	HPT T.Reinker	GerAF	L.F104	NK
4796	15.01.81	1/LT T.Alafakis	Gree	F5	OC	4870	06.07.81	LT/CDR G.L.Stubbs	USN	Int	NK
4797	20.01.81	LT/COL M.R.Plummer	USMC	Phant	OC	4871	09.07.81	S/L R.L.Dixon	RAF	Phant	NK
4798	20.01.81	LT/COL J.A.Marshall	USMC	Phant	OC	4872	09.07.81	F/O	RAF	Phant	NK
4799	21.01.81	1/LT K.S.Callicutt	USAF	Phant	OC			M.R.L.Syndercombe			
4800	21.01.81	CAPT A.Bready	USAF	Phant	OC	4873	14.07.81	CAPT C.R.Glaeser	GerAF	L.F104	NK
4801	23.01.81	WO G.Ciccarelli	Italy	MB326	NK	4874	14.07.81	2/LT R.Dietl	GerAF	L.F104	NK
4802	23.01.81	CAPT V.Angeli	Italy	MB326	NK	4875	17.07.81	FL/LT I.P.Kenvyn	RAF	Jag	NK
4803	24.01.81	CAPT P.Flannery	USAF	Phant	OC	4876	21.07.81	CAPT N.R.Koeck	USAF	Phant	NK
4804	24.01.81	MAJ D.M.Carson	USAF	Phant	OC	4877	21.07.81	CAPT C.A.Schmitz	USAF	Phant	NK
4805	26.01.81	FL/LT R.J.Lawley	RAF	Phant	OC	4878	22.07.81	Booth	USAF	Phant	NK
4806	29.01.81	MONS Witt	Civ	Alpha	NK	4879	23.07.81	LT C.H.Leach	USN	Prowl	NK
4807	23.02.81	LT/COL R.T.Swope	USAF	Phant	NK	4880	23.07.81	LT/CDR W.C.Alpeter	USN	Prowl	NK
4808	23.02.81	CAPT J.A.Roy	USAF	Phant	OC	4881	23.07.81	CDR W.D.Joslin	USN	Prowl	NK
4809	01.03.81	FL/LT R.Prest	Oman	Jag	OC	4882	23.07.81	FL/LT J.Wild	RAF	Light	NK
4810	01.03.81	F/O S.Waring	Oman	Jag	OC	4883	24.07.81	S/L Barnett	RAF	Jag	NK
4811	02.03.81	CAPT K.W.Smith	USAF	Phant	OC	4884	25.07.81	LT A.J.Howard	USN	Prowl	NK
4812	02.03.81	CAPT J.F.Sullivan	USAF	Phant	NK	4885	25.07.81	CDR D.B.Sehlin	USN	Prowl	NK
4813	04.03.81	CAPT W.H.Christian	USAF	Phant	OC	4886	25.07.81	LT/CDR R.C.Christian	USN	Prowl	NK
4814	04.03.81	CAPT G.A.Loughran	USAF	Phant	OC	4887	25.07.81	LT T.S.Robinson	USN	Prowl	NK
4815	15.03.81	CADET G.M.Dua	IndAF	Kiran	OC	4888	30.07.81	AP/O G.D.Trezona	RAF	J.Pro	NK
4816	17.03.81	CAPT Jousset	Fr AF	Myst	OC	4889	04.08.81	CAPT W.Daberkow	GerAF	L.F104	NK
4817	17.03.81	MR J.Stewart-Smith	RN	Hunt	OC	4890	10.08.81		Pak	Mir	OC
4818	25.03.81	FL/LT T.Muhajer	Pak	SY.F6	OC	4891	10.08.81	F/SGT Bury	Fr AF	Mir	NK
4819	27.03.81	SGT F.Keller	Switz	Venom	OC	4892	13.08.81	Classified			
4820	03.04.81	W/C D.S.B.Marr	RAF	Hunt	OC	4893	14.08.81	CAPT P.U.Ribbe	Chile	Hunt	NK
4821	07.04.81	CAPT Galan	Spain	Mir	OC	4894	15.08.81	CAPT M.Pena	Hond	Myst	NK
4822	07.04.81	CAPT Compagny	Spain	Mir	OC	4895	17.08.81	O/LT U.Ahrens	GerAF	L.F104	NK
4823	07.04.81	2/LT Reirhan	Libya	Mir	OC	4896	19.08.81	LT S.D.Sanders	USN	Prowl	OC
4824	08.04.81	R.A.Nachmanowiks	Braz	MB326	OC	4897	19.08.81	LT/CDR M.S.Williams	USN	Prowl	OC
4825	14.04.81	S/L D.H.Milne-Smith	RAF	Jag	OC	4898	19.08.81	LT J.H.Mallory	USN	Prowl	OC
4826	15.04.81	CAPT M.R.Dixon	USAF	Phant	NK	4899	21.08.81	HPT E.Blind	GerAF	Phant	NK
4827	15.04.81	CAPT C.G.Sallee	USAF	Phant	NK	4900	24.08.81	FL/LT P.Tabassam	Pak	SY.F6	OC
4828	15.04.81	1/LT D.Viera	USMC	Phant	OC	4901	25.08.81	O/LT H.Schmidt	GerAF	L.F104	NK
4829	16.04.81	FL/LT S.Adhikari	IndAF	Jag	OC	4902	25.08.81	FL/LT M.D.Beech	RAF	Harr	OC
4830	24.04.81	LT R.T.Phillips	USN	F14	OC	4903	26.08.81	O/LT Z.S.Bauer	GerAF	L.F104	OC
4831	24.04.81	LT/CDR R.L.Kimmel	USN	F14	OC	4904	07.09.81	LT W.R.Mnich	USN	F14	NK
4832	30.04.81	CAPT D.R.Ziegler	USAF	Phant	OC	4905	07.09.81	LT C.E.Nangle	USN	F14	NK
4833	30.04.81	CAPT R.L.Neese	USAF	Phant	OC	4906	08.09.81	F/O N.G.F.Alexander	AusAF	Mir	OC
4834	08.05.81	LT Bournique	Fr AF	Myst	OC	4907	14.09.81		Pak	Mir	NK
4835	08.05.81	CPAT D.N.Rwashdeh	Fr AF	Mir	OC	4908	23.09.81	FL/LT Southwold	RAF	Bucc	OC
4836	12.05.81	Gummel	USAF	Phant	OC	4909	23.09.81	FL/LT S.T.Logan	RAF	Bucc	OC
4837	12.05.81	Muldoon	USAF	Phant	OC	4910	25.09.81	LT/CDR D.R.Thomas	USN	Phant	OC
4838	21.05.81	1/LT D.Baumann	Switz	Mir	OC	4911	25.09.81	LT/CDR	USN	Phant	OC
4839	26.05.81	FL/LT J.Mardon	RAF	Harr	OC			C.T.Springfels			
4840	27.05.81	LT T.Gressmman	GerAF	Phant	NK	4912	29.09.81	LT K.C.Ayers	USN	F14	OC
4841	01.06.81	CAPT C.L.Blackman	USAF	Phant	OC	4913	29.09.81	LT R.B.Bell	USN	F14	OC
4842	01.06.81	LT/COL R.E.Venkus	USAF	Phant	OC	4914	01.10.81	FL/LT A.Singh	IndAF	Kiran	NK
4843	01.06.81	CAPT Salomon	Fr AF	Mir	OC	4915	01.10.81	CADET A.Singh	IndAF	Kiran	NK
4844	01.06.81	FL/LT I.P.Kenvyn	RAF	Jag	OC	4916	02.10.81	ASP T.Digbandjoa	Togo	MB326	OC
4845	01.06.81	FL/LT D.Webb	RAF	Jag	OC	4917	07.10.81	WO R.Farraj	Iraq	Myst	OC
4846	01.06.81	FL/LT T.Muhmood	Pak	SY.F6	OC	4918	08.10.81	A.Tsaklis	Gree	L.T33	NK
4847	09.06.81	FL/LT E.J.Whitaker	RAF	Bucc	OC	4919	09.10.81	TEN T.Jativa	Ecuad	S.Mas	OC
4848	09.06.81	LT/JG R.Wright	USN	Crus	OC	4920	09.10.81	LT R.Penaherrera	Ecuad	S.Mas	OC
4849	10.06.81	LT Audoit	Fr AF	Mir	OC	4921	10.10.81	C.Pallis	Gree	L.T33	NK
4850	10.06.81	MAJ Arnoux	Fr AF	Mir	OC	4922	13.10.81		Mor	Mir	EA
4851	13.06.81	MAJ C.W.Holmes	USMC	Phant	OC	4923	14.10.81		Mor	Mir	EA
4852	13.06.81	1/LT F.J.Welsh	USMC	Phant	OC	4924	20.10.81		Col	Mir	OC
4853	15.06.81	LT R.A.Falcao	Port	F.G91	OC	4925	21.10.81	S/L I.G.Aubrey-Rees	RAF	Hunt	OC
4854	16.06.81	LT Volto	Fr AF	Jag	NK	4926	21.10.81	FL/LT D.Oakley	RAF	Hunt	OC
4855	17.06.81	Classified				4927	21.10.81	FL/LT S.B.Prescott	RAF	Jag	OC
4856	17.06.81	Classified				4928	22.10.81	P/O P.B.Smith	RAF	J.Pro	NK
4857	17.06.81	Classified				4929	05.11.81	MAJ B.Newham	SA	Mir	NK
4858	17.06.81	Classified				4930	05.11.81	CMDT S.Venter	SA	Mir	NK
4859	19.06.81	LT G.F.Tritt	USN	Crus	NK	4931	15.11.81		AusAF	Mir	NK
4860	25.06.81	CAPT K.E.Yowell	USAF	Phant	OC	4932	30.11.81	CDT Ali	Kuw	Mir	NK
4861	25.06.81	1/LT D.Williams	USAF	Phant	NK	4933	01.12.81	FL/LT D.K.Wakefield	RAF	Hunt	OC

No.	Date	Name	Force	Type	Cause
4934	01.12.81	FL/LT R.E.Lotinga	RAF	Hunt	NK
4935	03.12.81	LTA C.K.Tan	Sing	S.Mas	OC
4936	08.12.81	LT/JG P.Fisher	USN	F14	NK
4937	08.12.81	LT S.L.Saunders	USN	F14	OC
4938	15.12.81		Iraq	Mir	EA
4939	15.12.81		Iraq	Mir	EA
4940	18.12.81	LT T.W.Tiller	USAF	Phant	NK
4941	19.12.81	CDR W.H.Switzer	USN	F14	NK
4942	19.12.81	LT/JG D.Barenak	USN	F14	NK
4943	30.12.81	LT Perra	Venez	Mir	OC
4944	31.12.81	R.Emeri	Switz	Vamp	NK
4945	07.01.82	FL/LT P.Bennett	RAF	Hawk	OC
4946	20.01.82	LT/CDR T.S.Heath	USN	F18	OC
4947	22.01.82	LT/CDR R.Pinnell	USN	Prowl	OC
4948	22.01.82	LT M.Rickenbacker	USN	Prowl	OC
4949	22.01.82	LT/CDR J.Powell	USN	Prowl	OC
4950	22.01.82	LT T.Wood	USN	Prowl	OC
4951	26.01.82	MR Lindsay	USA	Moh	NK
4952	04.02.82	LT/COL W.D.Carr	USMC	Int	NK
4953	04.02.82	COL K.C.Bateman	USMC	Int	NK
4954	06.02.82	LT T.J.Davis	USN	F14	NK
4955	06.02.82	LT G.Gayax	USN	F14	NK
4956	10.02.82	F/O S.Mohan	IndAF	Marut	NK
4957	11.02.82	Classified			
4958	12.02.82	CAPT J.E.Bull	USMC	Int	NK
4959	12.02.82	1/LT J.J.Spegle	USMC	Int	NK
4960	25.02.82	FL/LT M.S.McGeown	RAF	Canb	OC
4961	25.02.82	FL/LT T.J.B.Tucker	RAF	Canb	OC
4962	26.02.82	CAPT Kundu	Kenya	Hawk	OC
4963	26.02.82	CAPT Ndeti	Kenya	Hawk	OC
4964	28.02.82	O/LT D.Kall	GerAF	L.F104	OC
4965	03.03.82	MAJ R.L.Myer	USAF	Phant	OC
4966	03.03.82	MAJ Ryad	Iraq	Mir	OC
4967	06.03.82	LT Kandalec	USN	F14	OC
4968	06.03.82	LT Spilman	USN	F14	OC
4969	15.03.82	Classified			
4970	15.03.82		Tunis	MB326	OC
4971	15.03.82		Tunis	MB326	OC
4972	15.03.82		Tunis	MB326	OC
4973	16.03.82	P/O F.H.Sikander	Pak	SY.F6	OC
4974	17.03.82	FL/LT R.Sears	RAF	Hunt	OC
4975	17.03.82	MR J.Leng	Civ	Hunt	OC
4976	19.03.82	MAJ W.L.Miller	USAF	Phant	NK
4977	19.03.82	CAPT M.A.Christensen	USAF	Phant	NK
4978	31.03.82	1/LT J.W.Williams	USMC	Phant	OC
4979	31.03.82	1/LT M.J.Flood	USMC	Phant	OC
4980	05.04.82	CAPT R.W.Bundschuh	USAF	Phant	OC
4981	05.04.82	CAPT W.C.Welde	USAF	Phant	OC
4982	07.04.82	P/O Bilal	Pak	SY.F6	NK
4983	14.04.82	S/L George	RAF	Phant	OC
4984	14.04.82	S/L Slocum	RAF	Phant	OC
4985	14.04.82	LT/COL Courteille	Fr AF	Mir	OC
4986	14.04.82	CAPT C.Sirot	Civ	Alpha	NK
4987	21.04.82	HPT P.Heidmann	GerAF	L.F104	OC
4988	22.04.82	P/O A.Yadav	IndAF	Hunt	NK
4989	22.04.82	FL/LT D.M.McIntyre	RAF	J.Pro	OC
4990	22.04.82	CDR A.Prakash	RAF	J.Pro	OC
4991	26.04.82	ASP Wurtz	Fr AF	Jag	OC
4992	01.05.82	1/LT Perona	ArgAF	Mir	EA
4993	05.05.82	S/L S.N.Garg	IndAF	Marut	NK
4994	06.05.82	CAPT R.M.Turner	SA	Imp	OC
4995	13.05.82	FL/LT C.Robinson	RAF	Hunt	OC
4996	13.05.82	1/LT T.R.Trueblood	USN	Prowl	OC
4997	13.05.82	LT C.G.Elcock	USN	Prowl	OC
4998	13.05.82	LT R.C.Perkins	USN	Prowl	OC
4999	14.05.82	CAPT Perret	Fr AF	Mir	OC
5000	14.05.82	CDT Moisset	Fr AF	Mir	OC
5001	15.05.82		Pak	Mir	OC
5002	15.05.82	2/LT J.M.Bell	USAF	Phant	OC
5003	15.05.82	CAPT M.E.Sams	USAF	Phant	OC
5004	17.05.82	LT/CDR D.Poole	RN	S.Har	OC
5005	20.05.82		Braz	Mir	NK
5006	20.05.82		Braz	Mir	NK
5007	20.05.82	P/O Z.Malik	Pak	SY.F6	NK
5008	21.05.82	1/LT Senn	ArgAF	Dag	EA
5009	21.05.82	CAPT Benitez	ArgAF	Puc	EA
5010	21.05.82	MAJ Tomba	ArgAF	Puc	EA
5011	21.05.82	CAPT Donadile	ArgAF	Dag	EA
5012	21.05.82	MAJ Piuma	ArgAF	Dag	EA
5013	21.05.82	FL/LT J.Glover	RAF	Harr	EA
5014	21.05.82	LT Luna	ArgAF	Dag	EA
5015	24.05.82	MAJ Puga	ArgAF	Dag	EA
5016	24.05.82	CAPT Diaz	ArgAF	Dag	EA
5017	25.05.82	FL/LT D.S.Griggs	RAF	Jag	NK
5018	26.05.82	LT/COL Chiaretio	Arg N	MB326	NK
5019	26.05.82	LT/COL Mazorra	Arg N	MB326	NK
5020	27.05.82	S/L R.D.Iveson	RAF	Harr	EA
5021	28.05.82	LT Cruzado	ArgAF	Puc	EA
5022	28.05.82	LT Arganaraz	ArgAF	Puc	EA
5023	29.05.82	LT/CDR G.M.Broadwater	RN	S.Har	OC
5024	30.05.82	S/L J.J.Pook	RAF	Harr	EA
5025	01.06.82	FL/LT Mortimer	RN	S.Har	EA
5026	11.06.82	FL/LT Turner	RAF	Jag	OC
5027	12.06.82	FL/LT A.K.Mathur	IndAF	Marut	OC
5028	13.06.82	CAPT Pastrain	ArgAF	Canb	EA
5029	14.06.82	LT/CDR G.Sottile	USN	F14	OC
5030	14.06.82	LT E.R.Riley	USN	F14	OC
5031	14.06.82	CAPT G.B.Molinaro	Civ	MB339	OC
5032	14.06.82	MR R.Durione	Civ	MB339	NK
5033	16.06.82	CAPT Elizeu	Fr AF	Mir	NK
5034	16.06.82	ASP Vegas	Fr AF	Mir	NK
5035	17.06.82	FL/LT N.Maddox	RAF	Bucc	NK
5036	17.06.82	FL/LT J.Jolly	RAF	Bucc	NK
5037	21.06.82	FL/LT A.Bashir	Pak	SY.F6	OC
5038	22.06.82	LT/JG S.E.Sheely	USN	Phant	OC
5039	22.06.82	LT B.E.Koenig	USN	Phant	OC
5040	06.07.82	CDR J.H.Findley	USN	Phant	OC
5041	07.07.82	O/LT F.Genge	GerAF	L.F104	OC
5042	13.07.82	CAPT W.B.Hankins	USMC	Phant	NK
5043	13.07.82	GOH T.Chuen	Sing	S.Mas	OC
5044	13.07.82	CAPT K.H.Yick	Sing	S.Mas	OC
5045	20.07.82	MR Costain	Civ	F86	OC
5046	28.07.82	FL/LT N.J.Demery	RAF	Hawk	NK
5047	30.07.82	LT/JG C.M.Rowell	USN	Prowl	NK
5048	30.07.82	LT/CDR C.E.Thompson	USN	Prowl	NK
5049	04.08.82	HPT H.Renger	GerAF	L.F104	OC
5050	04.08.82	CADET A.Golani	IndAF	Kiran	NK
5051	05.08.82	G/CAPT P.D.Oulten	RAF	Hunt	OC
5052	05.08.82	FL/LT M.B.Stoner	RAF	Hunt	OC
5053	08.08.82	S/LT T.S.Tomar	Ind N	Kiran	OC
5054	09.08.82	MR T.O.Pimental	Civ	Tuc	NK
5055	09.08.82		Mor	Mir	OC
5056	09.08.82	MR R.K.Moraes	Civ	Tuc	NK
5057	15.08.82		Venez	Mir	OC
5058	18.08.82	1/LT C.A.Dunn	USAF	Phant	OC
5059	18.08.82	CAPT D.J.Bohac	USAF	Phant	OC
5060	18.08.82	LT C.T.Peterson	Den	L.F104	OC
5061	21.08.82	CAPT R.C.White	USAF	Phant	OC
5062	21.08.82	CAPT W.W.Taylor	USAF	Phant	OC
5063	23.08.82		Switz	Hunt	OC
5064	26.08.82	O/LT E.Sudmeyer	GerAF	L.F104	OC
5065	07.09.82		Pak	Mir	NK
5066	09.09.82	LT P.C.McMillan	SA	Imp	OC
5067	09.09.82	CAPT F.J.Sevenster	SA	Imp	NK
5068	13.09.82	FL/LT D.S.Griggs	RAF	Jag	OC
5069	14.09.82	LT A.E.Lippert	USN	Phant	OC
5070	20.09.82	LT D.E.Berry	USN	F14	NK
5071	20.09.82	LT K.L.Norris	USN	F14	NK
5072	20.09.82	FL/LT P.Braithwaite	RAF	Bucc	OC
5073	20.09.82	FL/LT D.R.Major	RAF	Bucc	OC
5074	27.09.82		Mor	Mir	EA
5075	27.09.82	Classified			
5076	28.09.82	CAPT Dias	Spain	Mir	OC
5077	29.09.82	W/C Lovett	RAF	Jag	OC
5078	11.10.82	LT Hamri	Mor	Mir	OC

No.	Date	Name	Force	Type	Cause	No.	Date	Name	Force	Type	Cause
5079	11.10.82	S/L K.Chaudhary	Pak	SY.F6	NK	5153	29.04.83	J.J.Grunberg	Fr AF	Etend	OC
5080	12.10.82	O/LT B.Bode	GerAF	Phant	NK	5154	01.05.83	LT Perona	ArgAF	Mir	NK
5081	12.10.82	HPT A.Turmer	GerAF	Phant	NK	5155	02.05.83	LT/CDR C.Stencil	USN	F18	OC
5082	18.10.82	MAJ Gendreau	Fr AF	Myst	OC	5156	03.05.83		Pak	SY.F6	NK
5083	19.10.82	MR I.Somers	Zaire	MB326	OC	5157	03.05.83	FL/LT S.K.Brown	RAF	Harr	OC
5084	19.10.82		Zaire	MB326	OC	5158	05.05.83		USAF	Phant	OC
5085	20.10.82		Switz	Hunt	NK	5159	05.05.83		USAF	Phant	OC
5086	20.10.82	FL/LT G.J.Rawles	RAF	Hawk	OC	5160	14.05.83	LT/CDR J.G.Stevenson	USN	Phant	OC
5087	20.10.82	MAJ D.Fetzer	GerAF	L.F104	OC	5161	14.05.83	LT M.H.Knighton	USN	Phant	OC
5088	22.10.82	1/LT G.D.Yoder	USMC	Phant	OC	5162	16.05.83	MR R.M.Carter	RN	Hunt	OC
5089	22.10.82	CAPT K.E.Kitchens	USMC	Phant	OC	5163	31.05.83	Classified			
5090	27.10.82	SGT Poirier	Fr AF	Mir	OC	5164	31.05.83	Classified			
5091	01.11.82	Classified				5165	03.06.83	SGT/CH J.M.Girbe	Fr AF	Mir	OC
5092	01.11.82	Classified				5166	04.06.83	FL/LT Humayun	Pak	SY.F6	OC
5093	03.11.82	FKPT H.Muller	Ger N	L.F104	OC	5167	04.06.83	LT/CDR R.Johnson	USN	Phant	OC
5094	05.11.82	CDT Gaudemarie	Fr AF	Mir	OC	5168	08.06.83	1/LT Gresham	USAF	Phant	OC
5095	06.11.82	W/C P.T.Squire	RAF	Harr	OC	5169	08.06.83	1/LT Ambs	USAF	Phant	OC
5096	15.11.82		Libya	Mir	NK	5170	13.06.83		Fr N	Crus	NK
5097	15.11.82		Libya	Mir	NK	5171	13.06.83	P/O Riaz-Ul-Haq	Pak	SY.F6	NK
5098	15.11.82	LT/COL Amberg	Fr AF	Mir	OC	5172	14.06.83	O/LT W.Frank	GerAF	L.F104	OC
5099	07.12.82	O/LT M.Doetzer	GerAF	L.F104	OC	5173	14.06.83	O/LT L.Schonecker	GerAF	L.F104	OC
5100	10.12.82		USAF	Phant	NK	5174	15.06.83	LT S.Hargreaves	RN	S.Har	NK
5101	10.12.82		USAF	Phant	OC	5175	16.06.83	FL/LT B.Robinson	RAF	Jag	OC
5102	10.12.82	LT A.A.Stapa	SA	Imp	OC	5176	16.06.83	FL/LT S.Dalton	RAF	Jag	OC
5103	21.12.82	Classified				5177	17.06.83	CAPT R.G.Leary	USAF	Phant	OC
5104	29.12.82		Chile	Mir	OC	5178	17.06.83	1/LT R.L.Toms	USAF	Phant	OC
5105	29.12.82		Chile	Mir	NK	5179	18.06.83	L/V M.Mezencev	Fr N	Crus	OC
5106	07.01.83	MAJ A.Vincent	USAF	Phant	OC	5180	22.06.83	CAPT N.J.Halvgaard	RAF	Jag	OC
5107	07.01.83	T.S.Hong	USAF	Phant	NK	5181	28.06.83	1/LT J.Wright	USMC	Int	OC
5108	11.01.83	CAPT C.W.Strong	USMC	Phant	OC	5182	11.07.83		USAF	Phant	OC
5109	11.01.83	1/LT T.M.Sweeney	USMC	Phant	OC	5183	11.07.83		USAF	Phant	NK
5110	11.01.83	F/O Abbasi	Pak	SY.F6	NK	5184	18.07.83	O/LT H.Schmidt	GerAF	L.F104	NK
5111	19.01.83	F/O J.L.Cutinha	IndAF	Ajeet	NK	5185	18.07.83	HPT G.Berg	GerAF	L.F104	OC
5112	21.01.83	LT K.Fox	RN	S.Har	OC	5186	26.07.83		USAF	Phant	OC
5113	29.01.83	LT G.S.Maneklala	IndAF	Kiran	OC	5187	26.07.83		USAF	Phant	NK
5114	29.01.83	FL/LT A.G.Patil	IndAF	Kiran	OC	5188	27.07.83	LT G.Ribiere	Fr AF	Jag	OC
5115	01.02.83	CAPT Meilhan	Fr AF	Mir	OC	5189	29.07.83	FL/LT Philips	RAF	Hawk	OC
5116	04.02.83	Classified				5190	29.07.83	FL/LT Monaghan	RAF	Hawk	OC
5117	08.02.83	F/O Javed	Pak	SY.F6	OC	5191	29.07.83	LT Hameed	RAF	Hawk	OC
5118	17.02.83	CAPT F.Troglio	Italy	L.F104	OC	5192	29.07.83	FL/LT Mason	RAF	Hawk	OC
5119	18.02.83	C.Petinaris	Gree	Phant	NK	5193	29.07.83	LT/CDR R.Sheppard	RAF	Hawk	OC
5120	18.02.83	A.Krikonis	Gree	Phant	NK	5194	02.08.83	S/L J.Kindler	AusAF	Mir	OC
5121	23.02.83	FL/LT D.Oakley	RAF	Harr	OC	5195	04.08.83	CW3 G.J.Stein	USA	Moh	OC
5122	27.02.83	F/O K.Singh	IndAF	Hunt	OC	5196	04.08.83	S/SGT G.Hines	USA	Moh	NK
5123	28.02.83	LT/JG L.P.Gmoch	USN	F14	OC	5197	08.08.83	MAJ A.Annibali	Italy	MB339	OC
5124	28.02.83	LT G.B.Holthus	USN	F14	OC	5198	08.08.83	S/LT M.Orlandi	Italy	MB339	OC
5125	03.03.83	Classified				5199	08.08.83	LT/JG R.Dewar	USN	F14	OC
5126	07.03.83	FL/LT B.R.Iddon	RAF	Jag	OC	5200	08.08.83	CDR J.Luthman	USN	F14	OC
5127	07.03.83		Ecuad	Mir	OC	5201	08.08.83	LT N.Takate	Kuw	Mir	NK
5128	08.03.83	I.G.Tanase	Rom	Orao	NK	5202	08.08.83	CAPT K.Omar	Kuw	Mir	NK
5129	17.03.83	LT/JG W.E.Thiel	USN	F14	OC	5203	10.08.83	Classified			
5130	17.03.83	LT W.G.Welch	USN	F14	OC	5204	10.08.83	Classified			
5131	17.03.83	LT/JG C.V.Browne	USN	F14	OC	5205	11.08.83	FL/LT Evans	RAF	Bucc	OC
5132	17.03.83	CDR J.M.Sumnick	USN	F14	OC	5206	12.08.83	Classified			
5133	22.03.83	FL/LT M.A.Leakey	RAF	Harr	OC	5207	12.08.83		Ghana	MB326	NK
5134	30.03.83	FL/LT J.T.O'Halloran	AusAF	Mir	OC	5208	15.08.83		Iraq	Mir	NK
5135	30.03.83	CADET Dharwarkar	IndAF	Kiran	NK	5209	16.08.83	ASP S.Maurin	Fr AF	Jag	NK
5136	30.03.83	F/O A.Tanvir	Pak	SY.F6	OC	5210	17.08.83	ASP Plasse	Fr AF	Alpha	NK
5137	04.04.83	LT/CDR C.J.Tinker	USN	Phant	OC	5211	18.08.83		USAF	Phant	OC
5138	04.04.83	LT J.L.Walsh	USN	Phant	OC	5212	18.08.83	W.Hermandorfer	USAF	Phant	OC
5139	05.04.83		USAF	Phant	OC	5213	22.08.83	Classified			
5140	05.04.83		USAF	Phant	OC	5214	22.08.83	Classified			
5141	05.04.83	Costa	Fr AF	Mir	NK	5215	22.08.83	1/LT J.M.Stevenson	USMC	Prowl	OC
5142	12.04.83	CAPT C.A.Smal	SA	Mir	OC	5216	25.08.83	CAPT G.B.Habbested	USMC	Prowl	OC
5143	19.04.83	F/O J.L.Jackson	RAF	Jag	OC	5217	25.08.83	CAPT D.F.Tomaino	USMC	Prowl	OC
5144	21.04.83	SGT P.P.Inman	RAF	Hawk	NK	5218	25.08.83	CAPT J.J.Cuff	USMC	Prowl	OC
5145	25.04.83	CAPT A.M.Alvarez	Spain	Phant	OC	5219	26.08.83	LT L.G.Traynor	USN	Int	OC
5146	25.04.83	CAPT R.N.Medina	Spain	Phant	OC	5220	26.08.83	LT/CDR	USN	Int	OC
5147	26.04.83	FL/LT G.Preston	RAF	Hawk	OC			F.L.Vandeman			
5148	26.04.83	Classified				5221	30.08.83	LT/CDR G.A.Donato	USN	F14	OC
5149	28.04.83	CAPT G.B.Habbested	USMC	Prowl	NK	5222	30.08.83	LT G.S.Dobson	USN	F14	NK
5150	28.04.83	CAPT J.F.Scheiner	USMC	Prowl	NK	5223	04.09.83	Classified			
5151	28.04.83	MAJ D.H.Jacobs	USN	Moh	OC	5224	04.09.83	LT P.Badin	Fr AF	Alpha	OC
5152	28.04.83	CAPT J.J.Cuff	USMC	Prowl	OC	5225	09.09.83	CAPT Bastida	Spain	C.101	OC

No.	Date	Name	Force	Type	Cause
5226	09.09.83	CAPT Juez	Spain	C.101	OC
5227	09.09.83	TEN P.Manzoni	Italy	L.F104	OC
5228	15.09.83	TEN A.Casamatti	Italy	L.F104	OC
5229	19.09.83	F/O I.J.McLean	RAF	Jag	OC
5230	27.09.83	FL/LT N.Nickles	RAF	Torn	OC
5231	30.09.83	CAPT R.Gutzmer	GerAF	Phant	OC
5232	30.09.83	1/LT D.Gans	GerAF	Phant	OC
5233	07.10.83		Peru	Mir	NK
5234	07.10.83	FL/LT J.S.Dhillon	IndAF	Kiran	NK
5235	10.10.83	CW4 C.Spriegel	USA	Moh	NK
5236	10.10.83	SFC S.Greenleaf	USA	Moh	NK
5237	11.10.83	CDE V.Estela	Spain	Mir	OC
5238	13.10.83	FL/LT P.Sharma	IndAF	Kiran	OC
5239	13.10.83	S/LT N.Singh	IndAF	Kiran	OC
5240	18.10.83	CAPT M.E.Condra	USMC	Int	NK
5241	18.10.83	MAJ R.S.Nasby	USMC	Int	OC
5242	19.10.83	FL/LT A.K.Bugnait	IndAF	Jag	OC
5243	20.10.83	MAJ O'Hara	RN	S.Har	OC
5244	28.10.83	S/L G.Thurston	RAF	Torn	OC
5245	31.10.83	A.Taou	Togo	MB326	OC
5246	10.11.83		Pak	Mir	OC
5247	11.11.83	LT D.P.Jancarski	USN	F14	OC
5248	11.11.83	LT/CDR O.L.Wright III	USN	F14	NK
5249	14.11.83		Pak	SY.F6	OC
5250	15.11.83	Classified			
5251	17.11.83	FL/LT R.Poots	RAF	Bucc	OC
5252	17.11.83	CAPT W.Buckley	USMC	Phant	NK
5253	20.11.83	Classified			
5254	20.11.83	LT T.G.Allen	USN	Phant	NK
5255	20.11.83	LT/CDR R.W.Johnson	USN	Phant	NK
5256	21.11.83	FL/LT L.J.Betts	RAF	J.Pro	OC
5257	21.11.83	FL/LT G.O.Riddett	RAF	J.Pro	OC
5258	21.11.83		USAF	Phant	OC
5259	21.11.83		USAF	Phant	NK
5260	21.11.83	E.V.Laboureur	Fr N	Etend	OC
5261	23.11.83	MR W.Lawton	Civ	P	OC
5262	29.11.83		Pak	Mir	NK
5263	04.12.83	LT R.O.Goodman	USN	Int	EA
5264	06.12.83	CAPT B.Mettmann	GerAF	Phant	OC
5265	06.12.83	MAJ H.Peitzmeier	GerAF	Phant	NK
5266	07.12.83	S/LT Chuet	Fr AF	Mir	NK
5267	12.12.83	CNE Conrad	Fr AF	Mir	NK
5268	22.12.83	T/COL V.Pastore	Italy	L.F104	NK
5269	09.01.84	1/LT P.K.Schmerder	Ger N	Torn	OC
5270	09.01.84	CAPT Hansen-Hagge	Ger N	Torn	OC
5271	11.01.84	LT W.C.Davis	USN	Int	OC
5272	11.01.84	LT/JG M.W.Beach	USN	Int	NK
5273	17.01.84	S/L T.N.Allen	RAF	Jag	OC
5274	18.01.84	LT/JG D.P.Rouse	USN	F14	OC
5275	18.01.84	LT/CDR T.R.Brown	USN	F14	NK
5276	23.01.84	CAPT L.Angelopoulos	Gree	Mir	OC
5277	24.01.84	1/LT Tesmer	GerAF	L.F104	OC
5278	24.01.84	CAPT Zabler	GerAF	L.F104	NK
5279	06.02.84	FL/LT F.P.Smith	RAF	Torn	NK
5280	06.02.84	S/L I.Travers Smith	RAF	Torn	OC
5281	07.02.84	F/O G.T.Bagwell	RAF	Hawk	OC
5282	18.02.84	CAPT D.Kline	USAF	Phant	NK
5283	21.02.84	P/O K.Shankar	IndAF	Kiran	NK
5284	21.02.84	FL/LT R.Stephen	IndAF	Kiran	NK
5285	01.03.84		USAF	Phant	NK
5286	01.03.84		USAF	Phant	OC
5287	05.03.84		Chile	C.101	NK
5288	06.03.84	FL/LT T.J.Nolan	RAF	Phant	NK
5289	06.03.84	FL/LT R.Newton	RAF	Phant	NK
5290	08.03.84		Switz	Hunt	OC
5291	08.03.84		Switz	Hunt	OC
5292	12.03.84	ADJ Bury	Fr AF	Mir	OC
5293	13.03.84	CAPT D.Holdsworth	SA	Mir	NK
5294	13.03.84		Pak	Mir	OC
5295	16.03.84	LT/CDR Watson	RN	S.Har	OC
5296	20.03.84	LT Pernod	Fr AF	Jag	OC
5297	20.03.84	CNE D.E.Saxce	Fr AF	Mir	OC
5298	21.03.84	CADET V.Sivaraman	IndAF	Kiran	OC

No.	Date	Name	Force	Type	Cause
5299	21.03.84	CADET Vishvakarma	IndAF	Kiran	NK
5300	22.03.84		USAF	Phant	OC
5301	22.03.84		USAF	Phant	NK
5302	27.03.84	LT Salhen	Libya	Mir	OC
5303	02.04.84	LT/JG G.G.Sigler	USN	Phant	NK
5304	08.04.84	FL/LT S.Yar	Pak	SY.F6	OC
5305	11.04.84	FL/LT S.Atwal	IndAF	Jag	OC
5306	15.04.84	Classified			
5307	26.04.84	FL/LT J.Barden	AusAF	Mir	OC
5308	26.04.84	S/LT J.P.Conlan	AusAF	Mir	NK
5309	03.05.84	FL/LT T.J.McCormick	AusAF	Mir	OC
5310	08.05.84	CADET Anselm	Sing	S.Mas	OC
5311	08.05.84	LT M.Lim	Sing	S.Mas	OC
5312	08.05.84	LT G.Moraitis	Gree	F5	NK
5313	09.05.84	MR J.M.Saget	Civ	Mir	OC
5314	10.05.84	Classified			
5315	14.05.84	CAPT L.Eyharts	Fr AF	Jag	OC
5316	17.05.84		USAF	Phant	NK
5317	17.05.84		USAF	Phant	NK
5318	23.05.84	1/LT W.E.Harvey	USAF	Phant	OC
5319	23.05.84	CAPT K.B.Harrison	USAF	Phant	NK
5320	24.05.84	FL/LT M.Hale	Oman	Hunt	OC
5321	01.06.84	Grossette	Fr AF	Mir	OC
5322	01.06.84	CAPT M.Quarantelli	Civ	AMX	OC
5323	01.06.84		USAF	Phant	OC
5324	01.06.84		USAF	Phant	NK
5325	01.06.84		USAF	Phant	NK
5326	01.06.84		USAF	Phant	NK
5327	01.06.84	S/L G.Singh	IndAF	Jag	OC
5328	03.06.84	FL/LT N.Gilchrist	RAF	Harr	OC
5329	05.06.84	Classified			
5330	11.06.84	LT Outsios	Gree	Phant	NK
5331	11.06.84	LT Giannaros	Gree	Phant	NK
5332	15.06.84	LT B.Massimo	Italy	L.F104	OC
5333	02.07.84	HERR D.Thomas	GerAF	F.G91	OC
5334	10.07.84	1/LT R.Dietl	GerAF	L.F104	OC
5335	10.07.84	LT D.W.Yip	USN	Prowl	NK
5336	10.07.84	LT/JG E.P.Sullivan	USN	Prowl	NK
5337	10.07.84	LT/CDR K.L.Blanford	USN	Prowl	NK
5338	10.07.84	LT R.Hummel	Ger N	L.F104	OC
5339	12.07.84	LT D.B.Stansbury	USN	Int	OC
5340	12.07.84	LT J.W.O'Donnell	USN	Int	OC
5341	12.07.84	S/L D.M.Jones	RAF	Jag	OC
5342	12.07.84	S/L A.E.Boxall-Hunt	RAF	Torn	OC
5343	12.07.84	FL/LT T.S.Cave	RAF	Torn	OC
5344	13.07.84	CAPT L.Astyk	USMC	Int	OC
5345	13.07.84	1/LT M.A.Shumway	USMC	Int	OC
5346	15.07.84	LT/JG S.D.Bailey	USN	F14	OC
5347	15.07.84	LT P.M.Chalk	USN	F14	OC
5348	16.07.84	CNE O.V.Olivera	Braz	Mir	OC
5349	18.07.84	FL/LT J.Plumb	RAF	Torn	OC
5350	18.07.84	W/C J.B.Grogan	RAF	Torn	OC
5351	19.07.84	K.Iatridis	Gree	Phant	NK
5352	19.07.84	G.Geroulis	Gree	Phant	NK
5353	26.07.84	CNE C.A.Silva	Braz	Mir	OC
5354	01.08.84	CAPT F.J.Klauser	USMC	Phant	OC
5355	01.08.84	1/LT D.L.Godfrey	USMC	Phant	OC
5356	07.08.84	FL/LT P.V.Dishpandi	IndAF	Jag	OC
5357	07.08.84		USAF	Phant	OC
5358	07.08.84		USAF	Phant	OC
5359	08.08.84	LT/CDR F.H.Brown	USN	Phant	NK
5360	08.08.84	1/LT J.Baumgarten	GerAF	L.F104	OC
5361	17.08.84		USAF	Phant	NK
5362	19.08.84	FL/LT P.Humphreys	RAF	Phant	OC
5363	22.08.84	S/L J.Froud	RAF	Jag	OC
5364	24.08.84	S/L J.P.Joshi	IndAF	Hunt	OC
5365	30.08.84	P/O Fazal	Pak	SY.F6	NK
5366	31.08.84	FL/LT P.Lees	RAF	Hawk	OC
5367	04.09.84	LT D.B.Root	USN	F14	OC
5368	04.09.84	LT/CDR J.J.Destafney	USN	F14	NK
5369	08.09.84	CW3 R.R.Stevens	USA	Moh	OC
5370	08.09.84	E6 J.W.Armstrong	USA	Moh	NK
5371	11.09.84	MAJ A.M.Ali	Qatar	Mir	OC
5372	19.09.84	COL Reboul	Kuw	Mir	OC

No.	Date	Name	Force	Type	Cause
5373	05.10.84	MAJ M.Holquist	USAF	Phant	OC
5374	05.10.84	CAPT S.Pitotti	USAF	Phant	NK
5375	11.10.84	Classified			
5376	13.10.84	D.Vasilakopoulos	Gree	F5	NK
5377	19.10.84	CAPT H.J.Zabler	GerAF	L.F104	OC
5378	20.10.84	P/O N.Singh	IndAF	Kiran	NK
5379	20.10.84	Classified			
5380	25.10.84	FL/LT P.Hamilton	RAF	Hawk	OC
5381	25.10.84		USAF	Phant	OC
5382	25.10.84		USAF	Phant	NK
5383	25.10.84	FL/LT T.Roche	RAF	Hawk	OC
5384	26.10.84	LT R.J.Morgan	USN	Prowl	OC
5385	26.10.84	LT G.L.George	USN	Prowl	NK
5386	26.10.84	LT/CDR W.J.Donovan	USN	Prowl	NK
5387	26.10.84	LT/CDR C.E.Elcock	USN	Prowl	NK
5388	26.10.84	FL/LT Shaukat	Pak	SY.F6	NK
5389	29.10.84		Japan	Phant	OC
5390	29.10.84		Japan	Phant	OC
5391	07.11.84		USAF	Phant	OC
5392	07.11.84	FL/LT N.W.Willey	RAF	Hawk	OC
5393	07.11.84	P/O M.G.Ball	RAF	Hawk	OC
5394	07.11.84		USAF	Phant	NK
5395	08.11.84	FL/LT M.D.Hale	RAF	Light	OC
5396	08.11.84	S/L G.Williams	RAF	Torn	OC
5397	08.11.84	FL/LT E.Smith	RAF	Torn	OC
5398	15.11.84	Classified			
5399	15.11.84	Classified			
5400	21.11.84	1/LT R.E.Loomis	USMC	Int	OC
5401	21.11.84	MAJ R.C.Koch	USMC	Int	NK
5402	27.11.84	MAJ A.Jawad	Kuw	Mir	NK
5403	29.11.84	FL/LT I.Wilkes	RAF	Harr	OC
5404	01.12.84	LT S.R.Collier	RN	S.Har	OC
5405	10.12.84	CW3 J.T.Bailey	USA	Moh	OC
5406	10.12.84	E4 J.Zellmar	USA	Moh	NK
5407	11.12.84	CAPT D.A.Jones	USMC	Phant	OC
5408	12.12.84		Iraq	Mir	NK
5409	12.12.84	S/LT R.A.Schwab	RAF	Hawk	OC
5410	12.12.84		Iraq	Mir	NK
5411	13.12.84	LT J.O.Coulson	USN	Prowl	NK
5412	13.12.84	LT/CDR S.B.Westover	USN	Prowl	NK
5413	13.12.84	CDR R.C.Christian	USN	Prowl	OC
5414	13.12.84	LT S.Clinco	USN	Prowl	NK
5415	14.12.84	F/O K.Pirzada	Pak	SY.F6	NK
5416	21.12.84	S/LT A.Thomas	Fr AF	Alpha	OC
5417	07.01.85		Peru	MB339	OC
5418	07.01.85		Peru	MB339	OC
5419	15.01.85	CAPT A.J.Botha	SA	Imp	NK
5420	25.01.85	CAPT Selwan	Iraq	Mir	NK
5421	29.01.85		Pak	Mir	NK
5422	30.01.85		Abu D	Mir	OC
5423	31.01.85	1/LT L.Dannnemann	GerAF	Phant	OC
5424	31.01.85	CAPT A.Scharbach	GerAF	Phant	NK
5425	31.01.85	1/LT U.Zaydowicz	GerAF	Phant	OC
5426	01.02.85	MAJ L.Romano	Italy	MB339	OC
5427	04.02.85	A.G.Calleja	Spain	C.101	NK
5428	04.02.85	CDTE E.L.Menchon	Spain	C.101	NK
5429	07.02.85	CAPT R.D.Silva	Spain	Phant	OC
5430	07.02.85	TE G.L.Marquez	Spain	Phant	NK
5431	08.02.85	O/LT F.Genge	GerAF	L.F104	OC
5432	11.02.85		SA	Mir	OC
5433	18.02.85	F/O K.B.McCann	RAF	Harr	OC
5434	18.02.85	LT S.S.K.Shabouni	Libya	Mir	NK
5435	18.02.85	CAPT R.Gorath	Ger N	L.F104	OC
5436	11.03.85	CDR D.G.Strong	USN	Crus	OC
5437	13.03.85	W/C Chandrashkar	IndAF	Hunt	NK
5438	13.03.85	W/C K.S.Mandla	IndAF	Hunt	NK
5439	16.03.85	A.Ilias	Gree	L.F104	NK
5440	18.03.85	1/LT E.Siegmann	GerAF	Phant	NK
5441	18.03.85	1/LT E.Quintus	GerAF	Phant	OC
5442	19.03.85		Peru	Mir	NK
5443	22.03.85	CAPT M.Bauhuin	USAF	Phant	OC
5444	22.03.85		USAF	Phant	NK
5445	23.03.85	1/LT R.Dresbach	GerAF	L.F104	OC
5446	25.03.85	Classified			
5447	27.03.85	D.A.Othman	Abu D	Mir	NK
5448	31.03.85	LT M.Demuch	USN	F14	OC
5449	31.03.85	LT M.B.Boyd	USN	F14	NK
5450	01.04.85	F/O G.Brough	RAF	Jag	OC
5451	03.04.85	LT Koenig	Fr AF	Mir	NK
5452	03.04.85		ArgAF	Mir	NK
5453	09.04.85		USAF	Phant	OC
5454	15.04.85	Classified			
5455	15.04.85	Classified			
5456	16.04.85	LT Desiles	Fr AF	Mir	OC
5457	16.04.85	LT Accard	Fr AF	Mir	NK
5458	17.04.85	P/O A.Crosby	RAF	Hawk	OC
5459	19.04.85	MAJ Kajihara	ArgAF	Mir	NK
5460	30.04.85	LT/CDR D.H.Jaggers	USN	Phant	OC
5461	30.04.85	LT/CDR A.L.Cook	USN	Phant	NK
5462	08.05.85	CAPT Binas	Gree	Mir	OC
5463	08.05.85	CDT Petter	Belg	Mir	OC
5464	09.05.85	ENS F.Hoff	Fr N	Crus	OC
5465	10.05.85	E6 D.W.Margraitz	USA	Moh	NK
5466	10.05.85	MR P.Tucker	USA	Moh	NK
5467	21.05.85	M.O'Conner	USAF	Phant	NK
5468	21.05.85	J.C.Fitts	USAF	Phant	OC
5469	21.05.85	C.Kidd	USAF	Phant	NK
5470	21.05.85	R.Peloetier	USAF	Phant	OC
5471	22.05.85	CAPT L.Plessis	SA	Mir	NK
5472	28.05.85	LT Abdeffalam	Libya	Mir	OC
5473	28.05.85	LT Najib	Libya	Mir	OC
5474	28.05.85	F/O A.J.Quaife	AusAF	Mir	OC
5475	28.05.85		Braz	Tuc	NK
5476	29.05.85	LT Heurtebise	Fr AF	Mir	NK
5477	04.06.85	LT/COL D.Kenny	Can	F18	OC
5478	05.06.85	2/LT F.A.Nemran	Kuw	Mir	NK
5479	14.06.85	FL/LT M.D.Hayter	RAF	Bucc	OC
5480	25.06.85	CAPT Okeilly	Spain	Mir	OC
5481	03.07.85	J.J.Dewall	Belg	Mir	OC
5482	03.07.85	CAPT E.Lemercinier	Belg	Mir	NK
5483	03.07.85	P/O P.Lindsey	NZ	S.Mas	NK
5484	09.07.85	F/O I.J.Baston	RAF	Jag	OC
5485	15.07.85	CAPT C.J.A.Dahl	Col	Mir	NK
5486	16.07.85	G.Dritsakos	Gree	L.F104	NK
5487	17.07.85	CAPT P.L.Haake	USMC	F18	OC
5488	17.07.85	1/LT M.P.Bishop	USA	Moh	OC
5489	21.07.85		Iraq	Mir	EA
5490	31.07.85	S/L M.Banerjee	IndAF	Ajeet	OC
5491	01.08.85	LT/JG W.J.Cain	USN	Int	OC
5492	01.08.85	LT E.C.Anderson	USN	Int	NK
5493	05.08.85	S/L N.Sadiq	Pak	SY.F6	OC
5494	14.08.85	FL/LT Khizar	Pak	SY.F6	NK
5495	19.08.85	P/O S.C.Collcott	AusAF	MB326	OC
5496	21.08.85	Classified			
5497	21.08.85	Classified			
5498	22.08.85	CAPT C.Kempis	SA	Imp	OC
5499	28.08.85	CAPT Tagba	Togo	Alpha	OC
5500	28.08.85	CAPT Ayeva	Togo	Alpha	NK
5501	03.09.85	Classified			
5502	09.09.85	LT P.A.White	USAF	Phant	NK
5503	17.09.85		Gree	Mir	NK
5504	19.09.85	FL/LT C.Penrice	RAF	Light	OC
5505	26.09.85	FL/LT M.Brown	RAF	Hawk	OC
5506	26.09.85	FL/LT P.Applegarth	RAF	Hawk	OC
5507	26.09.85	FL/LT K.Watson	RAF	Hawk	OC
5508	03.10.85	MAJ A.Kreuzinger-Janik	GerAF	L.F104	OC
5509	07.10.85	F/O Friday	RAF	Jag	OC
5510	07.10.85	P.Dimitros	Gree	Phant	NK
5511	07.10.85		Gree	Phant	NK
5512	15.10.85	F/O C.P.Yadav	IndAF	Ajeet	OC
5513	17.10.85	FL/LT J.S.Walia	IndAF	Jag	OC
5514	06.11.85		USAF	Phant	NK
5515	06.11.85		USAF	Phant	NK
5516	08.11.85	FL/LT S.Shah	IndAF	Ajeet	OC
5517	15.11.85	MR K.Grubbs	Civ	P	NK
5518	03.12.85	ENS E.V.Hays	Fr N	Etend	NK
5519	13.12.85	F/O L.S.Bachher	IndAF	Hunt	OC

No.	Date	Name	Force	Type	Cause
5520	18.12.85	P/O T.Chaudhry	Pak	SY.F6	NK
5521	26.12.85	CAPT T.Spicer	USAF	Phant	NK
5522	26.12.85	CAPT G.Wiggam	USAF	Phant	NK
5523	27.12.85	FL/LT Abid	Pak	SY.F6	NK
5524	31.12.85	FL/LT T.A.F.Mullen	Oman	Jag	OC
5525	01.01.86		Iraq	Mir	NK
5526	03.01.86	CAPT Olivier	Fr AF	Jag	NK
5527	07.01.86	FL/LT I.K.Ferguson	RAF	Phant	OC
5528	07.01.86	FL/LT S.C.Williams	RAF	Phant	OC
5529	10.01.86	LT G.B.Sala	Italy	L.F104	NK
5530	14.01.86	COL G.Walston	USAF	Phant	OC
5531	14.01.86	MAJ B.Beezley	USAF	Phant	OC
5532	03.02.86		Sing	Hunt	NK
5533	11.02.86	CAPT D.M.Moss	USAF	Phant	OC
5534	14.02.86	LT/CDR T.Lorenzo	USN	F14	OC
5535	14.02.86	LT R.J.Sklenka	USN	F14	OC
5536	15.02.86	CAPT G.Waskowsky	USAF	Phant	OC
5537	15.02.86	CAPT H.Ruizramos	USAF	Phant	OC
5538	18.02.86	LT/JG S.R.Young	USN	Int	OC
5539	18.02.86	LT J.T.Casey	USN	Int	OC
5540	21.02.86	S/L Y.R.Rane	IndAF	Ajeet	OC
5541	26.02.86	A/COM T.K.Sen	IndAF	Ajeet	OC
5542	03.03.86	S/UFF T.Fassler	GerAF	L.F104	OC
5543	03.03.86	CAPT W.Wild	GerAF	L.F104	OC
5544	04.03.86	F/O A.Zaheer	Pak	SY.F6	NK
5545	05.03.86	MAJ W.A.Rosenthall	USAF	Phant	OC
5546	05.03.86	MAJ R.Patchett	USAF	Phant	OC
5547	12.03.86	MAJ G.Berg	GerAF	Torn	OC
5548	12.03.86	LT H.Ottl	GerAF	Torn	OC
5549	13.03.86	LT R.V.Mills	USN	F14	OC
5550	13.03.86	LT T.A.Powell	USN	F14	OC
5551	18.03.86	MAJ A.Biagetti	Italy	L.F104	NK
5552	26.03.86	CDR C.F.Zullinger	USN	F14	OC
5553	26.03.86	LT R.Samolovitch	USN	F14	OC
5554	27.03.86	LT M.Etcheberry	Fr AF	Jag	NK
5555	03.04.86	2/LT A.K.F.Maktoum	Dubai	Hawk	NK
5556	07.04.86	LT/JG K.F.Hancock	USN	Prowl	OC
5557	07.04.86	LT/CDR R.H.Millar	USN	Prowl	OC
5558	07.04.86	LT A.J.Wineland	USN	Prowl	OC
5559	08.04.86	CMDT S.Larroque	Fr AF	Alpha	OC
5560	13.04.86	LT H.J.Collins	USN	F14	OC
5561	13.04.86	LT J.C.Sadler	USN	F14	OC
5562	16.04.86	LT/CDR A.B.Sinclair	RN	S.Har	OC
5563	21.05.86	CNE Hendel	Fr AF	Mir	NK
5564	25.05.86	SGT A.Ball	RAF	Vamp	OC
5565	25.05.86	S/L D.Marchant	RAF	Vamp	OC
5566	27.05.86	FL/LT A.C.Bharali	IndAF	Jag	OC
5567	06.06.86	V.Nass	GerAF	Phant	NK
5568	06.06.86	MAJ J.Kupsch	GerAF	Phant	OC
5569	06.06.86	F/O D.Bryson	RAF	J.Pro	OC
5570	06.06.86	S/L R.Lindo	RAF	J.Pro	OC
5571	06.06.86	FL/LT B.Iddon	RAF	J.Pro	OC
5572	09.06.86	1/LT	USAF	Phant	OC
5573	09.06.86	CAPT	USAF	Phant	OC
5574	12.06.86	LT M.Fenner	SA	Imp	OC
5575	12.06.86	CAPT B.Barnard	SA	Imp	OC
5576	12.06.86	MAJ J.E.Garrett	SA	Imp	OC
5577	16.06.86		Japan	Phant	OC
5578	16.06.86	MAJ R.Di Labbio	Italy	L.F104	NK
5579	16.06.86		Japan	Phant	OC
5580	16.06.86		Japan	Phant	OC
5581	16.06.86		Japan	Phant	OC
5582	17.06.86	FL/LT G.A.Humphreys	RAF	Harr	OC
5583	18.06.86	LT B.J.Zerbey	USAF	Phant	NK
5584	18.06.86	LT/JG F.R.Kara	USN	F14	OC
5585	18.06.86	LT M.L.Cunniff	USAF	Phant	OC
5586	20.06.86	LT/CDR W.T.Lebeda	USN	F14	OC
5587	20.06.86	LT/CDR T.F.Nagelin	USN	F14	NK
5588	20.06.86	MAJ J.Branch	USMC	Phant	OC
5589	20.06.86	MAJ J.Sluder	USMC	Phant	OC
5590	20.06.86	MAJ J.Stover	USMC	Phant	OC
5591	20.06.86	MAJ F.Rademacher	USMC	Phant	OC
5592	25.06.86	CAPT A.P.Delferriere	Belg	Mir	OC
5593	27.06.86	LT/JG J.M.Greene	USN	Prowl	OC
5594	27.06.86	LT K.D.Fink	USN	Prowl	NK
5595	27.06.86	LT K.A.Lipscomb	USN	Prowl	NK
5596	27.06.86		Braz	Mir	NK
5597	28.06.86	CAPT V.P.Higgins	USMC	Int	NK
5598	28.06.86	CAPT R.J.Racine	USMC	Int	OC
5599	01.07.86		USAF	Phant	OC
5600	01.07.86	M.Hefferly	USAF	Phant	OC
5601	03.07.86	F/O R.Walters-Morgan	RAF	Phant	NK
5602	03.07.86	FL/LT C.V.J.Heames	RAF	Phant	NK
5603	07.07.86	F/O M.Cable	RAF	Hawk	NK
5604	13.07.86	LT/CDR J.R.Powell	USN	Prowl	OC
5605	13.07.86	LT/JG R.D.Sandlin	USN	Prowl	OC
5606	13.07.86	LT/JG D.J.Shea	USN	Prowl	NK
5607	13.07.86	LT R.E.King	USN	Prowl	NK
5608	14.07.86	Classified			
5609	14.07.86	Classified			
5610	15.07.86	FL/LT R.G.Bees	RAF	Light	OC
5611	25.07.86	SGT G.Lombardo	Italy	F.G91	OC
5612	04.08.86	CAPT A.Corselli	Italy	L.F104	NK
5613	05.08.86	MAJ L.D.Valdes	Venez	Mir	OC
5614	05.08.86	CNE W.C.Soteldo	Venez	Mir	OC
5615	05.08.86	CNE O.P.Escolona	Venez	Mir	OC
5616	10.08.86	FL/LT T.Muqtadar	Pak	SY.F6	NK
5617	13.08.86	LT/JG M.R.Brown	USN	F14	OC
5618	13.08.86	LT/CDR B.W.Clingan	USN	F14	OC
5619	14.08.86	G.M.Stoica	Rom	Swift	NK
5620	15.08.86	Classified			
5621	15.08.86		Iraq	Mir	NK
5622	15.08.86	Classified			
5623	20.08.86	CDT Kerforn	Fr AF	Mir	OC
5624	20.08.86	LT Imbert	Fr AF	Mir	OC
5625	22.08.86	CADET K.Srinivasa Rao	IndAF	Kiran	OC
5626	23.08.86	LT J.J.Ziegler	USN	F14	OC
5627	23.08.86	LT J.A.Firanzi	USN	F14	NK
5628	03.09.86	CDR S.J.Carro	USN	F14	OC
5629	11.09.86	CC V.Johannart	Fr N	Etend	OC
5630	18.09.86		Iraq	Mir	NK
5631	23.09.86	1/LT S.A.Colyer	USMC	Phant	NK
5632	23.09.86	CAPT R.H.Rives	USMC	Phant	NK
5633	24.09.86	LT M.Goncalves	Port	F.G91	OC
5634	24.09.86	CAPT B.De Sousa	Port	F.G91	OC
5635	25.09.86	LT S.Philip	Fr AF	Mir	NK
5636	16.10.86	Classified			
5637	16.10.86	Classified			
5638	18.10.86	LT A.Samdan	Kuw	Mir	NK
5639	20.10.86	T.G.O'Reilly	USAF	Phant	OC
5640	28.10.86	CAPT J.R.Borin	Braz	Tuc	NK
5641	29.10.86	Classified			
5642	03.11.86	FL/LT D.Findlay	RAF	Hawk	OC
5643	12.11.86	F/O T.R.Ellis	AusAF	MB326	OC
5644	18.11.86	LT/COL M.Lynch	USAF	Phant	NK
5645	19.11.86	CAPT	USAF	Phant	OC
5646	19.11.86	LT/COL	USAF	Phant	NK
5647	21.11.86	FL/LT E.Ahmed	Pak	SY.F6	NK
5648	02.12.86	S/L E.J.Wyer	RAF	Torn	NK
5649	02.12.86	FL/LT J.Magowan	RAF	Torn	OC
5650	07.12.86		Dubai	MB326	NK
5651	10.12.86	FL/LT R.P.Lewis	RAF	Torn	OC
5652	10.12.86	FL/LT A.M.Randall	RAF	Torn	OC
5653	15.12.86	CAPT P.M.Merryman	RAF	Hawk	OC
5654	15.12.86	FL/LT O.J.Tholen	RAF	Hawk	OC
5655	16.12.86	LT S.Singh	Ind N	Kiran	OC
5656	03.01.87	LT M.Valen	USN	F14	OC
5657	03.01.87	LT/CDR J.W.Orrison	USN	F14	OC
5658	14.01.87	MAJ L.E.Brandy	USMC	Phant	OC
5659	14.01.87	CAPT J.Ashford	USMC	Phant	OC
5660	14.01.87	1/LT R.S.Pandis	USMC	Int	NK
5661	21.01.87	LT R.Dietrich	USAF	Phant	OC
5662	21.01.87	LT J.Johnson	USAF	Phant	OC
5663	26.01.87	T.Becos	Gree	L.F104	NK
5664	04.02.87		Iraq	Mir	OC
5665	07.02.87	LT/COL P.Sullivan	USMC	F18	OC
5666	11.02.87	MAJ L.Stracciari	Italy	F.G91	NK

No.	Date	Name	Force	Type	Cause	No.	Date	Name	Force	Type	Cause
5667	12.02.87	LT/CDR D.Anderson	USN	F18	OC	5741	20.08.87	CMDT B.Berthaud	Fr AF	Jag	OC
5668	13.02.87	Le Roux	SA	Imp	NK	5742	24.08.87	LT Buffar-Morel	Fr AF	Mir	OC
5669	17.02.87	CAPT Gerrard	Fr AF	Mir	OC	5743	25.08.87	Classified			
5670	27.02.87		Iraq	Mir	NK	5744	29.08.87		Iraq	Mir	EA
5671	28.02.87		Iraq	Mir	NK	5745	07.09.87	F/O J.Hancock	RAF	Phant	OC
5672	06.03.87	CAPT E.Lemercinier	Belg	Mir	OC	5746	07.09.87	S/L T.Riddell	RAF	Phant	OC
5673	11.03.87		Peru	Mir	NK	5747	08.09.87	ENS R.Lekey	USN	F18	OC
5674	12.03.87	MAJ D.Boatright	USAF	Phant	OC	5748	08.09.87	LT A.C.Cuellar	USN	F18	OC
5675	12.03.87	MAJ R.Siegfried	USAF	Phant	OC	5749	15.09.87		Iraq	Mir	NK
5676	16.03.87		Mor	Mir	NK	5750	15.09.87		SA	Mir	EA
5677	16.03.87	FL/LT P.J.Batten	AusAF	Mir	OC	5751	15.09.87	S/L Gil	IndAF	Mir	OC
5678	16.03.87	N.Fifas	Gree	L.F104	NK	5752	20.09.87	LT J.G.Speer	USN	F14	OC
5679	16.03.87		Gree	L.F104	NK	5753	20.09.87	LT M.D.Conn	USN	F14	OC
5680	18.03.87	FL/LT R.B.Lennon	RAF	Light	OC	5754	21.09.87	MAJ Stacey	Can	F18	OC
5681	20.03.87	LT W.Mnich	USN	F14	OC	5755	22.09.87	1/LT R.Spouse	USAF	Phant	NK
5682	20.03.87	CDR J.R.Davis	USN	F14	OC	5756	22.09.87	CAPT M.Ross	USAF	Phant	NK
5683	24.03.87	LT M.Peinemann	GerAF	Phant	OC	5757	23.09.87	LT J.Morrison	USN	Int	OC
5684	24.03.87	CAPT G.Theis	GerAF	Phant	OC	5758	05.10.87	A.Elias	Gree	Phant	NK
5685	26.03.87	P.Kueng	Switz	Hunt	NK	5759	09.10.87	CAPT J.R.Adams	USMC	F18	OC
5686	29.03.87	N.Rigas	Gree	Phant	NK	5760	15.10.87	LT O'Meara	RN	S.Har	OC
5687	29.03.87	P.Nanis	Gree	Phant	NK	5761	20.10.87	CAPT D.A.Friedt	Can	F18	OC
5688	30.03.87	FL/LT J.A.Hill	RAF	Torn	OC	5762	21.10.87	R.Fabre	Fr AF	Mir	NK
5689	30.03.87	FL/LT J.P.Moloney	RAF	Torn	OC	5763	23.10.87	CAPT J.A.Kolp	USMC	Int	OC
5690	03.04.87		AusAF	Mir	NK	5764	23.10.87	R.L.Leggee	USMC	Int	OC
5691	10.04.87	Classified				5765	27.10.87	CAPT H.D.Moser	USMC	Phant	OC
5692	14.04.87	LT C.A.Boyajian	USN	F18	OC	5766	27.10.87	1/LT A.C.Aver	USMC	Phant	OC
5693	14.04.87	LT G.R.Penfield	USN	F18	OC	5767	01.11.87	CADET V.Saxena	IndAF	Kiran	OC
5694	15.04.87	LT M.Quinlan	USN	Prowl	OC	5768	01.11.87	S/L A.J.S.Sandhu	IndAF	Kiran	OC
5695	15.04.87	CDR W.F.Headridge	USN	Prowl	OC	5769	02.11.87	R.W.Gale	USAF		OC
5696	15.04.87	LT R.E.Smith	USN	Prowl	OC	5770	05.11.87	K.Tzitzios	Gree	Phant	NK
5697	23.04.87	CAPT N.Hunerbein	GerAF	Phant	NK	5771	05.11.87	G.Liberis	Gree	Phant	NK
5698	04.05.87	CAPT D.Beseit	Can	F18	NK	5772	10.11.87		Iraq	Mir	NK
5699	04.05.87	CAPT K.Gethards	Can	F18	NK	5773	11.11.87	FL/LT M.R.Sharman	RAF	Harr	OC
5700	12.05.87	ENS A.Hux	USN	Int	OC	5774	16.11.87	1/LT T.A.Drechsler	USMC	F18	OC
5701	12.05.87	LT/JG R.Rabuse	USN	Int	OC	5775	16.11.87	S/L T.Miller	RAF	Hawk	OC
5702	16.05.87	S/L R.U.Haq	Pak	SY.F6	NK	5776	16.11.87	FL/LT M.J.Newbury	RAF	Hawk	OC
5703	25.05.87	D.Thalassis	Gree	L.T33	NK	5777	19.11.87	Craenenbrouck	Belg	Mir	OC
5704	03.06.87	W/C A.V.B.Hawken	RAF	Torn	OC	5778	19.11.87	Boudringhien	Belg	Mir	NK
5705	03.06.87	W/C N.R.Irving	RAF	Torn	OC	5779	25.11.87	S.Lialiaris	Gree	Phant	NK
5706	04.06.87	CAPT S.T.Perkins	USMC	F18	OC	5780	26.11.87	CAPT G.Montironi	Italy	F.G91	OC
5707	10.06.87	LT/COL Bricka	Fr AF	Mir	OC	5781	02.12.87	CAPT Y.Guerrere	Fr AF	Mir	OC
5708	10.06.87	LT Lascoureges	Fr AF	Mir	OC	5782	02.12.87	S/LT M.Leclercq	Fr AF	Mir	OC
5709	12.06.87		ArgAF	Dag	NK	5783	03.12.87	MAJ H.Oelkers	GerAF	Torn	OC
5710	16.06.87	FL/LT H.U.Haq	Pak	SY.F6	NK	5784	03.12.87	CAPT C.Kunert	GerAF	Torn	OC
5711	17.06.87	FL/LT N.J.Campion	RAF	Torn	OC	5785	12.12.87		Venez	Tuc	OC
5712	17.06.87	FL/LT J.S.Head	RAF	Torn	OC	5786	12.12.87		Venez	Tuc	OC
5713	01.07.87	FL/LT D.K.M.Chan	RAF	Light	OC	5787	28.12.87	CAPT J.A.Sinclair	SA	Mir	NK
5714	07.07.87	ASP P.Bourdier	Fr N	Etend	OC	5788	30.12.87	Classified			
5715	08.07.87	L.C.Simon	Fr AF	Mir	OC	5789	14.01.88	LT F.Demonsais	Fr AF	Mir	NK
5716	10.07.87	LT/CDR V.L.Toalson	USN	F18	OC	5790	18.01.88	S/LT Huillier	Fr AF	Mir	NK
5717	15.07.87	LT J.A.Winnefield	USN	F14	OC	5791	18.01.88	STDT Chaisse	Fr AF	Mir	NK
5718	15.07.87	LT J.R.Wood	USN	F14	OC	5792	21.01.88	MAJ G.Chico	Ecuad	Mir	NK
5719	15.07.87	Classified				5793	22.01.88	C.Sturn	Fr AF	Mir	OC
5720	16.07.87	A.Ilias	Gree	L.F104	NK	5794	28.01.88	LT/JG D.T.Morgan	USN	F18	OC
5721	20.07.87	CAPT J.P.Pinaar	SA	Imp	OC	5795	03.02.88	Classified			
5722	21.07.87	FLT R.Radhish	IndAF	Ajeet	OC	5796	14.02.88	CMDT T.J.Schroeder	SA	Imp	NK
5723	26.07.87	LT Y.S.Brot	Fr AF	Alpha	NK	5797	15.02.88		Iraq	Mir	NK
5724	27.07.87	S/L Walker	RAF	Torn	OC	5798	18.02.88	CDR F.Garbani	Fr AF	Alpha	NK
5725	27.07.87	FL/LT Lloyd	RAF	Torn	OC	5799	18.02.88	LT M.Chavand	Fr AF	Alpha	NK
5726	27.07.87	COL G.Marinzi	Italy	MB326	OC	5800	18.02.88	C.D.Finney	USAF	Phant	NK
5727	27.07.87	CAPT U.Donati	Italy	MB326	OC	5801	18.02.88	S.N.Kohler	USAF	Phant	NK
5728	27.07.87	1/LT J.B.Wright	USMC	Int	OC	5802	20.02.88	Classified			
5729	27.07.87	MAJ J.M.Vizzier	USMC	Int	OC	5803	10.03.88	FL/LT R.Crispin	AusAF	MB326	OC
5730	03.08.87	FL/LT D.Hume	AusAF	MB326	OC	5804	25.03.88	LT N.A.Filippone	USN	F14	OC
5731	03.08.87	FL/LT B.Heslin	AusAF	MB326	OC	5805	25.03.88	LT E.P.Lampela	USN	F14	NK
5732	04.08.87	MAJ J.F.Thornell	USMC	Int	OC	5806	30.03.88	F/O T.D.Robinson	RAF	Torn	OC
5733	04.08.87	MAJ E.B.Stewart	USMC	Int	OC	5807	30.03.88	FL/LT S.P.Townsend	RAF	Torn	OC
5734	06.08.87	L.Bosch	SA	Cheet	OC	5808	01.04.88	CAPT J.Bellot	Fr AF	Mir	NK
5735	06.08.87	F.Viljoen	SA	Cheet	OC	5809	04.04.88	CAPT T.Ganiko	USAF	Phant	NK
5736	12.08.87	LT/JG G.A.Scheel	USN	F14	OC	5810	04.04.88	COL T.Grimsley	USAF	Phant	NK
5737	12.08.87	LT M.M.Hodge	USN	F14	OC	5811	05.04.88	S/L F.L.Atkins	AusAF	MB326	NK
5738	17.08.87	LT S.Richardson	USN	F14	OC	5812	05.04.88	A.Richardson	AusAF	MB326	NK
5739	17.08.87	LT M.Manazir	USN	F14	OC	5813	11.04.88		RAF	Light	NK
5740	20.08.87	MR F.Jouslin	Fr AF	Jag	OC	5814	14.04.88	COL S.C.Ferreira	SA	Imp	NK

No.	Date	Name	Force	Type	Cause
5815	16.04.88	CAPT K.Griesel	SA	Imp	NK
5816	27.04.88	W.R.Burks	USAF	Phant	NK
5817	27.04.88	LT/COL R.J.Bath	USAF	Phant	NK
5818	28.04.88	MAJ J.Molina	Peru	Mir	NK
5819	28.04.88	S/L J.R.Blythe-Wood	Somal	Hunt	NK
5820	04.05.88	CNE P.Charaix	Fr AF	Mir	NK
5821	10.05.88	LT/JG N.S.McEachern	USN	F18	OC
5822	12.05.88	F.G.E.Amian	Spain	Mir	NK
5823	12.05.88	J.T.Albert	Spain	Mir	NK
5824	13.05.88	R.F.Passfield	RAF	Hawk	OC
5825	13.05.88	A.Threadgould	RAF	Hawk	OC
5826	18.05.88		Peru	Mir	NK
5827	18.05.88	MAJ J.Avila	Peru	Mir	NK
5828	25.05.88	LT C.C.Wen	Sing	Hunt	NK
5829	01.06.88	CNE J.P.Castel	Fr AF	Mir	NK
5830	07.06.88	LT J.M.Clament	Fr AF	Mir	OC
5831	10.06.88	CAPT V.Schoenwinkle	Belg	Mir	NK
5832	14.06.88	LT/CDR Braithwaite	RN	Hunt	NK
5833	16.06.88	CAPT H.Borges	Port	F.G91	NK
5834	24.06.88	S/L P.J.Collins	RAF	Hawk	OC
5835	27.06.88	LT R.Sharma	Ind N	S.Har	OC
5836	27.06.88	CDR S.K.Damle	Ind N	S.Har	OC
5837	05.07.88	1/LT G.Borowiak	GerAF	Phant	NK
5838	05.07.88	CAPT J.Vergin	GerAF	Phant	NK
5839	02.08.88	FL/LT D.Johnson	RAF	Phant	NK
5840	02.08.88	N.S.Hacke	RAF	Phant	NK
5841	02.08.88	P.D.Ford	USMC	F18	OC
5842	12.08.88	C.Speziali	Italy	MB339	NK
5843	17.08.88	Classified			
5844	17.08.88	Classified			
5845	18.08.88	FL/LT P.W.Leach	RAF	Harr	OC
5846	25.08.88	F/O A.A.Al-Baluchi	Oman	Hunt	OC
5847	25.08.88	STDT Tazerny	Mor	Mir	OC
5848	28.08.88	S/L Abid	Pak	SY.F6	NK
5849	07.09.88	1/LT J.O.Black	RAF	Jag	OC
5850	08.09.88	LT/CDR M.A.Bruder	USN	F14	OC
5851	08.09.88	LT J.A.Abrams	USN	F14	OC
5852	10.09.88	CAPT D.Aloisi	Italy	L.F104	NK
5853	12.09.88	LT/CDR J.Barnett	USN	F14	OC
5854	14.09.88	FL/LT Arshad	Pak	SY.F6	NK
5855	15.09.88	LT/COL Gianelli	ArgAF	MB326	NK
5856	15.09.88	LT/COL Rodamo	ArgAF	MB326	NK
5857	18.09.88	M.Seegmuller	Somal	Hunt	OC
5858	18.09.88	Classified			
5859	22.09.88	LT C.P.Liptak	USN	F14	OC
5860	22.09.88	LT/CDR J.H.Russell	USN	F14	OC
5861	26.09.88	FL/LT V.Satyamurthy	IndAF	Kiran	NK
5862	26.09.88	LT M.S.Helwig	USN	F14	NK
5863	26.09.88	LT/CDR R.C.Sweeney	USN	F14	NK
5864	29.09.88	J.Parliaris	Gree	Mir	OC
5865	07.10.88	MR S.Ishmael	Civ	F18	OC
5866	16.10.88	LT Afif	Jord	Mir	OC
5867	18.10.88	LT F.L.T.Lines	RAF	Phant	OC
5868	18.10.88	FL/LT Fryer	RAF	Phant	OC
5869	05.11.88	CAPT M.Bates	SA	Imp	NK
5870	07.11.88	CAPT I.A.Ortiz	Spain	F18	OC
5871	09.11.88	CAPT Genty	Fr AF	Mir	OC
5872	10.11.88	CAPT J.K.Chepkwony	Kenya	Hawk	NK
5873	10.11.88	CAPT T.N.Giati	Kenya	Hawk	NK
5874	14.11.88	CMDT R.Masson	SA	Imp	OC
5875	15.11.88	FL/LT G.R.S.Reddy	IndAF	Hunt	NK
5876	07.12.88	Classified			
5877	07.12.88	Classified			
5878	16.12.88	LT P.Tikkanen	Finl	Hawk	OC
5879	16.12.88	LT J.F.Campbell	USN	F14	OC
5880	16.12.88	LT/JG M.Jakonen	Finl	Hawk	OC
5881	16.12.88	LT/JG D.A.Guerrieri	USN	F14	OC
5882	03.01.89	M.Markstaller	USAF	Phant	NK
5883	09.01.89	FL/LT Moulds	RAF	Phant	NK
5884	10.01.89	F/O Rashid	Pak	SY.F6	NK
5885	10.01.89	F/O A.S.Khan	Pak	SY.F6	NK
5886	12.01.89	S/L Sikander	Pak	SY.F6	NK
5887	27.01.89	LT W.J.Van Der Merwe	SA	Imp	NK
5888	06.02.89	M.K.Shing	Sing	S211	OC
5889	06.02.89	CPT B.Y.S.Meng	Sing	S211	OC
5890	10.02.89		USAF	Phant	OC
5891	27.02.89	HANNU Toumela	Finl	Hawk	OC
5892	27.02.89	Laitinen	Finl	Hawk	OC
5893	28.02.89	STDT C.Aube	Fr AF	Mir	NK
5894	08.03.89	F/O W.K.Owen	RAF	J.Pro	OC
5895	08.03.89		Pak	Mir	OC
5896	13.03.89		ArgAF	Mir	NK
5897	14.03.89	LT G.W.Fouche	SA	Imp	NK
5898	15.04.89	1/LT Hamdan	Abu D	Hawk	NK
5899	15.04.89	CAPT A.L.Sumati	Abu D	Hawk	NK
5900	18.04.89	LT/JG T.M.Cooper	USN	F14	OC
5901	18.04.89	LT C.C.Cinnamon	USN	F14	OC
5902	19.04.89	FL/LT V.Satyamurthy	IndAF	Kiran	NK
5903	19.04.89	F/O Haroon	Pak	SY.F6	NK
5904	20.04.89	SBTE H.D.Jorge	Ecuad	S.Mas	OC
5905	20.04.89	SBTE W.E.H.Zurita	Ecuad	S.Mas	OC
5906	20.04.89	TEN C.H.E.Torres	Ecuad	S.Mas	OC
5907	20.04.89	TEN Y.R.M.Fernando	Ecuad	S.Mas	OC
5908	24.04.89	S/L C.J.Bagnell	RAF	Phant	OC
5909	24.04.89	FL/LT R.A.H.Watson	RAF	Phant	OC
5910	26.04.89	1/LT R.Karlstedt	GerAF	L.F104	OC
5911	26.04.89	Classified			
5912	26.04.89	CAPT M.Reinhold	GerAF	L.F104	OC
5913	26.04.89	Classified			
5914	02.05.89	CAPT W.H.Van Zyl	SA	Imp	NK
5915	02.05.89	CAPT K.A.Fryer	SA	Imp	NK
5916	08.05.89	LT K.T.Houck	USN	F18	OC
5917	09.05.89	CDR J.B.Godwin	USN	F18	NK
5918	12.05.89	S.P.Aland	USAF	Phant	NK
5919	23.05.89	Classified			
5920	23.05.89	Classified			
5921	25.05.89	G.Zafiriou	Gree	L.F104	NK
5922	05.06.89	Classified			
5923	05.06.89	Classified			
5924	08.06.89	G.Konstadopoulos	Gree	L.F104	NK
5925	12.06.89	MAJ R.E.Schmidle	USMC	F18	OC
5926	13.06.89	CPT R.T.Fernandez	Spain	Mir	OC
5927	13.06.89	LT/COL A.Delgado	Spain	Mir	OC
5928	14.06.89	LT M.H.Seymour	RAF	Hawk	OC
5929	17.06.89	CMDT Rojaf	Chile	Mir	NK
5930	20.06.89	CAPT Price	RAF	Harr	OC
5931	20.06.89	S/TEN M.Piccoli	Italy	Torn	OC
5932	20.06.89	TEN G.Di Zenzo	Italy	Torn	OC
5933	22.06.89	LT/CDR D.C.Conrad	USN	F18	OC
5934	22.06.89		Iraq	Mir	NK
5935	28.06.89	CNE Perrin	Fr AF	Mir	NK
5936	04.07.89	FL/LT N.Burn	RAF	Torn	OC
5937	04.07.89	FL/LT B.Hodgson	RAF	Torn	OC
5938	05.07.89	LT Gomez	Spain	Mir	NK
5939	05.07.89	CMDT A.Celleni	Spain	Mir	NK
5940	06.07.89	S/L G.Yapp	RAF	Phant	NK
5941	06.07.89	LT/CDR D.Worden	USAF	Phant	OC
5942	06.07.89	MAJ W.C.Gallegos	USAF	Phant	OC
5943	08.07.89	F/O Shafqat	Pak	SY.F6	NK
5944	20.07.89	S/L Hartley	RAF	Torn	OC
5945	20.07.89	FL/LT Ewer	RAF	Torn	OC
5946	21.07.89	FL/LT D.S.Sully	RAF	Torn	NK
5947	24.07.89	LT/CDR C.L.Mitchell	USN	Prowl	OC
5948	24.07.89	LT S.I.Molter	USN	F14	OC
5949	24.07.89	LT D.E.Crisp	USN	F14	OC
5950	27.07.89	1/LT D.J.Weinberg	USAF	Phant	OC
5951	27.07.89	T.Canter	USAF	Phant	OC
5952	03.08.89	FL/LT P.Szypula	AusAF	MB326	NK
5953	03.08.89	FL/LT S.Jackson	AusAF	MB326	NK
5954	03.08.89	LT T.I.McCormick	USN	F14	OC
5955	03.08.89	LT C.A.Cox	USN	F14	OC
5956	04.08.89		Iraq	Mir	NK
5957	16.08.89	S/LT Greven	Fr AF	Mir	NK
5958	27.08.89	Classified			
5959	27.08.89	Classified			
5960	31.08.89	CAPT E.P.Delange	SA	Imp	NK
5961	11.09.89	V.Balcoucas	Gree	L.F104	NK

No.	Date	Name	Force	Type	Cause	No.	Date	Name	Force	Type	Cause
5962	14.09.89	W/C Wright	RAF	Torn	OC	6034	17.05.90	LT S.B.Bongart	USN	F14	OC
5963	14.09.89	S/L Lawton	RAF	Torn	OC	6035	17.05.90	COL F.Visconti	Venez	Mir	NK
5964	23.09.89	S.Brancaccio	Italy	MB326	NK	6036	17.05.90	LT P.Hirson	Fr AF	Mir	OC
5965	02.10.89	MAJ G.Serhal	Leb	Hunt	OC	6037	17.05.90	LT D.Blenard	Fr AF	Mir	OC
5966	02.10.89	LT C.R.Bartolett	USN	F18	OC	6038	17.05.90	ASP L.Artuso	Fr AF	Mir	OC
5967	04.10.89	LT P.Simmonds-Short	RN	S.Har	OC	6039	17.05.90	LT S.A.Winfrey	USN	F14	OC
5968	05.10.89	S/L Imran	Pak	SY.F6	NK	6040	28.05.90	S/TEN D.Mirabelli	Italy	MB326	NK
5969	06.10.89	LT R.C.Walker	USN	F14	OC	6041	05.06.90	LT/CDR M.T.Francis	USN	F14	OC
5970	06.10.89	LT R.S.Schrader	USN	F14	OC	6042	05.06.90	LT/CDR R.C.Dale	USN	F14	OC
5971	23.10.89	LT Richardson	Fr AF	Jag	NK	6043	14.06.90	CPT B.E.Alaoui	Mor	Mir	OC
5972	07.11.89	CDR H.D.Starling	USN	Int	OC	6044	22.06.90	CAPT J.M.G.Labajo	Spain	C.101	OC
5973	07.11.89	LT C.S.Eagle	USN	Int	OC	6045	22.06.90	2/LT E.L.Gonzalez	Spain	C.101	OC
5974	14.11.89	LT D.J.Williams	USN	F14	OC	6046	27.06.90	F/O G.Jackson	RAF	Canb	NK
5975	14.11.89	LT/JG J.T.Burns	USN	F14	OC	6047	11.07.90	Classified			
5976	16.11.89	LT/CDR M.Aringhoff	Ger N	Torn	OC	6048	26.07.90		USAF	Phant	OC
5977	16.11.89	1/LT H.Kraft	Ger N	Torn	OC	6049	26.07.90	W.Lujan	USAF	Phant	OC
5978	23.11.89	S/TEN M.Dasta	Italy	F.G91	NK	6050	26.07.90	CAPT Guagneux	Fr AF	Mir	OC
5979	01.12.89	LT M.F.Auckland	RN	S.Har	OC	6051	01.08.90		IndAF	Jag	OC
5980	04.12.89	LT/CDR	USN	Int	OC	6052	01.08.90		IndAF	Jag	OC
		P.M.Culbertson				6053	03.08.90	CMDT J.M.Dall'Aglio	Fr AF	Mir	OC
5981	04.12.89	LT E.T.Hobbs	USN	Int	OC	6054	14.08.90	W/C Buckler	RAF	Torn	OC
5982	05.12.89	M.Ritola	Finl	Hawk	NK	6055	14.08.90	LT J.J.O'Doherty	USN	F18	OC
5983	11.12.89		Arg N	Etend	OC	6056	14.08.90	CDR J.P.Merrill	USN	F18	OC
5984	12.12.89	2/LT B.G.Chalebgwa	Bots	S.Mas	OC	6057	15.08.90	LT W.C.Davis	USN	Int	OC
5985	12.12.89	MAJ C.Lempaletse	Bots	S.Mas	OC	6058	03.09.90	CMDT P.Lahens	Fr AF	Mir	NK
5986	12.12.89	CPT D.Pujol	Fr AF	Mir	OC	6059	04.09.90	CAPT S.G.Abdulla	Dubai	Hawk	OC
5987	12.12.89	CPT Hartel	Fr AF	Mir	OC	6060	04.09.90	LT H.O.Al-Mansoori	Dubai	Hawk	OC
5988	20.12.89	W.S.Cameron	USAF	Phant	OC	6061	05.09.90	Classified			
5989	20.12.89	G.E.Barrentine	USAF	Phant	OC	6062	05.10.90	STDT P.Pomagalski	Fr AF	Mir	OC
5990	04.01.90	CAPT R.Galvan	ArgAF	Puc	OC	6063	10.10.90	LT P.Clary	Fr N	Etend	OC
5991	09.01.90	FL/LT I.J.McLean	RAF	Torn	OC	6064	15.10.90		Spain	Mir	OC
5992	09.01.90	FL/LT N.Johnston	RAF	Torn	OC	6065	17.10.90	S/L A.D.Stevenson	RAF	Harr	OC
5993	16.01.90	S/L C.P.Roberts	Oman	Hunt	OC	6066	18.10.90	S/L Anderson	RAF	Torn	OC
5994	16.01.90	W/C A.W.Al-Baluchi	Oman	Hunt	OC	6067	18.10.90	S/L Walker	RAF	Torn	OC
5995	22.01.90	LT/CDR J.L.Wilson	USN	Int	NK	6068	20.10.90	CMDT R.P.Keet	SA	Cheet	OC
5996	22.01.90	LT/CDR F.R.Cordell	USN	Int	OC	6069	27.10.90	MAJ C.Willen	Venez	Mir	OC
5997	23.01.90	CAPT C.Moseley	USMC	F18	OC	6070	06.11.90	LT/CDR D.Brown	USN	Int	OC
5998	24.01.90		USAF	Phant	NK	6071	06.11.90	LT J.Hoyt	USN	Int	OC
5999	24.01.90		USAF	Phant	NK	6072	07.11.90	M.Adinolfi	Italy	AMX	NK
6000	06.02.90	F/O Aziz	Pak	SY.F6	NK	6073	07.11.90	LT W.Hallburg	USN	Int	OC
6001	14.02.90	CAPT M.R.K.Edwards	SA	Mir	OC	6074	07.11.90	LT B.Vail	USN	Int	OC
6002	15.02.90	CDR D.R.Miller	USN	F18	OC	6075	15.11.90		AusAF	MB326	OC
6003	15.02.90	Tanvir	Pak	SY.F6	OC	6076	06.12.90	B.Viviani	Italy	MB326	OC
6004	23.02.90	FL/LT	USMC	F18	OC	6077	17.12.90	LT J.M.Qualls	USN	F14	OC
6005	27.02.90	CAPT J.J.Rooney	USMC	Phant	OC	6078	17.12.90	LT M.J.Mealy	USN	F14	OC
6006	27.02.90	LT/COL S.C.Erickson	USMC	Phant	OC	6079	30.12.90	LT T.Brumfield	USN	Prowl	OC
6007	06.03.90	CPL U.C.Peyer	Switz	Vamp	OC	6080	30.12.90	LT J.Meier	USN	Prowl	OC
6008	13.03.90	R.E.Tucker	USAF	Phant	OC	6081	30.12.90	LT S.Schwing	USN	Prowl	OC
6009	15.03.90	J.M.Romero	ArgAF	Mir	OC	6082	30.12.90	LT/JG S.Dyce	USN	Prowl	OC
6010	19.03.90	MAJ G.Mills	USAF	Phant	OC	6083	31.12.90		Rom	Orao	NK
6011	19.03.90		USAF	Phant	OC	6084	31.12.90		Rom	Orao	NK
6012	29.03.90		Iraq	Mir	NK	6085	31.12.90	Classified			
6013	29.03.90		Iraq	Mir	NK	6086	31.12.90		Rom	Orao	NK
6014	31.03.90	FL/LT M.Panging	IndAF	Hunt	OC	6087	08.01.91	FL/LT G.J.Williams	RAF	Phant	OC
6015	31.03.90	LT/CDR Henderson	USN	F18	OC	6088	08.01.91	F/O G.A.Winwright	RAF	Phant	OC
6016	10.04.90	MR R.Lea	RN	Hunt	OC	6089	17.01.91	FL/LT A.Nichol	RAF	Torn	EA
6017	11.04.90	CAPT D.Eguiguren	Ecuad	Mir	OC	6090	17.01.91	FL/LT J.Peters	RAF	Torn	EA
		Burneo				6091	18.01.91	CAPT Burke	USAF	Phant	NK
6018	17.04.90	CAPT R.Decoste	Can	F18	OC	6092	18.01.91	J.Galindez	USAF	Phant	NK
6019	23.04.90		USAF	Phant	OC	6093	18.01.91	F/CAPT M.Cocciolone	Italy	Torn	EA
6020	30.04.90	FL/LT Simpson	RAF	Torn	OC	6094	18.01.91	MAJ G.Bellini	Italy	Torn	EA
6021	30.04.90	FL/LT S.D.Lungley	RAF	Phant	OC	6095	18.01.91	LT R.Wetzel	USN	Int	NK
6022	30.04.90	FL/LT Barnfield	RAF	Torn	OC	6096	18.01.91	LT J.N.Zaun	USN	Int	EA
6023	01.05.90	ENS V C.Jacob	Fr N	Etend	OC	6097	19.01.91	FL/LT R.Stewart	RAF	Torn	EA
6024	03.05.90	LT H.L'Her	Fr AF	Mir	NK	6098	19.01.91	FL/LT D.Waddington	RAF	Torn	EA
6025	06.05.90	LT DVS P.Jego	Fr N	Crus	NK	6099	20.01.91	S/L P.Batson	RAF	Torn	OC
6026	09.05.90	1/LT J.A.Barber	USMC	Phant	OC	6100	20.01.91	W/C M.Heath	RAF	Torn	OC
6027	09.05.90	LT W.A.Latif	RAF	Hawk	OC	6101	21.01.91	LT L.Slade	USN	F14	NK
6028	09.05.90	CAPT T.P.Hewitt	USMC	Phant	OC	6102	21.01.91	LT D.Jones	USN	F14	NK
6029	15.05.90	CAPT J.A.Moore	USAF	Phant	OC	6103	24.01.91	F/O S.Burgess	RAF	Torn	NK
6030	15.05.90	CAPT D.Scott	USAF	Phant	OC	6104	24.01.91	S/L R.Ankerson	RAF	Torn	NK
6031	17.05.90	LT Blanco	Venez	Mir	NK	6105	24.01.91	LT H.E.Overs	USN	F18	OC
6032	17.05.90	CR/CH R.L.Hatten	USAF	Phant	OC	6106	29.01.91	CAPT C.Kopp	USAF	Phant	OC
6033	17.05.90		USAF	Phant	OC	6107	29.01.91	R.B.Ricarte	USAF	Phant	OC

No.	Date	Name	Force	Type	Cause
6108	04.02.91	STDT Ducas	Fr AF	Jag	NK
6109	11.02.91	LT/CDR S.V.Parsons	USN	Int	OC
6110	11.02.91	LT L.L.Heid	USN	Int	OC
6111	13.02.91	LT/COL A.Tzanavaras	Gree	Mir	OC
6112	13.02.91	CAPT P.Louis	Fr AF	Alpha	OC
6113	15.02.91	FL/LT R.Clark	RAF	Torn	EA
6114	15.02.91	LT/CDR J.Williams	USN	Int	NK
6115	15.02.91	LT T.L.Fox	USN	Int	OC
6116	28.02.91	CAPT A.Barandi	USA	Moh	OC
6117	28.02.91	Classified			
6118	28.02.91	SPC Littleton	USA	Moh	OC
6119	28.02.91	Classified			
6120	08.03.91	CAPT	USMC	F18	OC
6121	08.03.91	MAJ	USMC	F18	NK
6122	14.03.91	S/LT Moutoussamy	Fr AF	Jag	NK
6123	20.03.91	CAPT D.S.Domoso	Chile	Hunt	OC
6124	30.03.91	CAPT J.R.Kregel	USAF	Phant	OC
6125	30.03.91	CAPT J.Norman	USAF	Phant	OC
6126	23.04.91	Classified			
6127	23.04.91	E.Roussis	Gree	L.F104	NK
6128	23.04.91	CAPT R.Ripamonti	Italy	L.F104	NK
6129	23.04.91	Classified			
6130	10.05.91	CAPT P.J.S.Ruiz	Spain	C.101	NK
6131	10.05.91	LT Mitchell	RN	S.Har	NK
6132	10.05.91	S/L P.Mason	RAF	Torn	OC
6133	10.05.91	FL/LT Woods	RAF	Torn	OC
6134	27.05.91	Classified			
6135	28.05.91	S/LT B.Guillomon	Fr AF	Jag	OC
6136	29.05.91	FL/LT S.Bell	RAF	Harr	OC
6137	31.05.91	TEN L.Bellini	Italy	AMX	NK
6138	17.06.91	CMDT I.C.Jones	SA	Cheet	OC
6139	29.06.91	LT T.Taylor	USN	F14	OC
6140	29.06.91	LT R.Maddock	USN	F14	OC
6141	08.07.91	LT W.H.Goodale	USN	F14	OC
6142	08.07.91	LT G.W.Huiet	USN	F14	OC
6143	12.07.91	LT M.M.Gautreaux	USN	F18	OC
6144	16.07.91	T/COL M.Lodovisi	Italy	MB326	NK
6145	16.07.91	LT R.A.Wucker	USN	F14	NK
6146	16.07.91	T/COL C.Landi	Italy	MB326	NK
6147	16.07.91	LT J.Whatley	USN	F14	NK
6148	19.07.91	LT J.Musaus	USN	Int	NK
6149	19.07.91		USMC	Int	NK
6150	19.07.91	1/LT L.K.Jarvis	USMC	Int	OC
6151	02.08.91		Mor	Mir	EA
6152	15.08.91	1/LT J.Asanger	GerAF	Torn	NK
6153	15.08.91	CAPT Albrecht	GerAF	Torn	NK
6154	20.08.91	CDR	USN	F18	OC
6155	21.08.91	J.R.Stipo	USAF	Phant	OC
6156	21.08.91	W.Jacoby	USAF	Phant	OC
6157	23.08.91	F/O G.Harley	RAF	Torn	NK
6158	23.08.91	F/O M.Entwhistle	RAF	Torn	NK
6159	24.08.91	LT	USN	F18	OC
6160	27.08.91	ENS DV N.Houel	Fr N	Etend	OC
6161	27.08.91	CPT I.G.Cirugeda	Spain	Mir	NK
6162	29.08.91	W/C W.Pixton	RAF	Jag	OC
6163	02.09.91	A.Katsibras	Gree	Phant	NK
6164	02.09.91	C.Lainopoulos	Gree	Phant	NK
6165	06.09.91	T/COL F.G.Aarns	Italy	L.F104	NK
6166	06.09.91	TEN CPL U.Gentilini	Italy	L.F104	NK
6167	12.09.91	FL/LT A.Edwards	RAF	Torn	OC
6168	12.09.91	W/C J.Ball	RAF	Torn	OC
6169	16.09.91	Classified			
6170	16.09.91	LT A.Lim Seng Tong	Sing	Hunt	OC
6171	18.09.91	LT R.A.Labranche	USN	Int	OC
6172	18.09.91	LT T.L.Fox	USN	Int	OC
6173	19.09.91		Jugo	Orao	NK
6174	25.09.91	CADET K.Saunders	RAF	Harr	OC
6175	25.09.91	S/L A.D.Stevenson	RAF	Harr	OC
6176	26.09.91	MTR E.Gruzynski	Fr N	Etend	NK
6177	30.09.91	FL/LT M.Zanker	RAF	Harr	OC
6178	06.10.91	CDR M.R.Groothousen	USN	F18	OC
6179	09.10.91	CAPT H.C.Dewey	USMC	F18	OC
6180	16.10.91	LT R.C.Angus	SA	MB326	NK
6181	17.10.91	LT C.Qesterle	USN	Int	OC
6182	17.10.91	LT/JG D.H.Waterman	USN	Int	OC
6183	19.10.91	K.Elias	Gree	Phant	NK
6184	19.10.91	F.Kabiotis	Gree	Phant	NK
6185	31.10.91	LT/CDR D.Henschel	Ger N	Torn	OC
6186	31.10.91	O/LT M.Gohler	Ger N	Torn	OC
6187	31.10.91	LT/CDR K.Seemann	Ger N	Torn	OC
6188	07.11.91	CAPT A.Scali	Italy	L.F104	OC
6189	07.11.91	S/TEN F.Majerna	Italy	L.F104	OC
6190	26.11.91	LT J.Scott	SA	Imp	OC
6191	04.12.91	CDR L.A.Fox	USN	F18	OC
6192	05.12.91	LT	USN	Int	OC
6193	05.12.91	LT	USN	Int	OC
6194	13.01.92	LT D.T.Armstrong	USN	F14	OC
6195	13.01.92	LT J.V.Stauffer	USN	F14	OC
6196	29.01.92	CAPT J.I.P.Diez	Spain	Mir	NK
6197	04.02.92	ENS DV Toussaint	Fr N	Etend	NK
6198	04.02.92	CAPT R.Valotti	Italy	AMX	OC
6199	05.02.92	L.A.Bath	SA	Mir	OC
6200	06.02.92	LT B.Bardischewski	Ger N	Torn	OC
6201	06.02.92	LT A.Hug	Ger N	Torn	OC
6202	15.02.92	FL/LT S.Clayton	RN	Hunt	OC
6203	15.02.92	CMDT Chaukai	Qatar	Mir	NK
6204	21.02.92	LT J.W.Nolan	USN	F14	OC
6205	21.02.92	LT B.Merrill	USN	F14	OC
6206	02.03.92	LT Torechio	Fr AF	Mir	OC
6207	13.03.92	S/L V.Jain	IndAF	Kiran	NK
6208	13.03.92	CADET S.Chowdhary	IndAF	Kiran	OC
6209	15.03.92	LT R.Schultz	USN	F18	OC
6210	15.03.92	S/L K.F.Lodhi	Pak	N.A5	NK
6211	19.03.92	LT V.M.Verges	USN	Prowl	OC
6212	19.03.92	CDR T.R.Miller	USN	Prowl	OC
6213	19.03.92	LT C.B.Becker	USN	Prowl	OC
6214	19.03.92	LT J.P.Hogan	USN	Prowl	OC
6215	21.03.92	H.F.Josehf	Chile	C.101	NK
6216	21.03.92	G/CAPT F.Sharp	AusAF	PC9	OC
6217	21.03.92	FL/LT R.J.Thacker	AusAF	PC9	OC
6218	05.04.92		Iran	Phant	EA
6219	05.04.92		Iran	Phant	EA
6220	08.04.92	Benitez	Ecuad	Mir	NK
6221	23.04.92	FL/LT Akmal	Pak	Ch.F7	OC
6222	29.04.92	W/C S.P.Singh	IndAF	Kiran	OC
6223	29.04.92	FL/LT J.D.Pillai	IndAF	Kiran	OC
6224	10.05.92	CAPT Cketby	Abu D	Mir	NK
6225	12.05.92	FL/LT P.Harrison	RAF	Tuc	OC
6226	12.05.92	FL/LT W.Hinmers	RAF	Tuc	OC
6227	13.05.92	LT S.M.Thompson	USN	F18	OC
6228	15.05.92	LT/CDR J.R.Muir	USN	F18	OC
6229	18.05.92		Pak	Mir	NK
6230	24.05.92	Classified			
6231	24.05.92	Classified			
6232	28.05.92	LT P.N.Wilson	RN	S.Har	OC
6233	29.05.92	CAPT T.E.Turner	USMC	F18	OC
6234	01.06.92	CDT Testaut	Fr AF	Mir	OC
6235	04.06.92	LT O.P.Honors	USN	Hawk	OC
6236	09.06.92	R.Monza	Italy	MB326	OC
6237	14.06.92	CAPT Reboul	Fr AF	Jag	OC
6238	23.06.92	Z.Vasilios	Gree	L.F104	NK
6239	13.07.92	A.Ioannou	Gree	F5	NK
6240	13.07.92	T.Zisios	Gree	F5	NK
6241	20.07.92	CAPT C.I.I.Krauel	Spain	Mir	NK
6242	07.08.92	FL/LT C.R.Huckstep	RAF	Harr	NK
6243	08.08.92	LT H.Hamon	Fr AF	Mir	NK
6244	25.08.92	T.G.Neagoe	Rom	Orao	NK
6245	25.08.92	D.C.Cosaceanu	Rom	Orao	NK
6246	03.09.92	LT N.Martidis	Gree	L.F104	NK
6247	30.09.92	FL/LT Blair	RAF	Hawk	OC
6248	01.10.92	LT/COL T.Pennington	USMC	F18	OC
6249	01.10.92	MAJ D.P.Yurovich	USMC	F18	OC
6250	07.10.92	G.Kormentzas	Gree	Mir	NK
6251	10.10.92	MR B.Sandberg	Civ	Tuc	NK
6252	16.10.92	LT/CDR J.Kesterson	USN	F14	OC
6253	16.10.92	LT/CDR G.R.Mickle	USN	F14	OC
6254	17.10.92	FL/LT F.A.Baig	Pak	N.A5	OC

No.	Date	Name	Force	Type	Cause	No.	Date	Name	Force	Type	Cause
6255	20.10.92	FLT T.Sueksamet	Thail	PC9	NK	6325	08.09.93	LT D.Fitzgerald	USN	Int	OC
6256	20.10.92	FLT T.Tamoon	Thail	PC9	NK	6326	13.09.93		Gree	Mir	NK
6257	20.10.92	CNE J.V.Vidal	Spain	Mir	OC	6327	13.09.93	LT C.M.Ortega	USN	F14	OC
6258	26.10.92	CAPT F.G.Buergo	Spain	C.101	OC	6328	13.09.93	LT T.M.Schrantz	USN	F14	NK
6259	26.10.92	2/LT A.G.Hevia	Spain	C.101	OC	6329	15.09.93	LT O.Nemes	Fr AF	Jag	OC
6260	27.10.92	FL/LT S.L.Singleton-Turner	NZ	S.Mas	OC	6330	15.09.93	Classified			
						6331	15.09.93	Classified			
6261	01.11.92		Pak	Mir	NK	6332	16.09.93	CDT P.Mimy	Fr AF	Jag	OC
6262	01.11.92	CAPT J.Rupp	USMC	F18	OC	6333	16.09.93	CNE V.De Gournay	Fr AF	Jag	OC
6263	01.11.92	MAJ E.B.Cassaday	USMC	F18	OC	6334	22.09.93	LT Torres	Braz	Tuc	OC
6264	07.11.92	FL/LT Taimuri	Pak	Mir	NK	6335	22.09.93	MAJ Crispim	Braz	Tuc	OC
6265	18.11.92	Moreno	Col	Mir	NK	6336	22.09.93	CADET A.M.C.Santos	Braz	Tuc	OC
6266	20.11.92	E.Michelet	Fr N	Etend	NK	6337	27.09.93		Pak	Mir	NK
6267	22.11.92	CDR E.Wattam	USN	F18	OC	6338	07.10.93		Zimb	Hawk	OC
6268	26.11.92	D.Bratsios	Gree	Mir	NK	6339	07.10.93		Zimb	Hawk	OC
6269	15.12.92	LT J.Burns	USN	F14	OC	6340	13.10.93	A/MAN S.Gyde	NZ	MB339	NK
6270	15.12.92	LT G.S.Hilliard	USN	F14	OC	6341	13.10.93	P/O C.J.Forster	NZ	MB339	OC
6271	17.12.92	LT J.A.B.Castano	Spain	Mir	NK	6342	14.10.93		Pak	N.A5	OC
6272	23.12.92	LT/CDR J.A.Summers	USN	F14	OC	6343	15.10.93	CAPT S.A.Whitley	Spain	C.101	OC
6273	18.01.93	LT/CDR K.B.Menz	USN	F14	NK	6344	15.10.93		Spain	C.101	OC
6274	18.01.93	LT/JG T.J.Hooper	USN	F14	NK	6345	21.10.93	FL/LT L.Taylor	RAF	Torn	OC
6275	19.01.93	CAPT Rudolph	GerAF	Torn	OC	6346	21.10.93	FL/LT S.Walker	RAF	Torn	OC
6276	19.01.93	CAPT Brosch	GerAF	Torn	OC	6347	18.11.93	LT K.D.Martin	USN	F14	OC
6277	25.01.93	LT P.Hooper	USN	F14	OC	6348	18.11.93	LT J.C.Daus	USN	F14	OC
6278	25.01.93	LT/CDR C.R.Dickerson	USN	F14	OC	6349	22.11.93	F/O P.K.Pareek	IndAF	Jag	NK
6279	12.02.93	Afonso	Civ	Etend	NK	6350	23.11.93	S/L J.Fernie	RAF	Harr	OC
6280	17.02.93	D.Leatherwood	USAF	Phant	OC	6351	17.12.93	MAJ J.C.Jumper	USMC	F18	OC
6281	17.02.93	M.Wells	USAF	Phant	OC	6352	05.01.94	LT P.N.Wilson	RN	S.Har	NK
6282	25.02.93	MAJ Shahab	Kuw	Mir	NK	6353	07.01.94		Kenya	Hawk	OC
6283	11.03.93	Classified				6354	07.01.94		Kenya	Hawk	OC
6284	11.03.93		Chile	Mir	NK	6355	18.01.94	LT Hart	Fr AF	Mir	OC
6285	11.03.93	Classified				6356	26.01.94	Classified			
6286	14.03.93		Kenya	Hawk	OC	6357	27.01.94	FL/LT K.S.Kumar	IndAF	Mir	OC
6287	22.03.93	LT P.N.Benvenuto	USN	Int	OC	6358	12.02.94	CDR S.L.Saunders	USN	F14	OC
6288	22.03.93	LT D.P.Quigley	USN	Int	OC	6359	12.02.94	LT/CDR M.W.Ullrich	USN	F14	OC
6289	23.03.93	MR B.Lehmann	Switz	Hunt	OC	6360	21.02.94	O/LT O.Queloz	Switz	Mir	OC
6290	31.03.93	CNE Despres	Fr AF	Mir	NK	6361	22.02.94	LT R.H.Lucas	USN	F14	OC
6291	06.04.93		Venez	Mir	NK	6362	22.02.94	LT J.W.Strobel	USN	F14	OC
6292	12.04.93	LT Vincotte	Fr AF	Mir	NK	6363	06.03.94	CAPT T.L.Gilbreath	USAF	Phant	OC
6293	13.04.93	LT/JG R.Gourley	USN	F14	OC	6364	08.03.94	1/LT D.A.Taylor	USMC	Prowl	OC
6294	13.04.93	LT J.Jacober	USN	F14	OC	6365	08.03.94	CAPT C.W.Smith	USMC	Prowl	OC
6295	14.04.93	LT D.E.Dugan	USN	Int	OC	6366	08.03.94	CAPT C.P.Hawn	USMC	Prowl	OC
6296	14.04.93	EX/OFF J.W.Jacobs	USN	Int	OC	6367	13.03.94	CDR E.G.Shankar	Ind N	S.Har	OC
6297	23.04.93	CAPT J.A.C.Von Solms	SA	Imp	OC	6368	17.03.94	S/L A.Sharma	IndAF	Kiran	OC
						6369	17.03.94	S/L R.Nambiar	IndAF	Kiran	OC
6298	23.04.93	LT S.L.Rennie	SA	Imp	OC	6370	27.03.94	Laporte	Fr N	Etend	OC
6299	29.04.93	Classified				6371	16.04.94	LT N.Richardson	RN	S.Har	EA
6300	29.04.93	LT K.Henderson	USN	F14	OC	6372	18.04.94	Maktoum	Abu D	Mir	NK
6301	29.04.93	LT/CDR S.Alexander	USN	F14	OC	6373	25.04.94		Dubai	Hawk	OC
6302	03.05.93	FL/LT S.M.Ali	Pak	Mir	OC	6374	06.05.94		ArgAF	Dag	NK
6303	03.05.93	2/LT S.Arvanitakis	Gree	Mir	OC	6375	02.06.94	Classified			
6304	07.05.93	LT L.A.Boxall	SA	Imp	NK	6376	02.06.94	Classified			
6305	21.05.93	LT Skaran	USN	F18	OC	6377	06.06.94	FL/LT S.Smiley	RAF	Torn	OC
6306	04.06.93	LT/CDR S.M.Dunwoody	USN	F14	OC	6378	07.06.94	FL/LT C.Chew	RAF	Torn	OC
						6379	09.06.94	MAJ A.D.Brand	SA	Cheet	OC
6307	10.06.93	CNE P.Lalois	Fr AF	Alpha	NK	6380	21.06.94	LT A.M.Taff	USN	F18	OC
6308	10.06.93	CNE P.Shisha	Fr AF	Alpha	NK	6381	29.06.94	LT C.M.Heath	USN	Prowl	OC
6309	14.06.93	Classified				6382	29.06.94	LT D.C.Eby	USN	Prowl	OC
6310	17.06.93	1/LT B.Close	USMC	Prowl	OC	6383	29.06.94	LT C.C.Sparks	USN	Prowl	OC
6311	17.06.93	CAPT K.T.McQuade	USMC	Prowl	OC	6384	29.06.94	LT C.J.T.Lee	USN	Prowl	OC
6312	17.06.93	CAPT P.F.Skopowski	USMC	Prowl	OC	6385	11.07.94	LT R.Arnold	USN	F14	OC
6313	26.06.93	F/O Auckland	RAF	Harr	OC	6386	11.07.94	LT/CDR D.Jennings	USN	F14	OC
6314	01.07.93	FL/LT Roberts	RAF	Hawk	OC	6387	18.07.94	Classified			
6315	01.07.93	FL/LT Day	RAF	Hawk	OC	6388	19.07.94	HPT A.Stumpf	RAF	Torn	NK
6316	06.07.93	MR C.Andskar	Swed	Vamp	OC	6389	19.07.94	FLT S.T.Petherick	RAF	Torn	NK
6317	08.07.93	Classified				6390	25.07.94	Classified			
6318	08.07.93	Classified				6391	25.07.94	Classified			
6319	20.07.93	LT R.D.Fuller	USN	F14	OC	6392	01.08.94	S/L D.H.Macleod	RAF	Torn	OC
6320	08.08.93	MR L.Radestrom	Swed	Grip	OC	6393	01.08.94	F/O I.Knott	RAF	Torn	OC
6321	30.08.93	Classified				6394	12.08.94		Ecuad	Kfir	OC
6322	08.09.93	LT/JG S.Gaze	USN	Int	OC	6395	16.08.94	MAJ E.G.Rosella	Spain	F18	OC
6323	08.09.93	CAPT A.Baur	USN	Int	OC	6396	17.08.94	LT/JG S.B.Inman	USN	Hawk	OC
6324	08.09.93	LT P.C.Gillis	USN	Int	OC	6397	26.08.94	LT J.Daus	USN	F14	OC
						6398	26.08.94	LT K.Martin	USN	F14	OC

No.	Date	Name	Force	Type	Cause	No.	Date	Name	Force	Type	Cause
6399	02.09.94		Gree	Phant	OC	6452	22.05.95	LT T.Parker	USN	F14	OC
6400	02.09.94		Gree	Phant	OC	6453	22.05.95	LT/CDR D.A.Burgoyne	USN	F14	OC
6401	14.09.94	Ricour	Fr AF	Jag	NK	6454	12.06.95	CAPT Viel	Fr AF	Mir	OC
6402	14.09.94	Bawejski	Fr AF	Jag	NK	6455	15.06.95	CAPT A.Day	Can	F18	OC
6403	19.09.94	FL/LT Ring	RAF	Torn	OC	6456	21.06.95	CAPT R.L.Paradis	RAF	Jag	OC
6404	19.09.94	F/O E.P.Moriarty	RAF	Torn	OC	6457	22.06.95	Classified			
6405	24.10.94	F/O M.D.Connolly	AusAF	MB326	OC	6458	22.06.95	Classified			
6406	24.10.94	F/O L.J.Pulford	AusAF	MB326	OC	6459	25.06.95	FL/LT S.Chauhan	IndAF	Jag	NK
6407	25.10.94	LT M.P.Klemish	USN	F14	OC	6460	04.07.95	Classified			
6408	29.10.94	CADET A.Dixit	IndAF	Kiran	OC	6461	20.07.95	Alech	Fr N	Crus	OC
6409	07.11.94	Classified				6462	10.08.95	S/LT I.Lambert	RAF	Hawk	OC
6410	07.11.94	Classified				6463	24.08.95	LT	USN	F18	OC
6411	07.11.94	CAPT P.J.Leroux	SA	Cheet	OC	6464	24.08.95	LT	USN	F18	OC
6412	18.11.94		USN	F18	OC	6465	25.08.95		GerAF	Torn	OC
6413	18.11.94		USN	F18	OC	6466	25.08.95		GerAF	Torn	OC
6414	01.12.94		Gree	Mir	NK	6467	25.08.95		GerAF	Torn	OC
6415	09.12.94	LT Negi	Ind N	S.Har	EA	6468	25.08.95		GerAF	Torn	OC
6416	15.12.94	LT D.J.Kistruck	RN	S.Har	OC	6469	29.08.95		Fr AF	Mir	EA
6417	21.12.94	LT/COL R.G.Leyden	USA	Moh	OC	6470	29.08.95		Fr AF	Mir	EA
6418	21.12.94	PF/C S.L.Lipscomb	USA	Moh	OC	6471	31.08.95	TEN A.Monaco	Italy	Torn	NK
6419	12.01.95	LT C.C.Enriquez	Spain	C.101	OC	6472	31.08.95	CAPT F.Vestito	Italy	Torn	NK
6420	12.01.95	CAPT P.Notti	Spain	C.101	OC	6473	14.09.95		RAF	Torn	OC
6421	13.01.95	LT T.B.Farley	USN	F14	OC	6474	14.09.95		RAF	Torn	OC
6422	13.01.95	LT E.Kost	USN	F14	OC	6475	20.09.95	LT/JG	USN	F14	OC
6423	13.01.95	LT P.Schirmer	USN	F14	OC	6476	20.09.95	LT	USN	F14	OC
6424	13.01.95	LT R.Kirkland	USN	F14	OC	6477	05.10.95	LT P.A.Kratzer	USMC	F18	OC
6425	15.01.95		Pak	Mir	NK	6478	05.10.95	1/LT T.A.Harp	USMC	F18	OC
6426	19.01.95	MR K.H.Lang	USAF	P	OC	6479	12.10.95	LT/COL C.Jara	Parag	MB326	NK
6427	07.02.95	GEN M.Ansaloni	Ghana	MB326	OC	6480	12.10.95	LT T.Farina	Parag	MB326	NK
6428	14.02.95	Classified				6481	20.10.95	LT/CDR C.Baylis	RN	S.Har	OC
6429	14.02.95	Classified				6482	24.10.95	M.G.Kreissl	GerAF	Phant	OC
6430	15.02.95	CAPT G.Alessandro	Italy	L.F104	NK	6483	24.10.95	E.Kistritc	GerAF	Phant	OC
6431	23.02.95		Gree	Phant	OC	6484	30.10.95	FL/LT McCarry	RAF	Torn	OC
6432	23.02.95		Gree	Phant	OC	6485	30.10.95	FL/LT Booth	RAF	Torn	OC
6433	01.03.95	S/L P.Benjawan	Thail	PC9	OC	6486	07.11.95	J.Tessier	Fr N	Etend	OC
6434	01.03.95	FL/LT S.Leaytip	Thail	PC9	OC	6487	08.11.95		SA	PC7	NK
6435	01.03.95	CAPT M.T.Manning	USAF	Phant	OC	6488	24.11.95	Classified			
6436	01.03.95	MAJ M.J.Leggett	USAF	Phant	OC	6489	27.12.95		Gree	Phant	NK
6437	09.03.95	CAPT Friedling	Fr AF	Mir	OC	6490	27.12.95		Gree	Phant	NK
6438	10.03.95	FL/LT D.J.Hazell	RAF	Torn	OC	6491	09.01.96	TEN M.Massimiliano	Italy	AMX	NK
6439	19.03.95		Pak	Mir	NK	6492	10.01.96		RAF	Torn	OC
6440	22.03.95		IndAF	Jag	OC	6493	10.01.96		RAF	Torn	OC
6441	23.03.95	CAPT V.C.Bateman	USN	F14	NK	6494	10.01.96		RAF	Torn	OC
6442	23.03.95	LT J.Seagle	USN	F14	NK	6495	10.01.96		RAF	Torn	OC
6443	29.03.95		Fr N	Crus	NK	6496	11.01.96		RAF	Torn	OC
6444	30.03.95	LT/COL V.David	Rom	Orao	NK	6497	11.01.96		RAF	Torn	OC
6445	30.03.95	MAJ V.Trofin	Rom	Orao	NK	6498	15.01.96	LT/CDR	USN	F18	OC
6446	12.04.95		Mor	Mir	NK	6499	17.01.96	LT K.Duggan	USN	F18	OC
6447	19.04.95	LT K.Coling	USN	F14	NK	6500	19.01.96		Fr AF	Mir	OC
6448	19.04.95	LT R.Byrnes	USN	F14	NK	6501	19.01.96		Fr AF	Mir	OC
6449	24.04.95	CAPT J.M.Jansen	USMC	F18	OC	6502	26.01.96	LV R.Olivier	Fr N	Etend	OC
6450	27.04.95	LT/CDR S.Bates	USN	F14	OC						
6451	27.04.95	LT M.Crawford	USN	F14	OC						

Martin-Baker Ejection History

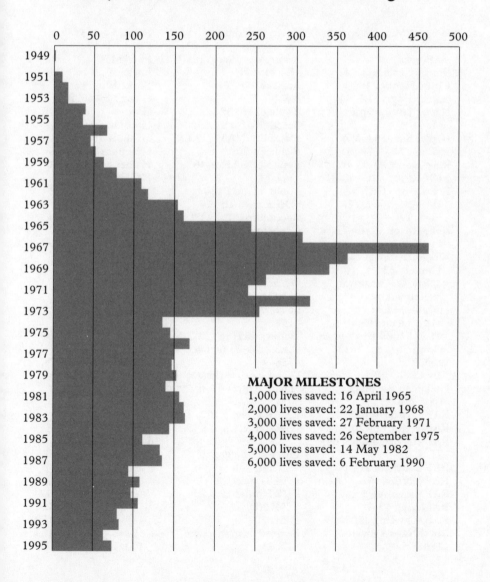

MAJOR MILESTONES
1,000 lives saved: 16 April 1965
2,000 lives saved: 22 January 1968
3,000 lives saved: 27 February 1971
4,000 lives saved: 26 September 1975
5,000 lives saved: 14 May 1982
6,000 lives saved: 6 February 1990

Index